Legal Nurse Consultant Procedure Manual (And More)

Katy Jones, MSN, RN

ISBN: 979-8-9943683-0-5

Cover design by: Katy Jones

Printed in the United States of America

Preface

Welcome to the Legal Nurse Consultant Procedure Manual (and More)—a resource crafted especially for legal nurse consultants, particularly those new to the field. When I first began my journey in legal nursing, I often wished for a single, reliable reference that could guide me through the maze of procedures, challenges, and best practices unique to our profession. This manual is the answer to that wish, transformed from the most essential content of my award-winning newsletter and website, LNCtips.com, expanded, and updated to reflect the evolving realities of legal nurse consulting.

Distinctive Features

Unlike other resources, this manual offers customizable procedures and real-world anecdotes not found elsewhere, making it indispensable for both new and experienced consultants. Every procedure is designed to be tailored to your specific situation—so no matter where you're starting from, you can adapt the steps to fit your workflow and caseload. This flexibility isn't just a feature; it's a lifeline for consultants facing the unpredictable challenges of the legal field.

What truly sets this manual apart is its blend of how-to guidance and practical wisdom. The "and More" woven throughout each chapter includes personal observations, industry standards, and time-saving tricks collected over years of experience. For instance, I remember stumbling through my first medical record review, overwhelmed by the volume and complexity. If only I'd had the step-by-step guide offered here—breaking down everything from organizing records to highlighting critical details for attorneys.

Specific Examples of What's Inside

- **Step-by-Step Guides:** Clear instructions for reviewing medical records, preparing reports, and communicating effectively with attorneys.

- **Case Studies:** Real cases with lessons learned, including navigating difficult attorney-client relationships and resolving complex liability questions.

- **Practical Tips:** Time-savers, sample documents, and wallet savers to streamline workflow and avoid common pitfalls.

- **Customizable Procedures**: Options to adjust and personalize each process, so you're never boxed into a one-size-fits-all approach.

- **Teaching Moments:** Anecdotes from my own journey—like the time I almost missed a key piece of evidence and what that taught me about diligence and persistence.

As you explore this manual, I hope you'll feel the warmth and support of someone who's been where you are. I've faced the same hurdles, second-guessed my findings, and celebrated the same victories. My goal is to offer not just procedures, but encouragement—helping you build confidence, sharpen your skills, and find joy in the unique role of legal nurse consulting. Think of this manual as your companion, teacher, and sounding board whenever you need guidance or reassurance.

Whether you're just starting out or looking to deepen your expertise, the *Legal Nurse Consultant Procedure Manual* is here to support you every step of the way—with exclusive content and a personal touch you won't find anywhere else.

Legal Nurse Consultant Procedure Manual (And More) ... 1

Katy Jones, MSN, RN ... 1

Preface ... 3

Chapter 1: Getting Started ... 14

Let's Talk: Choosing the Right Legal Nurse Consulting Program ... 15

Bedside Nurses and Legal Nurse Consultants: Two Unique Roles ... 16

Managing Deadlines: Navigating Time Pressures ... 17

Behind-the-Scenes: Lessons and Insights for New Legal Nurse Consultants ... 18

How the 5 Ws and 1 H Help Build a Medical Malpractice Case ... 21

Details vs. Minutiae in Legal Nurse Consulting ... 22

Focused Analysis ... 24

Preventing Analysis Paralysis: Four Steps for Legal Nurse Consultants ... 26

Starting Your Case Review: 3 Steps to Start Your Case Review ... 27

Commit to LNC Success: Navigating Your Path, One Step at a Time ... 29

Facing Overconfidence: How Legal Nurse Consultants Can Grow and Excel ... 31

Lessons from Nursing Orientation for New Legal Nurse Consultants ... 33

5 Ways New LNCs Can Overcome Desperation—and Build Confidence ... 36

Cognitive Reframing for Legal Nurse Consultants ... 38

4 Concrete Steps for Your First Attorney Meeting ... 41

Email Address Hierarchy for Legal Nurse Consultants ... 42

Chapter 2: Office Setup and Business Essentials ... 44

Computer Hardware Essentials for New LNCs ... 44

Software for Legal Nurse Consultants ... 46

4 Tips Every New LNC Should Know About Computer Troubleshooting ... 53

3 Time-Saving Computer Shortcuts Every LNC Should Know ... 55

Effective Document Organization for Legal Nurse Consultants ... 57

Legal Nurse Consultant Business Plan Worksheet ... 60

Sample Business Plan Worksheet ... 63

Common Legal Nurse Consultant Billing Blunders and Practical Solutions ... 68

Managing Deadbeat Clients and Payment Practices for LNCs ... 72

Mastering Letters of Understanding in Legal Nurse Consulting ... 74

Sample Letter of Understanding ... 76

The Effective Invoice: A Practical Guide for Legal Nurse Consultants ... 76

Sample Invoice 78
Chapter 3: Law Information for LNCs 80
Differences Between Medicine and Law: A Guide for New LNCs 80
Medical Malpractice Glossary – Explained Conversationally 83
It's a Party! 87
Understanding Key Legal Terms in Medical Malpractice Cases 89
Clarifying Hearsay and Testimony 90
Understanding Law Firm Roles: An Informational Guide for LNCs 92
Understanding Court Documents: A Simple Guide 95
Understanding Four Key Legal Deadlines: A Guide for LNCs 98
Understanding Pre-Litigation Requirements in Medical Malpractice Cases 101
Two Sides to Every Story: Justice, Truth, and Medical Malpractice 103
Understanding Two Defense Strategies 105
Understanding Medical Malpractice Defense: What Nurses Need to Know 107
Pyramiding / Stacking of Inferences in Legal Practice 108
Understanding Legal Case Resolution Methods 110
The Locality Rule and Standard of Care in Medical Malpractice for LNCs 112
The Blind Review Process in Radiology Case Evaluation 114
The CSI Effect in Medical Malpractice Cases 115
4 Things Jurors Don't Know 117
Medical Misconduct 118
Plaintiffs and Defendants Who Lie in Medical Malpractice Cases 120
Chapter 4 – Medical Records 123
Hospital Medical Records Chart Review: Best Practices for LNCs 124
Home Health Medical Records Chart Review: Best Practices for LNCs 127
SNF Medical Records Chart Review: Best Practices for LNCs 128
Sample Checklist: Tracking All Record Sources 131
Physician Office Records: A Practical Guide for LNCs 132
Understanding 3-D Medical Records: Essential Concepts for LNCs 134
Fraudulent Medical Documentation: Detection and Prevention for LNCs 137
3 Bad Habits with Medical Records 139
Electronic Medical Record Indexing: A Practical Guide for LNCs 141
HIPAA Compliant File Transfers 142

Deciphering Bad Handwriting in Medical Records: Strategies for LNCs.........146
Flippers, Organizers, & Page Turners 148
Chapter 5: Medical Research for Legal Nurse Consultants..........151
Internet Research Skills for Legal Nurse Consultants..........151
LNC Research Using the Wayback Machine 154
Comparing Google Scholar and PubMed for Legal Nurse Consultants............155
Evaluating Authoritative Journal Articles: Applying the CARS Checklist 158
Cyber Reputations and Background Investigations for LNCs..........160
Chapter 6: Case Analysis for Legal Nurse Consultants..........163
Medical Documentation Standards: Traditional and Electronic Records........163
Switch in Plaintiff and Defense Tactics 167
Understanding Nursing Documentation Standards 169
Effective Nursing Documentation: Legal Implications and Best Practices......170
Understanding Hindsight Bias 172
Accentuate Both the Positives and Negatives in Medical Case Analysis...........173
Understanding Mammograms in Medical Malpractice Cases 175
Teleradiology Medical Malpractice Guidelines: A Guide for LNCs 178
Anesthesia Record Analysis Made Simple 180
Reference Guide: Diary Analysis in Legal Cases 182
Pharmacy Record Analysis 185
Hospitalist Medical Malpractice..........186
Understanding EKG Reader Services and Their Legal Implications..........188
Craniosynostosis: Diagnosis, Treatment, and Legal Considerations 190
Perineural Invasion: Actionable Guidance for Legal Nurse Consultants 192
Genomics and Medical Malpractice: A Guide for LNCs..........194
Making Sense of Medical Bills: How LNCs Help Attorneys..........197
Profitability Case Analysis for Legal Nurse Consultants..........199
Cell Phones and Medical Malpractice: Lessons from Two Cases 201
"He Was Never Sick a Day in His Life" 203
Understanding Negligent Medical Referrals 205
ED Patient Boarding: Legal Nurse Consultant Review 207
Visual Acuity: Key Concepts, Abbreviations, and Legal Considerations..........210
Case Study Analysis: Medical Malpractice Claims in Newborn Care 212

Case Study: Analysis of a Defense Verdict in a Medical Malpractice Lawsuit..215
Chapter 7: Legal Nurse Consultant Reports 218
8 Kinds of LNC Reports 218
Medical Summary Guidelines for Legal Nurse Consultants 220
The Practical Guide to Writing Medical Summaries Quickly 224
Creating Medical Chronologies in Word: A Step-by-Step Guide for LNCs......230
Sample Case Example: Medical Chronology Table 231
Four Wrongs, Four Fixes 233
CaseMap Chronologies: A Guide for LNCs 235
Timelines vs. Medical Chronologies: A Practical Guide for LNCs 237
Sample Timeline 240
Medication Compliance Calendars: Utility, Limitations, and Legal Impact 241
Sample Calendar Report 243
Creating an Excel Chart from a Word Table for Medical Data Visualization ..244
Touch Charts: Visualizing Healthcare Interactions for Legal Cases 247
Sample Touch Chart 249
Treater, Provider, Fact Witness, and Cast of Character Lists 249
Sample Treater List 251
Effective Indexing in Legal Cases: A Guide for Legal Nurse Consultants 254
Sample Medical Records Index Entry: 254
Sample Radiograph Index Entry: 255
Sample Pathology Specimens Index Entry: 255
Sample Pleadings Index Entry: 256
Creating Medical Symbols with Macrons or Overstrikes in Microsoft Word ..258
Hyperlinking Electronic Medical Records: A Step-by-Step Guide 260
Attention to Detail: Four Tips for Polishing LNC Reports 262
Persuasive Use of Numbers in Legal Nursing 264
The Power of Analogies 266
Adding Images to Written Reports: Copyright, Fair Use, and Practical Steps 267
Sample Medical Summary with Image Added 269
Photo Chronology Accuracy in Legal Cases: Recommendations for LNCs......270
Tell Them a Story 272

Formatting Documents 275
Essential Adobe Acrobat Features for Legal Nurse Consultants 276
Wound Sizing in Written Reports: Practical Recommendations for LNCs 280
Chapter 8: Independent LNCs 283
Independent LNCs: Responsibilities, Realities, and Tips for Success 284
Setting Your Fee Schedule as an Independent Legal Nurse Consultant 286
4 Mistakes New Independent LNCs Make—and How to Avoid Them 289
Turning Mistakes into Success: Practical Advice for New LNCs 292
Why Do Independent LNCs Struggle? 294
Subcontractor LNC Opportunities 296
Chapter 9: Marketing and Networking for Expert and Independent LNCs 299
3 Lessons I Learned in Grade School—And How They Help LNCs Succeed 300
Overcoming Fear of Rejection: A Structured Guide for LNCs 302
Identifying Decision Makers / Influencers in Law Firms: A Guide for LNCs 304
Marketing Your LNC Services: It's Just Like Dating—Really! 307
Bullseye Marketing for LNCs: How to Hit Your Target Every Time 309
3 Creative Marketing Tips Every Legal Nurse Consultant Should Know 311
Creating Unbiased Marketing Materials for Legal Nurse Consultants 313
Email Marketing Made Easy: A Step-by-Step Beginner's Guide 316
Newsletter Marketing Tips for New Legal Nurse Consultants 318
Can Potential Clients Find You? 322
Inbound Marketing Strategies for Legal Nurse Consultants 324
Favicons: A Simple Guide for Legal Nurse Consultants and Website Owners 326
Three Practical Website Marketing Tips for Legal Nurse Consultants 328
Unlocking the Power of Website Analytics for LNCs 329
Testimonial Marketing for Your Legal Nurse Consulting Business 331
Discovery Marketing: Expand Your LNC Opportunities 334
Understanding Shop Lock: Why It Matters for Legal Nurse Consultants 335
Holiday Marketing Strategies for Legal Nurse Consultants 337
Networking for LNCs 339
The 30-Second Commercial for LNCs: Stand Out and Connect 340
Chapter 10: Expert LNCs 344
Locating Expert Witnesses: A Comprehensive Approach 344

Expert Legal Nurse Consultants: Pros, Cons, and Practical Guidance 346
Expert Legal Nurse Consultants Desirable Traits............349
Professional Credibility for Expert Legal Nurse Consultants 351
CVs for Expert Legal Nurse Consultants............353
Sample CV 354
Establishing Expert Legal Nurse Consultant Fee Schedules 356
Sample Fee Schedule 356
Unlocking Expert Recognition as a Legal Nurse Consultant............357
Expert Witness Selection Variables 360
Anatomy of an Affidavit............361
Sample Affidavit (Presuit Case)............362
Causation Affidavits............364
Sample Causation Affidavit 365
Understanding the Risks of Generic Affidavits in Medical Malpractice Cases 367
Four Key Reasons for Expert Disqualification in Medical Malpractice Cases .369
When an Expert's Not Qualified: Practical Guidance for LNCs 372
What Makes an Expert Witness Truly "Magical"? 374
Why are Some Experts Popular? 377
Why I Stopped Using Some Experts 378
Chapter 11: Depositions 380
Just the Facts – Deposition Preparation for Nursing Staff............380
Effective Depositions: Avoiding Absolutes in Healthcare Testimony............383
Sample Q&A: The Risks of Absolutes............385
Sample Q&A: Contextual Responses Reduce Perceived Negligence 385
Nursing and Expert Depositions............386
Navigating Deposition Challenges............388
Comprehensive Guide to Preparing for Video Depositions 390
Expert Witness Deposition Preparation Checklist 392
Understanding the Testimony Process: A Guide for New LNCs 394
The Unprepared Expert: Avoiding Common Pitfalls with Preparation 396
Deposition Data Banks............398
Deposition Summary Types: Guidance for New Legal Nurse Consultants......399
Sample Page-Line Summary (Product Liability Case) 400

Sample Narrative Deposition Summary (Product Liability Case)................402
Chapter 12: Launching A Legal Career—How to Land (and Keep) a Law Firm Job...406
Thinking About Becoming an In-House Legal Nurse Consultant?..................406
LNC Job Search: How to Find the Right Position for You..............................409
Nursing Positions in Law Firms...411
Launching Your Legal Career—A Nurse's Guide to Landing a Law Firm Job..413
Sample Resume Statements...415
8 Steps to Land That Law Firm Job: Let's Talk About It.................................416
How to Ethically Create an LNC Sample Work Product..................................418
Understanding Career Objectives for Legal Nurse Consultant Resumes.........421
Attorney-Friendly Legal Nurse Consultant Resumes: A Practical Guide........422
Sample Resume 1: Experienced Legal Nurse Consultant.............................425
Sample Resume 2: RN Seeking Independent LNC Role...............................426
Effective Cover Letters for Legal Nurse Consultants.......................................428
Sample Cover Letter...429
Successfully Mastering the In-House Legal Nurse Consultant Interview........431
Unique Value of LNCs: Distinguishing Clinical Expertise from Paralegals.....433
Recognizing and Addressing a Bad Fit as a Legal Nurse Consultant...............435
Four Reasons In-House Firms Fire LNCs—and How to Stay on Track...........438
Chapter 13: Law Firm LNC Skills...441
5 Proactive Strategies for Legal Nurse Consultants..441
Proactive Trial Preparation: A Step-by-Step Workflow for LNCs....................444
How to Become Your Firm's Best LNC Biller...448
ABA Billing Codes: A Simple Guide for Legal Nurse Consultants....................451
Expert Retention Process: Step-by-Step Guide with Checklist Linkage..........453
Streamlining Expert Contact Management: Practical Insights for LNCs.........457
Sample Expert Preferences Form..458
Expert Management in Medical Litigation: An Effective Tracking System.....460
Sample Tracking System...462
Expert Banks: Practical DOs and DON'Ts for Legal Professionals..................463
Nursing Licensure Issues: Lessons and Best Practices for Nurses and LNCs .466
Bates Stamping and Indexing for Legal Nurse Consultants............................469
Sample Index Table for Reference:...470

Best Practices: Working with Radiographs in Medical Malpractice Cases.......471
Tracking Pathology Slides 473
Effective Flagging and Tagging: A Practical Guide for LNCs 476
Medical Records Retrieval: A Guide for New LNCs..478
How to Acquire a Medical Record Abstract: A Clear Guide for All Readers....480
Supporting a Fired Colleague: Professional Boundaries and Communication482
Chapter 14: General LNC Skills 485
Three Rookie Mistakes 486
Understanding and Managing Conflicts of Interest in Legal Nursing 488
Sample Case Tracking Template 489
Patient Noncompliance: Legal Impact and Best Practices for LNCs 490
Critical vs. Analytical Thinking in Nursing 493
What Difference Did it Make? 495
How to Nail Down Timelines in Medical Malpractice Cases 497
Getting Started with Listservs: A Guide for New Legal Nurse Consultants.....499
Neurolinguistics for Legal Nurse Consultants 501
Working with Pro Se Litigants: Professional Boundaries for LNCs................503
Essential Communication Guidelines for Legal Nurse Consultants 506
Legal Plain Talk: Making Legal Language Understandable 509
Teaching Attorneys Medical Concepts: Guidance for LNCs............................511
Overcoming Roadblocks in Client Relationships 513
How to be a Benevolent Dictator 514
Using AI Tools in Legal Case Review: What Every LNC Needs to Know.........517
Redacting Documents 520
LNC Rigidity 523
The Typewriter LNC: Lessons on Embracing Technology in Legal Nursing ...524
How Long Will it Take? 526
4 Minutes a Day 527
Conquering Deadlines: A Practical Guide for New Legal Nurse Consultants ..529
Sample Assignment Tracking Checklist:...531
Sample Calendar Reminder Template: 532
5 Reasons for LNC Checklists..532
How to Set Up Tickler and Reminder Systems for Legal Nurse Consultants ..534

Look Ahead Day....536
LNC Cheat Sheets....538
Sample LNC Cheat Sheet....539
6 Ways to Find Information in the Chart....540
About the Author....542

Chapter 1: Getting Started

Beginning a career as a legal nurse consultant can feel both exciting and overwhelming. The transition from clinical nursing to consulting requires not only medical expertise but also an understanding of legal processes, attorney expectations, and the business side of independent practice. This chapter is designed to help you take those first steps with confidence. Think of it as your launchpad—providing the essential tools and mindset to move from "newcomer" to "prepared professional."

As a new legal nurse consultant, much of your early energy will be spent trying to secure that first case review. Yet the real question is: once you get the case, will you know how to analyze it? That's where this manual comes in. It begins by showing how legal nurse consulting differs from bedside nursing, and how my own daily experiences have shaped the guidance you'll find here. The aim is to build both confidence and competence in case analysis by exploring proven approaches that work in real practice.

If you've taken a legal nurse consultant course, you may have been given a few pages of medical records or a case study to analyze. Even after completing those exercises, many new consultants remain uncertain about how to evaluate an actual case. When I supervised new LNCs, I discovered that many simply didn't know *how* to analyze cases in a systematic way. To address this, I developed a variety of teaching methods, recognizing that different techniques resonate with different learners. In the following pages, you'll discover approaches such as the "5Ws and 1H," strategies for distinguishing details from minutiae, focused analysis methods, and step-by-step frameworks to prevent analysis paralysis and begin case reviews with clarity.

Beyond technical analysis, this chapter also explores the behavioral and attitudinal circumstances that can shape your early journey. We'll look at what it means to truly commit to LNC success, how to avoid the pitfalls of overconfidence or desperation, and how to reframe challenges constructively. You'll learn practical ways to manage orientation, handle expectations, and even structure professional communication—like email hierarchy—to project competence and professionalism.

This book assumes that you have taken a legal nurse consultant (LNC) course and know the basics of analyzing cases. Just in case you haven't taken an LNC course yet, you'll want to read the first article. And whether or not you've taken a course, by the end of this chapter, you'll have a clear framework for starting your journey, along with practical strategies to avoid common pitfalls and grow into a confident, capable legal nurse consultant.

Let's Talk: Choosing the Right Legal Nurse Consulting Program

Thinking about legal nurse consulting as a career? You're not alone! A lot of people start by asking, "Which LNC program is the best?" Honestly, that's not the most helpful question. Let's chat about why it's not and dig into the real questions that matter for your success.

First off, testimonials—those stories from other LNCs—can sound convincing, but they don't always reflect what happens in the real world. Instead of relying on someone else's experience, focus on what's right for you.

Here are the key questions you should ask yourself:

What's motivating me? Is it the promise of earning more money, or are you after professional growth or a new challenge? For example, if your main goal is financial, just know that very few nurses get rich as LNCs. But maybe you're seeking something new and meaningful—let your goals guide you.

- What skills do I have? Sure, your nursing background is important, but you'll also need sharp analytical skills and clear communication, especially when writing reports for attorneys. Picture yourself reviewing medical records and spotting what really matters, then explaining it in plain, organized language.
- How do I learn best? Some nurses thrive with online courses that fit their work schedules—like one nurse who studied after her night shifts. Others love the energy of in-person classes and the networking opportunities. Think about what helps you learn and connect best.
- What's my budget? Price is tricky. Maybe you know someone who got a ton out of an affordable program, while someone else swears by a pricey one. The main thing here: choose something you can afford and that delivers up-to-date, useful information. Don't stretch yourself thin for a high price if it doesn't offer more value and watch out for programs that just don't cover what you'll need.
- Are there any negatives? Do a quick online search for the program's name plus words like "complaints" or "scam" before you commit. Sometimes, a little research can save you a big headache down the road.
- Who's teaching? Ideally, you want instructors who are still working as LNCs today—not just folks who worked as LNCs years ago and have moved on. The field changes, and you'll benefit from up-to-date expertise.

All these questions are about YOU—your goals, your skills, your situation. Your answers will lead you to the program that's the best fit.

Quick Checklist: Compare LNC Programs

- Write down your main motivation for becoming an LNC.
- Note your preferred learning style (online, in-person, or hybrid).
- Set a realistic budget for your training.
- List any concerns about course quality or instructor experience.

Use this checklist to compare different programs and pick the one that will support you on your LNC journey!

Bedside Nurses and Legal Nurse Consultants: Two Unique Roles

For those exploring career paths in healthcare and beyond, it's important to understand the distinct roles of bedside nurses and legal nurse consultants (LNCs). Bedside nurses provide hands-on patient care in hospitals or clinics, closely monitoring, treating, and supporting patients during their stay. In contrast, LNCs use their clinical expertise in a legal setting, assisting attorneys with healthcare-related cases by interpreting medical records, offering expert opinions, and helping build or defend cases. While both professions rely on nursing knowledge, their day-to-day responsibilities and work environments differ significantly.

Comparing Core Competencies: Bedside Nurses vs. Law Firm LNCs

Let's explore how bedside nurses and LNCs apply key professional skills, highlighting similarities and differences through vivid scenarios. Though their settings differ, both roles require critical thinking, adaptability, and strong organizational abilities.

Setting Priorities: Making Quick and Informed Decisions

Both bedside nurses and law firm LNCs must know how to set priorities—but the ways they do so reflect their unique contexts. For instance, a bedside nurse starting a shift might immediately respond to a patient experiencing sudden chest pain, prioritizing rapid assessment and intervention to prevent complications. Meanwhile, an LNC in a law firm typically organizes tasks based on pressing legal deadlines. Imagine an LNC furiously reviewing records to compile a comprehensive medical chronology for an upcoming trial, ensuring every relevant detail is included for the attorney's review.

Setting priorities often goes together with managing deadlines—an essential skill in both professions.

Managing Deadlines: Navigating Time Pressures

The nature of deadlines differs between bedside nursing and legal nurse consulting, but both roles demand timely action. Bedside nurses face hourly or even minute-by-minute deadlines, such as preparing a patient for a CT scan at 10:00 AM or administering life-saving medication on schedule. Imagine a nurse juggling multiple medication rounds while ensuring a patient is ready for surgery. By contrast, LNCs encounter date-driven deadlines tied to legal proceedings. For example, an LNC may need to prepare a set of tagged medical records for a treater's deposition scheduled next Tuesday, or research and organize information ahead of a phone call with an expert witness the following morning.

As deadlines shift and new tasks emerge, both professionals must quickly adapt their workflow.

Managing New Assignments: Adapting to Changing Needs

When bedside nurses receive new patients, they perform crucial tasks such as admission assessments, educating patients about their care plans, and orienting them to the hospital environment. Picture a nurse welcoming a patient post-surgery, explaining pain management strategies and safety protocols. LNCs, depending on whether they work for plaintiff or defense law firms, adapt their procedures accordingly. Plaintiff-side LNCs might interview former patients to determine if they have viable cases, review medical records for patterns of care, or hire experts to support litigation. Defense LNCs, whose clients are healthcare providers, analyze case allegations and medical documentation, recruit expert witnesses, and draft reports for attorneys or insurance adjusters—usually without ever meeting the patient involved.

Integral to both roles is thorough documentation, which ensures accountability and continuity.

Documentation Practices: Ensuring Accuracy and Clarity

Meticulous record-keeping is vital for bedside nurses and LNCs alike, but their approaches and purposes differ. Bedside nurses document patient assessments, treatments, and responses in real time, creating a detailed chart that guides ongoing care and supports clinical decisions. Imagine a nurse updating a chart after administering a new medication and closely monitoring the patient's reaction. LNCs, on the other hand, produce work product like medical chronologies and case summaries. With multiple lawsuits on their desk, an LNC might update or create reports for 30 different cases in a month, rarely working on the same set of cases consecutively. Some cases may become "stagnant," sitting untouched for months until new developments arise.

Conclusion: Shared Foundations, Distinct Paths

In summary, bedside nurses and legal nurse consultants draw on similar foundational skills—priority setting, deadline management, adaptability, and documentation—but apply them in different ways based on their environments and responsibilities. Whether providing immediate patient care or supporting legal teams with clinical insights, both professions offer valuable and rewarding career options for those with a passion for nursing and a desire to make a difference in new settings.

Behind-the-Scenes: Lessons and Insights for New Legal Nurse Consultants

As a legal nurse consultant, my daily experiences became the foundation for the articles and resources I created. By sharing these behind-the-scenes stories, my goal is to offer practical guidance and relatable lessons to those new to the field of legal nurse consulting—helping you navigate the challenges ahead with greater confidence.

Turning Interviews into Opportunities: The Portfolio Article

One of my most impactful learning moments came during a law firm interview. Despite my background as an independent legal nurse consultant, the firm was searching for someone with direct law firm experience. I tried to explain my qualifications, but words alone weren't enough to convince them. That experience taught me a vital lesson: For new legal nurse consultants, it's not just what you say about your abilities, but how you demonstrate them.

Determined to stand out, I created a professional portfolio to showcase my skills and accomplishments. At my next interview, I presented the portfolio—a small binder full of sample reports. Although this firm also sought prior law firm experience, seeing my portfolio made all the difference. They offered me the position, choosing me over candidates with more experienced backgrounds. The takeaway? For those new to legal nurse consulting, building a strong portfolio can help you visually communicate your value and distinguish yourself during interviews and networking events.

Similarly, my interactions with new legal nurse consultants inspired me to create another set of articles focused on summarizing medical records efficiently.

Mastering Summaries: Teaching the 5Ws and 1H

While supervising and mentoring new legal nurse consultants, I noticed many were overwhelmed by the sheer volume of information in medical records. Distilling key facts into a concise summary proved challenging. Reflecting on my high school journalism class, I remembered the 5Ws and 1H approach—who, what, when, where, why, and how—to capture the essence of a story.

This technique became a cornerstone of my teaching. For new LNCs, learning to apply the 5Ws and 1H to medical case reviews can transform overwhelming data into clear, actionable summaries. The explicit takeaway here is that structured frameworks not only streamline your workflow but also boost your confidence and credibility when communicating findings to attorneys.

Building on this, I realized that efficient summarization was just one part of the bigger picture—new legal nurse consultants also needed to sharpen their analytical focus.

Bridging the Gap: Focusing Medical-Legal Analysis

I observed that many new LNCs, while excellent clinicians, naturally gravitated toward medical details and sometimes overlooked the legal aspects of a case. My experiences supervising these consultants revealed a crucial insight: Success in legal nurse consulting hinges on understanding how medical and legal elements intertwine.

To address this, I developed the Focused Analysis article, outlining practical steps for new LNCs to consider both perspectives. The lesson here is that by deliberately seeking out the legal context in each case, you position yourself as a more valuable team member and avoid missing critical information. For those new to the profession, this balanced approach is essential for comprehensive and effective case analysis.

As I continued supporting new LNCs, I realized that technical skills alone weren't enough—professional relationships and networking were equally critical for long-term success.

Networking: More Than Just Showing Up

One article was inspired by my observations at local chapter meetings of the American Association of Legal Nurse Consultants. I noticed two new LNCs who attended every dinner in their hospital uniforms, sitting together and rarely engaging with others. They never shared business cards, volunteered, or built connections, and over time, they stopped attending and never gained business from their efforts.

This experience taught me that successful networking is about active engagement and building relationships, not just attendance. For those new to legal nurse consulting, remember: Genuine connections foster opportunities. Approach networking events as chances to share your story, learn from others, and support your peers. Active participation can open doors that passive presence never will.

Even the creation of my website's logo offers a practical lesson for newcomers.

Details Matter: The Story Behind the LNCtips.com Logo

When designing the LNCtips.com logo, I wanted to visually reinforce the site's mission of supporting new legal nurse consultants. My inspiration came when an attorney handed me medical records highlighted in blue—a color that, when copied, obscures the underlying text. This experience reminded me of the importance of details that might seem small but have significant impact.

Figure 1 - LNCtips.com Logo

The yellow highlighter in the logo serves as a practical tip: For new LNCs, choosing the right tools (even something as simple as highlighter color) can make your work clearer and more effective. Blue, pink, orange, and other colors obscure highlighted information when copied; yellow doesn't. Don't overlook the little things—they can save time, prevent mistakes, and demonstrate professionalism.

Conclusion: Embracing Shared Experiences

Each of these stories—rooted in real-life challenges and solutions—demonstrates that the journey of a legal nurse consultant is filled with opportunities to learn and grow. For those new to legal nurse consulting, I hope these behind-the-scenes insights not only encourage you but also equip you with practical strategies for success. By embracing both the big lessons and the small details, you can build a rewarding and impactful career in this unique field.

How the 5 Ws and 1 H Help Build a Medical Malpractice Case

Have you ever wondered how legal nurse consultants (LNCs) break down a medical malpractice case? It's not that different from what journalism students learn on day one: Who, What, When, Where, Why, and How—the "5 Ws and one H." But for LNCs, these questions aren't just about telling the story—they're about building a solid legal argument. Let's walk through why each question matters so much in this context.

Who? You start by figuring out who everyone is in the case. Who is the plaintiff or their representative? Who are the defendants? Who were the caregivers or other key people? Why does this matter? Because identifying all the parties involved is essential for determining who might be responsible—and who could testify or be questioned. It's the starting point for determining liability.

What? What exactly happened? What led up to the event, and what happened afterward? This is where you lay out the sequence of events. Knowing "what" gives you the storyline, but it also helps you spot any breaches of duty or mistakes in the medical care. It's the foundation for arguing whether the standard of care was met.

When? When did it all take place? Setting the timeline is more important than it sounds. It helps you check if care was timely and appropriate. The "when" connects the dots between actions and outcomes.

Where? Where did the incident happen? Location sets the legal stage. Different places have different standards of care and rules, so "where" helps you know what guidelines to apply and where to find witnesses or evidence.

Why? Why did the event happen? Here's where causation comes in—a central legal concept. You need to show that the alleged mistake directly led to harm. For example, if a physician missed a diagnosis and the patient's condition got worse, you must prove that link. Causation means proving that the alleged deviation directly led to harm. For instance, if a missed diagnosis caused a patient's condition to worsen, this link must be established.

How? How did the event happen, and how did it affect the patient? This is about damages—the real-world effects on the patient. Damages refer to the actual harm suffered, whether that's a physical injury, emotional trauma, or financial loss.

Let's put this all into action with a real-world example. Imagine we're looking at the case of Mr. Dennis Grundy. Here's how the Ws and H play out:

- **Who?** Mr. Dennis Grundy, a 60-year-old patient. Also involved are staff at Cherry Oaks Medical Clinic, paramedics, ER staff at Lake Michigan Healthcare

System, Dr. Dona Milera (the physician in charge), and Susan Grundy (the patient's wife and personal representative). This helps us see who's who and who might be liable or provide testimony.

- **What?** He was treated for influenza, returned to the clinic with breathing problems, collapsed in the elevator, and died despite resuscitation efforts. Knowing these steps highlights possible mistakes or issues in care.
- **When?** All of this happened on February 13, 2025, after a week of treatment. The timeline helps us check the sequence and whether care was appropriate at each stage.
- **Where?** The events unfolded at Cherry Oaks Medical Clinic and continued at Lake Michigan Healthcare System's ER. This tells us what standards of care and rules might apply.
- **Why?** According to the autopsy, Mr. Grundy had ruptured diverticula, which led to peritonitis and his death. The underlying problem: possible errors during resuscitation, maybe because a new CPR protocol wasn't handled correctly. This is where causation comes in—we need to show how these alleged errors led to his death.
- **How?** There was confusion over a new CPR method; only one person knew how to perform it, but they were overridden by the physician. Because of this, Mr. Grundy's condition got worse, and he died. That's the damages part—what harm he suffered.

By asking these questions and connecting the answers, legal nurse consultants can make sure they're not missing anything critical and can build the strongest case possible.

Details vs. Minutiae in Legal Nurse Consulting

Legal nurse consultants know that details are important in the analysis of medical malpractice cases. However, new LNCs often mistake minutiae, those small trivial facts, for vital details. How can new LNCs tell the difference between details and minutiae? Let me tell you.

Details are the facts that make a difference in the case. They impact the outcome or help you understand what happened. Minutiae, on the other hand, are those pieces of information that don't change any legal or medical conclusions—basically, if it doesn't help answer the big questions, it's probably minutiae.

Why is this so tricky for new LNCs? Well, there are a few reasons:

- Context matters—a lot: Sometimes, the same fact can be crucial in one situation and totally irrelevant in another. For example, knowing that a patient has normal bowel movements is a detail in a colon cancer case, but it's just minutiae if the case is about a broken arm.

- We love medical details: Nurses are trained to look at every single aspect of a patient's health. It's second nature to want to know everything. But in a legal case, the interesting stuff isn't always the important stuff.
- Legal lens: Some new LNCs forget to look at things in terms of duty, breach of duty, causation, and damages—not just medical knowledge.

What's the solution to differentiating details from minutiae? As a new LNC, you can do a focused analysis. An even simpler solution is to write down what you're going to look for in a particular set of records. For example, let's look at a case in which the patient has a loss of function in her hand allegedly due to IV infiltration of a toxic medication.

- You'll look for the actions (or inactions) of the staff who inserted the IV and cared for the patient after the IV was inserted. You'll also review the medication orders and administration of medications. You'll determine how and when the patient's loss of hand function occurred. This is the meat of the case, where you'll focus on standards of care, causation, and damages.
- When you review records prior to the incident, look at them from the standpoint of the patient's condition and hand function. Did she have a history of venous problems? Did she have any problems with her hand prior to the incident? Did she ever receive OT or PT? You're looking for the baseline function of her hand.
- When you review records for dates after the incident, you'll focus on the patient's continued hand function. Did it improve, get worse, or stay the same? Medical records from PT, OT, vascular physicians, and Neurology are particularly important. You're looking for damages. You're also trying to determine whether the patient's condition has changed since the time of the original incident.

Now, here's where things get even more practical. Writing down what you need to look for helps keep your review from going off the rails. You could even use a checklist or template to stay organized. Here's a simple sample you can tweak for your own cases:

Case Issue	Relevant Details to Find	Sources/Records
Alleged Injury (e.g., IV infiltration, medication error)	Staff actions, timing of incident, symptoms, related orders	Nursing notes, physician orders, medication administration records
Pre-existing Conditions	History of related problems, baseline function	Admission assessments, therapy notes
Post-Incident Changes	Progression or improvement of injury, complications	Follow-up notes, therapy records, specialist consults
Legal Elements	Duty, breach, injury, causation	Summary sheets, incident reports

Figure 2 - Details vs. Minutiae Table

Here's a tip: before you dig into the records, fill out your checklist with the big issues and questions for the case. It'll help you zero in on the important stuff and avoid getting bogged down by minutiae.

Bottom line? If you can confidently tell the difference between what matters and what doesn't—and you use practical tools like these—you'll be way ahead in your case analysis as a new legal nurse consultant.

Focused Analysis

If you're just starting out as a legal nurse consultant, you might find it tough to zero in on the real issues of a case. Sure, as a clinical nurse, every bit of medical information matters for patient care. But when you're working on a legal case, it's a whole different ballgame—now, you need to put the spotlight on the details that matter to the case at hand. That's where your critical thinking and judgment come into play, and trust me, there's nothing more frustrating than sifting through pages of notes that don't make a difference.

Let's walk through an example. Imagine you're reviewing a case about an 80-year-old man in a nursing home. He has Alzheimer's, a history of prostate cancer, diabetes, heart disease, and he tends to wander. One day, he wanders off, gets hit by a car, and sadly, passes away from his injuries. So, what should your analysis focus on? Safety, wandering, Alzheimer's, and elopement—those are your key issues. While his other health conditions are important for his overall care, they're not central to the legal questions you're trying to answer.

Here's a little tip: jot down a brief synopsis of the main case issues before you dive in. It'll help keep you on track and can even be useful in your summary for the attorney. Think of it as your compass for the case. For instance, here's a sample synopsis, written by M. Lucero's work in the American Journal of Alzheimer's Disease & Other Dementias.

The last sentence was altered to include case-specific information. In this case, the patient was a resident in a nursing home.

Wandering is a behavioral problem of Alzheimer's patients. Serious safety problems for residents can result because they often wander into unsafe areas, handle unsafe objects, disassemble objects (exposing hazardous parts), or try to ingest inedible objects. In the institutional setting, these safety problems also raise significant issues of facility liability. Nuisance problems for institutional caregivers occur when residents rummage through the personal possessions of other residents, get into storage areas, walk away with nursing records, and get into the bed of another resident, sometimes with the resident in it. Residents who elope from the facility are often trying to go home. Elopement from the facility has led to the death of residents who have walked in front of cars and trains, which is what happened to Mr. Cowles when he was struck by a car and died from his injuries.

Now that you've nailed down your main case issues, let's talk about how to comb through the medical chart—step by step. You'll look at the whole chart, but you'll want to focus your energy on the sections that matter most for wandering and elopement.

Not sure where to start? Make yourself a "Where to Look" checklist. Here's one specifically for reviewing cases of wandering and elopement from nursing homes:

- Prior Records – Look for the date of Alzheimer's diagnosis, progression of dementia, and life expectancy estimates.
- Physician Orders – Scan for meds prescribed for Alzheimer's, any psychotropic drugs, or anything that might cause restlessness.
- Physician Progress Notes – Read all notes but pay special attention to anything about mental status or responses to wandering.
- MDS – Focus on sections C (cognitive patterns), D (mood), E (behavior), F (routine), I (diagnoses), N (medications), O (special procedures), and P (restraints).
- Care Plans – Hunt for goals and interventions that address wandering, like scheduled checks or environmental changes.
- Nursing Assessment, Nurses Notes, Monthly Summaries – Check for documentation about wandering, modifications to the environment, alarm devices, supervision, redirection, and anything listed in the Care Plan.
- CNA/ADL – Note if snacks were provided or how walks were supervised.
- Medication Administration Records – Look for cholinesterase inhibitors (like Aricept), NMDA inhibitors (like Namenda), and meds for agitation or anxiety.
- Restraints/Side Rails/Falls – Find evidence of restraints assessments, and confirm restraints were used only for medical reasons—not just to prevent wandering.

- Vital Signs/Weights/Intake and Output – Review weekly or monthly weights to flag any loss due to wandering.
- Dietary – Check for dietary assessments and progress notes to make sure nutrition was maintained, including supplements or snacks during wandering episodes.
- Social Services – Look for notes about social issues connected to wandering, efforts to make the room more homelike, and all family interactions.
- Activities/Recreational Therapy – See what diversional activities were offered.
- Other Reports – Review any incident/occurrence reports (if available), compare them to nursing notes, check inspection surveys, staff education on wandering/elopement prevention, policies, and procedures, staffing sheets for security assignments, alarm/police records, and even internet searches for media reports of missing residents. Compare these with the nursing notes to catch any inconsistencies or gaps.

When you've got your first draft, take a moment to review for extra information. Should you mention the resident's past heart disease, prostate cancer, and diabetes? Yes, but only include labs, x-rays, or related findings if they directly impacted or triggered the wandering or elopement—like an x-ray that reveals an injury causing restlessness. By focusing your report on what's truly relevant to the incident, you'll give attorneys clearer insights and stronger evidence for their case.

Three Essential Tips for Focused Analysis

1. Always start with a synopsis of case issues.
2. Review chart areas directly related to those issues.
3. Eliminate extraneous information from your report.

Preventing Analysis Paralysis: Four Steps for Legal Nurse Consultants

Analysis paralysis can affect both new and experienced legal nurse consultants. When reviewing medical records, it's easy to get stuck in the details, spending too much time researching, analyzing, and second-guessing your findings. This guide offers four clear steps to help you stay focused, work efficiently, and feel confident in your process.

Step 1: Remember Your Experience

You already have the skills to review medical records—it's a core part of nursing. Remind yourself that whether you're new or seasoned, your expertise is valuable.

Approach each case knowing you can identify the "4 Ds" of medical malpractice: Duty, Dereliction of Duty, Direct Causation, and Damages, as well as the medical details that matter.

Step 2: Research Efficiently

Set a clear time limit for researching the medical aspects of the case. Focus your research on understanding the relevant signs, symptoms, diagnosis, treatment, complications, and prognosis. Two focused hours are usually enough for most conditions. This keeps your process efficient and prevents getting lost in endless details.

Step 3: Take Action

Start reviewing the records, concentrating on the allegations, and recording your observations as you go. Trust your instincts to capture important information on your first read. If you hesitate about a detail, give yourself a few seconds to decide and move forward. This builds decisiveness and momentum.

Step 4: Refine Your Work

Review your notes or written summary. Remove any information that does not relate directly to the case. Make sure your findings clearly support or refute the allegations. If you need to check certain parts of the records again, do so, but avoid repeating unnecessary steps. Keep your work product clear and focused. "Work product" is a singular noun, like "family" or "group," which refers to multiple items. For LNCs, this includes medical summaries, chronologies, and other reports.

Stop over-thinking and start acting. You can do this!

Starting Your Case Review: 3 Steps to Start Your Case Review

Let's talk about how to get going as a legal nurse consultant, especially if you're looking at your first medical malpractice case and feeling a bit lost. Trust me, you're not alone—but with a clear structure and some handy definitions, you'll be ready to dive in. Here's how I walk new consultants through the process, with stories and quick takeaways after each step.

Step 1: Identify the Allegations

First things first: you need to know what's being claimed in the case. These allegations are the backbone of your entire review. If you're helping the person bringing the lawsuit (the plaintiff), the attorney should fill you in on the details—like what happened and why it's considered malpractice.

Let's clear up a couple of terms right off the bat:

- NOI (Notice of Intent; in some states): This is a formal heads-up sent to a healthcare provider, saying a lawsuit for medical malpractice might be coming their way. It lays out the basis for the claim.
- Affidavit or Certificate of Merit: This is basically a written, sworn statement—often from an expert or someone involved in the case—helping to back up those allegations.
- Complaint: The first formal legal document filed to start a medical malpractice lawsuit.

If you're working for the defense side (the person or team being sued), the attorney will often hand you an Affidavit or Complaint that spells out what's at stake.

Here's a real-life example: once, I reviewed eight years' worth of a cardiologist's medical records, hoping to figure out what the allegation was. Turns out, the issue was a simple mix-up—breast pain versus chest pain. If I'd known that from the start, I could have focused my review so much better.

- In summary: Always clarify the allegations before you jump into the records. It'll save you loads of time and frustration.

Step 2: Understand the Medicine

Next, make sure you're up to speed on the medical concepts that come up in the case. If you're not familiar with something—maybe it's a rare condition or a procedure you've never seen—don't hesitate to do some quick research. Google is your friend, and Google Scholar can fill in any gaps.

Let me share another story: I'd never worked with pediatric patients as a bedside nurse, but my law firm had cases about ependymoma, rickets, craniosynostosis, histiocytosis X—you name it. By looking up these conditions, I identified which symptoms a reasonable pediatrician should have noticed.

- In summary: Take time to learn about the medical issues in your case. It'll make your review much more effective.

Step 3: Review the Medical Records

Now you're ready to dig into the medical records. As you go through them, keep what I call the "4 Ds" of medical malpractice front and center:

- Duty: Did the provider owe a responsibility to the patient? If there was a provider-patient relationship, Duty was established. Thus, Duty is almost never a point of contention in medical malpractice cases.
- Dereliction of Duty: Was there a failure to meet that responsibility?
- Direct Causation: Did that failure directly lead to harm?
- Damages: What harm did the patient suffer?

People have different ways of tackling the records—some flip through quickly, some organize everything meticulously, and some go page by page. Whichever method you choose, always relate your findings to the 4 Ds.

- In summary: Review the records with the 4 Ds in mind so your analysis covers all the bases.

Recap: Simple Steps for Your Case Review

- Find and clarify the allegations. Ask for specifics and supporting docs (like NOI or Affidavit).
- Get smart about the medical details. Look up anything you don't know.
- Go through the records systematically, always thinking about the 4 Ds.

By following these steps—and learning from every case—you'll become a more confident, skilled legal nurse consultant. Remember, everyone starts somewhere, and your first case is just the beginning!

Commit to LNC Success: Navigating Your Path, One Step at a Time

So, you're thinking about shifting from bedside nursing to legal nurse consulting. Maybe you've taken a course, learned the basics, and started spreading the word about your new skills. Some LNC schools might have you believe you'll be an overnight success—but let's be real, for most of us, it's a journey. True success in this field means making a genuine commitment.

According to Lorie Brown, RN, MN, JD, there are five levels of commitment. Let's talk about the five levels of commitment, and how you can move up the ladder:

Level 1: Doing Nothing

Here's where a lot of folks start. Maybe you just wrapped up a legal nurse consulting course, got the "how-to" guide, and then—nothing happened. You might have made a few marketing attempts, didn't get results, and just stopped. We've all been there at some point. For instance, I knew an RN who simply froze after her training—she never even sent out her first email.

What can you do to shake this off? Pick one small, doable action, like reaching out to another LNC or updating your LinkedIn profile. Just get moving—because that's really all it takes to get unstuck.

Level 2: Wishing, Hoping, Wanting

Next comes wishing things would work out. I've heard it a hundred times: "I really want to become an LNC. If only you'd give me a chance!" But when I asked what steps they were taking, I usually got a blank stare, "I'm a quick learner," or "I'm a nurse, I can do anything." Wanting isn't the same as doing.

Want to level up? Turn that wish into a plan. Try researching three law firms this week or read a chapter of a legal nurse consulting book. Take one small step, and you'll start to move from dreaming to trying.

After all that wishing and hoping, some RNs decide to dive in and give LNC work a shot. Let's see what that looks like.

Level 3: Trying to See if You Like It

This is the "I'll give it a try" stage. I once knew an RN who joined a couple of online groups, read a bit, and waited for work to come to her. She didn't network, didn't seek out mentorship, and didn't work on new skills. And guess what? The opportunities just didn't show up. "Trying" can mean half-hearted effort, making excuses, or going through the motions. As nurses, did they "try" to correctly identify patients before surgery, or "try" to administer injections in the right location?

If you're stuck here, commit to purposeful action. Message a seasoned LNC for advice, join a professional event, or draft your own case summary, just for practice. Little by little, you'll build momentum and confidence.

Once you're moving, you might find yourself wanting to set some boundaries. Let's talk about how that plays out.

Level 4: Doing It Unless

Now you're really putting in effort—but with strings attached. You're all in, unless it means working full-time, visiting law offices, or juggling schedules with your RN job. For example, there was an RN who only worked as an LNC on weekends, but attorneys wanted weekday telephone conferences. Her limits shrank her opportunities.

Try this: See if you can relax just one restriction. Maybe offer to do telephone conferences during lunch hours or after work. Increasing your availability brings new possibilities.

Finally, let's look at those who really make it—no matter what.

Level 5: Doing Whatever It Takes

This is the "all in" stage. At my first AALNC chapter meeting, Cheryl, a seasoned LNC, told me the ones who succeeded did whatever it took, period. This level of commitment never includes excuses. I'm always surprised when I hear excuses such as "Attorneys won't hire me because of my age (or weight or other physical characteristics)." Take Jeffrey, for instance—he had trouble finding clients at first, but instead of quitting, he asked for feedback, updated his approach, took extra training, and even did volunteer projects to build his experience. He kept tweaking his strategy until things clicked. Eventually, he became the go-to expert in his field.

Want to reach this level? Commit to constant learning and adaptability. If something doesn't work, ask for feedback, change your plan, and try again. In the world of legal nurse consulting, persistence pays off.

Wrapping Up: Your Next Step

Wherever you are right now, know that you can keep moving forward. Start small, take action, and keep pushing your commitment a notch higher. With every step, you're that much closer to being a confident, successful legal nurse consultant—someone attorneys can truly rely on.

Facing Overconfidence: How Legal Nurse Consultants Can Grow and Excel

Let's talk honestly: overconfidence is a sneaky challenge in the world of legal nurse consulting. You might think you're ready to take on anything because you can type fast, navigate computers with ease, or write a decent report—but sometimes, reality gives us a wake-up call. And when we don't see our own blind spots, it's not just us who pay the price. Clients, attorneys, and even our fellow LNCs can all feel the consequences.

Lessons Learned: Real Stories from the Field

When I was an LNC supervisor at a law firm, I interviewed lots of LNC hopefuls who swore up and down they had top-notch skills. Some meant it. But once the real work started, it was clear that typing was slow, computer use was shaky, and reports? Let's just say spellcheck was working overtime. At first, I thought maybe they were fibbing to get hired. Now I realize, many just didn't know their true level.

And here's the rub: this overconfidence led to missed deadlines, messy reports, and frustrated attorneys. If you're an LNC, you know how one bad experience can make an attorney swear off hiring LNCs altogether—making it harder for everyone who comes after.

Finding the Root and Building Awareness

Now, it's tempting to point a finger at LNC schools. "You're a nurse! Attorneys need you!" they say—and yes, nurses have valuable expertise. But being a great nurse is just the starting point. Studies[1] show that overconfidence often travels together with not seeing your own shortcomings. That's why not every nurse is cut out for legal consulting (and that's okay).

Having seen firsthand how overconfidence can impact our profession, I realized that both education and self-awareness are crucial for success. This brings me to some practical steps you can take to ensure you're truly prepared for the demands of legal nurse consulting.

Practical Ways to Grow Your Skills (and Stand Out!)

- Self-Assessment: Be honest with yourself—take online skill tests or answer the test questions from resources like Legal Nurse Consulting: Principles and Practice.
- Mentorship: Connect with experienced LNCs. Find a mentor who's willing to give you real feedback, share their lessons learned, and help steer you away from rookie mistakes. Because you will be taking time away from their clients, expect to pay for mentorship opportunities.

[1] National Library of Medicine. https://pmc.ncbi.nlm.nih.gov/articles/PMC2702783/ (accessed December 2025).

- Keep Learning: Never stop growing. Workshops, webinars, new courses—keep your knowledge fresh and stay on top of legal and tech updates.
- Peer Review: Swap reports or case summaries with trusted colleagues. Honest and constructive critique can show you things you might never have noticed on your own.
- Show What You Can Do: When applying for jobs, share an original medical summary (not a class assignment) and be ready to show your typing and analytical chops. Build a portfolio that highlights your best work.

Learning From Each Other

Here's what I've found: sharing stories and seeking advice from others makes all the difference. When I was hiring, I looked for proof people could really do the job—not just take their word for it. Only about one out of every hundred applicants made it through. That might sound daunting, but it just means the field rewards commitment and self-improvement.

If you're worried you might be one of those overconfident LNCs—well, just asking the question shows real self-awareness. Whether you tend to be shy or more outgoing, don't be afraid to reach out for honest feedback from seasoned LNCs. And if you've got your own story or challenge to share, do it! We can all learn from each other's journeys.

Final Thoughts: Success Is a Journey, Not a Destination

Overconfidence doesn't have to set you back. Embrace feedback, seek out mentors, and keep learning. That's how you build real expertise—and how we can all raise the reputation of LNCs everywhere. Remember, your commitment to improving your skills is what sets you (and our profession) apart. Let's keep moving forward together!

Lessons from Nursing Orientation for New Legal Nurse Consultants

Do you remember your first RN job? Chances are good are that your employer provided an orientation for you. However, if you're like me, you received an initiation instead of an orientation. Let me tell you about my experience and why it relates to new legal nurse consultants.

When I was a new RN, I was very excited to get my first job as a staff nurse. I had worked as a nursing assistant in a hospital and nursing home during high school and college, and I had worked in a doctor's office one summer as a quasi-nurse. I expected the staff members to be as helpful to me as they had been in my other jobs. I was in for a surprise.

That first job was at a huge teaching medical center. Remarkably, there was no formal orientation program except for a ½-hour lesson on how to give medications. This was before unit dosing and Pyxis systems when pouring individual doses from huge bottles into medicine cups was the way it was done. The rest of the "orientation" was unit based, with each nursing unit determining what the orientation entailed. Unfortunately, my unit decided that it wasn't worth the effort to orient me or other new graduates. When I asked questions, the staff nurses told me that I was stupid.

"Stupid" seemed to be the favorite term of the staff. There were a lot of eye-rolling and deep sighs whenever I needed help. Today, the name for this behavior is "bullying". Back then, they termed it "sink or swim."

I learned to cope with this type of behavior because I:

• Wanted to become a crackerjack nurse. I was committed to doing whatever it took to attain my goal.

• Realized that I was the only person who had a stake in my success. I was the only one who could ensure that my "orientation" was successful.

• Listened to criticism without getting defensive. In my mind, some criticism was helpful ("There's a better way to do that"), and some criticism was not ("It's stupid to do it that way").

• Learned to calmly confront nurses who were disrespectful. ("I know that you don't mean anything by your comment, but I don't appreciate the word 'stupid.' Maybe you could show me a better way to do it.")

• Understood that no matter how it was phrased, some criticism was on target. I wasn't stupid, but there was a lot I didn't know. Because of that, I spent time in the hospital library after the end of every shift. I regularly read every nursing and medical journal available.

• Offered to help others. Whenever there was a skill to be learned or a type of patient condition that I was unfamiliar with, I offered to help with that patient's care. It was a rare person who turned down an offer to help. And after time passed and new RNs started on the unit, I helped them the way I had wanted to be helped.

Taking responsibility for my own orientation had some unintended consequences. I was one of the few nurses who frequented the hospital library; the other patrons were residents and attending physicians. I found out later that I had earned the reputation among the medical staff as being "that smart nurse." How ironic!

How Does This Relate to Legal Nurse Consulting?

Here's where my experience connects to legal nurse consulting. Just as I had to navigate an unsupportive environment as a new nurse, new legal nurse consultants might find themselves without any sort of formal guidance. You're stepping into a role where orientation is rare to non-existent, and you're left to figure things out for yourself. Sound familiar? If so, you're not alone—and you absolutely have the power to shape your own development.

Real-World Strategies for New LNCs

Let's get practical. Here are some strategies that helped me as a new nurse—and they work just as well for new LNCs:

- Commit to Success: Set clear goals for your journey as an LNC. That might mean dedicating time, energy, and even investing some money in courses or educational materials.
- Experiment and Adapt: If cold-emailing law firms isn't working, try joining online forums for legal nurse consultants, or attend industry webinars. Sometimes you have to try a few things before you find what works.
- Own Your Progress: Your success is yours to create. Don't wait for someone else to step in and save the day—reach out for help but make sure you're driving your own learning. Ask experienced LNCs for feedback on your reports or join a peer review group.
- Develop Core Skills: LNC work is about more than knowing medicine. If you don't type well, learn. If you don't write well, learn. If internet research is new to you, pick it up. And if you're unsure about creating written reports, take an online course or use and/or adapt the sample reports in this book. The more you know, the better you'll do.
- Network and Contribute: Don't be shy about volunteering—join an AALNC chapter, sign up for a committee, or help with a project. It's a fantastic way to meet people and discover new opportunities.
- Apply a Critical Filter: Before taking advice, ask yourself: Is the LNC who's advising me actively practicing and successful? If someone suggests a marketing trick, make sure it's worked for them recently.
- Leverage Technology: Get familiar with the software that's commonly used in medical-legal work. Online tutorials and short courses can help you get up-to-speed quickly.

Success Stories and Encouragement

Let me share something uplifting—a new LNC I knew volunteered for a committee in her local chapter and quickly built a network. That network helped her land her first consulting project. Another colleague took an online workshop in report writing, then got invited by a seasoned LNC to co-review a complex case. That opportunity kick-started a long-term partnership.

These stories aren't just exceptions—they're proof that initiative and community make a real difference. Even if your path feels uncertain, remember that lots of LNCs started out exactly where you are and have gone on to thrive.

Wrapping Up: You've Got This!

Starting out in legal nurse consulting can feel daunting, especially with little or no orientation. But by taking responsibility for your own learning and reaching out for support, you'll set yourself up for success. Stay flexible, embrace feedback, and keep building your skills. Your commitment—and your willingness to learn as you go—is what will set you apart. You really can do this!

5 Ways New LNCs Can Overcome Desperation—and Build Confidence

Starting out as a legal nurse consultant can feel overwhelming, especially when you're anxious to land your first client. That feeling is totally normal. In fact, a lot of us have been there. The problem is, if that urgency leaks into your marketing or the way you talk to potential clients, it could come across as desperation. But don't worry—I'm here to help you spot those signs and, even better, walk you through some concrete, step-by-step solutions so you can turn things around.

Spotting the Signs of Desperation

- Frustration: If you're comparing yourself to other LNCs who land clients instantly, it's easy to get discouraged. Potential clients might pick up on this frustration—sometimes before you even realize it yourself.
- Self-doubt: Ever catch yourself asking, "What's wrong with me?" when marketing doesn't work right away? You're not alone—but those thoughts can make it harder to show up with confidence.
- Asking for "a chance": If your pitch sounds like "Just give me a chance," you might accidentally focus more on what you lack than on what you offer.

- Offering to work for free: I know some people disagree, but volunteering your services (in a situation in which you should be paid) can actually signal to clients—and yourself—that you're not sure of your value. Attorneys may even wonder if you lack confidence or if you're not established in the field, which can really affect your credibility.
- Unfocused marketing: Sending out mass, generic emails might feel productive, but without a clear specialty, you can seem unfocused—and, again, a bit desperate for any case that comes along.

Let's Get Practical: Concrete Steps to Turn Things Around

Here's what you can do, starting today:

- Be a Skeptic with Testimonials: It's easy to think everyone else is an overnight success but remember—programs love to spotlight the rare instant wins. For most LNCs, it takes time to build up a client base. Trust your own process.
- Refocus Your Mindset: Instead of looking for a "chance," start with your strengths. Write down what makes you unique—maybe it's your clinical background, your attention to detail, or your research skills. These are your superpowers!
- Try This Targeted Marketing Plan:
    - Identify your top three strengths. What do you truly excel at or love most in nursing?
    - Research law firms that specialize in those areas. Check out their websites and the cases they handle.
    - Send personalized emails that highlight your relevant experience and how you can help them specifically. Make it about their needs, not just your availability.
    - Follow Up (But Don't Pester): After reaching out, a polite follow-up can show you're interested—just don't overdo it. Offer to answer questions or provide references.
- Get Out There and Network: Join professional associations, attend events, or participate in online groups. Building relationships makes you feel less isolated and opens doors to referrals.

Why Working for Free Can Backfire

I know it's tempting to offer free work when you're just starting out. But here's the thing: Attorneys may see unpaid work as a signal that you don't believe in your own abilities—or that you're not established yet. This can undermine your credibility. Plus, once you start for free, it's tough to break that expectation.

Let me share a quick story. Sarah M., a seasoned LNC, once did a free case review hoping it would turn into paid work. Instead, the attorney kept coming back for more freebies. When she finally set her fee, he moved on. That's when Sarah realized, "If I don't value my expertise, no one else will." So before offering free services, ask yourself: "Is this building my career, or just reinforcing my self-doubt?" Your time is valuable—spend it on meaningful connections, learning, and building up your portfolio.

You're Not Alone—Really!

It's completely normal to feel uncertain at the beginning. The truth? Every successful LNC once stood right where you are now. Take it from someone who's been there.

Remember, overcoming desperation isn't about hiding your enthusiasm. It's about channeling it into positive, confident action. Focus on your strengths, set boundaries, and use a targeted approach. You've got this—keep moving forward!

Cognitive Reframing for Legal Nurse Consultants

Let's talk about cognitive reframing—a practical tool that's all about changing the way you look at challenges. I first encountered reframing some years ago when I received a small raise. At first, I felt disappointed and undervalued by the modest increase—just 25 cents per hour. I remember telling my husband about it, expressing my frustration, and feeling that my hard work wasn't being fully recognized. His response shifted my perspective completely. He said, "If they took 25 cents per hour from your paycheck, it would seem like a lot of money." Suddenly, I realized I was focusing on what I expected but didn't get, rather than appreciating what I had received. That simple shift helped me see my situation in a new light, sparking a deeper appreciation and gratitude for the progress I was making.

For LNCs, reframing isn't about ignoring challenges—it's about finding new, more constructive ways to view them. For example, if a case review doesn't go as planned, instead of seeing it as a failure, you might reframe it as an opportunity to learn and improve your skills for future cases. You don't have to be a psychologist to benefit from this approach. Reframing your thoughts can help you feel more confident, connect with colleagues and clients, and enjoy your work as a legal nurse consultant even more. By shifting your perspective, you can reduce stress, build resilience, and approach challenges with renewed motivation—key factors for success as a legal nurse consultant.

If you're just starting out, you might sometimes feel discouraged, frustrated, or even alone, especially with all the effort you're putting into your new career. But here's the good news: those negative thoughts don't have to call the shots. When you change how you see things, you make room for growth, new opportunities, and progress.

Maladaptive Thought	Reframed Thought	Why This Helps
I don't have any support.	Reframing this as "I'm learning to function independently" empowers you to see growth in self-reliance.	When starting out as an LNC, it's common to feel isolated. It helps you view independence as a strength and encourages you to build your own support system.
Everything is so new that it's overwhelming.	Everything is so new that it's exciting. If I feel overwhelmed, I'll do one thing at a time instead of thinking about everything all at once.	Seeing new experiences as exciting turns anxiety into curiosity and tackling one thing at a time keeps things manageable.
It's hard to go from being comfortable with my nursing knowledge to being uncomfortable as an LNC.	Each day, I'll work on becoming more comfortable about my knowledge level.	This way, you allow yourself to grow gradually and show yourself some compassion instead of expecting perfection right away.
I don't know how to do things, such as writing an affidavit or completing a chart review.	I know how to use the internet, books, and other sources to help me with tasks such as these.	Reminding yourself of your research skills makes you feel more resourceful and encourages problem-solving.
If attorneys would just give me a chance, I know I could do this job.	I'm going to show attorneys and myself that I can do this job by creating work product samples.	Being proactive builds your confidence and proves your abilities to both yourself and others.
I'm getting no response to my marketing efforts.	I haven't gotten a response yet, but I'll continue to refine my marketing techniques.	This approach keeps you proactive and focused on improvement rather than feeling stuck.

Maladaptive Thought	Reframed Thought	Why This Helps
I don't know the legal nurse consulting field yet.	I'm getting better every day. I'm learning something every day.	Focusing on daily progress keeps you positive and motivated, turning uncertainty into opportunity.
If other people would do their jobs, I wouldn't have such a hard time doing mine.	I'm going to do the best job possible, even under these difficult circumstances.	Staying focused on what you can control helps you feel more resilient and less frustrated.
There's too much happening at once. I can't keep track of it all.	I'll get through this. I've gotten through difficult situations before, and I will now.	Looking back on past successes gives you confidence that you can handle what's in front of you now.
There are so many other LNCs. I don't know how to sell myself.	I'm an RN with a unique set of abilities and skills. There is no one else exactly like me, so I will capitalize on those unique abilities and skills to sell myself.	Embracing what makes you unique boosts your self-esteem and helps you stand out to potential clients.

Practical Tips for Reframing Your Thoughts

- Write down a negative belief and challenge it—list evidence against it or imagine how a trusted mentor would view the situation.
- Shape your reframed thoughts to fit your experiences and strengths. The more personal they are, the more impact they'll have.
- Try to use language that really resonates with you when you reframe your thoughts—this makes the new perspective feel more authentic and easier to adopt.
- Practice reframing your thoughts regularly. The more you do it, the more resilient and confident you'll become as you build your LNC career.

Remember, cognitive reframing isn't about pretending everything is perfect—it's about finding ways to empower yourself to move forward. Find the approaches that feel right for you, and trust that every small step is progress.

4 Concrete Steps for Your First Attorney Meeting

Landing your first case is a major milestone for new legal nurse consultants (LNCs) and it's easy to get caught up in marketing and networking. But when that long-awaited attorney meeting arrives, many LNCs feel suddenly unsure about how to present themselves and what to bring. The best way to avoid being blindsided is to prepare in advance with these four actionable steps, each illustrated by real-world examples and practical tips.

1. Decide What to Wear—Showcase Professionalism. It may sound basic, but your outfit speaks volumes before you even say a word. Consider this: Kenya, a new LNC, wore a navy-blue suit with a crisp white blouse and closed-toe black pumps to her first attorney meeting. She felt confident, polished, and was immediately taken seriously. A classic business suit—navy or charcoal—paired with a light blouse and simple accessories (avoid distracting jewelry), and neatly styled hair, sets the right tone. Remember: Attorneys expect to work with professionals, and your appearance can reinforce their confidence in you.
2. Build Your Attorney Binder—Bring Tangible Value. Imagine walking into the meeting with a well-organized binder, just like LNC Michael did. His binder contained several business cards, a one-page summary of his consulting services, testimonial sheets from colleagues or past employers, printed copies of his updated resume, and work product samples (see Step 4). Having these materials shows preparedness and makes it easy for the attorney to remember—and recommend—you. Pro tip: Use clear sleeves or tabs in your binder to keep everything neat and easy to flip through.
3. Update Your Resume—Highlight Relevant Expertise. Before her first meeting, LNC Jessica added a "Legal Nurse Consulting Skills" section to her resume, listing coursework, relevant continuing education, and her ability to analyze medical records. Even if you haven't worked on an LNC case yet, include transferable skills from your nursing background. Print several copies for your binder. Refer to sample resumes for inspiration, including the one discussed later in this book.
4. Prepare Work Product Samples—Showcase Your Analytical Skills. This is often the trickiest step, but also the most important. Attorneys want to see how you think: Can you organize complex medical facts? Spot key issues? Write clearly? If you've never worked on a real case, use de-identified examples from your work, or invent a hypothetical case based on your nursing specialty. For example, LNC Letty created a sample summary of medical records for a fictitious fall injury case, including a timeline, identification of critical events, and analysis of potential care issues. Why do attorneys value these? Because they offer a window into your expertise and working style. To get started, seek out sample templates

from the American Association of Legal Nurse Consultants (AALNC), your LNC training program, this book, or online resources.

Ready to take action? Start assembling your meeting materials today. Create a meeting preparation checklist to stay organized and set a date—maybe this week—to put your attorney binder together. Taking these concrete steps will help you walk into your first attorney meeting prepared, confident, and ready to win your first case. Every bit of preparation is a step closer to your LNC success!

Email Address Hierarchy for Legal Nurse Consultants

A professional email address isn't just a way to communicate—it's a powerful marketing tool and a signal of credibility. Attorneys and clients notice when your email looks professional, and it can make a strong first impression. Below is a hierarchy of email address types, with each option's pros and cons to help you choose the best fit for your legal nurse consulting business.

YourFullName@YourBusinessName.com (e.g., BrendaSmith@SmithLegalSolutions.com is the most professional email address.. Pros: Most professional and credible. Instantly communicates your name, your business, and your website. Easy for clients to look up your qualifications online. Variations (e.g., FirstName@, FirstInitialLastName@, LastName@) are equally effective. Cons: Requires purchasing a custom domain and setting up email hosting, but many web hosts offer step-by-step guides to make this simple.

Using an email address like **YourBusinessName@YourInternetMail**

Service.com (e.g., SmithLegalSolutions@gmail.com) is the next most effective email address. Pros: Shows your business name, which is better than a personal address. Easy to set up and free with most email providers. Cons: May suggest that your business doesn't have its own website or domain, which could seem less established to potential clients.

YourName@YourInternetMailService.com (e.g., BrendaSmith@gmail.com) is toward the bottom in terms of effectiveness. Pros: Simple, clear, and easy for people to remember. Suitable for personal use. Cons: Lacks business branding and credibility. Not recommended for professional communications when building your LNC practice.

InappropriateName@YourInternetMailService.com (e.g., ImaHotMama@gmail.com) is obviously the worst kind of email in terms of effectiveness. Pros: None for business purposes. Cons: Unprofessional and damaging to your reputation. Never use it for legal nurse consulting or any business communication.

How to Set Up a Custom Domain Email Address

1. Choose and purchase a domain name that matches your business (e.g., SmithLegalSolutions.com) from a trusted provider.
2. Select an email hosting service (your web host may include this option).
3. Follow your host's instructions to create your custom email address (like YourName@YourBusinessName.com).
4. Set up your new email on your preferred email client (Microsoft Outlook, Gmail, etc.).
5. Test your new address to ensure it works and update your website, business cards, and email signature.

By using a professional email address, you'll project expertise, reliability, and set yourself apart in the competitive legal nurse consulting field.

Chapter 2: Office Setup and Business Essentials

In this chapter, you'll discover how to set up your office with the essential computer hardware, software, and organizational strategies specifically chosen to support your daily tasks as a legal nurse consultant. These practical tips will help you work more efficiently and present a professional image to clients and attorneys. Next, you'll explore a sample business plan and worksheet designed to clarify your business goals and guide you in establishing a strong foundation for your consulting practice. By working through these resources, you'll be better equipped to make strategic decisions and achieve measurable results.

You'll also find solutions to common billing and client management challenges, along with sample documents such as a letter of understanding and an effective invoice tailored for legal nurse consultants. By mastering these strategies, you'll streamline your workflow and enhance client satisfaction as a legal nurse consultant. This chapter offers actionable guidance that connects each topic directly to your professional growth, making the material immediately relevant and motivating you to continue.

The chapter overview presents a clear and logical progression of topics, ensuring you know what to expect and how each section builds on the last. This structure makes the content easy to navigate and helps reinforce the practical value of each segment. Structured previews like this will continue at the start of each chapter, guiding you through the material and highlighting the benefits of each topic to your success as a legal nurse consultant.

This book focuses on core LNC skills and does not cover information typically addressed in legal nurse consultant courses, such as types of business entities, allowing you to concentrate on the tools and strategies that will truly elevate your professional practice.

Computer Hardware Essentials for New LNCs

A Practical Guide to Setting Up Your Home Office

As a legal nurse consultant (LNC), reliable computer hardware is fundamental to your success. You'll be typing reports, reviewing electronic medical records, and conducting online research daily. The right equipment makes these tasks easier and helps you present a professional image to clients and attorneys.

Choosing Your Computer: Desktop, Laptop, or Tablet?

- Desktop: Ideal for a home office—offers more computing power and value for your money. Desktops usually provide better performance and are easier to upgrade.
- Laptop/Tablet: Excellent for portability. If you anticipate working from multiple locations or need flexibility, a laptop or tablet is convenient, though they may offer less value for the price compared to desktops.

Choose the option that best fits your work style and workspace needs.

Essential Specifications: What to Look For

- Memory (RAM): RAM allows your computer to run multiple programs smoothly. At least 8 GB is recommended for basic multitasking; more (such as 16 GB) improves speed and handles larger tasks.
- Storage (Solid-State Drive, SSD): SSDs store your files and start your computer quickly. Aim for at least 500 GB of storage; 1 TB is ideal if you work with large files.
- Processor: The processor is your computer's "brain." Models such as Intel Core i3/i5 or AMD Ryzen 3/5 are sufficient for LNC work. A multicore processor helps with speed and efficiency.
- Ports: Ports allow you to connect monitors and other accessories. Common types include:
    - VGA: An older, blue-colored port.
    - DVI: A white port, less common on newer devices.
    - HDMI: Standard on modern devices, also used for TVs.

Having at least two video ports (any combination of VGA, DVI, or HDMI) enables you to set up dual monitors.

Monitor Setup: Enhancing Workflow

- Dual Monitors: Using two monitors lets you view medical records on one screen while typing reports on the other—greatly improving productivity and reducing errors. Or you could use a very large monitor 49 inches or greater.
- Compatibility: Ensure your computer's video ports match the outputs on your monitors. Check the box or the back of each monitor for details.
- Workspace Planning: Measure your desk to confirm both monitors fit comfortably.

Printers and Accessories: What You Need

- Laser Printer: Best for high-volume printing; toner lasts longer and is more cost-effective over time.
- All-in-One Inkjet Printer: Useful for scanning, copying, and occasional color printing (e.g., diagrams or photos in reports).
- Cables: Make sure you have the necessary cables for all devices. VGA cables may be included with new monitors, but DVI and HDMI often need to be purchased separately. You can find these at electronics stores or online.

Data Storage and Backup: Protecting Your Work

Online Backup Service: Instead of relying solely on external hard drives, consider subscribing to a reputable online backup service such as Carbonite. Automatic backups ensure your files are safe without requiring manual effort. When selecting an online backup service, ensure it offers end-to-end encryption and complies with HIPAA or other relevant data protection standards if you handle medical records. These criteria help safeguard sensitive information and maintain regulatory compliance. The personal version of OneDrive—which is typically included with a home computer—should not be used for files containing confidential patient information, such as medical records.

With these hardware essentials and practical considerations, you'll be well-equipped to handle your legal nurse consulting responsibilities efficiently and professionally. Investing in secure technology not only ensures smoother workflows and greater client confidence but also demonstrates your commitment to ethical standards and fosters long-term client relationships built on trust.

Software for Legal Nurse Consultants

HIPAA "2026 Requirements"

Before we talk about software, we have to discuss HIPAA (the Health Insurance Portability and Accountability Act) because, starting in May 2026, there may be major changes in requirements for software security. Because of HIPAA, there are certain precautions you should take in the selection of your software. As you know, HIPAA mandates that covered entities and their business associates safeguard patients' protected health information (PHI). If you work in a plaintiff law firm which represents no covered entity clients, HIPAA requirements don't apply to you. If you work in a defense law firm, the safeguards are likely already in place. However, HIPAA[2] updated its Security Rule in 2026, making it much stricter.

The stricter security measures will affect independent and expert legal nurse consultants in their choice of software. Some independent and expert LNCs question whether to install software (such as Microsoft Office 2024) to their local machines to safeguard PHI, or whether cloud-based subscription services (such as Microsoft 365 or Adobe Acrobat Pro) are acceptable. The answer depends, to some extent, on whether the LNC works for the defense or the plaintiff. Below is a table that explains standards for independent/expert LNCs working for the **defense**.

Safeguard Feature	**Locally Installed (Office 2024)**	**Cloud-Based (M365 + Copilot)**
Primary Responsibility	LNC (100%): You are the "IT Manager."	Shared: Microsoft secures the "pipes"; LNC secures the "faucet."
Encryption at Rest	Mandatory: Must use Full Disk Encryption (BitLocker/FileVault).	Managed: Microsoft encrypts the cloud; LNC must ensure local synced folders are encrypted.
Encryption at Rest	Mandatory: Must use Full Disk Encryption (BitLocker/FileVault).	Managed: Microsoft encrypts the cloud; LNC must ensure local synced folders are encrypted.
Encryption at Rest	Mandatory: Must use Full Disk Encryption (BitLocker/FileVault).	Managed: Microsoft encrypts the cloud; LNC must ensure local synced folders are encrypted.
Business Associate Agreement (BAA)	N/A to Software: Software is a tool; BAA is only needed for the firm hiring you.	Mandatory: **Must have an Enterprise/Business license** (E3/E5) to sign Microsoft's BAA.
Multi-Factor Auth (MFA)	Local Login: Required at the computer/Operating System level.	App Login: Mandatory for every login session to the M365 portal.
AI (Copilot) Privacy	N/A: No built-in AI; data stays on the hard drive.	Strict: Must disable "Web Search" and "Public Training" features within Copilot settings.

[2] HIPAA. https:// tinyurl.com/44vf9tp9 (accessed January 2026)

Safeguard Feature	Locally Installed (Office 2024)	Cloud-Based (M365 + Copilot)
Data Residency	LNC Site: Data lives physically in your home/office.	Cloud Data Centers: Must verify "US-Only" data residency in the M365 Admin Center.
Backup/Recovery	3-2-1 Rule: You must manually maintain off-site, encrypted backups.	Native: Built-in redundancy, but LNC must verify 72-hour restoration capability (2026 Rule).
Audit Logs	Limited: Basic Operating System logs show who logged into the PC.	Robust: Detailed logs show who opened, edited, or shared every file.

For independent and experts working for **plaintiff firms**, assuming that those firms have no covered entities as clients, HIPAA no longer applies. However, even if HIPAA doesn't apply directly, the independent/expert LNC is far from "off the hook." Instead of the HHS Office for Civil Rights (OCR) knocking on the door, there are different risks:

- State Privacy Laws: Many states (like California with the CCPA/CPRA or Texas with the Texas Medical Records Privacy Act) have privacy laws that are stricter than HIPAA and apply to anyone handling health data, regardless of whether they work for a "covered entity." See privacy laws for all states[3].
- Protective Orders: In most litigation, the court issues a Qualified Protective Order (QPO). This is a court order that dictates exactly how the expert must handle the data. Violating this is not a HIPAA fine; it is Contempt of Court, which can lead to sanctions against the expert and the law firm.
- Professional Ethics: As a nurse, the LNC is governed by their State Board of Nursing and the ANA Code of Ethics. Mishandling patient data—even in a legal context—can be viewed as "unprofessional conduct," putting their nursing license at risk.

In addition, there are other risks that plaintiff independent/expert LNCs face:

- Admissibility: If a defense attorney finds out that the LNC is writing reports on an unencrypted laptop in a coffee shop, the attorney can move to

[3] State privacy laws. https://tinyurl.com/r4dytcjw (accessed January 2026)

disqualify the LNC or strike their reports, arguing those methods are professionally unreliable.

- Future-Proofing: LNC's careers involve many cases. Next month, they might be hired by a firm representing a doctor (a covered entity). If they haven't set up their software environment securely now, they will be in violation the moment that new case starts.

As you can see, working for both the defense and plaintiff have implications for not only the safety and security of the plaintiff's PHI, but also for LNCs no matter for whom they work. Below is a summary of differences between defense and plaintiff requirements for LNCs as they pertain to privacy requirements.

Feature	**Working for a "Business Associate" Firm (Defense)**	**Working for a "Non-BA" Plaintiff Firm**
Primary Regulator	HHS (Federal Government)	State Courts / State Licensing Boards
Key Document	Business Associate Agreement (BAA)	Protective Order
Penalty for Breach	Federal Fines (up to 2M/year)	Contempt of Court / Malpractice / Loss of License
Software Setup	Must be HIPAA Compliant	Should be HIPAA Equivalent

There are other critical "2026" nuances. For locally installed software, such as Microsoft Office 2024:

The "Orphan Data" Risk: Because Office 2024 doesn't "talk" to the cloud, home-based LNCs are solely responsible for data disposal. When a case ends, you must use a "Secure Wipe" utility (NIST-level[4]) to delete the PHI. Simply hitting "Delete" or emptying the Recycle Bin is a 2026 compliance failure.

The Physical Threat: Your house/office is now a "data center." HIPAA requires physical safeguards (locking your office door, privacy screens) that are more scrutinized for local storage users.

For Cloud-Based (M365 with Copilot):

- [4] NIST. https://tinyurl.com/3tete376 (accessed January 2026)

- License Level Matters: You cannot use a "Personal" or "Family" M365 account. Microsoft will only sign a BAA for Business or Enterprise (E3/E5) tiers. Copilot in a personal or family account will learn from your data to improve its model—a massive HIPAA violation.
- Copilot Guardrails: Under the 2026 updates, if you use AI to summarize a medical record, you must ensure the AI output is manually verified. The OCR (Office for Civil Rights) has hinted that "hallucinations" in medical summaries that lead to privacy errors could be considered a lack of "data integrity."

Back to software. You'll want to know which computer apps will make your life easier and your work more professional.

Choosing the Right Office Suite: Practical Advice for Legal Nurse Consultants

Picking the best office suite software is a critical step for legal nurse consultants—your choice will shape how efficiently you work, how easily you collaborate, and how professional your reports look. We've already talked about Microsoft Office 2024. Here's a personalized breakdown to help you select the option that fits your needs.

Microsoft 365 Copilot: For Collaboration and Advanced Features

Microsoft 365 Copilot is popular for a reason. Its user-friendly interface makes it easy to jump in and start creating polished documents, spreadsheets, and presentations. You'll benefit from advanced features like track changes, robust formatting tools, and seamless integration with Outlook for email. Microsoft 365 Copilot also supports widely used file formats such as .docx, .xlsx, and .pptx, which means you can easily share and edit files with law firms and clients without worrying about compatibility or formatting issues. This suite is especially helpful if you routinely work with legal professionals who expect documents to be professional and accessible across different platforms.

Ideal for: Consultants who need powerful features, frequent collaboration, and compatibility with most clients. Tip: Make sure to download the full Microsoft 365 package to your hard drive—the online version is missing several advanced tools, and many helpful tips provided in this book won't work unless you're using the desktop version. The helpful tips will work in any desktop stand-alone or subscription version of Microsoft Office. In addition, you should never use any online version of Microsoft Office if you are writing about patients. Because online versions of Microsoft Office may store data on external servers that are not compliant with privacy regulations, using them for documents containing personal health information (PHI) could risk unauthorized access or breaches. Always use the desktop version for sensitive data to ensure compliance with privacy standards and protect confidential information.

Corel Office Suite: Advanced Tools with a Learning Curve

If you're seeking a budget alternative to Microsoft, Corel Office Suite may work for you. There are no subscriptions, and it offers some sophisticated tools, such as advanced spreadsheet functions and unique formatting options. However, its interface is less intuitive than Microsoft's, and features may be harder to find, especially if you're used to the Office layout. Corel can be powerful once mastered but expect to spend extra time learning its navigation and workflow.

Best for: Tech-savvy consultants who don't mind investing time to learn a new system, or those who need specific advanced features on a tighter budget. Note: Law firms used to use WordPerfect routinely, but most law firms have replaced it with Microsoft Office.

Google Docs: Simple, Collaborative, and Free—With Important Privacy Steps

If you're just starting out or working with a limited budget, Google Docs is an easy-to-use, free suite that covers basic word processing and document sharing, BUT it's not appropriate for creating reports with PHI from plaintiffs.

Who Should Use Google Docs? It's a smart choice for legal nurse consultants who want simplicity, real-time collaboration, and free basic tools—and who don't need complex formatting or privacy features for handling PHI.

Clear Setup Instructions

If you choose Microsoft 365 Copilot, download and install the desktop version on your hard drive. The web-based version is missing many advanced functions, and you'll get the best results by using the installed application for your legal nurse consulting projects. In addition, you should not use the web-based version if you are dealing with PHI.

PDF Tools

Next up: PDFs. You'll need tools that let you share documents without messing up your formatting.

- Adobe Acrobat Reader: Great for opening and viewing PDFs, but it can't create or convert documents to PDF.

- Adobe Acrobat Pro: If you want to create, edit, and convert files to PDF, this paid tool does it all. Your docs will look just right when you send them off to clients.
- Free Alternatives: Most computers let you "Print to PDF," or you can use a site like BentoPDF[5] for quick conversions without paying extra.

Tip: For most jobs, free PDF tools will do the trick. If you find yourself needing advanced features or handling lots of PDFs, consider upgrading to Acrobat Pro or using BentoPDF. While BentoPDF resides in your browser, your files are not processed in the cloud, making it a safe alternative to cloud-based subscription services.

Internet Browsers

Research, email, and cloud programs all start with a good browser. Which should you pick?

- Microsoft Edge: Ties in nicely with Microsoft products and works well for most basic surfing and research.
- Google Chrome, Mozilla Firefox, Safari: These are free and reliable. Chrome's super-fast and has tons of extensions. Firefox is great for privacy, and Safari is made for Mac users.

Tip: Choose the browser you like best or install a couple to cover your bases. Each has its strengths, so go with what feels comfortable.

Antivirus Software

This one's easy to overlook but trust me—your clients will not be happy if a virus sneaks into your emails. Keep your system protected!

- Built-in Options: If you're on Windows or Mac, you've already got solid antivirus protection that updates automatically.
- Third-Party Programs: Norton Antivirus and McAfee are popular paid choices with extra bells and whistles. If you want something free, AVG and Avast offer dependable basic protection.

Tip: Always keep your antivirus program up to date. If you want extra peace of mind, a third-party solution might be worth it, but the built-in options are a good place to start.

[5] BentoPDF. https://bentopdf.com/ Accessed January 2026

Wrapping Up

To run a smooth, professional legal nurse consulting practice, pick a reliable office suite (Microsoft 365 Copilot or Office 2024 is a safe bet), make sure you have PDF tools, use an internet browser you love, and don't skimp on antivirus protection. As you get busier, you might want to investigate special programs like CaseMap for organizing cases, but for now, focus on mastering these basics. Good luck, and happy consulting!

4 Tips Every New LNC Should Know About Computer Troubleshooting

It's no secret—I'm a bit of a computer geek these days. But I definitely wasn't born typing code or solving tech mysteries. When I first started using computers, I felt just as overwhelmed as many new legal nurse consultants do. Fortunately, a friend of mine who worked at a Help Desk in a big healthcare system shared three simple tips that transformed me from a computer novice into a semi-geek. I want to pass these on, so you feel more comfortable and empowered, too.

Tip #1: Use Your Software's Help Section (Step-by-Step)

When you run into a problem with a program—whether it's Microsoft Word, Adobe Acrobat, or WordPerfect—your first stop should be the software's built-in Help section. Here's how you can find and use it:

1. Open your program. Make sure you're looking at the main window of the software you're having trouble with.
2. Look at the top toolbar (menu bar). This is usually a row of words or icons at the very top of the window. Many programs have either a question mark icon (?) or the word "Help" up there.
3. Click on "Help" or the question mark. This opens a search box or a list of topics you can browse.
4. Type a few keywords about your problem. For example, if you want to know how to add page numbers, type "page numbers."
5. Read through the results for a solution. Don't worry if you don't see the answer right away—try a different keyword or check related topics.

If you can't find the Help section on your program's toolbar, try pressing the F1 key at the top of your keyboard. On some laptops, you may need to hold down the Fn key while pressing F1. This is a shortcut that opens the Help menu in most Windows programs.

I remember feeling lost the first time I couldn't figure out a simple feature. Using the Help section made me feel like I had a tech expert right there on my screen.

Tip #2: Master Google Searches by Refining Your Keywords

If the Help section doesn't give you the answer, don't worry—the internet is your next best friend. One of the biggest lessons I learned is that if you're having a problem, chances are someone else has had it (and solved it) before you.

Here's how to get the best help from Google, step by step:

1. Go to Google.com in your web browser.
2. Type a short phrase describing the problem. For example, start with "problem tables wordperfect borders."
3. If you don't see what you need, try changing your search terms:
4. Next, try "WordPerfect table border missing."
5. Still no luck? Try "how to add borders in WordPerfect tables."
6. Keep adjusting your keywords. Small changes—like adding or removing words—can make a big difference in the search results. This helps you find more relevant solutions.
7. Check the results carefully. Good answers can come from the software manufacturer's website, user forums, or blogs written by other computer users.

I remember trying to format a table in WordPerfect and almost giving up, but with a few tweaks to my search, I found a step-by-step guide on a user forum. That "aha!" moment felt like winning a mini-lottery.

Tip #3: Build Your Own Personal Help Folder

This next tip is a real time-saver. My computer-geek friend told me that the most common frustration at the Help Desk was people calling with the same question repeatedly because they didn't remember the solution. I've been there myself! When I upgraded from Windows 10 to Windows 11, I could never remember the new way to take a screenshot.

Here's how you can avoid repeating mistakes and create your own quick-reference resource:

1. Whenever you solve a problem, write it down. For example, I realized that pressing Windows key + Shift + S takes a screenshot in Windows 11.
2. Copy and paste the solution into a blank document. Include a brief description so you'll know what problem it solves.
3. Save the document with a clear name (like "How to Take Screenshots").

4. Keep all these documents in a folder called "Help" or "Computer Tips." The next time you forget how to do something, you'll have your very own help desk at your fingertips.

Trust me—after the third time I forgot how to take a screenshot, my Help folder saved the day and saved me lots of frustration.

Tip #4: Enlist Copilot's Help

If you're using Microsoft products with Copilot, you can take advantage of its features to organize your content or tidy up your documents. Here's a straightforward process for getting started:

1. First, highlight the text you want to fix.
2. Next, right-click on the selection and choose Copilot from the menu.
3. Follow the prompts to request writing suggestions or formatting help.

For example, I've struggled with misaligned bullet points—sometimes some bullets are indented farther than others even though they should match. Using Copilot, I was able to ask for help aligning my bullets, and it worked well.

But Copilot's capabilities go beyond bullet alignment. It can also help you rephrase sentences for better clarity, summarize lengthy paragraphs, or adjust the tone of your writing to be more formal or conversational. Whether you need editing, organization, or stylistic improvements, Copilot offers helpful tools to make your document shine.

Final Thoughts: Sometimes Simple Is Best

I promised these tips would be simple, and they really are. The best part? You don't have to be a computer expert to use them. With a little curiosity and your own growing list of solutions, you'll be more confident and ready to handle any tech hiccup that comes your way. Remember, everyone starts as a beginner—and every "geek" was once a little lost, too.

3 Time-Saving Computer Shortcuts Every LNC Should Know

Simple steps to boost your productivity, reduce frustration, and avoid common tech pitfalls

Ever find yourself endlessly clicking and searching for files, or panicking after an accidental deletion? You're not alone—these everyday computer frustrations slow us all down. Thankfully, with a few easy shortcuts and tools, you can save time, reduce stress, and keep your work safe. Here are three practical computer shortcuts I use in my legal nurse consulting practice, presented in a clear, step-by-step format to help you work smarter, not harder.

Tip #1 – Instantly Find Files with Desktop Search Tools

Summary: Desktop search tools let you quickly locate files, emails, and websites on your computer—no more aimless clicking or digging through folders.

Imagine this: You're at the supermarket, lost in the aisles, until a friendly stock clerk guides you straight to what you need. Desktop search tools work the same way for your computer, instantly finding documents or emails—even ones you forgot you had.

1. Download and install a desktop search tool such as Everything or Anytxt Searcher from their official websites.
2. Let the tool index your files and emails. For best results, leave your computer on for a while at first so it can scan everything in the background.
3. Type your keyword into the search box (for example, part of a file name or an Outlook email subject).
4. Select your result from the list and open it right away. I particularly like Anytxt Searcher because I can search for any word within a file, not just the file name. For instance, when I'm preparing a report and need to quickly locate a specific quote or technical term buried in my research notes, this feature saves me from opening dozens of documents one by one.

Benefit: Using desktop search tools means you spend less time hunting for files and more time focusing on what matters—no more lost documents or wasted minutes!

Tip #2 – Automate Your Research with Google Alerts

Summary: Google Alerts automatically sends you email updates about the latest news, job postings, or any topic you choose—so you never miss an opportunity.

Picture this: Instead of checking dozens of websites for legal nurse consultant jobs or industry news, imagine an assistant who emails you whenever something important pops up.

1. Go to google.com/alerts in your web browser.
2. Enter keywords that match what you want to track (like "legal nurse consultant jobs" or "LNC case studies").
3. Adjust your alert settings (such as frequency and sources) to fit your needs.
4. Create as many alerts as you want—you can edit or delete them any time if you get too many (or too few) results.

Benefit: With Google Alerts, valuable information comes straight to your inbox, saving you time and keeping you ahead in your career.

Tip #3 – Undo Accidents and Save Your Work Automatically

Summary: Keyboard shortcuts like Ctrl+Z (undo) and Ctrl+S (save) help you recover from mistakes and protect your work from unexpected disasters.

Imagine: You've just spent hours on a report—and with one wrong click, it's gone. That sinking feeling is all too familiar, but it doesn't have to be the end of the world.

1. If you accidentally delete or change something, press Ctrl+Z (or Cmd+Z on a Mac) to instantly undo your last action. Repeat if needed.
2. Turn on AutoSave in Microsoft Word if you're comfortable saving files to OneDrive (File > Options > Save > AutoSave).
3. If you prefer saving files locally, enable AutoRecover (File > Options > Save > Save AutoRecover information every 1–2 minutes).
4. Get in the habit of pressing Ctrl+S (Cmd+S for Mac) every few sentences to manually save your progress.
5. Consider buying a UPS (uninterruptable power supply) for battery backup, so your work is protected even during power outages.

Benefit: These simple steps help you avoid losing hours of work and keep your projects safe from accidental clicks, crashes, or power failures. Peace of mind is just a keystroke away!

Conclusion

By making these shortcuts part of your daily routine, you'll breeze through tasks, stay organized, and prevent those all-too-common computer headaches. Try one tip today—the time you save (and the stress you avoid) will quickly add up!

Effective Document Organization for Legal Nurse Consultants

A Practical Guide to Colorizing and Folderizing Paper and Electronic Files

As a new legal nurse consultant (LNC), you'll quickly discover that your cases come with a mountain of documents—whether in paper or electronic form. Medical malpractice, nursing home, and other complex cases can produce thousands of pages, making efficient organization essential for your productivity, accuracy, and peace of mind. This guide walks you through clear, step-by-step methods for organizing both paper and electronic documents, using real-world examples and practical strategies tailored to your needs.

Colorizing Paper Documents: Step-by-Step Methods

Colorizing is a powerful method for organizing paper documents. Our brains process color faster than text, making it easier to locate what we need quickly. Many law firms rely on color-coded systems to manage hundreds of files—here's how you can do the same in your home office.

1. Choose Your Color System: Decide how you'll use color to organize documents. For example, assign a color to each client, function, or priority.
2. Gather Supplies: Purchase colored file folders, colored dots, or labels from your local office supply store.
3. Apply Color Coding: I prefer to use an expandible file folder as mentioned in #4 below. Alternatively:
    - Use blue folders for medical research.
    - Use yellow folders for correspondence.
    - Use white folders for expert information.
    - Use green folders for invoices or financial documents.
    - Use red folders for urgent projects.
4. Organize by Priority or Function: Place projects with looming deadlines in red folders and those with lower urgency in yellow. Alternatively, create a color-coded expandable file folder for each case, using different colors for research, correspondence, work product, and invoices inside.
5. Maintain and Update: Regularly check your folders and update color coding as cases evolve.

Concrete Example: Imagine searching for a cardiac expert's file: Instead of sifting through hundreds of manilla folders, you simply look for the three white folders dedicated to expert information. This saves time and reduces frustration.

Parallels Between Paper and Electronic Organization

Just as color-coded folders make paper documents easy to locate, clearly labeled folders and subfolders in digital systems serve the same organizing purpose. Both strategies create visual cues—whether through color or labels—that help you find information instantly. Adapting these methods to electronic files ensures your digital workspace is just as manageable as your physical one.

Folderizing Electronic Documents: Numbered Steps for Email and Word Processing Organization

Folderizing Your Email Inbox

1. Create Folders for Each Client (Attorney) with subfolders for each case: In your email system (Outlook, Gmail, etc.), create a new folder or label named for each client. For Outlook, right-click on the Inbox and select "New Subfolder." For Gmail, use the "Labels" feature.
2. Sort Incoming Messages: Once you read and act on an email, move it to the appropriate client folder.
3. Use the Reading Pane: If available, use the Reading Pane to preview emails quickly and decide whether to open, move, or delete them.
4. Delete Unwanted Messages: Regularly remove non-essential emails from your Inbox to keep it clutter-free.
5. Declutter Gradually: If your Inbox is overflowing, commit to moving or deleting a handful of emails each time you check your messages. Spending just 10 seconds per session can steadily reduce inbox overload.

Folderizing Word Processing Documents

1. Create Main Folders for Each Client: In your file system (Windows, OneDrive, Google Drive), create a main folder named for each client.
2. Add Subfolders for Each Case: Within the client's folder, create subfolders for each individual case or matter.
3. Save Work Product by Category: Store medical research, correspondence, invoices, and other documents in clearly labeled subfolders.
4. Maintain Consistent Naming: Use standardized folder names and file naming conventions to ensure easy retrieval.

When finished, your folders and subfolders will be organized by client and case, mirroring the clarity and efficiency of your color-coded paper system.

Case Scenario: Organizing a New Case from Start to Finish

Let's walk through how a legal nurse consultant might organize a new medical malpractice case using both colorizing and folderizing techniques:

1. Receive Documents: The LNC receives paper records, electronic files, and emails related to a new cardiac case.
2. Colorize Paper Documents:
    - Assign the cardiac case to a blue expandable folder.
    - Place medical research in light blue folders inside.
    - Correspondence goes into yellow folders.

- Invoices into green folders.
   - Expert witness files into white folders.
3. Folderize Electronic Documents:
   - Create a Case folder with the name of the case on your computer or cloud storage.
   - Add subfolders: "Medical Research," "Correspondence," "Invoices," "Expert Witness."
   - Save all related word processing documents and PDFs to the correct subfolder.
4. Organize Email:
   - Move all incoming and outgoing case-related emails to this folder after reading and responding.
   - Maintain the System: Periodically update folders, remove outdated items, and ensure new documents are filed promptly.

By following these steps, the LNC is able to quickly find cardiac case documents, emails, and notes whether working at the office or remotely, and is always ready for meetings or deadlines.

Conclusion: The Benefits of Effective Organization

Mastering colorizing and folderizing techniques empowers you to work more efficiently, reduce stress, and impress clients with your professionalism. Whether you're managing a handful of cases or a rapidly growing practice, creating visual cues and clear systems for both paper and electronic files ensures you can always put your hand on the information you need. Start building your organizational habits now—and enjoy the confidence and productivity that comes with a well-ordered workspace.

Legal Nurse Consultant Business Plan Worksheet

A Practical Guide for New LNCs

Whether you're launching your first consulting practice or refining your vision, this business plan worksheet is designed to guide you through each step of business planning in a clear and supportive way. A written business plan helps you clarify your goals, map out your services, and plan for growth—even if you're new to business concepts. Don't worry if you're unfamiliar with any sections; hints and examples are provided throughout, and you can skip items now and return as you gain experience.

Business Description

Instructions: Use this section to describe your business basics. Fill in the blanks as best you can on the worksheet at the end. If you're unsure, review the provided hints or leave items blank for now.

- Location: Will you work from home or another setting? Example: ☑ I will work from my home.
- Business Address: Example: 123 Parmenter Lane, Lesser Main, OH 43099
- Business Name: Example: Somerville Legal Nurse Consulting LLC
- Business Structure: Choose the setup that fits you. Example: ☑ Sole proprietorship. Hint: If you're starting solo, sole proprietorship is common. Other structures (LLC, corporation, etc.) may require legal support.
- Scope of Work: Check all areas you intend to practice in. Example: ☑ Medical malpractice, ☑ Personal injury. Hint: Specialized areas, such as life care planning or toxic torts, often require additional training or certification. Focus on areas that match your expertise as a nurse.
- Consulting Services: How will you assist clients? Example: ☑ Reviewing/analyzing medical records, ☑ Providing expert witness testimony.

My goals for this business are:

Write your business goals below. Example: To provide expert medical record reviews to personal injury attorneys and build a reputation for accuracy and reliability in my region.

Market Analysis

Instructions: Identify your ideal clients. Select only a few to start—narrow focus helps you use your resources wisely.

- Potential Clients: Choose the types of clients you want to serve. Example: ☑ Plaintiff attorneys, ☑ Insurance companies. Hint: Marketing to attorneys and insurance companies requires tailored materials; start with one or two types for best results.
- Other Clients: Add additional client types as needed. Example: ☑ Hospitals

Competitive Analysis

Instructions: Understand your competitors and what makes your services unique. Use online searches, join professional organizations, and check social media for insights.

- Professional Organizations: Which groups will you join to learn and connect? Example: American Association of Legal Nurse Consultants (AALNC)
- Social Media Groups: Example: Legal Nurse Consultants Network on LinkedIn
- Competitor Pricing: Example: $150 per hour
- Competitor Marketing: How do your competitors attract clients? Example: Networking at legal conferences and maintaining an active LinkedIn profile
- Your Unique Value: What sets you apart? Example: I offer faster turnaround on case reviews and flexible scheduling.
- Experience Comparison: Example: My competitors have more experience than I do, but I bring fresh clinical insights and dedication.

Marketing Plan

Instructions: Define how and where you'll promote your services. Choose strategies that fit your budget and comfort level. For new LNCs, networking and social media are often cost-effective starting points.

- Geographic Area Served: Example: ☑ The city in which I reside. Hint: Starting locally may be more manageable and less costly than national or international reach.
- Organizations/Social Media: Who will you contact or connect with? Example: Local Bar Association, attorneys on LinkedIn
- Pricing Strategy: Example: $125 per hour
- Target Firm Size: Example: ☑ 1-2 practitioners, ☑ 3-10 practitioners. Hint: Smaller law firms may be more open to hiring outside consultants compared to larger firms with in-house LNCs.
- Marketing Tactics: Choose what fits your resources. Example: ☑ Networking (in person), ☑ Social media, ☑ Website. Hint: Direct mail and cold calling can be costly and/or less effective for new LNCs. Networking and building your online presence are recommended starting points.

Management Plan

Instructions: Outline who will manage the business and staffing plans. Most new LNCs start as sole owner and employee.

- Ownership: Example: ☑ I will own the business
- Partners/Employees: Will you have partners or hire help? Example: ☑ I will not have a partner in the business. Hint: Many LNCs start alone; you can add staff or subcontractors as your business grows.

- Starting Salary: Example: $40 per hour. Work Hours: Estimate your schedule. Example: I will work 10 hours per week to start, increasing to 20+ hours/week as the business grows.
- Full-Time Transition: Example: ☑ I eventually plan to work full-time in the business.
- Accounting: Will you use an accountant? Example: Smith & Co. CPAs. Hint: Using an accountant is wise if you plan to incorporate or hire staff, but optional for sole proprietors.

Financial Plan

Instructions: Plan your business finances, including costs and break-even expectations. Don't worry if you can't answer everything now; update as your business progresses.

- Bank: Where will you set up your business account? Example: First National Bank.
- Start-Up Costs: Estimate your initial expenses and attach a breakdown. Example: $2,500 total (computer, marketing materials, website).
- Break-Even Date: When do you expect your income will cover expenses? Example: 04/01/2026 (aspirational). Hint: Keep detailed records of all income and expenses. Your actual break-even date may shift as your business develops.

Final Tips - Remember, this worksheet is a living document. Update it as you learn more about your business and the legal nurse consulting field. Start simple, set realistic goals, and seek support from LNC organizations and peers.

You're building a foundation for success—one step at a time!

Sample Business Plan Worksheet

Fill in the blanks to the best of your ability and check the boxes that apply. You may leave some areas blank until you have more knowledge about your business.

Business Description

☐ I will work from my home. (Check if true.)

My business address will be: ______________________

The name of my business will be: ______________________

The business structure will be:

☐ Sole proprietorship

☐ Corporation

☐ Limited liability company

☐ Partnership

☐ S corporation

The scope of my work will include (check any that apply). Tip: New LNCs may not be qualified for every scope listed below—for example, life care planning usually requires additional training.

☐ Medical malpractice

☐ Personal injury

☐ Product liability

☐ Long-term care

☐ Workers' compensation

☐ Risk management

☐ Case management

☐ Insurance

☐ Toxic torts

☐ Forensic (criminal)

☐ Regulatory compliance

☐ Life care planning

☐ Other: ______________________

I plan to consult by: (Check all that apply.)

☐ Reviewing / analyzing medical records

☐ Surveying facilities for violations of regulations

☐ Reviewing / analyzing billing records

☐ Providing expert witness testimony

☐ Attending compulsory / independent medical evaluations

☐ Creating reports and summaries of medical records

☐ Researching medical literature

☐ Identifying cost estimates for future medical needs

☐ Drafting legal documents such as Affidavits

My goals for this business are:

____

____

Market Analysis

My potential clients are: (check all that apply). Tip: Marketing to different kinds of entities may require different techniques, more time, and more money. It's easier to get started if you limit the type of potential clients, at least when starting out.

☐ Defense attorneys

☐ Plaintiff attorneys

☐ Insurance companies

☐ Physicians

☐ Hospitals

☐ Free-standing surgery centers

☐ Surgery centers in physician offices

☐ Assisted living facilities

☐ Long-term care facilities

☐ Other: _____________________

Competitive Analysis

I will learn more about my competitors and colleagues by joining __________________ (name) professional organization and ____________

My consulting products differ from my competitor by

____

My competitors have __ more or __ less (choose one) experience than I do.

I am different from my competitors in the following ways:

____

Marketing Plan

The geographical area that I will serve is: (check all that apply).

☐ The city in which I reside

☐ The county in which I reside

☐ The state in which I reside

☐ National

☐ International

I will market members of the following organizations and / or social media:

____

My pricing strategy is to charge: $________ per hour.

I will target firms/organizations of the following size (check all that apply). *Tip: Larger practices are more likely to have in-house LNCs.*

☐ 1–2 practitioners

☐ 3–10 practitioners

☐ 11–50 practitioners

☐ Greater than 50 practitioners

I will use the following marketing tactics (check all that apply). *Tip: Consider the cost when choosing marketing strategies.*

☐ Direct mail

☐ Cold calling

☐ Telemarketing

☐ Networking (in person)

☐ Networking (virtual)

☐ Social media

☐ Blog / email campaigns

☐ Website

☐ Press releases

☐ Other: ____________________

Management Plan

Indicate your ownership and staffing plans by checking the boxes that apply and filling in the blanks.

☐ I will own the business.

☐ I will have a partner in the business.

☐ I will be the only employee in the business.

☐ I plan on hiring employees. (State type of employee and approximate date of hire: ______________________)

☐ I plan on hiring independent contractors. (State type of contractor and approximate date of hire: ______________________)

My starting salary will be ________________ per _________ (hour or week).

I will work _________ (number of hours) per week to start.

I will work _________ (number of hours) per week as the business grows.

☐ I eventually plan to work full-time in the business (check if true).

I will use_____________________________ (name) as my accountant for the business. Tip: Not all LNCs use an accountant for their businesses, but it's helpful to do so for tax purposes.

I will use_____________________________ (name) as my attorney for the business. Tip: Not all LNCs use an attorney for their businesses, although it's wise to do so if the LNC is setting up a partnership or corporation.

Financial Plan

Indicate your financial arrangements and projections by filling in the blanks below.

☐ I will use _______________________ as my bank for the business.

☐ I plan to spend $_________ on start-up costs. (Attach a copy of a breakdown of your start-up costs.)

☐ I plan to break even by (date): ______________________

Tip: Most business plans require a profit and loss statement, which lists the amount of income minus expenses. You may not be able to identify your break-even date until you have income. Keep scrupulous records of your expenses and income.

Common Legal Nurse Consultant Billing Blunders and Practical Solutions

How to Avoid Costly Errors and Build Trust with Clients

Accurate billing is essential for every legal nurse consultant (LNC), especially when starting out. Precise, transparent invoices not only ensure you get paid for your hard work, but they also build trust and credibility with clients. Unfortunately, several common billing mistakes can result in reduced payments, delayed compensation, or even non-payment. By understanding these pitfalls and implementing practical strategies, you can safeguard your income and reputation. Below, we identify the most frequent billing blunders faced by new LNCs, explain how to avoid them, and provide actionable checklists to help you put each solution into practice.

No Retainer

One of the most frequent mistakes new LNCs make is beginning work without securing a retainer—a pre-paid fee that shows client commitment and covers an initial block of hours. Without a retainer, you risk clients delaying payment or, in rare cases, not paying at all. For example, imagine you start reviewing medical records for a new attorney client but receive payment months after the project ends, causing financial strain.

Solution: Always require a retainer before starting any work. Seasoned LNCs often collect a retainer for every case, while some reserve this practice for new clients or those without a solid payment history.

Example Scenario: You set a retainer equal to four hours of work for a new law firm client. The client pays upfront, demonstrating commitment and ensuring you're compensated for initial services.

- Checklist:
- Define your retainer policy for all clients.
- Specify the retainer amount (e.g., 4 or 8 billable hours).
- Include retainer terms in your engagement agreement.
- Do not begin work until the retainer is received.

Once your payment is secured with a retainer, the next critical step is to accurately track your time to ensure precise billing for every activity related to your cases.

Inaccurate Tracking of Time

Failing to keep detailed records of your work hours can lead to underbilling or disputes with clients. As a new LNC, it's easy to lose track, especially when juggling activities like internet research, phone calls, and case reviews. Consider a scenario where you spend hours on various tasks but, at the end of the week, struggle to reconstruct your time, potentially missing out on billable hours.

Solution: Record your time as you go. Use a dedicated notebook, digital timer, or time-tracking app to log each activity in real time.

Example Scenario: You keep a log next to your computer and jot down start and end times for each task—such as "Medical record analysis: 2:00–3:30 PM," "Case-related emails: 3:30–4:00 PM."

- Checklist:
- Choose a time-tracking method (paper, app, spreadsheet).
- Log each activity immediately after completion.
- Review and total hours daily to prevent omissions.
- Reconcile tracked hours with client invoices monthly.

Vague Billing

Generic or repetitive billing entries, like "review of medical records," can confuse clients and appear as duplicate charges. Instead, specificity helps clarify what you did and justifies your fees. For instance, repeatedly billing for "analysis of records" may lead to questions about the value provided.

Solution: Clearly describe each service and reference relevant dates or patient details.

Example Scenario: Instead of "analysis of medical records," you bill "analysis of April 2025 admission records from Fair Oaks Medical Center for abdominal pain evaluation."

- Checklist:
- Use descriptive language for each billing entry.
- Include admission dates, facility names, and purpose of analysis.
- Differentiate between "review" and "analysis" where appropriate.
- Double-check for duplicate or vague descriptions before invoicing.

Infrequent Billing

Delaying invoices until a case closes can result in lost payments and cash flow problems. Imagine sending your bill months after the case has settled, only to find the client is unwilling or unable to pay.

Solution: Bill regularly—ideally, at the start of each month or after every significant interaction with the case.

Example Scenario: After each review session or meeting, you send an invoice on the first of the following month, maintaining a steady income stream and clear records.

- Checklist:
- Establish a routine billing schedule (e.g., monthly, after each task).
- Set calendar reminders for billing dates.
- Invoice promptly after case interactions.
- Track outstanding invoices and follow up as needed.

Block Billing

Grouping multiple activities into a single time entry, known as block billing, obscures how time was spent and can raise concerns about inefficiency or padded invoices. For instance, combining record review, research, and a phone call into one 6.5-hour entry leaves clients guessing.

Solution: Itemize each activity separately on your invoices.

Example Scenario: Your invoice lists "telephone conference: 0.5 hours," "internet research: 0.75 hours," and "medical record analysis: 5.25 hours," giving the client a clear breakdown of your time.

- Checklist:
- List each task individually with corresponding hours.
- Review invoices for grouped entries before sending.
- Provide brief descriptions for each activity.
- Respond to client questions about billing promptly.

Jargon

Using medical abbreviations or technical terms in invoices can confuse non-clinical readers and lead to delays in payment. For example, billing for "DVT eval via Doppler" may stump an insurance adjuster unfamiliar with the terminology.

Solution: Spell out all but the most common medical abbreviations and use layperson-friendly language.

Example Scenario: Rather than "EKG for CHF," write "electrocardiogram performed to evaluate congestive heart failure."

- Checklist:
- Review billing entries for uncommon abbreviations or jargon.
- Use plain English descriptions whenever possible.
- Include brief explanations for complex procedures.
- Verify clarity with a non-medical colleague if unsure.

Training

New LNCs often need extra time to learn case review techniques or software, but clients shouldn't pay for your learning curve. For example, if you're unfamiliar with chronology software and spend eight hours on a task that should take five, billing for all eight hours is unfair.

Solution: Adjust your billed hours downward to reflect only the time a competent, experienced consultant would require.

Specific Example: You spend eight hours creating your first medical chronology using unfamiliar software. Recognizing your inexperience, you decide to bill only five hours—a reasonable amount for the number of medical records—while noting the learning process for your own improvement.

- Checklist:
- Identify tasks requiring new skills or tools.
- Research reasonable timeframes for similar tasks.
- Reduce billed hours to reflect industry standards.
- Document your learning for future efficiency.

Billing Non-Billables

Clients generally won't pay for administrative or clerical tasks like filing, scheduling, and invoice generation. Attempting to bill for these tasks can lead to disputes or rejection of your invoice. For example, including "medical record organization" on your invoice may get flagged as non-billable by some clients.

Solution: Familiarize yourself with each client's billing guidelines and avoid invoicing for clerical or administrative activities.

Example Scenario: You clarify with the client whether organizing medical records is billable. If not, you exclude it from your invoice and focus only on substantive consulting work.

- Checklist:
- Review client billing guidelines before invoicing.
- Exclude clerical and administrative tasks from bills.
- Confirm billable status of borderline activities, like record organization.
- Keep separate records for non-billable time.

Conclusion

Avoiding billing blunders is key to your success as a legal nurse consultant. By securing retainers, tracking time accurately, providing specific billing descriptions, invoicing regularly, itemizing activities, using clear language, adjusting for training, and respecting client billing rules, you'll build stronger client relationships and ensure prompt payment. Implement these practical steps and set yourself up for lasting professional success.

Managing Deadbeat Clients and Payment Practices for LNCs

A Practical Guide to Client Selection, Payment Terms, and Professional Communication

Starting out as a legal nurse consultant, it's natural to want to secure any client who comes your way. While most clients in the legal field are professional and courteous, not all are easy to work with or reliable when it comes to payment. Understanding the types of problematic clients and proactively establishing clear payment practices will help protect your business, your time, and your income.

The Empty Promisor: Recognizing Unrealistic Promises

Some attorneys may attempt to negotiate your fees by promising a high volume of future cases in exchange for significant discounts or even free work. These "Empty Promisors" rarely deliver on their assurances and may simply move on to another consultant willing to work for less. To safeguard your interests, never accept compensation below what is fair and sustainable for your practice. Reserve unpaid work exclusively for legitimate volunteer opportunities, such as assisting organizations like Legal Aid. Always refer to your fee schedule and uphold your value as a legal nurse consultant.

The Abusive Attorney: Identifying and Responding to Bullying Tactics

Occasionally, you may encounter an attorney who becomes hostile or resorts to intimidation when asked to honor agreed-upon payments. This behavior is a deliberate tactic to avoid paying for services rendered. If you face abusive conduct, document every interaction, seek to communicate with another representative within the firm, and consider pursuing payment through formal channels such as small claims court if necessary. Importantly, recognize these patterns early and choose not to engage with such clients in the future. There are many reputable professionals who will value your expertise and treat you respectfully.

The Pokey Payer: Addressing Payment Delays

Some clients, while polite, consistently delay payment without valid reasons. It's important to distinguish between legitimate delays—such as those common with defense law firms awaiting insurance reimbursements—and unexplained postponements. For Pokey Payers, consider offering flexible payment methods like credit cards or PayPal to expedite transactions. If payment is late, follow up with the firm's accounts payable department, confirm invoice receipt, and request payment timelines. If delays persist, send progressively firmer reminders and refrain from accepting new projects until outstanding invoices are settled. As a last resort, consider enlisting a collections agency or pursuing legal remedies.

Preventative Measures: Establishing Clear Payment Terms Upfront

Preventing payment issues begins with clear communication and solid agreements. Here are best practices and sample contract clauses to include when onboarding new clients:

- Define Services and Fees: Clearly outline the scope of work and associated fees in writing.
- Specify Payment Schedules: Indicate when invoices will be issued and when payments are due (e.g., "Invoices are due within 30 days of receipt").
- Detail Accepted Payment Methods: State which payment options are available (e.g., check, credit card, PayPal).
- Include Late Payment Penalties: Add clauses such as, "Payments not received within the stated period will incur a late fee of $X per week."
- Require a Signed Letter of Understanding: Both parties should sign a letter that summarizes billing practices and consequences for late payment.

Tips for Communicating Payment Expectations with New Clients

- Discuss Payment Terms Early: Address payment schedules, methods, and penalties during your initial consultation.
- Share Written Policies: Provide clients with a written summary of your billing practices and expectations.
- Encourage Questions: Invite clients to ask about any aspect of your payment terms to ensure mutual understanding.
- Confirm Agreement in Writing: Obtain a signed agreement or letter of understanding before beginning work.
- Be Professional and Direct: Approach the topic confidently and clearly, reinforcing that these practices protect both parties.

Conclusion: Building a Successful Practice with Clear Boundaries

Managing difficult clients and establishing robust payment practices are essential skills for legal nurse consultants. By recognizing red flags, setting clear expectations, and communicating proactively, you can minimize payment issues and focus on building rewarding professional relationships. Remember, you deserve to work with clients who respect your expertise and honor their commitments—don't hesitate to stand firm on your policies and value.

Mastering Letters of Understanding in Legal Nurse Consulting

How to Clarify Terms, Set Expectations, and Strengthen Professional Relationships

Congratulations on landing your first client! Before you begin reviewing medical records or diving into case analysis, it's essential to formalize the terms of your spoken agreement with the attorney. A letter of understanding is a written document that outlines these terms, ensuring that both you and your client are clear on the scope, expectations, and logistics of the assignment. This practice not only prevents misunderstandings but also establishes your professionalism as a legal nurse consultant.

Clarification of Key Terms

Legal nurse consulting often involves terminology that can be confusing if left unexplained. Here are brief definitions of some important terms you may encounter or need to include in your letter of understanding:

- Work product: Refers to the materials, reports, or analyses that you prepare for the attorney as part of your consulting services. This may include case summaries, timelines, or research findings.
- Expert retention: Means that you are formally engaged as an expert on the case, which may require you to provide opinions, testify, or offer specialized knowledge.
- Subcontracted employee: A person hired by you to assist with specific tasks related to the assignment. This individual works under your direction but is not directly employed by the attorney.

Essential Elements to Include in the Letter

To avoid potential misunderstandings, your letter of understanding should address the following points:

- Nature of the assignment: Clearly state the type of work you will perform, such as medical record analysis, billing review, expert retention, work product creation, or internet research.
- Deadlines: Include specific deadlines for each phase of the assignment to ensure timely completion.
- Fees: Detail your fees as they relate to the assignment. Even if you have a separate fee schedule, reiterate your charges here for transparency.
- Billing practices: Explain your billing procedures, such as invoicing intervals, payment terms, and expectations for client payment.
- Use of subcontracted employees: If applicable, indicate whether you will employ others to assist with the work and clarify their role.

Conclusion: Professional Benefits and Call to Action

Using letters of understanding is a hallmark of professional legal nurse consulting. They foster clear communication, minimize disputes, and demonstrate your commitment to ethical business practices. By outlining the assignment details, fees, deadlines, and roles, you present yourself as a reliable and organized consultant, which builds trust and credibility with attorneys.

Don't wait—adopt the practice of drafting a letter of understanding for every assignment. This simple step will enhance your reputation, safeguard your interests, and set the foundation for successful collaborations in your legal nurse consulting career.

Sample Letter of Understanding

Below is a sample excerpt to help you visualize the structure and content of a professional letter of understanding:

Dear (Attorney Name):

Thank you for speaking with me today. I appreciate the opportunity to consult on your case.

As agreed, my Emergency Department / Home Health RN employee will perform the following services at a rate of *(specify amount)* per hour:

- Medical record analysis to determine deviations in standards of care.
- Medical chronology related to the allegations we discussed.

I will also supply you with the name of a board-certified Emergency Department physician for a fee of *(specify amount)*. The physician will bill you directly for their review of the medical records.

A retainer of *(specify amount)* is due when you send the pertinent medical records via mail or file sharing service.

If analysis of the records requires more than 4 hours, I will get your approval for any additional time. I will bill in in ¼-hour increments, and payment will be due upon receipt of the invoice.

I understand that you need the analysis on or before *(date)*.

Thank you again for this opportunity. I look forward to working with you.

Sincerely,

The Effective Invoice: A Practical Guide for Legal Nurse Consultants

How to Create Invoices That Ensure Prompt Payment and Promote Your Services

A well-crafted invoice does more than just request payment—it also reinforces your professionalism and can help you grow your business. This step-by-step article will guide you through creating effective invoices by organizing key information into clear sections: Required Information, Payment Details, and Marketing Tips. Each section includes actionable instructions and sample templates to make the process easy and effective.

Required Information

Start by ensuring your invoice includes all the essential details needed for prompt processing. These elements help your clients identify and approve your invoice without delays.

- Label Clearly: Title your document as "Invoice." This may seem obvious but omitting it can cause confusion and delay payment.
- Date: Add the date you are mailing or emailing the invoice.
- Contact Information: List your business name, your name, mailing address, phone number, and email. Provide the same for your client's contact (e.g., attorney, secretary). In the "To" section, include your client's name, title, company, and mailing address.
- Case and File Details: For legal or consulting work, include the case name, file number, and (if relevant) insurance claim number. This helps your client's accounting team match your invoice to the correct project.
- Tax Information: If your services are taxable, note the applicable tax (e.g., gross receipts tax in New Mexico). If your client requires a W9 IRS form, mention if it's been provided or attach it as needed.

Payment Details

Help your clients process payments quickly by clearly outlining your payment terms, summarizing services, and offering flexible payment options.

- Payment Terms: State your terms (e.g., "Net 30 days"). Reference your fee schedule if applicable.
- Services Provided: Itemize the work completed with specific details (e.g., types of services, dates, people involved).
- Line Items and Totals: List the amount due for each service and show the total.
- Payment Options: Offer multiple payment methods to speed up processing. State acceptable options (e.g., check, PayPal, Venmo, credit card).

Marketing Tips

Transform your invoice into a marketing tool by showcasing your brand, highlighting your range of services, and encouraging future business or referrals. Every invoice is a touchpoint with your client—make it count!

- Add Your Logo: Placing your logo at the top of the invoice reinforces your brand and adds professionalism.
- List Additional Services: Briefly mention other services you offer to spark interest in future collaboration.
- Highlight Discounts or No-Charge Items: List discounts as separate line items and note any no-charge services. This demonstrates added value and encourages goodwill.
- Include a Thank-You Note: Express your appreciation to foster a positive relationship.
- Encourage Referrals: Add a gentle suggestion for referrals or testimonials.

Conclusion

An effective invoice is clear, detailed, and professional. By organizing your invoices with these sections and incorporating marketing strategies—like adding your logo, listing additional services, and showing appreciation—you not only ensure prompt payment but also build lasting business relationships. Use the provided template and examples to upgrade your invoicing process today and turn every invoice into an opportunity for growth.

Sample Invoice

Shamanda Leeder Consulting

The Leader in Legal Nursing

Date: 10/23/2025
Invoice #107
To:
Jan Mann, Assistant to BF Way, Esq.
Way Reilly & Reilly
148 Sovenia Drive
Linkland, FL 39894
555-555-5555

RE: Johns v. Nelson Hospital
Your Case # 998745

Insurance Claim # 749980

Hours	Description	Fee
0.25	Review of Complaint	$25.00
2.75	Analysis of Nelson Hospital records 6/17/25 – 9/19/25	$275.00

1.25	Analysis of Med Examiner records, autopsy report 9/19/25 - 9/29/25	$125.00
0.5	Social Media research on plaintiff, Sharilynn Fender New Mexico has an obligatory Gross Receipts Tax, which is levied on all professional services. This tax is passed along to the customer, like a sales tax. The tax is noted on my fee schedule, which I have already provided to you. If paying by check, please remit payment to the address listed below. PayPal, Master, Card, Visa, Zelle, and Venmo payments are also accepted. Thank you; we appreciate your business! Please send payment within 21 days of receiving this invoice. There will be a 1.5% interest charge per month on late invoices. Let us find your experts! We offer a full-service expert locating service!	NO CHARGE
	Subtotal	$425.00
	Gross Receipts Tax (7%)	$29.75
	Total	$454.75

If you're satisfied with our services, please consider referring us to colleagues!

Shamanda Leeder · PO Box 608 · Tesma, NM 39894 · Phone/Fax 555-555-1212 · SLC@email.com

Chapter 3: Law Information for LNCs

In Chapter 3, we're diving into a variety of topics that every Legal Nurse Consultant (LNC) should know—everything from the basics of law and courtroom language to legal theories and case strategy. If you're looking for an in-depth review of medical malpractice elements, like duty, breach, causation, and damages, you won't find it here; that was covered thoroughly in your LNC class.

To start, we'll look at how Medicine (and Nursing by association) stacks up against the field of Law. You'll quickly see these worlds operate very differently. Once we've established that foundation, we'll transition into exploring the contrasts between Criminal Law—the kind you see dramatized on TV—and Civil Law, which is where most LNC cases take place (trust me, it's not like TV at all).

Next, we'll break down common legal terms and court jargon. I'll also share a bit about the roles within law firms—plus, a personal confession: when I started out, I tuned out a lot of this in my LNC course. That came back to haunt me when I landed my first law firm job and didn't know what a "matter" was or what all those abbreviations meant. Consider this your chance to avoid my embarrassment!

As we continue, you'll learn about what hearsay really means, key legal theories like "Two Sides to Every Story," SODDI, the Empty Chair and United defenses, as well as the concept of Pyramiding of Influences. We'll also touch on how cases get resolved.

Finally, we'll cover some unique topics that probably didn't come up in your training—things like locality, blind reviews, the CSI effect, what jurors aren't told at trial, medical misconduct, and why both plaintiffs and defendants sometimes bend the truth.

Remember, no one expects you to know it all right away. Learning the ropes is a process, and you're not alone. Let's get started!

Differences Between Medicine and Law: A Guide for New LNCs

Real Scenarios, Definitions, and Tips—In Plain Language

Are you just starting out as a legal nurse consultant? If so, you probably learned in your LNC training about how the legal process works—and you understand that Medicine (including Nursing) and medical malpractice Law are two very different worlds. But just how different are they? Let's explore together.

How Medicine and Law Approach Things—With Examples

Let's start with Medicine. Imagine life as a journey: patients enter the system at birth, leave at death, and interact with healthcare providers every so often—sometimes for a quick checkup, sometimes for something more serious. Law is different. Some people never encounter the legal system at all, but if they do, it's usually because something's gone wrong—like a medical malpractice case. From there, it's a very structured process: cases get screened and either close quickly or may go all the way to trial.

As a legal nurse consultant, you'll team up with attorneys to review specific cases. Sometimes you'll get to know the plaintiff or defendant, but often you'll just be working behind the scenes, helping attorneys understand medical records and facts.

Teamwork vs. Competition: A Quick Story

Here's something you might recognize: Medicine is all about teamwork. For example, during a code blue in a hospital, nurses and doctors work side-by-side—every second counts, and everyone's focused on saving a life. Now, contrast that with Law. Picture a courtroom: it's the plaintiff's team against the defense, each side trying to prove their version of what happened during that same code blue. The case is literally named after this conflict—"Plaintiff Name v. Defendant Name." One side wins, and one side loses.

Your job as an LNC is to work with the attorney to get the best possible outcome for your client, whether they're the plaintiff or the defendant.

Communication: What You Need to Know (and Ask!)

In Medicine, the health care team can be big—sometimes dozens of people for a single patient. They communicate constantly, in writing and out loud, keeping everyone in the loop about the patient's care. In Law, teams are often much smaller. Sometimes it's just an attorney and their secretary. Other attorneys work with partners, associates, paralegals, legal nurse consultants, and other support staff. Some law firms have formal meetings; others swap info quickly, whenever necessary.

Here's a practical tip for you:

- Ask your supervising attorney early on whether they prefer email updates or phone calls and clarify how often they expect to hear from you.
- Find out whether they want detailed reports or just the highlights and follow up if you're not sure. Some attorneys may even have a preferred format; if so, ask them to give you / send a template, if possible.

- Don't be afraid to take the initiative and check in if you haven't heard anything in a while.

Figuring out the attorney's preferences up front will help you communicate like a pro.

Contemporaneous vs. Retrospective—What Does That Mean?

Here's some jargon you'll run into. In Medicine, everything happens in real time. That's what "contemporaneous" means: you treat the patient and document things as they happen—like recording vital signs or giving medication right when it's needed.

Law, by contrast, is "retrospective," which simply means looking back at what happened. Attorneys already know the outcome (for example, whether a patient had a good recovery or suffered harm), and then they work backward to figure out if the medical care met the standards. As an LNC, you'll have the benefit of hindsight, but you'll need to review records by imagining what the providers knew at the time.

A Little Drama—and What "Depositions" Are

Medicine is dramatic in real life—think about the birth of a baby, a life-saving surgery, or a patient's death. Law has its own drama, but it's more like a stage play. Attorneys set up depositions and trials to influence witnesses or sway the jury's opinion. "Depositions" are formal interviews where witnesses answer questions under oath as part of the discovery phase of a legal case.

Here's how you can help: as a legal nurse consultant, you might prepare witnesses and experts, explaining the dramatic moments of the legal process—like what to expect in a deposition or trial, and how to present themselves confidently.

Bridging the Gap

Understanding these differences will help you work smarter as a legal nurse consultant. You'll see how attorneys operate, make your expertise shine, and feel more prepared to handle whatever comes your way.

Don't forget: ask questions, stay proactive, and use your medical knowledge to clarify the facts. That's how you'll bridge the gap between Medicine and Law—and become truly indispensable.

Medical Malpractice Glossary — Explained Conversationally

A Friendly, Practical Guide to Legal Terms for Everyone

Are you new to medical malpractice law or just feeling overwhelmed by all the legal jargon? This guide is here to help! Instead of dry definitions, you'll find clear explanations and real-world examples to make these terms easy and approachable. Let's walk through some of the key phrases and abbreviations you'll encounter, so you can navigate medical malpractice cases with confidence.

Key Legal Terms in Medical Malpractice

Matter

A matter is a case in a lawsuit. Examples: Smith v. Jones and Morgan v. North American Hospital are both matters.

Count

In the legal world—especially in medical malpractice—a Count is a section within a Complaint (the document that starts a lawsuit) that outlines a specific act of alleged negligence by an individual or entity. Each count tells the story of what one person or organization supposedly did wrong. Example: Imagine a patient sues a hospital, claiming that both Dr. Smith and Nurse Lee contributed to their injury. The Complaint would have two counts: one for Dr. Smith's alleged mistake and one for Nurse Lee's. If the hospital itself is also accused, that's another count.

Cause of Action

A Cause of Action is a legal term that describes the reason for the lawsuit—the specific set of facts that gives the plaintiff (the person suing) the right to seek a legal remedy.

Direct Comparison: "Count" and "Cause of Action" often mean the same thing, but the preferred term changes from state to state. Whatever the label, both describe separate claims of negligence within the lawsuit.

Requests

A Request in medical malpractice law is usually a formal demand for information or documents, such as asking the other party to provide medical records. Example: The patient's attorney asks the hospital for all records related to the surgery. The hospital can either agree and send the records, or object, which may lead the lawyer to ask the judge to step in.

Claimant

A Claimant is the person or party making a claim—usually the patient who believes they were harmed. Example: In some states, you're called a "claimant" before you officially file a lawsuit. Once you file, you become the "plaintiff."

Consortium

Consortium refers to the rights of married partners, like companionship and affection. If an injury affects these, the uninjured spouse can file for "loss of consortium." Example: A husband severely injured by malpractice can no longer share the same relationship with his wife. The wife may claim "loss of consortium" as part of the lawsuit.

Certified

The term Certified can mean two things in medical malpractice cases:

- Certified Mail: Sending important legal documents via certified mail means the sender gets a dated receipt as proof that the documents were delivered. Example: A hospital mails a copy of medical records to a patient's attorney using certified mail, ensuring there's a record of delivery.
- Certified Copy: This means a true, exact copy of the original document, often with a statement attesting to its completeness and accuracy. Example: A medical records supervisor provides a certified copy of the patient's chart, confirming it matches the original medical records.

Demand

A Demand is when the plaintiff formally asks the defendant for compensation. Example: The patient's attorney sends a demand letter to the doctor's insurance company, asking for $250,000 to settle the case.

Personal Representative

A Personal Representative is someone (often a spouse or adult child) appointed to handle the estate of someone who has died—and to file lawsuits on their behalf. Example: If a patient dies because of alleged malpractice, their spouse can act as the personal representative and file a claim.

Wrongful Death

A Wrongful Death claim argues that the patient died because of a healthcare provider's negligence. The family's personal representative files this claim to seek compensation for lost earnings and emotional support. Example: A son files a wrongful death claim after his mother dies due to a medication error in a nursing home.

Trial Orders

A Trial Order is a court document that sets important deadlines and the trial date for the case. Example: The judge issues a trial order stating the case will go to trial on 06/10/2026, and that all evidence must be exchanged and depositions completed by 01/10/2025.

Notice

A Notice is a written communication informing someone about an important step in the case, like an intent to sue or scheduling a deposition. Example: In some states, before filing a lawsuit, the patient must send a notice to the doctor explaining they intend to sue for malpractice.

Video Deposition

A Video Deposition is testimony recorded on video, often when a witness might not be able to attend the trial. Example: A patient who is gravely ill gives a video deposition so the jury can see their condition, even if they cannot appear in court.

Standards of Care

Standards of Care are the generally accepted rules or guidelines that medical professionals are expected to follow in given situations. Example: If a hospital policy requires nurses to check vital signs every hour but a nurse skips a check, this could be considered a failure to meet the standard of care.

Statute of Limitations

The Statute of Limitations is the deadline for filing a lawsuit. Example: If your state gives you two years to file a medical malpractice claim, you must file within two years from the date the alleged error happened.

Statements: Sworn, Unsworn, and Affidavits

These are all ways of making a statement about what happened, but there are important differences:

- Sworn Statement: Made under oath—can be used in court.
- Unsworn Statement: Not made under oath—not used as evidence.

- Affidavit: A written, sworn statement used as evidence.

Example: A nurse gives a sworn statement about her actions during surgery, while a patient may submit an affidavit describing their experience.

Common Abbreviations in Medical Malpractice Cases

Legal Parties

- D. — Defendant: The person or organization being sued. Example: Dr. Jones is the defendant accused of making a mistake.
- PL — Plaintiff: The person who starts the lawsuit. Example: The patient claiming harm is the plaintiff.
- OC — Opposing Counsel: The lawyer for the other side. Example: If you're suing a hospital, their lawyer is the opposing counsel.
- RC — Records Custodian: The person responsible for keeping official records. Example: The hospital's RC certifies that the medical records are complete and accurate.

Documents and Procedures

- Meds or The Meds — Medical Records: Documents showing the care provided. Example: Lawyers review the meds to see what treatment a patient received.
- RFP / RTP / RPD — Request for Production / Request to Produce / Request for Production of Documents: Example: The plaintiff sends an RFP asking the hospital to provide all emails about the surgery.
- PD — Pre-Deposition: A meeting to prepare a witness before their official deposition. Example: The attorney meets with the nurse before her deposition to discuss what to expect.
- Stip — Stipulation: An agreement between both sides on certain facts, so they don't need to argue about them in court. Example: Both sides agree that certain medical photos are authentic and don't need further proof.

Case Milestones

- SOL — Statute of Limitations: The filing deadline for a lawsuit. Example: In a medical malpractice case, the SOL might be two years from the incident.
- DOI — Date of Incident: The day the alleged malpractice happened. Example: The DOI is the day surgery went wrong.

Legal Symbols

- π (Pi): The Greek letter Pi symbolizes the plaintiff in legal documents. Typewritten as π, it may also appear as handwritten versions resembling II or ∏.

Example: In a case caption, you might see "π v. Δ," indicating plaintiff versus defendant.

- Δ (Delta): The Greek letter Delta represents the defendant. A handwritten triangle is commonly used as shorthand for defendant. Example: "π v. Δ, No. 22-101" refers to a plaintiff suing a defendant in case number 22-101.
- § (Section symbol): Known as the "double S," this symbol refers to a section of a document, such as statutes or legal codes. Example: "§ 12" means section 12 of a statute. In a citation, you might see "Cal. Civ. Code § 51."
- §§ (Sections symbol): Doubling the section symbol means "sections." Example: "§§ 12-15" refers to sections 12 through 15.
- ¶ (Pilcrow): Known as the paragraph symbol, it identifies a specific paragraph in legal citations. Example: "¶ 4" points to paragraph 4 of a legal document.
- & (Ampersand): Commonly used as the "and" sign, its technical name is ampersand. Law firms often use it in their company names and legal shorthand. Example: Jones Jones & Jones is a typical firm name, using the ampersand to link partners.

Conclusion

Getting comfortable with these terms makes legal documents much less intimidating. If you come across a word or abbreviation you don't understand, don't hesitate to ask for clarification. The best glossaries—like this one—give you straightforward, practical definitions and real-life examples to help you feel at home with the language of medical malpractice law.

It's a Party!

A Practical Guide to Parties in Legal Cases

It's a party! Unfortunately, it's not the kind of party in which you whoop it up with your friends. In legal terms, a Party is a person or entity involved in a lawsuit. I'm sure you know that there are two kinds of parties—plaintiffs and defendants. But if you're a new legal nurse consultant, do you know the variations in parties and how they're styled in court documents?

In medical malpractice, the patient is the plaintiff, the person filing the suit. But in some situations, that's not the case. For example, when the injured patient is a child, the parent(s) can sue on behalf of the child. In that situation, the plaintiffs are styled as in this example: Leroy Samuels and Jennifer Litgow, as parents and natural guardians of Leroy Samuels, Jr.

When the patient is married and is injured in such a way that it results in loss of consortium (which refers to the loss of companionship and other benefits of a family relationship), the plaintiffs include both partners. In that case, the plaintiffs are styled as in this example: Robert C. Baker and David L. Baker, his husband.

When the injured patient dies, a legally appointed personal representative (a person appointed by the court to manage the estate of someone who has died) or executor is listed as the plaintiff as seen in this example: Jackson LeBeau, as Personal Representative of the estate of Lisa LeBeau, deceased.

In some states, minor children can be named as plaintiffs when their injured parent dies as a result of alleged medical malpractice. In such situations, they would be listed as seen in this example: Jackson LeBeau, as Personal Representative of the estate of Lisa LeBeau, deceased, and on behalf of Justin LeBeau, Kaylee LeBeau, and Michelle LeBeau, the surviving minor children of Lisa LeBeau.

What about defendants? Plaintiffs can sue individual or multiple practitioners, organizations, and corporate entities. Here's an example of defendants in a medical malpractice case involving a newborn injured at birth: Northeast General Hospital, L.P. d/b/a Northeast General Hospital, Lars Medival, MD, Woman's OB/GYN Services of Newton P.A., Leslie Stimpson, MD, Leslie Stimpson, MD, P.A. d/b/a The Meadows OB/GYN, Sara Brothers, ARNP, Casey Caswell, RN, and Newton Radiology, L.C. As you can see, the defendants in this lawsuit include several individuals, several organizations, and the corporate entities of the organizations.

Of course, the exact wording of court documents can vary from state to state.

Summary of Key Points

- Plaintiffs can include individuals, parents on behalf of children, spouses, personal representatives, and minor children depending on the circumstances.
- Defendants may be individual practitioners, organizations, or corporate entities, and sometimes multiple entities from different organizations are named.
- Legal terms such as "loss of consortium" (loss of companionship and relationship benefits) and "personal representative" (appointed to manage a deceased person's estate) are important to understand.
- Always check your state's specific requirements for how parties are styled in court documents.

Understanding Key Legal Terms in Medical Malpractice Cases

A Practical Guide for Legal Nurse Consultants

Legal nurse consultants (LNCs) play an essential role in bridging medical knowledge and the legal process, especially in medical malpractice cases. Understanding fundamental legal terms—such as order, stipulation, and petition—enables LNCs to communicate more effectively with attorneys and navigate case documentation with confidence.

Let's Start with Orders

An order is a directive issued by an authority figure. While medical professionals are familiar with medical orders written by physicians or advanced practice nurses, in the legal setting, orders come exclusively from the presiding judge.

Legal orders are written or verbal commands from a judge, expressing decisions about objections, trial procedures, or rulings on complex issues. Example: During a trial, if an attorney objects to certain evidence, the judge might issue an order either sustaining or overruling that objection. Case Study: In a medical malpractice case, the judge may issue an order requiring the hospital to produce specific patient records within a set timeframe. This ensures both parties have fair access to critical information.

Next, Let's Discuss Stipulations

A stipulation is an agreement between the attorneys representing the parties in a case. Unlike orders, stipulations originate with the attorneys—not the judge—and are often used to streamline proceedings.

Attorneys may stipulate to facts or evidence, such as the amount of lost wages or the admissibility of medical records. Strategic considerations: Attorneys may choose not to stipulate to certain points—like expert credentials—so that those details are presented to the jury. Example: In a medical malpractice case, both sides agree that the provider's medical records can be admitted without the records custodian appearing in court. Hypothetical Scenario: Suppose the plaintiff and defendant attorneys stipulate that the patient's surgery date is accurate, allowing them to focus on disputed facts rather than spend court time proving this detail.

Finally, Let's Look at Petitions

The term petition can refer to different things depending on the context.

- Everyday (Public) petitions: These are requests for support on issues—typically seen online or in public places—where individuals collect signatures to influence organizations or laws.

Transitioning to the legal realm, it's important to understand that a legal petition has a distinct meaning.

- Legal petitions: In medical malpractice cases, a petition is a formal written request submitted to the court by attorneys, usually seeking judicial intervention or a court order. Examples:
    - Requesting an extension of the statute of limitations for filing a lawsuit.
    - Asking for a continuance (postponement) of a hearing.
    - Seeking dismissal of the case for procedural reasons.

Hypothetical Scenario: In North Carolina, a plaintiff's attorney files a petition to extend the statute of limitations by 120 days before the deadline passes, providing the client more time to gather evidence.

Note: In some states, the initial complaint filed in a lawsuit is referred to as a petition.

Conclusion: Relevance for Legal Nurse Consultants

Orders, stipulations, and petitions are everyday occurrences in medical malpractice litigation. By understanding these terms and their practical uses, LNCs are better equipped to interpret case documents, discuss legal processes with attorneys, and contribute valuable expertise to the legal team.

Clarifying Hearsay and Testimony

A Guide for Legal Nurse Consultants

Understanding the difference between hearsay and testimony is essential for legal nurse consultants (LNCs), especially when reviewing medical-legal cases. It's common for new LNCs to wonder if patient or family statements that differ from medical records are considered hearsay. In legal practice, when a person shares their version of events during a deposition or trial, it is considered testimony—a valid form of evidence, just like the medical records themselves. But what exactly is hearsay, and how does it affect court proceedings?

Definition and Legal Application of Hearsay

Hearsay refers to an out-of-court statement offered to prove the truth of the matter asserted, typically made by someone other than the witness testifying. For example, imagine a nursing home case where a sister wants to testify that her now-deceased brother told her he saw a nursing assistant hit their mother. Because the brother—not the sister—witnessed the event, and the sister is only repeating what he said, the court would classify this as hearsay. In contrast, if the sister herself witnessed the incident and testified about what she saw, that would be direct testimony—not hearsay.

Why Hearsay Is Generally Inadmissible—and Its Exceptions

Hearsay is usually inadmissible in court because it prevents all parties from questioning the person who originally made the statement. The legal system requires that witnesses be available for cross-examination—where attorneys can assess their credibility and accuracy under oath. In the nursing home scenario, the deceased brother cannot take an oath, provide testimony, or answer questions on cross-examination, making it impossible for the parties to evaluate the reliability of his account.

However, there are exceptions to this rule. If the brother had given a sworn deposition before he passed away, and made a statement about the incident, his testimony would be admissible because all parties would have had the opportunity to question him. This exception exists because the deposition allows for cross-examination and a fair evaluation of the witness's credibility.

Case Scenario: Nursing Home Example

To illustrate, consider the nursing home case described above. If the sister testifies about what her brother told her, that's hearsay and is typically excluded. If she testifies about what she personally observed, that's direct testimony and is admissible. If the brother's statement was recorded during a deposition, it may also be allowed in court.

Bridging Evidence Types: Importance in Case Review

Distinguishing between hearsay and testimony is crucial when reviewing cases. This helps LNCs understand which evidence may be presented in court and which may be excluded, ensuring that the case evaluation is thorough and legally sound.

Reliability of Medical Records vs. Testimony

Sometimes, medical records may seem more reliable than the testimony of plaintiffs or their families. For instance, if an alleged incident occurred, but there are no physical marks or injuries documented in the medical records, and the family did not report the incident to nursing home administration or state authorities, it may indicate that the family's version of events is less accurate than what is reflected in the records.

Role of LNCs in Identifying Discrepancies

When reviewing cases for merit, it is the LNC's responsibility to identify and highlight discrepancies between witness statements and the medical records. Attorneys then decide whether these differences will impact their decision to pursue the case.

Applying Case-Based Examples to Other Legal Concepts

As you continue to learn about legal principles, using real-world scenarios like the nursing home example can help clarify other concepts relevant to legal nurse consulting. This approach not only deepens understanding but also strengthens your ability to provide valuable insights during case reviews.

Understanding Law Firm Roles: An Informational Guide for LNCs

Clarifying Key Positions, Responsibilities, and the Distinct Contributions of Paralegals and Legal Nurse Consultants

For legal nurse consultants (LNCs) and law firm staff, understanding the structure and roles within a law firm is essential for effective collaboration and workflow. This guide provides a consolidated overview of common law firm positions, grouped and presented with clear definitions, core responsibilities, and practical examples. It also offers a direct comparison between paralegals and LNCs to highlight their unique contributions to the legal team.

Partners

Definition: Senior attorneys who own and share profits (equity partners) or have elevated status within (non-equity partners) the firm. Main Duties: Oversee firm management, participate in major decisions, and may handle complex cases or attend trials. Example: An equity partner leads trial strategy and sits on the firm's management committee.

Associates

Definition: Attorneys employed by the firm who are not partners. Main Duties: Work on assigned cases, conduct legal research, prepare pleadings and discovery requests, attend hearings, depose witnesses, and prepare for trial. Example: An associate drafts a motion for summary judgment and argues it in court.

Accountants/Bookkeepers

Definition: Financial professionals managing the firm's fiscal operations. Main Duties: Pay bills, generate invoices, monitor cash flow, and process payroll. Example: An accountant ensures timely payment of expert witness fees to avoid case delays.

Administrators/Office Managers

Definition: Staff responsible for business operations, human resources, and facility management. Main Duties: Coordinate employee benefits, manage recruiting and onboarding, handle HR and facilities issues. Example: An office manager oversees the recruitment and onboarding of new paralegal staff.

Clerks

Definition: Support staff performing a range of clerical and case-related tasks.

- File Clerks: Organize and maintain legal documents to ensure access and prevent loss. Example: Files deposition transcripts for future reference.
- Law Clerks: Typically, law students, assist attorneys with legal research and draft memoranda. Example: A law clerk drafts a memo on recent changes in medical malpractice law.
- Subpoena Clerks: Draft, file, and track subpoenas to obtain records for cases. Example: Monitors the status of subpoenas for medical records in an active case.

Information Management

Definition: IT specialists responsible for supporting the firm's technology infrastructure. Main Duties: Manage computer hardware and software, ensure data security, and provide user support. Example: Troubleshoot network connectivity issues before an electronic court filing deadline.

Legal Assistants

Definition: Administrative professionals (formerly called legal secretaries) supporting attorneys with routine and specialized tasks. Main Duties: Schedule appointments, review mail, type legal documents, answer calls, maintain files, manage calendars, and sometimes perform paralegal tasks. Example: Prepares a draft client letter for attorney review and approval.

Paralegals

Definition: Professionals assisting attorneys with substantive legal work under attorney supervision. Main Duties: Conduct legal research, draft motions and pleadings, prepare discovery documents, and assist with deposition and trial preparation. Example: Summarizes deposition testimony and drafts interrogatory responses for attorney review.

Legal Nurse Consultants (LNCs)/Nurse Paralegals

Definition: RNs with legal training who support attorneys by focusing on the medical aspects of cases. Main Duties: Review and analyze medical records, advise attorneys on medical issues, locate medical experts, conduct medical research, interview fact witnesses, and assist with medical aspects of deposition and trial prep. Example: Identifies discrepancies in a patient's chart that are critical to a malpractice claim.

Comparison: Paralegals vs. Legal Nurse Consultants

Summary: While both roles support attorneys, paralegals focus on legal research and documentation, whereas LNCs specialize in interpreting medical information and advising on clinical aspects relevant to legal cases.

Office Services

Definition: Staff handling high-volume document reproduction and distribution. Main Duties: Copy, scan, and distribute mail, medical records, and legal documents; manage internal office deliveries. Example: Scans thousands of pages of records for digital use in litigation.

Receptionist

Definition: Front-desk staff managing client interactions and communications. Main Duties: Answer and forward calls, sort mail, greet visitors, coordinate conference rooms, and perform administrative tasks. Example: Welcomes a client and directs them to the appropriate conference room for a deposition.

Typist/Word Processor

Definition: Professionals dedicated to transcribing dictation and typing legal documents. Main Duties: Transcribe attorney dictation, produce formal correspondence, and format legal briefs. Example: Transcribes dictated notes into a formal appellate brief.

Conclusion

Understanding each law firm role, their duties, and how they interact is critical for efficient teamwork and case management. Recognizing the distinct contributions of paralegals and legal nurse consultants ensures that both legal and medical expertise are fully leveraged for the best outcomes in legal practice.

Understanding Court Documents: A Simple Guide

Breaking Down Legal Terms and Processes for Everyone

Navigating the world of court documents can be confusing, especially if you don't have a legal background. This guide will walk you through the different types of court documents, explain what each one does in plain English, and show you how they fit together in a real court case. We'll use easy-to-understand language and real-world examples so you can follow along with confidence.

Pleadings: Starting the Legal Conversation

The first step in almost any court case is filing documents called pleadings. You can think of pleadings as the official paperwork that starts and shapes the lawsuit. Here's what you might see:

- Complaint: This is the document that kicks off the case. It's filed by the person (the plaintiff) who is making the claim, and it lists their reasons and accusations. For example, if someone believes a hospital made a mistake that caused harm, the complaint explains what happened and why the hospital is responsible.
- Answer: The person or group being sued (the defendant) files this document. It's their official response to the complaint, where they agree, disagree, or add more details. Imagine the hospital replies by saying they followed all proper procedures, or that the events didn't happen as described.
- Reply: Sometimes, after the defendant responds, the plaintiff needs to reply again—especially if the defendant mentioned something new. This document lets the plaintiff address any fresh issues.

- Counterclaims, Cross-claims, and Amended Pleadings: These are ways for parties to add new complaints, respond to each other, or update information as the case moves forward. For example, if the hospital thinks someone else is responsible, they might file a cross-claim against another doctor involved in the case.

Once the initial pleadings are filed and everyone knows the main issues, both sides need to gather facts and evidence to support their arguments. This brings us to the next phase: discovery.

Discovery Documents: Gathering Information

Discovery is the process where both sides exchange information and collect evidence. The goal is to make sure there are no surprises at trial—everyone has a fair chance to see the facts. Here are the most common discovery documents:

- Interrogatories: These are written questions that one side sends to the other. The person who receives them must answer honestly and under oath. Example: "List every doctor who treated the patient during their hospital stay."
- Requests for Production: This is a formal request for documents or physical evidence. One side asks the other to hand over specific items that might help prove their case. Example: Asking the hospital for all medical records, X-rays, or insurance policies related to the patient.
- Depositions: These are interviews where lawyers ask witnesses questions, and everything is recorded word-for-word. The person answering is under oath, just like in court. Example: A nurse might be asked to describe what happened during a patient's surgery.

After all the evidence is gathered, both sides may want the judge to make decisions before a trial starts. This is where motions come in.

Motions: Asking the Judge to Decide

A motion is simply a formal request for the judge to make a ruling on a specific issue. Here are a few common types, explained in everyday terms:

- Motion in Limine: This is a request made before the trial to keep certain information or evidence out of the jury's sight. In plain language: One side is asking the judge to prevent certain evidence from being shown to the jury before the trial begins. For example, they may want to block a witness from discussing sensitive medical details they think are unfairly damaging.
- Motion to Dismiss (with or without prejudice): This asks the judge to end the case early for a legal reason. With prejudice means the case is permanently closed

and can't be brought up again. Without prejudice means the plaintiff can try again later, maybe after fixing a problem with their paperwork. Example: If a lawsuit is missing key details, the defendant might ask the judge to dismiss it until those are fixed.

- Motion for Summary Judgment: This requests that the judge decide the case right away, without a trial, because there's no disagreement about the important facts. For example, if both sides agree on what happened but disagree on the law, the judge might rule without a jury trial.

Now that you know the main types of court documents, let's look at a real-world example to see how all these pieces fit together.

Sample Discovery Document Explained

Imagine you're reading a court document called a "Request for Production." This is a discovery document where one side asks the other for specific evidence. Here's how to understand the parts of a sample document:

- Jurisdiction and Venue: This information is usually at the top and tells you which court is handling the case and where it's happening. Example: "Circuit Court, Palm Beach County, FL" means the case is being heard in a local Florida court, not a federal one. This lets everyone know the rules and location for the case.
- Case Number: Each case gets a unique number, often including the year and month it was filed. This helps everyone track the case and find documents. Example: "62 2025-CA 000458 XX17 (06)" tells you the case was filed in June 2025.
- Parties: This section lists everyone involved in the lawsuit. You'll see names like the plaintiff (the person bringing the case) and the defendants (the people or companies being sued). In our sample, the plaintiff is a wife acting for her late husband, and the defendants include a hospital, several doctors, and their business associations.
- Style or Caption: The "style" or "caption" is the heading that includes the jurisdiction, case number, and parties. Every court document needs this at the top.
- Title and Presenting Party: Next, you'll see the name of the document and who is making the request. Example: Dr. Wolske and his professional association are asking Jupiter City Hospital for documents.
- Body: This is where the specific requests or demands are listed. In our example, the hospital is being asked to supply medical records, X-ray films, and copies of their insurance policies.

- Certificate of Service: This section confirms that copies of the document have been sent to everyone involved, usually by mail. Example: A statement says that all attorneys received a copy on a certain date.
- Attorney Information: The document lists the law firm, address, phone numbers, and the lawyer's name and bar number.
- Service List: This final list shows which attorneys officially got the document, ensuring no one is left out.
- To obtain the Sample Request for Production[6], refer to the footnote below.

By understanding these parts, you can see how each court document fits into the larger legal process. From the first complaint to final motions, each step is designed to keep the process fair and organized, making sure everyone knows what's happening and has a chance to tell their side.

Bringing It All Together

Court cases might seem overwhelming, but they follow a set order: pleadings start the process, discovery gathers the facts, and motions help shape the trial. By breaking down legal terms and using real examples, anyone can learn to read and understand court documents with confidence. If you ever need to review a legal paper, remember to look for the basics—who's involved, what's being asked, and how the process moves forward.

Understanding Four Key Legal Deadlines: A Guide for LNCs

Making Legal Timing Clear and Practical for Nurse Professionals

Let's face it—nurses are experts at juggling deadlines. You're always keeping track of when to assess patients, give medications, or start treatments, because being on time can make all the difference for patient care. But did you know attorneys have their own set of critical deadlines too? Missing one could mean the difference between winning and losing a case. If you're a legal nurse consultant (LNC), it's super important to know what these deadlines are and how they affect your work. So, let's break down four main

[6] Sample Request for Production. https://tinyurl.com/mk8vntdh (accessed December 2025).

types of legal deadlines, explain some key terms, and share practical examples—so you'll feel confident handling these issues in your role.

1. Statute of Limitations

The statute of limitations is a law that sets a deadline for filing a lawsuit after something like an injury occurs. Miss this deadline, and the chance to sue is usually gone for good.

For LNCs, knowing the statute of limitations helps you figure out if a claim is still viable, especially when you're looking at older medical records or consulting on possible cases.

For example, many states say you have two years from the date of injury to file a medical malpractice claim. If the injury isn't discovered immediately, some states allow an extra year or two from the date it's found. Timeframes for kids can stretch until their 18th birthday, depending on where you are.

But wait, there's another deadline to know about—the statute of repose. It's like the ultimate cutoff for some claims.

2. Statute of Repose

The statute of repose is a stricter law that sets a final deadline for filing a claim, no matter when the injury was discovered. Unlike the statute of limitations, this one doesn't pause ("toll") if the injury isn't apparent. Once the deadline passes, that's it—even if you just found out about the problem.

Let's look at Florida, where both statutes are in play for medical malpractice. Adults generally have two years from the incident or when the injury's discovered, but never more than three to five years from the actual date of the incident, depending on the state stature. For instance, if an instrument was left in a patient during surgery on July 3, 2021, and found on July 2, 2025, the patient can still file a claim—just under the four-year mark. But if it's found on July 4, 2025, the four-year deadline has passed. If there was fraud or a cover-up, Florida might extend the window by two more years, for a maximum of six years.

3. Discovery Deadlines

So, what's a discovery deadline? During a lawsuit, both sides get a chance to gather facts, ask questions, and swap documents. Discovery deadlines are basically the time limits for getting all that done. Think of it as the "window" you must respond to requests for records or answer interrogatories (written questions).

Why should LNCs care? Well, you might be asked to help keep track of these deadlines—making sure the attorney gets all the medical records and your expert analysis on time. Miss a discovery deadline and you could lose out on using important evidence.

Here's a simple example: The law firm might have 30 days to answer interrogatories from the other side, or 45 days to hand over medical records. But keep in mind, every state sets its own deadlines, so you'll want to check the rules wherever your case is.

Once discovery wraps up, it's time to focus on trial deadlines as the case moves closer to court.

4. Trial Deadlines

Trial deadlines are different—they're set by the judge as the case heads to trial. These are the dates when certain tasks must be finished, like submitting a pretrial plan or setting up mediation.

For LNCs, this means helping prepare expert reports, organizing records, or making sure everything is ready to be submitted by each deadline. Staying organized and ahead of these dates keeps the legal team moving forward.

Picture this: If the trial is scheduled for January 28, 2027, you might need to help get the pretrial plan by September 24, 2026, attend mediation by October 24, 2026, and hire and identify witnesses to disclose them by November 15, 2026. It's all about keeping track of what's due and when.

Why Deadlines Matter—and Your Role as an LNC

If legal deadlines get missed, the case could be thrown out, or the attorney might even face legal malpractice charges. That's why, as an LNC, you could be responsible for calculating discovery and other key deadlines—using online calculators can make this easier. Whether you're working in-house, independently, or as an expert, staying clear about your deadlines and communicating with your legal team is vital to delivering the best results for clients.

Understanding Pre-Litigation Requirements in Medical Malpractice Cases

A Guide for Legal Nurse Consultants

For legal nurse consultants, navigating the legal landscape of medical malpractice claims requires more than understanding the courtroom process. Pre-litigation requirements—steps mandated by law before a formal lawsuit is filed—play a crucial role in shaping the direction and outcome of these cases. Recognizing and comprehending these prerequisites is essential for providing effective support to attorneys and healthcare professionals alike.

Semantics and Key Terms

In the context of pre-litigation, terminology often shifts depending on the stage of the process. The individual initiating a claim is typically called the Claimant during pre-litigation and referred to as the Plaintiff once litigation begins. Those facing a potential lawsuit are known as Prospective Defendants before a suit is filed, and simply Defendants after. In everyday conversation, these terms may be used interchangeably, but understanding the distinctions helps clarify roles during each phase.

Expert Affidavit / Certificate of Merit

One of the most common pre-litigation requirements is the Expert Affidavit or Certificate of Merit. This is a formal statement, usually prepared by a qualified expert, certifying that the facts of the case have been reviewed and that the proposed lawsuit has merit. In many states, the Claimant must secure this affidavit before proceeding, while in others, the Plaintiff's attorney files it alongside the initial Complaint. This requirement helps prevent frivolous claims and ensures that the case is grounded in professional medical judgment.

Once the expert affidavit is addressed, another important requirement in many states is the Notice of Intent (NOI).

Notice of Intent (NOI)

The Notice of Intent serves as formal notification to Prospective Defendants that a medical malpractice claim may be filed. Its purpose is to allow parties an opportunity to resolve the matter outside of court and to set the stage for further investigation and negotiation. States vary in their requirements for the NOI. For example, Florida law stipulates that the NOI must be accompanied by an expert affidavit, a list of healthcare providers who treated the Claimant within two years of the alleged negligence, and an authorization for Prospective Defendants to obtain relevant medical records.

After filing the NOI, the process moves into the investigation period, a critical phase for both legal nurse consultants and attorneys.

Practical Scenario for Legal Nurse Consultants: Florida Investigation Period

To illustrate the impact of these requirements, consider the role of a legal nurse consultant in Florida during the presuit investigation period. After the NOI is submitted, the Prospective Defendant has 90 days to investigate the claim and determine liability. During this time, legal nurse consultants often assist attorneys by organizing and analyzing medical records, identifying relevant providers, and preparing documents for informal presuit discovery. This discovery can include written questions (interrogatories), requests for document production, and unsworn statements—like depositions, but not under oath and inadmissible at trial. By ensuring that all pertinent information is gathered efficiently, legal nurse consultants help facilitate a thorough and timely investigation.

Investigation Period

The Investigation Period refers to the defined timeframe in which Prospective Defendants review the claim, collect evidence, and decide on a response. For example, Florida mandates a 90-day investigation after the NOI is received. In contrast, the discovery phase during actual litigation is much longer and more formal, often lasting years. Legal nurse consultants play a key role during investigation by supporting attorneys in record review, timeline construction, and communication with medical experts.

Beyond investigation, states may require additional steps before a case proceeds to litigation.

Other State-Specific Requirements

Several states have unique pre-litigation procedures. In Idaho, Claimants must file a specific form and request pre-litigation hearings. Utah, along with over 15 other states, requires cases to be reviewed by pre-litigation panels composed of attorneys, physicians, and laypersons, who evaluate the merit of the claim. Additionally, more than half the states, including South Carolina, mandate alternative dispute resolution measures such as mediation or settlement conferences to encourage early resolution.

Conclusion

For legal nurse consultants, understanding the nuances of pre-litigation requirements is vital to their role in medical malpractice cases. These procedural elements not only shape the early trajectory of a claim but also determine how consultants can best support attorneys and clients. Staying informed about state-specific rules, such as those outlined by the National Conference of State Legislatures, ensures that legal nurse consultants remain valuable contributors throughout the process.

Two Sides to Every Story: Justice, Truth, and Medical Malpractice

Contrasting Perspectives and the Challenge of Fairness

I once watched a compelling documentary series that explored the story of a man convicted of killing a woman, narrated from the perspective of the defense. As the narrative unfolded, I began to question whether justice had truly been served in this case. The defense's version raised doubts and suggested the possibility of an injustice. Seeking a more complete understanding, I listened to a podcast that examined the same events from the prosecutor's viewpoint. Hearing the prosecutor's arguments provided me with greater insight into the rationale behind the conviction. The stark contrast between these accounts highlighted how the same set of facts can be interpreted in dramatically different ways, depending on the viewpoint.

Just as in the criminal case, medical malpractice lawsuits often hinge on how each side interprets the same set of facts. These cases reveal the complexities of determining fault and the subjective nature of justice when multiple plausible narratives emerge from a single set of circumstances.

Case Description: Arden Trevino's Medical Journey

To illustrate, consider the example of Arden Trevino, a wealthy and prominent businessperson with a history of low back pain. He was undergoing evaluation for his symptoms and had recently received an MRI of his lower back. Eight days after the MRI, Mr. Trevino experienced a severe back spasm while picking up his Sunday newspaper, describing the sensation as if "something snapped" in his lower back. He sought care at Medical Memorial Hospital, where he was seen by his friend, Dr. Huey Johansen, an orthopedic surgeon.

Dr. Johansen ordered a cervical MRI, which was never performed for unclear reasons, and reviewed the recent lumbar MRI showing severe lumbar stenosis at L3-L4 and L4-5. Although Mr. Trevino expressed a desire for surgery, Dr. Johansen recommended trying an epidural steroid injection first. Dr. Garth Hamrick, a pain management anesthesiologist, performed an intralaminar epidural steroid injection at L3-L4 under fluoroscopy a few hours later.

Several hours after the injection, Mr. Trevino noticed scrotal numbness and difficulty urinating. He contacted another friend, Dr. Eddy Cline, a neurologist, who was not on call but came to the hospital, examined Mr. Trevino, and ordered a STAT spinal MRI. Despite multiple attempts, Mr. Trevino could not tolerate the procedure, so Dr. Cline ordered CT scans of the cervical and lumbar spine, which revealed multi-level degenerative changes.

Early the next morning, Dr. Johansen performed surgical decompression of Mr. Trevino's spine. After surgery, Mr. Trevino had numbness in his left foot. A STAT MRI revealed a large posterior disc extrusion at L3-L4 compressing the cauda equina. Mr. Trevino was taken back to surgery for an L3-L4 discectomy. Despite these interventions, he was left with a permanent left foot drop and persistent numbness in the scrotal and buttocks areas.

Plaintiff's Theory: Claims of Negligence

Mr. Trevino filed a lawsuit against Medical Memorial Hospital and Drs. Johansen, Hamrick, and Cline. The plaintiff's theory of the case included several key claims:

- Medical Memorial Hospital was vicariously liable for the actions of the physicians.
- Dr. Johansen failed to monitor the patient adequately intraoperatively and postoperatively, delayed performing lumbar decompression, and performed the surgery negligently when he finally operated.
- Dr. Hamrick did not sufficiently inform Mr. Trevino of the risks associated with epidural steroid injections and performed the injection despite Mr. Trevino's spinal stenosis.
- Dr. Cline should have consulted an anesthesiologist for monitored anesthesia care (MAC) to ensure the MRI could have been completed.

Defense Theory: Counterarguments and Expert Opinions

The defense offered a different interpretation of the events:

- Dr. Johansen maintained that both surgeries were timely and appropriate. His expert suggested that the extruded disc causing the foot drop was a complication triggered by the initial decompressive surgery—an outcome that could not have been foreseen or prevented.

- Dr. Hamrick argued that epidural spinal injections are common treatments for spinal stenosis and produced a signed consent form detailing the risks, which Mr. Trevino had acknowledged.
- Dr. Cline asserted that all feasible steps had been taken to obtain adequate imaging, and that the previous MRI and CT scans provided sufficient information to guide care.
- Medical Memorial Hospital supported the positions taken by the individual defendants.

Verdicts and Outcome

Ultimately, Dr. Johansen and the hospital reached confidential settlements with Mr. Trevino. The case proceeded to trial against Drs. Hamrick and Cline, both of whom received verdicts in their favor. The personal relationships between Mr. Trevino and his physicians were also irreparably affected.

Reflection: Justice, Truth, and the Complexity of Fault

This outcome underscores the profound challenge of determining fault in complex medical cases. Both the plaintiff and defense constructed plausible, evidence-backed narratives from the same set of facts, and the jury's decisions hinged on which version was deemed more convincing. The case illustrates that justice, especially in medical malpractice suits, is rarely straightforward. The truth is often multifaceted, shaped by expert opinions, incomplete information, and the inherent uncertainties of medicine.

For those seeking fairness, this case is a poignant reminder that legal outcomes do not always provide clear answers about what "should" have happened. Instead, they reflect the intricate process by which our system weighs conflicting accounts and expert testimony. Recognizing the limitations and ambiguities inherent in such determinations can foster a deeper appreciation for the complexities of justice, and a more nuanced understanding of how truth is pursued—and sometimes eludes us—in the courtroom.

Understanding Two Defense Strategies

SODDI vs. Empty Chair Defense in Medical Malpractice Cases

Defense attorneys often rely on strategic approaches to shift liability away from their clients. Two notable defenses are the SODDI defense—an acronym for "Some

Other Dude Did It"—and the empty chair defense, each with distinct applications and implications. Both defenses aim to shift blame away from the defendant.

The primary difference between these strategies lies in the nature of the party being blamed and the type of case. The SODDI defense is commonly used in criminal proceedings, where attorneys suggest that an unidentified individual committed the crime. In contrast, the empty chair defense is prevalent in civil litigation, notably medical malpractice, where blame is assigned to a specific but absent physician, nurse, hospital, or organization.

In criminal cases, motives are central to establishing guilt, making the SODDI defense a viable tactic. However, motives do not play a role in medical malpractice litigation, which focuses on negligence and causation rather than intent. Given this distinction, attorneys must employ different strategies to defend their clients in these cases.

The empty chair defense works by highlighting the negligence of an absent party who is not currently named in the lawsuit. This missing party might be a former defendant who settled before trial, a potential defendant omitted due to the statute of limitations, or someone not named for financial or strategic reasons. For example, a plaintiff may choose not to sue an uninsured physician and instead target the hospital, which has greater financial resources.

Throughout the trial, defense attorneys use the empty chair defense by describing the absent party as the true source of the plaintiff's injuries. Expert witnesses may testify about the role the missing defendant played, and the defense can ask for the absent party's name to be included on the verdict slip. A verdict slip is the form the jury uses to record its decisions, including how responsibility is divided among parties. To apportion fault means to decide what percentage of responsibility each party has for the plaintiff's injuries. This allows the jury to assign fault among all relevant parties, even those not present in court. For example, if there are four defendants listed—including one empty chair—and the jury assigns 25% of the fault to the empty chair, the plaintiff's compensation is reduced by that percentage. The person named as the empty chair does not pay anything because they are not officially part of the lawsuit..

Overall, the empty chair defense provides a powerful tool for shifting liability in medical malpractice cases, potentially reducing the damages awarded to plaintiffs.

Understanding Medical Malpractice Defense: What Nurses Need to Know

A Supportive Guide to Legal Terms and Strategies in Healthcare Lawsuits

It's easy for nurses to feel uneasy when they hear about lawsuits involving doctors, hospitals, and nursing staff. There's a common misconception that if a nurse is named alongside physicians and their hospital in a lawsuit, the nurse will be "thrown under the bus." But this fear isn't often realized, and knowing a few legal basics can help ease those concerns.

Legal Terms: Who's Who and What's What

Let's clarify some important terms. A plaintiff is the person who brings a lawsuit—they're the ones claiming harm and seeking compensation. On the other side, defendants are those being sued; this can include nurses, doctors, and hospitals. Occasionally, you'll hear the term conspiracy of silence. This refers to the perception that medical professionals protect each other by not admitting fault, making it harder for plaintiffs to prove their case. Understanding these terms can make the legal landscape less intimidating.

What Is the United Defense Strategy?

So, what really happens during a lawsuit? Instead of pointing fingers, most defendants—including nurses—work together in a united defense. This strategy means all defendants present a shared front, which reduces the risk of a verdict against them. If everyone starts blaming each other, it gives the plaintiff an advantage, almost like admitting someone did something wrong while others ignored it. The United Defense tactic is different than the Empty Chair tactic, in that there is no unnamed party to blame.

Real-World Example: Sticking Together

For instance, imagine a patient sues both a nurse and a doctor after a surgical complication. Both may present a shared defense showing that standard procedures were followed, rather than blaming each other. This united approach often makes it difficult for juries to believe every defendant was negligent and can lead to a verdict in favor of the healthcare team.

What Do the Numbers Say?

The united defense strategy works well in many cases. According to research, between 80% and 90% of jury verdicts in medical malpractice cases favor the defendants. Even more reassuring, nearly 97% of these claims are settled out of court, meaning most never reach a trial.

Encouragement for Nurses: You're Not Alone

Plaintiff attorneys sometimes call the united defense a conspiracy of silence, but both sides use strategies to support their clients. The key takeaway for nurses? If you're ever involved in a lawsuit, it's much more likely that all defendants, including you, will stick together and present a united defense. So next time this topic comes up among your colleagues, you can reassure them: you're not alone, and you won't be thrown under the bus.

Pyramiding / Stacking of Inferences in Legal Practice

A Guide for Legal Nurse Consultants

An inference is a logical conclusion drawn from evidence and reasonable assumptions. In legal contexts, pyramiding or stacking of inferences refers to building one assumption on top of another, where each step relies on the previous inference rather than direct evidence. This approach can undermine the strength of an argument because it increases speculation and decreases reliability.

Case Example: Step-by-Step Analysis

Consider the following scenario: A 62-year-old male patient visits his primary care provider (PCP) and learns that his blood pressure is 200/100. The PCP prescribes a medication for the blood pressure, refers the patient to a specific cardiologist, gives him the name and phone number of the cardiologist, and instructs the patient to return in one week. The patient returns to the PCP's office one week later and learns that his blood pressure is 170/99. The patient has filled the prescription but has not made an appointment with the cardiologist because the patient thought the PCP was going to make it for him. Because of the misunderstanding, the PCP asks his appointment clerk to contact the cardiologist. The clerk obtains an appointment for the patient for the next day due to a cancellation of one of the cardiologist's patients. Unfortunately, the patient dies in his sleep that night. The medical examiner lists the cause of death as cardiac arrhythmia. His wife considers filing a wrongful death or medical malpractice lawsuit against his primary care provider (PCP). Her reasoning involves several inferences:

1. If the PCP had made the cardiologist appointment at the first visit, the patient would have seen the cardiologist before the arrhythmia occurred. Analysis: This assumes the cardiologist had an available appointment before the fatal event. There is no direct evidence supporting this; it is possible no such opening existed.
2. If the patient had seen the cardiologist, the cardiologist would have diagnosed the cardiac arrhythmia. Analysis: This presumes the arrhythmia was present, detectable, and diagnosable at the time of the hypothetical visit. There is no evidence confirming the condition could have been identified during that specific appointment.
3. If the arrhythmia had been diagnosed, the cardiologist could have prevented it. Analysis: This assumes immediate and effective intervention was possible but does not account for the time required for testing, patient cooperation, or the effectiveness of available treatments.
4. If the arrhythmia had been prevented, the patient would still be alive. Analysis: This step assumes that prevention was certain and that no other factors contributed to the patient's death. There is no direct evidence guaranteeing this outcome.

Each inference depends on the truth of the previous one, without direct evidence at each step. This chain of assumptions illustrates how pyramiding of inferences can introduce uncertainty into legal reasoning.

Practical Strategies for Legal Nurse Consultants

- Map Reasoning Steps: Break down the argument into individual steps or links, showing how each conclusion is reached.
- Check for Direct Evidence: For each step, ask: Is there concrete evidence supporting this inference, or is it based on another assumption?
- Document Concerns: Make notes about where evidence is missing or where an inference relies on speculation rather than facts.
- Discuss Alternatives: Bring up other possible explanations or outcomes with the legal team to ensure all perspectives are considered.
- Stay Informed: Research your state's rules on pyramiding of inferences in civil litigation, as some states prohibit this approach.

Conclusion: Importance for LNCs

Recognizing and addressing pyramiding / stacking of inferences is essential for legal nurse consultants. By ensuring that each step in an argument is supported by direct evidence and not simply built on prior assumptions, LNCs help strengthen legal cases and support sound decision-making.

Understanding Legal Case Resolution Methods

A Practical Guide for New Legal Nurse Consultants

As a new legal nurse consultant, it's important to understand the different ways a medically related lawsuit can come to an end. While some cases are resolved in court, there are several other possible outcomes. This article will introduce you to key case resolution methods, define important legal terms, and provide practical examples to help you grasp how these processes work in real-world scenarios.

Summary Judgment: A Case Closed Without Trial

One way a lawsuit can end is through summary judgment. Summary judgment means the judge decides the case based on the facts presented, without a trial. The judge reviews all evidence and determines if there is any genuine dispute that requires a jury's decision. If not, the case can be resolved right then and there. In medical malpractice cases, this outcome often favors the defense, especially if they can show that no malpractice occurred or that any harm suffered was a known complication of a medical procedure. For example, if the defense demonstrates that the plaintiff's injuries were expected side effects of the surgery, the judge may grant summary judgment in favor of the defense, ending the case before it reaches trial.

Settlements: The Most Common Case Outcome

In addition to summary judgment, cases may also end through settlement, which is the most frequent resolution method. A settlement occurs when the plaintiff agrees to close the case in exchange for money from the defense. This approach is often a win for the plaintiff and is usually less expensive for the defendant (or their insurance company) than going through a full trial. For instance, if a plaintiff is willing to settle for $25,000, it's often more practical for the defense to pay the settlement rather than spend $100,000 on a trial, even if the defendants believe they could win.

Dismissal Types: With Prejudice vs. Without Prejudice

When a settlement is reached, the case is typically dismissed with prejudice. Prejudice in this context means that the plaintiff loses the right to bring the same claim against the defendant in the future. In contrast, if a case is dismissed without prejudice, the plaintiff retains the right to refile the lawsuit in the future—for instance, if new evidence emerges related to the dispute. However, defendants rarely agree to dismissals without prejudice, as it leaves the door open for future litigation.

Alternative Dispute Resolution: Mediation and Arbitration

Beyond settlements, alternative dispute resolution (ADR) methods like mediation and arbitration offer other paths to closure. Alternative dispute arbitration refers to ways of resolving disputes outside of the courtroom, with the help of a neutral third party. In mediation, the mediator helps both sides communicate and negotiate but does not have the authority to make a binding decision. The process is often successful in helping parties reach a mutually agreeable solution. For example, a mediator might guide a plaintiff and defense toward compromise in a medical malpractice case, leading to a quicker and less stressful resolution.

Arbitration is another ADR method, but here the arbitrator acts more like a judge. After hearing both sides, the arbitrator makes a final decision about the outcome, which is binding and permanent. Arbitration is typically used when both parties have agreed in advance, often through a contract, to resolve their disputes in this manner.

Trial: The Traditional Path to Resolution

If none of these options work, a case may end by going to trial. During a trial, the plaintiff and defense present their arguments before a jury, which decides the outcome. While some medical malpractice trials result in large awards for plaintiffs, most end in a verdict for the defense. In fact, up to 90% of medical malpractice trial verdicts[7] favor the defense. Even so, it's common for cases to settle at the last minute—right before trial or even during trial—because the defense may worry about the unpredictability of the jury. For example, if jury members appear more interested in witness personalities than the facts, the defense may choose to settle to avoid the risk of an unfavorable verdict.

Conclusion: Why Resolution Methods Matter

Understanding these various case resolution methods—summary judgment, settlements, dismissal types, ADR, and trials—is essential for legal nurse consultants. Being familiar with these terms and processes will help you navigate the legal landscape and support your clients more effectively. Every lawsuit is unique, but knowing the options available can make your work smoother and more informed.

[7] Verdicts. https://pmc.ncbi.nlm.nih.gov/articles/PMC2628515/(accessed January 2026).

The Locality Rule and Standard of Care in Medical Malpractice for LNCs

A Clear Guide to Key Concepts, Historical Context, and Modern Practice

Medical malpractice cases rely on several foundational concepts. The standard of care refers to the level of caution, attention, and judgment that a reasonably competent healthcare professional would exercise under similar circumstances. The locality rule is a legal principle that historically required the standard of care to be determined by the practices of healthcare providers in the same community or locality, rather than nationwide. Access to care means the availability of medical services, specialists, and facilities to patients within a particular community. Understanding these terms is essential for legal nurse consultants (LNCs) as they review and analyze malpractice cases.

History of Locality Rules: Early Practices and Challenges

Originally, the standard of care in medical malpractice was defined by the locality rule. In the past, there were no widely accepted guidelines from professional organizations or standardized education for healthcare providers. As a result, courts relied on community standards to determine whether a provider met the appropriate standard of care. This meant that expert witnesses had to come from the same or a nearby community, which often proved difficult—many experts were reluctant to testify against colleagues they knew personally, and smaller communities had fewer potential experts.

Transition to National Standards: Current Practices and Implications

Currently, most states have shifted away from the strict locality rule, favoring national standards of care. The widespread development of professional guidelines and the regulation of healthcare professions have made it possible to apply a consistent standard across different regions. While the standard of care is now generally recognized as a national benchmark, legal nurse consultants must remember that access to care—the availability of services and resources—can still vary greatly between communities.

For example, consider rural versus urban hospital settings. A rural hospital may only have a mobile MRI unit available one or two days a week, while an urban hospital may offer MRI services 24/7. If a patient at a rural hospital requires an urgent MRI, it is not a deviation from the standard of care if the MRI is unavailable on that particular day, given the community's resources. However, it would be a deviation if the hospital and physician failed to transfer the patient promptly to a facility with MRI capabilities.

Similarly, access to specialists can differ. In rural areas, patients might wait days or weeks to see a cardiologist, whereas urban centers often have multiple specialists available on short notice. The national standard of care requires that healthcare providers act reasonably within the limits of their available resources, not that every hospital offers identical services. Emergency services also vary; some rural hospitals and even many urban hospitals may not have immediate access to trauma surgeons. In those cases, the standard of care is met by stabilizing and transferring patients as needed.

In Contrast: Tennessee's Unique Statute

Despite the national trend, Tennessee maintains a statute closely aligned with the traditional locality rule. In Tennessee, a testifying expert must practice in Tennessee or one of its bordering states—Kentucky, Virginia, North Carolina, Georgia, Alabama, Mississippi, Arkansas, or Missouri—unless there is no other qualified expert available. This requirement persists even though Tennessee courts acknowledge that national and community standards of care are representative of each other. For legal nurse consultants, this means you cannot testify as an expert in Tennessee unless you live in Tennessee or a bordering state, unless an attorney files for—and the court grants—a waiver.

Conclusion: The Ongoing Relevance and Misunderstanding of Locality

While the locality rule has largely faded in importance across the United States, it remains a factor in specific jurisdictions and is often misunderstood. Legal nurse consultants must be aware that although national standards of care prevail, the realities of access to care and the unique statutes of certain states like Tennessee can affect malpractice cases. When reviewing cases, LNCs should carefully consider how community resources, specialist availability, and emergency services shape the standard of care in each scenario.

The Blind Review Process in Radiology Case Evaluation

Accessible Guidelines for Legal Nurse Consultants and Healthcare Legal Professionals

When reviewing medical malpractice cases, it's important for Legal Nurse Consultants (LNCs)—registered nurses with expertise in healthcare and law—to understand the case allegations. This helps them focus on key issues efficiently. However, there is an exception known as a blind review, which means examining case evidence—such as radiology images—without knowledge of the specific allegations or patient outcomes. The goal of a blind review is to promote objectivity and prevent bias in the evaluation process.

Why Blind Reviews Matter in Radiology Cases

Blind reviews are especially valuable in cases involving missed radiology findings, such as undetected cancers on mammograms, fractures on x-rays, or organ injuries on CT or MRI scans. Research shows that radiologists who know what problem to look for often find it immediately, sometimes overlooking other possibilities. For example, a radiologist familiar with a missed diagnosis may focus solely on that area. Blind reviews avoid this bias by ensuring the expert examines the images without any preconceived notions.

A 2010 study published in the American Journal of Radiology demonstrated that radiologists reviewing imaging without knowledge of clinical outcomes were less likely to identify previously missed findings. The study concluded that using radiologists who are "blinded" to case details is more objective when evaluating standard of care in legal matters.

Actionable Steps for Legal Nurse Consultants: Implementing Blind Reviews

- Remove references to case allegations: When communicating with radiology experts, avoid mentioning specific allegations or suspected findings.
- Send only imaging studies initially: Provide the radiologist with the relevant images first, without accompanying medical records or outcome details.
- Request an unbiased opinion: Ask the expert to review the images and report findings—without guidance on what to look for.

- Follow up with additional records: After the expert gives an initial opinion, supply any necessary medical records or case background for further review.
- Confirm attorney preference: Not all attorneys want a blind review, and not every case requires one, so check with legal counsel before proceeding.

Maintaining Objectivity in Legal Proceedings

During depositions, expert radiologists may be asked whether a blind review was performed. If not, opposing attorneys may question the expert's impartiality. By excluding case allegations when sharing information with experts, LNCs help maintain objectivity and strengthen the credibility of the expert's testimony.

The CSI Effect in Medical Malpractice Cases

Legal Terms Explained and Practical Impacts

The CSI Effect describes how popular television shows like "Crime Scene Investigation" have shaped public expectations of evidence in legal cases. While this phenomenon began in criminal law—where jurors now expect to see high-tech forensic proof—it also influences medical malpractice trials, but in unique ways. Understanding these effects is essential for anyone interested in the legal system, especially those unfamiliar with legal terminology.

Key Legal Terms Defined

- Standards of care: This refers to the level of competence and diligence reasonably expected from medical professionals in treating patients. For example, a doctor is expected to act as most other qualified doctors would under similar circumstances.
- Causation: In legal terms, causation means proving that the defendant's actions directly led to the plaintiff's injury. The plaintiff must show that the harm would not have happened without the defendant's conduct.
- Inflammatory: Evidence is considered inflammatory if it is likely to provoke strong emotional reactions from jurors, potentially leading them to form opinions based on emotion rather than facts. For instance, graphic photographs of injuries can sometimes be seen as inflammatory.

First CSI Effect: Juror Desensitization to Demonstrative Evidence

One major impact of the CSI Effect in medical malpractice cases is that jurors have become less affected by demonstrative evidence, such as photographs of injuries. In the past, attorneys might have objected to showing graphic images, arguing they were too inflammatory—meaning they could unfairly influence jurors' emotions. Today, however, jurors are accustomed to seeing extreme injuries on TV and often view such photos with a detached, matter-of-fact attitude.

This shift tends to benefit the defense, as jurors may not "connect" with the plaintiff or feel empathy for their suffering. Plaintiffs now face the challenge of making their injuries and experiences feel real and significant to jurors who are desensitized by media exposure. To overcome this, plaintiffs' attorneys may rely on compelling testimony, personal stories, or even video interviews with the patient and their loved ones. For example, a plaintiff might share a heartfelt account of how their injury has changed daily life, helping jurors understand the human impact beyond the clinical photos.

Second CSI Effect: Use of Teaching Aids to Explain Evidence

Another aspect of the CSI Effect in medical malpractice is the expectation that complex evidence will be explained visually, like how forensic TV shows use animations and graphics. Jurors now want to see how things work, and teaching aids—like models, diagrams, or timelines—help clarify medical details. For instance, in a case involving a bulging spinal disc, a model of the spine showing how the disc presses against the spinal cord can make the injury easier to understand. Similarly, a timeline that maps out key medical events—such as when symptoms first appeared, when treatment was given, and when complications arose—can help jurors follow the case's progression and better grasp causation.

Both plaintiffs and defendants can use these teaching aids to educate the jury and support their side of the story. Clear visuals and structured explanations not only make abstract legal concepts accessible but also ensure that jurors base their decisions on understanding rather than assumption.

Conclusion: The Double-Edged Impact of the CSI Effect

The CSI Effect has changed how evidence is perceived and presented in medical malpractice cases. Juror desensitization to graphic images poses challenges for plaintiffs, who must work harder to build empathy and connection. At the same time, the rise of teaching aids and visual explanations offers new strategies for both sides to clarify complex issues and educate jurors. By understanding these dynamics and using concrete examples, attorneys can help jurors make informed and fair decisions.

4 Things Jurors Don't Know

Some Facts Aren't Shared with the Jury

When attorneys try medical malpractice cases, jurors listen to evidence and expert opinions presented by both the plaintiff and defense attorneys. However, there are several important facts that attorneys typically do not share with the jury during the trial. These legal limitations exist to protect the integrity of the process, but they can also affect how jurors interpret the case. Here are four things jurors are not told:

1. Prior Defendants in the Case. To begin with, jurors are not informed about all individuals or entities originally named as defendants in the case. For example, imagine a plaintiff's case originally involved seven defendants—a hospital, an Advanced Registered Nurse Practitioner (ARNP), a physician assistant, and four physicians. If the hospital, ARNP, physician assistant, and two physicians settled out before trial, only two physicians might remain as defendants. Attorneys are often prohibited from mentioning the existence of these prior defendants because of statute or case law. Statutes are written laws passed by legislatures, while case law refers to legal principles established by court decisions. Not knowing about prior defendants can lead jurors to assume the remaining defendants bear all responsibility, even though others were previously involved.
2. Another important fact often withheld from jurors involves settlement amounts from other defendants. Building on the previous point, attorneys often do not inform jurors that five defendants settled or disclose the amounts paid by each. The rules about whether settlement agreements can be shared with the jury—known as admissibility—depend on state law. Admissibility refers to whether evidence is allowed to be presented in court, and settlement agreements are legal documents outlining terms for resolving cases without a trial. If jurors are unaware of prior settlements, they might overestimate the financial responsibility of the remaining defendants.
3. Transitioning to another common juror question, insurance coverage information is frequently withheld as well. Jurors often wonder if the defendants have insurance to cover any potential verdict, but in some states, statutes prohibit attorneys from sharing this information. Sometimes, jurors could still find out via public records, like Florida's practitioner profile, which shows how much medical malpractice insurance doctors and ARNPs carry and details about prior settlement amounts. If jurors do not know about insurance coverage, they

may perceive the financial impact of a verdict as greater or less than it truly is, which can influence their decision-making.

4. Lastly, another area kept confidential from jurors concerns attorney compensation. Plaintiff attorneys generally receive a percentage (often 33–40%) of any jury award. Jurors are usually not told how much the plaintiff firm will be paid if a verdict favors the plaintiff. Not knowing this may affect how jurors view the plaintiff's motivations or the scale of the award, potentially impacting the outcome.

In summary, while these limitations are designed to protect the fairness of the trial, they can also shape how jurors interpret evidence and reach decisions. Understanding what is not shared with jurors highlights the complexity of the legal process in medical malpractice cases.

Medical Misconduct

Key Legal Definitions and Applications

Understanding the distinctions between types of medical misconduct is essential for legal nurse consultants involved in malpractice cases. Medical misconduct encompasses more than simple negligence and can have significant legal implications depending on the state and circumstances. Below, we break down the key legal concepts and show how they apply in real-world scenarios.

Comparative Definitions of Medical Misconduct

The following terms are commonly used in medical malpractice litigation. While they are sometimes used interchangeably, each has a distinct legal meaning:

- Gross Negligence:
  - Michigan: Defined as "conduct so reckless as to demonstrate a substantial lack of concern for whether injury results."
  - Georgia: The absence of slight diligence.
  - Florida: Often equated with reckless disregard, healthcare conduct that creates an unreasonable risk of injury, affecting the life or health of another. In Florida, proven reckless disregard may entitle plaintiffs to punitive damages.
- Willful and Wanton Misconduct:
  - Occurs when healthcare providers knowingly take actions that could harm a patient and proceed regardless of the risk.

- Requires clear and convincing evidence that the provider understood the likelihood of injury.

Statutory Protections for Emergency Providers

To better understand how these definitions impact medical malpractice cases, it is important to consider statutory protections for healthcare professionals, especially in emergency settings. For instance, Florida's Good Samaritan Act provides immunity for emergency responders unless their actions demonstrate reckless disregard for patient safety. This means that a paramedic who performs a necessary procedure correctly, even if complications arise, is typically protected from lawsuits. However, failing to act when necessary—such as not establishing an airway for a patient in respiratory failure—may remove this protection.

Georgia's statutes are even more stringent; patients cannot sue Emergency Department providers unless gross negligence is proven. This heightened threshold has led to many unsuccessful lawsuits, but some exceptions exist.

Case Example: Gross Negligence in Georgia

To illustrate the application of gross negligence in practice, consider the case of Abdel Samed v. Dailey. In this situation, a patient required immediate surgery by a hand specialist, but the hospital failed to transfer him to an appropriate facility for almost ten hours. The resulting damages included amputation and chronic pain. The Georgia Supreme Court found that the actions of the Emergency Department staff and physician constituted gross negligence, highlighting the importance of timely and appropriate care.

Willful and Wanton Misconduct: An Illustrative Anecdote

Transitioning to willful and wanton misconduct, this category involves a conscious disregard for patient safety. A notable example comes from New York, where an obstetrician intentionally carved his initials into a patient's abdomen following a Cesarean section. This act was so egregious that, beyond civil liability, the physician faced criminal assault charges, clearly demonstrating the severe consequences of willful and wanton misconduct.

Practical Application for Legal Nurse Consultants

As you review medical records, it is vital to distinguish between ordinary negligence and more serious forms of misconduct. Look for patterns or actions that suggest a substantial lack of concern for patient safety, unreasonable risk-taking, or a knowing disregard for the potential for harm. Identifying these situations early can aid attorneys in determining whether the criteria for gross negligence or willful and wanton misconduct are met, ultimately influencing the direction and success of malpractice litigation.

Plaintiffs and Defendants Who Lie in Medical Malpractice Cases

Plaintiffs Who Lie: Motives, Methods, and Detection

In medical malpractice litigation, the credibility of plaintiffs can significantly impact case outcomes, especially when dishonesty is uncovered. Although rare, instances of plaintiffs providing false information to their attorneys can have severe consequences for both legal teams and the integrity of the judicial process. Understanding the reasons behind such behavior and the means of detecting deception is crucial for attorneys and legal nurse consultants (LNCs).

Plaintiffs may be motivated to lie to obtain financial compensation or to penalize healthcare professionals for perceived mistakes or unsatisfactory health outcomes. These lies may take several forms, including exaggerating injuries, misrepresenting the sequence of events, or falsely implicating multiple healthcare providers. One warning sign is when a plaintiff insists that every provider involved was incompetent. For example, a more credible statement would specify individuals and details, such as, "Dr. Silan told me my CT scan was normal. His assistant was there too, the one with red hair and freckles." In contrast, broad statements implicating everyone, like, "I asked every doctor and every nurse about my CT results, and they all said it was normal," raise suspicion.

LNCs can support attorneys by carefully comparing prospective plaintiffs' statements with the medical records. This verification process helps confirm or refute the truthfulness of the claims and ensures that attorneys are working with accurate information. If LNCs participate in plaintiff interviews, it is critical for them to collect facts and to instruct potential plaintiffs to promptly inform attorneys of any changes in their medical condition.

A common type of plaintiff dishonesty involves injuries that have been resolved after the lawsuit has begun—often unbeknownst to either party's attorneys. One effective method for defendants to assess the true status of a plaintiff's injuries is through a defense medical exam (DME). A DME is a physical examination conducted by a physician selected by the defense, designed to provide an objective assessment of the plaintiff's injuries. The DME can either corroborate the plaintiff's claims or reveal discrepancies, such as evidence that an alleged injury has been resolved.

Another investigative tool is surveillance of the plaintiff's activities. For instance, in one case, a 56-year-old woman claimed permanent disability and loss of employment after a dog bite and subsequent infection. However, surveillance video captured her walking without a cane, skipping, and dancing with her granddaughter—contradicting her testimony of disability. The implication for attorneys and LNCs is clear: corroborating injury claims with concrete evidence is essential, and surveillance can be a decisive factor in uncovering dishonesty.

In another example, a plaintiff nicknamed "Walking Wanda" asserted she was a permanent paraplegic. Yet video evidence showed her walking with a cane. When presented in court, the case was dismissed, and the plaintiff was found to have attempted to defraud the court. Defrauding the court refers to deceitful conduct that undermines the judicial system. These anecdotes underscore the importance of thorough investigation and the value of objective evidence in legal proceedings.

Defendants Who Lie: Distinct Motivations and Tactics

After exploring how plaintiffs may misrepresent facts in medical malpractice cases, it is equally important to consider how defendants can also be dishonest and the unique motivations behind their actions. With defendants who lie, their actions can unravel a defense case and result in serious professional and legal consequences.

Defendants may lie for various reasons, including fear of losing their reputation, job, or professional credentials (such as RN, MD, or RRT). Others may struggle with admitting mistakes or view all lawsuits as baseless, hoping that dishonesty will cause the case to "go away."

One way that defendants may be dishonest is by manipulating medical records. Manipulation can involve adding or removing documents from the record, particularly handwritten notes. For example, in a case involving an internist accused of failing to refer a patient with a persistently low white blood cell count, the physician removed hematology lab reports from his office chart. The discrepancy was discovered by comparing the records provided to attorneys with those previously given to the patient. This example highlights the importance of cross-referencing documentation and the vigilance required of legal teams and consultants.

Another tactic is documenting medical information after the fact, rather than contemporaneously. Contemporaneous documentation refers to recording medical details at the time care is provided, or shortly thereafter, to ensure accuracy and reliability. In legal cases, contemporaneous records are critical because they reflect real-time events and are less susceptible to alteration. For instance, in a case involving several physicians, a nurse, and a patient who died after being coded, the nurse documented all events only after her shift ended. Electronic time stamps revealed the documentation was completed hours after the actual events. Further investigation showed phone records did not match her claims about notifying physicians. The lesson here is that delayed documentation can be detected and often signals attempts to cover up errors or misrepresent facts.

Verbal testimony is another area where defendants may be dishonest, often resulting in a "he said, she said" scenario. In such instances, medical records become indispensable for verifying the sequence of events and supporting or refuting witness statements.

In summary, dishonesty—whether by plaintiffs or defendants—can have disastrous consequences for medical malpractice cases. For attorneys and legal nurse consultants, understanding the motives and tactics behind these actions, recognizing red flags, and relying on objective evidence like DMEs, surveillance, and contemporaneous documentation are critical for building strong, credible cases.

Chapter 4 – Medical Records

Medical records form the foundation of case analysis for legal nurse consultants (LNCs), and understanding their diverse formats is essential for effective review. This chapter provides a comprehensive overview of medical records originating from hospitals, skilled nursing facilities (SNFs), home health agencies, and physician offices, highlighting their unique characteristics and relevance to LNC practice.

We begin by examining hospital and home health records, which are most often provided as fully paginated electronic documents. These records typically require minimal reorganization; however, LNCs must remain vigilant in verifying completeness. Comparing the chart sections described in this chapter with the actual records ensures that no critical information is missing.

Transitioning to hybrid systems, SNFs and physician offices frequently present a mix of electronic and handwritten documentation. This hybrid approach introduces notable challenges. For example, a patient's medication administration record might be electronically generated, while physician orders from the same admission are handwritten on paper. In practice, an LNC may locate electronically stored lab results but struggle to find a corresponding physician's handwritten order, which could be misfiled or overlooked entirely. Such inconsistencies demand a meticulous review strategy and an awareness of where critical documents may be housed.

The chapter then explores advanced topics, including "3D medical records" and fraudulent documentation. A 3D medical record is an approach to chart review that layers audit trails—allowing LNCs to reconstruct the sequence of events with greater clarity and context. In contrast, fraudulent documentation refers to deliberate actions to falsify, alter, or omit information within the medical record. For instance, a staff member might add progress notes after the fact to cover up an error or remove pages to conceal evidence of substandard care. Recognizing these issues is critical for accurate case analysis and legal integrity.

Finally, the chapter previews how LNCs interact with medical records in practice. We will discuss common pitfalls—such as overlooking handwritten elements, failing to index complex records, and sharing documents in ways that may compromise HIPAA compliance. Strategies for deciphering poor handwriting and three distinct methods for approaching medical record review will also be addressed, equipping LNCs with actionable best practices.

By following these structured steps, LNCs can navigate the complexities of medical record review, anticipate common obstacles, and apply advanced analytical tools to deliver thorough and reliable case support.

Hospital Medical Records Chart Review: Best Practices for LNCs

Reference Guide to Chart Organization and Section Review

Ensuring a hospital chart is complete is essential for accurate case analysis. Legal Nurse Consultants (LNCs) play a critical role in reviewing medical records, verifying that all necessary sections are present, and identifying any missing or incomplete documentation. This guide provides a structured overview of hospital medical record organization and actionable tips for LNCs during chart review.

General Organization of Electronic Medical Records

Most hospital records are now managed electronically, streamlining organization compared to traditional paper charts. Electronic records are typically paginated and exported as PDF files for legal requests, such as authorizations or subpoenas. For best results, maintain the original pagination and section order when reviewing electronic files. LNCs should ensure that all chart sections are present and clearly note any missing or incomplete areas in their reports. If working in a law firm or other organization, follow the entity's standard procedures to request the missing records.

Restricted Access Records

Certain documents in the hospital chart may be stored with restricted access, sometimes referred to as "the legal button." These can include signed consents, living wills, durable power of attorney forms, photo IDs, and insurance cards. If you notice that sections like the admission face sheet or consents are missing, it may indicate restricted access. Always document any inaccessible or missing records in your report and request the missing records.

Hospital Chart Sections: Logical Order

1. Admission
    - Admission Face Sheet: Contains patient demographics, admitting physician, diagnosis, and insurance information.
    - Consents: Includes consents for admission, treatments, or surgeries.
    - Inventory Sheet: Tracks patient belongings during the stay (not always available).
    - Living Will & Durable Power of Attorney: Legal documents, if completed, may be present.

- Photo ID & Insurance Cards: Copies may be included or restricted.
- Transfer Forms: Created when a patient is transferred to another facility.

2. Emergency Department Records
    - Physician and nursing notes
    - Treatment plans and orders
    - Medications administered
    - Progress reports and admission decision making
    - Laboratory results
    - Vital signs
    - Radiology impressions
    - Emergency department consent form (if applicable)
3. History and Physical (H&P)
    - History of Present Illness (HPI)
    - Medical, surgical, and family history
    - Medication lists and allergies
    - Review of Systems (ROS)
    - Vital signs, height, and weight
    - Physical examination notes
    - References to lab and radiology results
    - Diagnoses and plan of care
4. Consultations
    - Specialist or healthcare professional notes, either as a separate section or integrated into Progress Notes.
    - Multiple consultant entries may be found throughout the chart, especially when the patient is followed over time.
5. Orders
    - Physician and healthcare professional orders input into the electronic system.
6. Progress Notes
    - Daily documentation by physicians and other professionals, such as therapists, social workers, or case managers.
    - Electronic progress notes may contain repetitive information.
7. Radiology Tests/EKGs
    - Results may be in a dedicated section or integrated elsewhere.
    - Be alert for hyperlinks or scanned documents indicating diagnostic tests; verify that results (e.g., EKGs, Code Blue records) are included and properly located. See image of a scanned document with a hyperlink as shown.

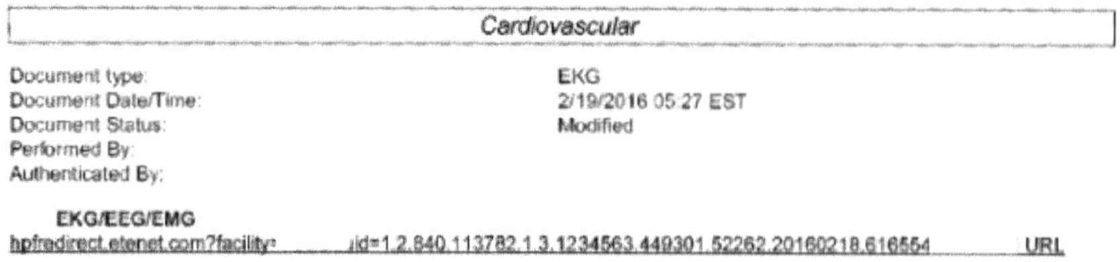

Cardiovascular

Document type:	EKG
Document Date/Time:	2/19/2016 05:27 EST
Document Status:	Modified
Performed By:	
Authenticated By:	

EKG/EEG/EMG

hpfredirect.etenet.com?facility= id=1.2.840.113782.1.3.1234563.449301.52262.20160218.616554 URL

Figure 3 - Scanned EKG with Hyperlink

8. Surgeries and Procedures
   - Operative reports
   - Pathology reports
   - Anesthesia records
   - Intraoperative and PACU documentation
9. Nursing Assessment and Care Plans
   - Initial and ongoing nursing assessments
   - Care plans for patient management throughout the stay
   - Flow Sheets and Nursing Notes
   - Extensive documentation of physical assessments, vital signs, pain levels, intake and output, and other treatments
   - Supplemental notes regarding patient condition and communication
10. Medication Administration Records (MARs)
    - Details of all scheduled and PRN medications administered during the hospital stay
11. Discharge Summary
    - Admission and discharge diagnoses
    - Summary of hospital course
    - List of problems and test results
    - Disposition details (e.g., discharge home or another facility)

Actionable Tips for Legal Nurse Consultants

- Verify that each chart section listed above is present and complete.
- Note any missing, incomplete, or restricted-access sections in your report.
- Pay special attention to scanned records, hyperlinks, and repetitive electronic entries to ensure all relevant results and documentation are available.
- Document any issues with accessibility or missing information for legal or case review purposes.

Home Health Medical Records Chart Review: Best Practices for LNCs

Reference Guide to Chart Organization and Section Review

Most home health records are now maintained in electronic format. Because electronic systems typically arrange records automatically by date, additional manual organization is usually unnecessary. Whether records are maintained electronically or on paper, organizing home health medical records by category and then in chronological order is essential for clarity and completeness.

With paper medical records, legal nurse consultants will find that Home Health records include some unique categories, such as OASIS assessments, that other organizations do not have. OASIS assessments are standardized data collection tools required for Medicare reimbursement and help track patient outcomes over time. Including these documents is critical for demonstrating care quality and compliance. As with all medical records, Home Health charts are organized first by category and then in chronological order. LNCs can use the categories below to organize Home Health records or modify the order to fit individual preferences (unless pages are already paginated).

For instance, when reviewing a chart for a patient admitted in January, begin with the intake forms, followed by the initial plan of treatment, and then proceed to physician orders and OASIS assessments in chronological order. This systematic approach ensures all key components are addressed and supports a thorough legal review.

Administration

- Photo ID and insurance information, including insurance verification intake (referral) and Medicare secondary payer worksheet
- Consents, including release of information, photo consents, client service agreement
- Re-certification information
- Living Will (This form may have been signed prior to intake.)
- Durable Power of Attorney (This form may also have been signed prior to intake.)
- Authorization for Payment, Insurance Screening Form
- Patient Rights

Plan of Treatment

- History and Physical
- Primary and secondary diagnoses
- Medical necessity

Physician Orders

Outcome and Assessment Information Set (OASIS) Assessments

- Including discharge OASIS with progress summary

Supervisory Visits

Clinical Notes

- Nursing Notes
- Home Health Aide Notes

Rehab

- Physical Therapy, Occupational Therapy, Speech Therapy Notes

Notes from Other Disciplines

Medication Profile

Labs / X-Rays / EKGs / Other Tests

This clear structure makes it easy for users to navigate the records and ensures comprehensive chart review. When expanding or updating this guide, continue to integrate new sections in a similarly logical manner to maintain clarity and thoroughness.

SNF Medical Records Chart Review: Best Practices for LNCs

Reference Guide to Chart Organization and Section Review

Maintaining complete and well-organized Skilled Nursing Facility (SNF) records is crucial for legal nurse consultants (LNCs), especially since SNFs often use a mix of electronic and hand-written documentation. This hybrid system can make the record review process complex, as documents may be scattered, duplicated, or missing. A systematic approach, supported by concrete tools like checklists and clear organizational strategies, helps ensure you don't overlook critical information.

Paper nursing home records can be much more complex and more time-consuming for Legal Nurse Consultants to organize than other types of medical records. Because the resident's stay might be months or years, nursing home records are often voluminous. Many nursing homes don't have a medical records department so when the chart is thinned, the thinned records may be stored "as is" and not put into order of any kind. Since the records may be thinned numerous times over the course of the resident's stay, the records can be very mixed up by the time the LNC receives them. The LNC must put the forms in chronological order.

SNF records have different chart sections than other organizations and the contents may be different from their hospital counterparts. Below are categories that can be used to determine if SNF records are complete. The categories and order can be altered to LNC or attorney preference.

Administrative Information: Include the admission face sheet, insurance, consents, inventory, and advanced directives (e.g., DNR forms and power of attorney documents). Example: Place Mrs. Smith's DNR order and admission consent directly after her face sheet.

Prior and Hospital Records: Group all hospital transfer forms and ER records together, separating them from the SNF chart. Example: If there's a stack of hospital discharge papers, sort them by admission and then note type (e.g., progress notes, nurse's notes) and then chronologically within each type.

Orders: Keep monthly SNF pre-printed orders at the front, followed by telephone orders (even if several months are summarized on one sheet), then miscellaneous signed orders. Tip: Telephone orders often aren't in order—sort them as best as possible.

Physician/Consultant Notes: Print and file electronic notes as-is, followed by hand-written notes in date order. Group consultant notes by specialty (e.g., dental, podiatry, psychiatry).

MDS/CAA Forms: Arrange Minimum Data Sets (MDS) and Care Area Assessments (CAA) in chronological order, with each CAA placed immediately after its corresponding MDS. Tip: Use the MDS Assessment Reference Date for dating, not the signature date.

Care Plans: Place care plans in chronological order, starting with the initial 24-hour plan, then the comprehensive plan by day 21, and subsequent updates. Indicate whether goals were achieved and interventions adjusted. Example: If Mrs. Smith's fall prevention goal was met, document the outcome and any updated interventions.

Nursing Assessment/Notes: Start with the admission assessment, then any re-admission forms, followed by ongoing nursing notes in chronological order. Place quarterly updates and skin summaries at the end of this section, unless directed otherwise.

MARs/TARs: Separate Medication Administration Records (MARs) from Treatment Administration Records (TARs) unless they are part of a set. File each by month, keeping narcotic sheets and behavior/side effect records immediately behind the relevant month's MAR.

Decubitus/Skin Reports: Sort by scale (e.g., Norton/Braden), then bi-weekly checks, then wound reports grouped by wound site, with photos directly following documentation for that site.

Fall/Restraint/Side Rail Assessments: Group each assessment type together, arranging documents chronologically within each group.

Vital Signs/Weight/I&O: These may be on the TARs. If not, group by type—vital signs, weights, intake & output—all in chronological order.

Miscellaneous Assessments: Place any forms that don't fit other categories here (e.g., pain assessments, neurological checks).

Therapies: Start with screening sheets (if present), then group by discipline - physical therapy (PT), Occupational Therapy (OT), Speech Therapy (ST), Respiratory (RT), keeping each discipline's notes together and in order. Place swallow studies after ST.

Restorative Nursing: Be careful, as these records can look like nursing notes. File separately from therapy notes and only if present.

Dietary: Begin with the initial assessment, followed by narrative notes, food consumption sheets, and notification slips in chronological order.

Activities (Recreational Therapy): Start with the initial assessment, followed by quarterly updates, then narrative notes.

Social Services: Begin with the initial assessment, followed by quarterly updates and other updates as needed.

Lab Results: File by specimen collection date, ensuring all results are from the SNF stay, not prior hospitalizations.

X-rays/EKGs: Place all imaging and test reports from the SNF stay together, with other studies (e.g., EMGs) behind x-rays.

Suppose you receive records for a resident, Mrs. Smith, whose stay includes both paper and electronic documentation. Here's how you might organize her chart:

1. Inventory and Label: Start by sorting all records by type and format (e.g., electronic printouts, original paper documents).
2. Checklist Review: Use your checklist (example below) to confirm which sections are present. For example, you find paper MARs for January–March, but electronic MARs for April–June.
3. Chronological Order: Within each section, combine paper and electronic documents in chronological order. For example, in the "Physician Progress

Notes" section, insert the handwritten electronic notes from January, then follow with printed progress notes from February, and so on.

4. Group by Section: Assemble documents into the main chart sections (see Quick-Reference Table below). Example: All "Lab Results"—whether scanned from paper or printed from an EHR—are placed together in chronological order by specimen collection date.
5. Flag Missing Items: If your checklist reveals missing records (e.g., no transfer forms from a hospital admission), note these gaps for follow-up.

This method ensures a comprehensive, easy-to-navigate chart, even when dealing with a mix of formats.

Sample Checklist: Tracking All Record Sources

To streamline the process, use a checklist to track every source of records collected and reviewed. This prevents missed documents and makes it easier to identify gaps. Below is a sample SNF Record Source Checklist you can adapt for your cases:

- Resident Name: ___________________________
- Admission Dates: ___________________________
- Record Sources (check as received):
- ☐ Admission face sheet
- ☐ Insurance/consents
- ☐ Advance directives (DNR, POA, Living Will)
- ☐ Inventory sheet
- ☐ Prior hospital records
- ☐ Transfer forms (hospital & SNF)
- ☐ Physician/Consultant notes
- ☐ Orders (monthly, telephone, miscellaneous)
- ☐ MDS/CAA forms
- ☐ Care plans
- ☐ Nursing assessments/notes
- ☐ Medication Administration Records (MARs)
- ☐ Treatment Administration Records (TARs)
- ☐ Decubitus/skin reports
- ☐ Fall/restraint/side rail assessments
- ☐ Vital signs/weight/I&O
- ☐ Miscellaneous assessments
- ☐ Therapy notes (PT, OT, Speech, Respiratory)

- ☐ Restorative nursing
- ☐ Dietary
- ☐ Activities (Recreational Therapy)
- ☐ Social Services
- ☐ Lab results
- ☐ X-rays/EKGs/other studies
- ☐ Other: ______________________________

A thorough, organized SNF chart is essential for effective legal nurse consulting. Using a checklist, grouping documents by section and date, and adapting your approach to match the case's needs will save time and ensure accuracy. Refer to the quick-reference table during your review for efficient, consistent results.

Physician Office Records: A Practical Guide for LNCs

Improving Record Requests and Overcoming Hybrid Chart Challenges

Physician office records are essential for legal nurse consultants (LNCs) when evaluating cases. Understanding the typical components of these records helps ensure you request and receive a complete chart.

- Patient Demographics: Name, date of birth, employment, contact details, and a copy of a photo ID.
- Insurance Information: copy of insurance card, including provider name, address, and phone number.
- Problem List: Current and past diagnoses.
- Family History: Conditions in close relatives, focusing on genetic factors and major illnesses (e.g., diabetes, heart disease, cancer). Specialists may ask about family issues relevant to their field.
- Medications: List of current and past prescriptions, including both electronic and handwritten forms.
- Diagnostic Reports: Lab results, radiology, and other test outcomes.
- Allergies: Medication and environmental allergies.
- Records from Other Physicians: Referrals and correspondence with other providers.
- Treatment Records: Office procedures such as injections, suturing, and EKGs.

- Office/Progress Notes: Exam findings, referrals, diagnoses, and follow-up plans. Some electronic systems use colored bullets to highlight abnormal (black) or normal (white) values for quick reference.

Hybrid Records: Challenges for Legal Nurse Consultants

Physician office records can be challenging to review because they may be incomplete, especially in small practices with limited staff training in records management. The records are often hybrid medical records, a combination of paper, scanned, and computer-generated records. Hybrid records present a unique challenge for LNCs because hybrid systems are designed for physicians and office staff, not legal professionals. This mismatch means that crucial documents may be missing or stored in multiple formats and several locations. Some staff only produce the paper chart, while others pull only computer-generated records, leading to gaps in the documentation.

Practical Insights: Case Studies and Solutions

One recurring issue is inconsistent production of records. For example, an office might send only medical assistant forms, which include patient height, weight, and vital signs, but omit dates or staff names. In one case, I noticed missing dates and usernames on several forms. After further inquiry, I discovered a different form with the same data, plus the missing identifiers. This taught me to always look for alternate records with more complete information.

Another common pitfall is overlooking records stored in separate locations—like faxes, phone messages, or copies of identification cards kept outside the main chart. Staff may not consider these parts of the official record. Visiting the office and working directly with the responsible employee helps reveal where additional data is stored and what screens on the computer are used or skipped in practice. *Note: Visiting the office is permitted for defense law firm employees only if the law firm represents the physician and the visit is specifically requested by their attorney.*

Checklist for LNCs: Steps for Requesting Complete Records

- Ask if both paper and electronic records are maintained.
- Verify the storage location of all paper records—are they centralized or dispersed?
- Request copies of all scanned documents and clarify which records are scanned.

- Ensure all record types are included: faxes, phone messages, lab work, referrals, prescriptions, insurance forms, test results, authorizations, and pharmacy refill requests.
- Review all available screens in the computer program that generates electronic medical records, not just those used daily by staff.
- Check multiple formats of similar data (e.g., forms with and without dates/user names) and request all versions.
- List each required record type explicitly on authorizations and subpoenas and follow up if specifics are ignored.
- Collaborate with staff to address misunderstandings about what constitutes a "complete" chart.

Conclusion

Thorough review and proactive collaboration with office staff are key for LNCs seeking complete physician office records. By understanding the hybrid nature of modern records, using a systematic checklist, and addressing staff misconceptions, you can minimize missing information and strengthen your legal case analysis.

Understanding 3-D Medical Records: Essential Concepts for LNCs

An Accessible Guide to Audit Trails, Metadata, and Practical Applications in Electronic Medical Records

Medical records have evolved significantly over the years. In the past, patient information was recorded on two-dimensional sheets of paper—simple 8.5 by 11-inch documents. The information on the page was WYSIWIG (What You See Is What You Get) – nothing but the information written on the page. Today, electronic medical records (EMRs) add a new level of depth, that I call "3-D medical records." These modern records contain much more information, offering a richer and more complex picture of patient care. For legal nurse consultants, this evolution means looking beyond the surface of scanned documents or PDFs to uncover additional, valuable information.

Defining 3-D Medical Records: Added Depth and Data

"3-D medical records" is a term I use to describe the expanded scope of information available in electronic medical records compared to traditional paper charts. This "third dimension" includes not just the clinical notes, but also digital footprints and communication logs that provide context and accountability. In other words, these records are more than just digital versions of paper—they're dynamic repositories of information, interactions, and access history.

Audit Trails: What They Are and Why They Matter

An audit trail is a digital log that records who accessed the electronic chart, when they did so, and what actions they performed. In the context of EMRs, audit trails are invaluable for tracking the flow of information and ensuring the integrity of records. They help identify who viewed or modified a chart and can reveal patterns that may indicate alterations or unauthorized access.

Hospitals typically use sophisticated audit trail systems due to the complexity of inpatient care. These systems not only log access times and user identities but also detail what sections of the chart were viewed—such as "Patient Lookup," "Visit Navigator Template," or "Chart Review – Imaging." In contrast, physician offices often use simpler audit trails that track appointment dates, arrival times, and basic access information, but may not specify exactly what information was reviewed.

Case Study: Using Audit Trails to Verify Record Alterations

Imagine a scenario where a patient's outcome is being questioned in a legal case, and there are suspicions that the medical record was changed after the fact. A legal nurse consultant (through the law office they're working with) can request the audit trail from the hospital's EMR system. By reviewing the audit trail, the consultant could see that Nurse Smith accessed the chart at 2:00 PM, made an entry in the "Medication Administration" section, and then Dr. Jones accessed and edited the same section at 3:15 PM. If there is evidence that the medication entry was altered after the event, the audit trail provides a transparent timeline of who made each change, supporting or refuting claims of record tampering.

Metadata in Secure Texting Apps: What It Means and Why It Counts

Legal nurse consultants should also be aware of metadata, especially as it relates to secure communication apps used in healthcare. In this context, metadata refers to background information about a message—such as the sender, recipient, date, time, and whether the message was delivered or read. While the content of a text message might be a medication order, the metadata documents the circumstances surrounding the communication.

For example, a secure, HIPAA-compliant texting app like emitrr[8] allows providers to send orders or updates via text, and its metadata ensures each message is traceable. This can be important if there's a dispute about whether a nurse received a critical instruction. The metadata would show exactly when the message was sent, received, and opened, providing objective evidence in a legal review.

Additional Data Sources: Software Examples and Their Roles

Beyond audit trails and communication logs, other software tools supplement the information in EMRs. For instance, some hospital systems use programs like Intellinx, which tracks user activity and provides an extra layer of audit information alongside the main EMR software, such as EPIC. These tools can reveal patterns of access and interaction that might not be visible in the EMR alone, helping consultants reconstruct the full story of a patient's care.

Guidance for Legal Nurse Consultants: When and How to Seek 3-D Record Elements

While electronic records offer a wealth of information, it's not always necessary—or practical—to request every possible data element from every provider. Legal nurse consultants should work closely with attorneys to decide which parts of the 3-D medical record are relevant, focusing on the provider or facility where the patient's injury or event occurred. For peripheral providers, a case-by-case assessment can help determine whether detailed audit trails or communication logs are truly needed.

Conclusion: The Importance of Understanding Electronic Records

As the healthcare industry continues to move beyond paper, understanding the full scope of electronic medical records is essential for legal nurse consultants. By mastering concepts like audit trails, metadata, and supplemental software, consultants can uncover critical evidence, ensure the integrity of records, and provide informed guidance in legal cases. Embracing these digital tools means being better equipped to navigate the complexities of modern healthcare documentation.

[8] emitrr. https://emitrr.com/ (accessed December 2025).

Fraudulent Medical Documentation: Detection and Prevention for LNCs

A Practical Guide for Legal and Healthcare Professionals

Fraudulent documentation in medical records poses significant risks to the integrity of patient care, legal proceedings, and the reputation of healthcare providers. When medical charting is intentionally altered or falsified, it can compromise evidence, mislead attorneys, and jeopardize fair outcomes in litigation. Legal nurse consultants (LNCs) play a crucial role in uncovering such misconduct and ensuring proper documentation standards are upheld.

How Fraudulent Documentation Occurs

Fraudulent documentation may arise before a lawsuit is formally filed. Consider the following scenario: A patient requests a copy of their medical records from a healthcare provider, using a standard authorization. Unbeknownst to the provider, these records are then submitted to a plaintiff law firm for review. Weeks or months later, the law firm submits a second records request—this time on official letterhead, again with patient authorization. The provider, now aware that legal scrutiny is imminent, may review the chart and decide to "clarify" previous entries or add new notes that portray their actions more favorably.

For example, a provider might insert a late entry stating, "I discussed all risks in detail and the patient agreed to proceed immediately," even if such a conversation was not documented contemporaneously. In some cases, these additions are dated as late entries; in others, particularly with paper records, entries may be backdated to appear as if they were written earlier. While electronic medical records (EMRs) have audit trails to deter backdating, intentional alteration remains possible and constitutes fraudulent documentation.

Identifying Discrepancies

Detecting fraudulent documentation requires a systematic comparison of all medical record versions. Legal nurse consultants should be vigilant for red flags such as:

- Inconsistent Entries: Differences between copies of the same record obtained at different times, especially new notes or altered wording.
- Late or Addendum Notes: Entries labeled as "late entry" or "addendum" that provide excessive detail or justification for care decisions.

- Backdating: Handwritten notes with dates that do not match the sequence of care, or digital entries with suspicious time stamps.
- Mismatched Signatures or Handwriting: Signatures or writing styles that differ from the original entries.
- Audit Trail Discrepancies: In EMRs, audit logs showing edits or additions made after the initial patient encounter.

For example, if the initial record copy obtained by the patient lacks mention of a risk discussion, but the subsequent version includes it, this discrepancy warrants immediate investigation.

The Role of Legal Nurse Consultants

Legal nurse consultants are instrumental in reviewing medical records, identifying fraudulent documentation, and supporting attorneys. Their responsibilities include:

1. Comprehensive Record Review: LNCs obtain all available versions of the patient's records, including those provided through patient and attorney authorizations.
2. Cross-Referencing: They meticulously compare each version for differences in content, dates, and signatures.
3. Audit Trail Analysis: For electronic records, LNCs review audit logs to identify when entries were created, modified, or deleted.
4. Identifying Red Flags: LNCs look for the indicators outlined above, using checklists and timelines to track inconsistencies.
5. Reporting Findings: LNCs prepare detailed reports for attorneys, highlighting discrepancies, summarizing findings, and explaining the potential impact on the case. They may create side-by-side tables or annotated copies of records to illustrate their findings clearly.

For instance, if a provider's late entry appears only in the second set of records or the audit trail confirms it was created after the initial records request, the LNC should document this timeline and alert the attorney to potential spoliation of evidence.

Best Practices and Prevention Tips

To prevent or detect fraudulent documentation early, healthcare providers and legal professionals should adopt the following best practices:

- Timely and Accurate Charting: Healthcare providers should document care contemporaneously and avoid making after-the-fact entries unless absolutely necessary, always clearly labeling them as late entries with the actual date and time of entry.

- Maintain Record Integrity: Do not alter or backdate entries. For EMRs, ensure audit trails are preserved and accessible during legal proceedings.
- Respond Promptly to Multiple Requests: Defense attorneys and their LNCs should request all versions of records received by the plaintiff and compare for discrepancies as soon as possible.
- Education and Training: Regularly educate staff on the legal and ethical implications of documentation practices.
- Implement Checklists: LNCs should use standardized checklists when reviewing records to ensure all potential red flags are assessed.

Conclusion

Fraudulent documentation can have severe consequences for legal cases and patient safety. By understanding how such documentation occurs, applying systematic review methods, and fostering a culture of accountability, legal nurse consultants, attorneys, and healthcare providers can work together to detect and prevent fraudulent practices. Early detection and transparent reporting are key to upholding the integrity of medical records and ensuring just outcomes in litigation.

3 Bad Habits with Medical Records

We all have our little quirks—maybe it's sneaking ice cream during a late-night TV binge, leaving those pesky dirty dishes in the sink, or skipping the gym one too many times. Legal nurse consultants (LNCs) are no exception, and when it comes to handling medical records, a few bad habits can creep in. Thankfully, these missteps won't threaten your health, but they can certainly drain your most precious resource: time.

So, what are these common pitfalls, and how can you avoid them?

1. Reviewing Medical Records Without Knowing the Case

This is a classic rookie move. Eager new LNCs often jump headfirst into the records, hoping to grasp the details as quickly as possible. But imagine caring for a patient without knowing their nursing needs—pretty risky, right? Similarly, approach medical records as if they were a patient: have a thorough conversation about case allegations with the potential plaintiff, attorney, or attorney representative. Review any supporting documents (like a Complaint or Affidavit) before you start analyzing. Once you're clear on the allegations, conduct any necessary medical research to understand the standards of care involved. Only then should you dive into the records.

Once you've addressed this first habit, it's important to consider how you approach organization, as the next step can make or break your efficiency.

2. Reviewing Medical Records as You Organize Them

Just as a cluttered kitchen slows down dinner prep, disorganized medical records can hinder your efficiency and accuracy when reviewing case files. While it might seem efficient to read and organize simultaneously, this approach often results in poorly sorted paper documents, overlooked electronic records, or the need to re-read everything later—none of which is an effective use of your time.

For medical records, the best practice is to organize all documents first (if they even need organizing). Once everything is in order, proceed with a thorough review. This method ensures that nothing is missed and allows for a more focused analysis.

When dealing with electronic medical records, start with a quick scan to confirm that the chart is complete. By verifying completeness upfront, you avoid wasting time on partial or missing information.

Alternatively, you can choose to review the records in their current state or enlist a clerk to assist with organization. By teaching your organizational method to a clerk, you reduce the temptation to combine tasks and ensure a consistent system is maintained throughout the process.

In addition to organizing records efficiently, another common pitfall is getting stuck in the endless loop of re-reading documents.

3. Reviewing Medical Records Multiple Times

Sometimes, it's necessary to revisit records—maybe to refresh your memory before consulting with an expert or focusing on a specific issue. But beware the trap of reading records repeatedly just to "get a feel for them." If you find yourself caught in this cycle, you might be experiencing analysis paralysis. The good news? There are proven ways to break free:

- Set a time limit for each review session to keep yourself on track.
- Use a checklist to focus your attention and make sure you cover key points.
- Outline the key questions you want to answer before starting your review.
- Summarize your findings after each pass through the records to clarify your insights.

Try implementing one or more of these prevention techniques to make your review process more efficient and less overwhelming.

Breaking any bad habit takes effort, but the reward is well worth it: more free time for work and play—maybe even enough to finally tackle those dishes or enjoy a guilt-free bowl of ice cream. By recognizing and overcoming these habits, you'll streamline your workflow and set yourself up for success as a legal nurse consultant.

Electronic Medical Record Indexing: A Practical Guide for LNCs

How to Quickly Find What You Need in Thousands of Pages of Records

If you've ever spent hours combing through electronic medical records just to track down a single note or diagnosis, you'll know exactly how overwhelming—and time-consuming—it can be. I used to dread those marathon search sessions, especially when a case required me to locate documentation from a specific treater buried deep within a PDF. But after discovering some simple indexing techniques, I now find what I need in just minutes. Here's a step-by-step guide to help you do the same.

Step 1: Software Requirements—Choosing the Right PDF Tool

To efficiently index electronic medical records, you'll need a PDF program that supports full-text search and bookmarking. The paid versions of Adobe Acrobat (such as Adobe Acrobat Standard DC or Pro DC) work seamlessly for these tasks. If you don't have access to a paid Acrobat license, don't worry—there is an excellent free online tool called BentoPDF[9]. This free PDF software "lives" in your browser, but your files are never uploaded from your device, making it ideal for HIPAA compliance. The right tool can turn a tedious process into a breeze.

Step 2: Preparing Your Document—Ensuring Searchable Text

Before you start, check if your medical record PDF contains searchable text. Most modern records are already text-searchable, but sometimes you'll run into scanned images that aren't. If that's the case, you'll need to run an OCR (Optical Character Recognition) process. In Adobe Acrobat, look for "Scan & OCR" in the right-hand menu, then select "Recognize Text." Free tools like BentoPDF also offer basic OCR features. From personal experience, running OCR on a large file can take a while—sometimes I've

[9] BentoPDF. https://www.bentopdf.com/ (accessed January 2026).

let it run overnight. Just remember to save your document when it's done, so all your hard work is preserved.

Step 3: Searching Within the PDF—Accessing the Search Function

With your document open, it's time to search for the terms or names you need. In Adobe Acrobat, press Ctrl + Shift + F (or CMD + Shift + F on Mac) to open the advanced search box. If you're using BentoPDF use Ctrl + F for a simple search.

Step 4: Reviewing and Indexing Results—Bookmarking and Tagging Key Pages

Type your keyword or the treater's name into the search box and hit "Search." You'll see a list of all matches, each linked to its page in the document. Personally, this step transformed my workflow—what used to involve flipping through endless pages now takes just seconds. To keep things organized, you can bookmark important pages using Ctrl + B (or CMD + B on Mac) in Acrobat. For BentoPDF, scroll to Edit Bookmarks. For physical files, I like to tag printed pages with sticky notes to mirror my digital bookmarks. That way, my indexed pages are always easy to find, whether I'm working on-screen or with hard copies.

Conclusion: Indexing Made Effortless

Switching to efficient electronic indexing has saved me countless hours and made reviewing medical records far less daunting. By using the right software, ensuring your PDFs are searchable, and mastering simple search techniques, you'll be able to focus on what matters—supporting your clients and cases with speed and confidence. Even if you're new to digital tools, these steps make the process approachable and effective. Happy indexing!

HIPAA Compliant File Transfers

Some legal nurse consultants swear by DropBox, while others use Google Drive or iCloud. These cloud storage and file sharing services may offer security, but are they secure enough to protect the protected health information (PHI) in medical records? Let's take a closer look at which cloud services are HIPAA compliant, which are not, and the fees associated with different services.

As an LNC, you're likely to receive and/or send medical records electronically. The HITECH (Health Information Technology for Economic and Clinical Health) Act incentivized healthcare providers to switch from paper to electronic medical records, and it also mandates HIPAA (Health Insurance Portability and Accountability Act) compliance—requiring strict security measures for electronic records and imposing severe penalties for non-compliance. One crucial legal requirement for HIPAA compliance is a Business Associate Agreement (BAA) that outlines responsibilities for handling and protecting personal health information.

A covered entity is typically a healthcare provider, health plan, or clearinghouse directly subject to HIPAA. Legal nurse consultants and defense law firms often qualify as business associates if they handle PHI on behalf of covered entities, making them subject to HIPAA rules. Plaintiff law firms may not always be considered business associates unless they contract with covered entities to process PHI.

That's why it's important to understand the details of various cloud storage and file transfer sites. Below is a list of some of the most common platforms.

Platforms That Do NOT Meet HIPAA Requirements Out of the Box

Platform	**Reason for Non-Compliance**
Hightail	Does not offer HIPAA-compliant features or a BAA.
iCloud	Not HIPAA-compliant; Apple does not sign BAAs.
OneDrive (Personal)	Not covered under Microsoft's enterprise BAA; lacks necessary controls.
DropBox (Personal)	Does not offer HIPAA-compliant features or a BAA.

Platforms That CAN Be HIPAA-Compliant (With Proper Configuration)

Some platforms can be HIPAA-compliant if you sign a BAA and the platforms configure them properly with access controls, audit logs, and encryption. Even with a signed BAA and use of an approved platform, ongoing vigilance is required—regularly review security settings, update access controls, and audit logs to ensure continued compliance.

Platform	HIPAA-Compliant Plan(s)	Monthly Cost Per User	Annual Cost Per User	Notes
Box	Enterprise / Enterprise Plus	$35-$50	$420-$600	BAA required; HIPAA support only on Enterprise tiers; offers encryption, access controls, and audit logging.
DropBox Business	Business / Business Plus	From $15	~$180+	BAA required; must configure securely; includes two-factor authentication, advanced encryption, and admin controls.
Google Workspace	Business or Enterprise Plans	From $6-$18	~$72-$144	BAA included; includes Drive, Gmail, Meet, etc., but must be configured; only core services are HIPAA compliant.
OneDrive for Business	Microsoft 365 Business / Enterprise	From $6-$12	~$72-$144	BAA included; must configure properly, includes encryption and multifactor authentication.

And the Winner Is:

Platform	HIPAA-Compliant Plan(s)	Monthly Cost Per User	Annual Cost Per User	Notes
Sharefile	Premium / VDR / Industry Advantage	$25-$67.50	$300-$810	Turn-key—HIPAA support is built-in; BAA required; designed for secure file

Platform	HIPAA-Compliant Plan(s)	Monthly Cost Per User	Annual Cost Per User	Notes
				sharing with healthcare-grade protections.

Selecting a cloud storage and file sharing service requires thoughtful decisions. If you're only receiving medical records, you typically don't need to purchase anything—the sender will provide you with a secure download link. If you're sending records on behalf of the defense, you must use a HIPAA-compliant service, which will require investment to meet HIPAA and HITECH requirements. Encryption must be enabled both at rest and in transit. Plaintiff law firms aren't subject to the same HIPAA requirements as defense firms unless they act as business associates for covered entities.

Although this article focuses on file transfers, remember: never store medical records on your personal OneDrive account, as it violates HIPAA. Microsoft does not provide a BAA for personal plans, and storing PHI on personal OneDrive exposes sensitive information to unauthorized access and legal liability. Civil penalties can range from $100 to $50,000 per violation.

Sidebar: HIPAA Compliance Checklist for Legal Nurse Consultants (LNCs)

If you handle medical records, you handle risk. Use this checklist to ensure your file storage and sharing practices meet HIPAA and HITECH standards.

Secure Storage & Access

- Use HIPAA-compliant platforms: Box Enterprise, Dropbox Business, OneDrive for Business, ShareFile, or Google Workspace (with BAA).
- Sign a Business Associate Agreement (BAA) with any cloud service provider before storing PHI.
- Enable multi-factor authentication (MFA) on all accounts.
- Restrict access to PHI to authorized individuals only.

File Management

- Never store PHI on personal cloud accounts (e.g., personal OneDrive, iCloud).
- Regularly audit and remove outdated PHI from your systems.
- Maintain audit logs to track who accessed or modified files.

- Secure Sharing & Transmission
    - Use encrypted file transfer tools or secure client portals.
    - Avoid sending PHI via unsecured email or messaging apps.
    - Verify recipient identity before sharing any medical records.

For example, if you receive medical records via email, immediately transfer them to your HIPAA-compliant cloud storage or computer's hard drive, and delete the original message from your inbox.

Training & Awareness

- Stay current on HIPAA regulations and best practices.
- Train staff or collaborators on secure PHI handling.
- Document your compliance procedures and update them regularly.

Breach Prevention & Response

- Have a data breach response plan in place.
- Report unauthorized access or loss of PHI immediately.
- Keep records of all compliance efforts and incidents.

Reminder: Even if you're not a covered entity, you may be considered a business associate under HIPAA. That means you're legally responsible for protecting PHI.

Deciphering Bad Handwriting in Medical Records: Strategies for LNCs

Practical Approaches to Interpreting Illegible Documentation and Communicating Findings

Although electronic medical records are now standard, legal nurse consultants (LNCs) still encounter occasional handwritten documentation during medical record reviews. Interpreting these records is crucial for understanding standards of care, causation, and damages in legal cases. Illegible handwriting can obscure important details, making the LNC's expertise essential.

Challenges in Interpreting Medical Records

- Abbreviations and Terminology: Medical records often use numerous abbreviations and terms from Latin and Greek, many with multiple meanings (e.g., PT, DC).

- Inconsistent Grammar and Spelling: Punctuation and grammar are frequently overlooked, and spelling errors may further complicate interpretation.
- Legibility Issues: Handwritten notes, especially from physicians, can be difficult to read, even for experienced nurses and LNCs.

Grouped Strategies for Deciphering Handwriting

Compare Different Types of Documentation

- Review Typed Reports First: Start with consults, discharge summaries, histories/physicals, and computer-generated orders, which usually include the provider's name, specialty, and care plan. Use these as a reference for understanding related handwritten notes.
- Cross-Reference Similar Entries: When orders are written, check them against progress notes since one might be easier to read. If the orders are computer-generated, comparing them with progress notes helps streamline your work. Make sure the treatment plan is consistent throughout.
- Check Nursing Notes: Nurses may document which physicians were involved, which can help identify signatures or clarify context.

Use Context and Specialty Knowledge

- Consider the Note's Context: Focus on terminology relevant to the provider's specialty (e.g., respiratory terms for pulmonologists). Review nursing notes from the same period for additional clues.
- Prioritize Critical Records: Spend more time on documentation directly related to the case's main issues, such as primary care or cardiology notes for a patient with a fatal cardiac event.

Tools and Techniques for Deciphering

- Magnification: Use a magnifying glass for paper records, or the zoom feature in PDF software for electronic records.
- Identify Key Letters and Words: Find a clearly written letter (like "P") and use it to decode other words. Once you recognize a word (e.g., "Prilosec"), use its letters as a reference for others.
- Compare Multiple Notes: Reviewing all notes from the same provider in one sitting can reveal patterns or repeated words. Alternatively, take a break and revisit later with "fresh eyes."
- Seek a Second Opinion: Ask another LNC to review the handwriting for additional perspectives.

Communicating Findings to Attorneys

- Document Interpretation Attempts: Keep a clear record of strategies and resources used to interpret illegible handwriting, noting any words or sections that remain unclear.
- Assess Potential Impact: Highlight the possible significance of indecipherable sections, especially if they relate to key issues in the case.
- Suggest Additional Steps: Advise the attorney to consider actions like deposing the treating provider or obtaining a transcript when vital information is unclear.

Conclusion: The Value of Diligence and Collaboration

Deciphering handwritten medical records is a vital skill for legal nurse consultants. By using structured strategies, leveraging available resources, and communicating findings effectively, LNCs help ensure that legal teams have the clearest possible understanding of the medical facts. Thoroughness and collaboration remain key to overcoming the challenges of illegible documentation.

Flippers, Organizers, & Page Turners

Which Medical Record Reviewer Are You?

Are you a Flipper, an Organizer, or a Page Turner? These playful terms describe the different ways legal nurse consultants tackle the challenge of reviewing medical records. Let's dive into some real-life scenarios to see how each approach works in practice, why you might choose one method over another, and what you can do when you hit a snag.

Flippers: Zeroing in on Allegations First

Picture this: You're reviewing a case where a patient suffered a medication error during a hospital stay. As a Flipper, you start by pinpointing the main allegation—perhaps a wrong dose given on the night shift. You immediately flip to the medication administration records for the suspected date, then hop over to the nurse's notes, and finally scan the physician orders. Only after this targeted search do you circle back to get the full picture from the rest of the chart. This approach is especially handy when time is tight, or when you need to quickly confirm (or disprove) a specific claim.

However, Flippers sometimes risk overlooking context or missing details scattered elsewhere in the record. To avoid this, many Flippers use checklists for key chart sections or allegations, making sure nothing slips through the cracks. If you're a Flipper, consider creating a template checklist to track what you've reviewed and what still needs attention.

Organizers: Following the Timeline

Organizers are all about structure and sequence. Imagine you're working on a complex surgical case: a patient undergoes a cardiac bypass and then develops complications requiring interventions from cardiology, infectious disease, and nephrology. As an Organizer, you start at the front of the medical record—admission notes, pre-op assessments—and work your way forward, following the timeline as it unfolds. This method lets you trace how events unfolded, how different specialties communicated, and exactly when each intervention took place. When the chart is in chronological order, it's much easier to spot delays, missed handoffs, or patterns that explain the outcome.

But what if you're handed a stack of electronic records uploaded in random order? This can trip up even the most dedicated Organizer. One solution: use software tools to rearrange records by date and section before you begin your review. Some Organizers build their own digital "to-review" lists, marking off each section as they go to ensure nothing is missed, even when charts are a mess.

Page Turners: Embracing the Chaos

Sometimes, you have no choice but to be a Page Turner. Maybe you're reviewing a nursing home chart where lab results, physician notes, and therapy summaries are all mixed together, or you receive a PDF dump of electronic medical records with no logical order at all. The Page Turner starts at page one and works straight through to the end, regardless of the sequence. This thoroughness means you won't miss anything, but it can be slow and frustrating—especially when you're looking for a single event buried in hundreds of pages.

To make this process more manageable, Page Turners often take notes or flag pages as they go, creating a quick-reference index for later. Some also use digital bookmarks or sticky notes to mark sections that need a second look.

Which Reviewer Are You? Let's Find Out!

Do you mostly flip to the "good stuff," follow the chart's timeline, or power through page by page? Maybe you use all three approaches, depending on the case. Here's a quick quiz to help you discover your style:

1. When you start a new case, what's your first move?
    - A. Jump to the sections about the main allegation

- B. Begin at the first page and follow the entire timeline
    - C. Review each page in order, no matter how the record is organized
2. When charts are disorganized, you:
    - A. Hunt for the right sections, even if it takes some detective work
    - B. Try to reorganize them before reviewing
    - C. Just start reading and sort it out as you go

Mostly A's? You're a Flipper. Mostly B's? You're an Organizer. Mostly C's? You're a Page Turner. But remember—many of us blend these strategies, adapting as each case demands.

Chapter 5: Medical Research for Legal Nurse Consultants

When Legal Nurse Consultants hear "medical research," they might picture lab coats and test tubes. In reality, most LNCs need targeted research skills to support legal cases efficiently. This chapter is designed for Legal Nurse Consultants seeking practical research skills to enhance their effectiveness in legal cases. Whether you're investigating a complex timeline, verifying product information, or building a case strategy, mastering essential research techniques is critical for success.

We'll begin by exploring the core skills LNCs need to conduct effective internet research, including search basics, strategic approaches, and how to organize resources for quick retrieval. You'll see how these foundational abilities streamline information gathering and improve the accuracy of your case assessments.

Next, we'll examine how to use the Wayback Machine—a valuable tool for accessing archived websites—in product liability and other legal cases where historical web content can make a difference.

We'll also compare Google Scholar and PubMed, the two most widely used platforms for finding and obtaining medical research, and review how to evaluate the authority of journal articles. These skills help ensure you rely on reputable sources and present strong evidence in your analyses.

Finally, you'll learn how to conduct non-scholarly internet research, such as background investigations and cyber reputation checks, expanding your toolkit for uncovering crucial information relevant to legal matters.

By the end of this chapter, you'll have a practical set of research strategies that directly impact your effectiveness as a Legal Nurse Consultant—making your work more efficient, thorough, and credible.

Internet Research Skills for Legal Nurse Consultants

Practical Strategies and Case-Based Applications

While the term "research" often brings to mind experimentation, statistics, and strict scientific protocols, the approach taken by Legal Nurse Consultants (LNCs) is distinctly different. Unlike laboratory researchers who conduct experiments, LNCs focus on gathering and interpreting medical data relevant to legal cases. For LNCs, research means searching for and evaluating high-quality medical information that can clarify complex medical issues in a legal context.

LNCs depend on the internet for a variety of professional tasks. Whether locating journal articles, medical images, expert witnesses, statutes, licensure requirements, reference materials, or demographic data, strong internet research skills are essential. For instance, when preparing a case, an LNC might use online databases to find recent studies about a specific medical procedure or consult government websites for updated licensure requirements. For independent LNCs, online resources also support business operations and professional growth, making internet research a cornerstone of both casework and career development.

Browsers vs. Search Engines: What's the Difference?

Understanding the distinction between browsers and search engines is fundamental. A browser is software that allows you to access the internet. Examples include Chrome, Firefox, Microsoft Edge, and Safari. Think of the browser as the vehicle that gets you onto the internet highway.

A search engine, on the other hand, is a website you visit using your browser to find and rank information based on keywords you enter. Popular search engines include Google, Bing, DuckDuckGo, and Yahoo. Returning to the analogy: if the browser is your car, the search engine is your map, helping you navigate to your destination online.

In summary, a browser is the tool you use to access the internet, while a search engine is a website you visit through the browser to find the information you need.

Navigating Tabs and Address/Search Bars

Most browsers share a similar layout. At the top, you'll find tabs, which let you view multiple websites within a single window—each tab represents a different webpage. You can add a new tab by clicking the + sign, rearrange tabs by dragging them, and close tabs when they're no longer needed. However, keeping too many tabs open can slow down your computer, so some browsers like Chrome and Edge offer features to "sleep" unused tabs and save memory.

To visit a specific site, enter its address in the address bar. When you want to search for information, you can type keywords directly into the address bar or into the search bar on your preferred search engine's homepage.

Effective Search Strategies

Finding the right information quickly involves more than just typing a few words into a search bar. Here are strategies to enhance your search:

- Choose Specific Keywords: Use terms directly related to your topic or case. For example, in a medical malpractice case, keywords like osteoporosis, "vitamin d deficiency", fracture, “treatment guidelines” are more precise than general terms.
- Use Quotation Marks: Place quotation marks around a phrase (“vitamin d deficiency”) to search for those words in that exact order. This narrows results and filters out unrelated content.
- Combine Keywords: Enter multiple keywords to focus your search (e.g., osteoporosis "vitamin d deficiency" “treatment guidelines”).
- Add Refiners: Include words like guidelines, review, meta-analysis, or a specific year (e.g., 2022) to target recent or authoritative sources: osteoporosis "vitamin d deficiency" treatment guidelines 2022.
- Exclude Irrelevant Results: Use a minus sign to exclude certain terms (e.g., osteoporosis "vitamin d deficiency" -pediatrics if you want to avoid pediatric information).
- Evaluate Source Credibility: Prefer reputable websites, such as those ending in .gov, .edu, or .org—these are often government agencies, universities, or professional organizations. Examples include the National Institutes of Health (nih.gov) or the American Academy of Family Physicians (aafp.org). Always check the publication date and author qualifications when possible.

Additional Case Scenarios

- Verifying Medical Images: If you need to confirm the appearance of a specific medical condition, use keywords like osteoporosis x-ray image. Always verify images by checking the source—prefer medical journals, professional organizations, or academic institutions. Avoid using images from social media or forums unless you can confirm their reliability.
- Finding Expert Contact Information: To locate a potential expert witness, search for terms such as orthopedic surgeon expert witness or osteoporosis medical expert profile. Look for contact details on reputable association websites or academic faculty pages.

Bookmarking and Organizing Resources

When you find a helpful webpage you’ll want to revisit, save it as a bookmark (sometimes called a Favorite). In most browsers, click the star icon or press Ctrl+D (Windows) or Cmd+D (Mac) to bookmark a page. Organize your bookmarks into folders by topic (such as “Treatment Guidelines” or “Expert Witnesses”) for easy access later.

Conclusion: Mastering Internet Research

With these skills, you're well-equipped to perform effective and credible internet research as a legal nurse consultant. By understanding the difference between browsers and search engines, using strategic keywords, evaluating sources, and staying organized, you can efficiently support your cases with reliable information.

LNC Research Using the Wayback Machine

If you're of a certain age, you might remember Mr. Peabody, the genius cartoon dog from the classic Rocky and Bullwinkle television show. On the show, Mr. Peabody and his boy Sherman traveled through history using the WABAC (pronounced "wayback") machine. Similarly, the internet offers its own Wayback Machine, a tool that legal nurse consultants (LNCs) can use to explore previous versions of websites. How does this benefit you as an LNC? Let's find out.

Background

The Wayback Machine[10] is an internet archive that stores over 1 trillion web pages, some dating back to 1996. Because many websites are dynamic and change often, the Wayback Machine captures snapshots of web pages as they appear at different points in time. This enables LNCs to retrieve older versions of websites—including pages that have been altered or deleted. This feature is especially useful when researching product liability cases, where it's important to determine whether manufacturers made, changed, or removed explicit or implied promises to consumers.

How to Use the Wayback Machine

Now that you know what the Wayback Machine is, let's look at how to use it step-by-step. To access archived versions or deleted pages of a website, type the website's URL into the search box on the Wayback Machine's homepage and press Enter. You'll see a timeline with a bar graph covering the years from 1996 to the present. Select a year, and a calendar will appear with highlighted dates indicating when snapshots were taken. Clicking on a highlighted date will open the website as it appeared on that day. Be patient—the archived websites may take time to load. Most links work but might also open pages from different archived dates.

[10] The Wayback Machine. https://web.archive.org/ (accessed December 2025).

Limitations

The Wayback Machine has some important limitations to keep in mind. It does not archive interactive elements such as forms, login-required content, or dynamically generated pages, meaning users cannot submit information or view personalized content in archived versions. Additionally, it does not capture all content behind password-protected areas, including private pages on most social media sites like Facebook, X, and Instagram. As a result, the interactive and personalized features of these pages are typically unavailable in the archive.

Legal Aspects

Beyond its technical capabilities, the Wayback Machine also offers support for legal documentation. While it wasn't originally designed for legal purposes, the site provides a legal page outlining its policies for responding to information requests. The Wayback Machine can supply printed copies of archived web pages and a standard affidavit to establish authenticity. However, because it is a nonprofit organization with limited staff, the Wayback Machine prefers that attorneys request the opposing party to stipulate to the authenticity of documents retrieved from its archive.

By combining a little pop culture nostalgia with practical guidance, using tools like the Wayback Machine becomes both accessible and enjoyable. Staying curious and leveraging these resources can help LNCs uncover valuable historical information in their work. If you find the Wayback Machine helpful, keep the same spirit of discovery in mind as you explore other technical tools and resources!

Comparing Google Scholar and PubMed for Legal Nurse Consultants

A Practical Guide to Accessing Medical Literature

As a legal nurse consultant, accessing reliable medical literature is vital for supporting your work and assisting attorneys. Two popular platforms—Google Scholar and PubMed—offer different approaches to searching and obtaining medical research. This article provides a clear, side-by-side summary of their key features, followed by practical instructions and search examples to help you choose the right tool for your needs.

Quick Comparison: Google Scholar vs. PubMed

Criteria	**Google Scholar**	**PubMed**
Authority	Broad disciplines, less content vetting	Focuses on peer-reviewed biomedical journals
Cost	Many free articles; paid articles vary by publisher	Free articles; paid articles usually through libraries at a flat fee
Ease of Use	Very user-friendly; similar to Google search	Requires account setup; interface less intuitive
Full-Text Availability	Many free PDFs; some articles require payment	Free articles available; other paid articles accessed via interlibrary loan

Google Scholar: Features and Search Examples

Google Scholar[11] is a search engine for scholarly literature across various disciplines. It provides access to many free full-text articles. Articles may be labeled as “Free,” “PDF,” or sometimes have no identifier but are still accessible at no cost. To search, simply enter your terms—no need for quotation marks.

- Basic Example: Searching for renal failure yields over 3 million results.
- Refined Example: Adding a date range, e.g., renal failure 2022-2025, narrows results to about 2,260.
- Additional Scenario: Searching for type 2 diabetes 2020-2025 can focus on recent research, while stroke guidelines 2023 targets the clinical recommendations from that year.

You can see whether an article is free or available as a PDF immediately. For paid articles, you must obtain each from its publisher, which can be time-consuming if you need multiple articles from various sources.

[11] Google Scholar. https://scholar.google.com/ (accessed December 2025).

PubMed: Features and Search Examples

PubMed[12] (pubmed.gov) indexes the MEDLINE database and the US National Library of Medicine. It is more authoritative, focusing exclusively on peer-reviewed biomedical literature—making it a strong choice for high-quality, vetted research.

- Basic Example: A search for renal failure returns about 6,600 results.
- Refined Example: Searching renal failure 2022-2025 narrows results to just three, highlighting PubMed's strict indexing criteria.
- Additional Scenario: COVID-19 vaccines 2021-2025 will yield the most recent peer-reviewed studies, while pressure ulcer prevention guidelines focuses on best practices.

PubMed is not a full-text provider; it indexes articles and links out to publishers or libraries for access. Obtaining multiple articles is easier via institutional accounts and interlibrary loans, offering efficient and consistent pricing.

Step-by-Step Guide: Account Creation and Article Access in PubMed

1. Create an NCBI Account (PubMed): Go to pubmed.gov. Click on Login > Sign up > Create New NCBI Account. Enter your name, email, and password, then submit.
2. Set Up Library Access: Register with a university or medical library online. The library pays publishers for articles on your behalf and charges you a flat fee per article. You do not need to visit the library in person; all transactions occur via the internet and email.
3. Access and Download Articles: Return to PubMed and search for your topic. Download free articles directly. For paid articles, add them to your Clipboard, and submit a request for interlibrary loan to your registered library. Electronic copies are often delivered within an hour via email, regardless of publisher origin.

Additional Search Scenarios

- Google Scholar: Searching "pediatric asthma treatment 2021-2025" yields thousands of diverse articles, including guidelines and reviews.

[12] PubMed. https://pubmed.gov/ (accessed January 2026).

- PubMed: The same search may return fewer but more authoritative articles, focusing on clinical trials and peer-reviewed studies.
- Google Scholar: "opioid litigation outcomes" provides access to law, policy, and medical perspectives.
- PubMed: "opioid litigation outcomes" will focus on biomedical and public health research, generally fewer in number.

Conclusion: Choosing the Right Platform

For legal nurse consultants, Google Scholar offers broad access and ease of use, making it ideal for initial searches and interdisciplinary topics. PubMed provides highly vetted, peer-reviewed biomedical literature, best for in-depth clinical research and authoritative evidence. Your choice should depend on the scope of your query, the need for article quality, and your access requirements. When in doubt, consider starting with Google Scholar for breadth, then turn to PubMed for depth and rigor.

Evaluating Authoritative Journal Articles: Applying the CARS Checklist

A Structured Guide for Legal Professionals, Students, and Researchers

When asked to review an opposing expert's testimony, especially when the expert cites authoritative journal articles, it is essential to assess whether those sources are truly reliable. The CARS Checklist—Credibility, Accuracy, Reasonableness, and Support—offers a systematic approach for evaluating research sources. This guide details each element of the checklist and provides clear strategies and neutral examples for effective assessment.

1. Credibility

Start by determining if both the article and its journal are peer reviewed (also called refereed). Peer review typically indicates a higher level of scholarly scrutiny compared to non-peer-reviewed publications but be aware that journals may also contain non-peer-reviewed content such as editorials or letters. Examine the author's qualifications, including education, training, experience, and any disclosed affiliations or financial relationships. Consider whether funding or institutional ties could introduce bias, rather than making assumptions solely based on an author's employer. Additional signs of credibility include clear authorship, editorial oversight, and attention to detail (such as proper grammar and spelling).

2. Accuracy

Assess the timeliness of the information: medical and scientific fields evolve rapidly, so recent publications are generally more reflective of current standards and practices. Some foundational concepts may remain relevant over time (for instance, the role of sustained pressure in pressure ulcer development), but treatments and guidelines often change. Ensure that any cited research aligns with the timeframe relevant to the case at hand. Be cautious of articles that use absolute language ("always," "never") or provide vague details, as these can undermine accuracy.

3. Reasonableness

Evaluate the article's fairness and objectivity. A reasonable source presents information in a balanced manner without favoring a single viewpoint. Consider whether the author discloses any potential conflicts of interest, such as financial investments or institutional affiliations that might influence their perspective. Neutrality and transparency are key indicators of a reasonable and trustworthy source.

4. Support

Look for clear source citation and corroboration. Peer-reviewed articles typically include a bibliography or reference list, allowing you to trace the origins of the information. Assess whether these references are current and relevant; outdated sources may weaken the article's reliability. Additionally, confirm that any data or statistics can be independently verified through credible references.

Additional Review Steps

Beyond the CARS checklist, examine any notations or highlighted sections within the articles—experts may emphasize points that support their opinions. Cross-reference these highlights with the expert's deposition testimony to ensure their interpretation accurately represents the key findings of the cited work.

By systematically applying the CARS checklist and supporting your review with careful attention to potential biases and the quality of evidence, you can confidently assess whether the expert's cited journal articles are truly authoritative.

Cyber Reputations and Background Investigations for LNCs

Not all internet research is scholarly. As a legal nurse consultant, I periodically review online photos and social media content, including images of individuals in various stages of undress or engaging in questionable behavior. This activity is not a reflection of personal interest but a necessary part of investigating the cyber reputations of parties involved in medical malpractice cases. Understanding a person's online presence can provide valuable insight into their character, which may influence how a jury perceives them. If I react a certain way to someone's cyber reputation, it is likely that jurors may have a similar response.

Juries tend to relate positively to individuals who demonstrate strong community ties. Pictures of people participating in family activities, serving in civic organizations, or attending religious services typically foster goodwill. Conversely, images depicting risky behavior such as excessive drinking, drug use, or inappropriate attire can negatively affect a jury's perception. Therefore, whether representing the plaintiff or the defense, it is crucial to assess both your client's and the opposing party's cyber reputation. This investigation also includes searching for evidence that supports or refutes the specific allegations in the malpractice suit. For instance, in cases involving alleged surgical errors, online comments or photos may substantiate or challenge the claims.

Before delving into the research process, it is important to address the ethical considerations involved. If individuals have made their social media profiles and posts public, you are generally permitted to save, share, or print this information. However, if their accounts are private, professional ethics dictate that you should not attempt to gain access through deceptive means, such as sending a friend request solely to view restricted content. For this guidance, we are focused strictly on gathering information from public internet sources and social media profiles, rather than utilizing paid background check services that law firms might employ for factual data such as vehicle registrations or previous addresses. These services may not include online commentary or imagery.

To conduct thorough online searches, I primarily use platforms such as Google (including both Web and Images), Facebook, X, Threads, Reddit, and others. TikTok, while popular, has not yielded significant results in my experience, but many other social media sites may offer useful information. Facebook requires a free account to search for individuals; once registered, you can review public posts and photos on their "wall." These materials can be saved and printed if they are publicly visible. On X, reviewing a person's posts may reveal relevant information for the medical malpractice case. TikTok allows searches via phone numbers, usernames, or keywords.

Most readers are familiar with basic internet searches using Google, but it is also possible to search specifically for images. By clicking on "Images" in Google's homepage and entering identifying information, you may locate photos that individuals have attempted to remove. Google caches each webpage and image, storing backup copies that remain accessible even after the originals have been deleted. This enables access to content that might otherwise be unavailable.

Expanding Beyond Cyber Reputation: Investigating Criminal Backgrounds

In addition to analyzing social media profiles, it is also important to investigate any potential criminal history that may impact the case. Medical malpractice lawsuits are adjudicated in civil courts, but legal nurse consultants may need to determine whether parties have engaged in criminal activity. Previously, this type of investigation often required hiring a private investigator. Now, with the resources available online, legal nurse consultants can research the criminal background of individuals without incurring significant costs.

Websites such as Mugshots[13] offer information including arrest dates, charges, locations, and prison status. Some listings include trial dockets, with records extending back decades. To locate details, enter the person's name to receive results quickly. These resources have revealed significant information about parties in litigation and can also be used to verify the status of individuals via county sheriff websites. You can access your county's sheriff office by searching for "USA Cops[14]" or by using Google's search function.

County records provide additional criminal case information. To access these records, search for your county name followed by "clerk of court." Public records may be available through links such as "Look Up Your Court Case" or "Public Access Case Search." Input the party's name to identify all cases in which they were involved. The National Sex Offender[15] website is another useful resource, although it may not always yield relevant information for parties in litigation. Nevertheless, it can provide insight into the local community.

DirtSearch[16] is a comprehensive site for background checks. Enter the individual's name and location to begin your search. While results may take longer to process during certain times, DirtSearch offers thorough criminal and social media search capabilities.

[13] Mugshots. https://mugshots.com/ (accessed January 2026).
[14] USA Cops. https://www.usacops.com/ (accessed January 2026).
[15] National Sex Offender. https://nsopw.gov/ (accessed January 2026).
[16] Dirtsearch. https://dirtsearch.org/ (accessed January 2026)

Once you have gathered relevant information, provide it to your attorney for review. They may choose to conduct a more exhaustive paid background check or use the findings to inform case strategy. By conducting professional and diligent online investigations, you can offer valuable support to attorneys throughout the litigation process.

Chapter 6: Case Analysis for Legal Nurse Consultants

Legal nurse consultants (LNCs) play a vital role in the thorough analysis of medical records, going far beyond simply identifying documentation errors. In this chapter, we explore the complexities of case analysis for LNCs, emphasizing the importance of a systematic approach to reviewing a wide range of medical and legal scenarios.

We begin by outlining the standards, practices, and effectiveness of medical documentation, highlighting how proper recordkeeping can impact case outcomes. LNCs must remain vigilant for both strengths and weaknesses in documentation, taking care to avoid the pitfalls of hindsight bias while maintaining objectivity.

Through the examination of diverse malpractice cases—including mammograms, teleradiology, anesthesia records, diary and pharmacy record analysis, hospitalist involvement, and EKG reader services—you will learn essential strategies for dissecting complex clinical narratives. The chapter also delves into specialized topics such as rare pediatric disorders like craniosynostosis, the mechanisms of metastasis via perineural invasion, and the applications of genomics in case analysis.

To ensure comprehensive case evaluation, we discuss additional considerations such as interpreting medical bills, analyzing the profitability of cases, and understanding the role of cell phones and changing tactics in patient care. Topics like "never sick" claims, negligent medical referrals, ER patient boarding, and visual acuity assessments are explored to illustrate common challenges in legal nursing reviews.

Finally, we address key theories of the case and provide insights on the misdiagnosis of aortic dissection, demonstrating how LNCs can critically assess clinical decisions and outcomes. By integrating these diverse topics, this chapter equips you with the analytical tools necessary to identify, interpret, and present findings from a variety of legal and medical scenarios, ensuring your evaluations are both thorough and effective.

Medical Documentation Standards: Traditional and Electronic Records

Accurate and thorough documentation is a cornerstone of quality healthcare and a critical component in legal proceedings. For legal nurse consultants and healthcare professionals, understanding the nuances between documentation standards and hands-on patient care standards is essential, especially as electronic health records (EHRs) introduce new complexities. This article clarifies these standards, explores their legal implications, and provides actionable guidance for professionals working in today's evolving healthcare environment.

Traditional Documentation Issues

Defining Documentation Standards vs. Hands-On Patient Care Standards

Documentation standards refer to the professional and institutional requirements for accurately recording assessments, interventions, and outcomes in the patient's medical record. These standards ensure that all relevant patient care activities are logged in a timely, factual, and complete manner.

Hands-on patient care standards, on the other hand, pertain to the direct provision of medical or nursing care to patients, such as administering medications, performing procedures, or monitoring vital signs. These standards focus on the actual delivery of care, regardless of whether it is documented.

Legal Implications and the Role of Testimony

It is widely taught in nursing education and risk management that "if it wasn't documented, it wasn't done." However, this maxim oversimplifies the reality. In legal proceedings, evidence encompasses both written documentation—such as medical records—and sworn testimony from healthcare providers and patients. When discrepancies arise between the written record and provider recollections, it falls to the jury to determine which account is more credible.

While juries may give greater weight to contemporaneously written records, they are tasked with considering all available evidence. A lack of documentation may indicate a violation of documentation standards but does not automatically mean hands-on care was not provided. For instance, if a nurse turns a patient every two hours as required but does not record it, the nurse has failed to meet documentation standards but still has fulfilled the hands-on care standard. In such cases, providers can rely on their sworn testimony to establish that care was rendered.

Provider Responses and the Influence of Training

Legal nurse consultants working for plaintiffs often emphasize every lapse in documentation, extrapolating that missing documentation imply missing care. In contrast, those working for the defense may interview providers to clarify their recollection of events. Providers sometimes doubt their own memories, feeling constrained by "not documented, not done" training—even when they recall performing the care. It is important for consultants to reassure staff, explaining the distinction between failing to document (a record-keeping issue) and failing to provide care (a clinical issue).

Transitioning to Electronic Records

As healthcare systems adopt electronic health records, new challenges and legal strategies are emerging. Transitioning from paper-based to electronic documentation has shifted the landscape, prompting both plaintiffs and defendants to adapt their approaches.

Challenges with Electronic Records

One significant feature of many EHR systems is the use of self-populating fields. These fields are designed to streamline documentation by automatically filling in standard responses or checklists based on typical patient encounters. For example, a gastrointestinal (GI) review of systems might auto-populate with, "Denies appetite changes, weight changes, dysphagia, nausea, vomiting, hematemesis, bright red blood per rectum, melena, abdominal pain, colic, icterus, diarrhea, constipation, change in bowels, tenesmus, hemorrhoids, rectal pain, hernia."

If a patient reports any symptoms, the provider selects or highlights the relevant terms (often in bold or with visual indicators). If the patient denies all symptoms, no further action may be required, and the system records a blanket denial. While efficient, these features can inadvertently introduce inaccuracies if providers overlook or fail to ask each question individually.

New Plaintiff Strategies and Expanded Hypothetical Scenarios

Recently, plaintiffs have begun to challenge the assumption that documented care was performed, particularly when self-populating fields are involved. They may allege that, despite thorough electronic documentation, providers did not truly ask the questions or perform the assessments recorded. This shift is largely due to the prevalence of EHRs and the potential for automated entries to misrepresent actual interactions.

Consider the following expanded scenarios:

- Scenario One: Close Temporal Proximity. A patient visits his primary care provider (PCP), whose EHR system uses self-populating fields for the GI review. The record indicates the patient denied all GI symptoms. The next day, the patient presents to the emergency department with acute abdominal pain and is diagnosed with a ruptured diverticulum. In this case, the proximity of the two visits raises questions about whether the PCP's documentation accurately reflects what was asked or if the self-populated denial was entered without a thorough review. Upon investigation, the PCP recalls being rushed due to a high patient load and may admit to his attorney to relying heavily on the default entries, highlighting how workflow pressures can impact documentation accuracy.

- Scenario Two: Extended Time Interval. In a similar situation, the patient visits the ER two weeks after the PCP appointment. Here, it is less likely that the PCP's documentation was inaccurate, as GI conditions can develop or worsen over time. However, if the provider's notes are identical across multiple visits, it may suggest overreliance on self-populating fields rather than tailored patient assessments. Providers may respond by explaining their typical workflow, describing how they use templates but make adjustments when patients report new or changing symptoms.
- Scenario Three: Other Types of Self-Populating Fields. Beyond GI reviews, self-populating fields are common in documenting pain assessments, fall risk evaluations, or medication reconciliations. For example, a nurse may click "no allergies" by default, but if the patient reports a new allergy not listed in the system, this could lead to a discrepancy. Providers may later testify that they followed protocol but acknowledge that the system's defaults may not always capture nuanced patient responses unless actively modified.

In all these scenarios, patients (plaintiffs) may rely on their own testimony to claim that certain questions were never asked, while defendants use provider testimony to assert that care was rendered according to policy. The jury ultimately weighs the credibility of both sides.

Implications for Legal Nurse Consultants

Best Practices and Handling Inconsistencies

Legal nurse consultants must be vigilant in recognizing the limitations of both paper and electronic documentation. When reviewing records, it is important to:

- Identify patterns or inconsistencies between the patient's reported experience and the documented care.
- Assess whether self-populating fields or templates could have contributed to inaccuracies.
- Interview providers about their standard practices, use of EHR features, and recollection of specific patient encounters.

Guidance on Affidavits and Testimony

When forming expert opinions or affidavits, consultants should rely on sworn statements rather than unsworn reports when medical records conflict with plaintiff recollections. Defense attorneys increasingly challenge affidavits based on hearsay or staff recollections unless they are corroborated by the patient's own sworn testimony. Affidavits based on unsworn reports may be dismissed by courts or weaken the credibility of the case, potentially jeopardizing the outcome for the plaintiff. For example, I have seen affidavits that have stated, "According to the paralegal at the plaintiff's law firm, the plaintiff complained of pain..." This type of affidavit is unacceptable. An acceptable affidavit might state, "According to the affidavit of patient John Remoran, he complained of pain in his lower left side when he visited Dr. X on February 18, 2025," rather than relying on secondhand information.

Verbal testimony, when sworn, carries the same legal weight as written documentation. Legal nurse consultants should prepare to address cases where documentation and testimony conflict, especially as EHRs create new avenues for dispute.

Conclusion: Evolving Standards and Recommendations

The maxim "not documented, not done" is no longer sufficient in an era of electronic records and automated documentation. Legal nurse consultants and healthcare professionals must distinguish between failing to document and failing to provide care, understand the strengths and limitations of EHRs, and approach each case with a critical eye toward both written and verbal evidence. By staying informed and adapting to these evolving standards, professionals can better serve patients, providers, and the legal system.

Switch in Plaintiff and Defense Tactics

What it Means for Legal Nurses and Healthcare Providers

As discussed in the last article, electronic medical records (EMRs) have led to a fascinating shift in legal strategies during medical malpractice cases. Not long ago, plaintiff attorneys often argued, "If it's not documented, it's not done," insisting that missing chart notes meant missed care. Defense teams would counter with sworn testimony from nurses and doctors, filling in the gaps with their recollections. Now, the tables have turned. EMRs are so detailed—and yes, sometimes overwhelming—that plaintiff attorneys are questioning whether all that documented care happened. As a result, they're now relying more on sworn testimony to challenge what's in the record.

What does this shift mean for you as a legal nurse consultant or healthcare provider? For one, the credibility of both documentation and testimony will face greater scrutiny in courtrooms. We can expect future malpractice cases to dig deeper into the consistency, accuracy, and authenticity of the medical record. Could a perfect chart raise more suspicion than a messy one? Might a nurse's or doctor's sworn statement now carry more or less weight than before? This new reality calls for increased vigilance in documentation and a sharper eye for inconsistencies—because every detail, whether written or spoken, could become the battleground.

Let's revisit a case that I reviewed: A young man went to an Emergency Room because of left groin pain. Over the next several hours, the patient's pain subsided from 9/10 to 1/10. The ER physician diagnosed a small inguinal hernia, reduced the hernia, referred the patient to a surgeon, and told the patient to return to the ER if his pain returned. Two days later, the patient went to a different hospital with right testicular pain and had an emergency orchiectomy for torsion.

The plaintiff alleged that the ER physician at the first hospital should have diagnosed testicular torsion even though there was no evidence of a testicular problem found in the medical records. To bolster his argument, the plaintiff submitted a sworn affidavit that he was writhing in pain during his entire ER visit. He swore that he told the doctor and nurse that his pain was in his right testicle, not his left groin. In other words, he disputed everything that the doctor and nurse documented about his ER visit.

At first glance, the chart and the affidavit couldn't be further apart. But is it possible that something other than intentional misrepresentation is at play? People's memories fade, and acute pain or stress can cloud recall. Could the patient have misunderstood what he was asked or miscommunicated his symptoms? Did the staff perhaps focus so much on the obvious groin issue that they missed subtle clues about testicular pain? These are the questions that turn simple contradictions into complex puzzles.

As a legal nurse consultant, how would you approach such a situation? I would start by comparing the timeline and language in both the chart and the affidavit. Look for objective findings—vital signs, medication responses, imaging results—that support or challenge each account. Since I'm a defense LNC, I would interview other staff present during the visit to gather additional perspectives. Plaintiff LNCs would want to suggest to the attorney to depose the other staff. I would review hospital policies: Were pain assessments and communications documented according to standard practice? I would consider requesting security footage for context or checking for translation needs if language barriers might have played a role. The goal isn't just to pick sides but to help attorneys understand the full picture. Are you alert for subtle signs of error, oversight, or honest confusion? How can you help ensure the truth—and not just the best-prepared story—prevails?

This evolving legal landscape means your role as a legal nurse consultant is more critical than ever. With greater scrutiny on both records and recollections, your analytical skills and attention to detail can make all the difference. So, how will you rise to the challenge? Are you ready to dig beneath the surface and ask the tough questions?

Understanding Nursing Documentation Standards

Nursing Documentation Practices: Distinguishing "Shouldn't from "Don't"

In both clinical and legal contexts, it is crucial to distinguish why nurses shouldn't document every aspect of patient care and why they don't do so in practice. For those unfamiliar with nursing workflows, this distinction can clarify how documentation is approached and why certain actions may not appear in a patient's medical record.

Why Nurses Shouldn't Document Everything

Nurses shouldn't document every minor action or step performed during patient care, primarily due to time constraints and the need to maintain workflow efficiency. Documenting each detail—such as verifying medication labels or opening packaging—would be impractical and could detract from direct patient care. Professional guidelines, including those from state nursing boards and accrediting bodies like The Joint Commission, emphasize that documentation should be concise, relevant, and focused on information that impacts patient outcomes and safety. Excessive documentation of routine, non-clinically significant actions is discouraged as it can lead to information overload and reduce the clarity of the record.

Why Nurses Don't Document Everything

Contrary to the mantra, "If it wasn't documented, it wasn't done," nurses don't document every step because many routine actions are considered standard practice within the profession. For example, when administering medication, nurses typically record the time, route, and patient response. However, they may not document routine safety checks—such as confirming the patient's identity or verifying the dosage—because these steps are universally expected and embedded in nursing protocols. These unwritten practices are supported by professional standards and are assumed to be performed unless otherwise noted.

According to guidance from the American Nurses Association, nursing documentation should prioritize clinically relevant observations and interventions, as well as patient responses. The focus is on capturing meaningful information that directly affects patient care, rather than exhaustive records of every action taken during a shift.

For legal nurse consultants, understanding and explaining these documentation practices is essential when preparing attorneys for medical malpractice cases. By clarifying what constitutes standard nursing practice versus what is formally documented, LNCs help bridge the gap between clinical realities and legal expectations, ensuring that attorneys appreciate the context in which care is provided and documented.

Effective Nursing Documentation: Legal Implications and Best Practices

Enhancing Patient Safety and Reducing Liability through Clear Charting

Accurate and detailed nursing documentation is critical for patient safety and legal protection. The language nurses use in medical records can have far-reaching consequences, influencing not only clinical decisions but also potential legal outcomes. Vague charting, such as the phrase "will continue to monitor," often fails to communicate necessary information, putting both patients and practitioners at risk.

Common Pitfalls: Risks of Vague Charting

One of the most problematic habits in nursing documentation is relying on ambiguous statements like "will continue to monitor." This phrase may signal ongoing observation, but it often masks a lack of critical thinking or timely action. As a result, defense attorneys may struggle to justify the nurse's actions, while plaintiff attorneys find grounds for litigation.

Real-Life Example: Gradual Decline Missed in the ICU

Consider the following case from a surgical ICU: During a change-of-shift walking round, a nurse noticed a patient with a drooping right eye and mouth, a weak right upper extremity, and a flaccid right lower extremity—none of which were present the previously. The outgoing nurse had diligently charted hourly assessments but failed to recognize the subtle, cumulative changes. By the end of the shift, the patient had suffered a dramatic and irreversible stroke, illustrating the dangers of documenting subtle decline without intervention.

Documentation Standards: Guidance from the Joint Commission

According to the Joint Commission's guidelines, nursing documentation must be clear, timely, and accurately reflect the patient's status and interventions taken. Documentation should never be used as a filler or a substitute for clinical judgment and action. The Joint Commission emphasizes that vague statements like "will continue to monitor" do not meet standards for effective communication and can contribute to adverse events and legal exposure.(Joint Commission, "Documentation of Care, Treatment, and Services," 2024)

Recommended Actions: Steps for Meaningful Documentation

Instead of relying on vague charting, nurses should pause after each assessment and ask: "Has this patient's condition changed since the last shift?" If the answer is yes, the next question should be, "Is this change significant?" Significant changes require prompt notification of the provider and clear documentation of actions taken. This proactive approach not only improves patient outcomes but also provides legal protection.

Case Study: Paralysis from Missed Assessments

In another case, a nurse documented a patient's complaint of numb legs after an accident and wrote, "will continue to monitor." However, no further assessments were recorded during the twelve-hour shift. By the time the next nurse took over, the patient had become paraplegic. This scenario underscores how insufficient documentation and a lack of follow-up can result in severe consequences and potential breaches of the standard of care.

Best Practices: Actionable Advice for Nurses and Legal Nurse Consultants

To avoid documentation pitfalls, nurses should:

- Document specific observations and interventions, not just intentions to monitor.
- Recognize and record changes in condition promptly.
- Notify providers of significant changes and document the communication.
- Reference authoritative guidelines, such as those from the Joint Commission, to ensure compliance.
- Legal nurse consultants (LNCs) reviewing records should apply the same critical questions: Was there a change in condition? Was the provider notified? Were appropriate assessments performed?

Conclusion: Reinforcing the Need for Clear, Actionable Documentation

Precise, actionable documentation protects patients and nurses alike. By moving beyond vague charting and following established standards, nurses can ensure their records reflect both clinical vigilance and accountability. Ultimately, the goal is to safeguard patients' well-being and reduce legal risk through thoughtful, thorough documentation.

Understanding Hindsight Bias

The Role of the Legal Nurse Consultant

A retrospectoscope is a term used in the medical and legal fields to describe the act of evaluating a situation after knowing its outcome—a form of looking back with 20/20 hindsight. While this perspective can make it seem easy to identify what the correct diagnosis or plan of treatment should have been, it can also introduce bias into the analysis of medical cases, especially in the context of medical malpractice.

A Legal Nurse Consultant (LNC) is a registered nurse who applies their clinical expertise to assist attorneys in understanding medical records and healthcare issues that arise in legal cases. By interpreting complex medical information, LNCs help ensure that the legal process is informed by accurate medical insights.

Most attorneys and LNCs strive to approach each case with fairness and objectivity. The challenge, however, is to avoid the influence of hindsight bias. When reviewing a case after the fact—especially if a patient experiences a negative outcome or death—it can be tempting to scrutinize each detail through the lens of what is now known. This is not inherently problematic, as thorough analysis is essential. The problem can arise if an LNC unintentionally focuses only on information that supports a particular outcome, rather than considering all available evidence.

For example, suppose a patient presents with symptoms of confusion and dizziness. These symptoms are quite general and could indicate many different conditions. If the patient later experiences a stroke, it might be easy—using the retrospectoscope—to suggest that the confusion and dizziness were clear warning signs of a transient ischemia attack (TIA). A TIA is a temporary reduction in blood flow to the brain, which can cause stroke-like symptoms but typically resolves within minutes to hours. However, these symptoms could also be due to other causes such as hypoglycemia, dehydration, or a range of other disorders. Real-world examples like this highlight the importance of considering all potential explanations, not just those apparent in hindsight.

To avoid hindsight bias, LNCs should remember that healthcare providers make decisions based on the information available to them at the time—not on knowledge gained after the fact. Legal nurse consultants play a vital role in ensuring that case reviews are grounded in the realities faced by providers in the moment, which supports a fair and balanced legal process.

Accentuate Both the Positives and Negatives in Medical Case Analysis

Making Medical Terms Accessible for Legal Nurse Consultants

There's an old song with lyrics that go, "You've got to accentuate the positive, eliminate the negative." The song describes how to achieve happiness by focusing on the positive aspects of life while playing down the adverse ones. However, if you are a legal nurse consultant who is new to medical malpractice case analysis, you'd better not eliminate the negatives because they could be the crux of the case.

Analyzing medical malpractice cases requires careful attention to both positive and negative findings in patient records. While focusing on positive aspects may seem like a path to happiness, in the world of medical case review, ignoring negative findings can lead to missed critical information. For legal nurse consultants who are new to case analysis, understanding and accurately interpreting both positives and negatives is essential to building a strong case.

Defining Key Medical Terms

- PSA (Prostate-Specific Antigen): A blood test used to help detect prostate cancer by measuring the level of PSA, a protein produced by prostate cells.
- Osteopenia: A condition where bone mineral density is lower than normal, but not low enough to be classified as osteoporosis. It indicates an increased risk of fractures.
- Barium Enema: An imaging test where barium sulfate is introduced into the colon through the rectum. It helps highlight abnormalities in the large intestine on X-rays.

Here are a few questions to ask as you analyze the positives and negatives related to the allegations in your cases:

Test Interpretation

- Were test results misinterpreted as normal or negative when they were actually positive? For example, if a mammogram (an X-ray of the breast) is incorrectly read as negative, cancer may go undetected and worsen over time.
- Are the results dependent on how a physician or technician interprets the test? Some exams, such as bone density tests, require accurate data entry. If information is entered incorrectly, the results may not reflect the patient's true condition.
- Did the person interpreting the test consider the possibility of error and seek a second opinion or review?
- Did the ordering physician question unexpected results, or were they accepted without further investigation?

Patient Harm

- Did the patient experience harm due to a misread or misinterpreted test? For example, if a bone density test incorrectly reports osteopenia instead of osteoporosis, the patient may not receive aggressive treatment, leading to fractures.
- When did a physical finding become positive or abnormal? Consider a scenario where a 65-year-old man sues his physician for a delayed prostate cancer diagnosis. Did he have annual PSA (Prostate-Specific Antigen) tests? Were results explained to him? Were previous results within normal limits or did they rise gradually?
- Were there any delays in treatment due to missed or misunderstood test results?

Screening Guidelines

- Did the physician follow recommended screening protocols for early disease detection? For instance, a 54-year-old woman sues for failure to detect colon cancer. Was her family history considered? Did her doctor recommend a colonoscopy at age 45, or earlier if her family history was positive?
- Were other screening tests ordered, such as barium enema, CT colonography (a special type of CT scan for the colon), or fecal occult blood tests (which check for hidden blood in stool)?
- Did the patient follow medical recommendations, and were the results communicated clearly?

Case Scenarios: Impact of False Positives and Negatives

- False Negative Mammogram: A woman receives a negative mammogram result, although she really has early-stage breast cancer. The missed diagnosis allows the cancer to grow and worsen before it is finally detected, negatively impacting her prognosis.

- False Positive HIV Test: A patient receives a positive HIV test result but does not have the virus. This leads to unnecessary emotional distress and possibly unwarranted treatment.
- Incorrect Bone Density Test: A patient with osteoporosis is incorrectly diagnosed with osteopenia. Lack of proper treatment increases their risk of fractures and related complications.

Conclusion

When reviewing medical records in malpractice cases, it's crucial to pay attention to both positive and negative findings. Positive results highlight the presence of disease, while negative or normal findings can indicate the absence of disease. However, misinterpretation of these results—whether due to human error or test limitations—can have serious consequences for patient care. Legal nurse consultants should always accentuate both the positives and the negatives to ensure a thorough and accurate case analysis.

Understanding Mammograms in Medical Malpractice Cases

The Importance of Accurate Interpretation for Timely Breast Cancer Diagnosis

Accurate interpretation of mammograms is crucial in medical malpractice cases, especially those involving allegations of delayed or missed breast cancer diagnoses. As a two-time survivor of triple negative breast cancer, I have a deep, personal understanding of the stakes involved. Legal nurse consultants play a key role in helping attorneys navigate the complexities of mammogram classifications, required follow-up, and the consequences of errors in the diagnostic process.

Mammogram Classification: Screening vs. Diagnostic

Mammograms are generally classified into two types: screening and diagnostic. The imaging procedure itself is similar for both, but the context and follow-up differ. A screening mammogram is performed on patients who have no signs or symptoms of breast cancer. These patients typically leave the facility after their mammogram, and the images are interpreted later by a radiologist, with results sent by mail or through their healthcare provider.

In contrast, a diagnostic mammogram is indicated when a patient presents with symptoms such as a palpable lump, thickening, or unexplained breast pain. In these cases, the mammogram is read promptly, often while the patient remains onsite, allowing the radiologist to discuss findings and recommend immediate next steps.

The distinction between these classifications is not just procedural—it has significant implications for malpractice allegations. Errors in classification can lead to harmful delays in diagnosis and treatment.

Case Example: The Consequences of Misclassification

Consider the case of Ms. A, a 52-year-old woman who reported minor breast discomfort to her primary care provider. Her mammogram was incorrectly marked as a screening study, despite her symptoms. As a result, she left the imaging center without a same-day radiologist consultation. The radiologist reviewed her mammogram hours later, noted a subtle abnormality, and sent a routine follow-up letter. By the time Ms. A returned for additional imaging months later, she was diagnosed with stage III breast cancer. This delay, caused by misclassification, contributed to a more advanced disease and limited her treatment options.

BI-RADS Categories: Definitions and Significance

To standardize mammogram interpretations, radiologists use the Breast Imaging-Reporting and Data System (BI-RADS®), developed by the American College of Radiology. These categories guide follow-up recommendations and patient management:

- BI-RADS 0: Incomplete – More imaging or prior studies are needed before making a final assessment.
- BI-RADS 1: Negative – No evidence of cancer; routine screening recommended.
- BI-RADS 2: Benign – Non-cancerous findings; routine screening recommended.
- BI-RADS 3: Probably Benign – Findings are likely not cancer, but short-term follow-up is suggested.
- BI-RADS 4: Suspicious – Abnormality with a risk of cancer; biopsy should be considered.
- BI-RADS 5: Highly Suggestive of Malignancy – Strong suspicion of cancer; immediate action is necessary.
- BI-RADS 6: Known Biopsy-Proven Malignancy – Cancer already confirmed by biopsy.

The BI-RADS system ensures clear communication and sets expectations for next steps, reducing ambiguity in patient care.

Spot Compression Mammograms: Definition and Role

Sometimes, a mammogram reveals an area that appears questionable or unclear. In these cases, a spot compression mammogram is performed. This specialized imaging technique applies focused pressure to a small region of the breast, helping to distinguish overlapping tissues from true abnormalities. Spot compression can clarify ambiguous findings and determine whether further testing, such as ultrasound or biopsy, is necessary.

Common Allegations in Medical Malpractice

Many malpractice cases stem from two main pitfalls: misinterpretation of imaging and confusion over ordering additional studies. One frequent allegation is that a radiologist failed to recommend or order further imaging—such as spot compression, breast ultrasound, or breast MRI—after an unclear or suspicious mammogram. For instance, if a radiologist overlooks a subtle abnormality on a mammogram and does not recommend further imaging, this oversight may result in delayed diagnosis and subsequent legal action. Historically, regulations required only the treating practitioner to order additional studies, but this has changed, and radiologists now often initiate further testing to ensure timely care. However, insurance restrictions sometimes complicate this process by requiring no more than one breast imaging study per day, which can delay necessary follow-up tests and potentially impact patient outcomes. These limitations can hinder prompt decision-making and may force providers to prioritize studies, potentially increasing the risk of missed or delayed diagnoses.

Another recurring issue is the misreading of mammograms as negative or benign when a malignancy is present. If a patient is told to return in a year for routine screening but has an undetected cancer, the delay can allow the disease to progress to a more advanced and less treatable stage.

Conclusion: Impact of Errors on Patient Outcomes

Errors in mammogram classification and interpretation can have profound consequences for patients, leading to delayed diagnoses, more advanced cancer, and reduced chances of successful treatment. Legal nurse consultants and medical legal professionals must understand these processes, key terms, and the significance of timely follow-up to effectively advocate for patients and ensure accountability in breast cancer care.

Teleradiology Medical Malpractice Guidelines: A Guide for LNCs

Structured Steps for Investigating Teleradiologist Compliance and Supporting Attorney Education

Teleradiology, the remote interpretation of imaging studies, plays a crucial role in modern healthcare. However, just like on-site radiologists, teleradiologists are subject to medical malpractice claims if interpretations are inaccurate or guidelines are not followed. The American College of Radiology (ACR) has established specific standards for teleradiology to ensure quality and accountability. As a legal nurse consultant (LNC), your expertise is essential in determining whether these guidelines were met and in educating attorneys about the unique aspects of teleradiology malpractice cases.

Licensing Requirements

Proper licensure is foundational to teleradiology practice. LNCs should first verify whether the teleradiologist holds valid medical licenses in both the transmitting state (where the patient underwent the imaging study) and the receiving state (where the radiologist is located). Most states now require this by law, following ACR guidance. Sample LNC Scenario: When reviewing a case, you might ask: "Does the teleradiologist have an active medical license in the state where the imaging was performed and in the state where the interpretation took place?" Relevance to Malpractice: Practicing without appropriate licensure could invalidate a teleradiologist's authority to interpret studies and may strengthen a plaintiff's malpractice claim. Once licensure is confirmed, LNCs can proceed to other credential checks.

Certification and Privileges

Beyond licensure, teleradiologists should be certified by the American Board of Radiology (ABR) and hold staff privileges at each facility transmitting images for their interpretation. LNCs play a key role in verifying these credentials. Sample LNC Questions: "Is the teleradiologist listed as board-certified on the ABR website?" and "Does the teleradiologist have documented staff privileges at the originating facility?" Actionable Step: Use online resources, such as the ABR website for certification and state physician profile sites for malpractice insurance and privilege verification (if available). If information is unavailable, recommend that the attorney request it through discovery. Relevance to Malpractice: Lack of board certification or required privileges may indicate a failure to meet professional standards, increasing liability risk.

Case Example: An attorney questions whether a teleradiologist in a malpractice suit was properly credentialed. You, as the LNC, check the ABR website and confirm certification. Next, you review the facility's records and discover the teleradiologist lacks staff privileges at the transmitting hospital—a significant finding that could impact the case.

Quality Assurance

Participation in quality assurance (QA) programs ensures that teleradiologists adhere to the same standards as on-site staff. The ACR recommends that teleradiologists be involved in the originating facility's QA and quality improvement activities. Sample LNC Question: "Was the teleradiologist engaged in the facility's ongoing quality assurance or peer review process?" Relevance to Malpractice: QA involvement demonstrates professional accountability; absence may suggest systemic issues and contribute to liability if errors occur. Transitioning from credential checks to QA involvement helps ensure that teleradiologists are truly integrated into the facility's patient safety culture.

Communication Standards

Effective communication is vital—especially for emergent cases. Teleradiologists should be immediately available for consultation on urgent matters and must establish clear processes for communicating findings in non-emergent cases. Facility policies often dictate whether the teleradiologist's reading is preliminary, with a final interpretation by a local radiologist. Sample LNC Questions: "Was the teleradiologist available for immediate consultation when required?" and "What procedures were in place for relaying critical findings?" Actionable Step: Review facility policies and procedures related to teleradiology, which can be obtained through the discovery process. Relevance to Malpractice: Delays or failures in communication can directly impact patient outcomes and are frequent grounds for malpractice claims. This section of the ACR guidelines builds on prior guidelines by emphasizing the need for seamless interaction between remote and on-site staff.

Conclusion: The Importance of Comprehensive LNC Investigation and Education

Investigating teleradiology malpractice involves more than checking basic credentials—it requires a thorough review of licensure, certification, privileges, QA participation, and communication practices. By systematically addressing each guideline and asking targeted questions, LNCs provide invaluable support to attorneys and help uphold teleradiology standards.

Anesthesia Record Analysis Made Simple

Accessible Strategies and Practical Tools for Legal Nurse Consultants

When I first started as a legal nurse consultant, the sheer amount of information packed onto hand-written anesthesia records felt overwhelming. Even with electronic records, the challenge remained: so many details, so little space! But over time, I developed an easy, practical method to break down this intimidating task—and it's all about using simple, low-tech tools anyone can master.

Breaking Down Overwhelming Tasks

The secret to tackling big, complex jobs—like analyzing anesthesia records—is to break them into manageable pieces. Before I dive into any review, I mentally divide each record into clear sections. For anesthesia records, typical sections include:

- Monitors and equipment used during anesthesia
- Type of airway utilized
- Medications and anesthetic agents administered
- Vital signs and patient responses

This approach transforms the record from a chaotic blur into a series of manageable checklists.

Essential Tools for Analysis

- Marker (or Highlighter): Used to mark off reviewed information and prevent duplicate entries.
- Magnifier: Helpful for enlarging hard-to-read handwriting, small print, or intricate details.
- Guide (Ruler or Paper Edge): Keeps your place as you move through time increments, ensuring accurate data entry.

Anecdote: How Simple Tools Saved the Day

I once faced an anesthesia record where the vital sign boxes—just one-eighth inch wide—were packed with tiny numbers. Using my trusty magnifying glass, I enlarged the tricky sections. With a ruler, I lined up the five-minute increments to keep my review on track. As I entered each detail into my medical chronology, I highlighted it to ensure nothing was missed or duplicated. By the end, what started as a chaotic mess was transformed into a clear, minute-by-minute timeline. Those simple tools turned a daunting task into an organized, stress-free process.

Step-by-Step Review Process

I always make a copy (or printout) of the anesthesia record so I can annotate freely. I review each section one-by-one, creating a minute-by-minute medical chronology. For electronic records, digital magnifiers and highlighters can substitute for their physical counterparts.

Anesthesia records often use graphs with tiny boxes—each representing five minutes of patient data. My guide (a ruler or paper edge) helps me line up information within these intervals, while the magnifier ensures I don't miss any critical details. As I work, I highlight each item after entering it into my chronology, keeping my review organized and thorough.

Key Questions to Ask

As you review anesthesia records, consider these grouped questions to guide your analysis:

- Pre-Anesthesia Assessment: Was a pre-anesthesia assessment performed by an anesthesiologist or a Certified Registered Nurse Anesthetist (CRNA)? If a CRNA did the assessment, did an anesthesiologist review and co-sign? When did the assessment occur—was it right before surgery or several days earlier? Was a follow-up assessment done on the day of surgery? Did the assessment include a review of the patient's history, physical exam, lab results, and EKG (as needed)? Were significant findings noted?
- Patient Consent and Safety: Did the patient sign a consent form outlining anesthesia risks and benefits?
- Did anesthesia personnel note the patient's dentition (e.g., dentures, loose teeth)?
- Technical Classifications: What was the patient's ASA class (American Society of Anesthesiologists classification, a scale from ASA 1 for healthy patients to ASA 6 for brain dead patients)? What was the Mallampati score (a scale from Class 1, easiest to intubate, to Class 4, most difficult)?
- Type and Administration of Anesthesia: What type of anesthesia was used (general, spinal, regional, or monitored anesthesia care)? Who administered the anesthesia—CRNA, anesthesiologist, or both? Was an anesthesiologist present during induction and emergence?
- Were appropriate medications given in response to changes in vital signs?
- Did the patient recover sufficiently before transfer to the recovery room or ICU?

- Electronic Records: If reviewing electronic anesthesia records, do you have a copy of the anesthesia graph? Sometimes it's not included unless requested.

Additional Record Review

Don't stop at the anesthesia record. Review related documents such as pre-anesthesia forms, anesthesia orders, perioperative notes, and post-anesthesia recovery records. Pay close attention to crucial times: patient transport, anesthesia personnel start, induction, surgery start/end, and anesthesia end. If these times aren't in the anesthesia record, look for them in the operating room nursing notes or recovery room notes. Check if any incident times align with induction or surgery start.

Conclusion: Keep It Simple and Stay Organized

Analyzing anesthesia records can be challenging, but it doesn't have to be overwhelming. By breaking the process into sections, using simple tools, and asking the right questions, you'll turn a mountain of data into a clear, useful chronology. Remember, even low-tech solutions—like a marker, magnifier, and guide—can make all the difference. Stay curious, stay organized, and trust your process.

Reference Guide: Diary Analysis in Legal Cases

Structured Evaluation for Legal Nurse Consultants

I analyzed a diary case a few weeks after I started my career as a law firm LNC. It's the case that solidified my love of the role because my analysis of a diary helped the attorney win a difficult case at trial.

Our firm received this case after two other defense firms had told the adjustor that the diary written by the plaintiff's daughter would sink the case. Naturally, I read the diary first and was horrified, because there seemed to be some big lapses in the standard of care. However, as I read the diary, I entered the information into a medical chronology, and thought, hmmm. There seemed to be some big gaps between dates in the diary. So, instead of focusing solely on the negative parts of the diary, I looked for inconsistencies and context that suggested alternative explanations for the events described. I analyzed the diary from this new perspective and realized there were overlooked details that could support our defense. And, needless to say, I compared the diary entries to the facts in the medical records.

Not everyone keeps a diary, of course, but diaries written by patients or their family members can be influential pieces of evidence in medical malpractice and nursing home litigation. Depending on their contents and context, diaries may strengthen a plaintiff's claim or bolster a defense. As a legal nurse consultant, you are responsible for carefully reviewing these diaries to assess if they will benefit or harm your case. The following guide outlines a structured approach for diary analysis, connecting each evaluation step with practical examples to illustrate their impact on jury decisions.

Diary Analysis Criteria

Begin your analysis by examining the diary with specific evaluation questions. Each criterion helps clarify how the diary's content may be interpreted by a jury and supports your overall case review strategy.

- Timing of Diary Entries. Was the diary written contemporaneously with the events it describes, or was it created retrospectively? Accurate, timely entries often carry more weight, while delayed entries can introduce bias or inaccuracies. To assess timing, compare diary entries to a medical chronology and note discrepancies. Example: If a patient claims to have written diary entries at the time of events, but dates and details do not match medical records, this can discredit the writer in the eyes of the jury.
- Purpose Behind the Diary. Why was the diary written? Understanding the motive—whether as emotional release or for documentation—can influence its credibility. If possible, have someone from your law firm ask the writer directly, or address the question in deposition. Guidance: Diaries written primarily as therapy may be perceived differently than those intended for legal purposes.
- Gaps in Diary Entries. Are there unexplained gaps or missing periods in the diary? Significant gaps, especially during critical events, can raise questions about the diary's completeness or authenticity. Anecdote: In one case, a daughter's diary omitted six weeks when her mother was transferred to hospice. The inability to explain this gap led the jury to question her honesty, resulting in a defense verdict.
- Inclusion of Unrelated Information. Does the diary contain details unrelated to the case? Excessive unrelated content can undermine the diary's relevance and focus. Example: The daughter's diary mentioned her mother's pain six times but referenced visits to Kentucky Fried Chicken 12 times. This detail, when highlighted in court, diminished the plaintiff's case by suggesting misplaced priorities.
- Presentation and Tone of Facts. How are events and emotions described? A detached tone may be portrayed as cold by the defense, while strong emotional language might be viewed as "hot-headed" or, conversely, as justified outrage. Tip: Carefully note whether the diary's tone supports or detracts from your side's narrative.

- Evidence of Outside Influence. Does the language suggest legal or medical coaching? Phrases like "duty" or technical terminology may indicate that the writer received professional help, which can affect perceived authenticity. Sample Entry: "This is neglect and it is the duty of ABC Nursing Home to find out what happened..." Such wording is uncommon among laypersons and can signal outside influence.
- Use of Medical Records in Diary Composition. Was the diary written after reviewing medical records? Entries that mirror medical record language ("released," "personal car") may suggest post-hoc editing rather than personal recollection. Sample Comparison: "James was released and returned to ABC Nursing Home by personal car" versus "I drove James back to the nursing home from the ER."
- Actions Taken Beyond Writing. Did the writer take any steps other than documenting events—such as speaking to management or reporting issues to authorities or file a complaint with a state licensing agency? A diary without evidence of further action may be viewed as lacking genuine concern. Guidance: Juries may question whether the writer was truly affected if their only response were to write in a diary.

Applying the Analysis: Connecting Criteria to Case Outcomes

As you move through these evaluation steps, remember that each criterion connects diary content to its potential legal impact. By documenting your findings and relating them to real-world examples, you create a stronger, more defensible position for your side. Use color-coding or annotations to distinguish between contemporaneous and retrospective entries and always cross-reference diary details with official records.

Conclusion: The Value of Structured Diary Analysis

A thorough, organized analysis of patient and family diaries is essential in legal nurse consulting. By systematically evaluating timing, motive, content gaps, relevance, tone, outside influences, use of medical records, and the writer's actions, you ensure that diary evidence is clearly understood and effectively leveraged for your case. Real-world examples demonstrate how these details can sway jury decisions, underscoring the importance of a structured approach.

Pharmacy Record Analysis

Guidance for Legal Nurse Consultants

As a new legal nurse consultant, you may be tasked with analyzing pharmacy records for plaintiffs in medical malpractice cases. At first glance, these records may appear to be simple lines of data with limited relevance. However, a systematic approach can reveal critical information to support or refute case claims.

Step-by-Step Analysis Process

The initial step is to identify all medications listed in the records. While it is important to be thorough, keep in mind that not every medication will be relevant to the legal issues at hand. Focus on those drugs that relate to the plaintiff's allegations.

For example, in a case involving emotional distress, search for prescriptions such as anxiolytics or antidepressants that may indicate attempts to manage those symptoms. Similarly, in pain management cases, examine whether the plaintiff received and regularly refilled pain medications, which could validate claims of severe, persistent pain.

Once you have identified relevant medications, the next step is to review refill patterns to assess compliance. Consistent refills, typically every 30 days for scheduled medications, can suggest adherence to treatment, while gaps may point to potential non-compliance. For a visual representation, tools like a Medication Non-Compliance Calendar (see Reports chapter) can be helpful.

Following this, examine prescriber information to uncover possible gaps in the medical record. Pay attention to new or unfamiliar prescribers, noting their names and specialties. Discovering a new prescriber, such as an emergency medicine physician or hospitalist, may indicate an ER visit or recent hospitalization. If the pharmacy record includes prescriptions outside the known medical record timeline, alert the attorney so they can request updated records.

Additionally, consider other concrete scenarios, such as medication interactions or adverse effects. For instance, if the plaintiff alleges harm due to drug interactions, closely review pharmacy records for combinations of medications known to interact. Similarly, check for prescriptions that may have side effects relevant to the case allegations.

Be Aware of Potential Pitfalls

While conducting your analysis, there are several common mistakes and challenges to avoid. One frequent pitfall is missing records from smaller, independent pharmacies, as plaintiffs may use multiple dispensing locations. Defense firms often subpoena the largest area pharmacies, but overlooking smaller establishments could result in incomplete data.

Another challenge is interpreting gaps in medication refills. Not all gaps indicate non-compliance; legitimate reasons such as hospitalization, changes in treatment plans, or medication discontinuation should be considered. Ensure you correlate prescription dates with medical records and consult with the attorney about any inconsistencies.

Conclusion

By following these steps and staying alert to potential pitfalls, you can turn seemingly simple pharmacy records into a meaningful analysis for your attorney, strengthening your case through careful review and application of relevant examples.

Hospitalist Medical Malpractice

Key Findings and Guidance for Legal Nurse Consultants

Hospitalists are physicians dedicated exclusively to inpatient care, rather than seeing patients in outpatient office settings. As the attending physicians for hospitalized patients, hospitalists assume responsibility for medical decision-making during often complex and acute episodes of care. In recent years, the frequency of medical malpractice cases involving hospitalists has risen—a trend supported by a comprehensive study conducted by The Doctors Company in 2018.

The study highlights that hospitalists are more than twice as likely to be involved in cases with higher injury severity (72%) compared to other physician specialists (34%). This significant disparity underscores the unique risks associated with hospitalist practice and warrants closer examination of the underlying causes.

To understand the specific vulnerabilities in hospitalist care, it is important to review the main patient allegations identified in the study. The top two allegations were:

- Diagnosis-related issues (40%): These include failure to diagnose, delayed diagnosis, and incorrect diagnosis. The most frequently misdiagnosed or delayed conditions were intestinal disorders, vascular problems, stroke, myocardial infarction, sepsis, pulmonary embolism, spinal epidural abscess, lung cancer, pneumonia, endocarditis, and aortic conditions.

- Improper management of treatment (28%): This category refers to cases where the diagnosis was correct, but the management was flawed. For example, a hospitalist might correctly identify hypokalemia but fail to order potassium replacement.

Additional allegations included medication-related errors (10%), failure to treat (2%), delay in treatment or procedure (5%), and failure to monitor patient status (3%). These statistics illustrate the multifaceted nature of hospitalist malpractice risks and set the stage for analyzing contributing factors.

Transitioning from allegations to causative factors, the study identified several key contributors to patient injuries:

- Patient assessment issues (35%): These were attributed to failures in developing a differential diagnosis, delays in ordering diagnostic tests, and not integrating critical clinical information from test results or nursing observations.
- Poor communication among providers (23%): This included breakdowns in nurse-to-physician communication and failures by hospitalists to review essential information documented in the medical record.

Other contributing factors were related to the selection and management of therapy, communication between providers and patients or families, failure to obtain appropriate consults or referrals, and patient-specific factors. These findings point to recurring system and process issues that legal nurse consultants should be aware of when assessing hospitalist-involved cases.

Given these insights, what practical steps should legal nurse consultants take when reviewing hospitalist cases? A structured approach can help ensure that all relevant aspects are thoroughly evaluated. Consider the following checklist:

- Identify whether a hospitalist was the attending physician during the patient's hospitalization.
- Examine the medical record for evidence of timely and accurate diagnosis, especially regarding the high-risk conditions noted above.
- Assess whether treatment plans were appropriate and whether any errors or omissions in management contributed to the outcome.
- Investigate medication orders for potential errors or omissions by the hospitalist.
- Review documentation for delays or failures in performing necessary procedures or treatments.
- Check for adequate monitoring of patient status and prompt response to clinical changes.
- Analyze communication flows between the hospitalist, nursing staff, consultants, and the patient's family for lapses or misunderstandings.

- Verify whether consults or referrals were obtained when clinically indicated.
- Document any patient-specific factors that may have influenced outcomes and the hospitalist's response to these challenges.

Using this systematic approach, legal nurse consultants can more effectively identify areas of concern and support the legal process with evidence-based analysis.

Understanding EKG Reader Services and Their Legal Implications

A Practical Guide for Legal Nurse Consultants and Attorneys

Electrocardiograms (EKGs) are essential tools for monitoring a patient's heart activity, especially in hospital settings. Occasionally, medical malpractice cases arise when an EKG is performed shortly before a patient experiences a sudden cardiac event—such as a Code Blue—and unexpectedly passes away. Attorneys often include the cardiologists who interpreted these EKGs as defendants in lawsuits. However, those cardiologists are frequently removed from the case once the specific role of EKG reader services becomes clear. Understanding how EKG reader services operate is crucial for accurately determining liability.

What Are EKG Reader Services?

EKG reader services, sometimes called EKG reading panels or EKG panels, are groups of cardiologists who contract with hospitals to interpret EKGs performed there. These cardiologists take turns, or "rotate," covering EKG interpretation during assigned days. For example, if 50 EKGs are performed at a hospital in a single day, one member of the EKG reader service is responsible for reviewing and interpreting all 50 tests during that day.

A key process used by EKG reader services is called "batch reading." In batch reading, a cardiologist sits down and reviews many EKGs—often all tests conducted over a period of hours or an entire day—in one session. This means that EKGs are not evaluated immediately after each test is completed, but rather are read together at a later, scheduled time. As a result, there can be a significant delay—sometimes nearly 24 hours—between when an EKG is performed and when it is interpreted by a cardiologist.

STAT Consults vs. Routine EKG Interpretation

Another important distinction is between a STAT cardiology consultation and a routine EKG order. A STAT consultation is an urgent request for specialist input, typically made when a provider believes immediate interpretation of the EKG is necessary due to a suspected emergency. In these cases, a cardiologist will review the EKG right away and provide input on the patient's care. For example, if a patient presents with chest pain and a doctor is concerned about possible heart ischemia, a STAT consultation would be ordered, prompting near-instant review by a cardiologist.

In contrast, if an EKG is ordered as "stat" but without a formal request for a cardiologist consult, the ordering doctors—often in the Emergency Department or a critical care unit—interpret the EKG themselves. The cardiologist from the EKG reader service will later "overread" or double-check the EKG, but this review is not immediate and may happen hours later as part of the batch reading process.

Case Scenario: Timing and Liability in Practice

Consider this hypothetical scenario: A patient in the hospital has an EKG performed at 8:00 a.m. The test shows subtle abnormalities, but no STAT cardiology consult is ordered. At 10:00 a.m., the patient suffers a cardiac arrest (a Code Blue event) and unfortunately passes away. The hospital's EKG reader service cardiologist does not review the EKG until 2:00 p.m., as part of their scheduled batch reading. In this situation, the cardiologist did not have the opportunity to intervene before the cardiac event, making them unlikely to be liable for the patient's outcome.

Legal Implications and the Role of Legal Nurse Consultants

Understanding these procedures is vital when determining who should be named in a medical malpractice case. Legal nurse consultants play a key role in analyzing medical records to identify which providers were involved in a patient's care at critical times. To assess whether a cardiologist from an EKG reader service might be liable, the nurse consultant should check the date and time the EKG was interpreted. This information is often found printed on the EKG next to the cardiologist's name.

If no interpretation time is recorded, the consultant should determine whether a STAT cardiology consult was ordered. If such a consult occurred, the cardiologist likely reviewed the EKG before documenting their consultation, and the dictation time of the consult can provide evidence of this. If there was no STAT consult, it is probable that the EKG was only reviewed later as part of the batch reading process, making it less likely that the cardiologist was involved in the patient's immediate care before the adverse event.

By carefully reviewing the timing and nature of EKG interpretations, legal nurse consultants can help attorneys accurately identify responsible parties and focus their cases on those directly involved in the patient's care at the most critical moments.

Craniosynostosis: Diagnosis, Treatment, and Legal Considerations

What is Craniosynostosis?

Have you ever seen a baby wearing a helmet that fit close to their head? The helmets are used to correct some forms of craniosynostosis. Craniosynostosis is a condition present at birth where a baby's head develops an abnormal shape because the bones in the skull fuse together too early. This early fusion prevents the skull from growing normally and can affect both appearance and brain development.

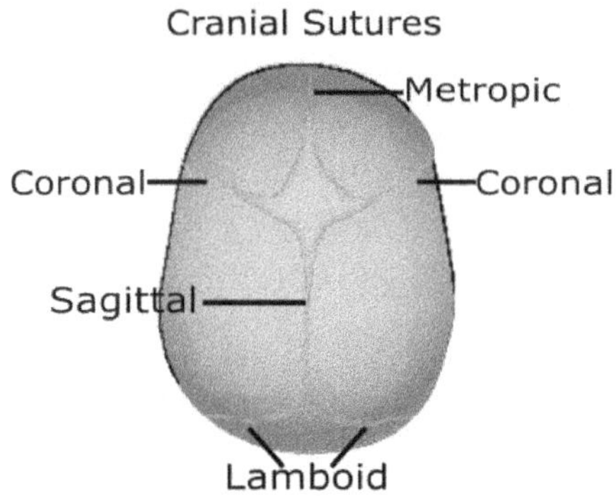

Types of Craniosynostosis

- Dolichocephaly (Scaphocephaly): When the sagittal suture (the seam running from front to back along the top of the head) closes prematurely, the skull grows long and narrow, creating an "elongated head" shape.
- Plagiocephaly ("Oblique Head"): Occurs when either a coronal or lamboid suture (seams on the sides or back of the head) closes early. This causes the head to flatten on the fused side of the suture and bulge on the opposite side, resulting in an uneven shape.
- Oxycephaly, Turricephaly, or Acrocephaly ("Cone Head"): If the coronal suture and another suture (such as lamboid) fuse too soon, the top of the head may appear pointed or cone-shaped.
- Pansynostosis: This is when three or more sutures fuse prematurely. Examples include:
    - Microcephaly: A condition where the head is abnormally small.
    - Cloverleaf Skull: A rare condition in which the skull grows in a cloverleaf shape.

Causes and Diagnosis

For most infants, the cause of craniosynostosis is unknown, but sleeping position and/or genetic factors may play a role in some cases. Parents or healthcare providers may notice an unusual head shape, which should prompt further evaluation. Diagnosis is typically confirmed through a head CT scan (a type of detailed imaging).

Treatment Options

- Surgery: Most children undergo surgery between 6 and 12 months of age. The procedure involves removing fused sutures and reshaping the skull.
- Cranial Helmet Therapy: In some cases, a special helmet can be used to gently mold the skull into a more typical shape without surgery.
- Delayed Diagnosis: If craniosynostosis is discovered after age two, treatment options may be more limited and less effective.

Legal Considerations for Nurse Consultants

When involved in a medical malpractice case regarding craniosynostosis, legal nurse consultants should:

- Determine if the diagnosis was made in a timely manner. Some forms, like pansynostosis, are obvious at birth.
- Gather photographs of the child from birth onward to help objectively document when craniosynostosis should have reasonably been recognized by a pediatrician.
- Identify any complications resulting from delayed diagnosis or treatment.
- Assess whether the child has met all developmental milestones.

Potential Complications

- Papilledema: Swelling of the optic nerve due to increased pressure inside the skull (can affect vision).
- Asymmetrical Orbit and Ear Placement: Eyes and ears may not line up normally because of bone growth changes.
- Malpositioning of Teeth: Abnormal growth can affect how teeth come in.
- Cognitive and Academic Impact: Research suggests that children with untreated single suture craniosynostosis may have lower IQs and perform worse on math tests compared to peers.

- Reference: Speltz, M.L., et al. "Intellectual and Academic Functioning of School-Age Children with Single-Suture Craniosynostosis." Pediatrics, 2015; 135(3): e615-e623.

Craniosynostosis can be a frightening diagnosis for parents, but understanding the condition, its treatment, and potential complications can empower families and professionals to seek the best outcomes.

Perineural Invasion: Actionable Guidance for Legal Nurse Consultants

Enhancing Legal Strategy and Patient Care Through Early Identification of PNI

Perineural invasion (PNI) represents a unique and often under-recognized pathway by which cancer spreads. For legal nurse consultants (LNCs), understanding PNI is critical because its presence can dramatically influence both the medical and legal aspects of a case. Early identification and proper management of PNI help guide attorneys in making informed decisions, impacting patient outcomes and legal strategy.

Definition of PNI: Distinguishing a Distinct Cancer Spread Mechanism

Traditionally, cancer is known to spread by invading nearby tissues or metastasizing through the bloodstream and lymphatic system. However, PNI occurs when cancer cells invade, travel alongside, or infiltrate nerves adjacent to the primary tumor. Unlike other forms of direct invasion, PNI can allow cancer to reach distant sites via nerve pathways. For instance, salivary duct carcinoma may progress from the primary site to cranial nerves or the brain stem through perineural routes.

PNI is most often found in cancers of the head, neck, prostate, biliary tract, stomach, rectum, and colon. The reason for this regional preference remains unclear, but its presence is associated with higher risks of local recurrence and a poorer prognosis.

Diagnosis of PNI: Pathological Identification and Detection Challenges

Diagnosing PNI requires a pathologist to examine slides for evidence of cancer cells within or around nerves. These nerves are typically too small to be detected by imaging studies, and patients may show no symptoms initially. As the disease progresses, pain or neurological deficits may emerge, highlighting the need for careful pathological review.

Because PNI is a pathological diagnosis, it is essential for LNCs to ensure that all relevant pathology slides are obtained and reviewed by an expert. This step is particularly important in cases involving anatomical regions prone to PNI or when recurrence has occurred.

Legal Implications for LNCs: Impact on Prognosis and Case Strategy

The identification of PNI can significantly alter a patient's treatment plan and long-term outlook, often necessitating more aggressive interventions, such as extensive surgery, chemotherapy, and radiation. For legal nurse consultants, recognizing PNI early allows for more accurate case evaluation, appropriate expert recommendations, and comprehensive future care planning.

Missed or delayed identification of PNI may affect legal arguments regarding standard of care, informed consent, and damages, making the LNC's role pivotal in assembling and interpreting medical evidence.

Action Steps for LNCs: Checklist for Suspected PNI

- Review all available pathology reports for evidence of perineural invasion.
- Recommend that the attorney retain an expert pathologist to interpret findings, especially in high-risk anatomical locations or if recurrence is suspected.
- Assess the patient's treatment history for aggressive interventions that may indicate PNI involvement.
- Advise the attorney on the need for additional experts, such as life care planners or economists, to evaluate long-term care and financial impact.
- Document neurological symptoms or pain that could suggest progressive PNI, supporting the need for further investigation.
- Ensure that all relevant medical records are collected, organized, and reviewed for comprehensive case analysis.

Case Study: The Impact of Early Identification

In a recent head and neck cancer case, PNI was not detected until the patient experienced a recurrence. The attorney, guided by an LNC, retained a pathologist who re-examined the original slides—previously interpreted as having clear margins—and found evidence of PNI. As a result, the patient underwent extensive surgery, including partial mandible removal and lymph node dissection, followed by chemotherapy and radiation. The LNC recommended hiring a life care planner to assess future reconstructive needs and an economist to determine financial damages. Early recognition of PNI in this scenario would have altered the initial treatment plan and legal approach, potentially improving both patient outcomes and case resolution.

Conclusion: Proactive Steps Enhance Outcomes

Perineural invasion poses complex challenges for both patient care and legal case management. By following a structured, actionable approach—reviewing pathology, recommending expert consultation, and assessing long-term needs—LNCs can play a vital role in early identification and effective advocacy. Prompt attention to PNI not only strengthens legal strategy but also supports optimal patient care and recovery.

Genomics and Medical Malpractice: A Guide for LNCs

Understanding Key Terms, Testing Types, and Legal Implications

Genomics has rapidly transformed the landscape of medical diagnosis and treatment, particularly in the context of medical malpractice. As genetic testing becomes more widely available, it is essential for legal nurse consultants and clinicians to understand not only the science behind these technologies but also their legal and ethical implications.

Types of Genetic Testing

Genetic testing encompasses a variety of methods that help identify risks for specific diseases and conditions. Historically, tests such as prenatal screening for Down syndrome and Trisomy 18, as well as newborn screening for phenylketonuria (PKU), have been routinely offered. These tests, similar to the well-known BRCA1 and BRCA2 gene tests for breast cancer risk, assess the likelihood of developing certain genetic disorders.

- Carrier Testing: Identifies individuals who carry a gene mutation that could be passed on to their children, such as those for sickle cell anemia or cystic fibrosis.
- Predictive and Presymptomatic Testing: Detects whether a person is at increased risk for diseases that may develop later, like some colon cancers or certain types of breast cancer.

- Pharmacogenetic Testing: Assesses how a person's genetic makeup affects their response to medications. For example, one patient with a genetic variant affecting drug metabolism switched to a more effective treatment after pharmacogenetic testing guided the change, resulting in improved health outcomes.
- Preimplantation Genetic Diagnosis: Used with in vitro fertilization to screen embryos for genetic abnormalities before implantation; this area raises important ethical questions.

Understanding Key Genetic Terms

- Exons: Exons are the coding regions of genes that contain instructions for making proteins—the building blocks and machinery of our bodies.
- Exome: The exome refers to the collection of all exons within a genome. Since exons comprise the protein-coding part of genes, studying the exome helps identify changes that may cause disease.
- Whole Exome Sequencing: This technique involves mapping the exome to detect mutations, such as duplications (extra copies) or deletions (missing segments) of exons. These mutations can disrupt normal function and result in disorders.
- Variant of Uncertain Significance (VUS): A VUS is a genetic change whose impact on health is not yet known. Because science has not concluded whether such variants are harmful or benign, they often require ongoing monitoring.

Advances in Genomics: Case Studies and Examples

The expansion of genetic testing means that many more genes are now tested beyond BRCA1 and BRCA2, including PTEN, CDH1, and PALB2. For instance, duplications or deletions in the PTEN gene can result in disorders like Cowden's syndrome. Alterations in the CDH1 gene may lead to several types of cancer, as can changes in the PALB2 gene.

A poignant example involves a friend with a mutation in the SMARCA4 gene—a cancer suppressor gene—who developed aggressive cancer and passed away within two months of first symptoms. This highlights the potentially life-altering consequences of genetic mutations and the importance of timely genomic analysis.

Pharmacogenetic testing also demonstrates the power of genomics: one individual's adverse reaction to a common medication was resolved when genetic testing suggested a more suitable drug, ultimately improving the patient's quality of life.

Legal Considerations in Genomic Medical Malpractice

Moving from testing methods to legal implications, genomics introduces several new considerations in malpractice claims:

- Failure to Order Genetic Testing: For example, a mother alleged that her pediatrician failed to advise her of the risk of a rare genetic disorder. Her child was ultimately diagnosed with the condition—resulting in blindness and developmental disabilities—after whole exome sequencing revealed a duplication of several exons.
- Failure to Act on or Misinterpret Results: Misunderstanding complex genomic reports, such as confusing the terms "genome" and "exome," can result in missed or incorrect diagnoses. Labs may be responsible for reporting errors, but providers are liable for interpretation and communication.
- Failure to Communicate or Follow Up on Findings: As standards evolve, providers are expected to recontact patients about new research, especially when initial results include a VUS. If patients do not return for scheduled follow-ups, they may miss critical updates on whether a variant has been reclassified as pathogenic.

Role of Legal Nurse Consultants

Legal nurse consultants play a pivotal role in reviewing medical records for evidence of appropriate genetic assessment. Key points include:

- Patient Background: Consider ethnic and family history, as some populations (e.g., individuals of Ashkenazi Jewish descent or African heritage) are at higher risk for certain genetic disorders.
- Referral to Geneticists: Assess if and when a referral was indicated and whether it was completed.
- Test Availability: Determine when relevant genetic tests became available. In one case, the physician could not have ordered a test that did not exist at the time, but a referral to a genetic specialist might have been warranted.
- Family History: Ensure that the provider obtained a thorough family medical history, as some genetic risks may not be immediately apparent.

Limitations and Future Directions

Despite its promise, genomics remains a developing science. Many mutations and their health effects remain unknown, which limits the certainty and scope of genetic testing. Standards of care in this field are evolving, and ongoing education is essential for both clinicians and legal nurse consultants.

In summary, a solid understanding of genomics—including basic concepts like exons, exome, and VUS—empowers legal nurse consultants and clinicians to better evaluate medical malpractice claims, ensure ethical care, and advocate for patients as science and the law continue to advance.

Making Sense of Medical Bills: How LNCs Help Attorneys

An Accessible Guide to Medical Bill Analysis in Legal Cases

Legal nurse consultants play a vital role in medical malpractice cases by carefully analyzing medical bills to determine the costs a patient, known as the Plaintiff, has incurred. Plaintiffs often claim these expenses resulted from alleged medical errors. Legal nurse consultants who also work as Life Care Planners use these bills to estimate the future medical needs and associated costs for the Plaintiff. However, examining medical bills goes far beyond simply listing expenses—it provides valuable insights into the case that can help attorneys build a stronger argument.

Defining Key Acronyms

- ICD (International Classification of Diseases): A global system used to classify and code all health conditions and diseases. It helps standardize the way illnesses are described in records and bills.
- CPT (Current Procedural Terminology): A set of codes used to describe medical, surgical, and diagnostic services. These codes allow for clear communication and billing of procedures across healthcare providers.
- DSM (Diagnostic and Statistical Manual of Mental Disorders): A manual that provides codes for classifying mental health conditions, making it easier to identify and bill for psychiatric diagnoses.
- NICU (Neonatal Intensive Care Unit): A specialized hospital department that provides intensive medical care for premature or seriously ill newborns.

Challenges in Reviewing Medical Records

Analyzing medical records can be tricky, especially when dealing with handwritten notes. For instance, psychiatrist records often feature handwriting that is so difficult to read that it resembles hieroglyphics, making it nearly impossible to decipher diagnoses or treatments. In these cases, reviewing DSM codes within the records can sometimes reveal key information about the patient's mental health diagnosis. On the other hand, psychologist records are usually neatly written and easy to interpret—it's almost as if penmanship is part of their training!

The shift to electronic medical records has resolved many handwriting issues but has introduced new challenges. Electronic records, especially for patients with extended hospital stays, can be overwhelming in volume. For example, when reviewing the records of a premature infant who spent 39 days in the NICU, I found thousands of pages with progress notes and test results scattered throughout. To locate when a cranial ultrasound was performed, I quickly searched the billing records for the CPT code 76506, which identified the date of the procedure. This shortcut allowed me to find the relevant study in the medical records almost immediately, saving time and helping the attorney address urgent questions.

Using Billing Codes: Streamlining Record Review

Billing codes do more than just clarify procedures—they can help resolve discrepancies and support case preparation. For instance, in another case involving a post-surgical patient, the attorney noticed a charge for a wound care procedure but couldn't find any documentation of it in the medical records. By referring to the CPT code in the billing statement, we confirmed the procedure was performed and located the nurse's notes in a separate section of the records. This helped the attorney demonstrate that the hospital provided necessary care, even though the documentation was initially hard to find.

Reasons to Analyze Medical Bills

- Identify all dates of service: Reviewing billing dates helps ensure you have a complete set of medical records from each provider. If there are bills but no corresponding records, you may be missing valuable information.
- Verify records for each service date: Medical bills may reveal procedures—like X-rays or lab tests—that aren't documented in the medical records. This highlights any gaps in the documentation.
- Discover all insurance companies involved: Billing records almost always list the patient's insurance company, which may differ from outdated information in medical records. Insurance company records can also point to additional healthcare providers.
- Identify all treating providers: Large medical groups often have multiple doctors involved in a patient's care. Billing records specify which physician saw the patient and when, clarifying exactly who provided treatment.

- Spot potential fraudulent charges: Unexplained billing for office visits, treatments, or tests without supporting medical records can be a sign of fraud. Careful review helps protect both legal and medical interests.

Conclusion: The Importance of Thorough Medical Bill Analysis

Medical bill analysis is more than just counting costs—it's a vital strategy for uncovering crucial details, clarifying discrepancies, and supporting attorneys in building strong cases. By understanding billing codes, addressing challenges in record review, and using bills to fill gaps and answer questions, legal nurse consultants make a meaningful difference in medical-legal investigations.

Profitability Case Analysis for Legal Nurse Consultants

As a new legal nurse consultant, you may initially think that plaintiff attorneys pursue medical malpractice cases solely based on the elements of professional negligence—duty, breach of duty, causation, and damages. However, plaintiff law firms also carefully analyze potential cases for profitability. Many plaintiff firms operate on a contingency basis, which means the law firm only gets paid if they win or settle the case. If the case is unsuccessful, the firm does not receive payment. This financial structure means that plaintiff firms are selective, only taking cases that show strong potential for a profitable resolution, even if professional negligence appears obvious.

Find the Deep Pockets

One common strategy is to identify "deep pocket" defendants—those with substantial financial resources or insurance coverage. A deep pocket defendant, such as a hospital or a large healthcare system, is likely to have a hefty insurance policy capable of paying large settlements or judgments. Vicarious liability is a legal concept that means an organization can be held responsible for the actions of its employees or members. For example, physician group practices can be vicariously liable for the acts of individual physicians, making the group a potential deep pocket. Similarly, hospitals may be vicariously liable for their staff, including emergency room doctors. In contrast, uninsured physicians are undesirable defendants unless they possess other significant assets.

Step-by-step recommendations for LNCs: When reviewing a case for merit, create a comprehensive treater list and, if indicated in the records, note which physicians belong to groups. Be sure to highlight any documentation showing a physician's uninsured status. Some states provide physician profiles that may include the amount of liability insurance carried.

Cast a Wide Net

Another key strategy by plaintiff firms is to cast a wide net by naming multiple parties as defendants in a lawsuit. This approach can be profitable if some defendants choose to settle early, perhaps because settling may cost less than defending the case through trial. Each settlement can help the plaintiff finance the ongoing litigation against other defendants. However, this strategy can increase costs for the plaintiff firm, as each type of defendant may require an expert witness with matching credentials, depending on state law. For example, in a case involving failure to diagnose a stroke in the emergency room, possible defendants include not only the ER physician and hospital, but also the radiologist, neurologist, neurosurgeon, and others. Each specialty would require its own expert.

Recommendation for LNCs: Develop a detailed treater list and conduct a thorough analysis to identify professional negligence by each potential defendant.

Find Liability for Big Damages

After considering the impact of damages, it's also important to recognize that plaintiff firms prioritize cases involving significant harm. Juries are often sympathetic and may award multi-million-dollar verdicts to plaintiffs who have suffered catastrophic injuries, such as brain damage in infants. Juries tend to believe that such tragic outcomes must be someone's fault, which can lead to substantial compensation even when it's unclear if there were medical errors.

Recommendation for LNCs: Identify every instance where providers failed to meet the standard of care and determine whether those failures caused or contributed to the medical catastrophe.

Assessing Client Attributes

After evaluating damages, it's also crucial to assess the attributes of the client. Plaintiff characteristics can influence jury sympathy and, ultimately, the profitability of a case. Juries may be less generous to clients viewed as greedy or as having contributed to their own injuries. For example, adult children suing a nursing home over a parent's death may seem unsympathetic if they rarely visited the parent. Similarly, clients with histories of drug abuse, non-compliance, alcoholism, or criminal backgrounds may not elicit sympathy.

Recommendations for LNCs: When meeting potential clients, take a thorough background history and assess their credibility and likeability. Pay close attention to the client's social history, especially if they are claiming lost wages—tax returns will be important. Marital status should also be checked, as divorced spouses may have limitations in filing lawsuits depending on state law. While reviewing medical records, note all instances of non-compliance. For nursing home cases, evaluate family relationships, including phone calls and visits by children or representatives.

In summary, consider these strategies when analyzing plaintiff cases. The practical information and recommendations you gather will help the plaintiff firm determine if a case is likely to be profitable, empowering you as a legal nurse consultant to play a vital role in case selection and review.

Cell Phones and Medical Malpractice: Lessons from Two Cases

What Every Legal Nurse Consultant and Healthcare Professional Needs to Know

Think back to your first cell phone—did you get it for safety, to stay in touch with family, or simply because everyone else had one? Now, imagine working in a busy hospital where cell phones are everywhere. Have you ever wondered how personal phone use at work could affect patient care—or even lead to a malpractice lawsuit?

Case Example 1: Cell Phones and Delayed Care in the ER

An elderly woman arrived at the ER with a high fever—104.6°F. She was accompanied by her husband and a neighbor. After triage, she waited for hours without seeing a doctor. The neighbor, growing anxious, went to the nursing station and found six staff members on their cell phones. When asked, one staff member claimed they were communicating with doctors, but the neighbor later told the patient's family that the staff were checking Facebook. Hours later, the husband saw a nurse reading on a tablet. It took 14 hours for a physician to admit the patient, and another four hours for antibiotics to be administered. Tragically, the patient died from sepsis. Her husband filed a malpractice suit, citing staff neglect.

Analysis: Here, cell phone use directly contributed to the perception—and reality—of staff inattention. The staff's personal phone activities not only delayed care but also created evidence that was pivotal in the legal proceedings. Cell phone records requested during the lawsuit showed that none of the usage was work-related. This data strengthened the plaintiff's case, making it clear that technology distracted staff from their duties. Legally, this raises questions about professional accountability and the ethical obligation to prioritize patient care over personal convenience. Ethically, it's a stark reminder that patient well-being must always come first, and personal distractions in clinical settings can have fatal consequences.

Case Example 2: Cell Phone Transcripts and Timely Communication

In another case, the wife of a deceased patient sued a hospital, a neurologist, and his neurology group, alleging that her husband—who suffered a stroke—wasn't treated promptly. Two nurses testified that they'd repeatedly called the neurology group's answering service, but the group insisted that only one call was received. The group provided transcripts of texts sent to the on-call physician's cell phone, showing that the only message received was about the patient's death. The plaintiff's attorney suspected the phone had been wiped, but a forensic examiner found no tampering or deleted messages. This confirmed the physician received just one text, leading the plaintiff to drop the neurologist and the neurology group from the case and focus on the hospital, which soon settled.

Analysis: In this scenario, cell phone records served as crucial evidence, clarifying communication timelines and responsibilities. The accurate transcript protected the neurology group from wrongful allegations, highlighting how proper documentation and transparency with technology can be a defense in malpractice cases. Legally, the integrity of cell phone records proved essential. Ethically, this case underscores the need for clear and documented communication—especially during emergencies. The outcome demonstrates that technology, when used correctly, can uphold professional standards and safeguard providers from unjust claims.

Implications for Legal Nurse Consultants: Best Practices for Cell Phone Evidence

So, what does this mean for legal nurse consultants? Cell phones are often part of the story in malpractice cases, and handling their evidence carefully is key. Here are concrete steps and best practices to follow:

- Identify Relevant Devices: Determine which staff used personal or work cell phones during the incident period.
- Request Detailed Records: Obtain call logs, text message transcripts, and app usage reports for the time frame in question.
- Verify Purpose of Use: Cross-check whether phone activity was work-related or personal.

- Document Timing: Note the exact time and length of calls or messages to align with critical events in the patient's care.
- Preserve Evidence: Advise clients to maintain the integrity of electronic records by avoiding deletion or modification.
- Consult Forensic Experts: When necessary, engage specialists to analyze phones for possible tampering or deleted data.
- Maintain Confidentiality: Ensure compliance with privacy laws and institutional policies when managing personal device records.
- Educate Staff: Recommend ongoing training about the legal risks of inappropriate cell phone use at work.

Conclusion: Cell Phones—A Double-Edged Sword in Healthcare

Cell phones can be both a help and a hindrance in the clinical setting. Used wisely, they facilitate communication and document care. Used carelessly, they distract from patients and create legal vulnerabilities. As a legal nurse consultant or healthcare professional, your approach to cell phone evidence can make or break a malpractice case. Ask yourself: Are you prepared to handle this digital dimension of modern healthcare? What steps will you take to ensure cell phone use supports—rather than jeopardizes—patient safety and legal compliance?

"He Was Never Sick a Day in His Life"

Lessons from a Medical Malpractice Case

When I hear someone say their loved one "was never sick a day in his life," I immediately get concerned. This phrase might sound reassuring, but in my experience, it often means the person never went to the doctor for routine checkups. Let me share a personal story and a medical malpractice case that highlight why this matters.

Personal Reflections: Skipping Checkups Isn't Always a Badge of Health

Growing up, my father was a family physician. He often warned that people who skip regular doctor visits can let small health problems grow into life-threatening ones. My own father-in-law was a brilliant nuclear physicist who believed he knew more about his body than any doctor ever could. He never went to the doctor—until three months before he died.

At that point, he developed ascites, which is a buildup of fluid in the abdomen, often a sign of serious liver disease. Doctors soon diagnosed him with Stage IVB liver cancer. Stage IVB means the cancer was very advanced and had spread to distant parts of the body. By the time he sought medical care, it was too late for effective treatment.

Case Example: One Man's Medical Journey

This personal experience shapes my perspective when I hear the phrase "never sick a day in his life" in medical malpractice cases. In one such case, the wife described her husband that way. He was 64, healthy, and active—swimming two miles in the ocean daily, running half marathons, and dancing often. But he hadn't seen a doctor since leaving the Army 40 years earlier.

He lost a significant amount of weight over a period of a few months. One day, he started having abdominal pain and didn't feel like eating. He went to the Emergency Department (ED), where tests found a mass in his colon—a blockage caused by abnormal tissue.

He was admitted to the hospital, and a gastroenterologist performed a colonoscopy the next day. A colonoscopy is a procedure where a doctor uses a camera to look inside the colon for problems. The doctor saw that the mass blocked almost the entire colon, leaving only a pinpoint opening.

Because the patient didn't have health insurance and was worried about costs, the gastroenterologist discharged him and arranged for a surgeon to see him the next day. The surgeon scheduled a colectomy—an operation to remove part or all of the colon—for the following week. The delay was necessary to get medical clearance since the patient hadn't seen a doctor in decades. Medical clearance means getting checked by another doctor, usually an internist, to make sure there are no hidden health risks before major surgery.

The internist evaluated him and found only borderline high blood pressure; otherwise, his lab tests were normal. The patient was cleared for surgery.

Medical Complications: How Things Took a Turn

The day before surgery, things changed dramatically. The patient developed a high fever, felt shaky, and collapsed at home. Paramedics rushed him to the Emergency Department. His condition got worse quickly, so doctors put him on a ventilator and moved him to the ICU with a diagnosis of sepsis, a life-threatening infection. The cause of the sepsis was undetermined but was thought to be due to either the mass or perforation from the colonoscopy.

A few days later, although his body stabilized, he remained unconscious and dependent on the ventilator. The surgeon believed surgery could help, but when he asked the patient's wife for consent, she refused. She signed a Do Not Resuscitate (DNR) order, had him removed from the ventilator, and stopped antibiotics. Sadly, the patient passed away.

Legal Resolution: The Malpractice Case

The patient's widow sued the hospital and all the doctors involved, claiming that delays in treatment contributed to his death. Ultimately, everyone settled the case at mediation for a small amount.

Conclusion: Key Takeaways for Patients and Families

This story offers an important lesson. In medical malpractice cases, the lack of regular care can complicate both treatment decisions and legal outcomes.

Firsthand experiences like mine—and the case described above—show that being "never sick a day in your life" is not always a good thing. In this case, some people might say that the biggest delay occurred due to the patient refusing to see doctors because, "He was never sick a day in his life."

Understanding Negligent Medical Referrals

A Guide to Legal Standards, Documentation, and Real-World Outcomes

Negligent medical referrals can significantly impact patient outcomes and raise important legal and ethical questions for healthcare providers. When a healthcare professional refers a patient to a specialist, the expectation is that the patient will follow through. However, complications arise when the patient does not act on the referral and later develops a serious or life-threatening condition. Determining whether this constitutes negligence depends on several factors, including the actions of the provider and the quality of their documentation.

Defining Key Legal Concepts

Standard of Care: The standard of care refers to the level of attention, caution, and skill that a reasonably competent healthcare provider would exercise under similar circumstances. It serves as the legal benchmark against which a provider's actions are judged.

Grounds for a Medical Malpractice Case: To successfully bring a medical malpractice case, the plaintiff (patient) must demonstrate that the healthcare provider's actions fell below the standard of care and that this failure directly caused harm or injury. In other words, not only must the provider's conduct be inadequate, but it must also be the cause of the patient's negative outcome.

Common Patient Claims

Patients who experience adverse outcomes after a referral often make several claims in malpractice lawsuits. Typical allegations include:

- The provider did not emphasize the risks of not seeing a specialist.
- The seriousness of my condition was not explained.
- If I had known my condition was potentially deadly, I would have acted sooner.
- The provider never actually referred me.
- The provider did not follow up to confirm I saw the specialist.

Evaluating Documentation

Documentation plays a crucial role in defending or substantiating claims of negligent referral. The strength of the provider's records often determines the outcome of a case. Below are examples of documentation practices, ranging from weak to strong:

- Weak Documentation: Vague chart notes such as "Refer to Ortho" or "Refer to Cardiologist." These entries lack details and may lead to disputes about what was communicated.
- Moderate Documentation: Faxing or calling referrals to specialists. While proactive, these methods are only effective if records are kept and confirm the referral occurred. In practice, specialist offices may discard referral information if patients do not contact them.
- Strong Documentation: Specific notes in the chart, such as "Refer to Dr. Bibner for Neuro exam," indicating both the referral and the reason for it were discussed with the patient.
- Stronger Documentation: Written prescriptions to a named specialist for a specified reason (e.g., "Refer to Dr. Makoto for elevated IOP" for glaucoma evaluation).
- Strongest Documentation: A copy of the prescription in the patient's chart, along with a note that the referral and its importance were discussed with the patient and the prescription was provided directly to the patient.

Case Scenarios and Outcomes

Consider the case of a patient with an enlarged lymph node who was referred to an ENT specialist but never went. When she returned almost two years later, she was diagnosed with incurable tonsil cancer. The patient argued that her physician should have called to ensure she saw the specialist, but courts found that such follow-up is not part of the standard of care. Other claims have had varying success, largely based on the thoroughness of the provider's documentation.

Documentation Quality	Typical Outcome
Vague referral notes	Cases may settle or be dismissed; higher risk for providers
Specific referral notes	Better defense; claims less likely to succeed
Documented discussion and prescription copy	Strong defense; most claims result in defense verdicts or dismissal

Conclusion

The deciding factor in negligent medical referral cases is often the quality and clarity of the referring provider's documentation. Providers who communicate clearly, document referrals thoroughly, and ensure patients understand the seriousness of their condition are far better positioned to defend against claims. For patients and healthcare professionals alike, understanding the importance of both the standard of care and detailed documentation can help prevent misunderstandings and promote safer, more effective referrals.

ED Patient Boarding: Legal Nurse Consultant Review

A Practical Guide to Understanding Responsibilities and Ensuring Safe Patient Care

Emergency department (ED) boarding occurs when a patient has been accepted for inpatient admission but remains in the ED due to a lack of available inpatient beds. This situation is widely recognized as problematic by hospital administrators, ED physicians, and staff. Boarding is not only distressing for patients, but it also increases the risk of delays in care and potential medical malpractice claims. Understanding how responsibilities shift among the care team during this period is essential for patient safety and legal compliance.

Role Handoff Process: Clear Responsibility Shifts During Boarding

The transition of responsibility during boarding involves three key roles: the ED physician, the attending physician or hospitalist, and the ED nurse. Clear communication and understanding of each role's duties are crucial to prevent lapses in care.

- ED Physician: Initially, the ED physician assesses the patient, orders diagnostic tests, starts treatments, and stabilizes the patient. Once the decision to admit is made, the ED physician communicates a thorough handoff report to the attending physician or hospitalist. After admission orders are entered, the ED physician's active role typically ends, unless re-engaged for emergencies or if ED nurses are unable to reach the attending / hospitalist.
- Attending Physician / Hospitalist: The attending physician or hospitalist takes over once they receive the ED physician's report and issue admission orders. These orders specify the inpatient unit, medications, monitoring, and interventions required. From this point, the hospitalist is responsible for the patient's ongoing care and medical decisions.
- ED Nurse: While the patient remains in the ED, ED nurses follow admission orders as appropriate. They provide ongoing monitoring, administer key medications, perform assessments (such as pain checks and vital signs), and report any changes in the patient's condition. However, ED nurses may not implement all interventions typically performed on inpatient units due to ED resource constraints.

As seen above, responsibility formally shifts from the ED physician to the hospitalist at the time admission orders are given. ED nurses retain bedside care until the patient is physically transferred to the inpatient unit but are limited in scope by ED capabilities and policies.

Common Malpractice Allegations: Scenarios and Risks During Boarding

Boarded patients are at increased risk for malpractice claims, often due to lapses or delays in care during the handoff and waiting period. Common allegations include:

- Delayed Treatment or Monitoring: For example, a patient with a spinal infection is boarded for several hours, during which neuro assessments are missed, leading to paralysis.

- Missed or Incomplete Medication Administration: Essential medications ordered by the hospitalist are delayed or not given at all, resulting in deterioration (e.g., missed antibiotics for sepsis).
- Lack of Timely Interventions: Interventions such as applying sequential compression because they are available on the nursing unit but not in the Emergency Department.
- Poor Communication: Changes in patient status are not promptly reported to the responsible physician, or confusion exists about who is accountable for new or worsening symptoms.
- Failure to Address Patient Needs: Prolonged boarding leads to missed nutrition, inadequate pain management, or delayed wound care.

Legal Nurse Consultant: Review Steps & Checklist

Legal nurse consultants (LNCs) play a critical role in evaluating whether the care provided to boarded patients met the standard of care. When reviewing medical records, LNCs should focus on the following key responsibilities:

1. Boarding Time. The Joint Commission (JCAHO) recommends that boarding times should not exceed four hours.
2. Timeliness of Critical Interventions: Were all important medications, tests, and treatments ordered by the attending physician administered promptly?
3. Appropriateness of Monitoring: Was the patient monitored according to the admission orders? For example, if neuro checks were ordered, were they performed and documented?
4. Communication of Condition Changes: Did ED nurses promptly report changes in the patient's condition? Was it clear which physician (ED or hospitalist) was notified?
5. Causation Assessment: Did the patient's harm result from delays or missed care during boarding, or would the outcome have been similar with immediate inpatient transfer?

By systematically answering these questions, legal nurse consultants can form a comprehensive assessment of the care provided during ED boarding and identify potential areas of liability or opportunity for process improvement.

Visual Acuity: Key Concepts, Abbreviations, and Legal Considerations

A Clear Guide for General Readers and Legal Nurse Consultants

Visual acuity is an essential measure of how well a person can see and distinguish details at specific distances. Accurate documentation of visual acuity is important not only for patient care but also in legal settings, especially when assessing damages in medical malpractice cases. This article provides an accessible overview of visual acuity, explains common abbreviations, and highlights the significance for legal nurse consultants.

Understanding Visual Acuity

Normal visual acuity is commonly referred to as 20/20 vision in the United States, which means a person can see at 20 feet what someone with standard vision should see at that distance. In other countries, the measurement might be expressed as 6/6, using meters instead of feet. Visual acuity is typically assessed using charts, with the Snellen eye chart being the most widely used. This chart displays rows of letters decreasing in size, each corresponding to different levels of vision such as 20/20, 20/25, 20/30, and so on.

The test is performed on each eye separately, with the right eye always measured and documented first. The results help determine if a person's vision is better or worse than average. For example:

- 20/200 vision: The patient can see at 20 feet what a person with normal vision can see at 200 feet (very poor vision).
- 20/10 vision: The patient can see at 20 feet what a person with normal vision can see at 10 feet (better than average vision).

Some charts use symbols, such as the tumbling "E," instead of letters, to help test children or individuals who cannot read.

Documenting Visual Acuity: Methods and Examples

When recording visual acuity, healthcare professionals note the results for each eye separately. In addition to the standard measurement (such as 20/20), documentation may include plus (+) and minus (–) signs to indicate accuracy or additional achievement:

- Minus sign (–): Indicates missed letters on a line. For example, "20/50–2" means the patient missed two letters on the 20/50 line.

- Plus sign (+): Indicates the patient read all letters on a line and one on the next smaller line. "20/50+1" means all letters were read on the 20/50 line, plus one on the next line.

Sample documentation entries:

- OD: 20/40+2 (Right eye saw all letters on the 20/40 line plus two on the next line)
- OS: 20/100–1 (Left eye missed one letter on the 20/100 line)

Common Visual Acuity Abbreviations

Visual acuity documentation includes several abbreviations. Here is a quick reference guide:

- OD (Oculus Dexter): Right eye
- OS (Oculus Sinister): Left eye
- OU (Oculus Uterque): Both eyes together
- VA or V: Visual acuity (general measurement)
- DVA or VAd: Distance visual acuity (measured at a distance)
- NV, NVA, VAn: Near visual acuity (tested by reading a card held 14–16 inches from the face)
- CC: With correction (using glasses or contact lenses)
- SC: Without correction (no glasses or contacts)
- PH: Pinhole (testing vision through a small hole, which reduces effects of refractive errors)
- CF or FC: Counting fingers (the examiner asks, "How many fingers do you see?")
- HM: Hand motion (can the patient detect hand movement?)
- LP: Light perception (can the patient sense light?)
- NLP: No light perception (complete blindness)
- CL: Contact lenses
- GL: Glasses

Legal Nurse Consultant Perspective

For legal nurse consultants, understanding visual acuity documentation is crucial in medical-legal cases. Mistakes in testing or recording visual acuity can raise concerns about the standard of care. More commonly, consultants analyze visual acuity results to assess damages, which may include decreased vision or blindness due to delayed referrals, missed diagnoses, or improper procedures.

Practical scenarios include:

- Reviewing visual acuity results before and after an incident to determine the extent of injury.
- Assessing whether documentation supports allegations of poor outcomes or negligence.
- Interpreting abbreviations and test results to clarify the patient's visual status for legal proceedings.

Conclusion

Accurate and clear documentation of visual acuity is vital for clinical care and legal analysis. Familiarity with standard abbreviations and test procedures helps healthcare professionals and legal nurse consultants interpret records effectively and advocate for patients.

Case Study Analysis: Medical Malpractice Claims in Newborn Care

Defining Key Terms, Evaluating Theories, and Exploring Case Implications

In medical malpractice lawsuits, both the plaintiff (the party bringing the claim) and each defendant (the party being accused) develop what are known as theories of the case. A theory of the case is an organized explanation, supported by facts and reasoning, that each side uses to clarify what happened, why it happened, and whether medical malpractice occurred. These theories guide how each party presents their arguments and evidence to persuade the court or jury.

Case Background: Medical Events and Key Terms Explained

This case centers on a full-term newborn who died five days after birth. After being discharged from the hospital two days post-delivery by her pediatrician, the parents were given written instructions to schedule a follow-up appointment for two days after discharge. Three days after leaving the hospital, the parents noticed the baby was not eating well and called the pediatrician’s office, which offered a same-day appointment. As the day progressed, the newborn developed shortness of breath and mottling (patchy discoloration) of her legs.

The parents attempted to drive her to the hospital of birth, unaware that it did not have a pediatric unit. During the drive, the baby stopped breathing, prompting a 911 call. She was transferred to a hospital with specialized pediatric care but died in the emergency room.

Due to the circumstances, the Medical Examiner performed an autopsy. The parents reported that the baby had been healthy until feeding issues developed on the day she died. The autopsy revealed the child died from a congenital heart defect, which means a problem with the heart's structure present at birth. However, the autopsy was poorly conducted, making it unclear whether the cause of death was hypoplastic left heart syndrome—a condition where the left side of the heart is severely underdeveloped—or aortic atresia, where the main artery carrying blood from the heart is blocked or absent.

Plaintiff's Theory: Arguments and Evaluation

After reviewing medical records, the plaintiff argued that the hospital and pediatrician were negligent based on a single elevated respiratory rate recorded on the day of discharge. The theory was that the slightly increased breathing rate should have led to the newborn remaining in the hospital for another day. If she had stayed, her subsequent feeding problems might have prompted further investigation, potentially revealing the heart defect.

Strengths: The plaintiff's theory highlights the importance of careful monitoring and erring on the side of caution when vital signs are abnormal, especially in newborns. It points to a missed opportunity for earlier intervention.

Weaknesses: The argument relies heavily on a single data point (the respiratory rate) and assumes that keeping the newborn longer would have led to a diagnosis, which is speculative. It does not account for the possibility that the heart defect may not have been detectable through routine observation or that other assessments were normal.

Hospital's Theory: Arguments and Evaluation

The hospital responded that one elevated respiratory rate was not enough to reflect the newborn's overall health. Other assessments were within normal limits, and the baby passed a four-extremity pulse oximetry test (a screening for congenital heart defects) with scores of 98-99%, which are considered normal.

Strengths: This theory is supported by comprehensive clinical data and screening results, suggesting that the discharge decision was based on standard medical practice and available evidence.

Weaknesses: It may underestimate the significance of subtle signs in newborns or overlook how rare conditions can evade standard screenings. The hospital's reliance on protocols could be viewed as insufficiently individualized for high-risk cases.

Pediatrician's Theory: Arguments and Evaluation

The pediatrician's position echoed the hospital's but added two points: First, the parents reported to the Medical Examiner that the baby fed well until the day of death, implying that an extra day in the hospital would not have revealed feeding problems. Second, if feeding problems had arisen and the parents had attended the recommended follow-up appointment, the pediatrician would have investigated further.

Strengths: These arguments emphasize the importance of parental observation and adherence to follow-up instructions and suggest that the care plan allowed for timely medical intervention if problems developed.

Weaknesses: The theory assumes that all parents would recognize and act on subtle changes in feeding or breathing, which is not always realistic. It also relies on the accuracy of the parents' recollections and the assumption that feeding issues would have been immediately evident.

Case Outcome: Settlement and Rationale

Despite the defendants' views that the plaintiff's theory was weak and based on speculation, neither the hospital nor the pediatrician wanted to risk going to trial. Both parties chose to settle during the discovery phase, likely due to the uncertainties surrounding the autopsy findings and the unpredictable nature of jury decisions in emotional cases involving newborns.

Conclusion: Lessons and Implications

This case illustrates the challenges in proving causation in medical malpractice claims, especially when rare conditions and incomplete documentation are involved. It highlights the need for thorough and accurate record-keeping, clear communication with families, and robust follow-up procedures. For healthcare professionals, careful attention to even minor abnormalities and consistent documentation can be crucial in defending clinical decisions. For families, understanding discharge instructions and promptly seeking medical care for concerning symptoms can be life-saving. Ultimately, the case underscores the complexity of medical decision-making and the importance of collaboration between caregivers, parents, and providers.

Case Study: Analysis of a Defense Verdict in a Medical Malpractice Lawsuit

An Analytical Review of Plaintiff and Defense Arguments in an Aortic Dissection Misdiagnosis Case

This case involved a 55-year-old male plaintiff who presented to the emergency department (ED) with abdominal pain. A physician assistant (PA) ordered an abdominal CT scan. The radiologist's preliminary report was negative, except for a finding of ectasia (widening) of the aorta. The patient was discharged but returned to another hospital twelve days later, where a CT revealed a large aortic dissection—a serious condition in which the inner layer of the aorta tears, allowing blood to flow between layers of the vessel wall. Surgical repair was complex and left the plaintiff with triplegia (paralysis of three limbs). The plaintiff sued the PA and supervising ED physician, seeking $27 million in damages. After an hour's deliberation, the jury found for the defense. The following analysis provides a balanced overview of both parties' arguments and the key factors influencing the verdict.

Plaintiff's Claims and Supporting Evidence

The plaintiff argued that the initial ED visit resulted in a premature discharge, given the presence of abdominal pain and a finding of ectasia on the preliminary CT. The plaintiff contended that the PA and supervising physician failed to recognize or act on early signs of an aortic dissection or to ensure timely communication of the final radiology report, which later noted borderline aneurysmal dilation (enlarged aorta) and a moderate amount of mural thrombus (a blood clot attached to the vessel wall). The plaintiff maintained that prompt recognition and intervention would have prevented progression to paralysis. Expert testimony for the plaintiff emphasized missed opportunities to diagnose and treat the aortic pathology, as well as alleged deviations from the standard of care. The plaintiff also raised concerns about the adequacy of discharge instructions and the lack of follow-up.

Acknowledging the Plaintiff's Position

The plaintiff's concerns centered on the possibility that the initial discharge was premature and that critical findings—such as aortic ectasia and mural thrombus—were not adequately communicated or acted upon. The plaintiff's expert testimony suggested a failure to adhere to the standard of care, emphasizing that earlier intervention might have prevented catastrophic injury. These arguments were supported by the sequence of events and the eventual diagnosis of aortic dissection.

Factors Influencing the Defense Verdict

1. Absence of Classic Symptoms and Reliance on Preliminary CT

A key reason for the defense verdict was the plaintiff's lack of classic symptoms of aortic dissection, such as tearing chest pain, tachycardia (rapid heartbeat), tachypnea (rapid breathing), or diaphoresis (sweating). The PA based the discharge decision on the preliminary CT report, which did not indicate acute pathology beyond ectasia. This context helped the jury understand that the clinical presentation did not strongly suggest a dissection and that the PA's actions aligned with standard ED practice. The defense successfully argued that, given the available information, the decision to discharge was reasonable.

2. Communication of Radiology Findings and Allocation of Responsibility

The final radiology report, dictated more than 24 hours after the ED visit, noted aortic ectasia to borderline aneurysmal dilation (3.7 cm) and a moderate mural thrombus. Importantly, the radiologist did not communicate these findings to the ED team or the patient. The defense attributed primary responsibility for the missed diagnosis to the radiologist, and the court agreed, instructing the jury that the radiologist's failure constituted negligence. This allocation of fault shifted focus away from the ED providers, weakening the plaintiff's case against them.

3. Plaintiff's Own Actions and Contributory Negligence

The jury was influenced by evidence that the plaintiff did not seek recommended follow-up care with a primary physician or specialist, despite worsening symptoms. Two days after discharge, his condition deteriorated significantly, yet he delayed seeking further medical attention for ten days, even after his wife urged him to return to the hospital. Both the defense and the plaintiff's own expert agreed that earlier intervention could have prevented paralysis. This contributory negligence likely diminished the jury's sympathy and reduced the perceived liability of the ED providers.

4. Credibility and Qualifications of Expert Witnesses

Expert witness credibility played a critical role. The defense's expert was an internationally recognized cardiothoracic surgeon with extensive experience and publications on aortic dissection, enhancing his authority and persuasiveness before the jury. In contrast, the plaintiff's expert was a retired surgeon with less relevant experience and no publications on the topic. The jury likely found the defense expert more credible, which strengthened the defense position and influenced the outcome.

5. Preparation and Clarity of Defendant Testimony

The PA and ED physician were well prepared and utilized the APE technique (discussed in another article in this book) to clearly explain their clinical reasoning and actions. They articulated the distinction between preliminary and final radiology reports and the standard process for communication and supervision in the ED. Their confident, logical testimony reassured the jury that their care was appropriate and within accepted standards, countering allegations of negligence.

6. Absence of the Plaintiff at Trial

The plaintiff's absence from the two-week trial affected jury perception. While his condition would have evoked sympathy, his failure to appear made it easier for jurors to focus on the facts and the law rather than emotional considerations. This absence diminished the emotional impact of the plaintiff's injuries and may have contributed to the defense verdict.

7. Persuasiveness of Closing Arguments

The defense attorneys delivered a logical, structured, and persuasive closing argument, systematically addressing key points and reinforcing their case. In contrast, the plaintiff's counsel presented a less organized, repetitive argument, repeatedly emphasizing the high damages demand rather than substantiating liability. The clarity and professionalism of the defense's closing likely reinforced jurors' confidence in their position.

Conclusion

This case illustrates the multifaceted nature of medical malpractice litigation, where clinical decision-making, communication failures, patient actions, expert witness credibility, and courtroom presentation all influence the outcome. While the plaintiff raised valid concerns about premature discharge and communication lapses, the jury found that the prevailing evidence and testimony supported a defense verdict.

Chapter 7: Legal Nurse Consultant Reports

As legal nurse consultants, one of our most valuable contributions lies in the reports we prepare. These documents are more than just paperwork; they are the bridge between complex medical records, and the legal strategies attorneys rely on. Each report type serves a distinct purpose, helping to clarify, organize, and communicate medical information in ways that strengthen a case.

Sometimes the task calls for a medical summary, a concise overview of a patient's history and treatment that highlights the essentials. Other times, a medical chronology is needed, carefully arranging events in date order to reveal patterns or timelines of care. Visual tools such as timelines and calendars can make key events easier to grasp at a glance, while Excel charts allow you to track trends or compare outcomes with precision. More specialized formats, like touch charts or treater/provider lists, help map the network of caregivers involved in a case. And when attorneys need quick reference, indexes provide a way to locate information efficiently within large sets of records.

Beyond choosing the right format, the way you craft these reports can save time and elevate clarity. Formatting tools—such as templates that automatically generate days of the week, or medical symbols that condense complex instructions—streamline the process. Hyperlinking information directly to electronic records ensures quick access for attorneys and colleagues. Clarity is further enhanced by polishing details, using numbers persuasively, and even drawing on analogies to make unfamiliar concepts more relatable. Practical techniques, like describing wound sizes in everyday terms, help non-medical readers visualize information accurately.

Finally, strong communication strategies bring your reports to life. Adding images where appropriate, saving photos with litigation in mind, and presenting case review findings in a clear, confident manner all contribute to reports that not only inform but persuade. In this chapter, we'll explore these report types and strategies in depth, giving you the tools to create documents that are both professional and impactful.

8 Kinds of LNC Reports

Legal nurse consultants (LNCs) must be familiar with different types of reports to effectively communicate crucial information to attorneys. As an employee in a law firm, I had the flexibility to create any report format that best illustrated case facts. Independent LNCs, on the other hand, may need to recommend the most suitable report type to their attorney clients. It's essential to remember that experts should not draft reports unless approved by an attorney, as some states consider these documents discoverable. Below are eight types of reports commonly prepared by LNCs for medical malpractice attorneys, along with their advantages and potential limitations.

1. Medical Summaries: These reports use full sentences to narrate the sequence of medical events, offering both a storyline and often an analysis of medical-legal issues. Well-written medical summaries give attorneys a rich understanding of the case's medical aspects. Strengths: Summaries are highly readable and provide context for events. Limitations: They may be less effective for quickly pinpointing specific dates or facts. Case example: A medical summary helped clarify the progression of symptoms in a complex case, guiding the attorney's strategy.
2. Medical Chronologies: These reports list events in precise date and time order, often in a table format, often using phrases instead of full sentences. Medical chronologies are especially helpful for attorneys who may struggle to interpret information scattered throughout a medical chart. Strengths: Chronologies provide a thorough, organized overview of all relevant events. Limitations: Their detail can sometimes overwhelm readers seeking only the most pertinent facts. Case example: A comprehensive chronology helped an attorney reconstruct the sequence of interventions during a critical care hospitalization.
3. Timelines: These reports focus exclusively on major events, often over a short period, and are typically presented along a horizontal axis. While some use "medical chronology" and "timeline" interchangeably, I differentiate them: timelines highlight only the most critical events. Strengths: Timelines are concise and ideal for visualizing pivotal moments. Limitations: Their brevity may omit valuable background information. Case example: A timeline was used to spotlight the sequence of emergency interventions in a wrongful death case.
4. Calendars: These are valuable tools for visually tracking key events over time. I've used calendars to highlight missed physician visits, the onset of urinary tract infections in nursing home patients, patterns of Emergency Department visits, and prescription pickup dates. Strengths: Calendars provide a straightforward, visual overview of patterns and gaps in care. Limitations: They may not capture the context behind each event, so additional narrative may be required. Case example: In one malpractice case, a calendar helped clarify the frequency of missed appointments, which was crucial for establishing a timeline of care lapses.
5. Excel Graphs: These graphs are excellent for visualizing changes in data over time. I've used them to depict a patient's weight loss over several months or the gradual increase in creatinine levels over two years. The best part is that creating these graphs doesn't require advanced Excel skills. Strengths: Excel graphs are user-friendly and make trends easy to spot. Limitations: If not carefully designed, they may oversimplify complex data or omit important details. Case

example: An Excel graph was instrumental in demonstrating the slow progression of kidney function decline, helping the attorney understand the timeline of the patient's condition.

6. Touch Charts: These illustrate staff interactions with a patient over time, ranging from minutes to months. Touch charts show the type of staff involved and the number of contacts with the patient. Strengths: They can clearly demonstrate patterns of care or neglect. Limitations: They may not reflect the quality or appropriateness of each interaction. Case example: A touch chart substantiated a family's claim that a patient was left unattended, supporting their litigation.
7. Treater/Provider Lists: Treater and Provider lists identify all relevant people involved in the Plaintiff's care. These lists provide attorneys with an accurate guide of who did what when. Strengths: Treater/Provider lists make it easy for attorneys to quickly reference and contact the individuals involved in a case, ensuring that no critical witness or provider is overlooked. They help streamline communications and can be invaluable for organizing depositions. Limitations: These lists may lack detailed context about each provider's involvement, and without careful documentation, important nuances—such as the significance of a particular interaction—can be missed. Additionally, if the list is not regularly updated, it may omit newly discovered or secondary care providers who played a role in the plaintiff's treatment.
8. Indexes: Indexes are organized lists of case-related items, such as imaging studies, medical records, or pathology slides. Early in my career, I provided these indexes to attorneys to help decide which items to send to experts; now, I often make those decisions myself. Strengths: Indexes streamline information and make case review more efficient. Limitations: They require careful organization and may be less useful if items are not clearly described or categorized. Case example: An imaging index helped an attorney quickly locate critical scans for submission to a radiology expert.

I'll continue sharing specific examples and practical insights for each report type in future articles to help demystify technical concepts and illustrate how these tools apply in real legal nurse consulting scenarios.

Medical Summary Guidelines for Legal Nurse Consultants

Instructional Guide for Clear, Structured Medical Summaries

Medical summaries serve as structured narrative reports detailing a patient's medical history and key events relevant to legal cases. Legal nurse consultants (LNCs) must create these summaries to assist attorneys in understanding medical facts and their implications for legal matters. Adhering to precise formatting and content guidelines ensures clarity, professionalism, and utility in legal settings.

General Formatting Guidelines

These tips are a combination of formatting from business reports and APA style. You can use another style if you prefer or if the attorney wants a specific format.

1. Use Easy-to-Read Fonts: Select Calibri, Verdana, Arial, Helvetica, Aptos, or Times New Roman in sizes 10–12. Clear fonts improve readability for legal teams.
2. Include a Footer: Center "CONFIDENTIAL ATTORNEY WORK PRODUCT" at the bottom of each page. This denotes the document's sensitive nature.
3. Add Page Numbers: Place page numbers in the bottom right corner. Facilitates document navigation and referencing.
4. Full Justification: Justify all text. Creates a polished, professional appearance.
5. Set Margins: Use 1 to 1.5 inch margins on both sides. Provides space for notes and maintains standard formatting.
6. Heading Format: Center and bold the summary heading as follows:
    - Name of Plaintiff v. Name of Defendant
    - File or Claim Number
    - Medical Summary and Analysis

Ensures immediate identification of the case.

1. Paragraph Spacing: Single-space paragraphs and insert one blank line between each. Improves readability and separation of ideas.
2. Indentation: Indent the first line of every paragraph. Distinguishes new paragraphs for easy review.
3. Spacing Between Sentences: Use two spaces between sentences. Law firms often prefer this traditional formatting for clarity.
4. Use Headings: Organize content with clear headings. Enhances document structure and helps readers locate information.

Content Structure

1. Review Plaintiff's Allegations: Examine all allegations and related documents. Ensures the summary addresses case-specific concerns.
2. Introduction Paragraph: Begin with an overview of the case, citing key facts and listing reviewed records. Provides context for the reader.

3. Summary of Allegations: Summarize plaintiff's claims and assess their merit. Guides the reader through the case's main issues.
4. Patient Diagnoses: Present a bulleted list of diagnoses and relevant details. Offers a quick reference to medical conditions involved.
5. Narrative Chronology: Detail key events in chronological order using brief paragraphs or bullet points. Clarifies the sequence of medical events.
6. Analysis Section or Integrate Analysis Within the Narrative Chronology: Include an analysis of medical/legal issues. Helps attorneys understand the connection between medical facts and legal implications.
7. Reference Medical Literature: Add relevant journal articles or internet research under appropriate headings or as footnotes. Supports medical findings with authoritative sources.
8. Recommendations: Conclude with recommendations regarding records, expert witnesses, and fact witnesses. Directs attorneys on next steps and additional services if applicable.

Number and Measurement Guidelines

Apply the following rules for numbers and measurements to maintain clarity and consistency. Write out numbers zero through nine; use numerals for 10 and above. Example: "Three days later, the patient developed symptoms." Example: "The medication was administered 12 times."

Do not begin or end sentences with numerals. Correct: "Twenty patients were admitted." Incorrect: "20 patients were admitted."

Abbreviate metric units after numerals, using lowercase and no period. Example: "The patient received 30 cc of saline." Example: "The incision measured 12.4 cm after surgery."

Write out non-metric units of measure. Example: "The wound was three inches wide." Example: "She lost five pounds."

Provide non-metric equivalents in parentheses when metric measurements are important to the case. Example: "The wound measured 8 cm long by 6 cm wide (3.1 inches long by 2.4 inches wide)." Example: "The rash measured 2.5 cm in diameter, about the size of a quarter." Helps readers unfamiliar with metric units. If measurements are not essential to the case, omit conversions. Example: "The patient's blood pressure was recorded as 140/90 mmHg."

Language and Abbreviation Use

- Acronyms and Abbreviations: Do not use periods in medical abbreviations (e.g., COPD, not C.O.P.D.). Ensures consistency and reduces clutter.
- First Use of Abbreviations: Write out the full medical term, then provide the abbreviation in parentheses. Example: "Mr. Smith had a cerebral vascular accident (CVA)." Because of the CVA, he had difficulty ambulating. Clarifies terminology for all readers.

Plural Abbreviations: Use a lowercase "s" without an apostrophe for plurals (e.g., IVs, not IV's). Distinguishes plural from possessive forms.

Limit Medical Abbreviations: Use abbreviations sparingly; avoid making the summary resemble a medical chart. Promotes clarity for non-medical readers.

Additional Tips

- Treater/Provider List: Consider listing names of organizations, physicians, and providers in a separate treater/provider list as well as the medical summary. Assists attorneys in identifying sources for additional records and depositions.
- Authorship References: Avoid using "I" or "the writer" unless your name appears on the report. Prevents confusion regarding authorship if the case changes hands.
- Layperson Language: Write for intelligent readers with limited medical knowledge. Ensures accessibility for all attorneys and jury members.
- Bates Stamps: Consider including Bates stamp numbers when referencing medical records if available. Facilitates quick retrieval of information.
- Drafting Process: Review medical records and draft observations as you read; finalize structure and format after identifying key facts. Improves accuracy and organization.
- Emphasize Key Sections: Prioritize the introduction and recommendations when writing and revising. These sections are most critical for case review.

Conclusion

Consistent adherence to these guidelines ensures medical summaries are clear, professional, and useful for legal analysis. By structuring content, applying standardized formatting, and providing concise explanations, legal nurse consultants enhance attorney understanding and support effective case resolution.

The Practical Guide to Writing Medical Summaries Quickly

Step-by-Step Instructions, Real Examples, and Solutions for Common Challenges

Let me start with a quick story: Years ago, I worked alongside a legal nurse consultant who was baffled by my speed at writing medical summaries. We were both on the same network and she'd often peek into my files to see how much progress I'd made. One day, while tracking my updates, she exclaimed, "So that's how you do it!" Her surprise made me realize that my process—which I'd fine-tuned over time—could help others, especially newcomers to medical summaries. If you've ever wondered how to tackle these time-consuming reports with confidence, read on.

Step 1: Type the Allegations Up Front

The very first thing I do is type the allegations directly into my summary. Why? Because keeping the allegations front and center ensures I stay focused on what matters most to the case. I normally use an easy-to-read font; to distinguish the medical summary in this book from the main article, I italicized the summary. Here's a sample of how I set the allegations up:

Patient: Lerner Smithe. Allegations: Failure to timely diagnose an ependymoma in a 13-year-old male by Dr. Stoudtver and Pediatricss4Us

Tip: If the medical terms or diagnoses are unfamiliar, I pause here for a quick internet search to get my bearings. This way, I don't waste time later.

Step 2: Review Medical Records and Start Summarizing Facts

Armed with the allegations, I dive into the medical records. My goal: pick out facts that connect directly to the allegations. I enter key details as I go, right into my summary file.

Patient: Lerner Smithe. Allegations: Failure to timely diagnose an ependymoma in a 13-year-old male by Dr. Stoudtver and Pediatricss4Us

July 30, 2022 – saw Adam Stoudtver , MD at Pediatrics4Us for backache. Came with mother – Was in a minor MVA 2 days ago. Back exam – tenderness around T8. No weakness, bowel problems, bladder problems, fever, weight loss, not limping, no radiation. Dx – back sprain. NSAIDs, return if not better or worsens.

August 8, 2022 - saw Dr. Stoudtver at Pediatrics4Us for continuing backache. Mother, No change in exam. Thoracic spine x-ray ordered, return in one week.

I used to jot these down on paper, but—confession time—that was double the work.

Step 3: Ditch the Paper—Go Digital for Speed

Here's an honest, slightly embarrassing admission: I clung to my paper notes like Linus and his blanket. I'd jot facts, cut up the paper, tape them in order, then type it all up. When I finally forced myself to skip the paper and enter information straight into the computer, it felt odd—but wow, did I save time. No more shuffling scraps or retyping. If you're still hanging on to pen and paper, I encourage you to give this a try—it's a game changer.

Step 4: Enter Facts Chronologically—Make Reordering Easy

I add facts as I encounter them in the records, always in chronological order. If I spot a detail that needs to slot between two others, I simply insert it right where it belongs. Note that I inserted information between July 30 and August 8, 2022, below.

Patient: Lerner Smithe. Allegations: Failure to timely diagnose an ependymoma in a 13-year-old male by Dr. Stoudtver and Pediatricss4Us

July 30, 2022 – saw Adam Stoudtver , MD at Pediatrics4Us for backache. Came with mother – Was in a minor MVA 2 days ago. Back exam – tenderness around T8. No weakness, bowel problems, bladder problems, fever, weight loss, not limping, no radiation. Dx – back sprain. NSAIDs, return if not better or worsens.

August 7, 2022, 2:00 p.m. – Telephone message from nurse at school. ***Was child in summer school?*** *Lerner is complaining of backache. Tylenol doesn't help. Stoudtver's response at 2;15 p.m.: Send to ER or will see here tomorrow if he's not acute.*

August 8, 2022 - saw Dr. Stoudtver at Pediatrics4Us for continuing backache. Mother, No change in exam. Thoracic spine x-ray ordered, return in one week.

If I'm unsure about something, I bold it or note it another color to revisit later.

Step 5: Review the Draft and Delete What Doesn't Matter

Here's a lesson from experience: Don't get attached to every note. After reviewing my rough draft, I delete any facts that aren't directly relevant to the allegations.

- Before Deletion:
- 01/10/2022: Patient presents to ER with severe back pain.

- 01/10/2022: Patient had a sandwich for lunch. (Irrelevant)
- 01/10/2022: Dr. Smith orders spinal x-ray.

After Deletion:

- 01/10/2022: Patient presents to ER with severe back pain.
- 01/10/2022: Dr. Smith orders spinal x-ray.

It's much easier to delete short notes than carefully crafted paragraphs—so don't over-write at this stage.

Step 6: Transform Notes into Clear Sentences

Once I've trimmed the list, I flesh out the notes into complete sentences. Here's an example:

Patient: Lerner Smithe. Allegations: Failure to timely diagnose an ependymoma in a 13-year-old male by Dr. Stoudtver and Pediatrics4Us

On July 30, 2022, Lerner Smithe presented to Adam Stoudtver, MD, a pediatrician at Pediatrics4Us for a complaint of a backache. Lerner related that he was in a minor motor vehicle accident on July 28, which resulted in back pain. Dr. Stoudtver noted tenderness around the eighth thoracic vertebra (T8). However, the child had no signs of more severe causes of back problems such as weakness, bowel problems, bladder problems, fever, weight loss, radiation of the pain down the leg, or limping. Dr. Stoudtver diagnosed back muscle sprain, told the mother to give NSAIDs for pain, and instructed her to bring him back if he wasn't better. Muscle sprain is the most common cause of back pain in children, so Dr. Stoudtver's history, exam, diagnosis, and treatment plan were appropriate. However, he should have provided some parameters about when to return, such as a week or a few days, to the mother.

On August 7, 2022, at 2:00 p.m., Pediatrics4Us received a telephone call from Lerner's school nurse at summer school. The message was for Dr. Stoudtver, and it indicated that Lerner was complaining of a backache which wasn't relieved by Tylenol. Dr. Stoudtver responded at 2:15 p.m. that the nurse should either send Lerner to an emergency department or, if his symptoms weren't that acute, the parent(s) should bring Lerner to the office the next day. Dr. Stoudtver's response is standard for most office-based practices. In fact, many of them tell patients to call 911 if they're acutely ill. It's unclear if Dr. Stoudtver reviewed Lerner's chart before he responded because there was no mention of the fact that the child had been taking Tylenol instead of receiving NSAIDs.

On August 8, 2022, Dr. Stoudtver saw Lerner again at Pediatrics4Us for his continuing complaints of a backache. Lerner's mother accompanied him. The results of Dr. Stoudtver's exam were the same as the exam in July. Dr. Stoudtver ordered a thoracic spine x-ray and asked Lerner to return in one week for the results. Ordering the x-ray was a reasonable next step for a back pain work up. However, Dr. Stoudtver still didn't address the Tylenol/NSAIDs discrepancy.

This step is also where I check spelling—especially for tricky doctor names and Pediatrics spelled with a double-s.

Step 7: Add Analysis and Final Recommendations (If Needed)

If the attorney requests it, I include a brief analysis of the care provided or potential liability. Otherwise, I stick to the facts. I also write a conclusion and recommendations at the end.

Overall, it is doubtful that an expert would find that Dr. Stoudtver delayed Lerner's diagnosis and treatment. It would have been a huge leap to diagnose ependymoma at any of the three visits, particularly given the history of a recent car accident. Although Dr. Stoudtver should have given Lerner's mothers a definite time frame to return during the July 30, 2022, visit, Lerner returned less than 10 days later. While Dr. Stoudtver should also have addressed the Tylenol/NSAIDs discrepancy, it is doubtful that this would have resulted in an earlier diagnosis. In addition, providing pain medication as a first step, ordering an x-ray next, and then referring Lerner to a specialist is a reasonable approach to diagnosing the cause of back pain in an adolescent. It is likely that an expert will opine that once Dr. Stoudtver referred the patient to an orthopedist, the back pain workup was the responsibility of the orthopedist. Because eight months elapsed after Dr. Stoudtver last saw Lerner, it is recommended that you obtain the names and medical records of other providers to determine when and where the delay occurred. XYZ Legal Nurses would be happy to conduct an initial review of those medical records. If you choose to have an expert review the case, XYZ would be happy to locate experts with experience testifying in situations such as these.

Pro tip: Run a final spell- and grammar-check before finishing.

Step 8: Write the Introduction—Summarize Key Facts Up Front

I save the introduction for last, summarizing the most critical facts and findings. Attorneys love having key information at the start.

As you know, Lerner Smithe was 13-years-old when he presented to Adam Soudtver, MD at Pediatrics4Us on July 30, 2022, with complaints of back pain. After reviewing the Pediatrics4Us records, it is apparent that there were a few inconsequential deviations in Dr. Stoudtver's care. However, it is likely that an expert will find that Dr. Stoudtver used a reasonable and timely approach to his workup of Lerner's back pain. It is also likely that an expert would opine that any delay in the diagnosis of Lerner's ependymoma occurred after Dr. Stoudtver referred Lerner to an orthopedist.

Here's What the Complete Medical Summary Looks Like

(Minus a few pages and some formatting.)

As you know, Lerner Smithe was 13-year-old when he presented to Adam Soudtver, MD at Pediatrics4Us on July 30, 2022, with complaints of back pain. After reviewing the Pediatrics4Us records, it is apparent that there were a few inconsequential deviations in Dr. Stoudtver's care. However, it is likely that that an expert will find that Dr. Stoudtver used a reasonable and timely approach to his workup of Lerner's back pain. It is also likely that an expert would opine that any delay in the diagnosis of Lerner's ependymoma occurred after Dr. Stoudtver referred Lerner to an orthopedist.

On July 30, 2022, Lerner Smithe presented to Adam Stoudtver, MD, a pediatrician at Pediatrics4Us for a complaint of a backache. Lerner related that he was in a minor motor vehicle accident on July 28, which resulted in back pain. Dr. Stoudtver noted tenderness around the eighth thoracic vertebra (T8). However, the child had no signs of more severe causes of back problems such as weakness, bowel problems, bladder problems, fever, weight loss, radiation of the pain down the leg, or limping. Dr. Stoudtver diagnosed back muscle sprain, told the mother to give NSAIDs for pain, and instructed her to bring him back if he wasn't better. Muscle sprain is the most common cause of back pain in children, so Dr. Stoudtver's history, exam, diagnosis, and treatment plan were appropriate. However, he should have provided some parameters about when to return, such as a week or a few days, to the mother.

On August 7, 2022, at 2:00 p.m., Pediatrics4Us received a telephone call from Lerner's school nurse at summer school. The message was for Dr. Stoudtver, and it indicated that Lerner was complaining of a backache which wasn't relieved by Tylenol. Dr. Stoudtver responded at 2:15 p.m. that the nurse should either send Lerner to an emergency department or, if his symptoms weren't that acute, the parent(s) should bring Lerner to the office the next day. Dr. Stoudtver's response is standard for most office-based practices. In fact, many of them tell patients to call 911 if they're acutely ill. It's unclear if Dr. Stoudtver reviewed Lerner's chart before he responded because there was no mention of the fact that the child had been taking Tylenol instead of receiving NSAIDs.

On August 8, 2022, Dr. Stoudtver saw Lerner again at Pediatrics4Us for his continuing complaints of a backache. Lerner's mother accompanied him. The results of Dr. Stoudtver's exam were the same as the exam in July. Dr. Stoudtver ordered a thoracic spine x-ray and asked Lerner to return in one week for the results. Ordering the x-ray was a reasonable next step for a back pain work up. However, Dr. Stoudtver still didn't address the Tylenol/NSAIDs discrepancy.

Overall, it is doubtful that an expert would find that Dr. Stoudtver delayed Lerner's diagnosis and treatment. It would have been a huge leap to diagnose ependymoma at any of the three visits, particularly given the history of a recent car accident. Although Dr. Stoudtver should have given Lerner's mothers a definite time frame to return during the July 30, 2022, visit, Lerner returned less than 10 days later. While Dr. Stoudtver should also have addressed the Tylenol/NSAIDs discrepancy, it is doubtful that this would have resulted in an earlier diagnosis. In addition, providing pain medication as a first step, ordering an x-ray next, and then referring Lerner to a specialist is a reasonable approach to diagnosing the cause of back pain in an adolescent. It is likely that an expert will opine that once Dr. Stoudtver referred the patient to an orthopedist, the back pain workup was the responsibility of the orthopedist. Because eight months elapsed after Dr. Stoudtver last saw Lerner, it is recommended that you obtain the names and medical records of other providers to determine when and where the delay occurred. XYZ Legal Nurses would be happy to conduct an initial review of those medical records. If you choose to have an expert review the case, XYZ would be happy to locate experts with experience testifying in situations such as these.

Common Pitfalls—and How to Avoid Them

- Including Too Many Irrelevant Details: It's tempting to document everything but focus on facts that support or refute the allegations. Solution: Ask, "Does this detail relate directly to the case?" If not, out it goes.
- Writing Full Paragraphs Too Soon: Jumping to full sentences before you know what's important can waste time. Solution: Stick to short, factual notes until you've reviewed all the records and trimmed the excess.
- Hesitating to Delete: It's tough to cut content you've spent time on it. Solution: Remember, less is more. Your summary should be concise and targeted.
- Getting Lost in Medical Jargon: Not everyone will know all the medical terms. Solution: Use plain language or brief explanations for technical terms.
- Skipping Spelling and Grammar Checks: Even the best summary loses impact if riddled with errors. Solution: Always do a final review.

Conclusion: Give This Method a Try

Medical summaries can be daunting, especially for beginners, but with this process, you'll find they're much more manageable—and even a little satisfying to complete. My switch from paper to digital, focus on the allegations, and willingness to hit the delete key made all the difference for me. Try these steps, adapt them to your workflow, and see how much time (and frustration) you save. Happy summarizing!

Creating Medical Chronologies in Word: A Step-by-Step Guide for LNCs

Instructions and Practical Examples for New LNCs

Medical chronologies are essential reports prepared by legal nurse consultants (LNCs) to document and organize key medical events in legal cases. A well-structured medical chronology helps attorneys and other professionals quickly understand the patient's medical history and case details. As a new LNC, mastering the creation of clear, accurate medical chronologies will make you a valuable asset to your team and clients.

Overview

- Legal nurse consultant (LNC): A registered nurse who applies clinical expertise to legal cases.
- Medical chronology: A timeline summarizing important medical events, treatments, and provider notes relevant to a case.
- Chronologies must be clear, consistent, and easy to follow.
- Tables in word processing software (such as Microsoft Word) are commonly used for organizing entries.

Step-by-Step Instructions for Creating a Medical Chronology in Word

1. Open a New Document: Go to File (top left), click New, then select Blank Document.
2. Choose Page Orientation: Click the Layout ribbon at the top of the page. Select Orientation, then choose Portrait or Landscape. (Landscape gives more space, but Portrait is common.)
3. Enter Case Information and Title: Type the case name, e.g., Jensen v. Jessup Community Hospital.
4. On the next line, type the report title, e.g., Medical Chronology.

5. Optionally, add the date and file number on the following lines.
6. To center these lines: Highlight your case information. Click the Home ribbon, then the Paragraph section, and choose Center. Alternatively, press Ctrl + E on your keyboard.

Prepare for Table Creation:

1. Press Enter twice after your case information to add a space.
2. Click the Home ribbon, then Paragraph section, and select Left Justification for the next section. Alternatively, press Ctrl + L on your keyboard.
3. Insert Your Table: Go to the Insert ribbon at the top of the page. Click Table. In the pop-up, select the size you want (for example, 4 columns wide × 2 rows long). You can add more rows later.
4. Label Table Headers (the top row): Type header labels in the top row: Date / Time, Organization, Medical Record, Facts. Use the Tab key to move between cells.
5. Style Your Table: Select your table. Go to Table Design and choose a style such as Plain Table 1 for alternating row colors (optional).
6. Adjust Column Widths: Hover over the vertical lines between columns, click, and drag them to resize so contents fit neatly. For example, you probably want more space in the Facts column.

Add Chronology Entries: Fill in each row with relevant case information. Press Tab at the end of a row to add new rows as needed.

Sort by Date and Time: To keep events in order, select the entire table, go to Table Layout, and click Sort.

Highlight Key Details: Bold important terms (e.g., medications and allergies) for visibility. Add comments in italics or use a separate Comments column if preferred.

Add or Delete Rows: Right-click on any row, then select Insert (or Delete) Rows Above or Insert (or Delete) Rows Below to add new entries.

Review for Clarity and Consistency: Ensure all abbreviations and terminology are defined and used consistently throughout your chronology.

Sample Case Example: Medical Chronology Table

Below is a realistic example, demonstrating a patient's reaction to an antibiotic prescription. This can be adapted for simple or complex scenarios.

Date / Time	**Organization**	**Medical Record**	**Facts**
3/12/25	Glenellen View Offices	Office Visit	Samual Stone, MD. Patient cut right ring finger on metal bracket. Bacitracin applied. Return to clinic in one week.
3/21/25 2247	Jessup Community Hospital	Triage Record	Janetta Forsom, RN. Patient states he's allergic to Penicillin.
3/21/25 2339	Jessup Community Hospital	ER Nursing Notes	Linda Barnes, RN. Cut his right ring finger two weeks ago. Right ring finger edematous. Yellow drainage from the wound.
3/21/25 2359	Jessup Community Hospital	ER Physician Notes	David Lancaster, MD. Incision and drainage of right ring finger – large amount of purulent drainage. Wound cultured.
3/22/25 0005	Jessup Community Hospital	Discharge Instructions	Referred to primary MD for follow-up. Prescription written by Dr. Lancaster for ampicillin. *Ampicillin is a type of penicillin.*
3/22/25 1115	Walgreen's Pharmacy	Prescription Records	Ampicillin prescription filled. *No indication of penicillin allergy.*
3/23/25	Glenellen View Offices	Office Visit	Samual Stone, MD. Seen for hives all over body. *Hives indicate an allergic reaction, most likely from ampicillin.*

Customization Tips

- Adapt your table columns to suit the specifics of each case (e.g., add a Comments column).
- Use bold or italics to highlight critical information, such as allergies or adverse reactions.
- Sort entries chronologically for clarity.
- Adjust formatting and terminology based on attorney or workplace preferences.

- Complex cases may require additional columns for providers, medications, or outcomes.

Conclusion

Creating detailed, organized medical chronologies is an essential skill for every legal nurse consultant (LNC). By following these step-by-step instructions and adapting your documentation to the needs of each case, you will produce chronologies that support legal teams and improve case outcomes. Practice regularly, seek feedback, and always aim for clarity and consistency in your work.

Four Wrongs, Four Fixes

It's Easy to Make Medical Chronology Mistakes: Here's How to Fix Them

Four wrongs: wrong dates, wrong times, wrong caregivers, wrong information. These errors appeared in medical chronologies I inherited from another law firm. Several cases were transferred to my firm, and the chronologies came with them. Let's examine the mistakes made and four practical fixes to help you avoid similar issues.

The medical chronologies arrived in CaseMap format with linked records, allowing for detailed review. This made it easier to see the dates each entry was typed and which records were referenced. Here are some of the problems I found:

- One chronology included an infant born in 2024, but two entries were dated in 2023—months before the birth. Times were also entered incorrectly; for example, the child's newborn assessments were recorded at 6 a.m. and 10 a.m., hours before the actual noon birth.
- Some entries used erroneous dates from the medical records, simply copying a caregiver's mistake, which can occur in handwritten documentation.
- Entries for pathology reports were often dated one to three days late because the date reflected when the lab received the specimens, not when they were collected.
- Duplicate entries appeared, sometimes created on different days from separate sets of records. In some cases, duplicate entries listed different caregiver names.
- On certain dates, some entries included times while others did not. Mixing timed and untimed entries causes sorting problems in CaseMap and Word; untimed entries sort before timed ones, leading to confusion about the order of events.

It's easy to make these mistakes when handling large volumes of information, but four steps can help prevent and fix them:

1. Use judgment: If something looks out of place, investigate before finalizing. For example, the original chronology's creator noted that some dates didn't make sense but failed to correct them. Whenever I correct entries, I note that the medical records are misdated. For example: *Date of 1/3/24 is correct. Entry in medical records is incorrectly dated 1/3/23, which is before the infant had been born.*
2. Proofread entries: Review your chronology for errors in spelling, dates, times, and caregiver names. Proofreading catches problems like entries recorded before an infant's birth and duplicate or mismatched caregiver names.
3. Follow standard methods for dating and timing: For lab reports, use the specimen collection date and time. For critical lab results (such as blood cultures) also add a note indicating the date and time the results were received. If radiographs are critical to the case, use the times imprinted on the films. Otherwise, using the time of dictation for radiographs is usually sufficient.
4. Use event anchors to sort entries correctly: An anchor is a known event, such as an operative report at 10:10 a.m. In the example below, the patient's pathology report was followed by her ER visit and then surgery (the anchor).

Date & Time	**Report/Record**	**Fact Text**
Sat 02/22/2025	Surgical Pathology Report	Skin biopsy left foot – necrotizing vasculitis. Left great toe – gangrene and osteomyelitis.
Sat 02/22/25	ER Records	Seen for pain and swelling in left foot x 3 weeks. Left foot ischemia - ? vasculitis.
Sat 02/22/2025 10:10 AM	Operative Report	Dr. Felton Rensler. Skin biopsy dorsal left foot and amputation of left great toe for gangrene.

The entries should have ordered as ER Records, Surgical Pathology Report (because the biopsy was obtained during surgery), followed by the Operative Report (which was dictated after the end of surgery). And since pathology and surgical reports are timed, those times should have been added.

A medical chronology with wrong information is a jumbled mess. By using these four fixes, your chronologies will be accurate and reliable.

CaseMap Chronologies: A Guide for LNCs

Accessible Insights and Practical Examples for Everyday Use

CaseMap is a specialized litigation software frequently used by legal nurse consultants (LNCs) to organize and analyze medical chronologies. Unlike traditional word processing programs such as Microsoft Word, CaseMap is built as a relational database. A relational database is a system that stores information in multiple connected tables, allowing you to view, organize, and retrieve data in flexible ways—far beyond what a basic document can do. For example, while Word lets you create a list or table, CaseMap enables you to link related information, filter content, and display details in formats tailored to your needs.

Key Components of CaseMap

CaseMap operates through three main, interconnected spreadsheets:

- Facts Spreadsheet: This is where you build your medical chronology. Columns—called fields—such as Date & Time, Provider, Medical Record, Fact Text, and Linked Issues help you organize every detail. You can customize these fields to fit your case, adding or removing fields as needed.
- Objects Spreadsheet: Here, "objects" refer to people, organizations, documents, and other entities related to the case. For instance, all healthcare providers and institutions are listed, each with a "Short Name" for quick entry. When you type the first three letters of a short name, CaseMap automatically fills in the full name—saving time and reducing errors.
- Issues Spreadsheet: This sheet lists all the issues relevant to your case, such as questions of liability or causation. Each issue also has a short name for fast linking in the Facts spreadsheet.

CaseMap Features in Practice

One major advantage of CaseMap is its ability to automatically arrange facts in chronological order. When you add new facts, they appear at the bottom, but refreshing the spreadsheet instantly sorts everything by date and time—making it easy to follow the case timeline.

Unlike Word, where deleting a column permanently removes it, CaseMap allows you to simply hide fields. If you decide later that you need to see a field such as "Linked Issues" again, you can unhide the field with a click, ensuring nothing is lost. You can also rearrange columns by dragging them to new locations, helping you prioritize information based on your current needs.

Filtering is another powerful tool. Filtering means temporarily hiding all entries that don't match specific criteria. For example, if you're preparing for a deposition involving Dr. Lonnie Cray, you can filter the chronology to show only the facts related to him. Dr. Cray has records from three different places – his office, Central City Medical Center, and County Regional Hospital. Suppose there are 197 entries total; after filtering, you see just the 59 entries for Dr. Cray as shown below.

Facts (Search Results)			59 Records
Date	**Provider**	**Medical Record**	**Fact Text**
07/11/2023	Central City Medical Clinic	Office Note	Lonnie Cray, MD. Discus. with TL McCree, MD 500 mg Cytoxan IV...
08/10/2023	Comprehensive Insurance	Correspondence	Lonnie Cray, MD. In recs of County Regional Hosp. Regarding rash...
08/03/2024	County Regional Hosp.	Consultation	Javier Scotto, MD, refer by Lonnie Cray, MD. Hx:.

If you need to focus further, filter again by "County Regional Hospital" to narrow it to his 16 entries related to that facility. This targeted view is invaluable when organizing information for depositions or expert reviews.

Facts (Search Results) Filter Linked to County Regional			16 of 59 Records
Date	**Provider**	**Medical Record**	**Fact Text**
08/03/2024	County Regional Hosp.	Consultation	Javier Scotto, MD, referred by Lonnie Cray, MD. Hx:...
08/03/2024	County Regional Hosp.	History and Physical	Lonnie Cray, MD. Chief Complaint: Progressive...
08/03/2024	County Regional Hosp.	EKG	Ordered by Lonnie Cray, MD, read by Sally Mohic...

Tagging offers a different kind of focus. Tagging, in CaseMap, means marking entries with a label so you can easily identify them later. Unlike filtering, all entries remain visible, but tagged items stand out. For example, if you tag Dr. Cray's entries for a treater deposition, you can quickly see which facts pertain to him (the tag to the left of the date) while keeping the rest of the chronology for context.

Facts (Search Results) Tag Linked to Fact Text: "Lonnie Cray, MD"			197 Records - 59 Tagged
Date	**Provider**	**Medical Record**	**Fact Text**
11/28/2024	Central City Medical Clinic	Office Visit	Lonnie Cray, MD. Seen for steroid induced DM, achy...
12/15/2023	Tabatha McCree, MD	Office Visit	Continues to have leg spasms with wobbly sens...

02/03/2024	Central City Medical Clinic	Correspondence	From Lance Vonder to Lonnie Cray, MD. This ...

Direct Linking to Electronic Records

One of CaseMap's standout features is the ability to link directly to electronic medical records. A paperclip icon next to each entry lets you open the supporting document instantly. Even better, CaseMap can link to the exact page in a document, much like placing a sticky note on a physical chart. This is especially valuable when you, your attorney, or an expert need to quickly access critical evidence during case review or collaboration.

Reporting and Collaboration

For professional presentations, CaseMap's Report Books feature creates comprehensive, easy-to-read reports that include all your spreadsheets. These reports help you share case details with colleagues or legal teams, supporting informed decision-making.

CaseMap vs. Word: The Differences That Matter

While Word is great for drafting documents, CaseMap is designed for managing complex, interrelated case data. Its database structure, customizable fields, powerful filtering and tagging, and direct links to electronic records provide LNCs with tools that streamline case preparation and support more effective collaboration. For more information, you can visit the LexisNexis CaseMap website.

Timelines vs. Medical Chronologies: A Practical Guide for LNCs

Clarifying the Differences, Selecting Key Events, and Creating Effective Reports

Legal nurse consultants (LNCs) play a vital role in helping attorneys understand medical facts within the context of legal cases. One common request from attorneys is to produce a timeline or a medical chronology. Understanding the differences between these report types—and knowing when and how to use each—will help you deliver clear, effective, and objective reports that support case strategy and presentation.

Detailed Comparison: Timeline vs. Medical Chronology

Although the terms timeline and medical chronology are sometimes used interchangeably, they serve distinct purposes in legal cases. The table below highlights their key differences:

Aspect	Timeline	Medical Chronology
Focus	Key events related to specific allegations over a defined period	All pertinent medical care related to allegations, including condition before and after date of incident
Purpose	Highlight facts central to the case; often used as trial exhibits	Provide a comprehensive, objective record of medical history
Level of Detail	Selective and concise	Broad and thorough
Audience	Attorneys, jurors, judges—anyone needing a clear summary of critical events	Attorneys, clients—anyone needing full context of medical care
Format	Horizontal or vertical sequence of key facts over a defined time; may use tables or charts	Chronological list or table of all medical events related to allegations and other events.

- Timelines: Focus on a series of significant events tied to allegations, such as missed diagnoses or treatment delays.
- Medical Chronologies: Include information about events tied to the allegations as well as prior and succeeding events.

Example Scenarios: When to Use Each Report Type

Timeline Example Scenario:

A plaintiff claims that a hospital failed to treat a fever over a 20-hour period, leading to complications. The LNC creates a timeline showing only the temperature readings, patient mentation, and interventions directly related to the fever, omitting unrelated care.

Medical Chronology Example Scenario:

In a case involving alleged substandard care over several years, the LNC prepares a medical chronology listing every clinic visit, lab result, medication, and physician recommendation related to fevers. This provides a comprehensive history, allowing the attorney to track overall care and compliance.

Checklist: Selecting Key Events for Timelines

To create a focused and effective timeline, use the following checklist and guiding questions:

- What are the central allegations or issues in the case?
- Which events directly relate to those allegations?
- What is the relevant time frame to cover?
- Which facts are essential for the attorney or jury to understand?
- Are there patterns (e.g., repeated missed appointments) that support or refute the case theory?
- Does each included event contribute to the narrative or help clarify causation?
- Can unrelated details be omitted without losing clarity?

Before finalizing your timeline, ask yourself:

1. Is every event relevant to the case issues?
2. Does the timeline present information in a logical, sequential order?
3. Have you avoided adding unnecessary details?

Advice: Maintaining Objectivity and Clarity

- Present facts without interpretation or speculation.
- Avoid inserting opinions or drawing conclusions about causality.
- Use neutral language and consistent formatting.
- Check for accuracy and verify all dates and details against source records.
- Ensure the timeline is easy to read and visually clear, especially if used as a trial exhibit.

Practical Walkthroughs: Creating Timelines in Word

Step-by-Step: Timeline Creation in Microsoft Word

1. Open a new Word document.
2. Create a timeline by going to the Insert tab and clicking SmartArt.
3. In the Choose a SmartArt Graphic gallery, click Process, and then double-click a timeline layout.
4. Use text boxes and lines to highlight or connect events, focusing attention on crucial facts.
5. Enter dates/times and event descriptions in the appropriate text boxes.
6. Apply formatting (e.g., bold for key interventions, color for critical changes in patient status).
7. Review for clarity and ensure only relevant events are included.

Download a free Microsoft Word Timeline template to help get started quickly.

Conclusion: Using Timelines to Clarify Complex Events

Timelines are powerful tools for legal nurse consultants, enabling you to distill complex medical records into clear, focused reports. By understanding the differences between timelines and medical chronologies, selecting key events with care, and maintaining objectivity, you can help attorneys—and jurors—grasp the essential facts immediately. Use the practical steps and resources provided to create timelines that clarify even the most complicated cases.

Sample Timeline

The sample below was created by inserting SmartArt from the Insert menu, selecting Process, and then choosing Basic Timeline. The arrow was stretched, and additional circles were added to represent individual events. Finally, text boxes and connecting lines were inserted to clarify the relationship between each event and its place on the timeline.

The following timeline illustrates the sequence of events related to a medical case involving a young child. This timeline visually represents the key events leading up to and following the alleged failure to timely and effectively treat a fever, which resulted in alleged brain damage in the patient. Presenting the details in this format helps clarify the chronology and significance of each intervention or missed opportunity.

Timeline for Melissa DuBois 4/2/25 – 4/3/25

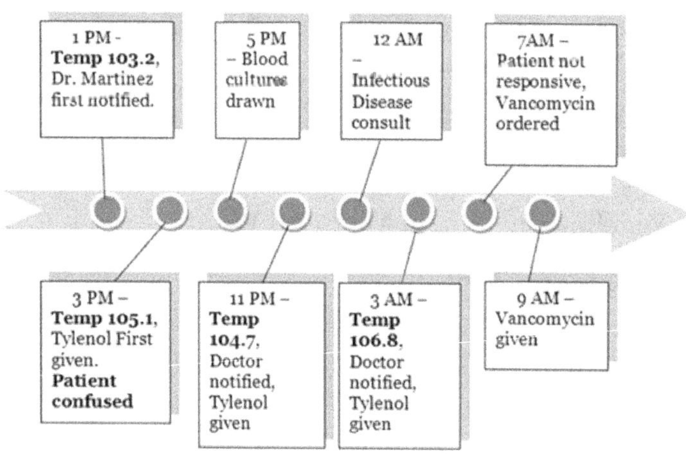

Figure 4 - Timeline

Medication Compliance Calendars: Utility, Limitations, and Legal Impact

Medication compliance calendars are increasingly used in legal cases to provide clear, visual evidence of gaps in patient care. By mapping missed prescription fills or appointments on a calendar, these tools allow attorneys and legal nurse consultants to quickly identify periods of non-compliance. The visual nature of calendars makes patterns—such as extended gaps between medication refills—more apparent than a chronological list or narrative summary, which can be especially valuable in complex cases.

Limitations and Challenges of Calendar Evidence

While medication compliance calendars offer objective visual summaries, they also present several limitations that must be acknowledged for balanced analysis. Importantly, pharmacy records indicate only when medications were dispensed, not whether the patient actually ingested the medication as prescribed. Additionally, pharmacy errors—such as incorrect record-keeping or mistaken entries—can affect the accuracy of calendar data. Patient self-reporting, which may be used to fill in gaps or explain missed fills, is subject to recall bias and may not always align with documented evidence. These factors mean that calendar-based evidence should be interpreted cautiously and supplemented with other forms of documentation when possible.

Step-by-Step Process for Creating Medication Compliance Calendars

1. Review Case Allegations: Begin by analyzing the specific allegations in the legal case to determine the relevant time frame and the nature of the alleged non-compliance.
2. Examine Medical and Pharmacy Records: Collect and review all applicable physician office and pharmacy records for the identified period, ensuring a comprehensive understanding of the patient's medication and appointment history.
3. Develop a Focused Chronology: Create a targeted chronology that includes only dates directly related to the allegations, such as missed office visits or prescription fills. Note any documented reasons for missed appointments, like hospitalizations, as these may explain apparent gaps.
4. Select an Appropriate Calendar Template: Choose a calendar template from Word, Excel, or online sources that best displays the data. Mark dates when

medications were filled or appointments attended to provide an objective visual summary.

5. Present and Interpret the Calendar: Use the calendar to highlight periods of adherence and non-compliance. Clearly indicate any limitations or data gaps, referencing supporting records or patient explanations where available.

Legal Impact: Influence on Strategies and Outcomes

In legal cases—particularly malpractice claims—medication compliance calendars can play a pivotal role. For instance, if pharmacy records show that a plaintiff filled prescriptions only three times in a year for a medication intended for daily use, a calendar can visually underscore significant gaps in adherence. Such evidence can support expert testimony by objectively demonstrating non-compliance, which may be relevant in establishing causation or contributory negligence. For juries, calendar visuals provide an accessible way to understand complex timelines, potentially swaying decisions by making non-compliance patterns unmistakable. However, attorneys and consultants must contextualize these visuals within the broader evidentiary record, noting limitations to avoid overstating their conclusiveness.

Instructional Approach for Other Evidence Presentations

This step-by-step methodology—beginning with case review, followed by focused record analysis, visual presentation, and careful interpretation—can be applied to other types of reports or evidence, such as appointment attendance charts or therapy participation logs. By maintaining a clear, structured approach, legal professionals ensure their evidence presentations are both compelling and balanced, ultimately supporting fair and informed case outcomes.

Sample Calendar Report

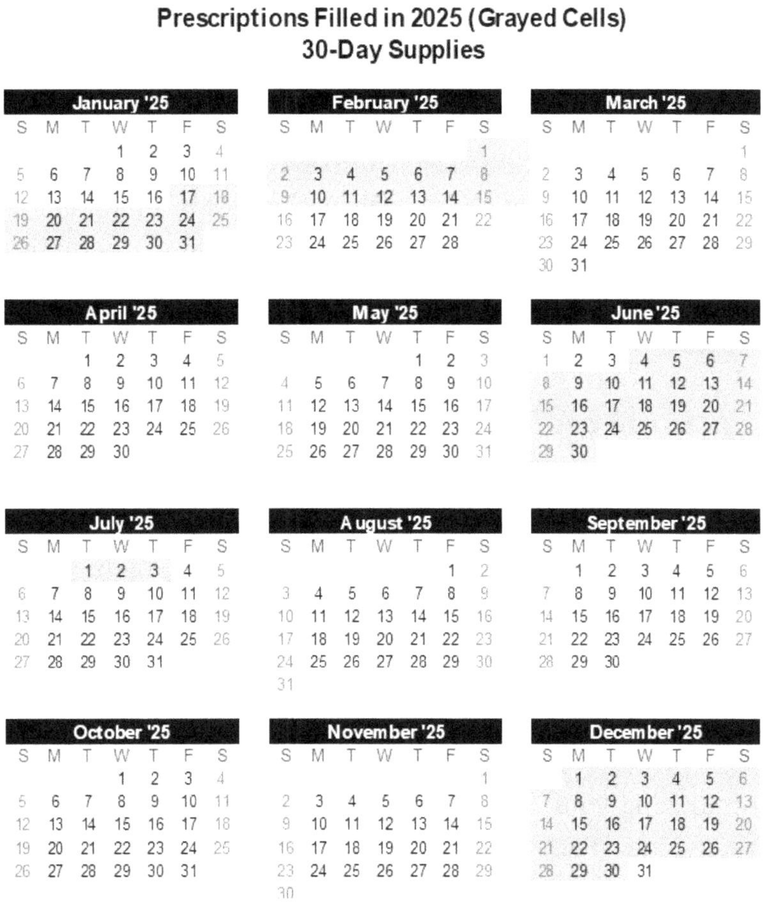

Figure 5 - Prescription Calendar

Conclusion

Medication compliance calendars offer clear, visual evidence that can clarify patterns of care in legal proceedings. While they are powerful tools for highlighting adherence or non-compliance, it is essential to recognize their limitations—including the inability to confirm medication ingestion, potential for record errors, and reliance on patient self-reporting. By following a structured, transparent process and acknowledging these challenges, legal professionals can maximize the value of calendar evidence while maintaining objectivity and credibility.

Creating an Excel Chart from a Word Table for Medical Data Visualization

For Legal Nurse Consultants and Beginners

Excel is a spreadsheet program that allows you to organize and visually present data for clearer analysis and reporting. Legal nurse consultants can use Excel charts to highlight trends in medical information, such as changes in a patient's laboratory values or weight over time. Importantly, you don't need advanced mathematical skills to create professional-looking charts—just a basic understanding of copying, pasting, and using Excel's charting tools.

What Is Creatinine and the Normal Creatinine Range?

Creatinine is a waste product produced by muscles and filtered out of the blood by the kidneys. Measuring creatinine levels helps assess kidney function. In healthy adults, the normal blood creatinine range is generally about 0.6 to 1.2 mg/dL, though this can vary slightly between laboratories. Values above this range may indicate impaired kidney function or acute kidney injury.

Step 1: Create Your Data Table in Word

Begin by organizing your data into a simple table in Microsoft Word, or you also enter data directly into Excel. For example, below is a table showing a patient's creatinine levels over several days. This format is ideal for use in narrative medical summaries or reports:

Date	Creatinine Level
2/27/24	1.1
2/28/24	1.8
3/1/24	2.7
3/2/24	2.8
3/3/24	3.9
3/4/24	4.4
3/5/24	4.9

3/6/24	5.2
3/7/24	6.7
3/8/24	7.8

Step 2: Copy the Table from Word

To transfer your data from Word to Excel:

1. Open your Word document containing the table.
2. Click and drag your mouse to highlight the entire table, including headers, or select the icon above the top left corner of the table, which highlights the entire table.
3. Right-click on the highlighted area and select Copy from the menu.

Step 3: Paste the Table into Excel

Next, open a new or existing Excel workbook:

1. Click into the cell where you want the upper left corner of your table to appear (for example, cell A1).
2. Right-click in that cell and choose Paste. Your table will appear in Excel, preserving its original structure.

Step 4: Create a Chart in Excel

Now that your data is in Excel, you can create a chart to visualize the trends:

1. Highlight all the cells containing your data, including the headers (e.g., Date and Creatinine Level).
2. Go to the Insert tab at the top of Excel.
3. In the Charts group, select Line (or Bar) Chart and choose your preferred style. A line chart is especially effective for showing changes over time.

Step 5: Annotate the Chart with the Normal Creatinine Range

To add context and make your chart more informative:

1. Insert a rectangle shape across the bottom of the chart to visually represent the normal creatinine range (0.6–1.2 mg/dL).
2. Add a text box labeling the rectangle as "Normal Creatinine Range: 0.6–1.2 mg/dL."
3. If needed, draw a line from the text box to the rectangle for clarity.

Step 6: Copy the Chart Back to Word

Once your chart is ready in Excel, you can easily include it in your narrative medical summary:

1. Click on the chart in Excel to select it.
2. Right-click the chart and select Copy.
3. Go to your Word document and click where you want the chart to appear.
4. Right-click and choose Paste. Your chart will appear in your report, ready to support your findings.
5. Your chart will appear in your report like this:

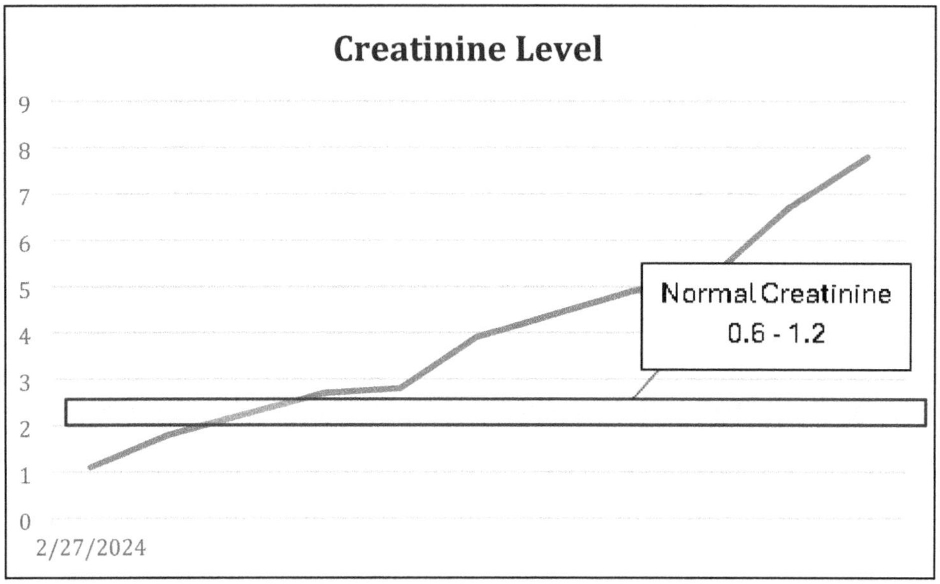

Figure 6 - Creatinine Level

Conclusion

By following these step-by-step instructions, you can efficiently transfer data from Word to Excel and create visually compelling charts. This approach helps legal nurse consultants and other professionals present medical data—like creatinine trends—in a way that is easy to understand and supports effective communication in reports and presentations. Taken on its own, the data in the above case appears to show a clear case of failure to diagnose and treat elevated creatinine and possible renal failure.

Touch Charts: Visualizing Healthcare Interactions for Legal Cases

Guidance for Legal Professionals and Healthcare Consultants

In litigation involving medical malpractice, nursing home neglect, or claims of inadequate staffing, allegations often arise that a patient or resident was left unattended for a certain period. Touch charts are effective visual tools that map out the number and type of healthcare providers who interacted with a patient during a specified timeframe, making patterns of care easy to interpret for legal professionals and healthcare consultants.

Defining Key Terms

- Coded: In healthcare, "coded" refers to when a patient undergoes cardiopulmonary resuscitation (CPR) for cardiac or respiratory arrest. If a patient was not "coded," it means CPR was not performed for such emergencies.
- Hash Marks: These are short vertical lines used to count occurrences. On a touch chart, hash marks tally each encounter a patient has with a caregiver, such as nurses, Certified Nursing Assistants (CNAs), physicians, or respiratory therapists.

Creating a Touch Chart

1. Review all relevant medical records for the specified time frame.
2. Document every instance of care provided, specifying both the type of care (vital signs, education, medication administration, assessments, hygiene assistance, etc.) and the caregiver involved.
3. Use hash marks to record each interaction by caregiver type.
4. Convert these tallies into a visual diagram, often formatted as a clock, calendar, or day planner, to clearly show the timeline and diversity of care.

Interpreting Touch Chart Results

When analyzing touch charts, look for patterns that reveal the quality and frequency of patient care:

- Long Gaps: Extended periods without any caregiver interaction may signal possible neglect or understaffing.

- Limited Caregiver Variety: If only one type of caregiver is present, this might indicate a lack of interdisciplinary attention, which can support claims of inadequate staffing.
- Frequent and Diverse Interactions: Numerous encounters involving different healthcare professionals typically suggest attentive and appropriate care.

Case Example: Using Touch Charts to Clarify Care Allegations

In one case I reviewed, a family alleged that their loved one was not "coded"—meaning she did not receive CPR for cardiac or respiratory arrest—and claimed that only one nurse attended to her in the last 22 minutes of her life. After a thorough chart review, I documented five nurse interactions, four CNA encounters, two physician visits, and one respiratory therapist session within that period. Using hash marks to tally these events and Microsoft Copilot to quickly create a touch chart, the visual evidence contradicted the family's claim. The touch chart demonstrated frequent and diverse caregiver involvement, providing a compelling visual rebuttal to allegations of neglect.

If this case had gone to trial, a professional graphics company could have further enhanced the touch chart for presentation to a jury or inclusion in a PowerPoint. The lesson learned is that touch charts can be invaluable in visually clarifying the actual care delivered, highlighting whether allegations of neglect or inadequate staffing are supported by the documentation.

Conclusion

Touch charts are powerful tools for legal nurse consultants and attorneys, transforming complex medical records into straightforward visual timelines. By defining key terms and guiding interpretation, these charts help clarify whether patients received proper care, ultimately supporting or refuting claims in legal cases.

Sample Touch Chart

Figure 7 - Sample Touch Chart

Treater, Provider, Fact Witness, and Cast of Character Lists

A Practical Guide for Legal Nurse Consultants

- Treater. The term "treater" refers to an individual who directly provides care to a patient. This typically includes doctors, nurses, therapists, or any healthcare professional who has hands-on involvement in the patient's treatment. Example: A nurse who administered medication during a patient's hospital stay is a treater.
- Provider. "Provider" can be used interchangeably with "treater" but often refers more broadly to both individuals and healthcare organizations involved in a patient's care. This may include hospitals, clinics, ambulance services, or home health agencies, in addition to the staff within those organizations. Example: General Hospital, as an institution, is a provider; its staff physicians and nurses are treaters.

- Fact Witness. A fact witness is a person who has firsthand knowledge of case events, whether they provided medical care or not. Fact witnesses can include treaters, family members, police officers, or others present during relevant events. These lists typically include the name and address of each witness. Example Scenario: If a patient's spouse testifies about the patient's physical limitations after an injury, the spouse is a fact witness. If a nurse testifies about the care she provided in the hospital, she is a treater.
- Cast of Characters. Used in tools like CaseMap, a "cast of characters" list encompasses all individuals and entities involved in a case, including treaters, fact witnesses, and expert witnesses. Example: The cast of characters might include the treating physician, the ambulance driver, the family member who witnessed the incident, the hospital where the patient was admitted, and a retained medical expert.

Types of Lists

- Treater/Provider List: Comprehensive listing of individuals and organizations involved in providing care to the patient.
- Fact Witness List: Names and addresses of all individuals with firsthand knowledge of relevant events, not limited to medical providers.
- Cast of Characters: Inclusive list of everyone involved in the case, including treaters, fact witnesses, and experts.

Reasons for LNCs to Create a Treater/Provider List

- Professional Differentiation: Few LNCs provide treater/provider lists proactively. Offering this service can set you apart and add value for your attorney clients.
- Completeness: Lists provided through the discovery process may be incomplete due to gaps in the healthcare system or patient memory. Creating your own ensures a more thorough accounting.
- Proactive Case Management: By generating these lists early, you can cross-reference treaters with subpoena or authorization logs and recommend additional record procurement if you work in a law firm. If you're an independent LNC, you can expand your consulting opportunities.
- Attorney Support: Providing clear, organized treater/provider lists streamlines the attorney's work, making your medical chronologies and summaries even more useful.

Methods for Creating Treater/Provider Lists

1. Prepare Your Workspace. Set up a dual-monitor system, if possible, or use a wide-screen monitor. Open the medical records on one screen and your report/table on the other.
2. Choose a Table Format. Create a table with columns such as "Name," "Role in Case," and "Found In Records Of." The "Found In Records Of" column is tremendously useful for depositions and trials. For instance, during a deposition, you might need to quickly confirm when and where a particular doctor's name is located. Imagine having to look through tens of thousands of pages of medical records, trying to locate a treater's name years after you first encountered it. This column allows you to look up names and correlate them to medical records in seconds.
3. It is easier to sort treater and fact witness names if their last names are written first as shown in the sample table entry below.
4. Method 1: Highlight and Extract. As you review each set of medical records, highlight every new name you encounter in your chronology or summary. After completing the review, copy and paste the highlighted names into your list table. Fill in the "Role in Case" and "Found In Records Of" columns for each entry. Remove the highlights once the information is transferred.
5. Method 2: Add Information on the Fly. When you first encounter a treater or provider name, immediately enter it into your list table. Also include where you found the names. Continue to add new names and details as you progress through the records. Periodically update the list as the case evolves and new records are received. Double-check for duplicates and clarify roles as more information becomes available.

Sample Table Entry

Name	**Role in Case**	**Found In Records Of**
Smith, Jane MD	Treating Physician	General Hospital Discharge Summary

By following these structured methods and understanding the distinctions between key terms, LNCs can create comprehensive, accurate lists that support both their own work and the needs of the legal team.

Sample Treater List

All samples in this book are customizable. The following Treater List differs from typical treater/provider lists in that it identifies staff from a single facility—Manorhouse

Skilled Nursing Facility (SNF). All names were sourced from Manorhouse SNF records, and the second and third columns have been repurposed as "Role in Case/Comments" to reflect case-specific notes.

This case involves allegations of negligence, including repeated resident falls and the development of sepsis stemming from a urinary tract infection (UTI). The comments in the second column highlight details relevant to these claims. Additionally, this Treater List documents inconsistencies in records concerning the resident's food intake. Identifying conflicting documentation is a common strategy in plaintiff cases involving skilled nursing facilities.

Rosswell Manorhouse Skilled Nursing Facility

Matter Number ROS-77

Treater List

Treater Name	**Role in Case/Comments**
Abbott, Mary, CNA	Day shift staff. Documented that Mrs. Rosswell was found on the floor on January 4, 2025
Baker, Beth, CNA	Night shift staff. Documented that Mrs. Rosswell ate 100% of all her meals in February 2025; conflicts with amounts documented by LPNs in Nursing Notes for that month.
Corrigan, Encita, CNA	Night shift staff
Davis, Maryann, LPN	Night shift staff
Entler, Enrique, CNA	Evening shift staff
Franks, Aiden, CNA	Day shift staff
Geneva, Sarah, CNA	Evening shift staff
George, Sally, CNA	Night shift staff
Hermanson, Hildie, LPN	Evening shift staff. Documented in Nursing Notes that Mrs. Rosswell ate only 25% of her dinner on February 8th, 2025. Also documented that Mrs. Rosswell was found on the floor on March 23, 2025
Johnson, Lynette, MD	Medical Director at Manorhouse; routinely saw Mrs. Rosswell

Treater Name	Role in Case/Comments
Kozak, Karen, CNA	Night shift staff
Lawry, Mary Beth, CNA	Day shift staff
Martin, January LPN	Wound care nurse at Manorhouse; failed to document condition of sacral decubitus, failed to inform physician of changes in decubitus.
Martinez, Felice, ARNP	Employed by Dr. Johnson; saw Mrs. Rosswell at Manorhouse.
Nathanson, Ima, CNA	Evening shift staff
Orvell, Erly, CNA	Day shift staff
Pierre, Lisette, CNA	Day shift staff
Quinn, Lettie, LPN	Day shift staff. Documented in Nursing Notes that Mrs. Rosswell ate only 50% of her breakfast and lunch on February 9th and 10th, 2025
Ransom, Diane, CNA	Evening shift staff
Rodriguez, Lula, RN	Director of Nursing; responsible for staffing levels at Manorhouse
Russell, Phillip, MD	Internist; Mrs. Rosswell's primary physician
Sampleton, Jesse, CNA	Evening shift staff. Documented that Mrs. Rosswell was found on the floor on April 10, 2025.
Sheldon, Marjory, CNA	Day shift staff
Sturgis, Deborah, CNA	Night shift staff
Tyler, Stella, LPN	Night shift staff. Documented foul-smelling urine on February 12, 2025, failed to inform physician of such.
Winkler, Suzanna, LPN	Day shift staff
Young, Melinda, CNA	Day shift staff
Yunis, Bella, CNA	Evening shift staff

Effective Indexing in Legal Cases: A Guide for Legal Nurse Consultants

Indexing plays a critical role in legal cases, allowing law teams to quickly locate, review, and interpret key documents and evidence. For legal nurse consultants (LNCs), understanding and customizing indexes can streamline case analysis and support efficient collaboration with attorneys. This article provides an overview of four essential types of indexes—medical records, radiographs, pathology specimens, and pleadings—complete with definitions, example entries, and practical guidance for tailoring indexes to specific case needs.

1. Medical Records Index

Medical records are comprehensive documents detailing a patient's medical history, treatments, diagnoses, and outcomes. Indexing these records helps legal professionals and LNCs track what has been received and where each record is located.

A typical medical records index includes the record type or source, dates of service, the location or storage number, and, when useful, the patient's diagnoses. Organizing the index alphabetically or chronologically can enhance accessibility, depending on the case's complexity.

Sample Medical Records Index Entry:

Provider	**Date of Service**	**Location Number**	**Diagnosis**
City Hospital	03/15/2025	MR-001	Fractured Femur
Smith Orthopedics	03/20/2025	MR-002	Post-op Infection

Tip: Always list your client's records first, then decide whether alphabetical or chronological order best suits your review process. Adding diagnoses to each entry helps quickly identify critical information.

2. Radiographs Index

Radiographs are images produced to visualize internal structures of the body, such as x-rays, CT scans, MRIs, and ultrasounds. Indexing radiographs ensures all imaging studies are accounted for and easily retrievable—a necessity given the volume and importance of these records in many cases.

A radiograph index usually lists the date of service, type of study, acquisition location, and the format (film or digital). LNCs may also include the time of study and the ordering physician when relevant, as this information provides context for the sequence of medical events.

Sample Radiograph Index Entry:

Date	Type	Location	Format	Time	Ordering / Reading Physician
03/16/2025	CT Scan	City Hospital Radiology	Digital (Disk 1)	10:30 AM	Dr. Allen / Dr. Flouta
03/17/2025	X-Ray	Medex Urgent Care Center	Film (2 films)	2:15 PM	Dr. Lee / Dr. Jensen

Tip: Note that digital radiographs maintain image quality when copied, while film images may degrade. Organize entries by date, location, or study type depending on what will most benefit your case analysis.

3. Pathology Specimens Index

Pathology specimens are samples of tissue, blood, or other bodily substances collected for diagnostic examination. Indexing these specimens involves tracking where and when samples were taken, as well as who was involved in their collection and interpretation.

A pathology specimens index typically records the date of service, body site, healthcare facility, and specimen number. Including the names of ordering and interpreting physicians can further clarify the chain of custody and analysis.

Sample Pathology Specimens Index Entry:

Date	Body Site	Facility	Specimen No.	Ordering Physician	Interpreting Physician
03/18/2025	Right Knee	City Hospital Lab	PS-005	Dr. Brown	Dr. Miller

Tip: Customizing the index with physician details allows for quick cross-reference with other records and adds clarity to complex diagnostic timelines.

4. Pleadings Index

Pleadings are formal documents filed with the court that articulate the parties' claims, defenses, and procedural motions throughout litigation. Indexing pleadings ensures that all filings are organized and easily accessible for reference during the case.

A pleadings index generally assigns a unique number to each document in ascending order, starting with the initial Complaint. Pleadings are typically filed in reverse chronological order—the most recent document appears first.

Sample Pleadings Index Entry:

Pleading No.	Date Filed	Title	Filed By
P-002	04/15/2025	Answer	Defendant
P-001	04/01/2025	Complaint	Plaintiff

Tip: While paralegals or legal secretaries often manage this index, LNCs may also index pleadings for their work. Include document numbers, filing dates, and parties involved for comprehensive tracking.

5. Medical Research Index

A medical research index serves as a comprehensive and organized list of all journal articles, books, and clinical references relevant to a particular case. For legal nurse consultants, maintaining a structured research index ensures that pertinent medical literature is readily accessible for case analysis and presentation.

Citation Formatting: Importance of Uniform Style Guides

Consistency in citation formatting is essential for professionalism and clarity. Applying a recognized style guide, such as APA or MLA, produces a uniform and polished index that meets the standards required by academic institutions and professional publications.

Challenges of Citation Rules

Citation style guides, including APA and MLA, contain detailed and sometimes complex rules that differ depending on the type of source (e.g., book, journal article, website), the number of authors, and the format in which the material was accessed (print or online). These rules can be challenging to remember, especially since they vary by source type.

Choosing Citation Generators: Criteria and Context

To streamline the citation process, legal nurse consultants can utilize free online citation generators, which automate the application of style guide rules. Selection of a citation generator should be based on the volume and type of sources to be managed:

- Zotero[17]: Ideal for managing many sources and organizing research libraries.
- Noodle Tools[18]: Suitable for educational settings and projects requiring collaboration.
- Citation Machine[19]: Efficient for quickly generating individual citations without creating a source library.
- Bibme[20]: Convenient for generating citations across various source types with a straightforward interface.

It is advisable to test both APA and MLA styles within the chosen generator to determine which format best suits the project's requirements. Once a style is selected, it should be used consistently throughout the index.

Copilot can also be used to generate Citations. Copy the text or webpage of the journal article or source you wish to cite. Paste the content or the URL into your Microsoft Word document. Then, select the relevant section and activate Copilot within Microsoft 365. Request Copilot to generate a citation in the desired style (APA or MLA). Carefully review the formatted citation, which will appear in the following style:

Berry, M. F. (2014). Esophageal cancer: Staging system and guidelines for staging and treatment. Journal of Thoracic Disease, 6(Suppl 3), S289–S297. Retrieved from https://pmc.ncbi.nlm.nih.gov/articles/PMC4037413/

Finally, copy and paste each citation into your index, arranging them in alphabetical order.

Formatting Citations: Creating a Hanging Indent

1. After pasting a citation, highlight the second and subsequent lines of the citation.
2. In Microsoft Word, press Control + T simultaneously to apply a hanging indent.
3. (For WordPerfect users, use Control + F7.)

[17] Zotero. https://www.zotero.org/ (accessed January 2026)
[18] Noodle Tools. https://my.noodletools.com/web2.0/express.html (accessed January 2026)
[19] Citation Machine. https://www.citationmachine.net (accessed January 2026)
[20] Bibme. https://www.bibme.org/ (accessed January 2026)

Organizing Citations: Table and Folder System

1. Insert a two-column table with invisible borders into your index document. Word can't format both a number and a hanging indent in a normal paragraph, but it can if the number is in one column and the citation is in the other.
2. Use the first column to assign a sequential number to each citation.
3. Enter the formatted citation into the second column.
4. Print and organize the research articles in a numbered, tabbed folder or binder, corresponding to the index. This system facilitates efficient retrieval of each referenced article during case preparation.

Conclusion: The Value of Individualized Indexes

For legal nurse consultants, effective and customized indexing is a foundational skill that enhances the clarity, efficiency, and quality of case review. By understanding the definitions, structures, and best practices for each index type, LNCs can ensure that every document is accessible and every detail accounted for—making them invaluable members of the legal team.

Creating Medical Symbols with Macrons or Overstrikes in Microsoft Word

A Step-by-Step Guide for Legal Nurse Consultants and Microsoft Word Users

Legal nurse consultants occasionally need to reproduce medical chart entries exactly as they appear, including specialized symbols for words like "with," "without," "before," "after," "every," and "except." These symbols are typically the letters c, s, a, p, q, and x with a line (a macron or overstrike) above each letter. Unfortunately, Microsoft Word does not include standard fonts that provide these overstruck letters. Using just the plain letters is not accurate, and drawing lines by hand is not professional. Fortunately, there is a straightforward way to create these symbols in Word using the Symbol menu and AutoCorrect feature. This guide provides clear, step-by-step instructions for both methods. *Note: This tip will not work in the online version of Word. Please download the Office Suite to enable Word's full potential.*

Step 1: Inserting a Letter with a Macron Using the Symbol Menu

1. Open your Microsoft Word document and place your cursor where you want the symbol to appear.

2. Type the letter you need (for example, a for "before").
3. Click the Insert tab at the top of the Word window (located next to the Home tab).
4. On the far right of the ribbon, click Symbol.
5. From the dropdown, select More Symbols...
6. In the Symbol dialog box, look toward the lower right for the Character code box.
7. Type 0304.
8. Next to "from:" ensure Unicode (hex) is selected.
9. Click Insert. The symbol should now appear, for example: ā.
10. Click Close to exit the Symbol dialog box.

After you have inserted the macron once, it will appear in the recently used list in the Symbol menu, making it quicker to insert for other letters.

Step 2: Repeat for Other Medical Symbols

Repeat the above process for each of the following letters: c ("with"), s ("without"), p ("after"), q ("every"), and x ("except"). For each, type the letter, then use the Symbol menu to add the macron as described.

Step 3: Setting Up AutoCorrect for Faster Typing

To save time, you can assign a keyboard shortcut using Word's AutoCorrect feature. This will allow you to type a combination (for example, a`) and have it automatically converted to ā.

1. Highlight one of the newly created symbols in your document (for example, ā).
2. Click the File tab in the top left corner of Word.
3. From the left column, select Options (located at the bottom).
4. In the Word Options window, select Proofing from the left menu.
5. Click the AutoCorrect Options... button on the right.
6. In the AutoCorrect window, under the "Replace" field, enter a shortcut you'll remember (for example, type a, then the backtick key [`], which is left of the 1 key for an "a" with macron).
7. In the "With" field, the selected symbol (e.g., ā) should already appear. If not, paste it here.
8. Click Add, then OK to save and close the AutoCorrect window.
9. Repeat this process for each symbol you need (for example, use c` for c̄, s` for s̄, etc.).

Example: To set up AutoCorrect for an "a" with a macron, enter a` in the "Replace" box and ā in the "With" box. Now, whenever you type a` and press space or punctuation, Word will automatically change it to ā.

Step 4: Testing and Using Your Shortcuts

To test a shortcut, type the shortcut you defined (for example, a`) and then press the spacebar. The corresponding symbol (e.g., ā) should appear in your document. Repeat this for all the medical symbols you set up. Once you become familiar with this technique, you'll find it much faster and more accurate for entering medical symbols in your reports.

By following these steps, you can efficiently create and use accurate medical symbols in your Microsoft Word documents, ensuring clarity and professionalism in all your legal nurse consultant reports.

Hyperlinking Electronic Medical Records: A Step-by-Step Guide

Save time and stay organized when managing medical records for legal cases

Has this ever happened to you? An attorney sends you a large batch of electronic medical records through a file-sharing site or on a flash drive. You create a medical chronology or summary, and then you're on the phone with your client. They ask you to look at a specific page, but you're struggling to find it quickly because the records are organized electronically and not in a simple stack of paper. This situation can be frustrating and time-consuming. Luckily, there's a practical way to solve this problem: adding hyperlinks to your report so you can jump directly to the exact page you need in the electronic records.

Why Hyperlinking Helps

You're probably familiar with internet hyperlinks—clicking a link takes you to a website. But in this context, hyperlinking means creating direct links from your report to specific files (or even specific pages) stored on your computer or your law firm's network. This makes it much easier to locate valuable information in electronic medical records while referencing your chronology or summary.

Step-by-Step: Hyperlinking to Electronic Medical Records in Microsoft Word

1. Save the Records: Download the electronic medical records onto your computer's hard drive or your firm's network. Make sure the records are saved in PDF format, which is standard for these types of documents.
2. Open Your Chronology: Launch Microsoft Word and open the chronology or summary document you've created. For this example, we'll use a chronology.
3. Locate the PDF Page: Open the PDF file containing the medical records. Use a PDF viewer (like Adobe Acrobat or the built-in Windows PDF reader) to find the specific page you want to reference.
4. Add a Column for Links: In your Word chronology table, insert a new column to the right of your current entries. This new column will hold the hyperlinks.
5. Enter and Highlight the Page Number: For each entry, type the relevant PDF page number into the new column. Highlight the page number you just typed.
6. Create the Hyperlink: Go to the Insert tab in the Word toolbar. Click Hyperlink (sometimes labeled as Link). In the dialog box that appears, choose Existing File or Web Page on the left. Navigate through your folders to find and select the PDF file you want to link to. Click OK to create the link.
7. Test Your Link: Hold down the Ctrl key and click the link you just created. The PDF should open, usually at the first page. Manually scroll to the page number listed in your chronology to view the exact information you need.

Troubleshooting and Limitations

- Access Issues: Hyperlinks to files on your computer or network will only work for users who have access to those files and locations. If you send the report to an outside attorney or client, they will not be able to open the links because the files are stored locally on your computer or organization's network.
- Printing and Sharing: Before printing or sharing your chronology, delete the column with hyperlinks and save the file under a new name. This prevents confusion for recipients who don't have access to your local files.
- Common Problems: If the link doesn't open, double-check that the file path is correct and that the PDF hasn't been moved or renamed. If you get an error message, the file may no longer be in its original location.

Alternatives and Cloud Sharing Tips

- Cloud Storage Solutions: If you want recipients to access the hyperlinks, consider uploading the PDF files to a secure cloud service (like ShareFile). Then, create hyperlinks to the shared cloud folder or specific files. This way, authorized users can access the documents from anywhere. However, this alternative may not be appealing to law firm employees. Law firms often manage numerous versions of medical records, which can lead to confusion, version control issues, and possibly increased storage costs. Adding another copy via cloud storage may exacerbate these problems rather than streamline access. Instead of cloud storage, exploring secure document management systems that allow direct linking without file duplication could be a more efficient solution for law firms.

- Protecting Sensitive Information: When using cloud storage, always check your organization's policies and ensure the sharing settings restrict access to only authorized individuals. Use password protection and encryption when appropriate. Never share sensitive medical records through public links.
- CaseMap Integration: For an even easier experience, applications like CaseMap allow you to create chronologies that link directly to the exact page in electronic medical records—no manual hyperlinking required.

Conclusion: Time-Saving Benefits and Encouragement

Hyperlinking electronic medical records in your reports may seem like an extra step, but it saves you and your team valuable time when referencing specific pages. The method is straightforward once you get the hang of it, and you can adapt it to fit your workflow—whether you're working solo or in a busy office. Try inserting hyperlinks into your next chronology and see how much easier it is to answer client questions, collaborate with colleagues, and keep your documentation organized. Remember, with a little setup, you'll never have to hunt for that elusive PDF page again!

Attention to Detail: Four Tips for Polishing LNC Reports

How Small Changes Can Enhance Clarity and Efficiency for Legal Teams

Attention to detail is a cornerstone of effective legal nurse consulting. Careful review of medical records and precise report writing can determine whether the plaintiff or defense prevails. While your reports may not decide the outcome of a case, a polished, well-structured document demonstrates your commitment to accuracy and professionalism—qualities highly valued by attorneys. Here are four practical tips to fine-tune your legal nurse consulting reports and help legal teams work more efficiently.

Tip 1: Use Proper Medication Naming Conventions

Begin each medication reference with the correct capitalization—brand names are capitalized, while generic names use lowercase. This distinction helps prevent confusion and ensures clarity in your reports. Why it matters: Attorneys and medical professionals rely on accurate medication identification to build timelines and clarify treatment details. Mixing up brand and generic names can cause misunderstandings or errors in case preparation. Example: Instead of writing "Dr. Anderson ordered 0.25 mg of Xanax," use "Dr. Anderson ordered 0.25 mg of Xanax (alprazolam) three times a day for the patient's anxiety." Both names in one entry make it easy for the legal team to cross-reference treatments. Scenario: A paralegal reviewing your chronology quickly identifies the correct medication when both brand and generic names are listed, saving time and reducing the risk of misinterpretation. Takeaway: Always capitalize brand medication names and use lowercase for generics; including both names in your reports streamlines communication and supports case accuracy.

Tip 2: Place Treater Names at the Beginning of Chronology Entries

Start each medical chronology entry with the treater's name to immediately identify the author of a record. Why it matters: Legal teams often review lengthy chronologies. Placing the treater's name first lets attorneys and consultants quickly determine who wrote the entry, saving valuable time during document review. Example: Instead of "Patient complained of chest pain. Dr. Smith," write "Dr. Smith: Patient complained of chest pain." This format streamlines identification. Scenario: While preparing for deposition, an attorney finds all relevant entries from a specific provider in seconds, thanks to your consistent formatting. Takeaway: Lead every chronology entry with the treater's name to promote quick, accurate identification by the legal team.

Tip 3: Refer to Medical Records by Their Exact Titles

Always use the precise title of each medical record when referencing documentation in your reports. Why it matters: Accurate record titles help legal teams locate specific documents efficiently, reducing time spent searching and minimizing errors in evidence review. Example: Instead of generically saying "nursing note," use "Nursing Narrative Report" if that's the actual title. This precision guides the legal team directly to the correct record. Scenario: During case review, an attorney needs to find the Medication Administration Record (MAR). Your report's exact terminology allows for quick document retrieval, preventing delays. Takeaway: Refer to each record by its official title to facilitate fast, error-free access to documentation.

Tip 4: Format Reports Using Full Justification

Type narrative reports, letters, and summaries in full justification to create a polished, professional appearance. Why it matters: Most law firms expect reports with flush edges on both sides for readability and consistency. Left justification leaves a ragged right edge, which can look unfinished and less professional. Scenario: An attorney shares your report with colleagues; the full justification immediately signals attention to detail and professionalism, reinforcing confidence in your expertise. Takeaway: Use full justification for all narrative sections in your reports but continue to use left or center alignment for tables to avoid excessive white space.

Conclusion

Implementing these four details—proper medication naming, treater name placement, accurate record titles, and professional formatting—enhances the quality and usability of your legal nurse consulting reports. By adopting these practices, you not only polish your work but also provide tangible benefits to legal teams, saving them time and supporting their ability to build strong cases.

Persuasive Use of Numbers in Legal Nursing

How Context, Analogies, and Storytelling Make Medical Data Accessible in Legal Settings

Numbers are a universal language in healthcare. Nurses routinely interpret vital statistics—such as a 62-year-old male patient standing 5'10", weighing 276 pounds, with a blood pressure of 180/114, LDL of 192, HDL of 36, and triglycerides of 521—to identify those at risk for cardiovascular events. Beyond the clinical setting, numbers are equally persuasive in legal contexts, helping attorneys and juries comprehend complex medical information. The key is transforming abstract data into relatable insights.

Making Numbers Relatable: Adding Context and Analogies to Statistics

Statistics can seem abstract, but familiar analogies make them tangible. For example, most people understand that eggs are sold by the dozen, have endured a three-day illness, and know there are 60 minutes in an hour, 24 hours in a day, and 365 days in a year. By framing medical statistics within these everyday experiences, legal nurses can bridge the gap between clinical data and layperson understanding.

Consider the incidence of a type of cancer called chordoma. This cancer is among the rarest in the United States, occurring in less than one person per million annually. To put this into perspective, being struck by lightning—a universally recognized rare event—happens to about one in 500,000 people each year. A cancerous chordoma is roughly twice as rare. Such comparisons help juries and attorneys grasp the extraordinary infrequency of certain medical conditions.

Storytelling with Data: Patient Scenarios and Step-by-Step Calculations

Storytelling transforms raw numbers into compelling narratives. Take, for instance, the standard of care for bedfast patients: clinical guidelines recommend turning these individuals every two hours to alleviate pressure on bony prominences and prevent decubitus ulcers. If a patient is hospitalized for three days—72 hours—she should be turned 36 times (72 hours ÷ 2 hours per turn). However, if records show she was turned only four times in that period, the deviation becomes clear. Instead of simply stating the numbers, walking the jury through the calculation illustrates the gap in care, making the abstract standard concrete and compelling.

Balancing Emotion and Fact: Objective Presentation of Medical Achievements

While numbers can evoke strong reactions, the narrative should remain grounded in factual clarity. For example, in a case involving delayed diagnosis of chordoma cancer, the legal nurse consultant might explain: "An internist typically sees 25 patients a day, 5 days a week, 50 weeks a year—totaling 6,250 patients annually. Over a 30-year career, that amounts to 187,500 patients. Given that cancerous chordomas represents a mere one-quarter of one percent of all cancers, and its incidence is less than one per million, it is commendable that the internist identified the abnormality so quickly. This outcome speaks to their diligence and expertise, especially considering that most physicians may never encounter such a case in their entire careers."

By coupling precise calculations with objective language, the achievement is highlighted without resorting to excessive emotion, maintaining credibility and persuasiveness.

Application: Using These Techniques in Legal Cases

Legal nurse consultants can leverage these approaches to make medical testimony accessible and convincing. Whether quantifying deviations from care standards or contextualizing rare diagnoses, integrating analogies, step-by-step calculations, and balanced storytelling empowers juries and attorneys to make informed decisions. For example, explaining that a patient should have been turned 36 times but was only turned four times paints a vivid picture of the care received. Comparing the rarity of a cancer diagnosis to the odds of being struck by lightning makes the abstract concrete.

Conclusion: Enhancing Persuasiveness and Clarity Through Numbers

Numbers, when paired with context and relatable analogies, become powerful tools in both nursing and legal communication. By telling stories with data and maintaining a balanced tone, legal nurse consultants can demystify complex medical concepts, making them accessible and persuasive for legal professionals, juries, and fellow nurses. This approach not only clarifies standards of care and rare events but also elevates the credibility of medical testimony in court.

The Power of Analogies

Harnessing the Impact of Analogies in Professional Communication

An analogy is a comparison between two things that share something in common but are otherwise quite different. One of the most common analogies in medicine is comparing the heart to a pump. While that analogy is familiar, my favorite has nothing to do with medicine, law, or legal nurse consulting. Instead, it involves a refrigerator, an oven, and a budget meeting—a story that highlights the power of using analogies in professional communication.

Back in the mid-1990s, I was a chief nurse executive trying to help my nursing directors manage their budgets. They were responsible for submitting budgets that addressed targets for census, nursing hours per patient day, total salaries, and salary hours per patient day for their nursing units. For some directors, translating staffing patterns into financial terms was a daunting task. To ease the process, I created an Excel spreadsheet—complex in design but simple for users. Directors could input their staffing pattern, and the spreadsheet would automatically generate projections for nursing hours, salary hours, and total salaries. If the numbers didn't align with budget expectations, they could adjust staffing and other parameters to meet projections. This eliminated endless meetings with the budget staff and let directors create budgets quickly and efficiently.

However, there was one major obstacle: the directors didn't have computers. To use the spreadsheet, they had to rely on computers belonging to non-nursing managers. At the next budget meeting, I requested computers for the nursing directors, fully expecting approval. To my surprise, the budget committee—comprised of administration and finance leaders—denied the request, worrying that nursing directors would "sit at their desks all day" using the computers.

After reflecting on the situation, I shared an analogy about refrigerators and ovens. A refrigerator runs all the time, while an oven is used sporadically. Yet both are essential in any kitchen. Financial staff used their computers like refrigerators—constantly. I explained that nursing directors would use their computers like ovens; they wouldn't need them all day, but when they did, it was essential to have them available immediately. Just as no one wants to go to a neighbor's house to cook, the directors didn't want to rely on other managers' computers.

At that moment, the analogy clicked for the budget committee. It was as if a light bulb went on above everyone's head. The president of the healthcare system smiled and said, "I think your nursing directors just got their computers."

This experience taught me firsthand how a simple analogy can transform a complicated discussion and make something abstract immediately understandable. Similarly, when collaborating with attorneys, you can use analogies to clarify medical concepts and bridge the gap between technical knowledge and practical understanding.

Summary: Just as the refrigerator and oven analogy helped the budget committee grasp the nursing directors' needs, using analogies can help attorneys quickly and effectively understand complex medical information. Attorneys often face challenges in making sense of anatomy, physiology, medical conditions, and treatments. By incorporating relatable analogies, legal nurse consultants can simplify these concepts for attorneys, who can then use them to help juries understand the complexities of medical malpractice cases.

Adding Images to Written Reports: Copyright, Fair Use, and Practical Steps

Incorporating images into your legal nurse consultant reports elevates their professionalism and clarity. A well-chosen photo or diagram can make medical concepts—like surgical techniques or anatomy—much easier for attorneys to grasp. Still, it's essential to use images responsibly and legally.

Understanding Copyright and Fair Use

Copyright is a law that protects the original work of creators, including photos, illustrations, and graphics. If an image is copyrighted, you must have permission or a license to use it in your report.

Fair Use is a limited legal exception that allows the use of copyrighted material without permission, usually for purposes like criticism, commentary, teaching, or news reporting. For example, quoting a short passage from a medical textbook in an educational seminar might qualify as Fair Use. However, Fair Use rarely applies to professional reports or work for clients—especially in legal or commercial settings. For your reports, assume that Fair Use does not cover image use and always secure proper licensing.

Using images found via search engines like Google, Bing, or Yahoo is risky. Many online images are copyrighted and using them without authorization is illegal and can result in fines or other penalties—even if you think the chance of being caught is low. To avoid these risks, always use images you have the rights to.

Recommended Image Sources and How to Access Them

- ShutterStock[21]: Offers a vast library of high-quality, royalty-free stock photos, illustrations, and diagrams. After creating an account, you can search by keyword (e.g., “surgical procedure” or “human anatomy”) and purchase images for a nominal fee. Download purchased images directly to your computer.
- iStock[22]: Similar to ShutterStock, iStock provides an extensive collection of affordable, royalty-free images. Register, search for medical or legal images, and pay per image or subscribe for broader access.
- Public Health Image Library (PHIL)[23] – CDC: A free resource specializing in public health and medical images. Visit the PHIL website, use the search bar to find images by topic (e.g., “surgical instruments” or “infection control”), and download images for use in your reports.
- MedPix[24] – NIH: Offers free, peer-reviewed medical images organized by diagnosis, organ system, and case. Go to the MedPix site, search or browse by category, and download images for educational and professional use.

[21] ShutterStock. https://tinyurl.com/y847fm9c (accessed December 2025).
[22] iStock. https://www.istockphoto.com/ (accessed December 2025).
[23] Public Health Image Library-CDC. https://phil.cdc.gov/ (accessed December 2025)
[24] MedPix-NIH. https://lhncbc.nlm.nih.gov/medpix.html (accessed December 2025)

Step-by-Step: Inserting and Formatting Images in Microsoft Word

1. Insert Image: Place your cursor where you want the image. Go to the Insert tab, click Pictures, navigate to your saved photo, and click Insert.
2. Resize Image: Click on the image. Drag a corner handle diagonally to adjust the size while maintaining proportions.
3. Add a Caption: Right-click the image and select Insert Caption. Type your descriptive caption (e.g., "Figure 1: Diagram of the surgical site") and click OK.
4. Align Image: Click the image, then select the Layout Options button that appears. Choose your preferred alignment (left, center, or right) to position the image within your report.
5. Format Text Wrapping (Optional): With the image selected, click Wrap Text on the ribbon and pick a style (e.g., "Square" or "Tight") to control how text flows around the image.

By following these guidelines, you'll enhance your reports with images that are both impactful and compliant with copyright law. Using reputable image sources and clear formatting ensures your work remains professional, legal, and easy for attorneys to understand.

Sample Medical Summary with Image Added

(I used Latin filler words in my report. Your report will be in English, I'm sure!)

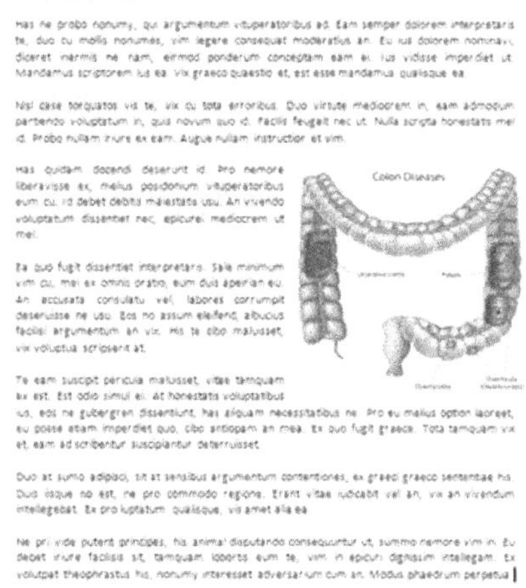

Johnson v. General Memorial Hospital

Medical Summary

Cu propriae dissentiet mea. Eam modus tacimates facilisis ei. Mei eu tritani interpretaris, et atqui dolor scripta mei. Et eum aperiam petentium incorrupte. Ad mei causae phaedrum, ut sed sonet percipit philosophia.

Has ne probo nonumy, qui argumentum vituperatoribus ad. Eam semper dolorem interpretaris te, duo cu mollis nonumes, vim legere consequat moderatius an. Eu ius dolorem nominavi, diceret inermis ne nam, eirmod ponderum conceptam eam ei. Ius vidisse imperdiet ut. Mandamus scriptorem ius ea. Vix graeco quaestio et, est esse mandamus qualisque ea.

Nisl case torquatos vis te, vix cu tota erroribus. Duo virtute mediocrem in, eam admodum pertinax voluptatum in, quis novum quo id. Facilis feugait nec ut. Nulla scripta honestatis mei id. Probo nullam iriure ex eam. Augue nullam instructior et vim.

Has quidam docendi deserunt id. Pro nemore liberavisse ex, melius posidonium vituperatoribus eum cu. Id debet debitis maiestatis usu. An vivendo voluptatum dissentiet nec, epicurei mediocrem ut mei.

Ea quo fugit dissentiet interpretaris. Sale minimum vim cu, mei ex omnis oratio, eum duis aperiam eu. An accusata consulatu vel, labores corrumpit deseruisse ne usu. Eos no assum eleifend, albucius facilisi argumentum an vix. His te cibo maluisset, vix voluptua scripserit at.

Te eam suscipit periculis maluisset, vitae tamquam ex est. Est odio simul ei. At honestatis voluptatibus ius, eos ne gubergren dissentiunt, has aliquam necessitatibus ne. Pro eu melius option laoreet, eu posse etiam imperdiet quo, cibo antiopam an mea. Ex quo fugit graece. Tota tamquam vix et, eam ad scribentur suscipiantur deterruisset.

Duo at sumo adipisci, sit at sensibus argumentum contentiones, ex graeci graeco sententiae his. Duo iisque no est, ne pro commodo regione. Errem vitae iudicabit vel an, vix an vivendum intellegebat. Ex pro luptatum qualisque, vis amet alia ea.

Ne pri vide putent principes, his animal disputando consequuntur ut, summo nemore vim in. Eu debet iriure facilisis sit, tamquam lobortis eum te, vim in epicuri dignissim intellegam. Ex volutpat theophrastus his, nonumy interesset adversarium cum an. Modus phaedrum perpetua

Figure 8 - Colon Diseases

Photo Chronology Accuracy in Legal Cases: Recommendations for LNCs

Introduction: The Importance of Photo Chronologies in Legal Cases

Photo chronologies are a vital tool for plaintiffs to document damages in lawsuits, especially in cases involving medical malpractice, personal injury, or nursing home claims. By contrasting images from before and after an alleged incident, these chronologies can provide powerful visual evidence. However, their effectiveness depends entirely on the accuracy of the photo dates and metadata.

Common Pitfalls: Incorrect Dating and Memory Errors

One of the most frequent mistakes in preparing photo chronologies is providing inaccurate dates for digital photos. These errors can occur if the camera's date stamp was set incorrectly, if photos are saved under misleading file dates, or if clients mistakenly recall when the pictures were taken. Such discrepancies can undermine the credibility of the evidence.

Case Study: Mastopexy Complications and the Role of EXIF Data

Consider the case of a plaintiff who suffered complications following a mastopexy (breast lift). She saw five different plastic surgeons—some took photos during consultations or additional procedures, while she herself documented her healing over several years. The plaintiff believed her most severe post-surgery photos corresponded with her visits to the original surgeon. However, this was incorrect. By extracting the EXIF (Exchangeable Image File Format) metadata from her digital photos, legal nurse consultants discovered that the troubling images actually coincided with appointments to the third and fourth surgeons. This revelation contradicted her testimony and called the entire photo chronology into question.

Next Steps: How to Verify EXIF Metadata

Verifying the dates and details of digital photos is straightforward and should be a standard step for all legal nurse consultants—both plaintiff and defense. To locate EXIF data:

- On a PC, right-click the photo file and select "Properties," then review the "Details" tab for the original date taken.

- On a Mac, select the photo in a Finder window, right click and select Get Info>More Info.
- For more comprehensive metadata, download an EXIF reader such as EXIF Pilot[25].

EXIF metadata provides not only the date and time the photo was taken but also information about the camera or device used.

Another Critical Consideration: Verifying Camera Type and File Format

Beyond date verification, it's essential to identify the device used to capture each image. EXIF data reveals whether a photo was taken with a smartphone or a standalone camera. If a phone was used, confirm whether the client still owns the device. If not, compare other photos from the same period to check for consistency in camera information—this can help validate the chronology. All original digital photos should be preserved on a flash drive as read-only files to ensure their integrity.

Best Practices: Handling and Storing Photo Evidence

When working with photo evidence, legal nurse consultants and defense teams should request original or true duplicate photos—ideally in JPEG or PNG formats—provided on a disk or USB flash drive. Avoid accepting photos that have been saved onto the plaintiff firm's computer, as this can alter metadata. Importantly, never accept PDF versions, which strip out crucial EXIF data.

Summary: Key Steps for Verifying Photo Chronology Accuracy

- Always verify the date and time of digital photos through EXIF metadata.
- Cross-check device information in EXIF data to ensure consistency.
- Request original or duplicate-original photo files in their native format (e.g., JPEG, PNG) via secure media.
- Never rely solely on clients' memories or unsourced file names for photo dating.
- Store evidence as read-only files to maintain authenticity.
- Avoid PDF conversions, which erase critical metadata.

By following these best practices, legal professionals can avoid common pitfalls and ensure the reliability of photo-based evidence in litigation.

[25] EXIF Pilot. https://www.colorpilot.com/exif.html/ (accessed January 2026).

Tell Them a Story

A Clinical Analogy for Legal Nurse Consultants

The ability to tell a story can significantly enhance your skills as a legal nurse consultant. As nurses, we're accustomed to documenting and verbally communicating with patients, families, and colleagues. But communicating with attorneys requires a different approach—one that prioritizes clarity, relevance, and strategic storytelling.

Think Like an ICU Nurse on Rounds

Imagine you're an ICU nurse giving a walking rounds report to the oncoming shift. You stop at bed nine and say, "This patient was just transferred from the step-down unit." What comes next?

If the patient were transferred because he coded due to a respiratory arrest, that's the first thing you'd say. You'd follow with the facts of the code, the interventions performed, and the fact that the patient is now on a ventilator. You wouldn't start with his age or admission diagnosis—you'd lead with the most critical information.

This is how attorneys want to hear your case review: start with the most important facts—the outcome and your opinion—then fill in the details.

The LNC's Story Structure

According to Aristotle, stories have a Beginning, Middle, and End. In legal nurse consulting, that structure still applies—but the order of delivery shifts depending on your audience.

The End (Start Here)

This is your opinion about the case. Attorneys want to hear this first so they can quickly assess whether the case is worth pursuing and where to focus their attention.

Example: "I believe that experts will find deviations in the standard of care for the ER physician, the hospital, the hospitalist, the cardiologist, and possibly the neurologist involved in this case. The healthcare providers failed to identify and treat an aortic dilation which led to an aortic dissection and death of the patient."

The Beginning

This includes the patient's demographic data, medical history, and reasons for seeking care. It sets the stage for understanding what led to the alleged malpractice.

Example: Bennett Sokolov, a 59-year-old white male, presented to the ER at Jedidiah Manion Hospital on October 17, 2023, with nausea, vomiting, dizziness, and upper abdominal/chest pain...

The Middle

This is the heart of the case—the negligence and resulting damages. It includes clinical decisions, missed opportunities, and deviations from the standard of care.

Example: Mr. Sokolov was admitted to the telemetry floor... An echocardiogram showed a dilated aortic root... There was no action on the echo results, and the patient coded and died later that day.

Why This Matters

Just like in ICU rounds, the order in which you present information matters. Nurses are trained to prioritize based on acuity. Legal nurse consultants must do the same—only now, the "patient" is the case, and the "oncoming shift" is the attorney.

By leading with your opinion and structuring your review as a story, you make your analysis more accessible, memorable, and actionable. You bridge the gap between clinical insight and legal strategy—exactly what attorneys need.

Case Review Template and Samples for Legal Nurse Consultants

R – Result First (Your Opinion):

A – Assessment of Care (Timeline & Analysis):

P – Patient Background (Demographics & History):

Reflect & Apply

Think of a recent case you reviewed. If you had to give a handoff to an attorney, what would you say first? Use the RAP structure to organize your thoughts.

Sample Case 1: Medical Malpractice – Delayed Diagnosis

R – Result First (Opinion)

I believe experts will find that the delay in diagnosing appendicitis led to a ruptured appendix and peritonitis. The ER physician and triage nurse failed to act on escalating symptoms and abnormal labs.

A – Assessment of Care

The patient presented to the ER with abdominal pain, nausea, and fever. Initial triage noted right lower quadrant tenderness, but the nurse documented it as "mild." Labs showed elevated WBC and CRP. No imaging was ordered for six hours. The patient deteriorated and was transferred to surgery with a ruptured appendix and abscess formation.

P – Patient Background

Shirley Lee, 34-year-old female, arrived at the ER on June 2, 2024, with abdominal pain and fever. She had no significant medical history and was otherwise healthy.

Sample Case 2: Nursing Home Neglect – Fall with Fracture

R – Result First (Opinion)

I believe experts will find that the facility failed to implement fall precautions despite known risk factors. The patient sustained a hip fracture due to inadequate supervision and environmental hazards.

A – Assessment of Care

The resident had a history of falls and was assessed as high risk. Care plans recommended bed alarms and hourly rounding, but documentation shows inconsistent implementation. On March 14, 2025, the resident was found on the floor with a displaced hip fracture. No staff witnessed the fall, and the bed alarm was not activated.

P – Patient Background

George Ramirez, 82-year-old male with dementia and Parkinson's disease, was a long-term resident at Willow Creek Nursing Center. He had a documented fall risk and required assistance with ambulation.

Conclusion

Mastering the art of storytelling is a vital skill for legal nurse consultants who aim to communicate effectively with attorneys. By adopting a clear and structured approach—beginning with the outcome, followed by a thorough assessment, and concluding with the patient's background—you ensure your findings are both impactful and actionable. This narrative strategy not only bridges the gap between clinical expertise and legal analysis but also strengthens your professional credibility in the legal arena. By telling the story of each case with precision and purpose, you contribute meaningfully to the pursuit of justice and improved patient care.

Formatting Documents

Oh, oh! That resume or report that you formatted so carefully might look terrible when your client opens it up from an email attachment. Legal Nurse Consultants need to be aware that electronic documents can look very different if the client doesn't use the same software as the one in which the document was created. And the client may never tell you that your report looks bad or downright bizarre. For example, here's a calendar format that I sometimes use to illustrate compliance with treatments and therapies. It was created in Microsoft Word and is supposed to look like this:

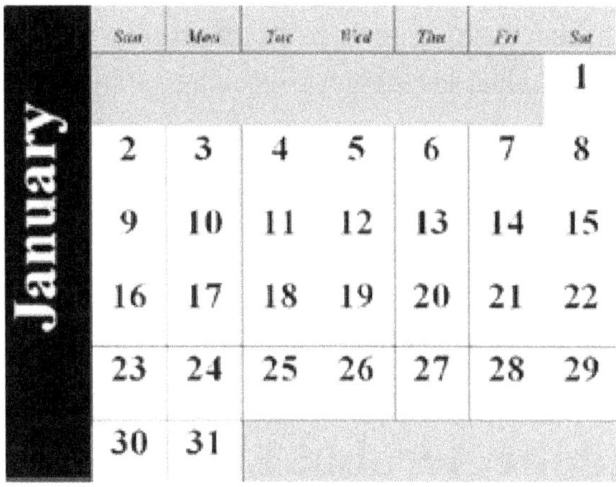

Figure 9 - Calendar in Word

But if the client uses WordPerfect instead of Word, the calendar looks like this instead:

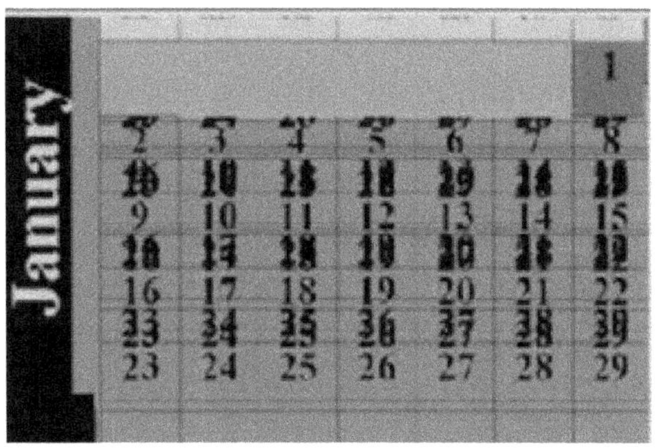

Figure 30 - Calendar Opened in WordPerfect

Sure, you could buy and use WordPerfect, but it's not just Word and WordPerfect that have problems "reading" each other's files. It happens with lots of different software. In addition to formatting changes, sharing documents in different software can sometimes affect embedded images, hyperlinks, or even document security settings. Converting to PDF helps address many of these issues as well. So, what can you do to prevent your resume or reports from looking like a mess? The answer is incredibly easy—convert the file to a portable document file (PDF) before you send it.

If you have Adobe Reader (and who doesn't?), you have probably read many files in PDF format. Converting a file to PDF preserves the document's formatting so that it can be viewed on any computer as long as the recipient has a PDF viewer, such as Adobe Reader.

You can print your document as a PDF right from Word. In Word, select File. Then choose "Print" from the menu. In the Printer dropdown, select "Microsoft Print to PDF" or "Save as PDF." Click "Print," and you'll be prompted to choose where you want to save your PDF file. In either case, select it to create a PDF of your document. This straightforward method makes saving your work as a PDF quick and easy—even if you're new to Word.

Creating PDF documents ensures your formatting stays intact and looks professional, no matter what software your client uses. Next time you finish a report or resume, take a moment to convert it to PDF before sending it out—your clients will appreciate the professional appearance!

Essential Adobe Acrobat Features for Legal Nurse Consultants

Step-by-Step Guide to Streamlining Electronic Medical Record Review

As a Legal Nurse Consultant, efficiently managing and reviewing electronic medical records is crucial. Adobe Acrobat offers several features—especially in its paid versions—that can significantly simplify your workflow. This guide breaks down seven key Acrobat features, providing clear, practical steps and tips for everyday use. Note: BentoPDF also has similar features, but they are configured in a different way that is very user-friendly.

General Best Practice: Always Save a New Copy First

- Before making any changes to a PDF, always save a new copy of the file.
- This protects the original document, allowing you to work freely and make edits without risk.
- Tip: Name your new file "PatientName_MedicalRecords_Edited.pdf" or something similarly descriptive.

Feature 1: Navigating the PDF

Available in: Both Adobe Acrobat Reader (free) and paid versions

- Use these methods to move through large medical records quickly:
- Scroll: Usc your mouse or trackpad to scroll through pages.
- Page Arrows: Click the up/down arrows in the Acrobat toolbar.
- Keyboard Shortcuts: Page Up (PgUp): Go to the previous page. Page Down (PgDn): Go to the next page.

Go to Specific Page: Enter the page number in the toolbar and press Enter. Example: Jump directly to page 45 for a specific lab result.

First/Last Page: If icons aren't visible, right-click the Page Arrows and add them. Keyboard shortcuts: Home (first page), End (last page).

Tip: If you're reviewing a 500-page medical record, learning these shortcuts saves considerable time!

Feature 2: Creating and Using Bookmarks

Available in: Paid versions of Adobe Acrobat

1. Open the side panel and check for existing bookmarks. If none, you can add your own.
2. Navigate to the page you want to bookmark.
3. Click the Bookmark icon (it looks like a ribbon or flag).
4. Select the New Bookmark option. It will appear as "Untitled."
5. Type a meaningful name, such as "Admission 03/18/2024," "H&P," or "Nursing Notes."
6. Repeat for each section you want to bookmark.
7. Practical Use: Bookmarking makes it easy to "jump" directly to key sections during case review or testimony.
8. Common Pitfall: Not all PDFs have bookmarks by default—creating your own ensures quick access.

Feature 3: Rotating Pages

For Paid Versions: Open your PDF in Acrobat. Go to Organize Pages (or Document > Rotate Pages in some versions). Select specific pages, even/odd pages, or all pages. Choose to rotate left or right as needed. Real-World Example: If a scanned EKG strip is sideways, use the rotate tool to make it readable before analysis. Tip: Double-check after rotating—sometimes only certain pages need adjustment.

Feature 4: Saving as Word and Using OCR

- Saving as a Word Document: Available in: Paid versions of Acrobat. Open your PDF. Go to File > Export To > Microsoft Word. Edit the document in Word as needed. In BentoPDF, scroll down to PDF to Word and select your file. Edit the document in Word as needed.
- Copying Text with OCR (Optical Character Recognition):
    - BentoPDF. For OCR, scroll down to OCR PDF and select your file.
    - Paid Adobe Versions: Open PDF > Tools > Scan & OCR > Recognize Text. Select the language/region (for best accuracy). After recognition, you can copy and paste text into Word.

Common Pitfall: OCR isn't perfect—watch for errors like "E" becoming "3." Tip: Always proofread OCR'd content, especially for medication names or critical dates.

Feature 5: Zooming In and Out

Available in: Both Reader and paid versions

- Keyboard Shortcuts: Ctrl + = to zoom in, Ctrl + – to zoom out

Other Methods: 1) Select a percentage from the zoom dropdown menu. 2) Click the magnifying glass, then drag a box around the area you want to enlarge.

Practical Scenario: Use zoom to review tiny print in physician orders or handwritten notes. Tip: Don't forget to zoom back out before printing or sharing!

Feature 6: Organizing Pages

Available in: Paid versions

1. Open the side panel and select "Pages" to view thumbnails.
2. Locate the page you want to move.
3. Click and drag the page to its new location.
4. When to Use: Organize unnumbered documents
5. Common Pitfall: Avoid moving numbered pages in large documents; it can cause confusion if page references no longer match.
6. Adding supplemental documents. I usually add supplemental documents at the end of numbered documents. For example, if I have 432 pages of Hospital A in numbered order for the May 19, 2025 admission, and Hospital A then sends an additional 12 pages for the same admission, I place the pages at the end of the May 19, 2025 admission to preserve the original numbered pages that had previously been sent to experts. This ensures that any references made by experts to specific page numbers remain accurate and consistent, preventing confusion

or miscommunication. The supplemental pages are labeled as "Supplemental 1-12" and placed after the original 432 pages, so it is clear which pages were part of the initial set, and which were added later.

7. In BentoPDF, select Duplicate and Organize. Select your file. Locate the page you want to move. Click and drag the page to its new location.
8. Tip: In lengthy files, make a list of page changes before you start to avoid getting lost.

Feature 7: Bates Stamping

Available in: Paid versions

1. Go to Tools > Edit PDF > More > Bates Numbering > Add.
2. Choose Output Options to set starting numbers.
3. Example: Start at 477 if your previous set ended at 476.
4. Customize the footer, including the case name if needed.
5. Click OK to apply Bates numbers.
6. Practical Advice: Electronic Bates stamping removes the need for leading zeros (e.g., 000001).
7. In Bento PDF, scroll down to Page Numbers. Select your file. Determine the position, format, and font size for the numbers, then click on Add Page Numbers. Note that all files will start with number one.
8. Tip: Always double-check your numbering sequence before distributing files. For more information on Bates stamping, see Chapter 13 article on Bates Stamping and Indexing.

Conclusion: Putting It All Together

Mastering these Adobe Acrobat features will make your work with electronic medical records faster, more accurate, and less stressful. Start by saving a new copy, then apply these tools as you review, organize, and prepare documents for your cases. The more you practice, the more second-nature these steps will become. Happy reviewing!

Wound Sizing in Written Reports: Practical Recommendations for LNCs

Introduction: Translation of Medical Measurements

When working as a legal nurse consultant, it's important to translate medical measurements into terms that attorneys and juries can easily understand. This guidance is specifically designed to help you prepare materials for legal professionals and lay audiences who may be unfamiliar with the metric system. By adapting your communication, you ensure that wound descriptions are clear, accurate, and relatable, reducing the risk of misinterpretation in legal settings.

As nurses, we are accustomed to measuring wounds precisely and recording their size in centimeters. However, in the United States, many jury members and attorneys may not be familiar with metric measurements. For instance, if you report a wound as 10 cm long, some may mistakenly imagine it as 10 inches instead of its actual length of about 4 inches.

To assist attorneys and help jurors visualize wound sizes more accurately in your reports, always describe wounds in both centimeters and inches. Additionally, consistently use analogies to familiar objects in your reports and testimony. This approach not only reinforces understanding but also makes medical information more memorable for non-medical audiences. Attorneys may even use these objects in court to provide a tangible reference for the jury.

The chart below matches common wound sizes in centimeters and inches with everyday objects, making abstract measurements more concrete. Consider expanding your descriptions with comparisons to additional familiar items, such as the diameter of a bottle cap or the width of a standard paperclip, to cover a wider range of scenarios. Due to rounding, some sizes appear more than once.

CM	Inches	Object
0.1 cm	0.04 inches	Grain of sugar
0.2 cm	0.08 inches	Pencil point
0.5 cm	0.2 inches	Pea
0.6 cm	0.2 inches	Pencil eraser
0.9 cm	0.4 inches	Ladybug

CM	Inches	Object
1.1 cm	0.4 inches	Diameter of AAA battery
1.4 cm	0.6 inches	Diameter of AA battery
1.6 cm	0.6 inches	Diameter of jeans button
1.7 cm	0.7 inches	Diameter of A battery
1.8 cm	0.7 inches	Dime
1.9 cm	0.8 inches	Penny
2.1 cm	0.8 inches	Nickel
2.4 cm	1 inch	Quarter
2.6 cm	1 inch	Diameter of C battery
2.7 cm	1.1 inches	Diameter of light bulb base
3.4 cm	1.3 inches	Diameter of D battery
4.3 cm	1.7 inches	Diameter of golf ball
6.4 cm	2.5 inches	Diameter of tennis ball
7.6 cm	3 inches	Diameter of soup can
9.2 cm	3.6 inches	Length of regular crayon
10 cm	4 inches	Diameter of drink coaster
15 cm	6 inches	Diameter of saucer
23 cm	9 inches	Circumference of baseball
29 cm	11.4 inches	Circumference of softball

If a wound measurement falls between the listed sizes, use an online metric conversion tool to find the equivalent size. You can still utilize the chart to provide analogies, for example: "The wound was 2.3 cm (0.9 inches) in diameter, slightly smaller than a quarter," or "The wound measured 6.1 cm (2.4 inches) in diameter, nearly the size of a tennis ball."

By consistently using these relatable comparisons in your documentation and testimony, you help ensure that wound descriptions are clear, easily understood, and memorable for everyone involved in the legal process.

Chapter 8: Independent LNCs

Independent legal nurse consulting has been both the starting point and the anchor of my career. I began on my own, spent years working within law firms, and—after retiring—occasionally returned to independent practice. In those early days, I was juggling multiple roles: pitching in at my husband's business, working ICU shifts, and trying to build my consulting work from the ground up. One of my first clients was an attorney who asked, "Can you sign an affidavit?" Without hesitation—and without enough information—I said yes. We discussed fees, and he handed me a stack of medical records to review.

As I dug into those records, I realized the case simply didn't hold up. The documentation was flawless and contradicted the client's claims. When I told the attorney the case wasn't viable, he was furious. He expected me to sign the affidavit regardless of the facts. That miscommunication damaged our working relationship, and he refused to pay the full agreed fee. I ended up settling for half, frustrated and disappointed, realizing that my eagerness to help had led to costly misunderstandings. Looking back, I wish I had established clear boundaries and confirmed case details before agreeing to any commitments. That lesson became the foundation for one of my most important practices: creating Letters of Understanding whenever I accepted assignments from attorneys (see Chapter 2 for a sample Letter of Understanding).

This chapter is designed to guide you through the essential principles I wish I had known from the start, so you can avoid common pitfalls and set yourself up for success as an independent LNC. Along the way, I'll share personal anecdotes that reinforce each lesson with real-world examples. You'll learn how to define the role of an independent consultant with professional objectivity, even when faced with client pressure. We'll explore strategies for setting fee schedules that reflect your expertise, managing client expectations with clarity, and turning early mistakes into stronger systems and communication practices. You'll also discover how to recognize red flags before committing to a case, protect your reputation and financial well-being, and consider subcontractor opportunities as a practical entry point into independent consulting.

By the end of this chapter, you'll not only understand what steps to take but also why they matter. My hope is that you'll feel confident and prepared to navigate the unique challenges of independent LNC work—armed with lessons I learned the hard way, and ready to build a career that is both sustainable and rewarding.

Independent LNCs: Responsibilities, Realities, and Tips for Success

Independent Legal Nurse Consultants (LNCs) operate "behind the scenes," supporting attorneys with their medical expertise without testifying at depositions or trials. As self-employed professionals, independent LNCs set their own fees and may collaborate with a handful of law firms or maintain a broader client base. Their work is highly varied, relying on both clinical knowledge and business acumen. Here's a closer look at the core responsibilities, illustrated with practical examples:

- Analyzing Medical Records: Independent LNCs are often tasked with receiving boxes or electronic files containing hundreds or thousands of pages of medical records. They systematically analyze these documents by date, provider, and event type, creating detailed chronologies, summaries, and timelines that highlight key treatments, hospitalizations, or changes in the patient's condition. For example, an LNC might summarize findings in a concise chronology for the attorney.
- Reviewing Cases for Merit: Attorneys rely on LNCs to help them determine whether a case is worth pursuing. This involves reading through the medical records to identify deviations from standard care, missed diagnoses, or causation issues. An LNC might, for instance, notice a delay in stroke treatment documented in the nursing notes, flagging this as a potential area of negligence that could form the basis of a lawsuit.
- Creating Reports: After analyzing the records, LNCs may prepare written reports that summarize their findings and opinions in straightforward language. These reports may include visual aids, like timelines or diagrams, to help the attorney and client understand complex medical issues.
- Locating Experts: LNCs may help attorneys find credible medical experts for testimony. This can mean searching professional association directories, contacting colleagues, or vetting potential expert witnesses for appropriate credentials and communication skills.
- Performing Medical Research: LNCs regularly research clinical guidelines, recent studies, or treatment standards relevant to the case. For example, if a case involves a rare post-surgical infection, the LNC might reference current CDC guidelines and medical literature to clarify whether the care provided met accepted standards.
- Attending Comprehensive Medical Examinations (CMEs) to report findings to hiring attorneys.

Real-World Scenario: Overcoming Marketing Challenges

When transitioning to independent practice, many nurses face the challenge of finding clients. Take the example of Lisa, a former ICU nurse who became an LNC. Initially, she struggled to secure cases despite her expertise. After attending local bar association meetings and offering free educational seminars to attorneys about interpreting medical records, Lisa began to receive referrals. Her persistence in networking and marketing paid off, and within a few years, she was regularly contracted by several law firms. This illustrates how consistent outreach and building relationships can help overcome the hurdle of marketing your services.

Advantages of Independent Legal Nurse Consulting

- Autonomy: You're your own boss, making all decisions about your business. This means you can tailor your practice to your interests and enjoy the satisfaction of seeing the direct results of your efforts.
- Flexible Schedule: You can choose how many cases to accept and set your own hours, allowing for better work-life balance or the ability to supplement your clinical income.
- No Dress Code: Much of the work can be done from home, so you have the freedom to dress as you like while working.
- Tax Benefits: Operating a home-based business offers potential tax deductions for eligible expenses, such as office space, internet, and even part of your vehicle if used for business. Always consult an accountant for guidance on deductions and compliance.

Disadvantages and Tips for Overcoming Common Obstacles

- Responsibility: The flip side of autonomy is that you bear all the risks. Every decision—from setting fees to managing client expectations—falls on you. Tip: Seek mentorship from experienced LNCs or join professional organizations to learn best practices.
- Irregular Income: Without a guaranteed paycheck, building a steady client base takes time. Many LNCs continue clinical work while ramping up their consulting practice. Tip: Budget conservatively and track your business growth to decide when it's safe to transition fully.
- Self-Motivation and Marketing: Success depends on your ability to market your services. Tip: Leverage your nursing network, attend legal seminars, and consider creating a professional website to showcase your expertise and services.

- Business Skills: Running a consulting practice means managing contracts, billing, and client communications. Tip: Take advantage of small business resources or online courses to strengthen your business management skills.

In summary, independent legal nurse consulting offers rewarding opportunities for nurses willing to learn new skills and embrace entrepreneurship. By understanding the realities of the role and preparing for common challenges, you can build a fulfilling and successful independent practice.

Setting Your Fee Schedule as an Independent Legal Nurse Consultant

Practical Strategies, Examples, and Steps for Success

Establishing an effective fee schedule is a foundational step for Legal Nurse Consultants (LNCs) entering the field. The right approach not only positions your services competitively but also ensures profitability and sustainability. Below, you'll find three tips for common fee-setting methods, each explained with practical scenarios, actionable steps, and a balanced look at their advantages and drawbacks. Use these insights to choose the strategy that best fits your professional goals.

Tip 1: Market Price Method

Description: The Market Price Method involves setting your fees based on what other LNCs in your region charge for similar services. This approach leverages prevailing industry rates to quickly establish your pricing structure.

Hypothetical Scenario:

Consultant A researches rates in her city and finds that most legal nurse consultants charge between $100–$130 per hour. She sets her initial rate at $120 per hour, hoping to attract clients by being competitive. However, some law firms expect lower rates due to their budgets, while others question the value at higher prices.

Actionable Steps:

- Research current hourly rates for LNCs in your geographic area and specialty.
- Contact professional associations or networking groups to determine if they will share typical fee ranges.
- List your anticipated business expenses (office supplies, marketing, etc.).
- Estimate your expected billable hours per month.

- Set your rate based on local market trends, adjusting as needed after initial client feedback.

Pros: Simple to implement; aligns with client expectations; offers a quick starting point.

Cons: May not cover your unique costs; could be too high or low for your market; relies heavily on external benchmarks.

Key Takeaway: The Market Price Method is best for quickly entering the market, but ongoing adjustments are crucial to ensure profitability and competitiveness.

Tip 2: The 3 Times Rule

Description: This method multiplies your current hourly wage by three to cover salary, benefits, and business expenses. It provides a straightforward formula for transitioning from employment to consulting.

Hypothetical Scenario:

Consultant B previously earned $40 per hour as a hospital nurse. Applying the 3 Times Rule, he sets his consulting rate at $120 per hour. He notices that some clients find his rate reasonable, but others balk, especially those accustomed to lower fees. He also realizes that his actual income is less than expected due to non-billable business activities such as networking and marketing.

Actionable Steps:

- Calculate your previous annual salary and divide by total hours worked to find your hourly wage.
- Multiply this wage by three to account for benefits and business expenses.
- List all anticipated operating costs and compare them against your projected income.
- Estimate how many hours per week/month you can realistically bill.
- Adjust your rate if it seems too high for your local market or if it doesn't meet your profit goals.

Pros: Easy calculation; ensures you account for more than just your salary; useful starting point for new consultants.

Cons: May not match what clients are willing to pay; doesn't factor in market trends or competition; can lead to unrealistic income expectations.

Key Takeaway: The 3 Times Rule offers a quick way to price your services but always validate your rates against market realities and actual billable hours.

Tip 3: Cost and Profit Model

Description: The Cost and Profit Model requires a detailed analysis of all your business and personal expenses, billable hours, and desired profit. This method is the most customizable and comprehensive, helping ensure your rates are both sustainable and competitive.

Hypothetical Scenario: Consultant C thoroughly tracks all her expenses—including software, travel, insurance, and living costs—and determines she needs to earn $80,000 per year to meet her financial goals. She divides $80,000 by her estimated 700 billable hours, arriving at an hourly rate of approximately $115. To optimize her fee schedule, she regularly reviews her expenses and profit expectations. For instance, she might reduce travel costs by attending fewer conferences or negotiate better rates for software subscriptions to lower her overall expenses. This approach keeps her rates both competitive and profitable. Note: A normal full-time job consists of 2,080 hours (calculated as 40 hours per week times 52 weeks per year). By identifying 700 billable hours, Consultant C is indicating she will spend about 34% of her time on billable tasks, with the remaining hours devoted to unbillable work or potentially another job.

Actionable Steps:

- List all personal and business expenses (travel, equipment, software, insurance, etc.).
- Determine your target annual income or desired profit.
- Estimate the total billable hours you can realistically work in a year.
- Divide your total expenses and desired profit by your estimated billable hours to calculate an hourly rate.
- Use online consulting rate calculators[26], such as those at ConsultingSuccess.com, to simplify the process and test different scenarios.
- Review and adjust your rate periodically as expenses or market conditions change.

Pros: Highly tailored to your financial needs; ensures all costs are covered; allows for flexible adjustments.

Cons: Requires more time, planning, and accurate record-keeping; may initially seem complex.

[26] Rate calculator. https://www.consultingsuccess.com/consulting-fees-calculator (accessed December 2025).

Key Takeaway: The Cost and Profit Model delivers the most personalized and sustainable fee schedule but requires diligence and ongoing review to stay aligned with your goals.

Conclusion

Setting your fee schedule as a Legal Nurse Consultant is a critical business decision. By understanding each method, considering practical scenarios, and following clear steps, you can choose the approach that best fits your needs. Regular review and adaptation will help ensure your fees remain competitive, profitable, and fair—laying the foundation for a successful consulting practice.

4 Mistakes New Independent LNCs Make—and How to Avoid Them

Practical, Step-by-Step Solutions for Launching Your Legal Nurse Consulting Business

We've all seen those tempting ads online: "Be your own boss!" "Work in your pajamas!" "Make $150- $175 an hour!" Sure, registered nurses can become successful independent legal nurse consultants. But the path isn't always as simple as it looks, and not everyone makes the transition smoothly. Let's make sure that's not you! Here are four common mistakes new LNCs make, along with practical, step-by-step actions and resources to help you avoid them. This guide is packed with real scenarios and actionable solutions—so you can confidently build your LNC career.

Mistake #1: Unrealistic Expectations and No Business Plan

Many LNCs dive into their businesses with dreams of big money or escaping bedside nursing—but no concrete plan for how to get there. Setting goals is great but achieving them takes strategy. That's where a business plan comes in: it's your roadmap from where you are now to where you want your business to be.

Don't worry if you're not a business plan expert. There's a free business plan worksheet in Chapter 2 in this book to guide you in asking the right questions about your new venture. To get started right now, here's a concise checklist of essential elements your business plan should cover:

- Target Market: Who are your ideal clients? (e.g., plaintiff or defense attorneys, insurance companies)
- Services Offered: What specific LNC services will you provide?

- Pricing Strategy: How will you set your rates? (Hourly, per-case, retainer?)
- Marketing Plan: How will you reach potential clients? (Networking, social media, presentations?)
- Financial Projections: What are your expected expenses and income for the first year?
- Operations Plan: How will you manage your workflow, communications, and records?

Sit down and fill out each item for your business idea. This checklist gives you clarity and focus, turning dreams into actionable steps!

Mistake #2: Making Assumptions About Not Getting Hired

New LNCs sometimes assume they aren't being hired because of personal factors ("I'm too old," "I'm too inexperienced," etc.), but these assumptions rarely reflect reality. Potential clients might not need your services at this moment, or maybe you haven't shown them the value of hiring an LNC.

Here's how you can get real answers and improve your chances:

- After a meeting or call, ask direct questions such as: "How do these services look to you?" or "Can you see yourself using a legal nurse consultant for your medical malpractice cases?"
- Listen carefully to their feedback—sometimes it's as simple as timing or budget, not personal at all.
- Keep a log of responses to spot patterns and refine your pitch.

Replace assumptions with actionable questions. You'll gain insights and possibly uncover opportunities you didn't know existed!

Mistake #3: Not Filtering Communication—A Real Scenario

Some new LNCs get so excited to prove their value that they forget to listen first. Imagine this: Ramona, a new independent LNC, meets with a law firm. As soon as the attorney describes a case, Ramona jumps in: "Oh, that case definitely has merit—you're likely to win!" The attorney thanks her and moves on. Ramona never hears back. Why? She gave away the key advice before being hired!

Here's how Ramona turned things around:

- On her next meeting with a different attorney, she asked thoughtful questions about the client's needs before offering any opinions.
- She practiced active listening—nodding, taking notes, and letting the client speak fully.

- Instead of giving away conclusions, she said, "I'd need to review the medical records in detail before providing any assessment."

Result: The attorney appreciated her professionalism and hired her for a comprehensive review. The lesson? Listen more than you talk, and don't solve the client's problem until you've officially partnered. Hold back on case merit discussions until you can review all the facts.

Mistake #4: Not Knowing When to Market—A Persistence Plan

Lots of LNCs put all their energy into an initial marketing blitz, then give up when responses don't pour in. The reality is, marketing is a marathon, not a sprint. Experienced sales pros know it can take a hundred "No's" to get one "Yes." Persistence is the key!

Here's your step-by-step plan for marketing with staying power:

1. Set aside dedicated time each week for marketing—no matter how busy you get.
2. Track your outreach efforts (calls, emails, networking events) in a simple spreadsheet.
3. Follow up with potential clients after initial contact; sometimes it takes several touches to get noticed.
4. Don't get discouraged—expect slow periods but keep going. Consistency builds credibility.
5. If you get more business than you can manage, explore hiring subcontractors to help with overflow.

Keep marketing whether you're just starting out or have a full caseload. The ones who succeed are the ones who don't stop!

By steering clear of these common mistakes—and taking practical steps to overcome them—you're setting yourself up for a rewarding, independent legal nurse consulting career. Remember, every successful LNC started where you are now. Stay focused, keep learning, and don't hesitate to seek out resources along the way. You can do this!

Turning Mistakes into Success: Practical Advice for New LNCs

Learn How to Grow Your LNC Career by Embracing and Resolving Errors

Mistakes are inevitable, especially in a field as complex and nuanced as legal nurse consulting. While nurses often fear errors due to their potential consequences in clinical settings, the LNC world offers more room for growth through trial and error. The key to building a successful legal nurse consulting career is not in avoiding mistakes, but in learning from them and responding proactively. This article will guide you through common pitfalls with both potential and actual clients and provide clear strategies for turning missteps into valuable experience.

Mistakes with Potential Clients: Recognizing and Correcting Early Missteps

As you begin your LNC journey, you'll encounter mistakes that primarily affect potential clients—those you hope to work with but haven't yet secured. These errors often stem from personal preferences, beginner misjudgments, or following advice that doesn't yield results. Understanding these common pitfalls is the first step toward improvement.

- Anecdote: One legal nurse consultant chose a logo that was intended to symbolize a phoenix, but it resembled a vulture to others. Although she liked her original design, she listened to feedback, invested in a new logo, and later landed her first client. This example highlights the importance of being open to constructive criticism and making business decisions based on market response.
- Following Ineffective Advice: Many new LNCs diligently implement recommendations from schools or peers but see little progress. For instance, if attorneys consistently reject your fees as too high, consider adjusting your pricing structure. If direct mail campaigns don't get results, experiment with web marketing or social media outreach.

Actionable Steps for Mistakes with Potential Clients:

1. Seek and listen to feedback from peers and potential clients.
2. Be willing to revise branding, marketing strategies, or pricing when needed.
3. If current approaches fail, consult with a marketing or business coach for expert guidance.

Shifting Focus from Prospects to Active Engagements

Once you begin collaborating with actual clients, mistakes can have greater impact on your reputation and business relationships. Transitioning from prospect management to client service requires a new level of professionalism and accountability.

Mistakes with Actual Clients: Navigating and Resolving Common Pitfalls

Treat mistakes that affect actual clients by making thoughtful business decisions. Don't cry, get angry, insist that you're right, or try to explain the reason for the mistake, even if your explanation seems reasonable. Remember, what feels like an explanation to you may sound like an excuse to your client. For example, consider how these explanations might be viewed from a client's perspective:

- "I had to charge you more than we agreed upon because it took me a lot longer than I thought it would." Your clients may think you're cheating them or that you failed to plan properly.
- "I wasn't sure how you wanted the work product formatted." Your client will wonder why you didn't ask for specifications in advance.
- "I haven't been feeling well for the last month." Your clients may feel sympathy, but they'll also question why you didn't communicate earlier, start work sooner, or agree to the project at all.
- "I can't turn in my summary because my printer ran out of ink and there wasn't any place open where I could buy an ink cartridge." Your client will likely view this as disorganization.
- "I had to work an extra shift at the hospital, so I didn't have time to review the case." Your clients may feel that their work is less important to you than your other commitments.
- "I missed the deadline because I was waiting for additional information." Your client might feel frustrated by the lack of proactive communication and wonder why you didn't notify them sooner.
- "I didn't respond to your email because I was overwhelmed with other tasks." Your client may perceive this as a lack of prioritization and question your reliability.

Instead, acknowledge the mistake, apologize sincerely, and offer a solution or corrective action to rebuild trust with your client. For example, you might say: "I realize I made an error in our agreement. Here's how I plan to resolve it for you." This demonstrates accountability and a commitment to client satisfaction.

By focusing on honest communication and taking responsibility, you reassure your client and maintain professionalism. If you miss a deadline or there's a lapse in communication, reach out promptly, admit the oversight, and outline your plan to make things right. These positive steps help preserve client relationships and reinforce your reliability as a legal nurse consultant.

Checklist: How to Respond When You Make a Mistake with a Client

1. Apologize sincerely—ideally in person or by phone, not just via email.
2. Take ownership of the error without making excuses or shifting blame.
3. Clearly communicate how you will fix the problem and follow through promptly.
4. Offer a tangible solution, such as a revision, refund, or expedited turnaround.
5. Learn from the experience by reviewing what went wrong and implementing safeguards for the future.

Conclusion: Growing Your Career Through Experience and Continuous Improvement

Legal nurse consulting is a new and challenging path for most registered nurses, and no one gets everything right the first time. By treating mistakes as essential learning opportunities, responding with professionalism, and continuously refining your approach, you'll set yourself up for long-term success. Remember, every error is a chance to build expertise and strengthen your business. Embrace the process, stay resilient, and let your experience guide the way to a rewarding LNC career.

Why Do Independent LNCs Struggle?

Four Common Pitfalls and How to Overcome Them

Starting out as an independent legal nurse consultant (LNC) is exciting—there's so much possibility, and most new LNCs are eager to be effective in this unique field. Yet despite the enthusiasm, many never achieve their goals. Some even leave the field without ever reviewing a single case. Let's break down the four main reasons why this happens and, even more importantly, how you can set yourself up for success.

1. Discomfort with Marketing

The biggest surprise for many new LNCs is how crucial marketing is to building a successful practice. It's common to believe that attorneys will come knocking as soon as you hang out your shingle, but the reality is quite different. When initial marketing efforts don't bring in clients, frustration sets in.

Many LNCs end up spending hours in support groups, LinkedIn groups, and listservs. These communities offer valuable learning and camaraderie, but they can also become a distraction from the core task—active marketing. For example, consider Mary Jo, an RN who became an LNC. She joined multiple online groups, participated daily, and learned a lot, but she didn't reach out to potential attorney clients. After six months, she still hadn't reviewed a single case.

Actionable Tip: For every hour you spend in a group, commit to at least an hour of direct marketing. That means reaching out to attorneys, networking at local bar associations, or following up with contacts. Try to market in some way every day. Remember, if you don't market, you won't make it—but if you do, your odds of success soar!

2. Discomfort with Business Aspects

Independent legal nurse consulting is more than just reviewing medical records—it's running a small business. Setting up an office, managing invoices and billing, tracking expenses, and understanding basic accounting can feel overwhelming, especially if you've never done it before.

Take Marco, for example. He was a skilled RN but had never created an invoice or tracked business expenses. He found himself disorganized and stressed, missing out on payments and opportunities.

Actionable Tips: Use the sample invoice form and letter of understanding in Chapter 2 to enhance your business skills. Don't be afraid to take short courses in bookkeeping or business management. If you prefer, hire a part-time bookkeeper or virtual assistant to manage administrative tasks, freeing you up to focus on your core strengths. The right support can make all the difference!

3. Lack of Understanding of the LNC Role

Many new LNCs think the job is all about reviewing medical records, but it's much more. You'll write clear, professional reports, communicate with attorneys and experts, and need strong organizational and research skills. Without these, thriving as an LNC is tough.

For instance, Latonya, an RN, was surprised by how much writing and communication her first case required. She realized she needed to brush up on her business writing and learn to present findings clearly.

Actionable Tip: If you're considering LNC work, try volunteering for a quality review committee at your hospital. This experience mirrors the process of analyzing records for attorneys and communicating findings—great practice for your future consulting role!

4. Having the Wrong Motives

Some RNs are drawn to legal nurse consulting for the wrong reasons—like the promise of high hourly rates ("Make $175 an hour!"), working less, or being their own boss. While these are attractive perks, they shouldn't be your only motivation. The reality is, the field requires hard work, resilience, and a genuine interest in bridging the worlds of nursing and law.

For example, Tomás entered the field hoping for quick money and more free time. When he realized that building a client base takes consistent effort, he became discouraged and eventually left.

Actionable Tip: Reflect on your reasons for becoming an LNC. If you're passionate about using your expertise to help attorneys understand medical issues and improve the legal process, you'll be more likely to stick with it—and succeed.

Subcontractor LNC Opportunities

A Possible Entry Point for New LNCs

Subcontracting can be an excellent entry point for new legal nurse consultants (LNCs). As a subcontractor, you take on temporary assignments from a legal nurse consulting firm, an independent LNC, or a temporary legal staffing agency. These projects are usually episodic and focused, such as reviewing medical records and creating a medical chronology for a specific case.

Employers often need subcontracting help on short notice, which means some may not require experience. Requirements can vary widely depending on the hiring firm and the project scope.

Effective Networking for Subcontractor Roles

Networking is key to landing subcontractor opportunities. Start by attending local AALNC meetings or joining online groups dedicated to legal nurse consultants. Platforms like LinkedIn,[27] Indeed,[28] and specialized forums (such as AALNC

[27] LinkedIn. https://www.linkedin.com/ (accessed December 2025.
[28] Indeed. https://www.indeed.com/ (accessed December 2025).

Community[29] or Nurse.com)[30] are excellent places to connect. Consider joining webinars or participating in online discussions to expand your reach.

For example, you might reach out to established LNCs on LinkedIn with a brief introduction and offer your availability for subcontracting work. Here's a sample message you could use:

Hi [Name of Contact], I'm a legal nurse consultant newly entering the field and interested in subcontracting opportunities. If you need assistance with medical record reviews or chronology preparation, I'd be glad to help. Please let me know if you have any upcoming projects or could use additional support. Thank you!

Additionally, join groups and participate in forums like AALNC Communities, Nurse.com's legal nurse consultant section, or attend webinars hosted by industry professionals. These venues allow you to briefly share your experience and let group members know you're available for subcontractor work.

Here's a secret about subcontracting: You may not need to rely solely on networking to secure jobs—simply sending your resume directly to legal staffing recruiters and expressing your interest in temporary positions can be effective. When reaching out to these recruiters, tailor your resume to highlight any relevant skills or experience, specify your availability for temporary assignments, and clearly state your interest in full-time temporary work. Sometimes, recruiters will hire LNCs with limited experience if you are available to work the number of hours they require (usually full-time for a few months).

Pay Rate Insights and Determinants

As of 2023, pay was often in the $45 to $50 per hour range, though rates can vary depending on your experience, the complexity of the project, and the type of employer. For instance, defense firms may offer lower rates due to their client contracts with insurance companies. Other factors influencing pay include the urgency of the assignment, your specialized skills, and the geographic region. Remember, while you may not earn as much as independent LNCs who secure their own clients, your time and expertise are valuable—avoid accepting assignments with extremely low compensation.

Contracts, Non-Compete Agreements, and Legal Guidance

Expect to sign a contract outlining the project scope and your rate of pay. Contracts might also include a non-compete agreement, which restricts you from marketing your

[29] AALNC Community. https://aalnc.org/community/ (accessed December 2025).
[30] Nurse.com. https://www.nurse.com/ (accessed December 2025).

services to certain clients for a specified period. It's important to review these agreements for reasonableness: avoid contracts that prohibit you from marketing to anyone or contracts without a clear time limit. If you are unsure about any part of a contract or non-compete agreement, consider consulting with an attorney familiar with employment law before signing.

If no formal contract is provided, request a letter of understanding detailing the work to be performed, payment terms, and deadlines. This is also a good time to ask if you can use the employer's name as a reference in your own marketing. Doing so signals your commitment to fulfilling the terms of the agreement and can help build your professional reputation.

Conclusion: You Can Succeed as an Independent LNC!

Every challenge you encounter is a chance to learn and grow. By embracing marketing, building business skills, truly understanding the LNC role, and having the right motivations, you can thrive in this rewarding field. Remember, you're not alone—tap into resources, seek out mentors, and keep moving forward. Your first case—and lasting success—could be just around the corner!

Chapter 9: Marketing and Networking for Expert and Independent LNCs

Starting out as a legal nurse consultant means entering a field where both your expertise and the connections you build are vital for success. While you may have learned marketing basics in your coursework, thriving as an independent or expert LNC requires more than traditional approaches. This chapter offers real-world guidance and supportive insights to help you move forward with confidence, showing you how to market your skills effectively and build relationships that sustain your practice.

We'll begin with the importance of relationship-building. Genuine connections not only expand your opportunities but also strengthen your reputation in the legal community. From there, we'll explore creative marketing techniques—identifying decision makers, tackling fears like rejection, and recognizing how the language you use shapes perceptions. You'll see how small adjustments in emails and newsletters can make a big difference in reaching legal clients.

Your online presence is another critical piece of the puzzle. A large section of this chapter is devoted to website optimization, including inbound marketing strategies, favicons, testimonials, and analytics. These tools will help you stand out in a crowded marketplace and ensure that attorneys can find and trust your services. We'll also introduce discovery marketing, an often-overlooked opportunity for independent LNCs, and show you practical steps to leverage it.

Finally, we'll turn to networking strategies. You'll learn how to refine your 30-second commercial for different audiences, market effectively around holiday times, and participate in online groups in ways that build credibility. Along the way, we'll discuss how to overcome the fear of rejection and how every interaction—whether successful or not—can contribute to your growth as a consultant.

By the end of this chapter, you'll have a toolkit of marketing and networking strategies that are both practical and encouraging. You'll be equipped not only to promote your services but also to build lasting relationships that support your career as a legal nurse consultant.

3 Lessons I Learned in Grade School—And How They Help LNCs Succeed

Turning Childhood Lessons into LNC Success—Let's Chat!

You know, sometimes our best business lessons come from the most unexpected places. For me, a lot of valuable insights came from my grade school days—yep, those days spent navigating recess, piano lessons, and a whole mix of classmates. Turns out, these simple childhood lessons can make a significant difference when you're starting out as a legal nurse consultant (LNC). Let me share three of them with you—and how you can use them to thrive as a new LNC.

Lesson 1: Relationship Building

Let's rewind to grade school. I made most of my friends during recess or after class—not while I was glued to my desk. Those genuine connections stuck with me for years. When you're a new LNC, building relationships can feel just as important—and it usually happens outside of formal work settings.

Here's the bottom line: To succeed as a new LNC, prioritize building relationships outside formal work settings by attending networking events and engaging on social media.

Wondering how to do that? Try joining local or online LNC groups, showing up at legal mixers, or diving into forums where attorneys spend time together. Reach out to attorneys on LinkedIn—just a friendly hello and a note about how you can support their cases. And if you meet someone at an event, don't forget to follow up. That's how the magic happens.

Just as building relationships is vital, developing your skills through consistent practice is equally important. They really do go hand in hand.

Lesson 2: Skill Development

Here's a story: When I was in grade school, I wanted to play the piano. I practiced like crazy for three years, got pretty good, and then one embarrassing recital ended it all for me (thanks to an itchy prank). But the big takeaway? Progress comes from practice—stop practicing, and your skills fade fast.

So, how does this help you? As a new LNC, commit to building your skills through regular, focused practice—especially when it comes to marketing and casework.

You can apply this lesson by reaching out to new clients regularly, refining your elevator pitch, and keeping your marketing materials fresh. Volunteer to do mock case reviews or summarize sample medical records for feedback. If your first case doesn't come quickly, don't let it get you down. Every effort counts, and every skill you sharpen gets you closer.

After you've built some relationships and started sharpening your skills, it's time to figure out what makes you stand out—and really lean into it.

Lesson 3: Self-Assessment

One thing I learned early in grade school is that everyone's different—some kids were athletes, some were bookworms, and some were just really great at making friends. As a new LNC, it's easy to focus on what you don't have, but it's much better to celebrate your unique strengths.

Your next move: Highlight your unique skills and experiences to set yourself apart in the LNC field—and use them in your marketing.

Not sure where to start? Here's a quick self-assessment checklist to help you pinpoint your standout qualities:

- Ask yourself: What clinical experiences set me apart?
- What feedback have I received from colleagues or patients?
- Which aspects of nursing do I excel at—patient education, case review, communication?
- Do I have specialized expertise (for example, skilled nursing facilities, wound care, emergency medicine)?
- What certifications, trainings, or language skills can I offer attorneys?

Once you've answered these, use them in your marketing. For instance, if you're a whiz at explaining medical conditions, let attorneys know you're great at breaking down complex info for juries. If you have tons of SNF experience, reach out to attorneys who manage resident rights cases and highlight your background.

Conclusion

It's funny how grade school can teach us lessons that stick with us for life—connecting with others, practicing new skills, and embracing what makes us unique. These aren't just nice memories; they're actionable strategies for your LNC journey. Build relationships, keep learning, and show off what makes you special. Every step forward is a win. You've got this!

Overcoming Fear of Rejection: A Structured Guide for LNCs

Fear of rejection can be more paralyzing than rejection itself, especially for new legal nurse consultants (LNCs) striving to establish their careers. When reaching out to attorneys and promoting LNC services, the possibility of being brushed off can discourage even the most determined professionals. However, you can overcome this fear by following a clear, structured process. Drawing on the insights of Geoffrey James[31], author of the world's most-visited sales blog, and Art Mortell[32], author of The Courage to Fail, here are four essential steps to stop letting rejection fear hold you back.

Step 1: Understand Why Rejection Hurts

Art Mortell identifies three specific situations that make rejection especially painful:

- Frequent rejection: While one or two rejections may seem manageable, facing 20 or 30 can feel overwhelming and hopeless.
- Personal rejection: Being rejected by a stranger is tough, but it stings even more when it comes from someone you know.
- Influential rejection: Rejection from someone you view as important—such as a well-connected attorney—carries more emotional weight than rejection from others.

Example: Sammie, a new LNC, sends out proposals to several attorneys. When she receives polite declines from two, she shrugs it off, but after the tenth "No," she begins doubting her own skills. Recognizing why these rejections hurt helps Sammie separate the emotional impact from her professional efforts.

Step 2: Determine Your Personal Rejection Fears

To address your fear, reflect on what makes rejection difficult for you:

- How many negative responses can you receive before taking it personally?
- How emotionally invested are you in each potential client?
- Does rejection from more influential attorneys affect you more deeply?

[31] Geoffrey James https://tinyurl.com/4stttvn2 (accessed January 2026).
[32] Art Mortell https://www.artmortell.com/ (accessed January 2026).

Example: Sammie realizes that after two rejections, she starts to feel discouraged. She notes that she feels especially hurt when a respected attorney turns her down, prompting her to consider how much weight she gives to others' opinions.

Step 3: Change Your Beliefs About Rejection

Geoffrey James suggests that the key to overcoming rejection fear is to change your perspective. Instead of viewing rejection as a personal failure, see each interaction as a new opportunity. Challenge your assumptions and reframe your thinking:

- Instead of dwelling on a negative response, remind yourself: "Every contact is a new opportunity. I can't change the past, only the future."
- If personal rejection is holding you back, tell yourself: "A business relationship that isn't worth risking isn't worth having."
- If influential rejection worries you, reframe it: "Coping with tough attorneys means I'm operating at a high level."

Example: After a disappointing call with a prominent attorney, Sammie repeats to herself, "This was just one call out of many. Next time could be different." She starts to see each "No" as a step closer to a "Yes."

Step 4: Reframe Negative Experiences

Transform rejection into a learning opportunity. Use every experience—positive or negative—to improve your approach and resilience.

Short Story: Sammie nervously calls another attorney after several rejections. This time, she receives constructive feedback instead of a simple "No." Instead of feeling defeated, Sammie thanks the attorney, makes note of the suggestions, and adapts her pitch for the next call. Over time, she discovers that her confidence and success rate improve as she reframes rejection as a natural part of growth.

Additional Expert Insight

As sales expert Brian Tracy notes, "The fear of rejection is the single greatest obstacle to success in sales and business. The more you experience rejection, the less it affects you." By viewing each rejection as practice, you build resilience and move closer to your goals.

Conclusion: Empowerment and Next Steps

Fear of rejection doesn't have to control your career as a legal nurse consultant. By understanding why rejection hurts, identifying your personal triggers, shifting your beliefs, and reframing negative experiences, you can turn setbacks into stepping stones. Act today—reach out, learn from each interaction, and remember that persistence is the key to success.

Identifying Decision Makers / Influencers in Law Firms: A Guide for LNCs

Understanding Roles, Authority, and Effective Marketing Strategies

To maximize your marketing success as a legal nurse consultant, it's essential to identify both decision-makers and influential staff within law firms. Decision-makers ultimately approve hiring and subcontracting, but non-decision-makers often shape outcomes through recommendations and gatekeeping. This guide presents common law firm roles, clarifies their decision-making authority, and offers tailored strategies for engaging each group effectively.

Partners

Definition: Partners are attorney owners of the firm and hold the highest level of authority.

- Decision-Making Influence: Primary decision-makers for hiring and subcontracting.
- May delegate some responsibilities to others, especially in larger firms.

Marketing Approach:

- Craft professional, concise materials that highlight your expertise and the value you offer. Request meetings or presentations to demonstrate your capabilities. Follow up with personalized communications that address the firm's specific needs.

Associates

Definition: Associates are attorneys employed by the firm, typically without ownership status.

- Decision-Making Influence: Generally, not final decision-makers unless delegated authority. May recommend vendors and services to partners.

Marketing Approach:

- Build relationships by providing valuable insights or resources relevant to their cases.
- Encourage associates to share positive feedback or recommendations with partners.
- Offer educational materials or lunch-and-learn sessions to demonstrate your expertise.

Administrators and Office Managers

Definition: Administrators and office managers oversee human resources and operations within the firm.

- Decision-Making Influence: Heavily involved in screening, interviewing, and evaluating candidates. Rarely make final hiring decisions but play a crucial role in the selection process.

Marketing Approach:

- Ensure your resume and materials are clear, well-organized, and tailored to the firm's needs.
- Respond promptly to inquiries and provide references or testimonials as requested.
- Express appreciation for their role in the process and maintain professional communication.

Legal Assistants (Secretaries)

Definition: Legal assistants support attorneys and function as gatekeepers for communications and materials.

- Decision-Making Influence: Do not make hiring decisions but control access to attorneys. Can facilitate or hinder your ability to reach decision-makers.

Marketing Approach:

- Be courteous and respectful in all interactions; their support can be invaluable.
- Provide clear, organized materials that are easy to review and pass along.
- Acknowledge their expertise and thank them for their assistance.

Legal Nurse Consultants and Nurse Paralegals

Definition: These are nursing professionals employed by the firm to provide medical expertise and case analysis.

- Decision-Making Influence: May be asked to review your credentials and make recommendations. Sometimes not involved in the hiring process at all.

Marketing Approach:

- Emphasize your collaborative spirit and willingness to support their work.
- Share case studies or outcomes that demonstrate your complementary skills.
- Ask for feedback and offer to connect for professional development or networking.

Bookkeepers and Accountants

Definition: Financial professionals who manage the firm's accounts and oversee budgeting.

- Decision-Making Influence: Rarely make hiring decisions for consultants directly. Advise decision-makers on budget constraints and affordability of services.

Marketing Approach:

- Be transparent about your fees and provide detailed breakdowns of costs.
- Highlight the return on investment and cost-saving benefits of your services.
- Offer flexible pricing options or packages to fit the firm's budget.

Engaging Influencers: Tips and Examples

While partners and attorneys make the final decisions, many staff members influence those choices. Here's how to engage these influencers positively:

- Build Rapport: Take time to understand each influencer's role and show genuine respect for their expertise.
- Provide Value: Share resources, articles, or tools that help them in their daily work (e.g., workflow tips for legal assistants, medical insights for nurse paralegals).
- Follow Up: Send thank-you notes or brief updates after meetings to keep communication open and positive.
- Request Feedback: Invite suggestions from influencers to improve your services or materials.
- Be Accessible: Respond promptly and professionally to inquiries from all staff, not just decision-makers.
- Example: If a legal assistant mentions a busy period, offer to adjust your follow-up timing. If an administrator requests specific documentation, provide it quickly and accurately.

Conclusion

Successfully marketing your legal nurse consulting services requires understanding both formal decision-makers and key influencers within law firms. By tailoring your approach to each role and fostering positive relationships with all staff, you can increase your chances of securing contracts and building lasting partnerships. A strategic, respectful, and informed approach sets you apart in a competitive market.

Marketing Your LNC Services: It's Just Like Dating—Really!

A Fun, Relatable Guide for Legal Nurse Consultants on Wooing Your Dream Clients

If you think marketing your legal nurse consulting (LNC) services is all business, think again—it's a lot more like dating than you might expect. Even if your dating days are behind you, those memories of first dates, awkward introductions, and finding "the one" can help you win over clients. Grab your marketing strategy—and let's dive in!

Finding the Ideal Date (Or Client!)

Remember the days when you had an image of your "perfect date"—maybe someone who loved hiking or could dance until midnight? You probably didn't ask out someone who preferred marathon gaming sessions over outdoor adventures. Dating was all about seeking someone who matched your vibe.

Marketing works the same way. Your potential clients are looking for their "perfect match"—someone who fits their needs and understands their challenges. Sure, you might feel ready to help any client, but they're looking for that special someone. So, let's get specific!

- Action Prompt: Take five minutes to jot down your strengths. What do you do better than anyone else? Are you an expert at deciphering complex medical records? Do patients love your clear, jargon-free explanations?
- Sample Questions to Ask Yourself:
  - What unique experience do I bring to the table?
  - Which type of cases would light me up the most?
  - What do my previous clients rave about?
  - Am I the "outdoor adventurer" of the LNC world, or the "book club aficionado"?

Write these down—they're your marketing secret sauce. Just like you'd describe yourself honestly (maybe with a dash of humor) in a dating profile, let these strengths shine in your marketing materials, website copy, and LinkedIn summary.

Appearances Matter (Dress to Impress)

We all know appearances matter on a first date. Imagine slipping into sweatpants and an old college t-shirt for dinner at a trendy restaurant—not exactly the way to make a good impression. Most of us spend extra time picking just the right outfit, making sure our hair is behaving, and—let's be real—checking for spinach in our teeth.

For your LNC business, appearances matter just as much. Think of your website and LinkedIn profile photo as your "first date outfit"—they should be polished, professional, and reflect your best self. A blurry, casual photo says, "I didn't care enough to dress up," while a crisp, friendly headshot is like wearing your best suit or dress. The same goes for your marketing materials and online presence; they should be informative and visually appealing. Otherwise, you risk getting ghosted by prospective clients before the conversation even starts!

Love at First Sight (Or Maybe After a Few Dates)

Sure, love at first sight happens, but most relationships require at least several dates before anyone's ready to meet the family or swap house keys. In marketing, landing a client is rarely a one-and-done deal. Sending a single email or mailing one brochure is like proposing marriage after appetizers—most people want to get to know you first.

Successful LNCs know that clients usually need several "dates" (emails, calls, meetings) before committing. Be patient, follow up, and remember: good things come to those who nurture relationships.

What Works for Some Doesn't Work for Others

We all know someone who met their soulmate in a crowded bar, while others swear by cozy bookshops, hobbies, or mutual friends. The point? There's no one-size-fits-all in dating.

The same is true for marketing your LNC services. Maybe you thrive at attorney conferences, networking like you're mingling at a friend's party and striking up conversations with mutual acquaintances. Or perhaps direct mail is your go-to, or LinkedIn messages are your "matchmaker." If one strategy isn't working—try another. There's a world of ways to connect with your ideal clients; don't be afraid to mix it up.

It's Not All About You (Don't Be That Date)

Remember those dates when the other person talked about themselves nonstop? You probably checked your watch or phone a lot. The best dates (and the best marketing) involve listening, learning, and responding to the other person's needs.

By necessity, your marketing materials tell prospective clients about you. But make sure you also address their challenges. Ask: What problems do my clients face? How can I help solve them? Your materials should show you're paying attention and ready to help—as if you're the date who asks questions and listens to the answers.

Conclusion: Keep Flirting with Your Marketing

Marketing your LNC services isn't just about selling—it's about building real, lasting connections. Stay conversational, keep things friendly, and don't be afraid to use humor and relatable analogies. When in doubt, remember: every marketing campaign should feel less like a sales pitch and more like an enthusiastic invitation to get to know each other better. Happy "dating"—and may you land the clients of your dreams!

Bullseye Marketing for LNCs: How to Hit Your Target Every Time

Actionable Steps and Real Success for New Legal Nurse Consultants

If you've ever played darts, you know the goal is to hit the bullseye—the tiny, red circle at the center of the board. That's where the highest score lives. Targeted marketing works the same way: the more precisely you aim, the greater your chances of winning new clients. For legal nurse consultants, focusing your marketing efforts on a specific audience can make all the difference.

Addressing Your Fears: Why Narrowing Your Focus Works

It's normal to worry that by zeroing in on a small group, you might miss out on other potential clients. But here's the truth: research shows that targeted marketing[33] is more effective by 54% compared to mass outreach. For example, Miriam, a legal nurse consultant who specialized in birth injury cases after years of working in labor and

[33] Targeted marketing https://tinyurl.com/3cnp5e2t (accessed January 2026).

delivery, saw her client base double within six months of refining her focus. By aiming for her "bullseye," Miriam became the go-to expert for attorneys in her niche—and her results reflect that.

Step-by-Step Guide: Hit the Target with Confidence

Let's break down the process into easy, actionable steps. Think of each step as moving your dart closer to the bullseye:

1. Identify Your Unique Experience. List your professional background and areas of expertise (e.g., labor and delivery, oncology, operating room). Ask yourself: "What types of legal cases am I most qualified to consult on?"
2. Define Your Ideal Client. Be specific about the type of attorney you want to work with (e.g., age, specialty, firm size). Consider their needs—what gaps can you fill based on your background?
3. Build Tailored Marketing Materials. Create a resume, website, and brochures that highlight your expertise in your chosen area. Emphasize how your skills benefit your target audience (e.g., providing expert insight, offering flexible consulting).
4. Locate Your Target Audience. Use online searches (e.g., "operating room medical malpractice attorneys") and directories like Martindale to find attorneys in your niche. Join professional groups and relevant communities on LinkedIn; consider starting your own group to attract your ideal clients.
5. Make Yourself Easy to Find. Update your webpage to clearly show your expertise and value. Use relevant keywords so your target clients can find you online. If you have one, invite your audience to subscribe to your newsletter or blog—place the invitation where they'll see it.

Checklist: Your Bullseye Marketing Plan

1. Pinpoint your professional specialty.
2. Describe your ideal client in detail.
3. Craft marketing materials that speak directly to your audience's needs.
4. Find your audience using online searches, directories, and networking.
5. Optimize your online presence for visibility and engagement.

Conclusion: Keep Throwing Darts—Expand Your Rings

Remember, every dart you throw at the bullseye strengthens your reputation in your specialty. Just like Miriam, you'll find that as attorneys recognize your expertise, you'll start getting opportunities in the outer rings—cases outside your original focus. Stay confident, keep your aim steady, and watch your client base grow as you master the art of targeted marketing.

3 Creative Marketing Tips Every Legal Nurse Consultant Should Know

How to Stand Out and Build Your Brand with Proven Industry Strategies

Have you ever noticed how TV beer commercials and perfume ads try to sell products you can't truly experience on the screen? You can't smell the perfume or drink the beer through your TV. In fact, in the U.S., advertisers aren't even allowed to show actors drinking beer in commercials. Despite these limits, these brands still manage to sell millions of products. Their secret? Creative marketing. As a legal nurse consultant (LNC), you can use these same techniques to make your services stand out in a crowded field.

Tip 1: Turn a Negative into a Positive

My interest in creative marketing started back in high school. There was a popular soap that advertised a "tingly" refreshing feeling after you washed with it. Later, I discovered that the tingly sensation came from a mild skin irritant—something that could be seen as a negative. Instead, the marketers turned it into a selling point. This is a notable example of flipping a perceived flaw into a unique benefit.

Legal nurse consultants can use this technique, too. Maybe you're new to consulting and worried about your lack of experience. Rather than hiding it, highlight your eagerness and fresh perspective. For instance: "Bringing the latest clinical knowledge and a keen eye to every case."

Tip 2: Promote an Atmosphere

Think about beer commercials again. They rarely focus on the drink itself. Instead, they create a feeling—camaraderie, quirky humor, or fun with friends. Perfume ads do something similar, often showcasing women as powerful, bold, and fashionable.

You can apply this to your LNC business by creating a mood around your brand. Is your approach compassionate and supportive? Are you the go-to expert for high-stress cases? Shape your marketing to reflect the atmosphere you want potential clients to experience.

Tip 3: Use Mascots and Logos

Insurance companies excel at this. We all know the Aflac duck, the Geico gecko, and Flo from Progressive. Travelers Insurance has its red umbrella logo, while Allstate is famous for its "good hands" symbol. These visuals become instantly associated with their brands and make them memorable.

As an LNC, your logo and visual identity can set you apart. Don't just copy the typical "scales of justice combined with a medical caduceus" logo—create something personal and meaningful to your background.

Applying Creative Marketing as an LNC: Tailoring Your Brand to Your Background

The worst thing you can do is blend in with everyone else. Many LNC websites use the same language and generic logos. Instead, build your brand around what makes you unique. Here are some ways to use your clinical experience to your advantage:

- OB Nurse: If you have years of obstetric experience, use imagery like a baby, a pregnant woman, or a mother and child in your logo. Use these visuals on your website, business cards, and all marketing materials. Choose colors that convey trust and warmth—the Omniconvert[34] website has great insights into persuasive colors. Target attorneys who manage "bad baby" cases and use a tagline like "Ready to review your OB cases!" or even "Practice limited to OB/GYN cases," turning your focus into a strength.
- Emergency Nurse: Highlight your ability to stay calm under pressure and quickly analyze fast-moving situations. Your logo might feature an EKG line, Star of Life cross, or even a stopwatch. Use phrases like "Swift, accurate case reviews for emergency and trauma litigation." Target attorneys who specialize in ER-related cases or trauma claims, emphasizing your experience in emergency environments.
- Oncology Nurse: Showcase your expertise in complex, protracted care cases. Your branding could feature a ribbon, a DNA helix, or imagery related to cancer awareness. Use a tagline such as "Your expert in oncology case reviews—bringing compassion and clarity to complex medical litigation." Focus your marketing on attorneys managing cancer misdiagnosis, treatment complications, or chronic care lawsuits.

[34] Omniconvert www.omniconvert.com/blog/color-persuasion/ (accessed December 2025).

- Surgical Nurse: Emphasize your meticulous attention to detail and understanding of the operating room. Consider a logo with surgical instruments or an OR scene. Use messaging like "Cutting through the details—expert surgical case reviews." Target attorneys involved in surgical error or malpractice cases and highlight your familiarity with surgical protocols and documentation.
- Medical-Surgical Nurse: Highlight your abilities to quickly address diverse populations of patient conditions using a wide range of skills. Consider a logo that shows a common theme in your day-to-day work – perhaps an IV, bandages, gloves, or scrubs. Use a tagline such as "Beyond the bedside—bringing expertise to medical litigation. Target attorneys who specialize in general hospital medical malpractice.

No matter your background, the key is to turn what might seem ordinary or even like a limitation into your strongest selling point. Share your story, just like brands do. Use creative marketing to establish a memorable brand and an atmosphere that reflects who you are and what you do best.

Conclusion: Stand Out with Creative Marketing

Creative marketing isn't just for big brands—it's a powerful tool for legal nurse consultants who want to make a lasting impression. By turning weaknesses into strengths, promoting a unique atmosphere, and developing a memorable logo or visual identity, you'll set yourself apart. Remember, your experience and story are your best assets. Use them to build a brand that attracts the clients you want and showcases your value in every interaction.

Creating Unbiased Marketing Materials for Legal Nurse Consultants

A Practical Guide for New LNCs to Appeal to Plaintiffs and Defendants

As a new legal nurse consultant (LNC), the way you present yourself in marketing materials can significantly impact your professional opportunities. Attorneys often scrutinize the language you use, and certain terms may unintentionally signal a preference for either plaintiffs (those bringing the lawsuit) or defendants (those being sued). Crafting unbiased marketing content helps you attract a broader client base and positions you as a versatile, professional resource.

Understanding Legal Terminology: Key Concepts Defined

- Merit: In legal terms, "merit" refers to the validity or strength of a case. Screening cases for merit means assessing whether the case has a legitimate basis and enough evidence to proceed.
- Damages: "Damages" are the losses or injuries claimed by the plaintiff and may include financial, physical, or emotional harm. Identifying damages involves reviewing records to determine what harm has occurred and its impact.
- Deviations: "Deviations" refer to departures from accepted standards of care in healthcare or nursing practice. Identifying deviations means finding places where medical staff may not have followed standard procedures.

How Language Signals Bias: Real-World Examples from LNC Websites and Social Media

Attorneys carefully examine the wording on your website, LinkedIn profile, and other marketing platforms. For instance, a defense attorney recently questioned a new LNC about terms on her website that appeared to favor plaintiffs. Here are some common phrases and how they may be perceived:

- Settle/Settlement: "Don't settle for less—settle for more." This language suggests that settlements (when the defendant pays the plaintiff to resolve the case) are always positive for plaintiffs. Defense attorneys may see this as biased since settlements are not always in their clients' best interests.
- Profits: "Maximize your profits. Discover hidden dollars in your case." Plaintiff attorneys may profit if the case payout exceeds expenses, but defense attorneys are typically paid a fixed amount regardless of case outcome. Using profit-focused terms may alienate defense clients.
- Screening for Merit: "Let me help your firm by screening cases for merit." Since only plaintiff attorneys review cases before filing lawsuits, this language is not relevant to defense attorneys.
- Deviations in Standards of Care: "Identify deviations in standards of care." This phrase assumes there are mistakes, which appeals to plaintiffs but may seem biased to defendants.
- Potential Defendants: "Identify and recommend potential defendants." Plaintiff attorneys seek out who to sue, while defense attorneys don't need this information.
- Damages: "Identify damages to strengthen your case." Damages are central to plaintiff cases but can weaken a defense strategy.

Unbiased Alternatives: Sample Phrases and Practical Suggestions

To make your marketing materials more inclusive, use language that addresses both sides. Here are practical examples and alternatives to the phrases above:

- Settlement: Instead of promoting settlements, say, "Provide objective analysis to support informed case resolution decisions," which applies whether the case settles or goes to trial.
- Profits/Costs: Replace "maximize your profits" with "help your firm efficiently manage case-related costs and resources," which is relevant to both plaintiffs and defendants.
- Merit/Review: Rather than "screening for merit," try "provide thorough review and analysis of medical records and case documents to inform legal strategy."
- Deviations and Adherence: Use "identify deviations and adherence to standards of care" to show you evaluate both compliance and noncompliance with medical standards.
- Potential Defendants/Providers: Instead of "potential defendants," say "identify all parties involved in patient care," which is neutral and useful for both sides.
- Damages/Contributing Factors: Adjust "identify damages" to "assess damages, contributing factors, and causation," making your services relevant for both plaintiffs and defendants.

Real-world example: An LNC LinkedIn profile states, "Objective medical record analysis supporting fair outcomes for all parties." This avoids signaling a preference and appeals to a wider audience.

Tailoring Messaging: Strategies for Targeting Plaintiffs, Defendants, or Both

Maybe you want to focus your marketing efforts on a specific audience. If so, tailor your messaging accordingly:

- Plaintiff-focused: Use terms like "case merit evaluation," "damages assessment," and "identifying deviations from standards of care." Be prepared to discuss your impartiality and expertise if asked.
- Defense-focused: Emphasize "cost analysis," "reviewing adherence to standards," and "identifying alternative causes or contributing factors."
- Inclusive approach: Clearly state in your materials, "Services available for both plaintiff and defense attorneys," and use balanced language as outlined above.

Conclusion: Actionable Steps for Revising Your Marketing Materials

1. Review your website, social media, and brochures for language that signals bias toward one side.
2. Replace terms like "settlement," "profits," and "merit" with more inclusive alternatives.
3. Provide examples of your impartial work for both plaintiffs and defendants.
4. State your commitment to objective, evidence-based analysis in all materials.

By using practical, unbiased language and clearly explaining legal concepts, you can position yourself as a trusted legal nurse consultant for a diverse range of clients. This approach not only broadens your business opportunities but also demonstrates your professionalism and understanding of the legal field.

Email Marketing Made Easy: A Step-by-Step Beginner's Guide

Practical Steps, Metrics Explained, and Personal Strategies for Success

Email is one of the most powerful tools professionals—like attorneys—use to connect, inform, and grow their network. In fact, about 95% of professionals rely on email for communication. While you could send emails directly from your regular inbox, using an email marketing service makes the process easier, more effective, and more professional. Let's break down why email marketing platforms are helpful and walk through exactly how to get started, even if you're brand new to the process.

Why Choose an Email Marketing Service?

Email marketing platforms such as Constant Contact, MailChimp, and IContact offer user-friendly templates that look great on any device—desktop, phone, or tablet. These services help you:

- Schedule messages in advance
- Avoid spam filters and sending limits.
- Analyze how your campaigns perform.

You'll also get insights into who opens your emails and which links get clicked, so you know what's working and where you can improve.

Getting Started: Step-by-Step

1. Research and compare services: Start by looking up popular email marketing platforms. Check out reviews—Business.com[35] has a great roundup, including free options. Focus on features like template variety and an easy-to-use drag-and-drop editor.
2. Sign up for an account: Once you've chosen a service that fits your needs and budget, go to their website and create your account. Most platforms make this process quick and straightforward.
3. Import contacts: Add your email list by typing in addresses or uploading a file. Alternatively, you can ask visitors to opt in via a signup form on your website. This helps grow your list with people genuinely interested in your content.
4. Select and customize a template: Pick a template that matches your brand. Use the editor to add your logo, photos, and colors so your emails are instantly recognizable to your audience.
5. Write your first campaign: Draft your message. If you're sending an informational email, use the same template for consistency and just swap out the topic each time.
6. Schedule and send: Write your content ahead of time and use the platform's scheduler to send emails at the best time for your audience—this way, you stay organized and never miss an opportunity.

Understanding Open Rates and Click Rates

Open Rate: This is the percentage of recipients who open your email. For instance, if you send your campaign to 100 people and 21 open it, your open rate is 21%. In the legal industry, the average open rate is about 22%. A higher open rate means your subject line and sender name are catching attention.

Click Rate: This shows the percentage of people who clicked a link within your email. For example, if 3 out of 100 recipients click a link, your click rate is 3%. The average in legal circles is about 3%. High click rates mean your content is engaging and encourages action.

Improvement Tips:

- Evaluate different subject lines to see which get more opens.
- Include clear, relevant links and calls-to-action for higher clicks.

[35] Business.com https://tinyurl.com/48u5enwx (accessed December 2025).

- Review your metrics after each campaign to learn what your audience prefers.

Personal Strategies: Boosting Engagement

From my own experience sending informational emails for a decade, I consistently achieved open rates two to three times above average, and my click rates were 10-15 times higher. Here's how:

- Teaser Paragraphs: I often started my emails with a short teaser—a sentence or two hinting at valuable information that could only be accessed by clicking a link. For example: "Discover the three critical steps for protecting your practice—click here to read the full article."
- Exclusive Content: I linked to longer articles, checklists, or videos on my website, making the email the gateway to deeper insights.
- Engaging Topics: Instead of generic updates, I shared tips, case studies, or answers to shared questions, ensuring each email delivered clear value.
- Consistent Branding: Using the same template built recognition and trust, so recipients were more likely to open and engage every time.

By mixing curiosity-driven teasers and practical resources, my audience looked forward to each message—and that's what increased my metrics.

Conclusion: Your Next Steps

Email marketing is a fantastic way to stay connected and build your professional reputation. Take it one step at a time: research platforms, set up your account, build your list, and create content your audience cares about. Monitor your results, experiment, and don't be afraid to share your expertise. With the right approach, you'll see your open rates, clicks, and engagement grow. Now, go ahead—get started and watch your email campaigns make an impact!

Newsletter Marketing Tips for New Legal Nurse Consultants

Practical Steps to Build Your Reputation and Connect with Attorneys

Newsletter marketing is a powerful way for Legal Nurse Consultants (LNCs) to build professional connections, educate attorneys, and grow your business. If you're just starting out and feeling unsure about what to write or how to engage your audience, these practical tips and concrete examples will help you create newsletters that get noticed and deliver real value.

Set Clear Goals for Your Newsletter

Begin by deciding what you want your newsletter to achieve. Are you hoping to attract new clients? Strengthen your name recognition? Position yourself as a go-to educational resource for attorneys?

- Example: If your goal is to educate attorneys, you might share brief case studies or explain complex medical terms relevant to legal cases.
- Example: If you want to bring in new clients, feature testimonials from satisfied attorneys or highlight the outcomes of cases you've consulted on (while protecting confidentiality).

Commit to Consistency

Regularly sending newsletters is crucial. Consistency keeps you top-of-mind for your readers and builds trust over time.

- Example: Choose a day—such as every Wednesday—and stick to it so attorneys learn to expect your updates.

Stay Disciplined

Publishing newsletters on a regular schedule helps you avoid procrastination. When you treat newsletter creation as a non-negotiable part of your routine, you're less likely to put it off.

- Tip: Mark your calendar for newsletter creation and sending dates, just like you would for client appointments.

Identify Your Audience

Take time to build a list of attorneys who would benefit from your expertise. The more relevant your content is to their needs, the more likely they are to read and engage with your newsletters.

- Example: Reach out to attorneys who specialize in medical malpractice, personal injury, or workers' compensation—areas where your clinical knowledge can add unique insights.

Provide Value with Every Issue

Your newsletters should offer useful information, not just promote your services. Attorneys appreciate practical insights they can apply to their cases.

- Example: Share brief explanations of medical concepts, recent developments in healthcare laws, or lessons learned from your clinical specialty.
- Example: If your background is in oncology, you could write about common cancer-related terms attorneys might encounter in medical records.

Sample Newsletter Excerpt: Oncology Focus

Subject: Understanding "Neoadjuvant Therapy" in Cancer Litigation

Dear Colleague,

In this issue, we spotlight "neoadjuvant therapy"—a term frequently found in oncology medical records. Neoadjuvant therapy refers to treatments like chemotherapy or radiation given before the main treatment, usually surgery, to shrink a tumor. Understanding this concept can be crucial in cases involving surgical outcomes or alleged delays in cancer treatment. If you have questions about interpreting oncology records, let me know—I'm here to assist!

Choose Topics That Matter

Write about subjects you know well and that align with your newsletter goals. Avoid unrelated personal interests unless you can connect them to your audience's needs.

- Example: Instead of describing your latest marathon, explain how stamina and discipline learned from running help you analyze complex medical records for legal cases.

Plan Ahead with a Topic List

Keep a running list of ideas for future newsletters. Update it whenever inspiration strikes and consult it when you're ready to write the next issue.

- Tip: Ask your attorney contacts what topics would help them most—you'll get fresh ideas directly from your audience.

Determine the Best Frequency

Send newsletters often enough to stay relevant, but not so frequently that your messages get ignored. Weekly, twice monthly, or monthly are common choices.

- Tip: Avoid more than one newsletter per week to prevent overwhelming your readers. On the other hand, don't wait more than a month between issues, or you risk being forgotten.

Stick to One Topic per Newsletter

Keep each newsletter focused on a single subject. This makes your message clear and easier for attorneys to digest. Quarterly newsletters with multiple topics are outdated and less engaging.

- Tip: Avoid sending newsletters as attachments—some recipients may not open them, even if they know you.

Brand Consistency Matters

Use your logo and website colors in every issue. Consistent branding helps attorneys recognize your business and builds your professional image.

Utilize Email Marketing Services

Consider using platforms like Constant Contact or iContact. These services offer professional templates, easy scheduling, and allow you to track how many people open your emails.

- Example: You can write your newsletter ahead of time and schedule it to be sent on your chosen date, even if you're busy with client work.

They also enable you to send thousands of personalized emails efficiently and without triggering spam filters.

Stay Compliant with the CAN-Spam Act

Your newsletters must include a valid physical postal address and a subject line that accurately reflects the email's content. This keeps your emails legal and professional.

Engage Readers with Multiple Calls to Action

Encourage your readers to interact with your newsletter in various ways. A clear call to action makes it easy for attorneys to take the next step.

- Offer a Discount: "The first hour of medical record review is FREE for clients who contact me at 555-555-1212 by the end of this week and mention this newsletter!"

- Invite Questions: "Reply to this email with your toughest medical record questions—your topic might be featured in our next issue!"
- Conduct a Survey: "Click here to answer a quick survey about what legal-medical topics you'd like covered in future newsletters."
- Encourage Sharing: "Know a colleague who would benefit from this newsletter? Forward it to them and help us grow our community!"

Conclusion: Start Building Your Newsletter Today

Newsletter marketing doesn't have to be complicated. By setting clear goals, providing valuable information, and engaging your audience, you'll strengthen your reputation as an expert Legal Nurse Consultant. Take the first step—plan your debut issue, commit to your schedule, and watch your professional network grow!

Can Potential Clients Find You?

Can potential clients find you? More specifically, can potential clients find your website? If you already have a website, congratulations—some independent legal nurse consultants don't, even though it's generally expected that every business has one. Potential clients often want to check you out online and may compare you to others in the field. Your website is a powerful way to showcase your most positive characteristics.

When potential clients search for your website, there are several ways they might find it:

- They can click on a link to your website from another site, such as the AALNC's LNC Locator.
- They might type your web address directly into their browser's address bar, although this is rare for unfamiliar websites.
- Most commonly, people use a search engine like Google, Microsoft Edge, or Safari, entering keywords to look for your website.

Meta data refers to information about your website—such as keywords and descriptions—that helps search engines understand what your site is about. Crawling is the process search engines use to scan your website's content, while indexing means that search engines add your site to their database so it can appear in search results.

To illustrate the importance of keywords and search engine optimization, consider this real-world example: In one week my website had 1,117 visitors. Of these, 51 (less than 5%) arrived from my email newsletter, and 180 (16%) already knew my website and typed the address directly into their browser. The remaining 886 (79%) didn't know about my site but found it by typing keywords into a search engine. This clearly shows how crucial keywords are for attracting new clients.

Meta data describes your web page in a way that's usually hidden from view, so you might not realize if your website lacks it. Without meta data, search engines—and therefore potential clients—are unlikely to find your site among the billion-plus websites on the internet.

Here's how you can check and improve your website's visibility:

- Check if your website has meta data. Right-click on your webpage and select "View Source" or "View Page Source," depending on your browser. Near the top of the page, look for a section that includes a description and keywords.
- Create a description and keywords if missing. Your description should summarize your qualifications, including your name, business name, title (legal nurse consultant), and actions you take in your business (e.g., analysis of medical records).
- Add this meta data using your website service's settings. If you built your own site with a service like GoDaddy, WIX, or Weebly, you'll need to create and publish the meta data yourself. Look for a Settings tab or use the Help section for guidance. If you have a website manager, ask them to include necessary meta data.
- Submit your site to search engines. Once you've added description and keywords, submit your website to search engines to speed up the process. For Google, ask your web manager to use Google Search Console; for Bing, Yahoo, and DuckDuckGo, use Bing Webmaster Tools. After submission, indexing can take anywhere from an hour to a month.

Steps to Improve Your Website Visibility:

- Check if your website has meta data by viewing the page source.
- Create a description and keywords if missing.
- Add meta data using your website service's settings.
- Submit your site to Google Search Console and Bing Webmaster Tools.

Once your website is indexed, your pages will be ranked and shown in search results. By adding a description and keywords, you dramatically increase the chances that potential clients can find your website—and, ultimately, find you.

Consider tracking your visitor statistics before and after making these changes or ask other consultants about their success stories to see the impact of search engine optimization firsthand. Sharing concrete results can further demonstrate how effective these steps can be.

Inbound Marketing Strategies for Legal Nurse Consultants

A Practical Guide to Attracting Your Ideal Clients

Inbound marketing is a powerful way for legal nurse consultants (LNCs)—both new and experienced—to connect with attorneys and law firms actively seeking their expertise. Unlike traditional marketing, which interrupts potential clients with unsolicited messages, inbound marketing draws clients in by providing valuable, searchable content. This guide explains how you can implement effective inbound strategies, illustrated with real-world examples and actionable tips.

Building Your Website

Your website is the cornerstone of your inbound marketing efforts. It's often the first impression potential clients will have of your services. Here's how to set up a site that attracts and converts:

- Choose a User-Friendly Platform: Opt for platforms like Wix or WordPress that make building and updating your site simple—even for beginners.
- Craft a Compelling Bio: Clearly highlight your nursing background and legal consulting expertise. For example: "With 15 years in critical care and 5 years consulting on medical malpractice cases, I help attorneys unravel complex medical records."
- Detail Your Services: List specific offerings, such as case reviews, expert witness reports, or chronologies. This helps clients understand exactly how you can help.
- Use Specialty Keywords: Incorporate terms attorneys are likely to search for, tailored to your niche. For instance, if you specialize in labor and delivery, mention "cerebral palsy case review," "shoulder dystocia analysis," or "birth injury litigation support."

Creating Targeted Content

Content marketing is essential for inbound success. By sharing your knowledge, you position yourself as a go-to expert. Here's how to leverage different types of content, with practical examples for LNCs:

- Blogs: Write short, informative posts that address common legal-medical questions. Example: "Five Key Signs of Missed Diagnosis in Pediatric ER Cases." Scenario: John, a pediatric LNC, writes monthly blog articles about recent trends in pediatric malpractice, attracting attorneys who specialize in child injury cases.

- White Papers: Offer downloadable guides or reports on complex topics. Example: "Understanding Electronic Health Record Audits in Malpractice Litigation." Scenario: Maria, an LNC skilled in orthopedics, publishes a white paper titled "Red Flags in Post-Op Infection Cases," which she shares with her LinkedIn network, leading to new client inquiries.
- Podcasts: Host or guest on episodes discussing legal-medical intersections. Example: "What Attorneys Need to Know About Pressure Ulcer Cases." Scenario: Steve, a long-term care LNC, interviews attorneys on podcast episodes, discussing recent case outcomes and how LNCs add value—expanding his reach to new contacts.
- Social Media Engagement: Share your content and insights on LinkedIn, Facebook, or X (formerly Twitter). Example: Post a quick tip about common documentation mistakes in surgical cases, then invite questions in the comments. Scenario: Lisa, who specializes in cardiology cases, participates in LinkedIn groups and shares case studies, building visibility among attorneys who follow those topics.

Integrating Traditional and Inbound Methods

While inbound marketing is highly effective, combining it with traditional tactics can maximize your reach. For example, direct mail can introduce your website or new blog to existing contacts. You might send a postcard or letter announcing your latest white paper, inviting recipients to download it from your site.

Case Example: After launching a new website, Mark, a surgical LNC, sent a personalized email to his attorney contacts with a link to his latest case study blog post. This outreach prompted several recipients to share the link with colleagues, expanding his network and generating new leads.

The key is to keep your name and expertise in front of clients—whether through online content, social media, or traditional channels.

Conclusion: Take Action and Stay Consistent

Inbound marketing empowers LNCs to attract clients already searching for their expertise. By building a professional website, creating targeted content, and smartly integrating traditional methods, you can stand out in a competitive field. Start with one or two strategies, track your results, and adjust as you learn what works best for you. Consistency is key—keep your content fresh and your name top of mind, and you'll see your client base grow.

Favicons: A Simple Guide for Legal Nurse Consultants and Website Owners

How to Easily Create and Add a Favicon to Your Website—No Tech Expertise Needed!

Have you ever noticed the little icon next to a website's name in your browser tab? Those tiny images pack a big punch when it comes to branding. They look like this:

Figure 41 - Favicons

They're each called a favicon—short for "favorites icon." While major companies like Target, Amazon, Google, Facebook, and LinkedIn all use favicons for instant brand recognition, surprisingly few legal nurse consultants (LNCs) do. If you want your website to stand out and be instantly recognizable, adding a favicon is an easy and effective way to do it.

What Is a Favicon and Why Should You Care?

A favicon is a small image (usually 16x16 pixels) that shows up in browser tabs, bookmarks, and favorites lists. Think of it as your website's tiny logo waving at visitors, helping them spot your site among a crowd of open tabs. Imagine a user switching between Target's and Facebook's sites—the favicon acts as a guiding light, helping them quickly find the right tab. Wouldn't you love for your LNC site to be just as easy to spot?

Brand Recognition: Big Brands and LNC Examples

Big brands never miss a chance to reinforce their image. Their favicons are instantly familiar. But when I checked a group of LNC websites, I noticed something: only a handful had favicons. The rest? Their tabs were blank or just showed the default browser icon, making it impossible to tell them apart. My own site uses a favicon, so it stands out right away—even when multiple LNC sites are open. Wouldn't you rather have your tab shine instead of blending into the background?

Step-by-Step: How to Create Your Own Favicon

Not a tech expert? No problem! Here's a simple guide to creating a favicon for your website:

1. Pick Your Image: Choose a logo, photo, or another image that represents your brand. Make sure it's clear and simple—detailed images can look blurry when shrunk down this small.
2. Check the Format: Your image should be in GIF, JPEG, or PNG format. Most computers and smartphones can save images in these formats.
3. Use an Online Favicon Generator: Go to a site like Favicon[36] favicon generator. Upload your image by clicking the "Choose File" or "Browse" button, then select your file and hit "Create Favicon."
4. Preview and Adjust: Look at the preview. If it's blurry or hard to recognize, try a different image or adjust the colors. Sometimes, using a bold background color and simple shapes works best.
5. Download Your Favicon: Once you're happy with the result, download the favicon file (usually named favicon.ico).

How to Add Your Favicon to Your Website

You've got your favicon—now let's get it onto your site.

1. If You Used a Website Builder: Platforms like GoDaddy, Wix, WordPress, or Blogger make this simple. Just search their help section for "favicon." For example:
    - On GoDaddy, there's an easy upload tool under "Site Settings."
    - For WordPress, use a plugin like "All in One Favicon" or check the "Site Identity" section in your customizer.
    - On Blogger, look for the "Favicon" option in your Site Layout settings.
2. Ask for Help If Needed: If a web developer created your site, just send them the favicon file and ask them to add it for you. They'll know exactly where to put it.

Not Sure? You're Not Alone!

Does this all sound a bit technical? That's totally normal! Many website owners find this part tricky at first, but once you've done it, you'll realize it's just another small step in making your brand stand out. And the best part? It's free and only takes a few minutes!

[36] Favicon. https://favicon.io/ (accessed December 2025).

The Finishing Touch for Your Brand

Are favicons absolutely essential? No. But they offer a subtle, professional boost that helps your site look polished and memorable. Now that you know what a favicon is—and how easy it is to add—why not take five minutes to give your website the "beacon" it deserves? Next time you visit a site, see if you can spot the favicon!

Three Practical Website Marketing Tips for Legal Nurse Consultants

Tip 1: Understand How Visitors Scan Websites

- Focus on Center of Page: Users look at the center first, not the top left as they would with printed material. Place your logo or menu in the top left but save key messages for central areas.
- Make Content Easy to Scan: Use headlines, summaries, bullet points, and bold text to guide the reader's eye.
- Emphasize Important Words: Highlight essential terms with bold text, not just headings. For example, Critical Care Experience or Case Review Savings.

Tip 2: Write Clear, Factual Content

- Avoid Marketing Fluff: Skip exaggerated claims and flowery adjectives.
- Use a Neutral, Conversational Tone: State facts about your expertise and services. Example: "Marcie Senko is an RN with over 30 years in Critical Care and Emergency Medicine."
- Back Up Claims: Only mention accomplishments you can support with statistics or testimonials. For instance, "I saved clients an average of 15% on case reviews last year."
- Practical Example: Instead of "XYZ Consulting provides comprehensive reviews that are economically advantageous," write "I can save you money on case reviews."

Tip 3: Optimize Website for Quick Results

- Put Important Information First: Use the inverted pyramid style—start with how you help clients solve their problems.
- Don't Make Visitors Wait: Avoid introductions that require clicking or waiting; get straight to the point.

- Use Search Engine Optimization Best Practices: Ensure pages load quickly, are mobile-friendly, and feature relevant keywords.
- Example of Optimized Headline:
- Before: "Welcome to the Website of XYZ Consulting"
- After: "Legal Nurse Consulting—Critical Care Expertise for Attorneys"

Example of Well-Optimized Introduction:

Before: "Welcome to our site. Click below to learn about our services."

After: "Get expert support on medical case reviews from a legal nurse consultant with 30+ years of experience."

Conclusion

Recognizing the differences between website and print marketing will help you build a website that attracts and keeps clients. Use these practical tips to make your online presence clear, credible, and client-focused.

Unlocking the Power of Website Analytics for LNCs

How Simple Data Can Transform Your Legal Nurse Consulting Business

Imagine these two scenarios for your legal nurse consultant (LNC) website:

In the first scenario, you launch your website and discover that visitors spend over 100 times more time on your site than they do on similar websites. In your first year, your site gets nearly 20,000 page views—while the average for similar sites is around 200. That's not just a little better—it's a night-and-day difference!

In the second scenario, you create a great-looking website for your LNC business and feel proud of what you've built. But here's the catch: you have no idea if anyone is visiting your site each day—or if your hard work is going unnoticed.

Which scenario would you choose for your business? I picked the first one, and I'm not guessing—those are real numbers from my own site, LNCtips.com. The secret wasn't just having a nice website or sending out newsletters. The difference was having information. In the second scenario, you're in the dark. In the first, you have clear, actionable data that helps you reach more potential clients and grow your business.

The Power of Analytics—Made Simple

So how do you get this kind of valuable information? The answer is website analytics. Analytics are tools that help you see what's happening on your site: how many people visit, which pages they like, what brought them there, and where they're from.

Three Major Benefits of Using Analytics

1. Monitoring: Analytics let you track, in general, who's visiting your site, what keywords brought them, how long they stay, and which pages they read. While you won't see names, you'll get great insights into what your visitors are looking for.
2. Refining Your Website: With analytics, you can make smart changes. For example, if almost no one uses your contact page, you can move your contact info to every page—which makes it easier for clients to reach you. If you see that your clinical expertise page is the most popular, expand it to get even more engagement.
3. Shaping Your Marketing Plan: Instead of guessing, you'll know what your potential clients care about and can tailor your site to fit their needs. For instance, if you see repeated visits to your review pages, you can add more detailed case breakdowns. This will help attract clients who are searching for those exact services.

Getting Started: A Simple Step-by-Step Guide

- Step 1: Go to Google Analytics[37] and sign up for a free account.
- Step 2: Follow the prompts to add your website. If you have a web manager, they can do this, but there are plenty of video and written tutorials if you prefer to do it yourself.
- Step 3: Connect your website to Google Analytics using the tracking code provided. (Most website builders have a place to paste this code.) Or you can ask your web manager to add your Google Analytics code.
- Step 4: Check your Google Analytics dashboard once a week. Look at how many people are visiting, which pages are popular, and where your visitors are coming from.

[37] Google Analytics. https://marketingplatform.google.com/about/analytics/ (accessed December 2025).

If you prefer alternatives, you can also try other free analytics tools like Matomo[38], Monster Insights[39] (great for WordPress websites), or OnePageGA[40] (touted as easier to understand than Google Analytics).

Conclusion: Use Analytics to Grow Your LNC Business

You can have a website that just sits there, or you can have one that actively helps your business grow. Website analytics take the guesswork out of your marketing and show you what's working. By taking a few simple steps to set up analytics, you'll be on your way to reaching more clients and making your LNC business stand out.

Testimonial Marketing for Your Legal Nurse Consulting Business

How to Use and Collect Authentic Endorsements to Grow Your Practice

Testimonials are among the most effective marketing tools available to legal nurse consultants. A compelling testimonial—a written or recorded endorsement from a client or professional contact—can help set your services apart and increase your credibility. If your goal is to attract more clients to your legal nurse consulting business, featuring authentic testimonials on your website and marketing materials is a highly practical strategy.

Why Testimonials Work

Testimonials have a powerful psychological impact on potential clients. Reading about the positive experiences of others often reassures prospects and encourages them to take action. For example, seeing a testimonial such as, "I made $100,000 working part-time from home as a legal nurse consultant!" can create an aspirational effect, making readers envision similar success for themselves.

There are two primary reasons testimonials are so effective:

- Testimonials imply a smart decision: When someone shares a positive result, it suggests that choosing your services is a wise move. For attorneys, endorsements

[38] Matomo. https://matomo.org/ (accessed December 2025).
[39] Monster Insights. https://www.monsterinsights.com/ (accessed December 2025).
[40] OnePageGA. https://onepagega.com/ (accessed December 2025).

from peers or clients indicate that collaborating with you is a sound business decision.

- Testimonials overcome objections: Potential clients often hesitate due to uncertainty or skepticism. Testimonials address these doubts directly. For example, "Using XYZ Legal Nurse Consulting saved my firm time and money. I never realized how valuable this service was until I tried it," helps reduce perceived risk and builds trust.

Understanding why testimonials are persuasive is the first step. Next, let's explore actionable strategies for collecting strong endorsements.

Ways to Collect Testimonials

- Ask satisfied clients directly: After completing a project, call or email your client to ask what they appreciated most about your service. Direct requests are often met with positive responses.
- Appeal for their help: A simple, honest request such as, "I wonder if you could help me by sharing your experience?" can motivate clients to provide a testimonial. People generally like to be helpful.
- Offer a small incentive: Consider providing a token of appreciation, like movie tickets or an ice cream coupon, as a thank-you for submitting a testimonial.
- Request video testimonials: Since attorneys are often comfortable speaking, a brief video endorsement can be especially persuasive when posted on your website.
- Add a testimonial submission form to your website: Make it easy for clients to share their thoughts by creating a prominent "Share Your Feedback" section or call-out box on your site.
- Use full names and credentials: Testimonials signed with full names and professional titles (e.g., "John Barrows, Esquire") carry more credibility than anonymous or abbreviated endorsements. Including photos also adds authenticity.
- Remind clients it benefits them too: Let clients know that their testimonial serves as free publicity for their practice or firm. You might even offer to link back to their website.
- Seek endorsements from non-clients, if needed: If you're new and don't have paying customers yet, ask former employers or colleagues to comment on your professionalism, reliability, or expertise. While not as impactful as client testimonials, these can still help build your reputation.

Sample Templates

Testimonial Template Example:

"Working with [Your Name/Company] was a seamless experience. Their expertise in medical-legal issues saved our firm significant time and resources. I highly recommend their services to any attorney seeking reliable legal nurse consulting." – [Full Name], [Title/Organization]

Email Script for Requesting a Testimonial:

Subject: Request for a Brief Testimonial

Dear [Client Name],

I hope you're doing well. I'm reaching out to ask if you'd be willing to share a short testimonial about your experience with my legal nurse consulting services. Your feedback would be invaluable to other attorneys considering similar support.

If you're comfortable, a few sentences about how my services benefited your firm would be greatly appreciated. Thank you in advance for your time and help!

Best regards,

[Your Name]

Authenticity and Ethics in Testimonial Marketing

Authenticity is critical in testimonial marketing. Only use genuine testimonials from real clients or professional contacts and never fabricate or exaggerate endorsements. Always obtain permission before publishing someone's testimonial, especially if it includes their full name, title, or photo. Transparency and honesty not only build trust but also ensure that your marketing practices are ethical and compliant with professional standards.

Conclusion

Incorporating authentic testimonials into your marketing strategy can significantly enhance your credibility and attract more clients to your legal nurse consulting business. By actively seeking endorsements, using practical collection methods, and maintaining high ethical standards, you'll create a stronger, more persuasive presence in the legal industry. Begin implementing these strategies today and watch the positive impact on your business growth.

Discovery Marketing: Expand Your LNC Opportunities

As a new legal nurse consultant, it's natural to focus your marketing efforts on case merit reviews in the pre-litigation phase—just like countless others entering the field. But by doing so, you're competing with thousands of peers and missing out on one of the most fruitful periods of a medical malpractice lawsuit: the Discovery phase.

The Discovery phase is not only the longest part of most cases but also where your expertise can make the greatest impact. In my practice, roughly 75% of my time was spent supporting cases in Discovery, reviewing far more medical records than I do before litigation even begins. Each set of records in Discovery requires careful analysis and professional judgment.

Anecdote: The Power of Discovery-Focused Consulting

Consider this example: While assisting an attorney during Discovery, I uncovered a previously overlooked set of radiology reports buried deep within the medical record stack. These records revealed a critical timeline inconsistency that ultimately shifted the direction of the case, leading to a favorable outcome for our client. This kind of pivotal contribution is possible only when you position yourself as an indispensable resource throughout the Discovery process.

Service Categories for the Discovery Phase

Record Review

- Review medical records obtained during Discovery to assess their relevance and significance to the case.
- Summarize complex medical records for attorneys and insurance adjustors (if applicable), making key information accessible and actionable.
- Identify additional records, radiographs, and pathology slides needed for a comprehensive case assessment.
- Create and update medical chronologies, summaries, timelines, and graphical reports to clarify the sequence of events.
- Develop indexes of radiographs and pathology slides for quick reference.

Expert Coordination

- Identify and recommend additional experts as the case develops.
- Locate and retain experts as needed, ensuring the attorney has the right team in place.

- Highlight additional treaters to interview or depose based on ongoing case findings.

Deposition and Litigation Support

- Identify key documentation from treaters and defendants in preparation for depositions.
- Draft medically relevant questions for both fact and expert witnesses.
- Attend witness preparation sessions, depositions, and independent or comprehensive medical evaluations (CMEs)to support the attorney directly.
- Summarize deposition transcripts and CME observations for quick attorney review.
- Draft interrogatories related to medical issues and create PowerPoint presentations for mediations, arbitrations, or trial presentations.

By targeting your marketing toward Discovery, you position yourself to provide a broader range of valuable services beyond the initial merit review. This approach not only sets you apart from most new LNCs but also allows you to become an essential partner throughout the legal process—bringing in more opportunities and maximizing your impact.

Don't limit your consulting practice to pre-litigation. The Discovery phase is packed with ways for you to contribute meaningfully, enhance case outcomes, and build lasting attorney relationships. Start marketing your services for Discovery today and unlock the full potential of your legal nurse consulting career.

Understanding Shop Lock: Why It Matters for Legal Nurse Consultants

Shop lock is a term you may not have come across before, but it's important for anyone running a small business—including legal nurse consultants. In simple terms, shop lock happens when you and your team are so busy working on current orders and projects that you neglect other essential parts of your business, such as sales and marketing. This can sneak up on you, especially when things seem to be going well, but over time, it can have a serious impact.

Everyday Examples of Shop Lock

Let's look at a classic example from a sign shop: the employees get so wrapped up in making signs for existing customers that nobody spends time reaching out to new clients or promoting the business. All attention is on production—nothing else gets done. That's shop lock. Just as a sign shop can lose out on new business by focusing only on current orders, legal nurse consultants face similar risks if they don't balance client work with ongoing outreach.

Now, consider how this might look for a legal nurse consultant. Imagine you've got a full calendar, working nonstop to review cases, prepare reports, and meet deadlines for your attorney clients. You get so caught up in the day-to-day work that you skip attending local networking events, ignore industry conferences, and forget to check in with previous clients. Before you know it, the pipeline for new cases starts to dry up, and your business growth stalls or even regresses.

In case you don't think this could happen to you, read this cautionary tale. My first law firm had an excellent relationship with an insurance company adjustor who sent our firm difficult cases from around the country. We won those difficult "unwinnable" cases.

Then, one day the adjustor was no longer at the insurance company. I don't know if he had been fired or if he died. All I know is that the partner didn't have the same close relationships with anyone else there. The partner also didn't have many cases from other insurance companies. The partner had to sell some of his assets, including his private jet, to keep the firm afloat. Within a few months, the firm went from 100+ employees to five – the partner, an associate, a paralegal, a secretary, and me.

Why Shop Lock Hurts Your Business

It's easy to get caught up in the excitement of a full workload, but only focusing on your core service—casework—can leave your business vulnerable. Without regular outreach and marketing, you risk having fewer new cases come in, and your client base may shrink over time. Think about your own business. Could you and your family personally survive if something happened to your main client? If you have employees, would you have to let them go? What assets would you have to sell to remain afloat?

Smart Strategies to Prevent Shop Lock

- Hire employees to help when you need it—bring on a secretary to manage routine tasks, another LNC to share the workload, or a marketing assistant to keep outreach going.
- Schedule regular marketing activities, like sending out newsletters, posting on social media, or updating your website.
- Set reminders to follow up with past clients, so you stay top-of-mind when they need your services again.

- Join professional associations or attend industry events to expand your network and meet potential clients.
- Outsource tasks that take up too much of your time, so you can focus on both casework and growing your business.

Remember, it's not just about doing great work—it's also about making sure people know you're available and ready to help. By keeping up with marketing and networking, you'll avoid shop lock and set your business up for lasting success. This week, choose one strategy from this list and put it into practice—whether it's reaching out to a past client or scheduling time for networking. Small steps now can safeguard your business for years to come.

Holiday Marketing Strategies for Legal Nurse Consultants

Distinctive and Actionable Ideas for Standing Out This Season

Although the winter holidays may seem far off, successful holiday marketing starts well in advance. By planning early, you can design unique strategies that make your legal nurse consultant business stand out and save valuable time during the busiest months.

Send a Gift

Show appreciation to clients who provide significant business by sending a thoughtful holiday gift. Options include homemade cookies or a small gift basket. To make a lasting impression, deliver your gift the week after Thanksgiving, when it's less likely to get lost among other holiday offerings.

Send a Holiday Message

Connect on a personal level by sending a holiday newsletter or card that highlights the human side of your LNC consulting business. Include photos of yourself working, share a recent success story, and thank clients for their role in your achievements.

Host an Event

Organize a gathering for clients and potential clients to foster relationships. Ideas include a pancake breakfast at a client's office, a cookie exchange, or a wine tasting party. Send invitations one or two months in advance as well as follow ups to ensure guests can save the date and anticipate your event.

Share Your Annual Accomplishments

Use a newsletter to showcase your successes from the past year, such as helping law firms secure positive verdicts or saving them money through your medical record reviews. This is a wonderful way to remind clients of your value and expertise.

Express Gratitude

Thank your existing clients by sending a Seasons' Greetings card. This simple gesture shows your appreciation and helps maintain strong relationships.

Offer Promotions and Discounts

Attract attention by running seasonal promotions or discounts. For example, you could offer a 10% discount on all medical record reviews booked during Valentine's week or run a Halloween-themed contest where the winner receives free consultation hours. Consider non-traditional holidays like Valentine's Day or Halloween, or create a promotion for each season—Spring, Summer, Fall, and Winter.

Send Cards—Affordable and Personalized Options

Choose from a variety of card options to suit your needs and budget:

- Discount Stores: Find packs of 20-30 generic cards at dollar stores for a budget-friendly option.
- Online Printing: Websites like Smilbox[41] let you design and print personalized cards from home.
- Customized Cards: Companies such as Zazzle[42] offer fully personalized cards without requiring large orders, with fast shipping.
- Bulk Professional Cards: For a large client base, companies like Cards Direct[43] provide quantity discounts and professional-looking cards.

Stand Out with Unique Ideas

Continue experimenting with innovative strategies, such as hosting themed events or sending gifts at non-traditional times. These memorable gestures help set your

[41] Smilebox. https://www.smilebox.com/ (accessed December 2025).
[42] Zazzle. https://www.zazzle.com/ (accessed December 2025).
[43] Cards Direct. https://www.cardsdirect.com/ (accessed December 2025).

business apart in a competitive marketplace and can be easily implemented by both new and experienced legal nurse consultants.

Networking for LNCs

Networking is a powerful way to build an independent legal nurse consulting business. In simple terms, it's about making connections with potential clients to buy and sell services. Through networking, prospective clients become familiar with you, which leads to trust and business relationships.

Business from networking doesn't happen overnight. Consistent contact is often needed, so many LNCs join groups or organizations. Active participation—such as attending meetings and volunteering—helps members get to know you and build trust. Some types of networking groups include:

- Professional Associations: Join groups related to your target market, like local Bar Associations. Many allow non-voting members.
- Business Referral Groups: Groups like BNI meet weekly, accept specific business owners, and require members to share leads and complete assignments.
- LNC Professional Groups: Associations such as the American Association of Legal Nurse Consultants offer educational meetings and networking opportunities. Getting involved locally or remotely by joining committees or volunteering strengthens connections.
- Online Networking: Platforms like LinkedIn and Facebook Pages help you connect with other LNCs and potential clients.

Summary: Select groups that can help your business and focus on active participation to build trust and meaningful relationships.

Do's and Don'ts of Networking

Networking is like a job interview in a social setting. Below are key behaviors to follow—and avoid—for effective networking.

Effective Networking Behaviors

- Go to events alone to encourage meeting new people.
- Shake hands firmly and maintain eye contact to show confidence and sincerity.
- Prepare a 30-second introduction about your work.
- Circulate and meet as many attendees as possible.
- Join tables with open seats – "Is this seat taken?"

- Ask about others' work and listen actively to find common ground.
- Bring business cards and exchange them with others.

Summary: Engage confidently, be prepared, and focus on genuine conversations to make lasting connections.

Ineffective Networking Behaviors

- Attending with friends can keep you in your comfort zone and limit new connections. Instead, challenge yourself to introduce yourself to at least three new people at each event.
- Sitting with friends or co-workers prevents networking with others. Choose a table with unfamiliar faces to expand your network.
- Not bringing business cards signals a lack of seriousness. Always carry enough cards to share with new contacts.
- Handwritten or crossed-out information on cards appears unprofessional. Prepare updated, professional cards in advance.
- Rambling when asked what you do suggests indecision about your LNC role. Practice a clear, concise introduction to confidently describe your work.
- Failing to ask about others can make you seem egotistical. Show genuine interest by asking questions about their work and listening actively.
- Limp handshakes suggest a lack of confidence or trustworthiness. Offer a firm handshake to convey professionalism.

Summary: Avoid comfort zones, always present yourself professionally, and ensure two-way communication to build credibility. Networking is essential for legal nurse consultants. Knowing which groups to join and how to participate effectively leads to business growth and professional relationships.

The 30-Second Commercial for LNCs: Stand Out and Connect

A Practical Guide for Creating Impactful Pitches to Attorneys, Insurance Professionals, and Healthcare Organizations

As an Independent Legal Nurse Consultant (LNC), your ability to captivate potential clients in just 30 seconds can open doors to new opportunities. Whether you're networking with attorneys, insurance professionals, healthcare organizations, or fellow LNCs, a well-crafted commercial positions you as a go-to expert and highlights the unique value you bring. This guide will help you create and tailor your commercial for maximum impact.

Essential Elements of a Strong 30-Second Commercial

- Your Name – Establish credibility from the start.
- Your Business Name – Reinforce your professional identity.
- Brief Description of Your Business – Clearly explain what you do and for whom.
- Unique Expertise – Emphasize certifications, specialized training, or areas of deep knowledge.
- Proven Results – Highlight your track record of uncovering critical evidence or achieving measurable outcomes.
- Audience Benefit – Directly link your services to the needs of your listener.

Strengthening Your Pitch: What Makes You the Expert?

To stand out, move beyond generic statements. Specify your clinical background, board certifications (e.g., LNCC), advanced training, or practical experience (such as testifying in court or reducing claim costs).

1. For Attorneys

My name is Susan Smith, president of Medical Legal Insights. I'm a Certified Legal Nurse Consultant with over 25 years of critical care experience and specialized training in forensic case review. I help attorneys achieve successful outcomes in medical malpractice and personal injury cases by meticulously analyzing medical records for overlooked errors and trends. My expertise will uncover crucial evidence, providing attorneys with clear, actionable reports that strengthen their arguments.

2. For LNC Networking

I'm Susan Smith, president of Medical Legal Insights. As an independent Legal Nurse Consultant eager to build my practice, I bring a strong foundation of nursing expertise and a passion for detail-oriented case support. I am available for subcontracting on complex cases that require thorough research and a fresh perspective. My commitment to professional growth includes ongoing education in legal nurse consulting and geriatric care. I am dedicated to supporting successful outcomes in medical malpractice and nursing home litigation from case intake through trial.

3. For Insurance Professionals

I'm Susan Smith, founder of Medical Legal Insights. With a solid background in nursing and recent coursework in claims review and risk management, I collaborate with insurance carriers to provide impartial, evidence-based analysis of medical claims. My developing expertise in identifying unnecessary treatments and clarifying causation helps insurers efficiently resolve claims and make well-informed coverage decisions. I am committed to supporting improved claims processes and accuracy for my clients.

4. For Healthcare Organizations

My name is Susan Smith, president of Medical Legal Insights. As a Legal Nurse Consultant with a strong clinical background and ongoing education in patient safety and hospital administration, I help healthcare organizations minimize legal exposure and enhance quality of care. I review incident reports, research system vulnerabilities, and recommend practical improvements to prevent potential litigation and regulatory penalties.

Adapting Your Commercial: Scenario-Based Examples

- At a Bar Association Networking Event (Attorney audience): "I'm Susan Smith with Medical Legal Insights. I help attorneys like you win tough medical cases by providing clear, evidence-based reviews that highlight critical issues in patient care. My advanced training and track record for uncovering hard-to-find evidence set me apart."
- Meeting an Insurance Claims Manager: "My name is Susan Smith. I work with insurance teams to streamline complex medical claims by offering objective analysis that identifies unnecessary services and supports fair claim resolutions."
- Introducing Yourself at a Hospital Risk Management Meeting: "I'm Susan Smith, a Legal Nurse Consultant with extensive hospital experience. I help organizations like yours spot and address risk factors before they become legal challenges."
- At an LNC Association Meetup: "Susan Smith, Medical Legal Insights. I'm available as a subcontractor for cases that need fast, thorough review, especially in elder care litigation. Let's collaborate for better client outcomes."

Checklist: Key Points for Your 30-Second Commercial

☐ State your name and business

☐ Clearly describe your role as a Legal Nurse Consultant

☐ Highlight your unique expertise (certifications, specialized experience, or advanced training)

☐ Share a proven result or specific impact

☐ Tailor your pitch to match the audience's needs

☐ Use clear, jargon-free language

☐ Invite further conversation or expressed willingness to help

Conclusion: Personalize and Practice for Success

Your 30-second commercial is your opportunity to showcase what makes you an exceptional Legal Nurse Consultant. Personalize your pitch for each audience, emphasize your specialized skills and results, and practice until your delivery is natural and compelling. The right introduction can open doors—make every second count!

Chapter 10: Expert LNCs

Stepping into the role of an expert legal nurse consultant is both an opportunity and a responsibility. Expert work places you at the intersection of medicine and law, where your testimony can influence case outcomes and shape legal strategies. To succeed in this arena, it's essential to understand not only the opportunities and challenges of expert work, but also the professional attributes, documentation, and strategies that will position you for credibility and success.

In this chapter, we'll explore the benefits and liabilities associated with expert testimony, highlighting the traits that make expert LNCs most desirable to attorneys. You'll gain practical guidance on crafting an impactful CV, developing a transparent fee schedule, and understanding the structure and purpose of affidavits—including causation affidavits. Along the way, we'll discuss common pitfalls, such as generic affidavits that fail to persuade, and the reasons experts sometimes become disqualified. We'll also examine the characteristics that distinguish highly sought-after "magical" experts from those whose behaviors may deter clients, giving you a clear picture of what attorneys value most.

But before we talk about *becoming* an expert, we'll spend some time on how to *locate* experts. Knowing where to find qualified professionals—and how to evaluate their credentials—can be just as important as developing your own expertise. Whether you're building your career or collaborating with other specialists, these insights will help you navigate the expert landscape with confidence.

By mastering these topics, you'll be well-equipped to build a reputable and rewarding career as an expert LNC, prepared to deliver testimony that is both credible and impactful.

Locating Expert Witnesses: A Comprehensive Approach

From Identifying Specialists to Securing Contact Information

Legal Nurse Consultants (LNCs), whether working independently or within law firms, play a crucial role in helping attorneys identify and connect with expert witnesses. These experts provide essential insights regarding standards of care, causation, and damages, and may range from generalists to highly specialized subspecialists. This guide presents an integrated, stepwise strategy that covers both finding the right expert and obtaining their contact details, removing duplication, and streamlining practical advice for professionals.

Step 1: Clarify the Attorney's Requirements

- Type of Expert Needed: Determine whether the case requires a nurse expert (e.g., critical care, OB, OR) or a physician/specialist in a specific field.
- Geographic Preferences: Attorneys may prefer local experts for convenience or jurisdictional rules, while others may prioritize national recognition.
- Existing Relationships: Check if the firm maintains an internal database of vetted experts—often the quickest and most reliable source.

Step 2: General Strategies for Locating Experts

- Tap Professional Networks: Other LNCs, colleagues, and listservs (e.g., LNCExchange) can be invaluable for referrals. Remember to reciprocate referrals.
- Use Expert Locator Tools: The AALNC Expert Locator is useful for finding RN experts across specialties.
- Hospital and Academic Websites: Review physician bios and faculty profiles to identify potential expert witnesses and their contact information.
- Ask Related-Field Experts: Consult with professionals in related fields to obtain recommendations for subspecialists.
- Search Online Directories: AMA DoctorFinder, state medical board profiles, and HealthGrades provide specialty, education, and licensing details.

Step 3: Advanced Strategies for Rare Subspecialists

- Leverage Professional Forums: Use platforms like LinkedIn groups and AALNC collaborations to reach experts in rare specialties.
- Conduct Literature and Guideline Searches: Use Google Scholar, PubMed, and clinical guidelines to find authors and contributors who are leaders in their specialty. Reach out to department administrators or use LinkedIn to connect if contact information is outdated.
- Explore Major Medical Center Directories: Teaching hospitals often list staff bios; if contact info is missing, call the hospital's main line or use networking platforms.
- Professional Organization Memberships: Access member lists (only using publicly available or authorized info) and request permission to post expert requests in forums.

- Commercial Expert Directories: Use these with discretion, considering attorney preferences and the perception of directory-listed experts.

Step 4: Practical Ways to Find an Expert's Email Address

Once you've identified a potential expert, obtaining their email address is often the fastest way to make contact. Use these ethical and effective methods:

1. Google Search: Combine the expert's name with "email" (e.g., "Dr. Jane Smith email") for quick results.
2. State Licensing Sites: For physicians, state board profiles (such as Florida Physician Profiles) may list email addresses.
3. Academic Publication Listings: Search PubMed for articles authored by the expert; contact information is often included for the first author.
4. Hospital and Personal Websites: Many experts' affiliated hospital or personal websites provide professional email addresses.
5. Listservs and Professional Associations: Join relevant listservs or use professional organizations' member directories to request contact details.
6. LinkedIn Messaging: Connect with and message experts directly via LinkedIn to request their professional email and CV.
7. Institutional Email Format Deduction: Use known email formats from the expert's institution to deduce their address (e.g., jsmith@xyz.net).
8. Expert Witness Directories: Some directories allow direct messaging to experts; use these ethically and consider attorney preferences.

Final Thoughts

Finding and contacting the right expert—whether a generalist or subspecialist—requires clinical insight, investigative persistence, and professional networking. By combining foundational and advanced search strategies with targeted contact methods, Legal Nurse Consultants can provide attorneys with credible, well-qualified experts who clarify complex medical issues and strengthen legal cases. Always respect privacy and use contact information responsibly and ethically for legitimate professional purposes.

Expert Legal Nurse Consultants: Pros, Cons, and Practical Guidance

An expert Legal Nurse Consultant (LNC) is a registered nurse who reviews medical-legal cases and provides testimony regarding the adequacy of another nurse's care. This specialized role brings unique benefits and challenges. Below, you'll find an expanded discussion of the pros and cons of becoming an expert LNC, complete with examples and actionable tips to support your decision-making.

Pros / Benefits

- Maintain Your Clinical Position: One significant advantage is that you can continue working in your current clinical role while taking on expert LNC work. In fact, many jurisdictions require that expert witnesses maintain recent, hands-on experience in the specialty area related to the case. For example, if you're testifying about ICU care, you may need to have worked in an ICU within the past year or so in most states. This not only ensures your expertise is current but also provides stability and benefits from your primary job while you explore legal consulting.
- Flexible Reporting Requirements: You don't always need advanced writing skills to serve as an expert. In some states, your oral testimony is sufficient—since written reports may be subject to discovery, and oral opinions can sometimes remain confidential until your deposition. In cases where written reports are required, law firms often assist with editing your report, ensuring it meets legal standards. You would review and approve any edits before submission, allowing you to focus on accuracy and clarity rather than legal formatting.
- Additional Income and Professional Recognition: Serving as an expert LNC can significantly boost your income. Compensation rates for expert nurse consultants typically range from $125 to $350 per hour for case reviews, with higher rates—sometimes $300 to $500 per hour—for depositions and court testimony.[1] In addition to financial rewards, expert LNCs gain professional prestige through recognition by peers, attorneys, and the court system. You might be asked to present at conferences, contribute to publications, or serve on advisory panels, further elevating your profile in nursing and legal communities.
- Combined Perks of Staff and Independent LNC Work: As an expert LNC, you enjoy the "best of both worlds"—a steady paycheck and benefits from your clinical role, plus the autonomy, variety, and intellectual stimulation of consulting. You set your own consulting hours, choose which cases to accept, and experience the satisfaction of supporting justice in healthcare while maintaining your nursing practice.

Cons / Liabilities

- Requirement to Testify: A major challenge of expert LNC work is testifying under oath, in depositions and/or in court. For many, the prospect of public speaking and being cross-examined by attorneys is intimidating. Preparation is key:

consider attending workshops on expert testimony, practicing with mock depositions, or observing legal proceedings to build confidence and competence.

- Ongoing Clinical Engagement: You cannot completely leave bedside or clinical practice. During depositions, you'll likely be asked, "When was the last time you worked with this patient population?" The ideal answer is "recently"—demonstrating your expertise is current. This means you must balance both roles, which can be demanding but is essential for credibility.
- Multiple Demands on Your Time: Expert LNCs must juggle clinical shifts, case reviews, and legal obligations. While you can often review records on your own schedule, meetings with attorneys, depositions, and trial dates usually occur during weekday business hours. Effective time management is crucial: use calendars to block out consulting time, communicate your availability clearly, and consider delegating some non-essential tasks. Setting boundaries with both your clinical and consulting commitments helps prevent burnout.
- Potential Organizational Resistance: Some employers, such as hospitals, may discourage or restrict your expert consultant work. They may worry about conflicts of interest, reputational risks, or divided loyalties—especially if you testify for plaintiffs in malpractice cases. In some instances, nurses have experienced subtle or overt pressure to stop consulting. To navigate these challenges:
    - Review your employment contract and policies regarding outside work.
    - Disclose your consulting role transparently, if required.
    - Avoid taking cases directly involving your own employer or coworkers. (It would be a conflict of interest anyway.)
    - Seek legal advice or join professional organizations for support if you encounter harassment or retaliation.

Building a network of supportive colleagues and mentors can also help you manage organizational pushback.

Actionable Guidance for Aspiring Expert LNCs

- Continue Learning: Read articles and books about expert witness roles, attend relevant workshops, and connect with experienced LNCs to understand the nuances of this field.
- Prepare for Testimony: Practice delivering opinions clearly and confidently. Consider mock depositions or joining local legal nurse consultant groups.
- Manage Time and Expectations: Plan ahead for busy periods and communicate proactively with both your clinical and legal teams about your commitments.
- Address Organizational Concerns: Know your rights, understand your employer's policies, and seek support if you encounter resistance.

If you're ready to explore becoming an expert witness, continue by reading the rest of the articles in this chapter to get a deeper understanding of the role, its requirements, and strategies for success. Preparation, networking, and ongoing education are key to thriving as an expert Legal Nurse Consultant.

1. Fees are for illustrative purposes only and are not meant to suggest a universal standard; actual rates may vary depending on the LNC's experience, geographic region, and the complexity of the case.

Expert Legal Nurse Consultants Desirable Traits

Key Qualifications and Attributes of Expert Legal Nurse Consultants

To excel as an expert legal nurse consultant (LNC), certain qualifications and attributes are essential. The following sections outline these desirable traits, with practical steps and recommendations to help you strengthen your professional profile and meet expectations in this specialized role.

Educational Background: Establishing Your Credibility

While holding advanced degrees can enhance your credibility as an expert LNC, remember that there are multiple paths to establishing expertise. Substantial clinical experience, combined with ongoing professional development—such as earning specialty certifications, participating in continuing education, and staying actively involved in your field—can effectively compensate for the absence of higher academic degrees. Present your unique qualifications confidently by highlighting your depth of knowledge and your commitment to remaining current in your specialty area. Tip: Regularly update your CV with new certifications, completed courses, or professional memberships to showcase your dedication to lifelong learning.

Clinical Knowledge: Demonstrating Subject Mastery

Beyond education, a thorough understanding of your clinical specialty is critical. Before accepting a case, carefully review the relevant allegations to ensure your expertise aligns with the issues at hand. Honest self-assessment is crucial; only take on cases where you can demonstrate genuine subject mastery. Overestimating your abilities may harm the outcome for all parties. Tip: Maintain a personal checklist of your clinical strengths and limitations to guide your case selection process.

Clinical Experience: Building a Strong Foundation

Another crucial factor is clinical experience. Depth and continuity of experience in a particular specialty generally carry more weight than broad but shallow exposure across multiple areas. Attorneys and courts often prefer expert witnesses with a history of focused practice. Tip: Highlight in your CV detailed examples of sustained involvement in your specialty, such as long-term positions, leadership roles, or advanced responsibilities.

Communication Skills: Translating Expertise for Non-Medical Audiences

Exceptional communication skills are vital for expert LNCs. You must be able to clearly explain complex medical concepts in ways that jurors and attorneys without medical backgrounds can easily understand. Effective strategies include avoiding medical jargon, using analogies or everyday language, and organizing your thoughts logically. For example, instead of saying "myocardial infarction," say "heart attack," and relate procedures to common experiences when possible. Practicing your explanations with non-medical friends or colleagues can help identify where further simplification is needed. Tip: After mock interviews or practice sessions, ask your listener to summarize your explanation to ensure clarity and understanding.

Employment Status: Staying Active in Your Field

Current employment in your area of expertise is highly valued. Attorneys and courts typically expect experts to be actively practicing, as this demonstrates ongoing familiarity with standards of care. In some states, you must be currently practicing or have worked within the past one to two years to qualify as an expert witness. When asked, "When did you last work in this field?" the ideal answer is "Recently" or "Yesterday." Retired nurses may face significant hurdles here. Tip: If you are transitioning between roles or working part-time, consider maintaining per diem or consulting positions to preserve your eligibility.

CV and Fee Schedule: Documenting Your Qualifications and Terms

Another fundamental requirement is a comprehensive CV and transparent fee schedule. Your CV should detail your education, certifications, employment history, speaking engagements, and publications. A clear fee schedule helps establish credibility and ensures transparency during the engagement process. Tip: Regularly review and update your CV, adding recent achievements or roles, and ensure your fee schedule matches current market rates and clearly states your terms.

Professional Credibility for Expert Legal Nurse Consultants

Ten Things NOT to Write on Your Expert CV, Social Media, or Website

As a legal nurse consultant, the way you present yourself online and in professional documents is critical to establishing your authority and impartiality. Attorneys, judges, and jurors scrutinize every detail you share—on CVs, websites, and social media—to assess your credibility as an expert witness. To ensure your professional reputation remains strong, it's essential to avoid common pitfalls that can inadvertently undermine your expertise or raise questions about your objectivity. Below are ten key mistakes to avoid when crafting your expert profile.

1. Do not claim you "help attorneys win cases." Stating on your CV or social media that you "help attorneys win cases" suggests you are willing to say anything to support your client, which can undermine your credibility as an impartial expert. How to fix it: Avoid any language that implies guaranteeing outcomes or acting as an advocate for attorneys. Rationale: In legal settings, experts are expected to provide unbiased opinions. Any hint that you'll do "whatever it takes" can damage your reputation and the case. Example: A nurse expert wrote on Facebook, "I always help my attorneys win!" At deposition, opposing counsel questioned her objectivity, weakening her testimony.
2. Keep blog and website content focused on your clinical expertise. Including unrelated topics such as cupcake recipes, animal husbandry, or celebrity trials confuses readers and raises doubts about your professional focus. How to fix it: Only post material relevant to your nursing specialty, like clinical updates or news about your field. Rationale: Unfocused content dilutes your authority and may prompt attorneys to avoid hiring you. Example: An expert's website with a mix of unrelated blog posts led a law firm to question her seriousness as a professional witness.
3. Avoid overstating your network or resources if not relevant. Listing "access to thousands of legal nurse consultants" can be questioned during deposition, especially if you are testifying as an individual expert. How to fix it: If you're acting as an independent LNC, this statement is acceptable. If you are an expert witness, remove it from your materials. Rationale: Attorneys and juries are interested in your personal qualifications, not your network size. Example: An

expert's claim of a vast network was challenged in court, distracting from her own credentials.

4. Use a CV, not a resume, for expert witness work. Resumes focus on employment history for job applications, while CVs detail clinical experience, education, awards, and publications pertinent to your expertise. How to fix it: Prepare a CV listing your professional qualifications rather than a job application-style resume. Rationale: A CV demonstrates your authority in your clinical specialty, which is what courts and attorneys need to see. Example: An expert using a standard resume was pressed in deposition about missing academic and clinical details.
5. List your full work history since graduation. Only including the last 10 years of experience leaves gaps that opposing counsel can exploit. How to fix it: Document your entire work history, starting from your nursing school graduation date. Rationale: Full disclosure prevents suspicion and demonstrates transparency. Example: An expert who omitted 15 years of her career faced intense questioning about what she was "hiding."
6. List job titles only—avoid detailed job descriptions on your CV. Providing synopses of each job invites unnecessary scrutiny and nitpicking in deposition. How to fix it: On your CV, list only your position titles and employers without descriptions. Rationale: Titles establish your experience without opening the door to debates over wording. Example: An expert's elaborate job summaries were dissected in court, detracting from her qualifications.
7. Exclude non-clinical hobbies and controversial affiliations. Mentioning activities like scuba diving or teaching controversial subjects can distract or alienate jurors. How to fix it: Limit resume content to clinical credentials; avoid personal or potentially divisive information. Rationale: Jurors may form negative opinions based on unrelated or controversial activities. Example: An expert listing membership in a political party on his CV invited antagonism by some jury members.
8. Do not include details about legal nurse consulting courses attended. Listing LNC coursework leads to questions about your motivations, the curriculum, and its relevance to your clinical expertise. How to fix it: Leave out LNC course details. Focus on your clinical background instead. Rationale: Attorneys want to know about your clinical, not legal, expertise. Example: An expert's lengthy explanation of her LNC course content detracted from her nursing credentials.
9. Be cautious about listing legal nurse consulting certifications. If your LNC credential isn't consistent with major certifying bodies, it may be challenged for authenticity. How to fix it: Consider omitting LNC credentials from your expert CV unless they are widely recognized and directly relevant. Rationale: Unfamiliar credentials can cast doubt on your overall qualifications. Example: An opposing

attorney questioned the value of a course-based certification, undermining the expert's authority.

10. Exclude certifications unrelated to nursing or clinical expertise. Credentials like "surfing instructor" do not strengthen your standing as a clinical expert and can confuse or distract attorneys and jurors. How to fix it: Only include certifications directly related to your area of clinical expertise. Rationale: Irrelevant certifications dilute your perceived expertise. Example: A non-clinical certification invited unnecessary questioning about its relevance during testimony.

As you refine your professional profile, remember that clear, focused, and relevant documentation enhances your credibility and effectiveness as an expert witness. For those serving as both independent LNCs and testifying experts, consider maintaining separate documents—a resume for consulting and a CV for expert witness roles.

CVs for Expert Legal Nurse Consultants

Creating a CV for Expert Legal Nurse Consultants

A CV (curriculum vitae) is a vital document for legal nurse consultants, serving as a comprehensive record of your professional journey. Unlike a resume, which is often tailored to a specific job and includes role descriptions, a CV catalogs your education, every position held since nursing school, conferences attended, all professional and academic presentations, grants received, publications, professional affiliations, certifications, honors, and awards. This thoroughness allows opposing counsel to verify your credentials during depositions, making accuracy and completeness essential.

Privacy Guidance: Protecting Your Personal Information

In the past, CVs commonly included details such as age, marital status, and children. Today, you only provide your name, city and state, phone number, and professional email address as personal information. When sharing your CV online or with unfamiliar parties, it's best practice to omit your full home address to safeguard your privacy.

- Suggested privacy statement for shared CVs: "Full address available upon request."

Formatting and Maintenance

A CV is structured as grouped lists, making it simple to update as you achieve new professional milestones. Keep digital copies for easy editing and set a reminder to review and add recent accomplishments every six months. Arrange your CV with personal information at the top, followed by the remaining sections in reverse chronological order (education, employment, etc.). Unlike resumes, CVs should not be customized for each audience; they serve as a complete and permanent record.

Key Differences: CV vs. Resume

- CVs are comprehensive and list all professional activities and achievements; resumes are concise and tailored to specific positions.
- CVs do not include job responsibility descriptions; resumes highlight experience through detailed descriptions of roles and accomplishments.
- CVs are not customized for each opportunity; resumes are often modified to fit the employer's requirements.
- CVs are used to verify credentials in legal contexts; resumes are used for job applications.

Sample CV

Below is a sample CV demonstrating how an expert legal nurse consultant organizes his credentials into grouped lists. Each section contains clear, specific details, and no job responsibilities are described, as is common in resumes. Note the inclusion of the "Publications" section, alongside guidance on privacy best practices.

Jackie Jensen, MSN, RN, LNCC

Address: Madisonville, WY. Full address available upon request

Phone: (555) 555-2345

Email: jackiejensen@email.com

Professional Experience

Pediatric Nurse Practitioner, Heart Transplant Coordinator, Pediatric Cardiology, University of Madisonville, Children's Hospital, Madisonville, WY - 2003–Present

Pediatric Nurse Practitioner, Pediatric Cardiology, Seminole Children's Heart Center, Carbondale, WY - 2000–2003

Pediatric Intensive Care RN, Saratoga University medical Center, Centerville, WY - 1997–2000

Pediatric RN, St. Francis Hospital, Evansville, WY - 1995–1996

Education

MSN – Nursing, Pediatric Nurse Practitioner / Pediatric Clinical Nurse Specialist Program University of Madisonville - 2002

BSN – Nursing, University of Madisonville - 1995

BA – Child Development, University of Madisonville - 1991

Licensure & Certifications

Registered Nurse – Florida

License #RN123456 - Active through 12/2026

Legal Nurse Consultant Certified (LNCC)

Certification #LNCC 78910 - Issued 2023

PALS and PICC Line Certified – 2001 to Present

Presentations

**Congenital Heart Disease for the Primary Care NP*, University of Madisonville, Madisonville, WY – 2004

*The Normal and Abnormal Heart—Review of normal and abnormal cardiac anatomy and physiology, Saratoga University Medical Center, Centerville, WY – 2003-2004

*Pediatric Review—anatomy and physiology, cardiac catheterization care, and medication review, Saratoga University Medical Center, Centerville, WY – 2002

**Introduction to Heart Transplantation lecture*, University of Madisonville, Madisonville, WY – 2000 - 2002

*Introduction to Interventional Cardiac Catheterization for Adults and Children with CHF, Seminole Children's Center, Carbondale, WY

Publications

Jensen, J. J. (2022). Pediatric Cardiac Nursing: Advances and Innovations. Journal of Pediatric Nursing, 37(4), 210-218.

Manuscript in Progress

Pediatric Cardiology for the Nurse Practitioner, 2nd ed., Lovick Lippman, Jared Smith, Samuel Lester, et al.—Chapter on Pediatric Heart Transplant - 2027

Establishing Expert Legal Nurse Consultant Fee Schedules

Expert legal nurse consultants (LNCs) should provide a fee schedule to the attorneys who hire them. This document outlines the charges for various expert activities and helps set clear expectations for both parties. Below are common elements included in a fee schedule, along with definitions to clarify key terms for those new to legal nurse consulting:

- Retainer: A retainer is an upfront payment that secures the consultant's services and is often applied toward initial case review hours. Some LNCs never charge a retainer, some require it only for new clients, and others request a retainer for each case. Typically, the retainer equals the consultant's charge for a set number of hours billed toward reviewing the case.
- Medical Records Review and Reports: This is the charge for the time spent analyzing medical records and drafting any reports. Billing increments are commonly 15 minutes.
- Conferences with Attorneys/Law Firm Staff and Conference Preparation: Fees for conferences are usually billed at the same rate as medical records review.
- Deposition Testimony: Deposition testimony refers to giving sworn evidence outside of court, usually as part of the discovery process. Often, LNCs charge for a minimum number of hours (e.g., four) and may require advance notice for cancellation. In some states, the attorney from the opposing side pays for deposition testimony, so experts often specify in their fee schedule that payment is required before or at the time of the deposition.
- Trial Testimony: Trial testimony involves presenting expert opinions during a trial. LNCs may charge a minimum number of hours (e.g., eight) and may include a statement regarding payment of travel/lodging expenses.

Sample Fee Schedule

For example, a fee schedule might state:

- Retainer: $1,000 (covers first 5 hours)
- Medical record review: $200/hour
- Deposition testimony: $275/hour (minimum 4 hours)
- Trial testimony: $430/hour (minimum 8 hours plus travel expenses)

The above fees are for illustrative purposes only and are not meant to suggest a universal standard; actual rates may vary depending on the LNC's experience, geographic region, and the complexity of the case.

LNCs are generally paid by the law firm that hires them, except for deposition testimony in some states. In those cases, the opposing attorney may be responsible for payment. Note: It is important to check local regulations, as some states require the opposing attorney to pay for deposition testimony. Legal nurse consultants should research their state's rules before finalizing their fee schedule to ensure compliance and avoid disputes.

Fee schedules should reflect the consultant's nursing and legal nurse consulting experience, as well as current market rates. If your legal nurse consulting course did not provide guidelines, consider researching online for sample fee schedules or joining organizations such as AALNC and its local chapter to connect with other legal nurse consultants. Be aware, however, that some consultants may hesitate to share their rates due to concerns about price fixing or competition.

Unlocking Expert Recognition as a Legal Nurse Consultant

Step-by-Step Strategies to Build Your Reputation and Get Retained

Are you ready to stand out as a legal nurse consultant but wondering why your phone isn't ringing yet? You're not alone—many aspiring experts feel overlooked despite having the right skills and temperament. The good news is, with a proactive approach, you can take control of your professional identity and become the go-to expert attorneys seek out. Let's break down actionable, practical steps to earn the recognition you deserve.

Step 1: Get Listed in Expert Directories—The Right Way

Expert directories like ALM, SEAK, or JurisPro can quickly boost your visibility—but let's be strategic. Follow the websites' guidelines, but these can make your profile shine:

- Craft a Compelling Profile: Highlight your credentials, specialty areas, and experience. Use clear, confident language that showcases your expertise and passion.
- Include Testimonials and Peer-Reviewed Work: Mitigate the "hired gun" perception by supplementing your profile with client testimonials, references, or links to articles you've published in reputable journals.

- Keep It Authentic: Focus on your real-world impact—describe cases you've worked on, results you've helped achieve, and your approach to consulting.

Please note that some attorneys may be reluctant to hire experts who pay for directory listings, as it can create the impression that the expert is primarily motivated by financial gain rather than objectivity. This perception may lead to concerns about the expert's impartiality and could impact your professional opportunities with certain law firms. If you want a free listing, check out the American Association of Legal Nurse Consultants (AALNC) LNC Locator. Membership is required, but it's a fantastic way to get noticed without paying for placement.

Step 2: Publish Articles That Prove Your Expertise

Publishing isn't just for seasoned writers—anyone can do it with a thoughtful, step-by-step approach:

- Identify Target Journals and Blogs: Look for peer-reviewed and professional publications in legal nursing, healthcare, or law. Don't overlook well-trafficked blogs and association newsletters.
- Review Submission Guidelines: Every publication has its own requirements. Read them carefully to tailor your article for acceptance.
- Collaborate for Impact: Team up with colleagues to co-author articles, share insights, and broaden your reach.
- Keep It Concise and Informative: Share practical tips, case studies, or emerging trends. Aim to educate and engage your audience.
- Promote Your Work: Share published articles on your LinkedIn profile, expert directory listings, and in professional groups.

Step 3: Speak Up—Join Speaker Bureaus and Present Your Expertise

Public speaking boosts your credibility and name recognition. Here's how to get started:

- Join Speaker Bureaus: Many organizations and associations offer free platforms for experts to present on topics in their field.
- Prepare Engaging Presentations: Focus on practical advice and real-world scenarios. Practice your delivery to build confidence.
- Seek Out Local and National Events: Start with small groups or workshops, then scale up as your reputation grows.

Step 4: Network—Connect with Attorneys and LNCs

Effective networking is about building authentic relationships:

- Attend Events and Join Listservs: In-person networking with attorneys and LNCs can lead directly to new opportunities. Online listservs—like LNCExchange[44] or Juris Educational Resource Knowledge for Legal Nurse Consulting[45] —are great for sharing knowledge and answering questions.
- Be Generous with Your Expertise: Respond to requests, share resources, and offer insights. This positions you as the go-to person in your specialty.
- Follow Up: After initial conversations, stay in touch with your contacts to nurture relationships.

Step 5: Optimize Your LinkedIn Presence

LinkedIn is a powerhouse for building your brand as an expert:

- Build a Strong, Clear Profile: Clearly state your expertise, credentials, and areas of specialization. Use a professional photo and headline.
- Connect Strategically: Search for attorneys, LNCs, and industry professionals. After connecting, offer to share your CV and start a conversation.
- Join and Contribute to Groups: Participate in discussions in LNC and attorney groups. Share your insights and answer questions to demonstrate your expertise.
- Share Valuable Content: Post articles, case studies, or tips related to legal nurse consulting to increase your visibility.

Conclusion: Take Action and Build Your Expert Reputation Today

Remember, becoming a recognized legal nurse consultant is all about consistent, proactive steps. Whether you're publishing, networking, speaking, or building your online presence, each action moves you closer to being sought after as the expert you already are. Stay motivated, keep learning, and embrace every opportunity to showcase your value—your next big case could be just around the corner!

[44] LNCExchange. https://lncexchange.com/ (accessed December 2025).
[45] The J.E.R.K LNC. https://www.thejerklnc.com/ (accessed December 2025).

Expert Witness Selection Variables

How Legal Nurse Consultants Select Expert Witnesses for Attorneys

Choosing the right expert witness is a critical part of legal nurse consulting. Attorneys have different priorities when seeking expert witnesses and understanding these preferences can help consultants make better matches. Here are three key variables to consider, along with practical examples:

1. Testifying Experience

Some attorneys prefer to work with experts who have a proven history in the courtroom. They believe that juries find these experienced experts credible. For example, an attorney might select a physician who has testified in multiple cases and is known for clear, persuasive testimony. In contrast, other attorneys prefer experts who are new to testifying in jury trials. They believe that less experienced experts may appear more genuine to juries. For instance, an attorney might choose a nurse who has never testified before, hoping the jury sees them as unbiased and authentic.

2. Plaintiff/Defense Mindset

Attorneys also consider whether an expert has experience working for both plaintiffs and defendants. Some look for healthcare providers who have testified on both sides, aiming to avoid any perception of bias. For example, an attorney might hire a medical expert who can point to previous work for both plaintiff and defense cases. On the other hand, some attorneys want experts who are firmly aligned with their side. For instance, a defense attorney may prefer an expert who has consistently supported defense positions and has never testified for plaintiffs.

3. Educational Qualifications

Expert credentials play a significant role for many attorneys. Some seek out experts with impressive academic backgrounds, such as a PhD for nursing experts or an Ivy League education for physicians. For example, an attorney might choose a nurse with a PhD to impress the jury with their academic background, while another might focus on a nurse's practical experience instead. In this case, the attorney may believe that hands-on expertise will make the expert's testimony more relatable and convincing.

Conclusion

Understanding these variables can help legal nurse consultants match the right expert to each attorney's unique needs.

Anatomy of an Affidavit

A Guide for Legal Nurse Consultants

Legal nurse consultants—whether serving independently, as expert witnesses, or as in-house professionals—are often called upon to prepare, review, or sign affidavits in medical malpractice cases. This guide outlines the structure and key components of an affidavit to help you confidently fulfill these responsibilities, with particular attention to how affidavits should be tailored depending on the case status.

Understanding Case Status: Presuit vs. Litigation

It's important to adjust the content and structure of your affidavit based on whether the case is in the presuit or litigation phase:

- Presuit Phase: In presuit cases, the affidavit should focus on your credentials (name, degrees, and professional qualifications) and a general statement of your opinion regarding the case. Do not include case numbers, court information, or detailed parties. The emphasis is on establishing your authority and providing a concise statement supporting or refuting the validity of the claim.
- Litigation Phase: If the case has moved into litigation, begin the affidavit with the case caption, including the court name, case number, and the names of the parties involved. This section precedes the title and clearly links your affidavit to the active legal proceedings. You should also include your credentials and a detailed statement of your expert opinion, as well as any other relevant procedural details as required by the court.

Step-by-Step Structure of an Affidavit

1. Title: Clearly state the type of document and identify the author, including name and educational credentials. For presuit cases, this comes after your credentials; for litigation, it follows the case caption.
2. Qualifications: Detail your educational background, certifications, relevant work experience, and active professional involvement. Reference your CV to demonstrate current expertise, as many states require that expert witnesses maintain active practice or teaching in their specialty.

3. Records Reviewed: List each medical record reviewed and the corresponding dates of service. This documents the sources you relied upon to form your opinion.
4. Factual Basis: Summarize the facts that support your professional opinion. This factual foundation is essential for establishing the validity of your conclusions.
5. Expert Opinion: State your opinion clearly, indicating whether the available facts support or refute a claim of medical malpractice.
6. Causation and Damages: If applicable, explain how a deviation from the standard of care resulted in damages to the patient, and describe how those damages were caused by the healthcare provider's actions.
7. Credibility Affirmation: Note if your expert opinions have never been disqualified in court, as this detail supports your credibility.
8. Certification: Include a statement certifying that you have never been found guilty of fraud or perjury and that you have read and verified the truthfulness of the affidavit.
9. Conclusion: End with the phrase "Further affiant sayeth naught" to indicate that you have nothing more to add.
10. Notarization: Sign the affidavit in the presence of a notary public to formally affirm or swear to the truthfulness of your statements.

This clear, step-by-step approach ensures that all critical elements are addressed in your affidavit, making the process straightforward and compliant with legal standards. While this guide is based on the format commonly used in Florida, requirements can vary by state. For additional guidance, consult reputable resources such as the National Conference of State Legislatures for state-specific laws, and always ask your supervising attorney for sample affidavits or certificates of merit previously drafted for similar cases.

Sample Affidavit (Presuit Case)

AFFIDAVIT OF ROSALINDA MATTHIESEN, MS RN

1. My name is Rosalinda Matthiesen, MS RN, and I am over the age of 18 and fully competent to testify as to the matters herein. I have been actively engaged in the practice of nursing within the five-year period immediately prior to the incident giving rise to this claim and am a Certified Wound Specialist. My qualifications are outlined in the attached curriculum vitae and made a part hereof. I am familiar with the standard of care as it pertains to the management of care in situations such as those that unfolded in this case.

2. I am an expert as defined by Florida Statute 766.202.

3. I have reviewed the medical records for Mallory Pledger:

    a. Central City Hospital – 7/31/2025 – 8/29/2025

b. Central City Rehabilitation Center – 8/29/2025 – 9/15/2025

4. The Central City Hospital records do not indicate any skin breakdown on Mrs. Pledger's sacrum before she was transferred to Central City Rehabilitation Center. The Central City Rehabilitation Center's history and physical and nursing assessment indicate that Mrs. Pledger's skin was intact. During her admission to Central City Rehabilitation Center, Mrs. Pledger developed a Stage III ulcer to her sacrum.

5. Based on my review of the above records, it is my opinion that, within a reasonable degree of medical probability, reasonable grounds exist to initiate a medical negligence claim against Central City Rehabilitation Center.

6. Based on my opinion, Central City Rehabilitation Center, through its nursing staff and nursing assistants, fell below the standard of care by failing to document skin assessments, failing to use pressure reduction devices, and failing to inspect, turn, and reposition Mrs. Pledger. As a result of Central City Rehabilitation Center's breach of the standard of care. Mrs. Pledger developed a Stage III pressure ulcer of her sacrum.

7. My opinion has never been disqualified in any court.

8. I certify that I have not been found guilty of fraud or perjury in any jurisdiction.

9. Under penalties of perjury, I certify that I have read the foregoing and that the facts stated in it are true.

FURTHER AFFIANT SAYETH NAUGHT.

____

ROSALINDA MATTHIESEN, MS, RN

The foregoing instrument was acknowledged before me this ______ day of ________ day of _________ 20___, by ____________________, who is (personally known to me) (or who has produced) ____________________ (as identification).

____

(Signature of Notary)

____

(Name of Notary typed, Printed or Stamped)

Causation Affidavits

A Guide for Legal Nurse Consultants

In medical malpractice cases, attorneys frequently ask experts to sign affidavits or certificates of merit. These affidavits and certificates are sworn statements that outline why the expert believes (or does not believe) a healthcare provider has fallen below the standard of care—that is, the accepted level of medical treatment—resulting in injury to the plaintiff. Occasionally, attorneys have specifically requested that I draft a causation affidavit, which is a sworn statement explaining whether the defendant's actions caused the patient's injury, for an expert to sign. Understanding the circumstances in which causation affidavits are used is important for legal nurse consultants, as these documents play a central role in medical malpractice litigation.

Causation affidavits are typically requested from defense experts in two main scenarios. The first scenario involves cases where the defendant clearly fell below the standard of care, but the patient's outcome was not affected by the defendant's action or inaction. It is important to remember that all four elements of negligence must be present in a medical malpractice case: duty, breach of duty (falling below the standard of care), causation (a direct link between the action and the injury), and damages (actual harm to the patient). If even one element is missing, medical malpractice did not occur.

For instance, consider a scenario where a missed diagnosis did not ultimately affect the patient's outcome. A patient underwent a mammogram that a radiologist misread as benign (not cancerous), but another physician diagnosed her with Stage 0 breast cancer (carcinoma in situ, an early and non-invasive cancer) a month later. In this situation, an expert's causation affidavit would state that it is more likely than not that the radiologist's missed diagnosis made no difference to the patient's treatment or prognosis. (If a longer period had passed and the patient was diagnosed at a higher stage, there would have been a stronger indication that the delay in diagnosis affected the stage of breast cancer and, consequently, the treatment and prognosis.)

Another scenario in which causation affidavits are important involves cases with more complex medical histories. For example, the family of a plaintiff with a complex medical history filed a Presuit claim (a formal notice required before filing a medical malpractice lawsuit in some states) against her rheumatologist for failure to refer the patient to an oncologist. This plaintiff had a positive anti-Hu antibody (a marker sometimes associated with certain cancers, such as small cell lung cancer). Her pulmonologist conducted extensive testing, including two PET/CT scans, which were negative.

The patient later developed a rash on her cheeks and other symptoms, which the rheumatologist diagnosed as systemic lupus erythematosus (an autoimmune disease). During one of her office visits with the rheumatologist, the plaintiff complained of pain after a fall in her bathroom. At subsequent visits, her pain level was zero out of ten. Nearly two years after her first visit with the rheumatologist and six years after her pulmonology workup, the plaintiff developed non-small cell lung cancer (a different type of lung cancer than initially suspected). The plaintiff's daughter alleged that since the plaintiff had once reported pain, the rheumatologist should have recognized this as a sign of non-small cell lung cancer and initiated a referral to an oncologist.

In this case, the attorney for the rheumatologist believed the allegations were unfounded and hired a rheumatology expert to sign a standard of care affidavit, confirming that the care met accepted standards. Additionally, an oncologist was retained to sign a causation affidavit, stating that the rheumatologist's actions did not cause the plaintiff's harm. Including these affidavits, which detail the specific case circumstances and outcomes, helps clarify the legal process and demonstrates how causation affidavits function in real-world medical malpractice litigation. Ultimately, the plaintiff's attorney declined to name the rheumatologist as a party in a lawsuit.

In summary, causation affidavits are crucial tools in medical malpractice cases for clarifying whether a provider's actions directly resulted in patient harm. Understanding when and how to draft these affidavits can help legal nurse consultants support expert witnesses and attorneys more effectively, ensuring that claims are evaluated fairly and accurately.

Sample Causation Affidavit

AFFIDAVIT OF PETER Z. JOHNSON, MD

1. My name is Peter Z. Johnson, MD, and I am over the age of 18 and fully competent to testify as to the matters herein. I am a physician licensed to practice medicine in the state of California and have been actively engaged in the practice of medicine within the three-year period immediately prior to the incident giving rise to this claim. I am also Board certified in Oncology and Hematology. In addition, I have a current Florida Medical Doctor Expert Witness license. My qualifications are outlined in the attached curriculum vitae along with my expert witness license certification and made a part hereof. Based upon my background, training, learning, and experience in the field of oncology I am familiar with the clinical presentation and the care and treatment of patients such as such as Lilith Sedgeway in situations such as those that unfolded in this case.

2. In that regard, I have been engaged by the law firm of Harder, Lester, and Monroe to review medical records and render an opinion as to whether there is a reasonable

basis to conclude that John C. Warren, MD and John C. Warren, MD, PA did not cause or contribute to injuries to Lilith Sedgeway. To that end, I have reviewed the Notice of Intent and the following records for Lilith Sedgeway:

A. John C. Warren, MD/Rheumatology Associates

B. Jessica Flicker, MD / Western Pulmonary & Sleep Specialists

C. Family Health Medical Center

3. Based upon my review of these records, as well as my background, training, learning, and experience in the field of oncology, it is my opinion that there is a reasonable basis to conclude that John C. Warren, MD and John C. Warren, MD, PA did not cause or contribute to cause injury to Lilith Sedgeway.

4. More specifically, in 2018 and 2019, Ms. Sedgeway had an extensive workup by Jessica Flicker, MD, a pulmonologist, for positive anti-Hu antibody, which is sometimes associated with small cell lung cancer. In January 2023. Dr. John C. Warren, a rheumatologist, saw Ms. Sedgeway for a butterfly facial rash and other complaints. After further testing, Dr. Warren diagnosed systemic lupus erythematosus.

5. Dr. Warren monitored Ms. Sedgeway's rheumatologic condition approximately every three months. At the six-month visit in July 2023, she complained of pain in her lumbar back after a fall in the bathroom. Dr. Warren offered to write a referral to an orthopedist, but the patient declined. At all subsequent visits, her pain level was zero over ten.

6. In September 2025, Ms. Sedgeway returned to Dr. Flicker with complaints of severe dyspnea and back pain. In October 2025, Ms. Sedgeway was diagnosed with adenocarcinoma, a type of non-small cell lung cancer, with metastasis to her ribs.

7. Untreated bone pain caused by metastasis from lung cancer is severe and unrelenting. Ms. Sedgeway's complaints of lumbar back pain to Dr. Warren occurred once and then never again. It is my opinion, to a reasonable degree of medical certainty, that Ms. Sedgeway's back pain at the July 2023 visit to Dr. Warren was musculoskeletal, not oncologic, in nature and did not merit a referral to an oncologist. Furthermore, Dr. Warren's alleged lack of an Oncology referral did not contribute to any injuries sustained by Ms. Sedgeway.

8. Based on the foregoing as well as my background, training, learning, and experience in the field of oncology, I am of the opinion, to a reasonable degree of medical probability, that the care and treatment or any alleged lack of care and treatment by John C. Warren, MD and John C Warren, MD, PA did not contribute to any injury the claimant sustained.

9. My opinion has never been disqualified in any court.

10. I certify that I have not been found guilty of fraud or perjury in any jurisdiction.

11. Under penalties of perjury, I certify that I have read the foregoing and that the facts stated in it are true.

FURTHER AFFIANT SAYETH NAUGHT.

____

PETER Z. JOHNSON, MD

The foregoing instrument was acknowledged before me this _________ day of _____ 20__ by ______________________, who is (personally known to me) (or who has produced) ____________________________ (as identification).

____

(Signature of Notary)

____

(Name of Notary Typed, Printed, or Stamped)

Understanding the Risks of Generic Affidavits in Medical Malpractice Cases

A Practical Guide for Legal Nurse Consultants and Medical Experts

Generic affidavits of merit are becoming increasingly common in medical malpractice litigation, especially in cases with multiple defendants. These affidavits typically use identical wording across different plaintiff experts, regardless of specialty or unique case facts. While templates and standardized formats can streamline the drafting process, the use of generic affidavits poses significant risks for legal nurse consultants (LNCs) and medical experts. This article explores two primary problems associated with generic affidavits, illustrates their consequences with examples and scenarios, and provides practical strategies for ensuring affidavit quality and expert credibility.

Problem 1: Lack of Independent Expert Opinion

A generic affidavit implies that each expert independently formulated the opinions and facts presented within the document. However, when multiple experts in a case—

such as an orthopedic surgeon, a vascular surgeon, an internal medicine hospitalist, and a cardiologist—sign affidavits containing identical language, it raises doubts about the authenticity and independence of their assessments.

For instance, imagine a malpractice case involving four physicians from different specialties. Each plaintiff expert submits a generic affidavit that outlines deviations in the standard of care for all defendants, using the same wording. Defense attorneys may argue that it is highly unlikely for four independent experts to arrive at identical conclusions and phrasing, undermining the credibility of the affidavits and potentially leading to their dismissal in court.

Implications: The perceived lack of independent analysis can damage the reliability of expert testimony, increase the risk of affidavits being challenged or discredited, and weaken the plaintiff's case overall.

Problem 2: Overstepping Specialty Boundaries

The second major problem arises when experts opine on matters outside their area of expertise due to generic affidavit wording. For example, if an orthopedic surgeon signs an affidavit critiquing the actions of a vascular surgeon, hospitalist, and cardiologist, this extends beyond the orthopedic surgeon's professional scope.

This issue is not limited to the specialties named above. Consider a hypothetical scenario where a pediatrician is asked to sign an affidavit addressing the actions of a neurosurgeon and an anesthesiologist. The pediatrician's lack of pertinent experience in those areas could be exploited by defense counsel, leading to the affidavit's exclusion or the expert's testimony being discounted.

Implications: Experts who opine outside their specialty risk having their testimony challenged for lack of qualifications, which can result in legal setbacks, exclusion of evidence, or damage to their professional reputation.

Case Study: The Impact of Affidavit Individualization

In a recent malpractice action, the plaintiff's legal team initially used generic affidavits for four experts. During pretrial hearings, defense counsel highlighted the identical wording and cross-specialty opinions, resulting in the affidavits being excluded and expert credibility questioned. The case stalled. Subsequently, the affidavits were revised: each expert's opinion was tailored to their specialty and reflected their unique assessment of the facts. The individualized affidavits were accepted, expert testimony was admitted, and the case proceeded, ultimately resulting in a favorable settlement for the plaintiff.

Practical Strategies for Legal Nurse Consultants and Experts

To avoid the pitfalls of generic affidavits, LNCs and medical experts should follow structured strategies:

- Use templates judiciously: While templates can standardize format, ensure that the core opinions and facts are customized to each expert's perspective and specialty.
- Document individualized expert opinions: Incorporate the exact phraseology used by experts during interviews or consultations.
- Verify tailored facts sections: Avoid duplicating case facts across affidavits; each should reflect the expert's own review and understanding of the case.
- Check for specialty boundaries: Confirm that the expert is only opining within their field of expertise. Do not include commentary on practices outside their specialty.
- Review before signing: Experts should carefully read the affidavit and ask questions such as:
  - Is this affidavit unique to my opinion and experience?
  - Does any section require me to comment on areas outside my specialty?
  - Are the facts presented based on my own review of the case?
  - Has this affidavit wording been used for other experts?
- Request revisions: If any part of the affidavit seems generic, or asks for opinions beyond the expert's scope, request modifications before signing.

Conclusion: Actionable Takeaways

Generic affidavits may seem like a time-saver, but they can undermine expert credibility and jeopardize medical malpractice cases. Legal nurse consultants and experts should prioritize individualized language, ensure opinions are within their specialty, and verify the accuracy of case facts. By following practical checklists and asking key questions, LNCs and medical experts can produce affidavits that withstand legal scrutiny and strengthen their professional reputation.

Four Key Reasons for Expert Disqualification in Medical Malpractice Cases

How Legal Nurse Consultants Can Protect Their Expert Status

Serving as an expert legal nurse consultant (LNC) in medical malpractice cases is a significant professional responsibility. Courts expect experts to meet specific qualifications, and failure to do so can result in disqualification, potentially impacting your ability to testify in the future. This article outlines four common reasons experts are disqualified, with practical examples, Q&A exchanges, and actionable advice to help you avoid these pitfalls.

1. Testifying Outside Your Scope of Expertise

Reason: Courts often disqualify experts who testify on matters outside their area of professional competence. Example Scenario: Imagine an office-based internist is asked to testify about the standard of care for anesthesiologists. Since anesthesiology is outside the internist's expertise, the court would likely disqualify this testimony.

Q&A Exchange:

Q: Are you qualified to speak on anesthesiology standards?

A: No, my experience is limited to internal medicine practices.

Prevention Tips:

- Review the case details carefully to ensure they align with your professional background.
- Understand your state's specific requirements for expert witness qualifications. Some states have highly structured criteria or residency requirements.
- Reference reliable summaries, such as SEAK's expert witness qualifications by state, before accepting a case.

2. Ignoring Relevant Testimony

Reason: Disregarding the testimony of other deponents or giving undue preference to written over oral evidence can lead to disqualification. Example Scenario: An LNC expert refused to consider nurses' oral testimony in a stroke case, claiming undocumented actions weren't performed. ("If it wasn't documented, it wasn't done.") However, the law values oral and written evidence equally.

Q&A Exchange – A better way to handle the nurses testimony:

Q: Do you have an opinion about the nurses' testimony?

A: Yes. The facts don't support some of their testimony.

Q: Are you calling the nurses liars?

A: Not at all. They documented their actions retroactively, and some activities weren't recorded as expected. The timeline in the documentation differs from their testimony, such as claiming the patient was resting at 3:00 a.m. when CT scan records show otherwise.

Prevention Tips:

- Always evaluate both written and oral testimony objectively and thoroughly.
- Address discrepancies respectfully, explaining your reasoning without dismissing witness credibility.
- Support your opinions with documented evidence and logical analysis.

3. Duty Conflict

Reason: If you have treated the plaintiff, you have a duty to the patient, which precludes testifying for the defense due to conflict of interest. Example Scenario: An LNC expert who previously cared for the plaintiff is asked to testify for the defense. This creates a conflict that the court will not permit.

Prevention Tips: Proactively identify and avoid conflicts of interest before accepting a case.

Actions for LNC Experts to Avoid Duty Conflicts:

- Review your professional history with all parties involved in the case.
- Ask the hiring attorney for a list of all plaintiffs and defendants.
- Check for prior treatment or consultation with any party in the case.
- Maintain a confidential record of all cases on which you have worked.
- Disclose any potential conflicts to the attorney before accepting the assignment.

4. Breach of Confidentiality

Reason: Working for both the plaintiff and defense on the same case violates confidentiality and will result in disqualification. Example Scenario: An expert inadvertently consults for both sides on a single case, risking exposure of confidential information and legal repercussions.

Q&A Exchange:

Q: Have you worked for both parties in this case?

A: Yes, but I was unaware they were on opposing sides.

Q: Are you aware this violates confidentiality?

A: I understand now and will ensure this does not happen again.

Prevention Tips:

- Keep a detailed list of all cases and associated hiring parties.
- Confirm the identity of the hiring party and their role in the case before agreeing to consult.

- Establish clear communication with attorneys regarding your current and previous engagements.

Conclusion: Best Practices for Maintaining Expert Eligibility

Legal nurse consultants play a vital role in medical malpractice litigation. To safeguard your expert status, always operate within your scope, evaluate all relevant evidence, vigilantly avoid conflicts of interest, and protect confidentiality. By following these best practices and remaining aware of state-specific requirements, you can minimize the risk of disqualification and maintain your professional reputation.

When an Expert's Not Qualified: Practical Guidance for LNCs

Understanding Legal Terms, Strategies, and Tools for LNCs

Expert witness qualifications are critical in medical malpractice cases. The credibility and experience of an expert can significantly affect the outcome of a trial, influencing how the jury perceives the testimony and, ultimately, the verdict. Legal nurse consultants (LNCs) play a vital role in evaluating expert credentials and ensuring compliance with federal and state requirements.

Legal Criteria for Expert Testimony

To testify in court, experts must meet specific criteria. Under the Federal Rules of Evidence, Rule 702, an expert must possess sufficient "knowledge, skill, experience, training, or education" to offer opinions. Many states set additional requirements, such as a mandate that the expert has practiced in the same specialty as the defendant within three to five years before the alleged malpractice, or that their experience includes clinical, consulting, or research work in the relevant field.

Many state statutes are strict, requiring expert witnesses to demonstrate recent, relevant experience in the same specialty. As an LNC, reviewing the CVs of opposing experts is a key responsibility to ensure they meet these statutory qualifications.

Three Attorney Strategies: Legal Definitions and Detailed Examples

1. Pre-Trial: Filing a Motion in Limine. A motion in limine is a formal request submitted to the court before the trial begins, asking the judge to exclude specific evidence—in this context, the testimony of an unqualified expert—from being

presented to the jury. If an LNC identifies deficiencies in an expert's credentials, the attorney may file a motion in limine, presenting evidence to the court about why the expert should not be allowed to testify. For instance, a defense attorney might file such a motion to exclude the plaintiff's surgery expert who lacks recent practice in the field.

2. During Trial: Strategic Non-Challenge and Highlighting Deficiencies. Sometimes, instead of immediately contesting an expert's qualifications, the attorney chooses not to challenge them directly. Instead, during cross-examination, the attorney highlights the expert's weaknesses. In closing arguments, the attorney contrasts these deficiencies with the strong credentials of the defense experts. For example, in a fractured hip case, suppose the plaintiff's expert is a general surgeon who completed an orthopedic residency 30 years ago but hasn't practiced orthopedic surgery since. During trial, the defense attorney brings out this lack of recent experience. In closing, the attorney emphasizes that the defense expert has spent the past 30 years actively practicing orthopedic surgery in a leading medical center. This contrast can strongly influence the jury's perception, leading them to view the plaintiff's expert as less credible or even as a "hired gun," potentially swaying the verdict in favor of the defense.
3. Post-Trial: Filing an Appeal. An appeal is a legal process where the losing party asks a higher court to review the trial court's decision. If the verdict was influenced by the testimony of an unqualified expert, the losing side can argue that the expert should not have been allowed to testify. For example, an appellate court may overturn a verdict if it finds that a defendant's nursing expert did not meet the required standards, such as not practicing in the same field or lacking the necessary skill level.

Role of Legal Nurse Consultants: Practical, Step-by-Step Guidance

Legal nurse consultants are essential in the expert review process. Here are actionable steps to follow:

1. Understand Relevant Statutes: Familiarize yourself with both federal and state laws governing expert qualifications. Summarize key statutes that outline specific requirements for expert witnesses in your jurisdiction.
2. Review Expert CVs Systematically: Use a checklist to evaluate whether opposing experts meet necessary criteria, such as recent practice in the specialty, appropriate licensure, and relevant education or training.
3. Document Findings: Clearly note any discrepancies or deficiencies in the expert's qualifications.

4. Communicate Effectively: Report your findings to the attorney promptly, providing detailed explanations and supporting documentation.
5. Prepare for Court Proceedings: Be ready to assist attorney with facts to draft motions.

Tools for LNCs: Checklists

- Expert Qualification Checklist:
- Has the expert practiced in the relevant specialty within the required time frame (e.g., last three to five years)?
- Does the expert have clinical, consulting, or research experience in the field?
- Is the expert currently licensed and certified?
- Does the expert's CV reflect compliance with state and federal statutes?

Conclusion: The Value of Thorough Review and Communication

Ensuring that expert witnesses meet all legal qualifications is crucial for the integrity of medical malpractice cases. Legal nurse consultants provide indispensable support to attorneys by conducting careful reviews, documenting findings, and communicating effectively. By using practical tools like checklists, LNCs can help safeguard the legal process and contribute to successful case outcomes.

What Makes an Expert Witness Truly "Magical"?

Lessons from the Field on Honesty, Insight, and Impact

Over the years, I've had the chance to work with hundreds of expert witnesses. Every so often, I encounter someone who seems to have almost magical powers—experts who can rescue a case teetering on the edge of disaster, much like a magician pulling a rabbit out of a hat. But what exactly do these "magical experts" do that sets them apart, and what can we learn from them?

Honesty and Factual Reporting: The Foundation of Credibility

First and foremost, magical experts are always honest and grounded in the facts. They don't shy away from sharing a complete summary of their findings, even when those findings include negative or inconvenient details. This approach stands in stark contrast to so-called "hired guns"—experts who will support an attorney's theory regardless of how far-fetched it appears.

This commitment to honesty is powerful because it builds credibility with judges, juries, and attorneys. When experts are transparent about both strengths and weaknesses in a case, their opinions carry more weight. In my experience, it's this integrity that lays the groundwork for true "magic."

Expert Insight and Nuance: Making Complexities Understandable

But magical experts don't stop at just reporting the facts. They use their knowledge to untangle complex issues and explain subtle details. Let me share an example: I once worked on a case involving a young woman who immigrated from Venezuela.

Two years after arriving in the U.S., she suffered several strokes, leaving her with movement and speech difficulties. The plaintiff's attorney brought in a neuropsychology expert who ran standard tests and concluded the woman was mentally impaired because of her strokes.

However, the defense's neuropsychology expert took a deeper look. He explained that these tests—while commonly used—may not be reliable or valid for someone with a different cultural or linguistic background. In other words, when tests are translated into another language, or used with someone whose education and life experiences differ from the norm, the results can be misleading. The "norms" the tests rely on might not apply, and the conclusions could be off base.

What made this magical expert effective was his ability to bridge the technical gap. He didn't just challenge the results; he educated everyone involved about why the testing process itself might be flawed for this patient. This kind of insight helps the legal team—and ultimately the court—understand the real issues, not just the surface-level findings.

Deep Knowledge: Clarifying Medical Details with Accessible Explanations

Another hallmark of magical experts is their deep understanding of medical literature and standards of care, which they can explain in plain language. Consider a case I worked on involving inflammatory breast cancer (IBC). For context, cancer "staging" is a way doctors describe how far cancer has spread. In IBC, all cases start at Stage IIIB because the cancer has reached the skin of the breast. Stage IIIC means it's spread to lymph nodes near the collarbone or inside the chest, and Stage IV means it has moved even further, to lymph nodes or organs farther away.

In this case, a surgical oncology nurse expert noticed that the plaintiff's cancer might have been incorrectly classified as Stage IV based on a PET scan showing activity in lymph nodes. The expert explained that proper staging at the time required a biopsy—

a small tissue sample—from the lymph nodes, not just the breast. If those lymph node biopsies had been negative, the patient's stage and treatment plan could have been entirely different, possibly affecting her outcome.

This expert's effectiveness came from making medical jargon understandable, highlighting how a single detail in the diagnostic process could change the entire course of a case. By translating complex protocols into clear explanations, the expert empowered everyone to grasp what was truly at stake.

Leveraging Professional Networks: Knowing the Players

Sometimes, magical experts seem to "work their magic" by knowing the experts on the other side. They might share insights about an opposing expert's reputation, work history, or patterns—such as whether an expert mainly testified for one law firm. These details can be invaluable when preparing for depositions, helping attorneys focus their research and questions more effectively.

The lesson here is that expertise isn't just about knowledge; it's also about relationships and awareness. Knowing the people involved adds another layer of strategy that can influence the direction of a case.

Resourcefulness: Sharing the Tools for Success

Finally, magical experts are generous with their resources. They regularly provide attorneys with relevant journal articles, guidelines, and literature that support their opinions. Some even go the extra mile by suggesting deposition questions for the opposing side's experts.

This willingness to share not only strengthens the legal team's case but also demonstrates true partnership. The best experts don't just answer questions—they equip their colleagues for success.

Conclusion: The Lasting Impact of Magical Experts

In summary, what makes an expert witness truly "magical" isn't supernatural—it's a combination of honesty, clear communication, deep knowledge, professional savvy, and resourcefulness. These experts transform complicated cases by making information accessible, offering strategic insights, and supporting their teams every step of the way. For legal professionals and general readers alike, the lessons from these magical experts are clear: value integrity, seek understanding, and always be willing to learn from those who make the difficult seem effortless.

Why are Some Experts Popular?

And Why It Can Cause an Unusual Problem

Are you a popular expert? If you have as much expert work as you want, that can be a good thing. However, being a popular expert might also cause an unusual problem for you. Here's the problem and how one expert fixed it.

In my experience, experts tend to become popular for two main reasons: 1) they're able to help attorneys craft a plausible theory of the case, and 2) they excel at explaining medical complexities in simple terms to juries. These qualities, while valuable to attorneys, can create a unique challenge for sought-after experts.

One issue is that attorneys may hire you not because they intend to use your services, but to prevent the opposing side from doing so—a tactic known as "tying the expert up." This means the expert is retained specifically to keep them unavailable to the other party. A retainer is an upfront payment that secures an expert's services for a case, whether or not the expert is ultimately called to testify.

For example, I know an expert who was very popular as a defense expert. He was a big, imposing, movie-star-handsome decorated veteran, and his reputation for presenting opinions clearly made him highly sought after. Plaintiff attorneys began hiring him, sending just a few pages of records and a small retainer check (typically $250 to $500), with no intention of ever calling him to testify. They considered the small investment worthwhile if it kept him off the defense's side.

Over time, the expert realized that being frequently hired but rarely called to testify was affecting both his professional reputation and his income stability. Instead of being recognized for his expertise, he was often sidelined, prompting him to rethink his fee structure and approach.

He responded by updating his fee agreement: he raised his retainer to a nonrefundable $10,000 and clarified in his fee schedule that until the retainer and records were received, he remained "free on the case." In other words, if another attorney contacted him and promptly sent a retainer and records, he would work for that attorney.

Is this expert still popular? Yes, he is, though he now primarily works for defense attorneys. Plaintiff attorneys usually aren't willing to pay the substantial non-refundable retainer unless the case has the potential for a large jury award.

Why I Stopped Using Some Experts

Key Lessons for Legal Professionals

Over the years, I've collaborated with many experts who were intelligent, knowledgeable, and helpful. Even so, there are compelling reasons why I no longer recommend certain experts for future cases. Below, I outline the main factors that have led me to discontinue working relationships, summarize each lesson, and share best practices for fostering positive expert partnerships.

1. Lack of Availability

Some experts are difficult to reach during normal business hours. While prioritizing patients is admirable, once an expert agrees to consult for a law firm, the firm becomes their client for the duration of the case. Inconsistent availability—such as limiting calls to narrow windows on weekends—makes effective communication impossible and disrupts case management. Key takeaway: Reliable availability during standard working hours is essential for timely collaboration. Best practice: Choose experts who set aside time for legal consultations and are responsive to the needs of the case. Clear communication expectations should be established up front, ensuring both parties can connect when needed. Experts who value accessibility contribute to stronger professional relationships and better outcomes.

2. Excessive Gatekeeping and Communication Barriers

Collaborating with experts who are overly shielded by staff can create unnecessary barriers. For instance, when a secretary filters all messages, important information may be delayed or lost. If an expert is not directly reachable, collaboration suffers. Key takeaway: Direct and open lines of communication are crucial for successful teamwork. Best practice: Engage experts who maintain straightforward communication channels. Direct access allows for prompt exchange of information, fostering trust and efficiency between the expert and legal team.

3. Unreasonable Payment Practices

Some experts require upfront payment for each subsequent record review, which deviates from standard practices. For example, unreasonable experts may require additional retainers for the same case for records sent on three different occasions. Typically, experts bill after completing their review or request a single retainer at the outset, rather than requiring separate advance payments for each new set of records. While retainers and invoices after services are appropriate, demanding advance payments for every new document undermines trust and complicates the financial relationship. Frequent advance payment requests can create uncertainty about costs and lead to administrative burdens, making it harder for both parties to plan and collaborate effectively. Key takeaway: Transparent, fair billing practices are necessary for professional integrity. Best practice: Work with experts who clearly outline their fee structures and adhere to industry norms. Consistent, reasonable payment terms foster mutual respect and simplify case administration.

4. Attitude and Professionalism

An expert's knowledge should be matched by professionalism and respect. Arrogance or elitism—such as refusing to communicate with non-attorney staff—can alienate the legal team and even negatively affect courtroom perception. Key takeaway: Humility and collaborative spirit are as important as expertise. Best practice: Select experts who treat all team members with respect and engage constructively in case discussions. Positive attitudes and collegiality strengthen relationships, enhance credibility, and ensure a smooth working process.

In conclusion, effective expert relationships are built on accessibility, open communication, fair business practices, and mutual respect. Legal professionals should seek experts who exemplify these qualities, as they are key to achieving successful outcomes and maintaining a productive, professional environment.

Chapter 11: Depositions

This chapter serves as a comprehensive guide for nursing staff and legal nurse consultants navigating the complexities of deposition preparation and testimony. Whether you're preparing to give a deposition, assisting colleagues, or supporting legal teams, this chapter addresses the most critical aspects of effective deposition practice. Beginning with practical strategies for preparing nursing staff, it examines the importance of using precise, non-absolute language and introduces the APE deposition technique to help witnesses remain composed and accurate. You'll also find guidance on preparing for video depositions, which require special considerations for professionalism and presentation.

To further support your success, this chapter provides an expert deposition preparation checklist and explains how to coordinate and manage scheduling, ensuring that all parties are ready for testimony. It highlights the risks and consequences of being unprepared, underscoring the need for thorough preparation. In addition, you'll learn about the value of maintaining deposition data banks for reference and ongoing education, as well as the differences between page/line and narrative deposition summaries—tools that streamline review and analysis.

With practical tips and best practices throughout, this chapter equips you with the knowledge and resources needed to approach depositions with confidence, integrity, and professionalism.

Just the Facts – Deposition Preparation for Nursing Staff

Effective Strategies and Sample Responses for Navigating Uncertainty

Quick! Tell me the year you got your nursing degree.

If you're like many nurses during their depositions, you might not remember the exact date you graduated or the specific year you received your certification—and that's completely understandable. If you find yourself uncertain about these details, it's okay to acknowledge that you do not recall. When this happens, remain calm and answer honestly. For example, you might say: "I do not recall the exact date at this time, but I can provide it after reviewing my records." This approach helps demonstrate your integrity and professionalism while ensuring your responses are accurate.

That's just one of the common queries that nurses flub during their depositions. As a legal nurse consultant who works for the Plaintiff, you may write deposition questions for nursing staff and other fact witnesses. If you work as an LNC for the Defense, you may help prepare nursing staff for their upcoming depositions. If you're an expert LNC, you'll also be questioned about this type of information.

Let's look at some factual questions likely to be asked during a nursing deposition for medical malpractice, nursing home, and other cases. To make preparation easier, the questions are grouped by topic so you can focus on one area at a time. For each section, I'll highlight some common stumbling blocks nurses encounter, along with tips or brief anecdotes on how to address them.

Personal Information

- What is your full name? What former names (such as maiden or name from previous marriage) have you used?
- What is your address? Former addresses? How long have you lived at each address?
- What is your Social Security number? Tip: Deponents can ask to respond to this question off the record so that the information isn't in a court document.
- What is your marital status? How many marriages have you had? What are the dates of your marriage?
- Common challenge: Many nurses do not remember the exact date(s) they were married. If unsure, you can say, "I do not recall the date at this time but can provide it after checking my records."

Education and Licensure

- What is your educational background? What year did you graduate? What degrees have you earned? What is the location of the schools?
- In my experience, many nurses are unable to provide their graduation date during their depositions. One nurse I worked with successfully prepared by bringing a summary of her education timeline, which helped her respond confidently. However, the summary should be shown to your attorney prior to the deposition because all information brought to your deposition is discoverable. If you aren't sure of the answer, you might say, "I do not recall the exact year at this time, but I can confirm it after reviewing my transcripts."
- Are you licensed or certified? (RN, LPN / LVN, CNA, etc.)
- What is the year of initial and renewal licensure/certification? How many times did you take the exam before you passed? In what states are you licensed/certified?

- Challenge: Nurses often forget renewal years or exam attempts. Preparing a brief written list ahead of time (if permitted by your attorney) can help. Remember: any notes you bring may be copied for the opposing side as an exhibit.

Employment History

- What is your current and past employment status? What are the names of employers? What are the dates of your employment?
- It's common to struggle recalling exact dates or employer details. One nurse overcame this by reviewing her resume and employment records before the deposition. If you need time to check records, say, "I do not recall the exact dates at this moment, but can provide them after reviewing my records."
- What is the title of your current position? What is the title of past positions? What are the responsibilities of each position?
- To whom do you report? Who reports to you?
- What types of patients do you work with now? What types of patients did you work with in past positions?

Why are nurses unable to respond to some of these questions? It's usually because they are nervous and unprepared. If you're an LNC working for the Defense, check with the attorney to see if he or she wants the nurse to write a brief list of answers to the above questions for use at the deposition. But recognize that any pieces of paper brought to the deposition by the nurse will be copied and supplied to the opposing side as an exhibit.

Be sure to ask nursing staff to answer all of these questions at pre-deposition conferences and be prepared to have more than one pre-deposition conference if the attorney agrees. Anticipating these common challenges and practicing your responses—even if you need to say, "I do not recall, but I can provide the information after reviewing my records"—can help normalize the experience and reduce anxiety.

Of course, these factual questions cover only demographic information. Deponents will also be asked about their role in the events leading to the allegation of medical malpractice.

Effective Depositions: Avoiding Absolutes in Healthcare Testimony

Guidance for Healthcare Professionals and Legal Consultants

Imagine being asked in court why you made a particular clinical decision—could your choice of words affect the outcome? The words healthcare professionals choose during depositions can shape how attorneys, juries, and judges perceive their actions. Simple language choices may unintentionally suggest negligence, even when care was appropriate. Absolutes refer to statements that leave no room for exceptions, while clinical judgment involves the thoughtful decision-making process healthcare professionals use in patient care. This article provides practical strategies for avoiding absolutes and communicating clinical judgment clearly in legal settings. Although the examples use staff nurses, this information also applies to LNC experts.

Avoiding Absolutes: Understanding the Risks

Absolutes are words like "never" or "always" that suggest an unwavering approach, such as, "I always give patients their medication on time." While this may sound reassuring, it can create problems if a situation arises where the statement is not true. For example, if a patient were in Radiology during their scheduled medication time, the nurse could not administer medication as usual. When witnesses answer deposition questions using absolutes, they commit themselves to a standard that may not fit every scenario, increasing the risk of appearing negligent if exceptions arise.

Attorneys for the opposing side often capitalize on absolute statements to challenge witnesses. If subsequent testimony deviates from the original absolute, it can imply negligence. For instance, if a nurse testifies that medications are "always" given on time, but documentation shows otherwise due to a patient being in Radiology, the nurse may appear negligent even if their actions were appropriate.

Nurses and other healthcare professionals are especially prone to using absolutes, often due to training that emphasizes strict adherence to procedures and documentation. However, clinical judgment requires flexibility and context-based decisions, making absolute statements inappropriate for many situations.

Summary: Using absolutes in depositions can inadvertently signal negligence and undermine the demonstration of professional judgment.

Alternative Phrases to Absolutes: Practical Examples

To avoid the pitfalls of absolutes, use language that reflects real-world variability and clinical reasoning. Here are expanded examples and a quick-reference bullet list:

- For the most part... – "For the most part, I administer medication within a half-hour before or after the time listed on the MAR."
- It depends on the circumstances... – "It depends on the circumstances when I give patient medications. For example, I administered meds after the patient returned from Radiology."
- My normal practice is... – "My normal practice is to give medications at the scheduled time or shortly before or after, but that isn't a strict rule."
- My routine is... – "My routine is to administer medications at the time listed on the MAR, unless special circumstances arise."
- What I usually do is... – "What I usually do is give patients their medications on time, but there are exceptions."
- Generally... – "Generally, I follow the procedure manual, but I apply clinical judgment as situations require."
- Typically... – "Typically, I consult with the attending physician if a patient's condition changes."

Summary: Using alternative phrases to absolutes allows witnesses to communicate their standard practices while acknowledging exceptions and professional judgment.

Context-Specific Examples: Beyond Nursing

The impact of deposition language choices applies to all healthcare professionals and a variety of legal cases. Consider these scenarios:

- Pharmacist: "My usual practice is to verify all medication doses, but in emergency situations, I may rely on verbal orders from physicians to expedite care."
- Physical Therapist: "Typically, I follow the prescribed therapy schedule, although I may adjust sessions if the patient experiences pain or fatigue."
- Respiratory Therapist in a negligence case: "For the most part, I check ventilator settings every hour, but in critical events, I prioritize immediate patient needs."
- Physician in a malpractice suit: "It depends on the circumstances when ordering diagnostic tests; sometimes I expedite tests based on emergent symptoms."

Summary: Context-specific examples show how healthcare professionals across disciplines can use flexible language to reflect clinical realities and reduce the risk of appearing negligent.

Answering "Yes" or "No": Risks and Recommended Approaches

One-word answers like "Yes" or "No" are also absolutes. While some attorneys advise clients to answer deposition questions succinctly, limiting responses to "Yes" or "No" can create misleading impressions. Consider these sample questions and answers:

Sample Q&A: The Risks of Absolutes

Attorney: Did Mr. Johnson develop a decubitus?

Nurse: Yes. I guess he wasn't turned often enough.

Here, the nurse's answer not only confirms the allegation but also suggests negligence. A simple "Yes" would have sufficed, but even that may need context.

Attorney: Does the hospital have a policy prohibiting diapering adult patients?

Nurse: Yes.

Attorney: Did you put a diaper on Mr. Johnson, even though the policy prohibits it?

Nurse: Yes.

Attorney: Did Mr. Johnson develop a decubitus on his back?

Nurse: Yes.

In this series, the nurse's "Yes" answers make it seem as if policy was violated and harm resulted, implying negligence.

Sample Q&A: Contextual Responses Reduce Perceived Negligence

Attorney: Did you put a diaper on Mr. Johnson, even though the policy prohibits it?

Nurse: Well, I put a diaper on Mr. Johnson at his and his wife's request. He wears diapers at home. I explained the policy, but they insisted. I checked his skin—there was no breakdown—and consulted with the nursing supervisor and physician. We felt it was in his best interest to continue as at home.

Attorney: Did Mr. Johnson develop a decubitus on his back?

Nurse: Yes, but the decubitus was on his upper back, not where the diaper was placed.

Here, the nurse's detailed, context-rich answers show thoughtful judgment and collaboration, shifting perception away from negligence.

Summary: Limiting responses to "Yes" or "No" can unintentionally suggest negligence; providing relevant context helps show sound judgment and adherence to best practices.

Key Takeaways and Practical Advice

- Absolutes like "always," "never," "yes," and "no" can commit witnesses to statements that may not reflect the complexity of clinical care.
- Alternative phrases allow healthcare professionals to acknowledge variability and use clinical judgment.
- Context-specific examples from various healthcare roles demonstrate broader applicability of these strategies in legal settings.
- Adding context to answers, especially beyond "Yes" or "No," helps clarify reasoning and reduces perceptions of negligence.
- Legal nurse consultants and healthcare professionals should reinforce these approaches when preparing for depositions, ensuring testimony accurately reflects reality and professionalism.

By understanding the impact of language in depositions and applying these practical strategies, healthcare professionals and legal consultants can protect both patient care and professional reputations.

Nursing and Expert Depositions

Th*e APE Deposition Technique*

The APE technique is a method used by deponents to tell their stories and to interrupt the flow of questions from the deposing attorney. It's a very effective technique for parties and experts in medical malpractice lawsuits who are being deposed by the attorney of the opposing party. Let me tell you what the APE technique is and why it's so effective. Spoiler alert. It's not about primates!

APE is an acronym that stands for Acknowledge, Pivot, Explain. The deponent acknowledges the opposing attorney's question by answering "Yes" or "No". Examples of Acknowledge include the following:

- Attorney - Are you a registered nurse?
- Deponent - Yes.
- Attorney - Are you licensed in the state of Florida?
- Deponent - Yes.
- Attorney - Were you employed by Madison Memorial Hospital on April 27, 2025?

- Deponent - Yes.
- Attorney - Were you assigned to care for the plaintiff, James Clarke, that evening?
- Deponent - Yes.

The opposing attorney has a rhythm going where he asks questions and the deponent (the nurse) answers with one word. The attorney wants the nurse to continue to answer "Yes" or "No" because it will make the nurse look negligent. If the nurse continued to only acknowledge the attorney's questions, that's exactly what will happen.

- Attorney - And Mr. Clarke's blood pressure was 102/48 at 9 p.m., correct?
- Deponent - Yes.
- Attorney - And you didn't notify the physician of this blood pressure reading?
- Deponent - No.
- Attorney - Mr. Clarke had a cardiopulmonary arrest during your shift, correct?
- Deponent - Yes.

By not notifying the physician of the patient's low blood pressure, the attorney is making the nurse look negligent. The attorney is also implying that the patient wouldn't have had a cardiopulmonary arrest if the nurse had notified the physician about the low blood pressure. Let's look what happens when the nurse acknowledges the question but pivots and takes control of the line of questioning. By doing this, the nurse explains her actions after acknowledging the attorney's last two questions.

- Attorney - And did you notify the physician?
- Deponent - No, not then. The rest of Mr. Clarke's vital signs were within normal limits. I don't notify physicians about random changes in vital signs. I look at the patient's entire clinical picture. His other vital signs were stable. I took his blood pressure again twenty minutes later, and his BP was 112/72, his pulse was 80, and his respirations were sixteen. He was hemodynamically stable.
- Attorney - Mr. Clarke had a cardiopulmonary arrest during your shift, correct?
- Deponent - Yes. Mr. Clark was stable until nearly the end of my shift. Then he decompensated over a period of about a minute and had a cardiopulmonary arrest. I immediately called a Code Blue, and one of the other nurses notified his doctor about the Code.

The nurse not only fully explained the evening's circumstances but likely threw the opposing attorney off his rhythm. For example, the attorney's question about the cardiopulmonary arrest no longer seems like it's in the correct sequence. A more logical question would have been to question the nurse about the meaning of hemodynamically stable.

Many deponents stop at acknowledging attorneys' questions. However, by pivoting and explaining, deponents can tell their stories and show that there was no negligence.

By pivoting and then explaining, the nurse not only clarifies the situation but also disrupts the attorney's rhythm and narrative. This approach gives the deponent the opportunity to fully explain the circumstances, providing a more accurate and fair account of their actions.

In summary, the APE technique empowers deponents to answer honestly while also sharing important context. By acknowledging, pivoting, and explaining, they can ensure their side of the story is heard and reduce the risk of being misrepresented.

Navigating Deposition Challenges

During a recent deposition—a formal legal proceeding where witnesses answer questions under oath—an attorney I worked with grew frustrated when a hospital nurse struggled to locate information in the printed version of electronic medical records. While her entries were marked, she couldn't easily find them on paper, as she was accustomed to digital recordkeeping. This confusion is common: printed electronic records often appear disorganized and repetitive, making quick reference difficult.

Understanding the Technical Hurdles

The attorney didn't assist the nurse during questioning, citing two reasons: he found the records hard to navigate himself, and helping could be seen as "coaching," which is not allowed in depositions. To streamline future depositions, I aimed to create a table of contents (TOC) for the medical chart.

A TOC in digital files typically uses PDF bookmarks, which are clickable links that help users jump to specific sections. These bookmarks can be exported and printed for easy navigation. However, the electronic medical records had been processed by an external company, whose embedded metadata—hidden information that organizes digital files—caused technical issues when exporting the bookmarks to Microsoft Word. Despite searching for solutions and testing several methods, the bookmarks didn't transfer properly.

Manual Problem-Solving and Persistence

When technology fell short, I resorted to a manual solution. Using a free template, I created a clear and organized table of contents by hand, listing each chart section and its page number. I also listed the pages that the nurse documented on. This approach, though time-consuming, ensured nurses and attorneys could quickly reference important information during depositions.

Reflection: Lessons in Adaptability

This experience reinforced the value of persistence and adaptability. While technology offers many shortcuts, it's crucial to have backup strategies and not hesitate to use traditional methods when needed. The manual table of contents now serves as a practical tool, and I encourage others facing similar challenges to consider both digital and hands-on solutions.

Final Table of Contents: SELDON HOSPITAL CHART (11/09/2025 – 11/12/2025)

CHART SECTION	PAGE
Admission Overview, Demographics	2
ED (11/09/2025)	5
Discharge Summary	17
Nursing Notes (Narrative)	52
Nurse Hamilton	54, 56, 58, 60, 61, 63, 136, 138, 154-156, 187-226
Nutrition Notes	68
Case Management / Social Work Notes	73
Orders and Results	80
Meds and Administration	136
Flowsheets Vital Signs, Assessments, etc.)	152, 154-156, 166-239
Respiratory Therapy	253
Scans (Wound Care Photos, EKGs, Misc)	295
ED (11/12/2025)	324

Comprehensive Guide to Preparing for Video Depositions

Best Practices for Legal Nurse Consultants and Attorneys

Preparing for a video deposition requires a higher level of attention and preparation than a traditional deposition. The primary reason is that video depositions become the jury's only opportunity to assess a witness's credibility, demeanor, and professionalism. Every action, tone, and appearance is recorded and later scrutinized, making it essential for both legal nurse consultants and attorneys to ensure that deponents, including experts, are thoroughly and effectively prepared for this unique setting.

Appearance: Presenting a Professional Image

- Attire: Choose professional, neutral-colored clothing that projects confidence and respect. Avoid bold patterns, stripes, or overly bright colors, as these can be distracting on camera. For example, a solid-colored blazer or jacket over a pressed shirt or blouse is usually appropriate. Consider clothing that reflects your role in the case—healthcare professionals might opt for clean, well-maintained scrubs or a lab coat, if that aligns with the image your legal team wants to convey. The key is to look polished, trustworthy, and appropriate for the situation, without relying on gender-specific expectations.
- Jewelry and Accessories: Keep jewelry minimal and quiet. Noisy or distracting pieces, such as charm bracelets or large earrings, can become a focal point on video. For example, a simple watch or stud earrings are preferable to statement pieces that could draw attention away from your testimony.
- Makeup and Grooming: If you choose to wear makeup, opt for a natural look that reduces shine without appearing overly done. Avoid heavy or dramatic styles, which can look exaggerated on camera. Ensure hair is neat and out of your face to avoid fidgeting or distractions.

In a video deposition, every movement and expression is recorded and scrutinized, making it crucial to maintain a composed and professional demeanor throughout. Distracting behaviors may cause the jury or attorneys to question your credibility or attentiveness, potentially affecting the outcome of your deposition. For example, if you fidget or seem disengaged, viewers may perceive you as less trustworthy or insufficiently prepared. Think of the Zoom meetings that you have attended where participants squirmed or fiddled with their hair; it most likely was very distracting!

Hand Placement: Rest your hands, lightly folded, on the table in front of you. This not only keeps your hands visible and avoids any suggestion of secretive behavior but also discourages nervous gestures such as fidgeting with jewelry or papers. For instance, absent-mindedly twisting a ring or tapping a pen can make you appear anxious or distracted. If you feel nervous, try taking a slow breath and refocusing your hands on the table to regain composure.

Posture and Stillness: Sit upright with both feet on the floor, maintaining a calm, steady posture. Avoid rocking your chair, shifting side-to-side, or making repetitive movements, as these can be distracting and may be interpreted as signs of discomfort or nervousness. If you notice yourself moving excessively, pause, adjust your posture, and remain still to project confidence.

Eye Contact: When answering questions, look directly at the camera rather than at the attorney or an off-screen person. This simulates eye contact with the jury and reflects honesty and engagement. For example, if you are asked a question, pause, gather your thoughts, and then address your answer toward the camera lens. If you accidentally look away, simply redirect your gaze back to the camera and continue calmly.

Facial Expressions: Maintain a neutral, approachable expression throughout the deposition. Avoid exaggerated reactions such as eye rolling, frowning, heavy sighs, or smirking—even if provoked by challenging questions. For example, if you disagree with a statement, remain composed rather than displaying surprise or disbelief. A slight, polite smile or attentive look can help project reliability and poise. If you catch yourself reacting strongly, take a moment to reset your expression before proceeding.

Device Etiquette: Turn off all electronic devices before the deposition begins. Refrain from checking your watch or glancing at your phone, as these actions may appear disrespectful or suggest you are preoccupied. If you accidentally interact with a device, apologize briefly and refocus on the deposition without drawing further attention to the incident.

Practice and Preparation: Ensuring Readiness

- Multiple Practice Sessions: Effective preparation often requires several rehearsal sessions. Use these opportunities to practice answering questions on camera, review appearance, and behavior, and address any areas for improvement.
- Videotaping Practice: Record practice sessions and review the footage with your legal team or consultant. Watching yourself on camera can help identify distracting habits, improve delivery, and build confidence.
- Consultant's Role: As a legal nurse consultant, you are essential to guiding the deponent through this process—offering constructive feedback, reinforcing best practices, and supporting the deponent in presenting their most credible and professional self.

Conclusion: Reinforcing Best Practices for Success

Thorough preparation for video depositions can significantly impact how the jury perceives deponents. By focusing on appearance, behavior, and rigorous practice, legal nurse consultants and attorneys can ensure their clients make a strong, trustworthy impression. Consistency and attention to detail are key to success in this high-stakes environment.

Expert Witness Deposition Preparation Checklist

Essential Documents, Definitions, and Practical Guidance for Deposition Success

Preparing thoroughly for your deposition as an expert witness is vital to presenting your qualifications and opinions clearly. The following checklist outlines what to bring, defines key legal terms, and explains the purpose of each item, ensuring you are fully equipped and confident for your deposition.

Checklist: What to Bring and Why

- Your entire file relating to the case: Gather all materials you have reviewed or produced. These documents may be referenced during questioning to support your opinions.
- All email, fax, memos, and other correspondence relating to the case: These communications can provide context for your involvement and may be requested to clarify your understanding or actions.
- Your CV (several copies): Your CV establishes your qualifications and may be referenced during questioning to confirm your expertise and experience.
- A copy of your retainer agreement: A retainer agreement is the contract outlining your engagement as an expert witness. This document clarifies your role, responsibilities, and compensation terms.
- All invoices and time records kept for the case: These documents may be requested to verify your involvement and compensation for your expert services.
- A list of all medical records sent to you by your attorney: Having a list ensures you can quickly reference what information you have reviewed. Your attorney may ask you to bring hard copies of specific records for discussion.
- A list of all depositions sent to you by your attorney: This list helps track prior testimony you have reviewed. Your attorney may request hard copies of certain depositions for reference.

- Any written reports that you have produced to your attorney: These reports document your findings and opinions. Bring copies to clarify any points or answer questions about your conclusions.
- If you are an author, a copy of all articles published in professional literature for the last several years (if relevant to the case): These publications may be used to assess your credibility or the basis of your opinions. If you have authored many articles, a list is acceptable.
- If you are an educator, a copy of all syllabi you have taught from in the last several years: Syllabi can demonstrate your teaching experience and subject matter expertise.
- A list or copy of the cover of any professional periodicals which you regularly receive: This shows your ongoing involvement in your field and awareness of current developments.
- Copies of any publications you believe are authoritative: These materials can support your opinions and may be referenced to justify your conclusions. Note: Check with your attorney about authoritative journals. They open the door for the opposing side to find information in those authoritative journals that contradict your opinion.

Pre-Deposition Conference: Definition and Preparation

A pre-depo conference is a meeting with your attorney before the deposition to review your materials and discuss case strategy. This session ensures you and your attorney are aligned on key issues and prepared for the types of questions you may face.

- Gather all the documents listed above, but do not provide them to the opposing side until your attorney has reviewed and approved each item.
- If your attorney does not initiate a pre-depo conference, request one. This can be conducted by phone, in person, or both.
- Before the conference, carefully review all relevant medical records, depositions, and other case materials.
- Ask your attorney if any case issues have changed and what hypothetical questions you should anticipate.

Final Preparation and Additional Tips

- Confirm with your attorney what you should bring to the deposition and clarify any last-minute questions.
- In many states, the plaintiff pays for your time during the deposition itself. Your attorney is typically responsible for covering your preparation time, including reviewing records and attending pre-deposition conferences.

- Stay organized and maintain clear records to facilitate effective testimony and communication with your legal team.

By following this checklist and understanding the purpose behind each item, you can approach your deposition with confidence and professionalism.

Understanding the Testimony Process: A Guide for New LNCs

Clarifying Payments and Procedures for Depositions and Trial Testimony

Welcome! If you're a new legal nurse consultant aiming to serve as an expert witness, you might have questions about how the testimony process works. This guide breaks down the key steps, clarifies payment distinctions, and offers practical tips—so you can feel confident and prepared as you begin your journey. For clarity, this explanation assumes you are engaged as an expert on behalf of the plaintiff in the matter. The procedures would be reversed if you were retained by the defense.

Where: Locations for Depositions and Trial Testimony

- Deposition Location: You'll usually be deposed in a convenient location near your home—this could be your office, the plaintiff attorney's office, a court reporter's office, or a rented conference room in your city.
- Trial Testimony Location: For county cases, you'll testify in the county where the case was filed, typically in a courtroom. Sometimes, the court may designate another area, such as a conference room, for testimony.

Who: Payment Details and Clarifying Examples

Payment for Trial Testimony: You are not paid to testify for the outcome of the case. Instead, you are compensated for your time and related expenses, such as travel and lodging, while you testify at trial. For example, if your testimony lasts two hours, you'll be paid your hourly rate plus any out-of-pocket expenses, regardless of which side wins the case.

Payment for Deposition Testimony: The attorney who schedules and conducts your deposition (usually the defense attorney if you're working for the plaintiff) pays you for your time spent in deposition. For instance, if the deposition is scheduled for three hours, you can request payment for those hours up front or at the time of the deposition.

While you are compensated for your time and expenses related to both depositions and trial testimony, you are not paid specifically for the act of testifying at trial itself, this ensures your impartiality as an expert witness.

How: Step-by-Step Deposition Scheduling

1. The opposing attorney's staff contacts your attorney's staff to request several possible dates for your deposition.
2. Your attorney's staff then checks with you for your availability and provides the dates to the opposing attorney's staff.
3. Both attorneys' staffs check their schedules to see if the attorneys are available on any of those dates.
4. If either attorney isn't available, the process starts over.
5. If both are available, the opposing attorney issues a written notice to all parties with the confirmed date, time, and location.
6. If there are multiple defendants (and attorneys), this process may be repeated several times until everyone can attend.

Trial Scheduling: What to Expect

The court sets aside a period—called a trial docket—for cases to be heard. Your attorney will check your availability for testimony during this period. If you're absolutely unavailable (for example, you're out of the country), your attorney can ask the court to reschedule. Otherwise, you'll be asked to testify on a specific date or within a short range of dates.

Conclusion: Moving Forward with Confidence

Remember, understanding the "where," "who," and "how" of the testimony process helps you approach your role as an expert witness with clarity and confidence. You're paid for your professional time and expenses, not for the outcome of the case. This distinction protects your credibility and impartiality. If you ever feel unsure, don't hesitate to ask questions—support is always available as you build your expertise!

The Unprepared Expert: Avoiding Common Pitfalls with Preparation

Actionable Strategies for Experts and Attorneys to Ensure Successful Testimony

Expert witness preparation is critical for a successful deposition or trial appearance. Whether you are a Legal Nurse Consultant (LNC) or an attorney working with expert witnesses, thorough preparation can be the difference between a credible, persuasive testimony and a disastrous one. The following real-world scenarios highlight common pitfalls experts face and, more importantly, provide clear, actionable steps for both experts and attorneys to avoid these mistakes.

Scenario 1: Deposition Materials Mishap

Consider the first expert, who arrived at his deposition with medical records annotated in the margins. When the opposing counsel requested to review these materials, the expert insisted they were "for my eyes only." Unfortunately, in the state where the deposition was held, all materials brought by the deponent must be shared with all parties. To make matters worse, his handwritten notes included derogatory comments about the plaintiff, such as "This guy sounds like a crack pot" and "He's a drug seeker." The expert was testifying for the plaintiff, so his own notes undermined his credibility and damaged his client's case.

Key Takeaway: Experts must understand and adhere to state statutes regarding materials brought to deposition or trial. Don't assume your personal notes are off-limits; what you bring may have to be disclosed.

- Before the deposition, consult with the hiring attorney to review all materials you intend to bring.
- Create and use a checklist of required deposition materials and review this together with the attorney ahead of time.
- Remove any informal or opinionated comments from your files; bring only clean copies with factual information.

Practical Advice for Attorneys: Proactively provide your expert with clear guidance on what is permissible and required regarding deposition materials. Hold a preparatory meeting to go through all documents together and ensure compliance with local rules.

Beyond materials, effective expert testimony often hinges on timely and transparent communication—especially when opinions evolve as new information emerges.

Scenario 2: The Perils of Poor Communication

The second expert appeared to be well-prepared to offer her opinions at deposition. However, she had not updated the attorney who retained her about changes in her assessment. A few weeks prior, after receiving additional medical records, she concluded that the plaintiff's damages were far more significant than initially thought. During her deposition (while testifying for the defense), she shared these updated opinions for the first time. The defense attorney was caught off-guard, having never been informed of this critical shift.

Key Takeaway: Experts must promptly communicate any changes in their opinions to the hiring attorney—well before testifying. Surprises in deposition can undermine the entire case.

- When new information leads to revised opinions, immediately schedule a call or meeting with the attorney to discuss these developments.
- Document all changes in writing and provide updated reports if required by local rules.
- For attorneys, establish clear expectations that experts should notify you of any opinion changes as soon as possible and create a process for reviewing these changes together before depositions or trial.

Clear, ongoing communication between expert and attorney helps ensure that everyone is prepared for what will be presented in testimony.

Accurate recollection and careful attention to case details are also essential for expert credibility. The risks of relying on memory alone are illustrated in the next scenario.

Scenario 3: The Dangers of Faulty Memory

The third expert confused facts from the current case with another, misstating the patient's gender and other key details during deposition. He relied solely on his memory and brought no case materials to prompt his recollection. The result was devastating: his credibility was destroyed, and the attorney was forced to find a replacement expert.

Key Takeaway: Experts should never rely purely on memory. Reference materials are essential, but they must be used appropriately.

- Bring a clean, unannotated copy of relevant medical records and a factual, chronological timeline of events for reference during deposition—verify with the attorney that these materials are permitted.
- Review all case facts and documents shortly before testifying to ensure accuracy.

- For attorneys, instruct your experts to use reference materials as permitted and clarify what they may bring into the deposition room.

Conclusion: The Common Denominator

In all three scenarios, the core issue was inadequate preparation and poor collaboration between the expert and the hiring attorney. To avoid these costly mistakes, experts should insist on a thorough preparatory meeting or phone conference before any deposition or trial. Attorneys should lead this process, ensuring compliance with legal requirements, alignment on opinions, and readiness to address case facts accurately. Together, these steps will help experts present clear, credible, and effective testimony every time.

Deposition Data Banks

Enhancing Expert Witness Assessment

As a legal nurse consultant, I routinely conduct background checks and internet research to evaluate the reputations of plaintiffs and defendants. When it comes to expert witnesses who are scheduled to testify, an additional layer of scrutiny is essential. This is where deposition data banks come into play.

Deposition data banks, such as TrialSmith[46] and LexisNexis Expert Research On-Demand (referred to here as LexisNexis[47]), serve as repositories for thousands of expert witness depositions. TrialSmith is exclusively used by plaintiff firms, while both plaintiff and defense firms can access LexisNexis. LexisNexis and TrialSmith help law firms assess expert witness credibility and identify grounds for impeachment. Understanding the function and scope of these data banks is crucial for legal professionals and expert witnesses alike, as they shape how expert testimony is evaluated.

To leverage these data banks, a law firm submits the expert's name and case details to LexisNexis or TrialSmith. For a fee, the firm receives reports on the expert's deposition history and published works. If no information is found, the fee is waived. This process allows attorneys to gather comprehensive background information, guiding legal strategy and witness preparation. Recognizing how this system works

[46] TrialSmith. https://www.trialsmith.com/ (accessed January 2026).
[47] LexisNexis. https://plus.lexis.com/erodlanding/ (accessed January 2026)

empowers professionals to anticipate how their own experts' testimony or opposing experts will be scrutinized.

Consider the following example: A defense firm requests a LexisNexis report on Dr. Jensen, an infectious disease expert, who is slated to testify for the plaintiff. Anticipating Dr. Jensen's opinion that the defendant's treatment of meningitis was substandard, the firm reviews his publications and prior testimony. If Dr. Jensen's statements or published work contradict his current position, these inconsistencies can be used for impeachment. Deposition data banks promote accountability and transparency by enabling parties to highlight discrepancies and ensure expert testimony aligns with documented standards.

The broader impact of deposition data banks extends beyond individual cases. They play a vital role in refining legal strategy, as attorneys can more effectively challenge or support expert witnesses. For experts, awareness of these resources encourages consistent, well-supported testimony and thorough preparation. The existence of deposition data banks reinforces the importance of accuracy, integrity, and clarity in expert witness contributions to legal proceedings.

Law firms should routinely consult deposition data banks to correlate expert testimony with evolving standards of care. While independent legal nurse consultants may not have direct access to these repositories, they can add value by reviewing reports provided by attorney clients and identifying inconsistencies. Ultimately, understanding and utilizing deposition data banks enhances the credibility of expert witnesses and strengthens legal outcomes.

Deposition Summary Types: Guidance for New Legal Nurse Consultants

Understanding Formats, Choosing Approaches, and Mastering Drafting Techniques

As a new legal nurse consultant, you'll quickly discover that drafting deposition summaries is a core responsibility that often overlaps with the work of paralegals. Depending on the firm, either role may take the lead in preparing these essential documents. It's important to understand not only how to create different types of deposition summaries, but also when and why each format is best suited for particular scenarios. This guide will walk you through the main summary types, their uses, and provide practical tips for drafting clear, reliable summaries that meet client needs.

Defining Deposition Summaries

A deposition summary is a concise, focused distillation of the main points from a deposition transcript. While there are various formats, two stand out for their distinct approaches: page-line summaries and narrative summaries. Each serves different purposes, and your choice should be informed by the client's preferences and the context of the case.

Page-Line Deposition Summaries

Description and Uses: Page-line summaries are highly structured and reference specific pages and lines from the deposition transcript. There are 25 lines on each page of deposition transcript. Each page-line entry pinpoints where in the transcript an important statement appears, making it easy for attorneys and legal professionals to cross-reference details or quickly locate testimony. This format is especially preferred when:

- Clients require precise citation of testimony for motions, briefs, or comparison with other depositions.
- Attorneys need to prepare for cross-examination or impeachment and want to easily reference exact wording.
- Cases involve complex facts or multiple depositions, making quick navigation and consistency critical.

Tip: Always format page-line summaries in a clear table and ensure page and line numbers match the official transcript. Accuracy is paramount.

Sample Page-Line Summary (Product Liability Case)

PAGE	LINE	SUMMARY
1	4	Is currently 71 years old, widowed. Was 70 years old at time of her surgery.
2	5-9	Retired in 2022 after being a school teacher for 35 years.
2	15-19	Was diagnosed with arthritis in both hips in 2019.
2	21-25	Her left hip has always hurt worse than the right.
6	14-15	After she retired, she became more physically active (dancing) and her left hip "started to degenerate" and she had increased pain.

PAGE	LINE	SUMMARY
7	11-13	Had a left hip prosthesis implanted on July 8, 2024. It was manufactured by Prosthesis Equipment, Inc.
8	2-5	Had pain from the start. The pain never went away after surgery. Describes pain as constant, sharp, stabbing, worse with activity.
10	20	Spoke with her surgeon, Jeffrey Mallin, MD about the pain at her first postop visit on July 15, 2024. Was assured that it would go.
11	14	Sometime in August 2024, the pain got to the point where she was unable to bear weight.
12	6-14	She had the prosthesis removed in August 2024 and replaced by one from a different manufacturer. She was told by Dr. Mallin that the original prosthesis had a vertical crack in it and that he's never seen anything like it before.
14	5-8	She's had a year of physical therapy with no end in sight for therapy, and she's never been able to walk correctly since the surgery. She still has pain constantly.
14	7-21	She uses a cane and walker in the house and wheelchair otherwise. Her social life has been severely limited since the surgery. She used to dance, attend church activities, and visit her friends. She's now "almost a shut-in."
17	15	She checked on the internet and found that vertical cracks were a problem in the equipment even before hers was implanted.
18	12-17	Dr. Mallin told her that the manufacturer did not inform him of equipment problems. Further, he inspected the equipment prior to implantation and there were no cracks.
18	21-22	She obtained a copy of her medical records and Dr. Mallin did indeed inspect the equipment.
19	46	She contacted her attorney, Mr. Arel, about the class action suit against Prosthetic Equipment, Inc.
20	13-19	She feels that the quality of her life has been ruined by Prosthetic Equipment, Inc. She feels that she should be compensated for her losses.

Annotation: Note how each entry is tied to a specific location in the transcript, making it easy for readers to verify and reference testimony. The structure is highly systematic, which supports detailed legal analysis.

Narrative Deposition Summaries

Description & Uses: Narrative summaries present deposition testimony in a flowing, story-like format, summarizing the key points and context in prose. This approach is ideal for:

- Clients who prefer a holistic overview, such as insurance adjustors or case managers.
- Situations where the main goal is to convey the logic, sequence, and impact of testimony rather than its exact wording.
- Cases where the summary will be used for settlement discussions, client updates, or internal team briefings.

Tip: Begin with demographic details, then highlight the most significant aspects of the testimony in a logical order. Remain neutral and objective throughout.

Sample Narrative Deposition Summary (Product Liability Case)

Dear Loretta,

On May 24, 2025, we deposed Sylvia Stringham. As you are aware, Ms. Stringham is part of a class action suit against our client, Prosthesis Equipment, Inc. Nelson Arel, Esquire represented Ms. Stringham. Darren Parmley, Esquire of our firm represented our client.

Ms. Stringham is currently 71 years old and a widow. She retired in 2022 after being a schoolteacher for 35 years. Ms. Stringham was diagnosed with arthritis in both hips in 2019, although her left hip has always hurt her more than the right hip. After her retirement in 2022, Ms. Stringham became more physically active, particularly with dancing. After several years of increased activity, her left hip "started to degenerate," which resulted in increased pain.

At the age of 70, she had a left hip prosthesis implanted on July 8, 2024. As you know, the prosthesis was manufactured by Prosthesis Equipment, Inc. Ms. Stringham relays that she had pain immediately from the start after the implantation. In addition, the pain never went away after surgery as one would expect. She described the pain as constant, sharp, and stabbing. The pain worsened with activity.

Ms. Stringham spoke with her surgeon, Jeffrey Mallin, MD, about the pain at her first postoperative visit at his office on July 15, 2024. Dr. Mallin assured her that pain after this type of surgery was common and would gradually go away. However, Ms. Stringham stated that the pain was so bad in August 2024 that she was unable to bear weight.

Because of the pain, Ms. Stringham had the prosthesis removed by Dr. Mallin in August 2024 and replaced by one from a different manufacturer. Dr. Mallin informed her that the original prosthesis had a vertical crack in it. He told her that he had never seen a crack in a prosthesis like this.

She testified that because of the prosthesis, she's never been able to walk correctly despite a year of physical therapy "with no end in sight." She is in constant pain. She uses a cane and a walker in her home and a wheelchair when she is outside the home. She testified that her social life has been severely limited since the surgery. She used to dance, attend activities at her church, and visit her friends. She describes herself now as "almost a shut-in." She feels that the quality of her life has been ruined by Prosthetic Equipment, Inc. and that she should be compensated for her losses.

She found out about the class action suit by happenstance. By searching the internet, she found out that vertical cracks were a problem with this device even before she had her surgery. She contacted Dr. Mallin to find out why he implanted a device that had a history of vertical cracks. He explained to her that he had been unaware of any problems because the manufacturer, Prosthetic Equipment, Inc. had not informed him of any problems with the device. In addition, he told her that he had inspected the device prior to implantation and there were no cracks in it.

Ms. Stringham then obtained a copy of her medical records and found a notation that Dr. Mallin had indeed inspected the equipment prior to implantation. At that point, she searched the internet again and found out about the class action suit. She contacted Attorney Arel about joining the class action suit.

We will continue our efforts and provide you with updates accordingly. Should you have any questions, please do not hesitate to contact us.

Regards,

Annotation: The narrative summary tells the story of the deposition in a logical, chronological sequence. Key facts are grouped thematically, making it accessible for readers seeking overall understanding rather than granular detail.

Comparing Page-Line and Narrative Summaries

Feature	Page-Line Summary	Narrative Summary
Structure	Tabular, references page/line numbers	Prose, organized by topic/chronology
Best For	Precise citation, legal motions, cross-referencing	Case overviews, adjustor reviews, internal briefings
Client Preference	Attorneys, paralegals, litigation teams	Insurance adjustors, managers, clients
Advantages	Accuracy, direct reference, easy comparison	Clarity, readability, narrative context
Potential Pitfalls	Omitting key lines, transcription errors	Loss of specific detail, risk of bias

Choose the format based on the client's needs and the intended use. When in doubt, ask your client or supervising attorney about their preference and any formatting requirements.

Drafting Tips and Common Pitfalls

- Focus on Accuracy: Double-check page and line references and ensure that facts are faithfully represented.
- Maintain Neutrality: Avoid adding personal opinions or interpretations. Summaries should reflect only what was testified.
- Stay Concise: Emphasize key points, but don't omit crucial context. Strike a balance between brevity and completeness.
- Double-Check References: Review the final summary against the transcript to catch errors or omissions.
- Clarify Ambiguities: If testimony is unclear, note uncertainties for the attorney's review rather than guessing or paraphrasing inaccurately.
- Watch for Jargon: Use straightforward language and avoid technical terms unless required by the client or case.
- Format Consistently: Use standard templates and ensure headers, tables, and paragraphs are clearly labeled.

Common Pitfalls: Overlooking minor yet significant testimony, misquoting the deponent, and failing to update summaries when transcripts are revised. Always review your work and seek feedback from experienced colleagues.

Annotated Examples: Key Structural Differences

- Page-Line Summary: Uses a table, each row tied to transcript location, ideal for pinpoint accuracy.
- Narrative Summary: Organizes testimony in logical order, emphasizing story and context, better for holistic understanding.

Refer to the paired examples above and consider which format best serves your client's objectives. Annotations highlight how structure shapes use: page-line for reference, narrative for context.

Conclusion and Next Steps

Mastering deposition summaries is a valuable skill for legal nurse consultants. By understanding the strengths and scenarios for each format, you'll be able to provide summaries that support your clients and legal teams effectively. Always communicate with your clients about their preferences, stay open to feedback, and strive for clarity and neutrality in every summary you draft. With practice and attention to detail, you'll soon become proficient in creating deposition summaries tailored to any legal situation.

Chapter 12: Launching A Legal Career—How to Land (and Keep) a Law Firm Job

Transitioning from nursing into the legal world can feel daunting, but it's also full of opportunity. Law firms remain the largest employers of legal nurse consultants, relying on LNCs to interpret medical records, support malpractice and injury cases, and provide insights that attorneys and paralegals without clinical training simply cannot. For nurses curious about exploring new horizons, the law firm setting offers a chance to apply your medical expertise in ways that directly impact litigation and client outcomes.

Imagine walking into a law firm interview with no prior legal background—armed instead with years of clinical experience and a fresh perspective that attorneys desperately need. Even if firms advertise for RNs with law firm experience, you don't need prior legal work to begin a rewarding career. What matters most is your ability to translate nursing skills into legal value, and this chapter shows you how.

We'll start by clarifying the difference between nurse paralegals and legal nurse consultants, so you know exactly which positions to target. From there, you'll discover the nursing skills that open doors in legal practice and follow a step-by-step plan to secure your first law firm position. You'll learn how to build an impressive portfolio, craft powerful career objectives, and tailor your resume and cover letters to stand out in the legal field. We'll also cover interview strategies, ways to present sample work effectively, and how to navigate setbacks with resilience.

By the end of this chapter, you'll have a clear roadmap for making the transition from nursing to law firm work. With practical tools and encouragement throughout, you'll be equipped to leverage your healthcare background, demonstrate immediate value to attorneys, and open new doors in the legal world.

Thinking About Becoming an In-House Legal Nurse Consultant?

A Friendly Guide for Nurses Curious About LNC Roles

Are you considering a career as a Legal Nurse Consultant (LNC) but feeling a bit daunted by all that it requires? Don't worry—you're not alone! Let's break down what this job is really about, what it takes to get there, and some practical steps you can follow. This way, you can decide if this path suits your skills and interests.

Responsibilities

So, what do in-house Legal Nurse Consultants actually do? In a nutshell, you'd be the medical expert on a legal team, helping attorneys make sense of medical issues in legal cases. Here's what your days might look like:

- Diving into Medical Records: You'll be reviewing patient records and looking for important details or inconsistencies. For example, if a law firm is handling a personal injury case, you might be the one spotting where a treatment timeline doesn't add up.
- Helping Shape Legal Strategies: Attorneys rely on your expertise to interpret medical info when they decide how to approach a case.
- Interviewing Clients: Sometimes you'll meet with clients to clarify their medical histories and piece together critical facts.
- Writing Reports: Expect to create clear, detailed reports for legal proceedings—think medical summaries and/or chronologies.
- Trial Prep Support: You'll help lawyers get ready for depositions and trials, preparing questions or exhibits that reference medical evidence.

You'll find LNCs mostly in law firms, but also in government agencies (like Medicare investigations), insurance companies, hospital risk management, and even forensic settings. Unlike independent LNCs, in-house folks don't testify in court or market themselves; you're an essential part of the team.

Pros and Cons

Every job has its ups and downs, right? Here's a quick rundown to help you figure out if in-house LNC work is a good fit.

Pros:

- Steady Paycheck: You'll get a regular salary and sometimes bonuses, especially in law firms or corporate settings.
- Better Work-Life Balance: Most positions are Monday–Friday and go by court schedules, so you'll often have more holidays off and minimal overtime.
- Good Benefits: Perks like health insurance are often as good as, or better than, what you'd get at a hospital.
- Job Security: Full-time means a consistent paycheck and hours.

Cons:

- Fewer Openings: These jobs are more competitive because there aren't as many of them as there are regular RN roles.
- No Overtime: Salaried positions don't pay extra for long hours, and the ceiling might be lower than for high-earning independent consultants.
- Less Flexible Scheduling: You won't get the three-day workweeks that some hospital nurses enjoy.

Balancing these pros and cons can help you figure out if you'd thrive in this kind of work environment.

Required Skills

Wondering what you need to get started? Here's a quick checklist:

- RN License: You'll need your nursing license, of course.
- Experience: Most employers want at least five years in clinical nursing—anywhere from hospitals to home health.
- Writing Skills: You'll be expected to write reports that are clear, concise, and grammatically spotless. Some places may ask for a sample summary before hiring you.
- Legal Know-How: Experience in a law firm or an LNC course is a big plus.
- Computer Skills: Being comfortable with tools like Word, PowerPoint, Adobe Acrobat, and even specialized billing software is important. You might need to put together a PowerPoint for trial or use Word for a medical chronology.
- Typing: You don't have to be a speed demon, but basic proficiency helps. If not, you can always brush up with a course.

To sum up, you'll need a mix of clinical experience, analytical thinking, and tech know-how.

Tips for Increasing Hirability

Now, if you're looking at this and thinking, "That's a lot," take heart! There are plenty of practical ways to make yourself a stronger candidate:

1. Take an LNC Course: This will build your confidence and credibility. You can find courses at colleges or through professional groups.
2. Showcase Relevant Experience: If you've ever reviewed charts for quality, peer review, or case management, highlight it in your resume. For instance, maybe you led a committee that reviewed cases and wrote up recommendations—put that front and center.

3. Build Your Portfolio: Have a few writing samples ready—mock reports, summaries, or analyses. Make sure they're typo-free and clear.
4. Brush Up on Tech Skills: Try free online typing programs or sign up for a local keyboarding class if you need practice.
5. Network Actively: Don't just attend local or virtual AALNC chapter meetings—get involved. For example, one nurse landed a job after volunteering on her chapter's newsletter committee; her dedication and organizational skills caught the right person's eye, and she got a referral.
6. Look for Mentorships or Externships: These might be unpaid (or even cost you), but the hands-on experience and networking are often worth it in the long run.

Conclusion

Becoming an in-house Legal Nurse Consultant is a great way to use your nursing experience in a brand-new setting. By understanding what the role involves, considering the pros and cons, and taking action to build the right skills and connections, you'll set yourself up for success. Take your time, prepare well, and remember—the legal world truly values nurses who are ready, motivated, and well-prepared.

LNC Job Search: How to Find the Right Position for You

Securing a Legal Nurse Consulting (LNC) position often requires a more focused and strategic approach than finding a traditional RN role in a hospital. To boost your chances of success, you must actively seek out opportunities and use a clear, organized job search plan. Below are consolidated steps to guide your journey:

1. Research and Target Prospective Employers

Identify organizations or law firms that interest you and gather detailed information about them. Nearly every organization now has a website you can review. For law firms, Martindale.com [48]is a valuable resource for learning about firms and their attorneys.

[48] Martindale. https://www.martindale.com/ (accessed January 2026)

2. Develop a Portfolio of Work Samples

If you're seeking an in-house LNC position, assemble examples of your work product. If you're new or lack direct experience, be transparent about your background and use the portfolio to showcase the type of work you're capable of producing. Refer to professional resources for tips on ethically preparing these samples.

3. Expand Your Professional Network

Evaluate your current affiliations and consider which new contacts you should add. In addition to connecting with attorneys, think about other potential clients. Join organizations like the American Association of Legal Nurse Consultants (AALNC) and your local chapter to access valuable contacts and job leads. When networking, introduce yourself professionally, briefly explain your background, and express your interest in LNC opportunities. LinkedIn is also an invaluable tool for connecting with other LNCs and attorneys.

4. Update and Expand Your Skills

To compete with established LNCs—especially for in-house roles—it's crucial to develop non-nursing skills such as:

- Report writing
- Understanding legal terminology and concepts
- Effective communication with attorneys
- Critical thinking for case analysis

5. Effective Job Search Strategies

- Network with LNCs and Attorneys: Other legal nurse consultants can be an excellent source of job leads, regardless of your desired role. If you don't know any LNCs, join your local or a remote AALNC chapter—some chapters share exclusive or unadvertised postings with members. Even if postings aren't available, members may know of employers seeking LNCs. When reaching out, clearly introduce yourself and mention your interest in open positions.

- Search Online Job Boards: For in-house positions, explore sites such as Monster,[49] CareerBuilder,[50], LawJobs,[51] Indeed,[52], and SimplyHired[53]. Use targeted search terms like "legal nurse" or "nurse paralegal" (in quotes) to narrow your results to relevant positions.

By combining targeted research, a strong portfolio, proactive networking, and continual skill development, you'll maximize your chances of landing the right Legal Nurse Consulting position. Stay persistent and professional—your efforts will position you for long-term success in this rewarding field.

Nursing Positions in Law Firms

Nurse Paralegal Versus LNC

When is a paralegal not a paralegal? As a new legal nurse consultant, you might feel hesitant about applying for nurse paralegal positions simply because you're not a paralegal. Have you ever skipped over a job ad because of its title? It's natural to feel unqualified or alienated by unfamiliar terminology. After all, you're an LNC, not a nurse paralegal. But could you be missing out on valuable job opportunities? The key is learning how to evaluate whether a nurse paralegal job is a fit for your LNC skills.

Paralegals typically work under the supervision of an attorney and often hold a degree or certificate in paralegal studies from an American Bar Association-approved program. Their responsibilities include conducting legal research, drafting documents, and helping with pleadings and discovery—tasks that aren't usually part of an LNC's role.

However, many attorneys use the term "paralegal" more loosely, viewing paralegals as anyone who assists them in their work. So, when they advertise for a "nurse paralegal," they may simply want a nurse to help with legal matters, regardless of formal paralegal qualifications. The American Association of Legal Nurse Consultants (AALNC) doesn't see LNCs as another category of paralegals, and I agree. Still, it's easy to see why attorneys might use the Nurse Paralegal title.

[49] Monster. https://www.monster.com/ (accessed December 2025).
[50] CareerBuilder. https://www.careerbuilder.com/ (accessed December 2025).
[51] LawJobs. https://lawjobs.com/ (accessed December 2025).
[52] Indeed. https://www.indeed.com/ (accessed December 2025).
[53] SimplyHired. https://www.simplyhired.com/ (accessed December 2025).

To complicate things, some nurse paralegal positions do require actual paralegal duties. So how can you tell if a nurse paralegal job is right for you? Next time you see a Nurse Paralegal position, take a closer look at the responsibilities before deciding whether to apply. Reviewing the ad or job description is the simplest way to evaluate a position.

- Nurse Paralegal Job Example 1: This may be the opportunity for you! This position will handle the litigation process for Insurance Defense / Medical Malpractice cases, including performing legal research, preparing and reviewing information pertaining to court cases and legal issues, reviewing documents, writing motions and pleadings. This person will provide the attorney with discovery, trial preparation, plus trial experience. Commentary: This ad clearly outlines tasks such as legal research and drafting motions—duties aligned with traditional paralegal roles, not typical LNC responsibilities. I wouldn't apply for this job because I wouldn't have the right qualifications.
- Nurse Paralegal Job Example 2: Top rated medical malpractice defense law firm looking for full-time RN/paralegal with wide range of nursing experience to organize and analyze complex medical charts and work closely with attorneys in analysis and evaluation of medical-legal issues, including standard of care and causation, medical research and retention of experts. Commentary: Despite the RN/Paralegal title, this ad describes responsibilities that match the expertise of an LNC, such as analyzing medical charts, medical research, and evaluating medical-legal issues. If I were looking for an LNC position, I would definitely apply for this one.

Have you ever wondered if you're passing up great opportunities just because of a job title? By comparing the actual responsibilities listed in ads, you'll know whether a position is right for you as an LNC, regardless of its title.

Summary: Steps for Evaluating Job Ads & Key Differences

In summary, always review the job responsibilities carefully and don't let titles discourage you from applying. Here's how to assess job ads and understand the differences between nurse paralegal and LNC positions:

1. Read the job description thoroughly—focus on listed duties, not just the title.
2. Identify whether the responsibilities align with LNC tasks (like medical chart analysis and medical-legal evaluation) or require traditional paralegal skills (such as legal research and document drafting).
3. Look for keywords that match your expertise as an LNC.
4. If in doubt, reach out for clarification or consider applying if the core responsibilities fit your background.

Remember, the main difference is that paralegal roles typically involve legal processes and documentation, while LNC positions rely on your nursing expertise to analyze medical issues within legal cases. Next time you see a Nurse Paralegal listing, take a closer look at the responsibilities—you might discover your next fantastic opportunity!

Launching Your Legal Career—A Nurse's Guide to Landing a Law Firm Job

Introduction: Overcoming the Experience Gap

Are you a new legal nurse consultant (LNC) wondering, "How can I get a law firm job when so many postings require law firm experience?" If that question feels familiar, you're not alone—and you're not out of options. While it's true that most new LNCs haven't worked directly in a law firm, you probably have valuable skills and experiences that law firms are looking for. With the right approach, you can highlight these strengths and position yourself as a top candidate. Let's explore how you can bridge the experience gap, confidently build your resume, and take the first steps toward a rewarding career as an LNC.

Why Law Firm Experience Matters

Law firms often prefer candidates with law firm experience because it means less time spent on training. However, what they're really seeking are professionals who understand medical record review, can communicate clearly, and have strong analytical abilities. Many nursing experiences translate directly to these requirements—even if you haven't worked in a law firm before.

Translating Experience: 10 Skills, Examples, and Scenarios

1. Independent Consulting. Scenario: Imagine you've worked as an independent nurse consultant, analyzing medical records for personal injury attorneys or insurance companies. For example, you might have organized complex charts and identified missing documentation for an attorney preparing a case. This shows your analytical ability and initiative. Resume Tip: "Served as an independent consultant, analyzing medical records for litigation support and preparing case summaries for attorneys."
2. Temporary LNC Positions. Scenario: Perhaps you took a three-month contract with a law firm to help review a surge of malpractice cases. During this time, you learned the firm's workflow and collaborated with attorneys to clarify medical

issues. This hands-on exposure is invaluable. Resume Tip: "Contracted as a temporary LNC, providing in-house support to a law firm by reviewing medical records and drafting preliminary reports."

3. Subcontractor Roles. Scenario: Maybe a senior LNC hired you to help review overflow cases. You completed record reviews, summarized findings, and flagged potential standard-of-care deviations. Whether on-site or remote, you gained direct experience in the core tasks law firms value. Resume Tip: "Subcontracted with established LNCs to review and summarize medical records, supporting litigation case preparation."
4. Peer Review Committees. Scenario: If you've participated in hospital peer review committees, you've already assessed cases for compliance with standards of care. For instance, you might have reviewed a patient's outcome after an adverse event and contributed to the committee's recommendations. Resume Tip: "Reviewed medical records for peer review committees to assess compliance with standards of care and identify areas for improvement."
5. Chart Audits. Scenario: Suppose you led a retrospective review of patient records to identify trends in medication errors. Step by step, you collected data, analyzed error rates, and presented your findings to improve patient safety. This is directly applicable to what LNCs do for law firms. Resume Tip: "Conducted retrospective chart audits to identify trends in medication errors and provided actionable recommendations."
6. Quality Assurance/Quality Improvement (QA/QI). Scenario: In a QA/QI role, you may have led initiatives to ensure your healthcare facility met quality benchmarks. For example, you might have developed and implemented new protocols after identifying gaps in care during audits. Resume Tip: "Led QA/QI projects to assess and enhance compliance with healthcare standards, improving patient safety and care quality."
7. Legal Aid Experience. Scenario: Volunteering with a legal aid organization, you might have collaborated with attorneys on cases involving domestic violence, reviewing medical reports, and explaining clinical issues. This experience hones both your record review and communication skills. Resume Tip: "Volunteered with Legal Aid, reviewing medical records for cases involving medical-legal issues and communicating findings to attorneys."
8. Management Positions. Scenario: As a nurse manager, you likely balanced staff schedules, prioritized competing demands, and communicated effectively with multiple disciplines. These organizational and leadership skills transfer directly to LNC work. Resume Tip: "Managed clinical teams, demonstrating strong communication, prioritization, and leadership skills in high-pressure environments."

9. Risk Management. Scenario: If you've worked in risk management, you've investigated adverse events, analyzed root causes, and recommended safety improvements. For example, you might have reviewed incident reports and developed strategies to prevent recurrence—skills that are critical in legal nurse consulting. Resume Tip: "Investigated adverse events and analyzed root causes as part of risk management team, recommending safety improvements."
10. Mentorship/Internship. Scenario: Through mentorship or internship, you worked alongside an experienced LNC—perhaps shadowing during case reviews or assisting with report preparation. This practical training helps you understand the expectations and workflow of legal nurse consulting. Resume Tip: "Completed mentorship with senior LNC, gaining hands-on experience in medical record review and litigation support."

Making Your Resume Stand Out: Step-by-Step Guidance

1. Review your work history and identify experiences that relate to LNC responsibilities—especially those listed above. On my first LNC resume, I wrote statements such as, "Primary responsibilities were patient care," then I listed information related to the legal field.
2. Write 1–2 specific bullet points for each relevant role, focusing on your achievements and the skills you used.
3. Use action verbs and clear language to describe your contributions.
4. Highlight transferable skills such as analysis, communication, organization, and leadership.
5. Tailor your resume for each job application, emphasizing the experiences most relevant to the position.

Using the example above, my first resume listed my responsibilities accurately as: Primary responsibilities were patient care. Served on critical care peer review committee to ensure compliance with standards of care for complex patients as well as identify areas for improvement.

Sample Resume Statements

- Reviewed medical records for peer review committees to assess compliance with standards of care.
- Served as an independent consultant analyzing medical records for litigation support.
- Conducted retrospective chart audits to identify trends in medication errors and recommended corrective action.

- Volunteered with legal aid, reviewing medical records for medical-legal cases and communicating findings to attorneys.
- Managed clinical teams, demonstrating strong communication and leadership skills.
- Completed mentorship with senior LNC, gaining hands-on experience in litigation case preparation.

Maintaining Motivation: Encouragement and Reminders

Remember, every step you've taken in your nursing career has given you skills that law firms value. You don't need to check every box on this list—just focus on what you have and present it confidently. The transition to legal nurse consulting is a journey, and your unique background makes you a strong candidate. Stay positive, keep learning, and believe in your ability to succeed!

Conclusion: Your Next Steps

With the right mindset and a thoughtfully crafted resume, you can demonstrate to law firms that you're ready for the challenges of legal nurse consulting. Identify your transferable skills, use concrete examples to showcase your experience, and don't hesitate to reach out for temporary or subcontractor opportunities. The door to your LNC career is open—walk through it with confidence!

8 Steps to Land That Law Firm Job: Let's Talk About It

Tips for Legal Nurse Consultants, Made Simple

So, you're looking for a position at a law firm. You send out your resume, but nobody calls you for an interview. Or maybe you get the interview, but not the job offer. What's going on? Honestly, I've seen so many Legal Nurse Consultants (LNCs) struggle with this. A lot of folks just don't know what steps they need to take. Let's walk through eight steps that can help you land that law firm job.

1) Think like an employer.

Here's the thing: most LNC candidates focus on what they want out of the job. Flip the script! If you start thinking like an employer, you immediately give yourself an edge. What are law firms looking for? The right mix of experience, skills, and attitude. They don't want to spend all their time training someone new, so they usually prefer LNCs who've already worked in a law firm. And naturally, they want someone with reasonable salary expectations.

2) Commit to finding a law firm job.

It's surprising how many people say, "I want to work in a law firm," but never actually do anything about it. If you're serious, you must take initiative: keep searching for openings and be ready to send your resume or interview anytime. For example, Jocelyn (an LNC I knew) set reminders to check job boards daily and told her friends she was looking—she eventually got two interviews.

3) Create a portfolio ahead of time.

Being "immediately available" isn't just about your schedule—it means having a portfolio ready to go. A portfolio is a collection of samples of your work, like medical chronologies or case summaries. These let law firms see how you analyze cases and present your findings. If you don't have samples prepared, someone else will—and you might lose out. Fun fact: a portfolio can level the playing field if you don't have prior law firm experience. If you're unsure how to start, we talk in Chapter 7 about Types of Reports.

4) Look for positions.

Network and let your colleagues know you're searching and check the internet regularly. Top places: Google (set up an alert), SimplyHired, Indeed, Monster, Career Builder. Don't forget local bar association job boards—those can be goldmines. LinkedIn is also great; just last week, one of my connections messaged me about an opening.

5) Tailor your resume for law firms.

I can't tell you how many resumes I've seen that look like the LNC is applying for a nursing job—not a law firm job. Employers want to know if you can analyze cases, not just your clinical background. Tailoring your resume means highlighting relevant skills—organization, analytical abilities, and familiarity with legal software. Here's an example: instead of listing only clinical tasks, talk about how you reviewed medical records for legal cases or worked with attorneys on case analysis. And write an employer-centric career objective (that means describing what you can do for them, not just what you want).

6) Tailor your cover letter.

Your cover letter is the first thing a law firm sees. Research the firm, then explain why you're a great fit. Craft your letter to address what the firm needs. Always ask for an interview at the end. If you haven't worked in a law firm before, consider including a sample from your portfolio—this gives employers a sense of your skills.

7) Interview like a pro.

Dress professionally, bring your portfolio, and print out extra copies of your resume. Practice answering common interview questions and focus on how you can help the employer. It's fine to ask about salary and benefits but save those questions for the end. Make sure you first ask about the role itself and the firm's needs.

8) Follow up.

After you've interviewed, send a thank-you email within 24 hours. Mention something specific about the interview that got you excited and remind them how your skills can help their firm. Let them know you're interested and eager to hear back.

That's it! Just follow these eight steps, and you'll be much closer to getting that law firm job. And to help you out, keep reading. I've got more information and some samples for you. Good luck—you've got this!

How to Ethically Create an LNC Sample Work Product

A Step-by-Step Guide for New Legal Nurse Consultants

As a new Legal Nurse Consultant (LNC), presenting a strong sample work product is vital to showcase your analytical skills and professionalism to prospective clients and employers. These samples—whether they are medical chronologies, summaries, timelines, calendars, or other reports—demonstrate your competence in interpreting medical records and addressing case issues. However, the process of creating your first samples can be challenging if you haven't yet worked on actual cases. *Note: The term "work product" is singular although it refers to multiple documents.*

The Wrong Way: Ethical Issues and Professional Consequences

It may be tempting to use a report written by another LNC or a sample developed during your LNC course as your own product. However, this practice is unethical and poses significant risks to your professional reputation. Representing someone else's work as your own is a breach of integrity that can undermine trust, damage your credibility, and may violate professional standards. In the legal community, your reputation is everything—being discovered using non-original work can have lasting negative effects, including being perceived as dishonest or incompetent. Integrity is the foundation of a successful LNC career, and authenticity in your samples is essential to establish yourself as a trustworthy expert.

The Right Way: Originality Demonstrates Integrity and Expertise

The correct and ethical approach is to create your own sample work products, even if they are based on fictionalized scenarios inspired by your real-world patient care experiences. This method not only maintains your professional integrity but also allows attorneys to see your genuine ability to analyze medical facts and produce clear, coherent reports. Originality in your samples is a direct reflection of your expertise and commitment to the highest standards of the profession.

Step-by-Step Guide: Ethical LNC Sample Work Product Creation

1. Start with Damages. Begin by identifying a situation from your workplace where a patient experienced a poor outcome. Imagine this outcome led to a lawsuit. Focus on the specific damages that resulted from the incident.
2. Create a Scenario. Develop a detailed scenario that incorporates a breach of duty and causation. Clearly illustrate how the breach led to the damages. Use fictional names, dates, and locations to protect privacy, and be thorough in your description of events before, during, and after the incident.
3. Draft Your Report. Organize your scenario into a professional report format, such as a medical summary or chronology. Ensure the document is clear, concise, and logically structured. Review sample templates online, in this book, or in specialized resources for guidance.
4. Proofread for Perfection. Carefully proofread your work for spelling and grammar errors. Use tools like Microsoft Word's spell and grammar check, or online resources such as Grammarly. Flawless writing reinforces your attention to detail and professionalism.

Practical Examples: Real-World Damages from Diverse Medical Settings

Below are some real examples of lawsuits from my practice. If you're having trouble thinking of a patient who has had a poor outcome, use one of these examples.

- Operating Room/PACU: Burns from cautery sparks, intraoperative deaths, or failure to monitor anesthesia.
- Med-Surg/ICU: Unexpected deaths, unreported changes in patient condition, medication errors, or pressure injuries.
- Emergency Room: Missed evolving strokes, delayed referrals, or missed infections.

- Home Health: Patient falls due to lack of safety measures, or delays in emergency interventions.
- Pediatrics: Late diagnosis of rare conditions, or critical incidents resulting in child fatalities.
- Dental: Implant failures, or development of jaw osteomyelitis.
- Physician Offices: Failure to refer urgently, delayed diagnosis, or falls in exam rooms.
- Radiology: Untimely communication of critical results, or misinterpreted imaging studies.
- Pathology: Mislabeling or misinterpretation of specimens.
- Nursing Home: UTIs, falls, wounds, dehydration, weight loss, elopement, or unexplained injuries.
- Pharmacology: Consequences of medication errors, such as tendon rupture from Levaquin or incorrect prescriptions.
- OB/GYN/Neonates: Maternal hemorrhage, unrecognized neonatal anomalies, or delayed cancer diagnosis.
- Plastic Surgery: Complications like poor wound healing or necrosis.

Think back to a challenging patient outcome in your career—how might you turn that into a sample scenario?

Checklist: Four Steps to Create Your LNC Sample Work Product

- Identify a poor patient outcome (damages) and imagine it as the basis of a lawsuit.
- Develop a scenario including breach of duty and causation, using fictional details.
- Write and format your report clearly and professionally.
- Proofread thoroughly to ensure your sample is error-free.

Conclusion: Integrity and Expertise Set You Apart

By following this ethical, step-by-step process, you will develop authentic LNC sample work products that reflect your genuine abilities. Maintaining originality not only demonstrates your integrity but also builds your reputation as a reliable and skilled consultant. Use your experiences, attention to detail, and commitment to excellence to set yourself apart in the legal nurse consulting profession.

Note: I created the original version of the above article for Legal Nurse Business.

Understanding Career Objectives for Legal Nurse Consultant Resumes

Making Your Resume Stand Out

If you're a registered nurse (RN) thinking about making the leap into legal nurse consulting at a law firm, starting your resume with a clear career objective is definitely a smart move. That objective is especially important when you're shifting from one field to another—it helps you highlight the skills you can bring with you and how they'll be valuable in your new role.

But here's the catch: most career objectives written by RNs for legal nurse consultant (LNC) jobs don't really grab employers' attention. Let me show you what I mean. A lot of RN resumes say something like, "Seeking employment in a professional organization that challenges me and has a rewarding environment."

So, what's wrong with that kind of objective? Well, let's break it down:

1. Seeking employment with a professional organization. This is way too general. If you're aiming for a job at a law firm, you should say so right up front. If you're trying to keep your options wide open, you might be hurting your chances. Law firm hiring managers can tell you're not fully committed to finding a job in their field and would settle for any "professional organization." The good news? If you have access to a word processor like Microsoft Word, it's easy to tweak your objective for each job you apply for—just specify that you want to work in a law firm.
2. Seeking challenging employment. This statement focuses on what YOU want. Law firms are much more interested in what THEY need in a candidate. Plus, they don't know you yet, so they can't guess what you'll find challenging.
3. Wanting a rewarding environment. Again, this is all about you. Law firms really want to know what you can do for their team, not what they can do for you. And anyway, they have no idea what you consider "rewarding"—maybe it's respect, maybe it's great benefits, maybe it's a big salary. It's too vague.

So, what's the right way to write a career objective? The best strategy is to spell out exactly how your RN skills and experience will benefit the law firm. Here's the career objective I used on my own resume years ago:

Seeking a legal nurse consultant position in a law firm that requires comprehensive knowledge of nursing and medical standards, superior analytic skills, and exceptional organizational and communication skills.

That's it! Even though I didn't have law firm experience, this objective (plus the rest of my resume) landed me an interview—at a firm that wanted candidates with law firm backgrounds. My objective made it clear that I had the skills and traits needed to excel as an LNC. And bringing a sample work product to the interview sealed the deal—I got the job!

When you're putting together your career objective, try to mirror it to the qualifications and requirements listed in the job posting. For example, if the job is full-time and on-site, tweak your objective to say: "Seeking a full-time on-site legal nurse consultant position in a law firm that requires..."

Please don't copy my career objective. After I published the career objective on LNCtips.com, I saw this exact wording on several other LNC resumes. Make your objective unique to you—showcase what makes you the best fit. You've got this!

Attorney-Friendly Legal Nurse Consultant Resumes: A Practical Guide

Introduction: What Attorneys Seek in LNC Resumes

Attorneys evaluating Legal Nurse Consultant (LNC) resumes look for clarity, direct relevance to legal casework, and strong analytical abilities. They want to easily understand your qualifications without deciphering medical jargon. Highlighting experiences that demonstrate attention to detail, objective analysis, and expertise in high-stakes clinical situations will set you apart. Tailoring your resume to reflect the needs and expectations of law firms greatly increases the likelihood of securing interviews.

Translating Nursing Experience for Legal Audiences

To make your qualifications accessible, describe nursing tasks in terms attorneys value—such as risk management, documentation accuracy, and adherence to protocols. Focus on how your role connects to legal issues, using plain language that emphasizes critical thinking and outcomes.

Attorney-Friendly Resume Checklist: Actionable Tips for LNCs

- Lead with relevant LNC or legal casework experience—place it at the top of your resume.
- Quantify achievements and describe measurable outcomes if possible (e.g., "reduced patient wait times by 30%").

- Use straightforward, professional formatting—limit to two pages and avoid excessive design elements.
- Emphasize experience with medical record review, case analysis, and compliance with clinical guidelines.
- Highlight leadership, teaching, and multidisciplinary team coordination (with specifics).
- Demonstrate analytical and organizational skills—mention quality improvement, risk management, or peer review roles.
- Include specialized expertise (e.g., pediatrics, oncology) relevant to legal cases.
- Proofread meticulously to ensure accuracy and consistency.

Problematic Nursing Phrases & Attorney Feedback

Below are some phrases that I shared with attorneys from my firm. The phrases are from resumes for LNC applicants, and I was interested in what the phrases meant to attorneys.

Phrasing	**Attorney Feedback**
Shared Governance	Unclear meaning; not recognized outside nursing.
Proctor for students	Can be misinterpreted; lacks clinical context.
Total patient care	Too general; attorneys seek specifics.
Nurse to patient ratios	Lacks context—are these ratios good or bad?
Foster staff participation in patient care	Vague term; needs concrete examples.
Mentored other nursing staff	Not specific about mentoring activities.
Precepted students	Terminology unfamiliar to legal audiences.
Fast-paced	Generic; doesn't highlight unique skills.
Developed a well-run unit	Attorneys want to know how and what results were achieved.

Expanded Before-and-After Phrasing Examples

- Instead of: "Administered IV medications," use: Managed patient care by administering medications, monitoring for adverse reactions, and ensuring adherence to medical protocols.
- Instead of: "Participated in SBAR communications," use: Communicated essential patient information to healthcare teams, supporting safe and effective care transitions.
- Instead of: "Responded to code blue," use: Led emergency interventions and coordinated response teams to deliver life-saving care.
- Instead of: "Managed wound vacs," use: Oversaw advanced wound care therapies using specialized equipment to promote healing and prevent complications.
- Pediatrics Example: Instead of: "Cared for pediatric oncology patients," use: Provided comprehensive care to children undergoing chemotherapy, closely monitoring for treatment side effects, and coordinating with multidisciplinary teams.
- Oncology Example: Instead of: "Administered chemotherapy," use: Delivered complex chemotherapy regimens, ensured compliance with safety standards, and educated patients and families on treatment protocols.
- Instead of: "Mentored other nursing staff," use: Trained new nurses on electronic medical record systems and best practices for medication administration.
- Instead of: "Precepted orientees," use: Supervised and evaluated nursing orientees, ensuring competency in patient care and documentation.
- Instead of: "Fast-paced," use: Effectively triaged emergencies and managed multiple priorities in a high-volume ER setting.
- Instead of: "Developed a well-run unit," use: Implemented workflow improvements that reduced patient wait times and enhanced team communication.

Sample Resumes for LNCs

Here are two sample resumes – one for an experienced LNC and one for a new LNC with no experience in the legal field. The two resumes have very little formatting; some sites like CareerBuilder and Indeed don't work well with formatting. However, if you're handing a resume to an attorney or emailing the resume directly to a law firm, you might want to "dress up" your resume a bit with bullets or download a resume template for a more polished look.

Sample Resume 1: Experienced Legal Nurse Consultant

Jennifer Lipson, BSN, RN, LNCC

Legal Nurse Consultant

723 Silverado Parkway
Mesna, FL 65890
247-xxx-xxxx | jlipson@XXXXX.com

Professional Summary

Motivated RN offering expertise in legal nurse consulting, cardiovascular care, and quality improvement. Adept at streamlining communication between hospital administration and external parties, with a proven record analyzing medical records and collaborating effectively with partners, associates, and other team members in a law firm specializing in complex medical malpractice cases.

Work Experience

Legal Nurse Consultant, 2023 – Present (Peoples and Narper, Mesna FL): Organized, summarized, and analyzed medical records. Evaluated case merit and strategy; developed chronologies and summary reports that contributed to successful trial outcomes. Coordinated with expert witnesses, facilitating review of cases and supporting effective deposition and trial preparation. Drafted targeted deposition and trial questions for expert and fact witnesses. Created PowerPoint presentations for mediations and trials, enhancing attorney presentations. Assisted attorneys with fact witness preparation, resulting in more confident and informed testimony.

Nurse Manager, 2020-2023 (Seldon Community Hospital, Seldon, FL): Collaborated with attorneys on malpractice cases; co-interviewed fact witnesses and contributed to successful legal outcomes. Led a team of 25 nurses, improving staff retention by 15% through targeted training and mentorship. Assisted in preparing interrogatories and witnesses for depositions and trials.

Assistant Nurse Manager, 2015 – 2019 (Seldon Community Hospital, Seldon, FL): Liaised between hospital administration and external attorneys regarding medical malpractice cases, streamlining communication and case resolution.

Staff RN / Charge RN, 2011 – 2015 (Seldon Community Hospital, Seldon, FL): Served as staff and charge RN in ICU, specializing in cardiovascular surgery and cardiac conditions. Member of the Quality Improvement Committee, analyzing nursing care for compliance.

Education

University of Florida, BSN in Nursing, 2011
Statewide, LNC Institute, Certificate as Legal Nurse Consultant, 2022

Certifications

American Association of Legal Nurse Consultants
Legal Nurse Consultant Certified (LNCC), 2024 – Present

Sample Resume 2: RN Seeking Independent LNC Role

John Sedgewick, BSN, RN

1919 El Camino Drive
New Bay, FL 37908
583-xxx-xxxx · JohnSedgewick@mail.com

Career Objective

Motivated RN seeking independent Legal Nurse Consultant opportunities with a firm that values comprehensive nursing knowledge and advanced analytical skills.

Professional Attributes

Extensive experience caring for patients with complex medical needs.

Knowledge of JCAHO and state health care regulations.

Skilled in explaining medical concepts clearly, both verbally and in writing.

Areas of Expertise

Burns, Shock Trauma, Cardiology, Respiratory, Stroke, Bariatric Surgery, Orthopedic Surgery, Neurosurgery, Urology, Geriatrics, Gastrointestinal, Cardiothoracic Surgery

Nursing Experience

Doctors' Hospital – New Bay, FL

Nurse Manager, Surgical ICU 2018 – Present: Led interdisciplinary peer review committee, identifying and correcting deviations from standards of care, which reduced incident rates by 12%. Oversaw situational review of sentinel events, collaborating with legal teams to ensure accurate reporting and resolution.

Staff RN 2011 – 2017: Assessed and treated critically unstable patients, consistently achieving rapid intervention benchmarks. Served on quality assurance committee, helping to decrease deviations in nursing care standards by 8%.

Staff RN, Telemetry 2008 – 2011: Cared for post-myocardial infarction and heart surgery patients; participated in hospital Safety Committee, contributing to a 15% improvement in safety compliance.

Education

Bachelor of Science in Nursing, 2008, Medical College of Georgia – Augusta, GA

University Legal Nurse Consulting Program, 2024 – Certificate as LNC

Certifications / Memberships

Basic Life Support, Current

Advanced Cardiac Life Support, Current

Certified by American Association of Critical Care Nurses

Member, American Nurses Association, 2008 – 2018

Member, American Association of Legal Nurse Consultants, 2024 – Present

Conclusion: Presenting Attorney-Friendly LNC Qualifications

Success as a Legal Nurse Consultant begins with a resume tailored to attorney expectations—concise, clear, and focused on legal relevance. Use specific, outcome-oriented language to describe your nursing experience, highlight analytical and organizational strengths, and showcase expertise that supports legal casework. By translating your clinical background into attorney-friendly terms and emphasizing the skills law firms value, you will stand out as a highly qualified LNC candidate.

Effective Cover Letters for Legal Nurse Consultants

How to Craft a Cover Letter That Gets You Noticed

What's more likely to land you an interview with an attorney—a cover letter or an awesome resume? If you guessed "awesome resume," you'd likely be mistaken. While a strong resume is essential, the cover letter is what motivates the attorney or hiring manager to read your resume and invite you for an interview. Cover letters are your first opportunity to sell yourself and your credentials. They let you highlight the characteristics that align with the firm's requirements and, most importantly, help you stand out from the competition.

How to Stand Out

Standing out is crucial because the competition for legal nurse consultant (LNC) positions is intense. For example, a recent CareerBuilder job ad attracted 75 applicants in a few hours—and that's just one job board. Hundreds more may have applied through other platforms. If your cover letter begins with "I'm interested in applying for the Legal Nurse Consultant position...," you'll blend in with everyone else. Instead, start your cover letter with a clear statement showing how you can meet the firm's needs.

Before you write, you need to understand what the firm is looking for in an LNC. Review job ads carefully—like those on Indeed—which often list key responsibilities and required skills. Match your opening sentence to the essential areas the firm has identified. This immediately demonstrates that you're a strong fit for the job.

Tip: Scan the job description for repeated keywords or skills. These are likely high priorities for the firm. For example, the CareerBuilder ad listed the following as essential skills:

- Strong attention to detail
- Able to organize, prioritize, and work under a tight schedule
- Able to multi-task and show flexibility in a fast-paced environment
- 1+ years of legal experience
- 3+ years of clinical experience

And it listed the following as essential job functions:

- Review medical records to identify key facts and issues
- Organize and synthesize information in preparation of summaries, chronologies, reports, spreadsheets, charts, logs, etc.
- Perform medical research and possess in-depth knowledge of medical terminology and principles

- Organize and prepare documents, exhibits, and other materials for use in discovery, hearings, or trials.

Tip: Use the first sentence of your cover letter to address one or more of these key requirements directly.

Research the Firm

Customizing your cover letter for each firm starts with research. Showing that you know the firm's major clients or recent achievements helps you connect your skills to their needs.

To research a firm, you can:

1. Visit their official website for background information and recent updates.
2. Read recent news articles or press releases about the firm.
3. Review their client list if available to understand their focus areas.

Sample Cover Letter Breakdown

A great cover letter doesn't just state your interest—it strategically matches your abilities to the firm's job ad. Here's how one RN with no prior LNC experience structured her cover letter and got an interview:

- In the first sentence, she explains how she can help the law firm with one of the essential job functions.
- She then mentions several skills listed in the job ad.
- She demonstrates that she's researched the firm and knows its major clients.
- She tells the recruiter or attorney why she's a good fit for the job.
- She attaches a sample medical summary to show she has the skills, even without legal experience.
- She explicitly requests an interview and, if being proactive, says she'll follow up on a specific date.

Let's put this structure into action with a full sample cover letter:

Sample Cover Letter

7946 Parkway Drive
My City, GA 55555
Cell: 555-555-5555
Email: sramirez@myemail.com

ABC Law Group
5986 Little Chute Road
My City, GA 55555

Dear Ms. Sellerstein,

I am a Registered Nurse with extensive experience reviewing medical records to identify key facts, issues, and deviations from the standards of care—an essential function your firm requires in a Legal Nurse Consultant. My background includes providing care for medically complex patients, where I routinely organize, prioritize, and multitask to ensure optimal outcomes. I have researched ABC Law Group and am impressed by your work with healthcare litigation clients such as LMN Hospital and MedTech Solutions. My skills in clinical documentation, patient assessment, and interdisciplinary communication directly align with the qualifications sought in your job posting. I am confident that my ability to analyze medical records and summarize findings would make me an asset to your team. Enclosed is a sample medical summary I prepared to demonstrate my ability to synthesize complex medical information for legal review.

I would appreciate the opportunity to discuss how my experience and skills can benefit ABC Law Group. I will follow up with your office on 10/09/2025 to discuss next steps.

Sincerely,

Sofia Ramirez

Key Takeaways

- Start your cover letter by addressing the firm's specific needs.
- Match your skills to the job ad using clear, targeted language.
- Research each firm and reference your findings in your letter.
- Provide evidence of your abilities (such as a medical summary) even if you lack direct LNC experience.
- End with a call to action—request an interview and consider stating when you'll follow up.

Tailoring your cover letter to each position increases your chances of standing out and landing an interview. Use the sample provided as a template, adapting it to highlight your unique strengths for every application.

Successfully Mastering the In-House Legal Nurse Consultant Interview

Introduction: Navigating the Unique Challenges of LNC Interviews

Securing an in-house Legal Nurse Consultant (LNC) position is a highly competitive endeavor that demands far more than clinical excellence. Unlike traditional nursing roles, LNC interviews require candidates to demonstrate fluency in legal concepts, an ability to bridge the gap between healthcare and law, and a clear understanding of how nursing acumen translates into legal value. Employers are meticulous in their selection, seeking professionals who can both interpret complex medical information and contribute meaningfully to litigation and case strategy. This guide offers a comprehensive roadmap for LNC candidates, including in-depth legal terminology, enhanced real-world scenarios, and strategies to articulate the unique role and value of LNCs within legal teams.

Expanded Legal Concepts: Key Terms and the LNC's Role

Understanding legal terminology is crucial for LNCs to communicate effectively with attorneys and support the litigation process. Below are essential legal terms and practical explanations of how LNCs contribute to each:

- Deposition: A deposition is a sworn, out-of-court testimony given by a witness or expert during the discovery phase of litigation. LNCs often prepare attorneys by summarizing medical records, identifying key facts, and formulating questions for medical witnesses. They may also serve as expert witnesses themselves, providing clinical explanations under oath.
- Discovery: Discovery is the legal process of exchanging evidence and information between opposing parties before trial. LNCs play a pivotal role by reviewing and organizing voluminous medical records, flagging missing documentation, and translating clinical data into timelines or summaries that clarify case strengths and weaknesses.
- Expert Witness: An expert witness is a professional qualified to offer opinions in their field of expertise during litigation. LNCs may serve in this capacity or assist in locating, vetting, and preparing other medical experts. Their clinical insight ensures that expert testimony aligns with medical standards of care.
- Interrogatory: Interrogatories are written questions submitted by one party to another, requiring formal written answers. LNCs assist attorneys by interpreting

medical jargon within interrogatory responses, ensuring accuracy, and identifying inconsistencies or omissions in opposing parties' statements.

By mastering these concepts and demonstrating their application, LNCs show they are not only medical resources but also valuable contributors to legal processes.

Sample Answers and Real-World Scenarios: Applying LNC Skills in Legal Contexts

The following sample questions, answers, and case studies illustrate how LNCs leverage their backgrounds to support legal teams:

- "Tell me about yourself." Strong Response: "With 20 years as a critical care nurse, I've specialized in complex chart reviews and patient advocacy. In my previous role, I collaborated with attorneys on a high-stakes malpractice suit, where I identified a subtle medication error that shifted the case's trajectory. My clinical analysis helped counsel prepare for deposition and ultimately led to a favorable settlement for the client. My passion lies in translating clinical complexities into actionable legal insights."
- "Can you describe a time you helped an attorney understand a complex medical issue?" Strong Response: "During a wrongful death case, I reviewed hundreds of pages of ICU documentation. The attorney struggled to piece together the timeline of interventions. I created a visual timeline highlighting each medication change, vital sign trend, and intervention. When the opposing expert claimed timely treatment, my analysis revealed a two-hour delay in antibiotic administration, which became a central argument during discovery. My work empowered the legal team to challenge the opposing side's narrative with confidence."
- "How do you prioritize tasks when working on multiple cases?" Detailed Example: "Recently, I managed three active cases approaching discovery deadlines. I established a triage system, consulting with each attorney to clarify priorities based on deposition schedules and upcoming interrogatories. By breaking down each case into actionable steps and leveraging project management tools, I ensured all critical summaries and chronologies were delivered ahead of attorney preparation meetings—even when new evidence was introduced last minute."
- "Describe a situation where you managed a tight deadline or shifting priorities." Scenario: "When a last-minute request for a medical expert summary arrived before a high-profile deposition, I reprioritized my schedule, coordinated with the legal assistant to obtain missing records, and synthesized a clear, concise report within 24 hours. The attorney credited my work with enabling a focused

line of questioning, which ultimately exposed inconsistencies in the opposing expert's testimony."

- "How do you handle working with a team of attorneys who may have different communication styles?" Illustrative Example: "In my current consulting practice, I support both litigation partners and associates—some prefer detailed written briefs, others opt for verbal debriefs. For one partner who favored succinct updates, I developed executive summaries with visual aids; for another, I provided annotated medical records. By seeking feedback and adjusting my approach, I ensured each attorney received the information in their preferred format, leading to more efficient case preparation."

Unique Value of LNCs: Distinguishing Clinical Expertise from Paralegals

Legal Nurse Consultants bring a unique blend of clinical expertise and legal acumen that sets them apart from paralegals. While paralegals possess strong legal research and procedural knowledge, they may lack the clinical background to interpret nuanced medical records, identify deviations from standards of care, or anticipate the medical implications of legal arguments. LNCs, as licensed healthcare professionals, decode complex medical data, spot subtle patterns, and provide context that shapes case strategy.

Attorneys rely on LNCs to translate medical jargon, summarize causation, and evaluate damages—functions that require both critical thinking and hands-on clinical experience. LNCs also serve as a bridge, ensuring that medical experts communicate effectively with legal teams and that legal arguments are grounded in accurate clinical realities. This dual perspective is invaluable in malpractice, personal injury, product liability, and other medically intensive cases.

Key Articulation Point for Interviews: "Unlike paralegals or attorneys, I bring firsthand clinical experience to the table. I don't just summarize medical records—I interpret them through the lens of current standards of care, anticipate how opposing experts might frame clinical events, and proactively identify gaps or strengths in the medical evidence that are critical to case outcomes."

Interview Preparation: Strategies and Typical Questions

1. Research the Firm: Understand its areas of practice, notable cases, and team structure. Tailor your responses to demonstrate alignment with the firm's values and needs.

2. Practice Legal Terminology: Use terms such as "deposition," "discovery," and "expert witness" confidently and accurately.
3. Prepare for Behavioral and Scenario-Based Questions: Illustrate your answers with specific examples that showcase your analytical skills, adaptability, and unique clinical insights.
4. Typical Interview Questions:
5. "Why do you want to work at this firm?" (Showcase genuine interest and long-term commitment.)
6. "Why did you become an LNC?" (Demonstrate passion for the intersection of law and medicine.)
7. "Where do you see yourself in five years?" (Express dedication to growing within the legal field.)
8. "What are your strengths and weaknesses?" (Be honest, self-aware, and solution oriented.)

Addressing Interviewer Reservations: Techniques and Model Responses

1. Listen and Clarify: If the interviewer expresses a concern, listen fully and ask clarifying questions if needed. Acknowledge and Connect: Recognize the concern and relate it to your transferable skills. Express Willingness to Learn: Demonstrate adaptability and eagerness to master new legal concepts or technologies.
2. Model Responses:
    - Lack of Legal Experience: "While I haven't worked directly in a law firm, my clinical background involved extensive chart review, policy interpretation, and multidisciplinary collaboration—skills central to the LNC role. I am committed to mastering legal procedures and have already completed continuing education in medical-legal consulting."
    - Employment Gaps: "During my career gap, I maintained my nursing license, completed legal nurse consulting coursework, and volunteered in case review projects. These experiences kept my skills current and demonstrated my commitment to ongoing development."
    - Unfamiliarity with Specific Software: "I haven't used [specific software], but I am proficient with multiple electronic health records and legal research tools. I enjoy learning new systems and am confident I can become proficient quickly."

Key Questions to Ask During Your Interview

- Who does this position report to, and what is the team structure?

- What are the primary responsibilities, including both legal and paralegal duties?
- Are there other LNCs on staff, or will I be establishing the role?
- Which attorneys will I support, and what are their expectations for the LNC position?
- What are the work hours, salary range, benefits, vacation policies, and dress code? (Discuss these after substantive role-based questions.)

Follow-Up: The Importance of the Thank-You Note and Final Strategies

Always send a brief, personalized thank-you email within three hours of your interview. Reference a specific moment from your conversation, reiterate your enthusiasm / excitement for the role, and restate the value you bring as an LNC. This step demonstrates professionalism, gratitude, and continued interest—qualities that leave a lasting impression.

Conclusion: Standing Out as an In-House Legal Nurse Consultant

Success in LNC interviews hinges on your ability to articulate the bridge you build between medicine and law. By mastering legal terminology, illustrating your value with detailed case studies, and clearly distinguishing your clinical insight from other legal professionals, you'll position yourself as an indispensable asset to any legal team. Prepare thoroughly, address challenges head-on, ask insightful questions, and follow up thoughtfully—you'll not only impress interviewers but also lay the foundation for a rewarding career as a Legal Nurse Consultant.

Recognizing and Addressing a Bad Fit as a Legal Nurse Consultant

Understanding 'Fit' in Legal Nurse Consulting

In the context of legal nurse consulting (LNC), "fit" describes how well your skills, personality, and work style align with a law firm's expectations and culture. Whether you're an in-house, independent, or expert LNC, your ability to function effectively hinges on more than just your clinical expertise; it's about how you're perceived by the firm, how your values align with theirs, and how comfortable you feel in your day-to-day role. Recognizing when you're a poor fit is crucial to your professional satisfaction and success.

Common Causes of a Bad Fit

A bad fit can stem from several sources, including:

- Culture: Differences in work environment preferences or communication styles.
- Values: Conflicting beliefs about ethics, work-life balance, or professional priorities.
- Job Content: Mismatches in job duties, workload, or required skills.
- Expectations: Diverging views on availability, responsiveness, or compensation.

New LNCs may overlook these factors in their eagerness to land a first case or position but acknowledging them early can help prevent frustration and burnout.

Signals of a Bad Fit

Internal Signals

1. Internal Signals Reluctance to Engage: You dread interacting with the law firm—perhaps you feel anxious before meetings or avoid answering calls and emails.
2. Mismatched Values: You notice discomfort with the firm's culture, such as tolerating inappropriate jokes or unprofessional behavior despite voicing concerns.
3. Identity Clash: Others see you differently than you see yourself; for example, you consider yourself thorough and energetic, but colleagues view your approach as overwhelming or out of sync with firm norms.
4. Declining Motivation: You struggle to give your best effort, find yourself distracted, or blame others for your loss of focus.

External Signals

1. Negative Feedback: You receive criticism that doesn't reflect your actual performance, such as being told your case analysis lacks support when you've been thorough, or feeling unfairly singled out by colleagues.
2. Unreasonable Expectations: The firm expects constant availability (e.g., 24/7 calls for expert LNCs) or flexibility in fees without respecting your business boundaries.

Strategies for Adapting to a Challenging Environment

If you suspect a misfit but want to improve the situation, consider these actionable steps:

- Seek Mentorship: Connect with a more experienced LNC or a trusted attorney within the firm. For instance, if you're struggling with the firm's workflow, a mentor can provide practical tips on navigating expectations or office politics.

- Communicate Openly: Schedule a meeting with your supervisor or point of contact to discuss your concerns. Use "I" statements and provide concrete examples (e.g., "I've noticed I'm not always clear on priorities for case reviews; can we review expectations?").
- Adjust Work Habits: Reflect on your work style and consider modifying your approach. For example, if you tend to be very detail-oriented and colleagues prefer concise summaries, try tailoring your reports to their preferences while maintaining accuracy.
- Set Boundaries: Clarify your availability and fee structure in writing. If a law firm expects you to answer calls at all hours, politely explain your working hours and stick to them.

Adapting can be challenging, but even small changes can improve your experience and demonstrate your willingness to be flexible and professional.

Tips for Transitioning Out of a Bad Fit

If adapting isn't feasible or feels unprincipled, it's wise to prepare for a transition:

- Network Proactively: Reach out to other LNCs, attend industry events, or join professional organizations like the American Association of Legal Nurse Consultants. Sharing your experiences can lead to referrals and job leads.
- Update Your Resume and Portfolio: Highlight your accomplishments and skills, focusing on experiences that demonstrate your adaptability and expertise. For example, include case studies that showcase your ability to deliver high-quality work under pressure.
- Seek Professional Support: Consider career coaching or peer support groups. Discussing your situation with others who understand the LNC field can offer valuable perspective and encouragement.
- Plan an Exit Strategy: Line up alternative contracts or employment before resigning. For instance, if you're an independent LNC, secure commitments from new attorney clients so you can transition smoothly.

One LNC, for example, realized after a year that her values didn't match her firm's aggressive litigation style. By gradually networking at national conferences, she landed a new position with a firm whose culture better matched her collaborative approach.

Conclusion

Recognizing a bad fit is not a personal failure; it's an important step toward a more satisfying and productive career. By staying alert to the signals, trying practical adaptation strategies, and preparing for a thoughtful transition if needed, you can ensure your work as a legal nurse consultant remains rewarding. Remember, every experience—positive or negative—can help guide your future choices and growth in the field.

Four Reasons In-House Firms Fire LNCs—and How to Stay on Track

Concrete, Step-by-Step Strategies for Legal Nurse Consultants to Thrive in In-House Firms

You've landed the LNC in-house firm job. Now let's make sure that you keep it. Working as a legal nurse consultant (LNC) in a firm brings exciting opportunities and unique challenges. While firings do happen, you can avoid common pitfalls by following clear, practical steps. Here are four key reasons in-house firms let LNCs go—and exactly what you can do to prevent these missteps, illustrated with both cautionary tales and encouraging examples of success.

1. Failure to Follow Firm Procedures: How to Ensure Compliance

In-house firms operate differently from hospitals, with individualized processes for everything from case file management to report formatting. Adapting quickly is crucial. Here's an actionable approach:

- Step 1: On your first day, request a written or verbal overview of the firm's processes for setting up case files, organizing medical records, and saving documents.
- Step 2: Create a personal checklist based on these procedures and refer to it before completing any task.
- Step 3: If a process seems unclear, ask a colleague or supervisor for clarification before making changes.
- Step 4: When asked to adjust your approach, make the change immediately and confirm with the requestor that the adjustment meets expectations.

Cautionary Example: An LNC who reorganized file folders without approval left an attorney unable to locate key documents and was terminated. Success Story: Another LNC noticed inefficiencies but first sought input from team members and leadership before suggesting any modifications. Her collaborative approach led to a process improvement initiative—and earned her praise.

2. Failure to Prioritize: Building a Weekly Routine

Effective prioritization is essential in a fast-paced firm. Use this simple weekly routine to keep yourself and your cases on track:

- Step 1: Every Monday morning, block off 30 minutes as your "Look Ahead" session.
- Step 2: Review your calendar for client meetings, depositions, trial dates, and special attorney requests for the week and month ahead.
- Step 3: List tasks by deadline and importance, then assign each a specific completion date and time.
- Step 4: Share your plan with your supervising attorney if needed to confirm priorities, adjusting as needed.

Cautionary Example: An LNC repeatedly missed deadlines for providing reports before client meetings and was let go. Success Story: By proactively scheduling her "Look Ahead" time, another LNC consistently delivered reports early, allowing attorneys to prepare thoroughly and leading to increased trust and repeat assignments.

3. Inability to Analyze Cases: Mastering Case Analysis Techniques

Strong case analysis skills set great LNCs apart. Rather than including all details, focus on what matters. Here's how to sharpen your analysis:

- Step 1: Read the case summary and identify the legal question (e.g., Was there nursing negligence in medication administration?).
- Step 2: Apply the 5 Ws and 1 H method:
- Who: Who was involved? (Patient, nurses, physicians)
- What: What happened? (Medication error, documentation gap)
- When: When did it occur? (Exact date/time of the incident)
- Where: Where did it happen? (Hospital unit, law firm context)
- Why: Why did it happen? (unclear protocols)
- How: How did it impact the case? (Patient outcome, damages)

Step 3: Summarize findings, highlighting only the relevant facts that answer the legal question.

Sample Analysis:

- Who: Ms. Smith, RN; Mr. Jones, patient
- What: Morphine dose administered at 2:00 PM
- When: 10/01/2025

- Where: Med/Surg Unit
- Why: Physician ordered repeat dose without updated assessment
- How: Patient experienced respiratory depression, requiring ICU transfer

Cautionary Example: An LNC who included excessive background details obscured the key issues and was eventually dismissed. Success Story: Another LNC mastered focused analysis using the 5 Ws and 1 H technique, producing concise summaries that helped attorneys pinpoint liability, leading to case wins and excellent performance reviews.

4. Attitude: Creating a Positive Impact

Your workplace attitude influences everything. Here are steps to foster professionalism:

- Step 1: Approach new policies and procedures with curiosity instead of criticism.
- Step 2: If you have concerns, raise them privately with your supervisor, using constructive language ("I'd like to understand the rationale behind this change" rather than "This is unnecessary").
- Step 3: Support colleagues by sharing resources and offering help when possible.
- Step 4: Celebrate team successes and express appreciation for feedback.

Cautionary Example: A paralegal publicly disparaged a new workflow and was let go. Success Story: An LNC who expressed openness and gratitude for feedback became a trusted team member, often chosen for high-profile assignments and included in decision-making meetings.

Conclusion: Actionable Steps for LNC Success

By following firm procedures, using a weekly prioritization routine, mastering focused case analysis, and maintaining a positive, collaborative attitude, you can avoid common pitfalls and create a thriving career as an LNC. Remember, every challenge is an opportunity to demonstrate your professionalism and dedication. With these step-by-step strategies, you'll be well-prepared to excel in any law firm environment.

Chapter 13: Law Firm LNC Skills

Working as a legal nurse consultant within a law firm requires more than clinical expertise—it demands adaptability, precision, and a deep understanding of how legal teams operate. Unlike independent practice, where you set your own pace and structure, law firm work places you in the middle of a fast-moving, collaborative environment. Attorneys rely on you not just for your medical knowledge, but for your ability to anticipate needs, manage records efficiently, and communicate findings in ways that support litigation strategy.

This chapter explores the essential skills that make you a valuable member of a law firm team. You'll learn how to navigate complex workflows, organize medical records for trial preparation, and contribute proactively to case management. From billing practices and expert retention to deposition support and document indexing, each section offers practical tools to help you thrive in a structured legal setting.

Whether you're new to law firm work or looking to refine your approach, this chapter will help you build confidence, avoid common pitfalls, and deliver consistent value to attorneys and clients alike. Let's dive into the skills that transform a nurse into a trusted legal consultant.

Before diving into specific workflows and billing practices, let's start with the mindset that sets successful law firm LNCs apart: proactivity.

5 Proactive Strategies for Legal Nurse Consultants

How to Move Beyond Crisis Mode and Add Value to Your Legal Team

When I first started as a legal nurse consultant (LNC) in a law firm, I noticed a stark difference between colleagues who were proactive and those who operated in a constant state of crisis. One nurse I worked with had twenty-five years of LNC experience, yet she often found herself scrambling at the last minute. She waited for assignments, responded to urgent requests, and spent her days "putting out fires." Watching her struggle convinced me that being proactive isn't just preferable—it's essential. Here are five actionable strategies, drawn directly from my own experiences, to help you become a proactive LNC and make a real impact.

1. Review Calendars Proactively

Early in my career, our law firm relied on secretaries to pass along notices of depositions, trials, and hearings to the LNCs. These notices were often scheduled weeks or even months ahead, providing plenty of time for thorough preparation. However, secretaries occasionally forgot to forward this critical information. One Monday morning, during our weekly office meeting, my reactive colleague discovered she was missing out on an important hearing scheduled for that week—information she should have received much earlier. She was understandably frustrated, racing to catch up and venting about the missed notice.

Instead of depending solely on others, I learned to take initiative by reviewing the firm's legal calendar myself. I'd not only look at the week ahead but scan a month or more in advance. This allowed me to proactively reach out to attorneys, offer support, request updated medical records, and prepare materials well before deadlines. By making calendar review a regular habit, you can avoid last-minute scrambles and ensure you're always prepared to assist your team.

2. Suggest Effective Report Formats

Attorneys appreciate clear, actionable information—but sometimes their requested formats aren't the most effective. In one nursing home case, I was asked to create a chronology of several years' worth of medication orders and administration records. After compiling the data, I realized that the traditional chronology was overwhelming and confusing, making it difficult to track medication trends over time.

I decided to try something different: using a calendar template in Microsoft Word, I mapped out when each medication was ordered and administered. The visual layout made patterns—such as gaps in administration or changes in orders—immediately obvious. When I presented this calendar to the attorney, she was thrilled. She mentioned that it "made the case so much clearer" and requested similar formats for future cases. The experience taught me that proactively suggesting alternative report formats can save time, reduce confusion, and strengthen your value to the legal team. Don't hesitate to propose new ways to present complex information, especially if it helps attorneys grasp the details quickly.

3. Create a Treater List While Reviewing Records

It's common for attorneys to ask for a list of physicians, nurses, and other treaters involved in a case. In my early days, I'd finish reviewing thousands of pages of medical records, only to be asked months later for a complete list of treaters—sending me back through stacks of documents and wasting valuable hours. To solve this, I started building a treater list as I reviewed each record. Every time I came across a new name or role, I added it to a running document.

This simple step paid off tremendously. When attorneys requested the list, I could deliver it within minutes instead of hours (or days). Keeping an organized, proactive treater list saves time, reduces headaches, and positions you as a detail-oriented consultant who anticipates needs before they arise. My advice: always compile your treater list as you go and update it regularly.

4. Change Your Attitude: Don't Wait for Settlements

Mindset matters. I once worked with a colleague who believed, "If you wait long enough, the case will settle." She used this as an excuse to delay her work, assuming she wouldn't need to provide a thorough report if the case resolved early. One time, she handed in a summary of the medical records at 11 p.m. the night before trial. The attorney told her, "This is useless to me now—I needed it a long time ago." Her procrastination not only caused unnecessary stress but also diminished her value to the team.

In contrast, proactive LNCs recognize that attorneys need information ahead of time to strategize and prepare. By providing summaries, chronologies, and analyses well before deadlines, you help attorneys do their best work—and you earn their trust. Adjust your attitude to anticipate needs, rather than waiting to be asked.

5. Know the Attorney's Style and Communicate Proactively

Attorneys, like everyone else, have their own work habits. Some are planners; others are last-minute workers. I've learned that understanding each attorney's style helps me anticipate their needs and deliver value at the right moment. For example, one attorney I worked with was notorious for requesting LNC services just days before a deposition. Instead of waiting to be asked, I'd check the legal calendar, note upcoming depositions, and send a quick email: "I noticed Dr. Smith's deposition in the Burns case is next week. Would you like a medical chronology or the records tagged ahead of time?" After learning that the attorney consistently preferred both a medical chronology and tagged records, I began gathering and preparing these materials ahead of time.

This proactive approach consistently helped attorneys by making their jobs easier. By tailoring your communication—whether by sending reminders, offering to prepare materials, or suggesting relevant reports—you demonstrate awareness and reliability. Take time to learn your attorneys' preferences and rhythms, then find ways to support them before they ask.

Conclusion: The Value of Proactive LNC Work

Functioning as a reactive LNC leads to stress, wasted time, and missed opportunities to shine. By proactively reviewing calendars, suggesting effective report formats, organizing treater lists, adjusting your mindset, and understanding attorney styles, you'll add genuine value to your legal team. These strategies, rooted in real-life experience, can help you shift from crisis mode to confident, proactive consulting. Start implementing them today—and watch your professional reputation and results grow.

Once you've embraced a proactive mindset, the next step is transforming your daily routines. Trial preparation isn't a last-minute scramble—it's a discipline that begins the moment a case lands on your desk.

Proactive Trial Preparation: A Step-by-Step Workflow for LNCs

Transforming Case Management with Practical Strategies and Concrete Examples

Trial preparation is often seen as a daunting process—one that many legal nurse consultants (LNCs) delay until a case is set for trial. In the United States, most medical malpractice cases settle before ever reaching a courtroom. As a result, it's common for LNCs to postpone trial prep, thinking, "If I wait long enough, this case might just disappear." While this approach may seem logical, it can create significant problems down the line.

The Problem with Last-Minute Preparation

When trial preparation only begins after a trial date is scheduled, chaos often follows. LNCs may find themselves spending weeks—or even months—frantically creating reports, gathering missing records, and trying to remember rarely used procedures. During this crunch time, other cases are neglected, causing a ripple effect of missed deadlines and increased stress throughout the firm.

For example, I once inherited 30 medical malpractice cases at a law firm, with 13 set for trial within the next 11 months. Tens of thousands of pages of medical records were waiting for review. The backlog was overwhelming, and the team was caught in a cycle of last-minute scrambling. This scenario is all too common for LNCs who rely on reactive rather than proactive strategies.

Shifting the Mindset: Treat Every Case as If It Will Go to Trial

The backlog wasn't really the fault of the LNC who had previously held my position. It's exceedingly difficult to break free from this stressful routine. To do so, I changed my approach. Instead of assuming cases would settle, I treated every new case as though it was destined for trial. The day I was assigned a case became the day I started trial preparation. This mindset shift transformed my workflow and reduced the pressure that came with impending trial dates. The more effort invested early in the case, the less panic and overtime required as trial approached.

Step-by-Step Workflow for Proactive Trial Preparation

1. Review Medical Records as They Arrive

Start by reviewing medical records as soon as they come in, rather than letting them pile up. For example, after receiving a new batch of documents, I quickly scan for admissions, surgeries, or critical test results, flagging any gaps or missing dates. This immediate review identifies issues early and helps prioritize next steps.

2. Identify and Obtain Additional Providers' Records

Next, as you review each record, note the names of other providers involved in the patient's care. With the attorney's approval, promptly request these records. This avoids the stressful, last-minute scramble to gather critical documents. For instance, if a hospital discharge summary mentions a specialist not previously on your radar, add that provider to your records request list immediately.

3. Develop a Treater List

After gathering provider information, create a comprehensive treater list. This document serves as a living record of everyone involved in the patient's care and later becomes the template for a fact witness list. Keep the list updated as new providers are identified.

4. Tag Important Pages in Medical Records

As you review, tag key pages in the medical records. For example, if you find a physician's progress note documenting a medication error, highlight and copy that page. I once tagged a set of operative notes that included a critical timeline error—these notes later became pivotal exhibits at trial. Tagging as you go ensures that important documents are easy to locate when needed.

5. Create a Medical Chronology and/or Summary

If you're just reading the medical records, you're wasting your valuable time. While reading the records, start building a medical chronology or summary. For example, read medical records on one monitor screen, and add information from the records on the other monitor screen. These documents help clarify the sequence of events and can be used to refresh the attorney's memory or assist new team members. For instance, a timeline showing when and how a patient's infection developed can be used to build a compelling narrative for trial.

6. Hire Experts Early and Send Them Pertinent Records

Next, identify and retain medical experts as soon as possible. Immediately send them only the most relevant records—don't wait until the last minute to send a mountain of documents. This approach gives experts time to thoroughly review the case and provide meaningful opinions.

7. Follow Up with Experts and Document Their Opinions

After that, schedule a phone conference with each expert to discuss their findings. This allows the attorney to strategize or, if the review is negative, seek another expert without delay. Summarize these conversations in a clear report for the trial team.

8. Create Pertinent Indexes

I used to be teased by another LNC about my indexes, but I always explained that spending time at the front end of the case saves ten times that amount of time at the end of the case. I didn't have to scramble at the last minute combing through files and letters finding information.

At the start of the case, create indexes for medical records. Update these as needed. For example, a medical record index with hyperlinks or page references saves hours when searching for specific entries.

9. Research Medical Conditions and Maintain a Research Index

Research relevant medical conditions early and maintain a research index. This resource can answer quick questions and support trial arguments. For instance, if the case involves a rare infection, gathering peer-reviewed literature upfront can strengthen your case.

10. Obtain and Index Radiographs and Pathology Slides

If radiographs or pathology slides are relevant, obtain them promptly and develop corresponding indexes. Send these materials to the appropriate experts early to avoid delays.

Ongoing Case Management

- Update the medical chronology, treater list, and all indexes as new records arrive.
- Regularly compare your treater list with the firm's subpoena or medical authorization log to confirm all necessary records have been collected.
- Prepare for depositions by tagging relevant provider documentation, Draft potential questions for both fact and expert witnesses as requested by the attorney.
- For living plaintiffs, obtain updated records from their primary care and other providers to ensure you have the latest information.
- Create visual aids—such as timelines, graphs, touch charts, and calendars—that clarify complex aspects of the case. These often become the foundation for demonstrative evidence at trial.
- Continue interacting with experts by sending them depositions and new medical records, and scheduling follow-up conferences as needed.

Practical Tips for Front-End Case Management

- Create Checklists and Templates: Develop and use checklists for each phase of case management, such as a "New Case Checklist" or "Deposition Prep Template." Update and refine these tools as you learn what works best for your practice.
- Schedule Regular Reviews: Set calendar reminders to review each case at regular intervals, even if no immediate deadlines exist. This keeps all cases moving forward and prevents last-minute surprises.
- Collaborate with Your Team: Share your checklists, templates, and findings with attorneys and paralegals to ensure everyone stays informed and aligned.

Conclusion: The Benefits of Proactive Preparation

By adopting a proactive, detailed approach to trial preparation, LNCs can reduce last-minute stress, avoid workflow disruptions, and ensure no case is neglected. Treating every case as if it will go to trial allows you to stay ahead of deadlines and increases your confidence in the courtroom. With effective task management, checklists, and collaboration, you'll deliver better outcomes for your clients—and turn trial preparation from a dreaded task into a manageable, even satisfying, part of your professional routine.

Strong workflows keep cases moving, but accurate billing ensures your contributions are recognized. Let's explore how to track your time with clarity and confidence."

How to Become Your Firm's Best LNC Biller

Practical Tips, Common Pitfalls, and Actionable Steps for Legal Nurse Consultants

Accurate billing is more than just a requirement for legal nurse consultants (LNCs)—it's a reflection of your professionalism, attention to detail, and commitment to your firm's success. Whether you're working at a plaintiff or defense firm, the way you track and document your time can impact your workflow, your reputation, and the revenue your contributions generate. I learned this firsthand as I navigated the world of law firm billing, transforming my approach through trial, error, and a few valuable lessons from colleagues.

My Journey: From Paper Forms to Efficient Billing

When I started as an LNC, billing was a foreign concept. Plaintiff firms often don't require time tracking since they work on contingency. (However, at the end of this article, I make a case for why you should keep track of your time no matter where you work.) Defense firms bill insurance companies meticulously for every minute spent. At my first defense law firm, I entered my own time using digital software, crafting detailed descriptions for each billing entry. It never occurred to me that someone else might input my time.

My second firm was a different story. There, my secretary was responsible for entering time, using a tablet of edge-glued forms with only two columns—case name and billing entries. I followed instructions and handed her my handwritten notes. The next day, I reviewed her entries and realized the descriptions were vague and didn't reflect the true scope of my work. I decided to write out my own billing descriptions but soon realized it would be far easier and more accurate to input everything into the computer myself rather than handwriting the billing entries. When I told my secretary, she was relieved; entering billing took her an entire day each month.

This shift was transformative. While my colleagues spent hours (or days) at month's end reconstructing their activities from calendars and memory, I documented tasks as I completed them—just as I would chart in nursing. Waiting until the end of the month to bill is like documenting patient care a month after it happens; it's inefficient and prone to errors.

Common Billing Mistakes—and How to Avoid Them

Through experience, I witnessed several common pitfalls that LNCs often encounter:

- Retrospective billing: Waiting until the end of the month to recall and record activities leads to forgotten tasks and incomplete entries.
- Vague descriptions: Billing entries that lack specificity do not accurately capture the work done and may be questioned by clients or auditors.
- Missed billable tasks: Overlooking time spent on substantive work, such as research or case analysis, reduces your reported productivity and your firm's revenue.
- Including non-billable activities: Tasks like scheduling meetings or transcribing notes should not be billed—these are typically considered secretarial work.

To avoid these mistakes, document each task immediately after completion, use precise and descriptive language in billing entries, and separate billable from non-billable activities. Contemporaneous billing ensures accuracy and completeness, while detailed descriptions provide transparency and value.

Digital Tools: The Game Changer

Initially, I tracked my time with handwritten notes, jotting down start and stop times. As technology advanced, I switched to digital time-tracking tools like Jibble[54], Clockify[55], and Toggl Track[56]. Using a timer app on my phone made it effortless to record time in six-minute increments, the standard for defense firms. This not only improved accuracy but also saved me time—no more deciphering scribbled times.

Switching to digital time tracking brought a new level of efficiency. I could quickly review my entries, generate reports, and ensure that every billable minute was accounted for. This reduced errors, eliminated redundant administrative work, and allowed me to focus on what mattered: supporting attorneys and clients with expert nursing insight.

[54] Jibble. https://www.jibble.io/ (accessed January 2026).
[55] Clockify. https://clockify.me/ (accessed January 2026).
[56] Toggl Track. https://toggl.com/ (accessed January 2026.

Key Steps to Becoming Your Firm's Best LNC Biller

- Track time contemporaneously: Document your activities as you complete them to ensure accuracy and avoid missed entries.
- Use detailed billing descriptions: Clearly explain each task, providing context and specificity for every entry. By proactively explaining the complexity and objectives of your review, you minimize billing disputes and reinforce your value as a detail-oriented LNC biller.
- In addition to providing detailed descriptions, consider how including page counts in your entries can impact billing transparency and reduce misunderstanding. Be mindful about adding the number of pages to your billing entries. If it's the firm's standard practice, continue to do so; otherwise, it's best to avoid it. Listing page counts often invites comparisons from firm administrators and adjustors. For instance, if you bill 1.2 hours to review 100 pages of Medical Records X but 4.7 hours for 100 pages of Medical Records Y, you might be asked to explain the time difference. Or the 4.7 hours might be cut to 1.2 hours automatically. To prevent such questions and actions, always clarify the scope of your review in your descriptions—such as, 'Review of Medical Records X to identify all entries by Nurse Hamilton in preparation for his deposition' versus 'Analysis of Medical Records Y, our client's records, from January through December 2025 to determine the sequence of medical events leading to plaintiff damages.
- Separate billable from non-billable tasks: Bill only for substantive work; exclude secretarial or administrative activities.
- Leverage digital time-tracking tools: Use apps like Jibble, Clockify, or Toggl Track to record time efficiently and accurately.
- Review entries regularly: Check your billing for completeness and clarity before submission.
- Take ownership of your billing process: Whenever possible, input your own time rather than relying on others to interpret your work.
- Learn from feedback: If your entries are questioned or revised, use the feedback to improve your future billing.

By embracing these strategies, you'll not only become your firm's best LNC biller, but also enhance your professional credibility and contribute greater value to your team. Accurate, efficient billing is within your reach; just take it one step at a time.

Accurately tracking your time and contributions is essential for success even in Plaintiff firms. This lesson became clear to me early in my career when I transitioned from a legal nurse consultant to a supervisory role at my first law firm. In addition to handling my usual casework, I found myself immersed in administrative responsibilities—writing policies and procedures, leading team meetings, and recruiting and training new nurse consultants. Because I was diligent about recording the hours I spent on each of these tasks, I could present a comprehensive log of my efforts when the firm asked everyone to summarize their annual contributions. As I compiled my time entries, I realized just how much I had accomplished: reviewing nearly 550 resumes, interviewing over 40 candidates, hiring and training a dozen new consultants, conducting multiple team meetings, and drafting several key policies. When year-end bonuses were awarded, my thorough time tracking paid off, and I received a significant bonus for my documented impact.

My experience illustrates how careful documentation not only showcases your value but can also lead to meaningful recognition. To make this work for you, establish a simple system—whether it's a spreadsheet or a reliable time-tracking app—and make it a habit to update your records consistently, ideally as you complete each task. By keeping your records current and detailed, you'll be prepared to demonstrate your contributions clearly and advocate for the recognition you deserve.

If you're working with defense firms or insurance clients, you'll need to understand ABA billing codes. These standardized tools help ensure your time is documented correctly.

ABA Billing Codes: A Simple Guide for Legal Nurse Consultants

Clear Steps for Billing Your Time and Expenses

ABA billing codes help defense law firms and their staff bill time in a consistent, standardized way. Most medical malpractice insurance companies require law firms to use these codes, so it's important for legal nurse consultants to know how they work. If you plan to work with defense law firms or medical malpractice insurance companies, understanding these codes will make your job easier.

Simplified Overview: How Billing Codes Work

ABA Codes[57] are part of the Uniform Task-Based Management System developed by the American Bar Association (ABA). For a complete list of ABA codes go to its website. The codes break down billable activities into clear categories, making it easier

[57] ABA Codes. https://tinyurl.com/mrytycvk (accessed December 2025).

for law firms and consultants to track work and expenses. There are three main groups of codes:

- L Codes – For legal tasks and stages of a case
- A Codes – For specific activities you perform
- E Codes – For reimbursable expenses

Attorneys, paralegals, and legal nurse consultants use both an L Code and an A Code when billing time. For example, if a physician client is accused of failing to monitor a patient's anticoagulation levels, resulting in a stroke, you would use specific codes for your tasks.

Step-by-Step Examples: Applying Billing Codes

Here are examples of common tasks and how to bill them:

- Consulting an Expert: Use L130 (Experts/Consultants) and A108 (Communicate - Other External). Description: "Phone call with cardiology expert about their opinion on plaintiff's anticoagulation therapy."
- Writing a Summary Report: Use L130 (Experts/Consultants) and A103 (Draft/Revise). Description: "Drafted summary of expert's review opinion on patient therapy."
- Reviewing Medical Records: Use L120 (Analysis/Strategy) and A104 (Review/Analyze). Description: "Analyzed medical records to determine anticoagulant dosing and lab results."

Guided Code Selection: Choosing the Right Codes

Choose the Appropriate L Code for the Stage of Litigation

L Codes represent the phase or type of legal work. Select the L Code that matches your task.

Case Assessment, Development, and Administration

Pre-Trial Pleadings and Motions

Discovery

Trial Preparation and Trial

Appeal

Choose Relevant E Codes for Reimbursable Expenses

E Codes are for costs you can be reimbursed for, such as copying, travel, or expert fees. Select those that apply to your work.

Document & Communication Expenses

Travel & Meals

Legal & Professional Fees

Select an A Code for the Activity Performed

A Codes describe the specific action you take, such as planning, researching, or communicating. Pick the A Code that best matches what you did.

Conclusion: Key Takeaways and Tips

- Use both L Codes and A Codes to bill your time. Pair them with a clear description of your task.
- Check with your client or law firm to confirm if you should use ABA billing codes, especially if you work independently for a defense firm.
- Only certain expenses are reimbursable—use E Codes for those. Organization of records is not reimbursed, nor is communication with others within the firm.
- ABA billing codes are not required for plaintiff law firms, experts, or independent consultants unless requested by your client.
- Keep your billing descriptions short and specific for clarity and accuracy.

With these steps and code lists, you are ready to bill your time as a legal nurse consultant.

Beyond your own work, law firm LNCs often manage expert retention—a process that demands legal awareness, precision, and strong communication."

Expert Retention Process: Step-by-Step Guide with Checklist Linkage

Ensuring Legal Compliance and Workflow Organization for Law Firms

Retaining expert witnesses is a critical component of case preparation in legal practice. A structured expert retention checklist ensures that all procedural, compliance, and communication steps are systematically addressed, reducing the risk of missed deadlines or overlooked requirements. Below, you'll find a clear, step-by-step guide that directly links each narrative explanation to its corresponding checklist item, highlights legal compliance, and offers suggestions for adapting the process to other jurisdictions or case types. The steps outlined here are tailored for civil litigation defense firms, but they can be easily adapted for plaintiff-side practices by shifting the emphasis to case intake procedures and enhanced client communication. For plaintiff firms, adjustments may include focusing on initial client interviews, obtaining authorizations, and ensuring early engagement with experts to support the plaintiff's claims.

Step-by-Step Expert Retention Process

1. Note Critical Deadlines and Pre-Litigation Requirements. In Florida, pre-litigation ("Presuit") rules impose stringent deadlines. The date Presuit ends is recorded at the top of the checklist (PRESUIT ENDS: 5/7/25). Missing this deadline can jeopardize the case by barring expert testimony or even resulting in case dismissal. Always calendar this date and set reminders.
2. Set Expert Review and Conference Deadlines. Identify the expert's review due date (REVIEW DUE: 3/20/25) and schedule a telephone conference well before Presuit ends (TELEPHONE CONFERENCE SCHEDULED: 3/23/25). Early scheduling allows time to secure a second expert if needed, especially if the initial review is unfavorable.
3. Verify and Obtain Expert Certificate. For experts without a Florida license, confirm certificate status (CERTIFICATE CURRENT UNTIL 3/1/26). Florida requires out-of-state physicians and dentists to obtain a certificate to testify. Failure to secure a proper certificate may render expert opinions inadmissible, risking case integrity. If the expert lacks the certificate, assist in obtaining the necessary credentials.
4. Submit Expert Information for Adjustor Approval. For defense firms, send the expert's CV and fee schedule to the insurance adjustor for approval (APPROVAL REQUESTED: 2/10/25; APPROVAL RECEIVED: 2/11/25). If the adjustor declines, promptly begin searching for alternate experts. Once approved, proceed to the next steps.
5. Send Thank You Letter and Retainer. After receiving adjustor approval, mail the thank you letter along with the retainer payment (THANK YOU LETTER MAILED: 2/13/25; RETAINER: $1,000, SENT WITH THANK YOU LETTER). This formalizes retention and sets clear expectations for the expert's engagement.
6. Mail Medical Records and Documentation. Include all necessary medical records with the thank you letter (MAIL MEDICAL RECORDS: MAILED WITH THANK

YOU LETTER) to facilitate the expert's review. Record the mailing date for tracking.

7. Add Expert to Internal Tracking System. Log the expert's details in your firm's expert bank or database (EXPERT BANK: ADDED 2/10/25) to maintain an organized record of all retained experts.
8. Ensure HIPAA Compliance and Business Associate Agreements (for defense firms only). Send the Business Associates Agreement (MAILED 2/16/25) and HIPAA Compliance Agreement (MAILED 2/12/25) to the expert. These documents ensure the expert's handling of protected health information is legally compliant. Record when agreements are received and follow up if necessary, as missing these steps may expose the firm to legal penalties. *Note: This step may not apply to Plaintiff experts.*
9. Gather Expert Preferences. Email the Expert Preferences Form *(see next article)* (EMAILED 2/12/25) to determine the expert's preferred format for receiving records and communication method. Note when the form is returned (RECEIVED 2/13/25).

Checklist Table: Tracking Actions and Dates

Checklist Item	**Status / Date**	**Received**
FLORIDA CERTIFICATION	CURRENT UNTIL 3/1/26	
APPROVAL REQUESTED	2/10/25	
APPROVAL RECEIVED	2/11/25	
THANK YOU LETTER	MAILED 2/13/25	
RETAINER	$1,000, SENT WITH THANK YOU LETTER	
MAIL MEDICAL RECORDS	MAILED WITH THANK YOU LETTER	
EXPERT BANK	ADDED 2/10/25	
BUSINESS ASSOCIATES AGREEMENT	MAILED 2/16/25	RECEIVED _____
HIPAA COMPLIANCE AGREEMENT	MAILED 2/12/25	RECEIVED _____

Checklist Item	Status / Date	Received
EXPERT PREFERENCES FORM	EMAILED 2/12/25	RECEIVED 2/13/25

Certificate and Compliance: Explanations and Consequences

- Certificate: Out-of-state medical experts must have a valid certificate to testify in Florida. Without it, their opinions may be excluded, weakening or undermining the defense.
- Presuit Deadlines: Missing the Presuit deadline can result in dismissal or inability to present expert testimony, ending the case before it reaches court.
- HIPAA/Business Associate Agreements: These agreements protect patient privacy and ensure compliance with federal law. Failure to execute them exposes the firm and expert to regulatory penalties.

Adapting the Checklist for Other Jurisdictions or Case Types

- Update Legal Requirements: Research local pre-litigation, certificate, and expert witness rules for your jurisdiction. Modify or add checklist items to reflect statutory or court-imposed deadlines and documentation.
- Adjust Approval Processes: Where insurance adjustor approval is not required (e.g., plaintiff firms or non-insured cases), omit this step and tailor communication for client or internal approval as needed.
- Customize for Case Type: For non-medical experts or other specialties, substitute relevant credential verification and compliance steps.
- Incorporate Electronic Systems: Consider digital checklists, automated reminders, and secure document portals to improve tracking and communication.

Conclusion: Organizational Benefits and Reminders

A detailed expert retention checklist, with each action directly linked to its narrative justification and tracked for completion, enhances legal compliance, reduces risk, and streamlines workflow. Regularly review and update your checklist to reflect changes in law, procedure, or firm practice. Always print and attach a hard copy to the case file for quick reference, ensuring all correspondence and critical steps are well-documented and accessible.

Streamlining Expert Contact Management: Practical Insights for LNCs

Organizing Preferences for Effective Communication and Medical Records Delivery

Managing expert contacts has become increasingly complex as my network has grown from just a handful to hundreds of professionals. Staying organized is crucial, especially when handling varying preferences for communication and medical records delivery. Over time, I've found that having a clear system not only benefits me but also ensures that experts receive information in the way that works best for them.

Adapting to Changing Preferences: From Hard Copy to Electronic Delivery

As my expert network expanded, so did their options for receiving medical records. While hard copies were once the standard, electronic formats—such as PDFs via file sharing platforms, CDs, and USB flash drives—have become increasingly preferred. Many law firms now favor electronic delivery because it's more efficient and cost-effective. From my experience, sending records electronically has streamlined the process and reduced delays, making it easier for both the firm and the experts involved.

Capturing Preferences: The Expert Contact Form

To keep track of these varied preferences, I use a contact form developed by my secretary. This form is sent to every expert we work with and helps us quickly identify whether they prefer hard copies or electronic records. If your firm has specific practices—like exclusively sending electronic records—you can easily modify the form to suit your needs. Including these options up front removes guesswork and helps everyone stay on the same page.

Communication Choices: Moving Beyond Telephone Tag

The form also asks experts to indicate their preferred method of communication. In the past, I spent a lot of time playing "telephone tag," leaving messages and waiting for return calls. Nowadays, most experts prefer email or text, allowing them to respond quickly on their smartphones without the need for lengthy conversations. This shift has saved me a considerable amount of time and made our exchanges much more efficient.

Address Details and Assistant Contacts: Enhancing Efficiency

Transitioning to other important details, the form includes sections for the expert's address and assistant contact information. Some experts want records sent to their home address, while others prefer their workplace. Additionally, having contact details for an expert's assistant can expedite critical tasks like conflicts checks, scheduling calls, and handling business associate agreements. I've found that involving assistants often leads to faster resolutions and smoother coordination.

Personal Experience: Real Benefits of a Structured Approach

I save the form in an electronic folder in the expert's name on my firm's network so that all firm members can access it. Implementing this form has truly simplified my workflow. Instead of struggling to connect with experts or wondering about their preferences, I can focus on the substantive aspects of their contributions—their expert opinions. The time saved and improved communication have allowed me to support our cases more effectively and build stronger professional relationships.

Conclusion: The Value of Organized Expert Management

In summary, organizing expert contact information and preferences is essential for legal nurse consultants and law firm staff. By adopting a streamlined form and embracing electronic options, you'll enhance efficiency, reduce miscommunication, and ensure that experts receive the information they need in the format they prefer. Small changes like these make a big difference in managing growing networks and keeping your workflow on track.

Sample Expert Preferences Form

Instructions for Completing the Expert Preferences Form

- Please fill out each section of the form as thoroughly as possible.
- Where options are listed, check all boxes that apply to your preferences.
- For address fields, indicate the exact location or method for delivery.
- Providing your assistant's contact details is optional but strongly encouraged to help expedite scheduling, records delivery, and communication.

Benefits of Completing This Form

By clearly indicating your preferences, you help us ensure records and communications are delivered promptly and efficiently, reducing unnecessary follow-up and allowing you to focus on your expert analysis. This process streamlines workflow for both parties and minimizes delays.

Name:	**Specialty:**
Medical Records Format (Check all that you prefer)	□ Hard copy – printed records □ Electronically – PDF format □ CD □ Flash drive □ ShareFile
Send Hard Copy Medical Records to: □ Home Address □ Office Address Send Electronic Medical Records Notification to: □ Email Address	______________________________ ______________________________ ______________________________ ______________________________
Your Assistant's Name:	
Your Assistant's Number:	
Your Assistant's Email:	

Expert Management in Medical Litigation: An Effective Tracking System

How a robust workflow tool saves time, reduces confusion, and improves accountability for law firms

Managing communications and document exchanges with many medical experts is a significant challenge for law firms managing complex medical malpractice cases. When I inherited some of these cases, I had to sort through letters to each expert to determine which records had been sent to them. As the number of involved experts increased, so did the risk of confusion, lost records, and inefficiencies with the potential to hinder case progress. Recognizing these challenges, our firm adopted a comprehensive tracking system that has transformed the way we coordinate with experts, streamlining our workflow and ensuring greater accountability throughout the litigation process.

Case Study Overview: Navigating Complexity in Medical Malpractice

To illustrate the scale and complexity of our work, consider a case involving multiple pediatricians, their employer, several pediatric ophthalmologists, an allergist, an eye hospital, a pediatrician from another practice, and a pediatric neurosurgeon. The patient—a four-year-old boy—presented with symptoms that led to visits with numerous specialists and a lengthy medical journey. Over several months, the child saw pediatricians for weight concerns, was referred to ophthalmologists for vision changes, visited an allergist for eye symptoms, and ultimately underwent a craniotomy for a suprasellar brain mass that left him blind and with diabetes insipidus.

The complexity of this case required us to retain eight experts, including specialists in pediatrics, pediatric ophthalmology, neuro-ophthalmology, neuro-oncology, gastroenterology, neurology, neurosurgery, and endocrinology. With different records and case materials mailed to each expert, managing communications became exponentially more challenging.

Connecting Case Complexity to Workflow Needs

The intricate web of specialists and the sheer volume of medical records—nearly 100,000 pages in this instance—highlighted the urgent need for a robust system to manage expert communications. Without a structured approach, it meant having to review every page of correspondence in the expert's folder, a tedious approach. Tracking what information had been sent, when it was sent, and to whom quickly became unmanageable, leading to repeated follow-ups and potential delays in expert reviews.

The Tracking System Solution: Implementation and Impact

To address these workflow challenges, our team developed a medical record tracking index—a centralized tracking system that logged every document sent to each expert, including the date of mailing and the specific records provided. This solution allowed us to efficiently monitor our communications with many experts, including those retained in just 10 days.

The system not only streamlined record management but also improved transparency and accountability. When an expert claimed to have not received records—a recurring issue in the past—I could quickly reference the index and respond, "We sent those records to you on March 29, 2025, but I'd be happy to send them again." This eliminated disputes and ensured that all parties had the documentation needed to proceed.

Demonstrating Effectiveness: Anecdotes and Metrics

Since implementing the tracking system, our staff has seen a measurable improvement in efficiency. For example, the volume of follow-up emails to experts regarding missing records dropped by 30%. Additionally, disputes over alleged missing documents—once taking days to resolve—can now be addressed within minutes by referencing the tracking log. In one memorable instance, a pediatric neurologist who regularly insisted on missing documents was provided immediate proof of mailing dates and record details, resolving the issue on the same day and allowing the expert review to locate the records and proceed without delay.

Conclusion: Lasting Benefits and Workflow Improvements

In summary, implementing an effective tracking system for expert communications has proven invaluable for our firm. It saved time, reduced confusion, and significantly enhanced accountability among staff and experts alike. Especially in complex cases with multiple defendants and a large volume of medical records, the system ensures that everyone stayed informed, disputes were minimized, and litigation proceeded smoothly. For law firms engaged in high-stakes medical malpractice cases, investing in such workflow tools is not just beneficial, it is essential for delivering results and maintaining professional standards.

Sample Tracking System

This case involved eight experts, but I deleted three columns—Neurology, Neuro-oncology, and GI—solely to fit the chart on the page. The removal of these columns does not affect the overall interpretation of the case, as their contributions were consistent with those of the remaining experts, ensuring that no essential information is missing.

PRUPOFF *v.* LLEVELOR PEDIATRICS, ARAPAHO & LUCKETT

MEDICAL RECORDS INDEX	**PEDS**	**NEURO - OPHTH**	**NEURO SURG**	**ENDO**	**OPHTH.**
Includes OUR CLIENTS – LLEVELOR PEDIATRICS, PCP, Underweight, Vision Problems ~ 1/18/20 – 8/5/24	3/29/25	4/5/25	12/6/25	12/22/25	12/21/25
CHILDREN'S EYE HOSPITAL Exotropia, Amblyopia ~8/27/24-12/8/24	3/29/25	4/5/25	12/6/25	12/22/25	12/21/25
JOHNSONVILLE PEDIATRICS Headaches ~9/10/23 – 1/5/24 ADDITIONAL RECORDS ~5/19/24	3/29/25 4/18/25	4/5/25 NO/LNC	12/6/25 NO/ATTY	12/22/25 NO/ATTY	12/21/25 4/18/25
CHILDREN'S PEDIATRIC OPTHALMOLOGY Eye Exams ~10/2/23 – 4/21/24 ADDITIONAL RECORDS ~ 5/19/24	3/29/25 4/18/25	4/5/25 4/18/25	12/6/25 NO/ATTY	12/22/25 NO/ATTY	12/21/25 NO/ATTY
ALLERGY & ASTHMA OF JOHNSONVILLE, Allergic Conjunctivitis ~11/3/24 – 1/10/25	3/29/25	4/5/25	12/6/25	NO/ATTY	NO/ATTY
JOHNSONVILLE HOSPITAL, ER, Vomiting~12/25/24	5/18/25	NO/ATTY	NO/ATTY	NO/ATTY	NO/ATTY

MEDICAL RECORDS INDEX	PEDS	NEURO - OPHTH	NEURO SURG	ENDO	OPHTH .
CHILDREN'S HOSPITAL OF JOHNSONVILLE (FULL ADMISSION), Craniopharyngioma ~2/4/25 – 2/15/25	3/29/25	4/5/25	12/6/25	12/22/25, DISCHARGE H&P, PATH ONLY	12/21/25, DISCHARGE MRI, PATH ONLY

Note: NO/ATTY and NO/LNC indicate that the attorney or LNC requested that records not be sent to specific experts.

Expert Banks: Practical DOs and DON'Ts for Legal Professionals

Step-by-step advice, real-world stories, and workflow tips for organizing your expert witness information

If you've ever worked on a case that required more than a handful of expert witnesses, you know how quickly things can get complicated. Early in my career, I only needed a few experts, and I kept their information in my head or scribbled in a notebook. But as my caseload grew, those methods failed me—I once spent hours chasing down a lost CV! That's when I realized the need for a systematic, digital expert bank. Think of it as your personal vault: a secure, organized place where you can quickly access every detail about your experts whenever you need it.

DO #1: Systematically Add Experts to Your Expert Bank

The most important habit is to make adding new experts part of your regular workflow. When I first started, I tried to catch up by adding all my experts at once—big mistake. It was overwhelming, and I missed details. I learned that consistency is key.

- DO: Add new experts as soon as you engage them. Enter their details into your expert bank right away, even if it's just the basics to start.
- DO: Set a recurring time to update your expert bank. For example, block 20 minutes every Friday afternoon to add new experts, review entries, and update documents.

- DO: Use a checklist for each expert:
    - Name, credentials, and specialty
    - Contact information
    - CV (with date in filename)
    - Fee schedule
    - Contracts and case list
    - W-9 form
    - Personal preferences or notes

DON'T: Rely on memory or try to batch-add experts only when you have spare time. I did this once before a trial, and I ended up forgetting to include critical contact details for two experts—one of whom was nearly impossible to reach at crunch time. Small, regular updates are much more reliable and far less stressful.

DO #2: Organize Folders with Clear Naming Conventions

When I first set up my expert bank, I created computer folders labeled by specialty—Pediatrics, Oncology, Pathology. It seemed logical until I encountered experts who fit multiple categories. I once spent half an hour searching for notes on an oncologist who was also a pathologist, only to find her information duplicated in two places, with updates in only one.

- DO: Create a separate folder for each expert. Use a precise naming convention: LastName, FirstName Credentials (Specialty). Example: Anderson, Megaly RN (Pediatric Neurosurgery Nursing).
- DO: Use your computer's search feature. When you need a Pediatric Neurosurgery Nursing expert, just type those terms into the search bar—your system will instantly pull up relevant folders.

DON'T: Duplicate expert information across multiple specialty folders. It leads to confusion and outdated records. Trust me—once, I sent an outdated CV to opposing counsel because I had two versions saved in different folders. One folder per expert keeps everything tidy and up-to-date.

DO #3: Save Documents in Word Format for Easy Searching

I used to save all my important documents as PDFs, thinking they were more professional. But when I needed to quickly find every expert I'd worked with from Akron, searching PDFs took forever—and sometimes didn't work at all. It was only after switching to Word files that everything clicked.

- DO: Save CVs, resumes, and case lists in Microsoft Word format whenever possible. Word automatically indexes all text, letting you search for any keyword in seconds.
- DO: Use the search bar to find experts by location, specialty, or any detail you remember (even if you forget their name).

DON'T: Default to saving everything as PDFs, unless necessary. Searching inside PDFs is slower and less reliable. I once spent an hour manually opening PDFs to find a fee schedule—never again.

DO #4: Keep All Versions of Important Documents

One time, an expert updated her fee schedule mid-case. I replaced the old file with the new one, thinking I was staying organized—until there was a dispute over which version was valid. Without the old schedule, I couldn't prove the timeline.

- DO: Store all pertinent documents in each expert's folder: CVs/resumes (with dates), fee schedules, contracts, W-9s, and preferences.
- DO: When updating a CV or fee schedule, never overwrite the old version. Instead, move outdated documents to a subfolder labeled "Old CVs and Fee Schedules."

DON'T: Delete older versions of documents. Keeping a clear record protects you in case of disputes about credentials or fees.

Conclusion: The Payoff for Smart Organization

By following these practical DOs and DON'Ts, you'll build an expert bank that grows with you—without the headaches. You'll save time, avoid costly mistakes, and always have the information you need at your fingertips. Stay consistent, keep it simple, and your expert bank will become one of your most powerful tools.

Building and managing an expert bank strengthens your ability to support attorneys with reliable resources. Yet even the most organized system depends on one critical factor: licensure. Without proper credentials, even the most qualified nurse or expert can be disqualified. That's why the next section turns to nursing licensure issues—an area where diligence and awareness protect both your credibility and your client's case.

Nursing Licensure Issues: Lessons and Best Practices for Nurses and LNCs

Understanding the Significance of Licensure, the Nurse Practice Act, and Legal Responsibilities Through Real-World Experiences

Nursing licensure is more than just a formality—it's a foundation for safe, ethical, and legal nursing practice. Yet I am continually surprised by how many nurses do not fully understand the laws and regulations outlined in their state's Nurse Practice Act (NPA), a legal document that defines the scope of nursing practice, sets educational and examination requirements, and establishes standards for professional conduct. Whether you're a staff nurse, administrator, or legal consultant, knowing the details of licensure can be the difference between professional security and facing serious consequences in a medical malpractice lawsuit.

Defining Key Terms

- Nurse Practice Act (NPA): The state law that governs nursing practice, specifying what nurses can and cannot do, licensure requirements, and disciplinary actions.
- Registered Nurse (RN): A nurse who has completed the required education and passed a national licensing exam, authorized to provide a wide range of patient care tasks and supervision.
- Licensed Practical Nurse (LPN): Sometimes called Licensed Vocational Nurse (LVN) in some states, an LPN completes a shorter training program than an RN and works under RN supervision, performing basic nursing care. In many states, LPNs can supervise CNAs.
- Legal Nurse Consultant (LNC): An RN with specialized training in legal matters who assists attorneys by reviewing medical records, evaluating nursing care, and analyzing licensure issues in legal cases.

Case Study: License Alteration

Let me share a story that highlights how easily licensure issues can arise. Years ago, I was a nursing administrator preparing for a Joint Commission accreditation survey—a rigorous process that ensures hospitals meet high-quality standards. To make sure all personnel were properly licensed, I asked every nurse to present their original license for verification. My Quality Assurance Director, an RN, handed in a photocopy instead. Upon closer inspection, the copy appeared altered. As it turned out, she had forgotten to renew her license and, instead of initiating the renewal process (which took weeks before online systems existed), she changed the expiration date on her old license to make it appear current. Ultimately, this act of license alteration was considered fraud, and she lost her job. Today, renewing a license online is quick and easy, but the lesson remains: shortcuts can have lasting consequences.

Case Study: Working Without Proper Licensure

Another incident that occurred many years ago involved an RN who had also forgotten to renew her license. She assumed she could simply work as an LPN until her RN license was reinstated. When I asked to see her LPN license, she admitted she didn't have one—she just thought she could "step down" into the role. However, licensure doesn't work that way. To legally perform LPN job responsibilities, you must hold a valid LPN license, regardless of your RN credentials. Fortunately, after calling the state board of nursing, I learned that proof of renewal payment—like a notation in her checkbook—was enough for her to continue working as an RN until her new license arrived.

Case Study: Staffing Patterns and Nurse Roles

In another hospital where I served as a nursing administrator, I discovered a potentially risky staffing pattern: on the night shift, the only RN in the entire hospital was the nursing supervisor. All other units, including intensive care, emergency, labor and delivery, pediatrics, and medical-surgical floors, were staffed by LPNs and nursing assistants. The prior administrator had addressed a nursing shortage by training LPNs to serve as charge nurses—a position with responsibilities such as patient assessment, supervising other staff, and delegation. However, according to the state's Nurse Practice Act, only an RN was allowed to perform those functions. Assigning LPNs to charge nurse roles placed them outside their legal scope of practice, exposing the hospital and staff to legal risk.

Similarly, in another facility, LPNs were working independently in intensive care units (ICUs) and leading teams on medical-surgical units—again, beyond what the state's Nurse Practice Act permitted. These scenarios illustrate how misunderstandings about roles and licensure can have serious implications for nurses and their employers.

Why Legal Nurse Consultants Are Essential

What do these stories mean for those of us involved in legal nurse consulting? Licensure problems are more common than most healthcare organizations realize. Even if licensure issues aren't central to a lawsuit, they can seriously undermine the credibility of the nursing staff involved. That's where the expertise of Legal Nurse Consultants becomes invaluable.

The Role of Legal Nurse Consultants: Responsibilities and Best Practices

As an LNC involved in a nursing malpractice case, your first duty is to verify the active licensure status of every healthcare professional relevant to the case—RNs, LPNs, and any certified personnel. Thankfully, every state now offers online license verification, making this task much more straightforward. Here are some best practices I recommend:

- Document Licensure Status: Make copies of licensure verification for all involved nurses. If you encounter a license that is out of date or otherwise problematic, immediately inform the attorney handling the case.
    - Defense Perspective: If you're working for the defense, request and review the personnel files for all implicated nurses, ensuring the files are up-to-date throughout the litigation.
    - Plaintiff Perspective: For plaintiff cases, start a file for all relevant personnel, print web pages verifying license status (with the date stamp), and suggest that attorneys formally request copies of the nursing staff's personnel files.
- Analyze Staffing Patterns: Request schedules, staffing assignments, and job descriptions for every role connected to the lawsuit. Compare these with the Nurse Practice Act to confirm that each nurse was practicing within their legal scope. Bring any discrepancies to the attorney's attention.

Conclusion: Ensuring Compliance and Protecting Credibility

Determining and documenting the licensure status of nurses in medical malpractice cases is a crucial function that Legal Nurse Consultants provide. By understanding the Nurse Practice Act, clearly distinguishing between RN and LPN roles, and proactively addressing licensure concerns, nurses and consultants can protect both patient safety and professional credibility. The stories I've shared underscore the importance of vigilance and integrity in licensure matters—lessons that benefit every member of the healthcare and legal communities.

Licensure highlights the importance of professional integrity and compliance. Once those foundations are secure, the focus shifts back to the practical mechanics of case management. One of the most essential—and often overlooked—tools in this process is Bates stamping and indexing. By mastering these organizational techniques, you ensure that every page of a medical record can be tracked, referenced, and presented with precision.

Bates Stamping and Indexing for Legal Nurse Consultants

Practical Guide to Document Numbering, Index Creation, and Common Pitfalls

Bates stamping is an essential technique in legal document management, especially for legal nurse consultants. By assigning a unique number to each page of every case document, Bates stamping enables quick review, easy retrieval, and clear referencing throughout case discussions and trials. This simple numbering system keeps everyone on the legal team organized and ensures specific pages can be found without hassle.

Mechanical vs. Electronic Bates Stamping: Side-by-Side Comparison and Examples

Method	How It Works	Pros	Cons	Example
Mechanical	Uses a self-inking numbering machine or pre-printed sequential labels applied manually to each page.	Simple, does not require electronic files or software.	Labor-intensive, can be slow for large volumes, risk of physical fatigue.	Stamping each document page by hand, e.g., Page 0001, 0002, etc.
Electronic	Applies numbers to digital files using software like Adobe Acrobat, which can also add case names or custom text.	Fast, efficient for large sets, allows customization, minimal physical effort.	Requires electronic documents and suitable software, may need reprinting after numbering.	Applying sequence to PDFs, e.g., ABC_Case_0001.pdf, ABC_Case_0002.pdf.

Creating and Using an Index: Step-by-Step Guide

An organized index is critical for tracking Bates number ranges, document sources, and brief descriptions. This helps you and your team know exactly where to find specific documents. Follow these steps to create an effective index:

1. Record Bates Number Ranges: As you stamp documents, note the starting and ending Bates numbers for each group.
2. Identify the Source: Specify the origin of the documents (e.g., hospital, clinic, insurance provider).
3. Add Descriptions: Include a concise description of each document set for quick identification.
4. Update Regularly: Revise your index whenever you add new documents or change Bates numbers.
5. Use a Table or Spreadsheet: Create your index in a format that's easy to search and update, such as Excel or a Word table.

Sample Index Table for Reference:

Bates Number Range	Document Source	Description
0001–0525	ABC Hospital	Emergency Room Records
0526–1347	DEF Clinic	Outpatient Visit Notes
1348–1450	XYZ Insurance	Claim Correspondence

- Always double-check Bates numbers when starting a new set.
- Keep a backup copy of your index in both physical and electronic formats.
- Update your index immediately after making changes to ensure accuracy.

Common Pitfalls and Tips: Advice for Avoiding Mistakes

New legal nurse consultants often encounter these common pitfalls when Bates stamping documents:

- Missing or Duplicate Numbers: Double-check that every page is stamped and that numbering proceeds sequentially. Skipped or repeated numbers can cause confusion later.
- Incomplete Stamping: Verify that no pages are missed—especially inserts, double-sided pages, or attachments.
- Electronic Backup Errors: Always create a backup copy of electronic files before applying Bates stamps. This protects original documents if you need to revert or correct mistakes.

- Inconsistent Indexing: Keep your index up to date as you stamp new documents. Delays and omissions can make tracking difficult.

Practical advice: Before beginning manual Bates stamping, run a quick test on blank pages to confirm your numbering sequence and method. For large sets, take breaks to avoid fatigue, and periodically verify your progress. For electronic stamping, save a pre-stamped copy in a secure location and use clear, consistent file naming conventions.

Conclusion

Bates stamping and proper indexing streamline document management for legal nurse consultants, making case review and retrieval much easier. By understanding both mechanical and electronic methods, following step-by-step indexing practices, and staying alert to common pitfalls, you'll be well prepared to handle legal documents efficiently. Use side-by-side comparisons and practical examples to simplify other legal processes you encounter in your consulting career.

Indexing documents is only part of the organizational puzzle. Legal nurse consultants also manage specialized materials like radiographs, which require careful management and technical understanding. The next section provides best practices for working with imaging studies, ensuring that you can support attorneys with clarity and accuracy in even the most complex cases.

Best Practices: Working with Radiographs in Medical Malpractice Cases

Organized Guidelines for Handling and Reviewing Radiographs

Radiographs—including x-rays, CT scans, MRIs, and other imaging studies—are often central to medical malpractice cases, especially those involving missed diagnoses or injuries from radiology procedures. Legal nurse consultants (LNCs) play a key role in collecting, organizing, and interpreting these images to support legal claims. Understanding radiograph formats and proper handling is essential for case accuracy and expert review.

Types of Radiograph Formats

Hard Copy Films:

- Physical films, typically viewed on a light box (e.g., chest, abdominal, limb x-rays).

- Bulky, difficult to store, and degrade in quality when copied.
- Rarely used today due to digital advances.

DICOM (Digital Imaging and Communication in Medicine):

- Standard digital format for medical imaging (used in CT, MRI, and more).
- Stored on CDs or flash drives, always provided with DICOM viewers (viewing software).
- Technical Definition: DICOM is a universal file format for medical images, designed to ensure image integrity and prevent unauthorized modifications.

Advantages of DICOM vs. Hard Copy Films

DICOM Images:

- Digital originals—quality does not deteriorate when copied.
- Cannot be altered or modified, ensuring authenticity for expert review.
- Preferred by radiology experts and recommended by the American College of Radiology.

Hard Copy Films:

- Lose image quality every time they are copied.
- Can be modified or scanned into less secure formats (PDF, JPG), which are not suitable for expert analysis.
- Not recommended for legal cases requiring high-quality, original (DICOM) images. In fact, the American College of Radiology [58] has recommended the use of original images for expert work since the early 2000s.

Differences Between Imaging Modalities

- X-ray: Uses radiation to produce images of bones and some tissues.
- CT (Computed Tomography): Combines multiple x-rays for detailed cross-sectional views.
- MRI (Magnetic Resonance Imaging): Uses magnetic fields and radio waves to visualize soft tissues.
- Ultrasound (US): Uses sound waves for images of organs, vessels, and tissues.
- Nuclear Medicine: Uses small amounts of radioactive material to assess organ function and structure.

[58] American College of Radiology. https://tinyurl.com/ye2x6jbc (accessed January 2026)

LNC Responsibilities in Obtaining and Handling Radiographs

1. Gather All Relevant Imaging Studies: Request every radiographic study related to case allegations (e.g., for a missed skull-based tumor, obtain all skull and brain imaging: MRI, CT, PET). Consider additional studies based on symptoms and injury types, such as swallow studies for tumor cases with swallowing issues.
2. Organize and Index Radiographs: Add all images to a primary index for easy cross-reference.
3. Verify Imaging Results Against Reports: Ensure every image aligns with its corresponding radiology report in the medical chronology or summary. Note and reconcile any time discrepancies between image timestamps and report times.
4. Provide DICOM Images to Experts: Mail (or use HIPAA-compliant filesharing application such as Nuance PowerShare) all applicable studies in DICOM format and reports in DICOM format to the radiology expert(s) for review.

Key Tips: Checklist for Working with Radiographs

- Assuming that they are important to your case, always request both radiology reports and original radiographs for your review.
- Request DICOM format for quality, authenticity, and expert review.
- Understand and distinguish between imaging modalities to ensure comprehensive case preparation.
- Keep a detailed index of all studies and cross-reference with corresponding reports.
- Double-check imaging timestamps and report times, noting any significant differences.
- Send only duplicate original (DICOM) images to expert witnesses.

Radiographs are one piece of the evidentiary record, but pathology slides present their own unique challenges. From chain of custody to future management, handling slides correctly safeguards both the integrity of the evidence and your professional credibility.

Tracking Pathology Slides

A Guide for Legal Nurse Consultants

Failure to diagnose and misdiagnosis of pathology slides are frequent allegations in medical malpractice litigation. Pathology slides are central to such cases, but they have a sneaky way of disappearing if you don't keep track of them. Losing these slides can seriously hinder legal investigations, compromise patient care, and make it difficult for either side to defend or refute malpractice claims. The absence of original slides may prevent a thorough expert review and can negatively impact the outcome of a case, underscoring the critical importance of maintaining accurate records and a secure chain of custody.

Types of Pathology Slides

- There are two main types of pathology slides: histology and cytology. Histology (also called histopathology) focuses on TISSUES. Histology slides contain tissue samples obtained through biopsy or surgery. These samples can be aspirates, such as those from fine needle aspirations of a thyroid gland, or masses removed during tumor surgery. The process involves slicing the tissue sample into very thin sections, placing them on slides, and staining them with dye for microscopic examination. To make the tissue firm enough for slicing, it is either frozen or treated with a fixative and embedded in paraffin wax. The preserved tissue in wax is referred to as a block, which allows for indefinite storage.
- Cytology (also known as cytopathology) Focuses on CELLS. Cytology slides contain free cells or small tissue fragments. Physicians collect cytology specimens by scraping, as in a Pap smear, or by extracting fluids such as pleural, cerebrospinal, peritoneal, urine, or sputum. Unlike histology samples, some cytology specimens do not produce a block, so their slides cannot be duplicated by recutting more tissue.

Challenges in Handling Pathology Slides

- Unlike medical records or radiographs, pathology slides are often irreplaceable and cannot be duplicated exactly. This creates unique challenges for legal nurse consultants (LNCs) managing such cases.
- When misdiagnosis or failure to diagnose is in question, both the plaintiff and defense typically hire pathology experts to review the slides. Although some labs scan slides digitally (which makes them permanently accessible), digital pathology is not yet the standard of care.
- Pathology laboratories are generally reluctant to release their original slides. When possible, they provide recuts—additional thin slices made from the original tissue block, which serve as substitutes for the original slides. While pathologists may consider recuts to be duplicates, technically they are not exact copies. Labs can distribute recuts to multiple law firms if enough tissue remains in the block.
- In cases where only original slides exist—such as with cytology slides which lack a block—the pathology lab will release the originals to a law firm for expert

review. These slides may be transferred between multiple law firms and pathology experts, sometimes involving several defendants. This repeated movement increases the risk of misplacement, breakage, or loss.
- Maintaining the chain of custody—chronological documentation of evidence—is essential in medical malpractice cases. Legal nurse consultants must track the movement of pathology slides in and out of the firm to establish a clear chain of custody.

Best Practices for Tracking and Chain of Custody

- If you need to send pathology slides to a local law firm or expert, draft a letter that specifies the date of transfer, a description of the slides, and the name and address of the receiving party. This letter becomes the foundation of your paper trail. Should the slides become misplaced, your documentation will aid in locating them.
- After drafting your letter, send the slides via a courier with instructions for the courier to obtain the printed name and signature of the receiver, along with the date of delivery. Ensure the courier returns this information to you. If sending slides to an out-of-town expert or law firm, use a mail service with tracking capabilities and require a signature upon delivery. Retain all tracking information in the case file or wherever the slides are stored.
- Once your firm's pathology expert has reviewed the slides, reverse the process. Do not rely on the expert to return the slides automatically. Whether the expert is local or out-of-town, arrange for the slides to be picked up and delivered back to you. Do not allow the expert to forward the slides to another law firm or pathologist, as this increases the risk of losing track of the slides.

The Future Management of Pathology Slides

The College of American Pathologists (CAP) has issued guidelines for Whole Slide Imaging (WSI). WSI is FDA-approved for use, but it is not yet the standard of care for pathology slide management. WSI offers several advantages, including faster diagnoses, no risk of broken slides, and, similar to DICOM (Digital Imaging and Communications in Medicine)—a standard for handling medical imaging information—there is no degradation of images over time. With WSI, Legal Nurse Consultants can send images to experts via a HIPAA-compliant internet site, eliminating the need for couriers or tracking services. By enabling faster diagnoses and removing the risk of lost or damaged slides, WSI can improve turnaround times and reduce errors in pathology, ultimately benefiting patient outcomes.

Conclusion

By implementing a thorough tracking system and maintaining a clear chain of custody, legal nurse consultants can safeguard irreplaceable pathology slides and minimize risks in medical malpractice cases.

Once specialized materials are accounted for, the next step is streamlining the review of medical records themselves. Flagging and tagging provide a practical system for highlighting key information, making it easier for attorneys to navigate complex charts and focus on the details that matter most.

Effective Flagging and Tagging: A Practical Guide for LNCs

Streamlining Medical Record Review with Clear Definitions and Actionable Strategies

Flagging and tagging medical records are essential practices in legal nurse consulting that enable attorneys to efficiently review, locate, and cross-reference critical documentation during depositions. By systematically organizing chart entries, Legal Nurse Consultants (LNCs) provide invaluable support to attorneys preparing for complex legal proceedings. This article outlines the key definitions, benefits, and practical steps for implementing an effective flagging and tagging system.

Defining Key Terms

- Deponent: A deponent is an individual—such as a treating physician, nurse, or other healthcare professional—who is scheduled to provide sworn testimony during a deposition. Their chart entries are closely examined by both plaintiff and defense attorneys before and during the deposition.
- Medical Chronology: A medical chronology is a detailed, organized timeline summarizing significant medical events and chart entries related to a case. It serves as a roadmap for attorneys to follow the sequence of care and highlight relevant documentation.

Flagging Process: Steps and Practical Examples

Flagging involves identifying and marking all documentation entries made by the deponent within the relevant medical records. For example, a nurse deponent's entries may appear only in hospital or nursing home charts, while a physician deponent might have documentation in multiple locations such as office notes, home health, pharmacy, or nursing facility records. Each set of records should be flagged accordingly.

1. Locate all chart entries authored by the deponent.
2. Highlight the date and the deponent's signature on each entry for quick identification.
3. Attach a colored flag (such as sticky flags from Post-It) to the page. Assign a unique color for each deponent—e.g., red for Nurse A, blue for Nurse B—to maintain clarity when multiple individuals are involved.

Practical Tip: Consistently use the same color for each deponent throughout all records. Create a simple reference key for color assignments and double-check all flagged entries to ensure accuracy and prevent confusion.

Tagging Process: Steps and Practical Examples

Tagging refers to labeling your medical chronology so that it corresponds directly with the flags placed in the physical or electronic records. This cross-referencing allows attorneys to seamlessly move between the summary and the original documentation.

1. In electronic chronologies (e.g., using CaseMap), add a colored tag or icon in the margin beside each entry related to the deponent.
2. In Word documents, identify all instances of the deponent's name and insert a checkmark symbol or electronic highlight for each occurrence.
3. Optionally, place a flag on the corresponding pages of the chronology that match the flagged entries in the medical record.

Practical Tip: When tagging, try to use the same visual cue (color, symbol, or highlight) as used in the original records. This consistency minimizes errors and streamlines attorney review.

Benefits for Attorneys: Why Flagging and Tagging Matter

A well-executed flagging and tagging system empowers attorneys to quickly locate, verify, and cross-reference essential medical record entries during depositions. This reduces time spent searching for information, helps attorneys formulate targeted questions, and improves overall case preparation. By enabling rapid access to key documents, LNCs support more effective and efficient legal proceedings.

Practical Tips and Common Pitfalls

- Be Consistent: Use the same color-coding and labeling conventions for each deponent throughout the case.

- Double-Check Entries: Review flagged and tagged entries to ensure accuracy and completeness; missed or misidentified entries can cause confusion during depositions.
- Document Your System: Provide a reference sheet or key explaining your flagging and tagging color codes for easy attorney reference.
- Stay Organized: Regularly update chronologies and flagged records as new information is received.

Conclusion

Flagging and tagging are tools for Legal Nurse Consultants supporting attorneys in medical-related litigation. By clearly defining terms, following consistent procedures, and embracing practical strategies, LNCs can enhance the efficiency, accuracy, and effectiveness of medical record reviews. Attorneys are encouraged to collaborate closely with LNCs to maximize the benefits of this systematic approach.

Of course, before records can be flagged or tagged, they must be obtained. Medical records retrieval is a foundational skill for LNCs, and mastering it ensures that your analyses are complete, timely, and legally sound.

Medical Records Retrieval: A Guide for New LNCs

Practical Strategies, Real-World Insights, and Actionable Tips

Retrieving medical records is a cornerstone task for some law firm employees impacting case timelines and outcomes. While it may seem straightforward, the process involves multiple steps, each with potential challenges. By understanding and organizing each phase, you'll ensure efficiency, minimize delays, and provide valuable support to your legal team. The person responsible for records retrieval varies by firm. It can be a subpoena clerk, a secretary, a medical records clerk, a paralegal, or a legal nurse consultant. In the following scenario, the LNC is the person responsible for obtaining medical records.

Step-by-Step Medical Records Retrieval Process

1. Identify Needed Records. Begin by clarifying which medical records are necessary for the case. Work closely with the attorney or legal team to create a targeted list—this may include hospital admissions, emergency room visits, clinic appointments, pharmacy records, or specialist consultations. As the case progresses, you will place additional names on the list. For example, in a post-

surgical infection case, you may need operative reports, wound care notes, and pharmacy dispensing logs.

2. Determine Provider Address. Finding the correct address for record requests can be surprisingly tricky. Providers may use corporate legal departments, off-site storage, or different addresses for record requests versus their main office. For instance, a national pharmacy chain like Walgreens usually requires requests to go to their corporate legal office, not the store location. Tips for success: Use state medical boards and provider directories for up-to-date contact information. Check provider websites for records request instructions. If uncertain, call the provider and document your conversation (date, time, and contact person). Don't hesitate to escalate: if you can't get an answer, ask for the medical records department or compliance officer. Real-world anecdote: One LNC found the correct address for a closed private practice by searching state licensure records and contacting a former office manager listed in online reviews.
3. Draft the Record Request. Prepare your request using a HIPAA-compliant authorization (for plaintiff cases) or a medical records subpoena (for defense cases). Use templates from your law firm, if available, since authorizations and subpoenas duces tecum are state specific. Always have the request reviewed by the supervising attorney before sending.
4. Obtain the Necessary Signature. Authorizations are typically signed by the patient (plaintiff), while subpoenas are signed by the defense attorney. Plaintiff attorneys often have clients sign several blank authorizations at the start of a case, streamlining later requests. Keep a log of all signed documents for easy tracking.
5. Mail the Authorization or Subpoena. Send the request to the provider using the verified address. For authorizations, standard mail or secure email may be used. For subpoenas, follow state-specific procedures: some require certified mail, others a Notice of Production from Nonparty. If using a process server, confirm delivery with a return receipt. Tip: Keep a record of all outgoing correspondence, including dates and tracking numbers.
6. Follow Up with the Provider. Providers usually have 10–15 days to comply, depending on state statutes. Delays are common, especially with smaller practices. Strategies for overcoming delays: Document each follow-up attempt (who you spoke with, when, and what was discussed). If calls go unanswered, escalate to the medical records supervisor or compliance officer. Send a polite but firm written reminder, referencing relevant regulations and original request dates. If needed, involve the attorney to apply additional pressure or file a motion to compel. Real-world example: After three unreturned calls to a long-term acute care hospital, an LNC documented each attempt and escalated to the hospital's compliance officer, resulting in same-day record release.

7. Log and Distribute Received Records. Once records arrive—usually in digital format—log their receipt, save them in the firm's designated folder, and notify the legal team. Double-check that all requested items are included. Share copies with all relevant parties, ensuring confidentiality and HIPAA compliance.

Conclusion

An organized approach to medical records retrieval not only streamlines your workflow but also demonstrates your professionalism as a legal nurse consultant. By anticipating challenges, leveraging available resources, and documenting every step, you will build strong relationships with your legal team and contribute meaningfully to case success. Persistence, attention to detail, and clear communication are your best tools—embrace them as you grow your LNC practice.

How to Acquire a Medical Record Abstract: A Clear Guide for All Readers

Understanding, Requesting, and Customizing Abstracts for Legal Cases

When attorneys are involved in medical malpractice cases, they sometimes need access to a summary of a patient's medical records. This summary is called an abstract. An abstract is a condensed version of selected medical records, providing key information to help attorneys quickly review details without requesting the entire chart.

Two other important terms often come up in this process:

- Authorization form: A document that gives permission for medical records to be released to a specific person or organization, commonly used by plaintiff attorneys.
- Subpoena: A legal order that requires an institution to provide medical records; commonly used by defense attorneys.

This guide will walk you through the process of acquiring a medical record abstract, making the steps clear and accessible for everyone, including those unfamiliar with legal or medical terminology.

Why Abstracts Vary: Seven Definitions

The definition of "abstract" can differ dramatically between healthcare providers. Here are seven examples of what different institutions consider an abstract:

1. Anything up to 50 pages (from a physician practice)
2. Immunizations, two years of office visits and lab information, and five years of radiology and diagnostic reports (from a pediatric practice)
3. Dictated physician reports such as cardiology, medical imaging, and pathology (inpatient setting)
4. Discharge summary, operative notes, and diagnostic testing (inpatient setting)
5. History of illness, discharge summary, test results, medications, hospital course, and discharge diagnosis (inpatient setting)
6. Discharge summary, history and physical, lab, pathology, operative reports, procedure notes, radiology reports, problem lists (inpatient setting)
7. Emergency room records, radiology reports, laboratory (inpatient setting)

As you can see, the term "abstract" can mean very different things depending on the provider. This variability makes it essential to clarify your needs before requesting records. Now, let's look at the two steps you should follow to ensure you get the right information.

Step 1: Determine the Information Needed

Every medical malpractice case is unique, and the information required may not be included in a provider's typical abstract. Abstracts also vary widely from one institution to another. The first step is to determine exactly what information you need. This usually involves discussing the case with the attorney or client to identify which records are most relevant.

For example, consider a case involving a pediatric inpatient who received an inappropriate medication. In this situation, you will need nursing notes, physician orders, progress notes, and medication administration sheets for the date of the incident and possibly for a few days before and after. Nursing notes and medication administration sheets are crucial in cases involving medication errors because they provide a detailed timeline of what was given to the patient, when it was administered, and by whom. Progress notes are also essential for damages. This information helps attorneys understand exactly how and when the error occurred, which is essential for building the case. You'll also want to include standard records like the history and physical exam and discharge summary.

Step 2: Review and Customize Authorization or Subpoena Forms

If the institution uses a pre-printed authorization form, your next step is to carefully read the form and check whether the abstract it describes includes all the information you need. If you're working for the plaintiff and the form is missing important information, add the specific documents you require—such as dates of service, types of records needed (e.g., medical or billing records), and any limitations on the scope of the request—and have the client (the plaintiff) sign the revised form (or use a pre-signed authorization form).

If the law firm uses its own authorization form instead, make sure it lists exactly the records you need for the case. For defense attorneys, a subpoena is typically required rather than an authorization form. In this case, ensure the subpoena is specific and includes all necessary information.

Conclusion: Recap of Steps for a Tailored Abstract

In summary, acquiring a medical record abstract that truly meets your needs comes down to two clear steps: first, clarify and identify the exact information required for your case; second, make sure your authorization form or subpoena is customized to request only the necessary records. By following these steps, you'll obtain an abstract that is tailored to your case and avoid wasting time on unrelated documents.

Supporting a Fired Colleague: Professional Boundaries and Communication

Practical Guidance for Workplace Professionals

When a colleague is fired and escorted out of the building, it can be difficult to know how to respond. You may want to support your former coworker, but it's important to balance empathy with professionalism. Thoughtful actions can help, but it's equally critical to respect boundaries and workplace policies. The following guidance clarifies when and how to reach out and offers practical templates and suggestions for ongoing support.

Clarifying Boundaries: Knowing When to Reach Out

Before contacting a fired colleague, consider the nature of your relationship and your role in the organization. Supervisors or managers should refrain from contacting former employees after termination to maintain professional boundaries and avoid legal or ethical complications. Such outreach may be misinterpreted, violate company policies, or interfere with post-termination processes. If you are unsure about reaching out, consider whether your contact could be misinterpreted or violate company policies. When in doubt, it's best to err on the side of caution and consult your HR department or firm administrator.

Risks of contacting former colleagues include potential breaches of confidentiality, misunderstandings about your intentions, or inadvertently sharing sensitive company information. Always respect both the company's privacy guidelines and the individual's need for space during a challenging transition.

Supporting Friends: Offering Empathy and Action

If the fired colleague is a friend, it's generally appropriate to reach out and offer a listening ear. Let them vent and express their feelings, as your friendship may be especially valuable during this tough time. Express your support by saying you're sorry and that you miss them at the workplace. Avoid telling them you know how they feel—even if you've experienced a similar situation—since the focus should remain on your friend's experience. Steer clear of unsolicited advice, but offer concrete help, such as searching for jobs together or reviewing their resume for relevance. Respect their privacy and avoid prying into the details of their termination.

Supporting Acquaintances: Writing a Thoughtful Note

For colleagues you respect but aren't close friends with, a note is an appropriate way to show support. Choose the medium that feels most comfortable—mail, email, or professional networking platforms like LinkedIn. A supportive note should include four key statements:

- Acknowledge your surprise or sorrow at their departure.
- Mention a quality or skill you appreciate about them.
- Express confidence in their future success.
- Wish them well in their next chapter.

Here is an example note suitable for various professions:

Dear ______,

I was sorry to hear that you are no longer with the firm. I have always appreciated your dedication and teamwork. I am confident that your skills will lead to new opportunities. Wishing you all the best in your next chapter.

Additionally, if your colleague is open to it, you might share resources such as job search websites or professional networking groups. Offering to stay in touch or meet for coffee can help maintain the relationship during their transition.

For example, a note to a former nursing colleague might read:

Dear ______,

I am sorry to learn that you are no longer with the firm. I always admired your breadth of knowledge and experiences. I believe your analytical abilities will serve you well in future roles. Best wishes in your new endeavors.

When Doing Nothing Is Appropriate

Sometimes, the best action is inaction—especially if you don't know the colleague well or never worked closely with them. For supervisors or managers, reaching out directly is generally inappropriate due to professional boundaries and possible legal risks. If you have no direct relationship or are uncertain about how your gesture might be received, it's acceptable to do nothing. However, don't let discomfort stop you from supporting colleagues with whom you shared a connection; this is a moment to set aside awkwardness and offer kindness.

Ongoing Support: Maintaining Relationships and Sharing Resources

Support doesn't have to end with a note or conversation. If your colleague is receptive, consider sharing helpful resources, such as job boards, industry contacts, or professional associations. Offering to stay connected—whether through social media, occasional emails, or coffee catch-ups—can make a significant difference during their career transition. Your continued support shows that professional relationships matter beyond the workplace.

Conclusion: Thoughtful, Respectful Support

Supporting a fired colleague requires both empathy and professionalism. By clarifying boundaries, choosing appropriate communication, and offering meaningful support, you can help former coworkers feel valued and encouraged as they move forward. Always act thoughtfully, keep company policies in mind, and focus on maintaining positive relationships throughout these challenging moments.

Chapter 14: General LNC Skills

Legal nurse consultants need a wide range of skills to function efficiently and effectively. The work demands not only medical expertise but also the ability to stay organized, communicate clearly, and adapt to the fast pace of legal practice. Over the years, I've relied on a variety of tools and strategies to keep myself on track, and my commitment to organization stems from a pivotal lesson early in my career.

At the time, the partner at my first law firm decided to merge with another firm in a different part of the state. The goal was to create a stronger, statewide presence. I was sent—alongside a paralegal and an attorney—to acquire that firm's medical malpractice cases, since their focus had been primarily personal injury. What we encountered when we walked through their offices was unforgettable. If there had been a television show called *"Hoarders: Law Firm Edition,"* it would have perfectly captured the chaos. Narrow pathways wound through stacks of files piled five feet high. Cabinets were jammed, with more files teetering on top, nearly reaching the ceiling. Every desk and chair was buried under mountains of paper taller than me. It took three of us an entire day to locate just eighteen medical malpractice files to bring back. That experience taught me, in the most vivid way possible, that strong organizational systems are not optional—they are essential for managing complex case files and delivering reliable results.

Organization is only one piece of the puzzle. Working within a law firm brings unique challenges and opportunities for legal nurse consultants. Unlike independent practice, where you set the pace and structure, law firm work requires adapting to the rhythm of attorneys, paralegals, and the broader litigation team. Success depends not only on your medical knowledge but also on your ability to integrate seamlessly into the firm's workflow, balancing precision with speed when deadlines loom.

In this chapter, we'll explore the general skills that make you indispensable in any setting. You'll learn how to manage medical records efficiently in high-volume cases, communicate findings in ways that resonate with attorneys, and maintain professionalism under pressure. We'll also look at strategies for building credibility, refining your organizational systems, and contributing insights that strengthen case preparation. By the end, you'll have a clear understanding of how to translate your nursing expertise into legal value—skills that will help you thrive whether you're working independently or within the structured, fast-paced environment of a law firm.

Three Rookie Mistakes

How to Avoid Them as a New Legal Nurse Consultant

We all begin our journey as legal nurse consultants (LNCs) with a strong foundation in nursing care and clinical procedures. However, most of us step into the LNC role with only a vague sense of how legal processes work. Let's face it—everyone starts as a newcomer, and rookie mistakes are common. The good news? You can sidestep these three classic pitfalls: misunderstanding law firm protocols, mismanaging expert responsibilities, and struggling with general organization—all of which we'll explore in detail. By understanding both the legal lingo and practical steps to stay organized and professional, you'll build confidence and avoid the errors that trip up so many newcomers. Let's dive in and learn how to make your transition into the LNC role smoother and more successful.

1. Sending an Expert the Firm's Only Copy of Records. Imagine this: An attorney is insistent—"Send the medical records to the expert right now!" You feel the pressure, so you package up the firm's only copy of an x-ray or crucial documents and ship them off. Now your firm is left empty-handed. Soon, you're scrambling to get the records back (awkward), or you're paying the healthcare provider for another set (expensive and avoidable).

   Checklist to Prevent This Mistake:

   - Never send out original medical records or radiographs—make a copy first.
   - If records are electronic (like a CD of x-rays), create a duplicate—it usually takes just a few minutes.
   - For paper records, scan or photocopy them before sending anything out. The extra effort now saves headaches later.
   - Or send records and DICOM films via a secure file-sharing website.
   - Communicate with the attorney: "I'll handle it right away," and then ensure the originals stay with the firm.

   This simple system protects your firm's interests and your professional reputation.

2. Writing Reports Without the Client's Knowledge. This one is tricky, because rules vary. Here's some legal language you'll hear often: The term 'work product' refers to materials prepared in anticipation of litigation that are generally protected from disclosure, while 'discoverable' means information that must be shared with the opposing party if requested. In-house LNCs often have the authority to write confidential reports at will, and these are usually considered protected work product. But if you're an expert LNC, especially in some states, anything you write—reports, emails, even notes in the margin of medical records—may be discoverable and could

end up in the hands of the opposing party. Laws differ by state, so always clarify expectations with your attorney client before you put pen to paper.

Checklist for Writing Reports:

- Before writing any report, always ask the attorney: "Is a written report required, and will it be discoverable?"
- Document any permissions or instructions you receive about report writing.
- Never bill for a report that wasn't authorized by your client.
- When in doubt, communicate! Transparency builds trust and keeps you out of trouble.

Taking these steps protects your relationship with your client and keeps you compliant with legal standards.

3. Ignoring or Forgetting Deadlines. As nurses, we know how vital deadlines are—medications must be given on time, and patient care can't wait. In healthcare, there's flexibility: a med can be given a bit before or after the scheduled time if the situation demands. But in the legal world, deadlines are much stricter. Terms like 'statutes of limitations' (the legal time limit to file a lawsuit) are firm, and missing them can have serious consequences, including professional sanctions for attorneys and lost cases for clients. I once heard about an LNC who relied on memory alone to track deposition dates—until a key deadline slipped by and the team had to scramble to recover. Don't let this happen to you!

Checklist to Stay on Top of Deadlines:

- Set up a 'tickler' or reminder system—use a calendar app, physical planner, or case management software.
- Record every legal deadline as soon as you learn it (statutes of limitations, discovery cut-offs, trial dates, etc.).
- Set reminders well in advance—try two reminders: one a week before, another a day before the deadline.
- Check your deadline calendar daily as a habit.
- Communicate upcoming deadlines to the attorney and confirm team responsibilities.
- With these steps, you'll always be ahead of the game—and never miss a critical date.

Every new LNC is still learning the ropes of the legal system. By understanding these legal terms and putting practical systems in place, you can avoid rookie mistakes and build a reputation for reliability and professionalism. You've got this!

Having explored the common pitfalls that trip up new legal nurse consultants, let's turn to a more nuanced challenge: navigating conflicts of interest with clarity and integrity.

Understanding and Managing Conflicts of Interest in Legal Nursing

Essential Guidance for Legal Nurse Consultants

Conflicts of interest are a critical concern for legal nurse consultants (LNCs), whether you serve independently, as an expert witness, or as part of a law firm. A conflict of interest arises when your professional obligations to two parties with opposing interests could compromise your impartiality. For example, if you agree to consult for the plaintiff and later switch to assist the defense in the same or related matter, your objectivity may be called into question. Proactively identifying and managing these situations is essential to maintaining credibility, avoiding disqualification, and upholding the integrity of both your work and the legal process.

Employment-Related Conflicts

Employment history and organizational affiliations often give rise to conflicts of interest. Understanding these scenarios is key to making ethical decisions in your consulting practice.

- Previous Care Provided to Plaintiff: If you have ever provided direct care to the plaintiff—even outside the scope of the current litigation, such as through home health services—this connection may compromise your objectivity. Case Example: In one case, an LNC who previously cared for a plaintiff was retained as an expert witness. The defense successfully argued for the consultant's disqualification, and the appellate court reversed the jury verdict due to the undisclosed prior relationship.
- Current or Past Employment with Defendant Entity: Working for a hospital or other healthcare organization named in the lawsuit—even if you did not directly care for the plaintiff—creates a conflict because of your employment ties.
- Affiliations with Parent or Subsidiary Companies: Employment with a parent company (for example, working for an entity within a large health system while another entity is the defendant) can also result in a conflict of interest, regardless of direct involvement in the care at issue.
- Switching Sides between Firms: If you move from a plaintiff firm to a defense firm (or vice versa), and both firms are involved in the same or related cases, you

must not participate in those cases at your new firm. An information barrier (sometimes called a "Chinese wall") should be implemented to prevent any sharing of case-specific knowledge.

Personal Relationship Conflicts

Personal relationships with parties involved in litigation can also compromise your impartiality. These connections should be scrutinized as carefully as employment ties.

- Relationships with Plaintiffs or Defendants: If the plaintiff or defendant is your neighbor, a fellow member of your religious community, or your personal healthcare provider, your ability to remain unbiased may be questioned.

Practical Tools for Avoiding Conflicts

To avoid conflicts of interest, LNCs should implement systematic approaches for screening cases and tracking professional engagements. Below are practical tools to help you stay organized and compliant.

Sample Case Tracking Template

Date	**Case Name**	**Plaintiff**	**Defendant**	**Attorney/Firm**	**Role (Review, Testify, etc.)**	**Notes**
MM/DD/ YYYY	Doe v. Hospital	Jane Doe	General Hospital	Smith & Partners	Review	Served as plaintiff's expert

Checklist for Vetting Potential Experts

- Have you ever provided care to any party in this case?
- Do you currently or have you ever worked for any involved healthcare entities or their parent companies?
- Have you reviewed cases or testified for or against any of the parties, attorneys, or law firms involved?
- Do you have any personal relationship with the plaintiff, defendant, or their representatives?
- Have you recently changed employers or firms that may be involved in this case?
- Is there any other factor that could be perceived as a conflict of interest?

Conclusion: Diligence and Integrity

Conflicts of interest can lead to disqualification as an expert and even reversal of jury verdicts. However, with diligence, clear procedures, and transparent communication, legal nurse consultants can avoid these pitfalls. By maintaining comprehensive records and systematically vetting all potential cases and experts, you protect your reputation and ensure that your contributions to the legal process remain above reproach.

Once we've established professional boundaries and ethical safeguards, it's time to examine a clinical issue that often complicates legal cases—patient noncompliance and its legal implications.

Patient Noncompliance: Legal Impact and Best Practices for LNCs

A Practical Guide for LNCs and Attorneys

Patient noncompliance—when a patient fails to follow medical advice, treatment plans, or follow-up instructions—plays a pivotal role in medical malpractice litigation. Its presence can significantly affect the strength of a claim, the strategies of both plaintiff and defense attorneys, and the ultimate legal outcome. For legal nurse consultants (LNCs), accurately identifying and reporting noncompliance is essential for objective case analysis and effective collaboration with attorneys.

Legal Impact of Noncompliance

When noncompliance is established, it can reduce or even bar damages awarded in a medical malpractice lawsuit. Many jurisdictions follow the doctrine of comparative negligence, which allows courts to apportion fault between the patient and healthcare provider. If a patient's actions—such as failing to attend follow-up appointments, ignoring medication instructions, or not pursuing specialist referrals—are found to have contributed to their injury, any award can be reduced proportionally. In some cases, clear evidence of substantial noncompliance may even discourage plaintiff attorneys from pursuing the case, as the likelihood of a favorable verdict or settlement diminishes.

Court Assessment of Noncompliance: Legal Standards and Use of Evidence

Courts assess patient noncompliance by examining whether the patient's actions (or inactions) were a proximate cause of the alleged harm and whether those actions were reasonable under the circumstances. The comparative negligence standard[59] is commonly applied, where a jury or judge determines the percentage of fault attributable to each party. Relevant legal precedents, such as Fritts v. McKinney, and similar state-level rulings, reinforce that a plaintiff's damages can be reduced in proportion to their contribution to the injury. Attorneys use contemporaneous medical record entries, pharmacy data, and documented provider instructions as evidence to demonstrate or refute noncompliance. Courts look for clear, objective documentation—such as missed appointments, failure to refill prescriptions, or ignored follow-up recommendations—to support findings of patient fault.

Attorney Strategies: Leveraging Evidence of Noncompliance

Attorneys defending healthcare providers often highlight noncompliance to shift or mitigate liability, using it as a key argument to reduce damages. Plaintiff attorneys, conversely, may seek to minimize or explain noncompliance, arguing that it was justified (e.g., due to lack of understanding or financial barriers) or not causally related to the alleged harm. LNCs support both sides by providing thorough, unbiased analysis of the medical records to clarify the presence, frequency, and impact of noncompliance, thereby shaping legal strategy and negotiations.

Identifying Noncompliance: A Systematic Approach for LNCs

To ensure comprehensive and accurate identification of noncompliance, LNCs should follow a structured review process. The following checklist outlines best practices:

- Step 1: Review All Provider Notes—Look for explicit documentation such as "No Show," "Missed appointment," or "Patient declined recommended treatment."
- Step 2: Examine Medication Records—List all prescribed medications, then cross-reference pharmacy records to identify gaps in initial fills and refills. Note any delays or omissions (e.g., "Prescription for isoniazid not filled until 3 weeks after order.").
- Step 3: Assess Follow-Up Compliance—Compare provider instructions for return visits or referrals with actual appointment dates. Look for entries like "Patient instructed to return in one month—did not return until five months later."
- Step 4: Evaluate Referral Completion—Check whether referrals to specialists or additional services were acted on. Obtain records from referred providers;

[59] Comparative negligence standard. https://tinyurl.com/5xn8rfcs (accessed January 2026).

absence of visits may indicate noncompliance (e.g., "Specialist notes: No record of patient appointment.").

- Step 5: Document Communication Barriers—Identify any evidence that the patient did not understand instructions, lacked resources, or faced other barriers, as these may affect legal interpretation of noncompliance.

Common Mistakes to Avoid: Do not assume noncompliance without objective documentation; avoid relying solely on provider impressions without supporting data. Failing to obtain all relevant pharmacy and specialist records can lead to incomplete analysis. Always distinguish between willful noncompliance and justified nonadherence (e.g., financial hardship, language barriers).

Case Examples and Sample Medical Record Excerpts

Example 1: Missed Appointments

A patient with diabetes was instructed to return for a follow-up in two weeks. The medical record states: "Patient instructed to return in 2 weeks for A1C check. No subsequent appointments scheduled; patient returned after 6 months with complications." This documented gap supports a finding of noncompliance.

Example 2: Failure to Fill Prescriptions

In a case involving tuberculosis treatment, the pharmacy records indicated: "Isoniazid filled 01/02/2025; next refill not until 03/15/2025. No refills for rifampicin or ethambutol after initial fill." Incorporating this data into a timeline or calendar visually demonstrates the patient's inconsistent adherence, strengthening the defense's argument.

Example 3: Ignored Referrals

A provider referred a patient to cardiology. The record shows: "Referral to cardiology placed 02/01/2025. No cardiology records available; specialist confirms patient did not schedule." This absence of follow-through may be a clear indicator of noncompliance unless the plaintiff chose to see a different cardiologist.

Reporting Noncompliance: Effective Methods for LNCs

LNCs should present noncompliance findings in a manner that is both clear and persuasive. Two effective methods include:

- Medical Chronology/Summary: Integrate instances of noncompliance directly into the timeline with explicit notes. Example: "04/10/2025—Patient instructed to follow up in 1 month; no return visit documented."

- Calendars and Visual Aids: Use color-coded calendars to display medication fill and refill patterns, making lapses immediately visible to attorneys and, ultimately, to juries.

Conclusion: The Value of Thorough and Clear LNC Reporting

Accurately identifying and clearly reporting patient noncompliance is crucial for LNCs supporting attorneys in malpractice cases. By applying a systematic review process, avoiding common pitfalls, and using objective evidence and compelling visuals, LNCs can provide attorneys with the robust analysis needed to assess case strength, guide negotiation, and present persuasive arguments in court. Thorough, clear documentation of noncompliance not only strengthens legal strategy but upholds the integrity of the litigation process.

With a deeper understanding of how noncompliance affects case outcomes, we now shift focus to the cognitive tools LNCs use to interpret complex medical narratives—critical and analytical thinking.

Critical vs. Analytical Thinking in Nursing

A Practical Guide for Legal Nurse Consultants

One of the strongest assets a legal nurse consultant (LNC) can bring to their work is the ability to think analytically. Analytical thinking is not just a step up from critical thinking—it's a natural evolution. While critical thinking equips nurses to react effectively in real-time patient care, analytical thinking builds on those skills to evaluate care retrospectively, especially when reviewing medical records for legal cases. For LNCs, understanding the distinction between these approaches is key to delivering thorough and reliable assessments.

Making the Distinction: How Analytical Thinking Builds on Critical Thinking

Critical thinking is foundational in nursing—it's the immediate, hands-on assessment and intervention that happens at the bedside. Nurses use critical thinking to gather data, spot problems, and respond quickly and appropriately to patient needs. Legal nurse consultant analytical thinking, however, takes those observations and actions a step further. It involves stepping back, evaluating the entire course of care, and determining whether the standard of care was met, especially in the context of a legal review. In short, analytical thinking is critical thinking applied in a structured, retrospective way, often with legal outcomes in mind.

Evolution of Skills: From Patient Care to Legal Review

Let's draw a direct comparison to make this evolution clear. In patient care, a nurse applies critical thinking to recognize a sudden drop in a patient's blood pressure, quickly assess contributing factors, and intervene to stabilize the patient. When that same nurse transitions to the role of a legal nurse consultant, analytical thinking comes into play. The LNC reviews medical records to determine if the nurse followed protocols, communicated effectively with the physician, and acted within the expected standards of care. The LNC then evaluates whether any failures led to patient harm, considering the four elements of medical malpractice: duty, dereliction of duty, causation, and damages.

- Critical Thinking (Real-Time Care): Quickly assessing symptoms, making decisions, and intervening to protect the patient.
- Analytical Thinking (Legal Review): Reviewing documentation, assessing whether care met standards, and determining links between actions and outcomes.

Expanded Examples: Applying Both Types of Thinking in LNC Cases

Hypotensive Patient: A nurse notices a patient's blood pressure dropping and responds promptly—a clear example of critical thinking. Later, as an LNC, you would analyze the records to see if the nurse's actions met the standard of care and whether any delay or omission contributed to patient harm.

Medication Error: Imagine a nurse catches a potential medication error—such as an incorrect dosage—and prevents administration, demonstrating critical thinking. As an LNC, you would review the medication administration records, compare actions to policies, and assess whether the error was avoided, if harm occurred, and if documentation reflects appropriate follow-up.

Postoperative Complication: Suppose a nurse identifies early signs of postoperative infection and initiates interventions to prevent escalation. In the LNC role, analytical thinking is used to review the timeline of care, evaluate whether symptoms were recognized early, if correct steps were taken, and whether communication with the surgical team was timely and effective.

Using practical, nursing-specific language and real-world scenarios helps clarify how these skills operate in different settings. Critical thinking gets patients the care they need in the moment; analytical thinking helps determine if that care was up to standard after the fact. Both are essential but understanding how and when to apply each is what sets strong legal nurse consultants apart.

As we refine our thinking strategies, we're better equipped to tackle one of the most pivotal questions in any malpractice case: causation. What difference did the alleged error actually make?

What Difference Did it Make?

Understanding Causation

Legal nurse consultants are typically astute at identifying deviations from standards of care and recognizing damages. However, analyzing causation—one of the four essential elements of medical malpractice—can be more challenging. An effective way to approach causation is to ask, "What difference did it make?" This question helps clarify whether a particular action or omission directly contributed to the patient's injury.

As a refresher, the four elements of medical malpractice are Duty, Breach of Duty, Causation, and Damages. Causation is the link between medical carelessness (a breach of duty) and patient injury (damages). If there is carelessness but no injury, there is no causation. Likewise, if there is injury but no carelessness, causation is not established. Let's apply this reasoning to a few examples, explicitly connecting the facts to the conclusions about causation.

It's important to note that while the "What difference did it make?" question is a helpful tool, causation is not always clear-cut in real-world cases. Sometimes, determining causation involves gray areas and disagreements among medical experts. In such situations, expert testimony or further investigation may be necessary to establish whether the care provided led to the outcome.

Lapse in Care?	**Damages?**	**What Difference Did It Make?**
The nurse administers Colace two hours later than scheduled.	The patient has a lethal myocardial infarction an hour after administration of the Colace.	Even though there was a deviation from the standard of care (administering the stool softener two hours late) and the patient suffered damages (the myocardial infarction), the timing of the Colace administration made no difference in the development of the MI; the two events are unrelated. Medical literature does not support a link between delayed administration of Colace and acute myocardial infarction, so the timing of the medication did not

Lapse in Care?	Damages?	What Difference Did It Make?
		contribute to the outcome. Therefore, there is no causation.
An ER nurse irrigates and dresses a deep laceration of a patient's right hand, following the physician's order and hospital policy.	The patient develops an infection at the wound site and ultimately loses the use of his hand.	What difference did it make that the nurse performed the procedure according to policy? Since the nurse's actions were appropriate and consistent with accepted standards, they did not contribute to the development of the infection. Thus, there is no causation. However, sometimes a patient's recollection of events ("Her hands were dirty!") can suggest causation, even when the medical records do not indicate a problem. In such cases, further investigation or expert review may be required to resolve disputes about causation.
A nursing assistant leaves a frail patient with dementia on the toilet.	The patient gets up from the toilet, urinates on the floor, slips on the wet floor, and breaks her hip.	What difference did it make that the CNA left the patient alone? In this instance, the damages—a broken hip—are directly linked to the CNA's actions. The patient's injury would likely not have occurred had she been properly supervised. Therefore, there is causation.

That's all there is to it. The next time you're evaluating causation, ask yourself, "What difference did it make?" This question-driven approach not only simplifies your analysis but also helps ensure you stay focused on the critical connections between care and outcome. When considering new scenarios or legal concepts, continue to use this question to maintain clarity and reinforce key ideas for yourself and your audience.

Once causation is established, the next step is often reconstructing the timeline. Let's explore how LNCs can build accurate, defensible chronologies that support legal arguments and clarify case progression.

How to Nail Down Timelines in Medical Malpractice Cases

Clarifying Terms and Steps for Legal Nurse Consultants

Timelines are essential in medical malpractice cases, as they help demonstrate the sequence of medical events and decisions. Although electronic medical records (EMRs) might seem to support accurate timeline creation, retrospective charting—when health care providers document after an emergency—can lead to discrepancies. Legal nurse consultants (LNCs) must rely on objective elements in the patient chart and other records to build a factual timeline. Using a case-based approach not only makes learning relatable but also enhances understanding, especially for new professionals. Below, we walk through a real-world example and define important terms along the way.

Case Example: Step-by-Step Timeline Reconstruction

A cardiologist admitted a patient with unstable angina (chest pain due to insufficient blood flow to the heart) to the telemetry unit. After a cardiac catheterization, results indicated the need for coronary artery bypass graft surgery (CABG), a procedure to improve blood flow to the heart. The cardiac surgeon scheduled the CABG for the next morning. During the early morning hours, the patient became hemodynamically unstable (experienced dangerous changes in blood pressure or circulation that threatened organ function).

The nurse contacted the cardiac surgeon, who ordered a stat CT scan and prescribed medications. Once the CT scan was complete, the nurse updated the surgeon and received orders for stat lab work. Shortly thereafter, the patient suffered a cardiac arrest but was successfully resuscitated by hospital staff. The nurse communicated with both the cardiac surgeon and the cardiologist, who came to see the patient. However, the patient arrested again and passed away before the physicians arrived. Documentation by the nurse, cardiac surgeon, and cardiologist each presented different timelines for when calls were made, orders given, and care provided.

Clarifying Terms

- DICOM (Digital Imaging and Communications in Medicine): A standardized format that embeds the exact time and details of medical imaging, such as CT scans, directly onto the image.
- Hemodynamically unstable: A medical condition in which a patient's blood pressure or circulation becomes dangerously abnormal, often requiring urgent intervention.

- MAR (Medication Administration Record): A chart or log that documents the timing and details of medications administered to a patient.

Checklist: Steps for Building an Accurate Timeline

1. Determine if the nurse used a hospital phone or their personal cell phone to communicate with physicians. Check phone records (with a subpoena if necessary) to verify the timing of communications between nurses and physicians.
2. Review the time stamps of orders for lab work, medications, and imaging—stat orders are usually entered immediately after physician contact.
3. Note when the lab technician drew blood; delays may indicate workflow issues.
4. If lab results were critical, compare notification times with phone records to confirm prompt reporting to physicians.
5. Review the actual imaging files in DICOM format to determine when CT scans started and ended and make allowances for patient transport time.
6. Check when the radiologist dictated the report or communicated critical findings, and cross-reference with phone records.
7. Examine the MAR to confirm that medications were given as ordered and without delay.
8. Compare all provider documentation with objective records to resolve discrepancies.

Key Takeaways and Recommendations

Establishing an accurate timeline in medical malpractice cases requires careful cross-referencing of objective records, such as phone logs, order entry times, lab and imaging data, and the MAR. Defining and understanding key terms ensures clarity and avoids confusion.

With timeline reconstruction under your belt, it's time to shift gears and explore how LNCs can build professional connections and stay informed—starting with the powerful tool of listservs.

Getting Started with Listservs: A Guide for New Legal Nurse Consultants

Understanding, Participating, and Staying Safe in Online Communities

Are you a new legal nurse consultant searching for expert advice, looking to understand standards of care, or curious about unfamiliar abbreviations? Want to stay informed about legislation that affects your practice? Listservs (note the lack of an "e" between the "v" and the "s") are valuable resources that can help with these challenges and much more. They connect you with a supportive community of peers who share knowledge, answer questions, and offer real-world insights. Two common LNC listservs at the time of this writing are LNCExchange[60] and The J.E.R.K. LNC[61]

What Is a Listserv? Key Terms Explained

A listserv is an automated email system that sends messages to all members who subscribe. Think of it as a group email discussion where you can read, ask questions, and share experiences with others in your field. Here are a few common terms you'll see in online communities:

- Lurking: This means reading posts without actively participating or posting messages yourself. It's perfectly fine to lurk—many newcomers do so to get comfortable and observe discussions before joining in.
- Flame: Flaming refers to posting hostile or insulting messages toward other members. If you disagree with someone, always respond politely and focus on sharing your perspective rather than attacking the person.
- Digest Feature: If you don't want to receive an individual email every time someone posts, you can choose the digest feature. With this option, you'll receive one or two emails daily that group together all posts from that time period, making it easier to manage your inbox.

How to Participate: Sample Scenarios and Questions

Listservs are great places to ask questions and learn from experienced legal nurse consultants. Here are examples of questions you might post:

[60] LNCExchange. https://www.lncexchange.com/ (accessed January 2026).
[61] The J.E.R.K. LNC. https://www.thejerklnc.com/(accessed January 2026)

- "Can anyone recommend study resources or tips for preparing for the LNCC exam?"
- "I'm new to reviewing medical records for legal cases. Are there checklists or templates others have found helpful?"
- "How do you handle situations when standards of care are unclear or not well defined?"

By asking practical questions like these, you'll get advice tailored to your needs and build connections with others in the community.

Listserv Etiquette: Social Rules and Best Practices

- Introduce yourself: When you join, share a brief overview of your professional background and interests.
- Always include your name: Sign your messages with your name, credentials, and any other relevant contact details. Make sure your email address is professional or neutral.
- Lurking is okay: Feel free to observe discussions until you're ready to contribute.
- Check archives before posting: Search the listserv's archives and files for answers to your questions. Many common topics, such as marketing your services or understanding LNC certifications, have probably already been discussed.
- Stay on topic: Post messages relevant to legal nurse consulting. For example, invitations to professional meetings are appropriate, but unrelated event promotions are not.
- Disagree respectfully: It's fine to have different opinions but avoid flaming (hostile or insulting messages). Respond courteously and explain your viewpoint.
- Avoid unnecessary responses: Instead of replying "Thank you" or "I agree" to the entire list, send these acknowledgments directly to the individual.
- Consider the digest feature: Use this option to receive grouped emails instead of individual ones for every post.
- Use clear subject lines: Make it easy for others to decide which posts to read by using descriptive email subjects.
- Express appreciation: If someone helps you, send a direct thank-you email.
- Don't self-promote: Avoid using the listserv to sell products or promote political or social causes, unless allowed by the group's rules.

Privacy and Protection: Staying Safe in Listservs

Many listservs are private, meaning their messages aren't searchable by the public. However, it's important to remember that your posts can be forwarded or shared outside the group (although that's usually against the listserv's rules). To protect yourself and your clients:

- Never share confidential information about clients, cases, or any details that could identify individuals or organizations.
- Avoid posting specifics that might connect you to a particular legal case or sensitive situation.
- Be cautious with personal information: Limit the amount of personal or professional data you share in your signature or posts.
- Think before you post: If you later serve as an expert on a topic you discussed, your listserv messages could be referenced. Stay factual and professional.

Conclusion: Join, Learn, and Connect

Participating in a listserv is an excellent way for new legal nurse consultants to learn, ask questions, and build a professional network. Start by observing, then join the conversation when you're ready. With a little practice and attention to etiquette, you'll find listservs to be a supportive, informative resource throughout your career.

Once you're plugged into the LNC community, you'll quickly notice how communication styles vary. That's where neurolinguistics comes in—helping you understand and adapt to both your own and your attorney's patterns.

Neurolinguistics for Legal Nurse Consultants

How LNCs Can Identify Their Own and Attorneys' Communication Tendencies

Neurolinguistics is the study of how language is represented and processed in the brain. In this context, we use it to refer to individuals' preferred methods of communication—visual, auditory, or kinesthetic.

The words we choose often reveal our communication tendencies. Some people are visually oriented, others prefer auditory methods, and a few favor kinesthetic (movement-based) communication. Understanding an attorney's neurolinguistic preferences can help you interact with them more effectively. I have some thoughts about which method attorneys usually prefer which I discuss later; see if you agree.

Let's explore the main characteristics of each communication style. While everyone uses a mix of these methods, most of us lean toward one more than the others. Here are some vivid examples to illustrate each type:

- Visual: People who prefer visual communication respond best to imagery such as photographs, movies, and magazines. They often think in pictures and visualize concepts mentally. In conversation, you might hear phrases like "I see," "Let's look at this," or "I can picture that." When giving directions, a visual communicator might say, "Turn left at the first stop sign, go straight until you get to Home Depot. Take a right and drive until you see the big pink building on the left." About 60% of people favor visual communication. For these individuals, charts, graphs, emails, letters, and other visual aids are most effective.
- Auditory: Auditory communicators focus on the spoken word. They appreciate precise language and often solve problems by talking things through. Listen for phrases like "I hear you," "Speak to me," or "Listen to this." Their directions tend to be detailed and verbal: "Go straight for a mile, then turn left. Stay on that street for three miles until you reach Seminole and Union Avenue. Turn right and drive for two blocks." About 30% of people prefer auditory communication. Conversations, lectures, phone calls, and voice mail work best with this group.
- Kinesthetic: Those who favor kinesthetic communication are attuned to physical sensations, movement, and gut feelings. They notice emotions and moods and might say things like "That performance was very moving," "That was a tense meeting," or "I'm going to walk away from that idea." Directions from a kinesthetic communicator might involve gestures, hand signals, and pointing. Only about 10% of people prefer this style. Demonstrations, samples, mock-ups, and tangible objects are most effective for kinesthetic communicators.

It can be challenging to identify someone's preferred communication style during conversation, since the focus is often on the message rather than the words chosen. However, with practice, you can start to pick up on these cues in dialogues with colleagues, friends, or family. For instance, pay attention to the language used in workplace debates or everyday exchanges. Once you determine someone's style, try mirroring it to improve understanding.

Which method do attorneys favor? My observation is that most prefer auditory communication. Civil case law is filled with language that reflects this tendency. For example, a medical malpractice case begins with a *Complaint*, followed by a *Summons* and an *Answer*. There are *interrogatories* (questions) and *testimony* at depositions. Attorneys attend *hearings* in court, file *objections*, and participate in trials packed with opening *statements*, *swearing in* of witnesses, more *testimony,* closing *arguments*, jury *instructions*, and finally, the verdict—a word rooted in "something *said* truly."

Of course, not every attorney prefers auditory communication. To determine an attorney's inclination, observe their behavior, listen to their words, and pay attention to their gestures and tone. Adapting your communication style to match theirs can enhance clarity and effectiveness in your interactions.

Communication becomes even more critical when working with pro se litigants. Let's explore how LNCs can maintain professionalism and clarity while navigating these unique relationships.

Working with Pro Se Litigants: Professional Boundaries for LNCs

A Neutral, Informative Guide to Navigating Pro Se Cases

"Pro se" is a Latin term meaning "for oneself" or "on one's own behalf." In the legal context, a pro se litigant is an individual who represents themselves in court without the assistance of an attorney. Legal nurse consultants (LNCs) may encounter pro se plaintiffs, particularly in medical malpractice cases, and it is important to understand the unique considerations and professional boundaries these cases present.

Challenges of Working with Pro Se Litigants

Working with pro se plaintiffs can present unique challenges for LNCs. Pro se litigants often lack formal legal training, which can result in misunderstandings about the litigation process, missed deadlines, incomplete documentation, or unrealistic expectations regarding outcomes and compensation. For example, some may file lengthy or unfocused complaints or have difficulty organizing the facts of their case.

Additionally, certain behaviors such as frequent, emotional communications or a tendency to allege conspiracies may complicate legal proceedings. These behaviors can be especially challenging when they interfere with the case's focus or the ability to collaborate effectively. It is important to approach each situation with professionalism and sensitivity, recognizing that these complications are not inherent to all pro se litigants but may arise in individual cases.

Why Plaintiffs Proceed Pro Se

Most plaintiffs choose to represent themselves in medical malpractice cases when they are unable to secure legal representation. There are several common reasons attorneys might decline to take a case:

- Lack of Merit: After reviewing the facts, attorneys (often with input from LNCs or expert witnesses) may determine that the healthcare providers met the standard of care or that there were no damages, making the case unlikely to succeed in court.
- Financial Considerations: Plaintiff attorneys frequently work on a contingency basis and must weigh the potential recovery against the costs of litigation. If damages are minor, the case may not be financially feasible for the attorney to pursue.
- Barriers to Success: Factors such as the plaintiff's background or specific behaviors may influence the perceived likelihood of success. For example, cases involving plaintiffs with complicated medical histories or behaviors that may be viewed unfavorably by juries can be more difficult to win.
- Attorney-Client Relationship Issues: Occasionally, an attorney may initially accept a case but later withdraw due to lack of cooperation or other challenges in working with the client.

Professional Boundaries for LNCs: Legal Advice vs. Permissible Guidance

A critical consideration for LNCs is the boundary between offering medical expertise and inadvertently providing legal advice, which is reserved for licensed attorneys. Practicing law without a license can have serious consequences; therefore, it is essential for LNCs to distinguish between permissible and impermissible activities.

What LNCs Can Do

- Summarize and analyze medical records and facts related to the case.
- Explain medical terminology and standards of care relevant to the clinical issues in question.
- Educate clients about the medical aspects of their situation, strictly without interpreting the law or suggesting legal strategies.
- Refer plaintiffs to appropriate legal or community resources for further assistance.

What LNCs Cannot Do

- Advise on the legal merits of a case (e.g., whether to file, settle, or pursue a claim).
- Recommend specific legal strategies or next procedural steps in litigation.
- Draft legal arguments, pleadings, or other documents intended for court submission.

- Interpret or apply the law to the plaintiff's individual circumstances.

For example, an LNC may provide a summary of what the medical records show regarding a patient's care but should not suggest whether the plaintiff should proceed with a lawsuit or how to respond to defense motions.

Guidance on Responding to Pro Se Plaintiffs

When approached by a pro se litigant seeking your services as an expert, it is important to maintain professional boundaries. If you are asked to provide services beyond your scope, such as evaluating the legal merit of the case or recommending next legal steps, politely decline and explain that these are matters for a licensed attorney. Instead, you can support pro se litigants by referring them to resources that may help them navigate the legal system.

Resource List with Explanations

- Legal Aid: These organizations offer free or low-cost legal assistance to individuals who qualify, focusing primarily on civil matters such as family law, housing, and sometimes medical malpractice. Legal Aid may also provide referrals to other resources or organizations if they cannot take the case.
- Court-Based Self-Help Centers: Many state courts operate self-help centers where individuals can access free workshops, informational materials, and assistance with court forms and procedures. These centers typically cannot offer legal advice but provide practical support for navigating court processes.
- Law School Legal Clinics: Law schools often run clinics where supervised students offer limited-scope legal help, such as reviewing documents or explaining legal rights. Services may be free or offered at a reduced cost.
- Pro Bono Programs: State and local bar associations may have pro bono (free) programs connecting individuals with volunteer attorneys for legal advice or representation. Assistance may be limited to specific aspects of a case, such as document preparation or court appearances.
- Online Resources: Websites such as LawHelp.org provide information on finding legal assistance, understanding legal rights, and accessing self-help materials across a variety of legal topics.

Conclusion: Best Practices and Maintaining Professional Boundaries

In summary, working with pro se litigants requires LNCs to adopt a neutral, supportive, and professional approach. By understanding the unique challenges these cases present and being clear about the limits of your professional role, you can provide valuable assistance without overstepping legal or ethical boundaries. Referring plaintiffs to appropriate resources ensures they receive the help they need while safeguarding your practice.

Whether you're working with attorneys or pro se clients, strong communication is non-negotiable. In the next section, we'll break down essential guidelines to help you avoid common pitfalls and build trust.

Essential Communication Guidelines for Legal Nurse Consultants

Clear Rules, Common Pitfalls, and Practical Scenarios for New LNCs

Starting out as a legal nurse consultant (LNC) can be exciting—and a bit overwhelming. One area that often trips up newcomers is understanding exactly how, and with whom, you can communicate during a legal case. The legal process sets strict boundaries for LNC communication, and crossing those lines—even unintentionally—can have serious consequences, including the risk of revealing confidential information, losing attorney-client privilege, or even being dismissed from a case. Based on my experience and observations, here's a straightforward primer for expert, in-house, and independent LNCs to help you avoid common mistakes and develop safe, effective communication habits.

Understanding Key Terms

- Certificate of Merit: This is a written statement prepared by an expert, such as an LNC, which confirms that a legal claim—often in medical malpractice cases—has merit based on a preliminary review of records. Its main purpose is to show that the case is not frivolous and warrants further action.
- Affidavit: An affidavit is a sworn written statement used in legal proceedings. LNCs may be asked to provide affidavits to formally assert facts or opinions relevant to a case, typically under oath. These documents serve as official evidence in court.
- Co-Defense: Co-Defense refers to multiple defense parties working together in a lawsuit, such as several hospitals or practitioners being sued in the same case. Communication among Co-Defense teams is common, but always subject to specific legal guidelines.

Expert LNC Communication Boundaries and Scenarios

If you're serving as an expert LNC, you have the flexibility to speak directly—verbally or through written correspondence—with members of the law firm that retained you, or with firms considering retaining you (as long as there's no conflict of interest). You can send Certificates of Merit and affidavits to these firms without concern since these serve specific legal purposes. However, for any other written communications—especially those that include your professional opinions—always consult with the attorney first. In some states, all written exchanges with experts must be shared with the opposing party, which could give them insight into changes in your opinion and affect the case's outcome.

Scenario: Suppose you receive an email from a paralegal at the opposing firm asking for your expert opinion. The correct response is to not reply directly. Instead, immediately notify the attorney at your retaining firm so they can address the situation. Direct communication with the opposing party can jeopardize your neutrality and may result in ethical or legal consequences. You can, of course, communicate with the attorney from the opposing side by answering questions at deposition and trial.

You should never communicate with other experts involved in the case unless you are specifically directed by your retaining attorney. You may, however, review transcripts of their depositions if provided by your law firm. Also, do not interact with anyone from the opposing party's firm. For example, if the opposing side wants to schedule your deposition, their secretary will contact your firm's secretary, who will relay the information to you—no direct contact is permitted. If you're a defense expert, avoid any interaction with the plaintiff unless you're a physician performing a court-approved medical exam. Even then, the exam is scheduled through the plaintiff's law firm.

Law Firm LNCs: Roles and Responsible Communication

Law firm LNCs can freely communicate with their own firm's attorneys and the experts they retain. Defense LNCs may also correspond with attorneys or LNCs from Co-Defense firms, primarily about sharing medical records or coordinating expert retention. Unless specifically authorized, LNCs should not reach out to anyone at the opposing firm.

Scenario: Imagine a Plaintiff law firm LNC receives a phone call from the defendant's office asking for medical records. The appropriate course is to politely decline and refer the caller to the supervising attorney, who will handle the request through official channels.

Plaintiff law firm LNCs can communicate directly with the plaintiff in both written and verbal forms. Defense law firm LNCs, on the other hand, must never contact the plaintiff directly except during depositions, where conversations should be limited to introductions. Violating these boundaries can lead to disciplinary action; for instance, I once witnessed a defense secretary lose their job after directly contacting a plaintiff to schedule a deposition instead of working through the plaintiff's attorney.

Independent LNCs: Limits and Scenarios

Independent LNCs are not law firm employees and do not testify as experts. Their communication is more restricted—they may only speak with those at their retaining law firm, and never with anyone from the opposing party. Independent LNCs often help coordinate with experts during and after retention but must never initiate contact beyond these limits.

Scenario: Suppose an independent LNC receives a LinkedIn message from an expert hired by the opposing party. In this case, do not respond. Instead, inform your retaining attorney about the contact and let them decide the appropriate next steps.

Why These Rules Matter

Improper communication exposes sensitive information, can result in loss of attorney-client privilege, and may even get you dismissed from a case or sanctioned by the court. Following these guidelines is crucial not only for protecting your reputation, but also for maintaining the integrity of the legal process and supporting your clients effectively.

By understanding these rules, you'll build trust with attorneys and avoid common communication pitfalls—setting yourself up for a successful career as a legal nurse consultant.

Strong communication skills set the stage for clarity, but legal language itself can still be a barrier. That's why the next section focuses on plain talk—translating complex legal terms into language that attorneys and clients can easily understand.

Legal Plain Talk: Making Legal Language Understandable

How Nurses and Legal Consultants Can Improve Communication

In your work as a nurse, you know how important it is to use plain talk when caring for patients. Nurses naturally adjust their language to match the listener's understanding, making complicated medical terms easy to grasp. For instance, while a nurse might document "sacral ecchymosis," with a patient, they'll simply say "bruise on your lower back." But when nurses step into the legal world—as legal nurse consultants (LNCs)—using plain talk can be more challenging, especially when speaking with experts or clients who aren't familiar with legal jargon.

Defining Legal Terms: Affidavit and Complaint

Let's look at an example I overheard between an expert and an LNC during a speakerphone call:

- LNC: I'm sending you the affidavit. You will have to execute the affidavit before May 9th.
- Expert: Execute the affidavit?
- LNC: Yes, you'll have to execute the affidavit before May 9th.
- Expert (jokingly): How should I execute it? Shoot it?

Here, the expert was puzzled by the word "execute." In legal plain talk, "execute" simply means "to sign." The LNC could have made things easier by saying, "You need to sign the affidavit before May 9th." Now, what's an affidavit? An affidavit is a written statement confirmed by oath or affirmation, used as evidence in court. It's not just a piece of paper—it's a statement that someone swears is true, and it usually must be signed in front of a notary public, who verifies your identity and watches you sign.

I'll admit, I've stumbled over legal language myself. I once told a client, "The plaintiff's attorney has filed a Complaint against you." The client was completely lost, even though I repeated what their attorney had said the day before. In legal terms, a Complaint is the formal document that starts a lawsuit. It's what someone files in court to say, "I'm suing you." If I'd said, "The patient has filed a lawsuit against you," or "The patient is suing you," the client would have understood right away.

Anecdotes: Real-Life Challenges and Solutions

These experiences taught me a valuable lesson: legalese can be confusing. After the incident with the Complaint, I made it a point to avoid legal jargon with clients and experts. I remember another time when an expert kept asking questions about terms I thought were straightforward. It reminded me that even professionals need clear explanations sometimes. Sharing simple definitions and everyday language makes everyone feel more comfortable and confident.

Actionable Strategies: Tips for Using Legal Plain Talk

1. Replace legal jargon with everyday words. Instead of "execute," say "sign." Instead of "Complaint," use "lawsuit."
2. Check for understanding. After explaining something, ask, "Does that make sense?" or "Would you like me to explain that further?"
3. Encourage clarification. Let people know it's okay to ask questions. I often say, "It's my job to make sure you understand this. Please let me know if anything I've said is unclear."
4. Share examples and stories. Anecdotes help illustrate complex ideas. By describing real situations, you make abstract concepts concrete.

Conclusion: The Value of Clear Communication

Whether you're a nurse, legal consultant, or expert, plain talk is essential. Clear communication builds trust, reduces confusion, and empowers everyone to make informed decisions. If you ever find yourself slipping into jargon, remember your audience and adjust your language. The goal is understanding, not impressing. And if someone jokes about "executing" a document, take it as a cue to clarify—and maybe share a laugh along the way. Plain talk isn't just good practice; it's the heart of great communication.

Once you've mastered simplifying legal language, the next challenge is explaining medical concepts to attorneys. This section offers strategies for bridging the gap between clinical knowledge and legal understanding.

Teaching Attorneys Medical Concepts: Guidance for LNCs

Strategies for Effective, Respectful Communication in Legal Cases

Clear and accurate communication between legal nurse consultants (LNCs) and attorneys is crucial for successful case outcomes. While attorneys are highly intelligent and experienced professionals, their medical knowledge may not always align with that of healthcare providers. As LNCs, our role is to bridge this gap, sharing essential medical information in a way that is informative, accessible, and respectful.

Anecdote: Atelectasis vs. Pneumonia

I once heard an attorney with 30 years of medical malpractice experience tell a group of new lawyers that atelectasis was another term for pneumonia. Atelectasis and pneumonia, however, are two separate medical conditions. Atelectasis refers to a collapse of part or all of a lung, whereas pneumonia is an infection of the lung tissue. This distinction is important because misidentifying these conditions can affect case strategy, expert testimony, and ultimately the outcome for the client. For instance, allegations of negligence may hinge on whether a lung collapse (atelectasis) was missed versus an infection (pneumonia), influencing how expert witnesses evaluate the standard of care and how damages are assessed.

This encounter reminded me that, regardless of experience, attorneys may not possess the same depth of medical knowledge as health professionals. Therefore, it's essential to communicate medical concepts clearly and thoughtfully.

Assessing Attorney Knowledge

To tailor your explanations appropriately, start by gauging the attorney's familiarity with the case and its medical aspects. I typically ask, "What can you tell me about the case?" The attorney's response helps determine their level of understanding. For example, if an attorney describes a client with a history of atrial fibrillation who suffered a cerebrovascular accident due to improper anticoagulation, I recognize a solid grasp of medical issues. Conversely, a description like "a heart condition that led to a stroke because he needed some medicine" signals the need for more detailed medical context.

Transitioning from assessment to explanation, always maintain respect for the attorney's expertise. Using qualifying phrases such as "As you know," or "I'm sure you know this" helps reinforce existing knowledge without appearing condescending. This approach is similar to how, in healthcare settings, one might ask a certified nursing assistant (CNA) if they have had a chance to do something rather than directly questioning whether a task was completed. By phrasing the question this way, you help maintain respect and avoid causing embarrassment, making the interaction more comfortable for everyone involved.

Communicating Medical Information

When discussing medical conditions, provide clear definitions and use lay terms alongside medical terminology. For instance, you might say, "This patient had diastolic heart failure, which some call a stiff heart. As you know, the left ventricle becomes thick and stiff, which makes it pump less effectively." This approach ensures accuracy while fostering understanding.

Encourage open dialogue by inviting questions. For example: "Please let me know if you'd like more details on any aspect of the medical history." This not only clarifies complex points but also demonstrates collaboration and respect for the attorney's perspective.

Using Abbreviations

Some medical abbreviations—such as IV, OB, ICU, OR, and ER—are widely recognized and typically do not require explanation. However, use abbreviations sparingly unless the attorney uses them first. For example, avoid substituting "PNA" for pneumonia unless you are certain the attorney is familiar with the term. Clear communication is paramount; when in doubt, opt for the full term.

Conclusion: Fostering Collaboration and Trust

Teaching attorneys about medical concepts requires sensitivity and adaptability. By assessing their knowledge, communicating clearly and respectfully, and being mindful of terminology, LNCs can provide valuable support. Remember to use phrases like "As you know" to reinforce their expertise and invite questions to maintain an open, collaborative dialogue. In doing so, LNCs help ensure attorneys have the accurate information needed to represent their clients effectively and ethically.

Clear communication with attorneys is vital, but client relationships bring their own challenges. Let's explore how independent LNCs can overcome common roadblocks while maintaining professionalism and trust.

Overcoming Roadblocks in Client Relationships

How Independent LNCs Can Avoid Communication Issues

Effective communication is at the heart of great client connections. Here are some bumps that can appear along the way:

- Missing Deadlines: If you miss a deadline, your client misses theirs too—which isn't ideal for anyone. Before you commit, chat with your client about the project details: how many records there are, what the deadlines look like, and whether they want a written or verbal report. Written reports usually take longer, so make sure you're comfortable with the timeline. Using project management apps or calendar reminders can really help keep everything on track.
- Business Call Challenges: Ever tried having a serious call with the dog barking or the TV blaring in the background? Not the best impression. For scheduled calls, ask a family member to watch the kids and pets so you can find a quiet spot. If you get a surprise call and it's noisy, it's perfectly okay to say, "Things are a little hectic here right now. Can we chat at 2:00 p.m. instead?"
- Slow to Respond: Waiting too long to get back to a client can be a deal breaker. Try to reply to client messages within a day or two. Setting up email notifications and blocking out time each day for correspondence makes it much easier to stay responsive.

Professionalism

Showing up as a professional builds trust—and keeps clients coming back. Watch out for these areas:

- Unprofessional Voicemail Greetings: Your voicemail is often your first impression. Instead of something playful, stick with a friendly but polished vibe, like, "Hello, you've reached [Your Name]. Please leave a message and I'll return your call as soon as possible."
- Limited Availability: If you're only free for calls at odd hours, clients might look elsewhere. Try to offer a couple windows during regular business hours for phone conferences. Scheduling tools can make finding a good time much easier for everyone.
- Typos and Grammar Errors: Mistakes in your written work can make clients wonder how careful you'll be with their cases. Turn on spelling and grammar checkers or use handy online tools like Grammarly or PaperRater. If you use the Word app from Microsoft 365, Copilot is excellent with formatting and polishing

your written work. Want to take it up a notch? Join a writing course or a peer review group to keep sharpening your skills.

Administrative Tasks

Smooth admin work helps everything run like clockwork. Here's what to keep in mind:

- Billing Mix-Ups: Inaccurate or messy invoices can erode trust quickly. Time-tracking software like Toggl or Invoice-Generator is a lifesaver for logging hours and generating precise bills. Double-check each entry and make sure your client has agreed to all charges before sending the invoice.
- Outdated Business Cards: Crossing out old info and scribbling a new phone number on your card just doesn't send the right message. Update your cards regularly so they're always current and stash a few extras in your bag or pocket for networking moments.

Conclusion: Keep Growing

Spotting these roadblocks and working to overcome them helps you build lasting client relationships and a strong professional reputation. Keep learning, pay attention to details, and stay open to feedback—your clients will notice, and your business will thrive.

Managing client relationships often requires assertiveness. The following section introduces practical dictation techniques—helping you communicate with precision whether you're working with a transcriptionist or voice recognition software.

How to be a Benevolent Dictator

How to Dictate Like a Pro

I'm not talking about creating a government in some other country. Instead, I'm referring to dictating your work product so that either a transcriptionist or voice recognition software can interpret it with few errors. If you are lucky enough to have a secretary, don't know how to type, are a slow typist, or have a physical disability that prevents you from typing, dictation may be the answer for you.

Let's first examine dictating for a human being, either a transcriptionist or a secretary, using a dictation machine. Here are some guidelines for using dictation machines:

1. Take a few moments to create an outline, even if it's just in your head, of what you want to say.
2. Don't eat, drink, or chew gum while dictating. Your transcriptionist or secretary will appreciate it, and you'll be able to pronounce words more distinctly.
3. Explain the purpose of the dictation and clarify how you want it formatted, c.g., "This is a medical summary for the Hardgrave case, #34-4437. Please put all headings in bold, use full justification for the paragraphs, and single space each paragraph with an extra line between paragraphs." If you're dictating a letter or a report that is familiar to your transcriptionist/secretary, you won't need to specify how you want the information formatted.
4. After you've given your instructions, say, "Start of dictation" and then begin to speak.
5. Make sure you identify punctuation and other formatting. For example: "New paragraph Mrs. Hardgrave comma her son comma and her daughter all lived together period. Janet Hardgrave open parenthesis formerly known as Janet Smith close parenthesis was diagnosed with liver cancer period." This would result in: Mrs. Hardgrave, her son, and her daughter all lived together. Janet Hardgrave (formerly known as Janet Smith) was diagnosed with liver cancer.
6. If you use a word that your secretary/transcriptionist might not understand, say the word, then spell it out.
7. Use the pause button if you're not sure what to say next.
8. Finish by saying, "End of dictation."

Quick Tips for Dictating to a Human Transcriptionist

- Outline your message
- Speak clearly—no eating or drinking
- State formatting instructions upfront
- Signal the start and end of dictation
- Identify punctuation and special formatting
- Spell out unfamiliar words
- Pause as needed to gather your thoughts

Proofread! I've seen words substituted in:

- Medical terminology – "entitled CO2" was substituted for "end tidal CO2." To avoid this mistake, verify that medical terms are spelled and used correctly.
- Homophones (words that sound the same but have different spellings) – "This lead to an infection" uses "lead," which is the present tense. The correct form is "This led to an infection," where "led" is the past tense. Double-check verb tense when using words that sound alike.

- Idioms (common phrases peculiar to a population) – "kit gloves" is a mishearing of "kid gloves," which means to handle something delicately. Similarly, "all intensive purposes" should be "all intents and purposes." Be mindful of idiomatic expressions and confirm their correct wording and spelling.

Now that we've covered dictating for a human transcriptionist, let's explore how these principles adapt when using voice recognition software.

The other way of dictating is through the use of voice recognition software, which turns your spoken words into text. There's a learning curve with any speech recognition software because you'll need to learn all the commands. Windows has free speech recognition software that can be accessed by going to the search bar on the bottom task bar and typing "speech recognition." For best results, use a headset microphone, set the microphone up to work with the software, and take the speech tutorial.

Unfortunately, Microsoft's old voice recognition software is not HIPAA compliant as it sends audio to Microsoft's cloud, unless it is configured to run offline, using Voice Access[62]. See Chapter 2 for a discussion on HIPAA when using medical software on your local machine. Another choice would be to use Dragon Medical One[63] software, which is used primarily as a transcription app.

Let's look at the eight points listed above and see how they might change when using voice recognition software. The commands I'm using are for the Windows speech recognition program:

1. Creating an outline is still important when you use speech recognition software.
2. Don't eat, drink, or chew gum because it will increase the error rate of your dictation.
3. You won't need to explain the purpose of the dictation, and you'll dictate your formatting as you go along. Use short phrases with brief pauses when you're formatting. For example: "medical summary (pause) select medical summary (pause) bold (pause) all caps (pause) center." These commands will type MEDICAL SUMMARY and center it on the page for you. After the speech recognition program learns your speech patterns, you'll be able to dictate longer phrases.
4. You won't need to indicate the start of dictation. Open the application (such as Microsoft Word) and place your cursor where you want to start. Then tell the software to "Start Listening" and begin talking. Or use the voice recognition software to open the application by saying, "Open Microsoft Word." The cursor

[62] Voice Access. https://tinyurl.com/mtjpks5n (accessed January 2026).
[63] Dragon Medical One. https://www.dragonmedical.us/ (accessed January 2026)

will appear at the top left of the document. You can move the cursor by saying "Enter," "Tab," "Center," and other commands.

5. You will need to identify all punctuation and all formatting, including new lines and paragraphs. See #5 above for punctuation and formatting examples; they're spoken the same way for speech recognition software.
6. If the software misspells a word such as "his team cytosis" instead of "histiocytosis," say, "Correct his team cytosis" and then spell out each letter of the correct word.
7. If you want the software to pause, say, "Stop listening." Say, "Start listening" when you're ready to dictate again. Or just don't speak if you want to pause. But don't talk on the phone or yell at your kids unless you want it transcribed on your work product.
8. You won't need to say, "End dictation" when you've finished speaking. You can save your dictation by saying, "Click file (pause) Save as (your file name) (pause) Save."

Quick Tips for Dictating to Voice Recognition Software

- Outline your message
- Avoid eating or drinking while dictating
- Use formatting commands as you go
- Clearly identify punctuation and formatting
- Correct errors as they occur
- Pause or resume dictation using voice commands
- Save your work with voice instructions

You can see that each type of dictation has its advantages and disadvantages. No matter which method you choose, you're now ready to be a benevolent dictator!

Dictation is one way technology supports LNCs, but AI tools are rapidly expanding the possibilities. In the next section, we'll examine how to use AI responsibly and effectively in case review.

Using AI Tools in Legal Case Review: What Every LNC Needs to Know

Artificial Intelligence (AI) is transforming the way legal nurse consultants approach medical case review. While AI offers impressive speed and organizational power, it also brings critical compliance concerns, especially around HIPAA regulations.

Understanding these requirements—and knowing how to work with AI safely and effectively—is essential for every legal nurse consultant.

Using AI is definitely in the future for legal nurse consultants. AI can currently help with reports (using no PHI), asking general questions (using no case facts), learning concepts/workflows, and editing text that contains no identifiable health information.

In the future, AI may become commonplace. Artificial intelligence tools, even when used on HIPAA-compliant platforms, should be viewed only as **support tools** in legal nurse consulting. AI may assist with record organization, pattern identification, or draft summaries, but it does not replace the legal nurse consultant's clinical judgment, analysis, or professional responsibility. All AI-generated output must be carefully reviewed and verified by the LNC before use or disclosure.

Legal nurse consultants remain fully accountable for the accuracy and integrity of their work. AI should not be used to form medical opinions, determine standard of care, assess causation, or reach legal conclusions. When PHI is involved, LNCs should ensure that any AI platform used is appropriate for regulated data and that its use complies with applicable laws, professional standards, and contractual obligations.

De-Identifying PHI: A Practical Example

Suppose you need to use a general AI tool, such as Chat GPT, Copilot, or Gemini, to format and edit a patient report, but you don't have a BAA or HIPAA compliant controls. You must first remove all Protected Health Information (PHI) [64]. Here's how:

1. Identify PHI: Scan the report for items like patient names, dates of birth, medical record numbers, addresses, and any other information that can directly or indirectly identify the patient.
2. Redact or replace: Delete these details or substitute them with generic placeholders (e.g., replace "Jane Doe" with "[Patient Name]").
3. Review for indirect identifiers: Make sure details like rare diagnoses or location specifics are also removed.
4. Process via AI: Use the AI tool for editing, formatting, or summarizing the de-identified report.
5. Restore PHI: After AI processing, manually insert the original PHI back into the document before finalizing.

[64] Protected Health Information. https://tinyurl.com/4hs85w83 (accessed December 2025).

It's a lot of work to de-identify and then re-identify information for reports. You will need to decide if it's worth your time and effort.

The guidance above—de-identifying PHI before using an AI tool—applies specifically to situations where you do not have a Business Associate Agreement (BAA) in place or the AI platform does not offer HIPAA-compliant controls. This would typically be the case when using general-purpose AI tools such as ChatGPT, Copilot, or Gemini in their standard configurations, which may not guarantee HIPAA compliance or secure handling of PHI unless configured as part of a HIPAA-compliant environment.

In contrast, if you are using a specialized healthcare AI platform like CorMetrix's app VerixAI[65], which provides HIPAA-compliant controls (such as end-to-end encryption, role-based access, audit logs, and a BAA), you do not need to de-identify PHI before processing. These systems are specifically designed to securely manage patient information and meet all regulatory requirements. Always confirm that the platform has the necessary safeguards and contracts in place before uploading any patient data.

In summary, de-identifying PHI is essential when using AI tools that do not provide HIPAA-compliant controls or a BAA. For platforms designed for healthcare and compliance, such as VerixAI, this extra step is not required.

AI in Legal Nurse Consulting: Actionable Scenarios

HIPAA compliant AI platforms can be used to organize and summarize patient information in medical summary or medical chronology format. It can also quickly identify and tag treater names, filter out irrelevant visits, and highlight important medical issues—tasks that would take hours manually. Still, double-check the AI's work to ensure nothing vital is missed or misrepresented. Of course, with new tools come new risks. Before relying on AI, it's important to understand its limitations—especially glitches and hallucinations that can mislead your analysis.

AI Glitches and Hallucinations: Real-Life Anecdotes

While AI is fast and convenient, it's not perfect. For example, I've experienced AI "hallucinations," where the tool confidently cited statistics about legal nurse consultants from a source that didn't exist. Always verify any AI-generated references or facts. Technical glitches can also occur—AI platforms may freeze, disconnect, or produce

[65] CorMetrix VerixAI. https://www.cormetrix.com/verixai (accessed January 2026).

errors, such as misspelling words in graphics or failing to respond. These hiccups are part of the current reality and require patience and backup plans.

Tip Box: What to Watch Out For When Using AI Tools

- Never expose PHI to AI tools without a BAA or HIPAA compliant controls in place.
- Always de-identify if using Chat GPT, Copilot, Gemini, or other AI services without HIPAA compliant controls and BAAs.
- Verify all AI-generated data, summaries, and references for accuracy.
- Be prepared for technical glitches—keep manual backup systems ready.
- Stay up-to-date on AI features and compliance requirements.

By following these steps and remaining vigilant, legal nurse consultants can harness the power of AI while maintaining compliance, accuracy, and client trust.

After exploring AI's potential and pitfalls, we return to a more familiar tool: Adobe Acrobat. This section highlights essential features that streamline medical record review and keep your workflow efficient.

Redacting Documents

The LNC's Role in Protecting Patient Privacy

As a new legal nurse consultant, you may be responsible for redacting documents. It's important to distinguish between correcting errors in medical records and redaction. While correcting errors in medical records ensures accurate documentation for clinical care, redaction is specifically used to protect patient privacy by removing identifying information from documents shared outside the clinical setting. As a nurse, you know there is a correct way to note errors in electronic records, which is to create a new entry, clearly explain the error, and provide the reason for the correction (e.g., wrong patient). For paper records, the proper way to note an error is to draw a single line through the entry and note that the entry was written in error. The purpose of the single line is so that the entry isn't obliterated and can still be read. In contrast, redacted documents have had parts of them obliterated so those parts can't be read.

Redaction means to edit a document, usually to remove information. In medical malpractice litigation, redaction is often used to remove the names of patients who aren't parties in the lawsuit. Documents that require redacting may not include medical records because those are specific to the patient whose case is in litigation. (Note: Some jurisdictions require plaintiff identifiers be redacted; other jurisdictions do not).

Instead, documents that need to be redacted are those that could violate the confidentiality of other patients. These types of documents include:

1. Sign-in sheets at doctor's offices. These are often used to infer that a physician saw so many patients on a particular day that the physician didn't spend enough time with the plaintiff to correctly make a diagnosis.
2. Schedules which include the names of other patients. For example, a schedule sheet for Radiology could be used to pinpoint the time a patient was in that department. An operating room schedule could be used to determine if a surgeon operated for an unusual length of time on a particular day or operated in an assembly line fashion on many patients that day, inferring carelessness by the surgeon.
3. OB delivery logs. Delivery logs can be compared to staffing assignment sheets to determine if staffing was adequate. For example, if several deliveries occurred at the same time, a plaintiff with a bad outcome may infer that the bad outcome was caused by inadequate monitoring by the delivery room nurses.
4. Staff assignment sheets. Staff assignment sheets may show patient names and can identify which staff members cared for the plaintiff. If the assignment sheets show that the staff member caring for the plaintiff was assigned to many patients, the plaintiff may infer that inadequate attention was paid to the plaintiff, resulting in a poor outcome.
5. Visitor logs that require the visitor to write which patient is being seen. These are often used in nursing home cases by the defense to show that family members rarely visited their relative. The defense may infer that family members started the lawsuit to gain money and not from concern about the patient.

Redacting documents is straightforward but still can be done incorrectly, as shown in the image below (the patient’s name is not real). As you can see, when the image is enlarged or viewed with a magnifying glass, the patient's name can be seen.

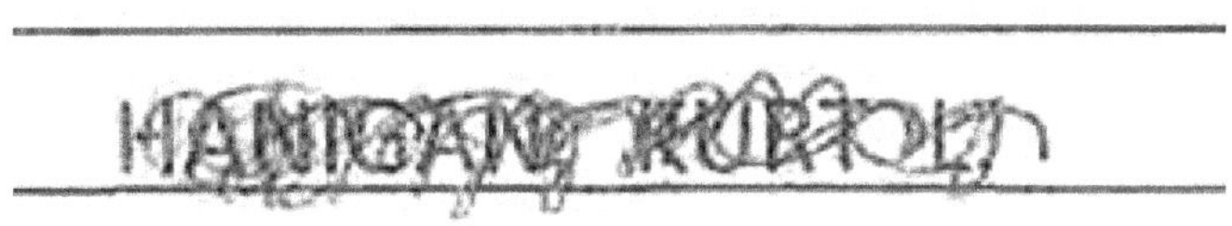

Figure 52 - Scratched Out Name

Other common mistakes include using basic image editing tools that only visually obscure information but do not remove it from the file or forgetting to check for patient names in document metadata. Always verify that redacted information cannot be recovered by viewing the document in different formats or with specialized software.

When using electronic redaction tools, always use the dedicated 'Redact' function rather than simply covering text with shapes or highlights, as these methods may leave underlying information accessible. After redacting, double-check by attempting to copy and paste or search for the redacted information to confirm it is completely removed.

Metadata is information embedded within a file that may include author names, document history, or hidden text. Before sharing documents, use your software's 'Remove Metadata' or 'Sanitize Document' feature to ensure no confidential information remains in the file properties.

What's the correct procedure to redact a paper document?

1. Make a copy of the document you're going to redact. The copy will be your working copy. Never redact an original document.
2. Use scissors, white correction fluid, white correction tape, or a black permanent marker to completely cross out the patient's name and any other identifying information such as a social security number or medical record number. If you use scissors, you will cut out names and other identifiers and you will need to shred the information you remove. In the example below, a black permanent marker was used.
3. At this point, the name may still show through if it's held to the light. To make sure that the name is not visible, make a copy of your working copy. This copy of your working copy will be the document that is provided to opposing counsel.

Your properly redacted document will look something like this:

Figure 63 - Redacted by Marker

If you want your document to look tidier than the example above, you can scan the document and electronically redact it using Adobe Acrobat Professional, Adobe Acrobat DC, or other redaction software, such as BentoPDF. For instance, to redact text in BentoPDF, scroll to 'PDF Editor', and drag your file to the drop zone. Select 'Redact' and highlight the text to redact. Click on the 'Redact' icon. Save your file 'as Medical_Records_Redacted or something similar. If you're using Adobe Acrobat, open the scanned document, click on the 'Tools' tab, select 'Redact,' and follow the prompts to permanently remove sensitive information.

Do not use online redaction software because uploading documents to third-party servers may compromise protected health information and violate HIPAA regulations. Always use locally installed software to ensure data security.

To remove metadata before sharing a document, you can select the 'Print to PDF' feature when printing. This will save the document as a new PDF file without the original metadata, making it safer to share.

Figure 74 - Redacted by Adobe

That certainly looks better. Once you've redacted your document, save it as a new PDF (so that no alterations can occur) before providing it to opposing counsel.

As a new LNC, you can now redact documents. And you can redact them correctly and professionally.

Mastering technical tools is one thing, but embracing change is another. The next section challenges LNCs to overcome rigidity and adapt to evolving practices.

LNC Rigidity

Breaking Through to Embrace Change

Legal nurse consultants (LNCs) have shown remarkable flexibility in their personal lives over the past decade or so. Many bank, shop, and communicate online, use cell phones for a variety of tasks, and stream their favorite shows on platforms like Netflix and Hulu. These examples highlight how readily we've adopted new technologies and habits outside of work. Yet when it comes to our professional practices as LNCs, many of us still struggle with rigidity and are slow to adapt to evolving methods in legal nurse consulting.

This resistance often stems from our nursing roots. Nurses are trained to follow strict procedures for good reason—deviating can compromise patient safety. The phrase "We've always done it this way" is a familiar refrain throughout our nursing careers. While this mindset is present in clinical settings, it can make us hesitant to embrace change in legal nurse consulting, especially when there's no one-size-fits-all procedure for tasks like reviewing medical records.

Looking back, I remember my own hesitation when electronic medical records began replacing handwritten charts. I insisted on organizing and indexing paper copies before reviewing them, believing this process helped me understand the case better. Even when my law firm transitioned to scanning records, I clung to my old methods, convinced I'd miss something important unless I had a neatly organized hard copy. But once I finally tried reviewing electronic records on my computer, I realized the format didn't change the information; it simply offered a new way to access it.

I'm not alone in this journey. Many LNCs I've spoken with have expressed similar initial resistance to electronic records but found that adaptation led to greater efficiency and improved organization. Industry trends show a growing preference for digital workflows, not just with medical records but also with communication. For example, I used to rely on phone calls to reach experts, spending countless hours playing "telephone tag." Now, I use email or even text messages—methods many experts prefer—which saves time and streamlines collaboration.

Concrete Steps for Embracing Change

- Experiment with one new technology at a time to avoid feeling overwhelmed.
- Seek out training opportunities or webinars to build confidence and skills.
- Share experiences and lessons learned with peers who have successfully adapted.

Ultimately, adapting to new technologies and methods is essential for LNCs to remain effective and relevant in a changing legal landscape. By overcoming rigidity and embracing innovation, we position ourselves—and our clients—for continued success.

Resistance to change can hold consultants back. The following section illustrates this with the "Typewriter LNC"—a cautionary tale about outdated habits and the importance of embracing technology.

The Typewriter LNC: Lessons on Embracing Technology in Legal Nursing

How Outdated Habits Hold Us Back and Why Modern Methods Matter

Have you ever noticed how easy it is to get stuck in old routines, even when new technology offers better ways to work? In legal nurse consulting, clinging to outdated habits can slow us down and make our jobs harder than they need to be. The tendency to do things "the way we've always done it" isn't just nostalgic—it can be a real barrier to efficiency and client satisfaction.

My College Process: Manual Methods and Challenges

Back when dinosaurs roamed the earth and personal computers were only a dream, I was in college facing the challenge of writing reports without the help of modern technology. Writing assignments by hand was normal, but when it came to formal reports, I relied on a labor-intensive method: first, I would gather all my material, jot down key concepts on paper, and then handwrite sentences and paragraphs. If something felt out of order, I literally cut out sections and taped them elsewhere on the page. My reports were a patchwork of handwritten notes and taped corrections. Only when everything was in the right place would I sit down at my typewriter to create the final version. It was time-consuming and far from efficient, but it was the best process I knew back then.

The LNC's Experience: Modern Parallels and Inefficiencies

Years later, this same approach resurfaced in my professional life. At my law firm, a seasoned legal nurse consultant (LNC) was given a tight deadline: prepare a report on a newborn's head circumference in just three hours. She reviewed the records, carefully wrote out her findings by hand, and submitted the handwritten report to the attorney. While the information was accurate, the attorney made it clear that handwritten reports were no longer acceptable. The next time, she typed the report—but her process was nearly identical to my college days. She reviewed records, jotted notes on paper, handwrote sentences and paragraphs, cut and taped sections, and finally typed everything into the computer. This method took two to three times longer than simply composing the report directly in a word processor as she reviewed the records.

Lessons Learned: Synthesis of Stories and Clear Takeaway

Both my college experience and the LNC's story highlight a powerful lesson: sticking to outdated work habits can hold us back, even when new tools are available. In both cases, the process was unnecessarily complex and time-consuming. The main takeaway for legal nurse consultants is clear—embrace technology and adapt your workflow. By creating reports as you review records and taking full advantage of computers for editing and organizing, you can save valuable time, produce higher-quality work, and deliver better results for your clients. Let go of the “we’ve always done it this way” mindset and be open to evolving your approach.

Conclusion: Call to Embrace Technology and Efficient Processes

As legal nurse consultants, our goal is to provide meaningful, timely, and accurate reports for our clients. By embracing new technology and continually updating our work processes, we not only increase our own efficiency, but also improve the results we deliver. The stories shared here remind us that vivid, relatable anecdotes can make lessons memorable—so keep telling your own stories as you grow and adapt. Let’s move forward together, leaving inefficient habits behind and making the most of the tools at our disposal for better outcomes and greater professional satisfaction.

Once you've embraced modern methods, efficiency becomes the focus. The next section explores how to realistically estimate review time and manage attorney expectations.

How Long Will it Take?

Factors Affecting Your Case Materials Review Time

"How long will it take?" Attorneys frequently ask this question when requesting record reviews. As a new legal nurse consultant, you might feel unsure about how best to respond. While there isn't a one-size-fits-all answer, I can help you prepare to answer attorneys confidently and effectively.

If there were a magic answer to this question, it would be, "It depends." Each case presents its own set of challenges, and every LNC brings unique experience and skills. To help you estimate your review time, consider asking yourself a few key questions about the case and your background.

First, reflect on your clinical experience in relation to the case type. For instance, if you typically work in obstetrics but are asked to review a critical care case, anticipate spending more time. You may need to study the patient's clinical condition as well as critical care guidelines to ensure thoroughness. This scenario is common for new consultants and underscores the importance of adapting to unfamiliar medical specialties.

Next, think about your experience as a legal nurse consultant. When you're new to the field, reviewing cases may take longer simply because the process is unfamiliar. As you gain experience, you'll find your efficiency improves and review times decrease.

Consider your current workload and competing responsibilities. For example, if you're scheduled to work five consecutive 12-hour shifts, finding time to tackle a new case may be difficult. Balancing casework with other job duties is a frequent challenge for new LNCs, so it's important to assess your availability honestly.

When speaking with the attorney, ask, "How many pages of medical records are there?" While charging by the inch or the number of pages isn't recommended, the number of pages directly affects the time required. Reviewing 10,000 pages is a very different undertaking than reviewing just 100 pages.

Additionally, inquire about the format of the medical records. Are they typed, electronic, handwritten, or hybrid? Handwritten records usually demand more time due to legibility issues. Typed reports—such as discharge summaries, consultations, or histories and physicals—are typically quicker to review. Electronic medical records are also typed, but may be duplicative, stretching a four-page flowsheet into 20 pages of similar information. Hybrid records combine these formats and can further complicate the review process.

Another crucial aspect to consider is whether the attorney expects a written or verbal report. A verbal report requires less preparation and can be delivered with informal notes. In contrast, a written report involves creating a grammatically correct, formally structured summary of your review, which is more time-intensive.

After collecting this information, always ask the attorney, "When do you need the results of my review?" Deadlines can drastically influence your ability to deliver a thorough and timely review. For example, if you're facing a short deadline, many handwritten records, and other work commitments, meeting the attorney's expectations may be challenging. Conversely, a longer timeline allows for a more comprehensive review, especially if you're adapting to unfamiliar records or specialties.

As you can see, the time required to review medical records depends on many variables. In truth, "It depends" may be the most accurate answer to the question, "How long will it take?" Your ability to assess these factors and communicate clearly with attorneys will help you provide realistic timelines and build trust as you grow in your role.

Summary - Main Factors Affecting Review Time

- Your clinical experience in relation to the case type
- Your experience as a legal nurse consultant
- Competing responsibilities and overall workload
- Number of pages of medical records
- Type of records (typed, electronic, handwritten, or hybrid)
- Whether a written or verbal report is required

Finally, we close with a practical reminder: small, consistent efforts add up. Just four minutes a day can transform your practice and keep you moving forward.

4 Minutes a Day

How to Adjust Your Attitude Toward Dreaded Tasks

Except for those who are rich and have full-time housekeepers, cooks, and gardeners, we all have chores and tasks around the house that we hate. Some of us hate mowing the lawn. Others detest doing the laundry or cleaning the toilet. My most despised chore was unloading the dishwasher and putting away the clean dishes and flatware. However, I no longer hate this task. In fact, unloading the dishwasher provided me with an insight that helps me as a legal nurse consultant. And I learned that if I spent just four minutes a day, I could perform an LNC task that I used to detest.

Here's how I changed my attitude about unloading the dishwasher. While I am grateful that I have a dishwasher, one day I was about to unload a dishwasher that was as full as it could be. The top and bottom racks seemingly held all the dishes and pans that my family owned. But the worst part was the flatware basket. I had always hated emptying the flatware basket, and this time it was jammed with utensils. I complained to myself about spending all my time removing the contents of the dishwasher. I said to myself, "I bet it'll take me 20 or 30 minutes to put this all away." I looked at the clock and started to unload the dishwasher. When I finished my hated chore, I looked at the clock again and was shocked. Only four minutes had passed. Four minutes!

I realized that, over the years, I had loathed a task that only took four minutes a day. The amount of time was probably less than four minutes, because the dishwasher wasn't overcrowded most days. I recognized that I had a distorted perception of the time it took me to perform tasks that I didn't like to do. I also understood that I had wasted my mental energy in anticipation of unloading the dishwasher. My attitude toward this chore changed instantly once I made these realizations.

This small shift in perspective didn't just change how I approach chores at home—it transformed how I handle challenging tasks in my legal nurse consulting work.

How does my experience unloading the dishwasher relate to legal nurse consulting? Like many LNCs, there are tasks that I love to do, and tasks that I have avoided. For example, I once worked for a plaintiff attorney who designated one of my responsibilities as reading the daily obituaries. I hated this task; I assumed that the attorney was trolling for potential clients, the families of the deceased. I had to determine if the patient died in a nursing home, assisted living facility, or hospital. If the patient died in one of those facilities and died unexpectedly or after a brief illness, I informed the attorney.

I hated reviewing obituaries and would always put it off. However, I thought about my dishwasher-unloading episode, and I told myself that I was only going to review obituaries for four minutes that day. I set a timer for four minutes, and again, I was surprised when I finished scanning obituaries in that amount of time. I felt invincible! I could face abhorrent tasks if I only had to spend four minutes a day on them. After that, it took me a little longer on some days—up to 10 minutes—but I learned not to stress about reading obituaries. After all, I was only spending four to 10 minutes a day on the task, which amounted to less than one percent (when I spent four minutes) to two percent (when I spent 10 minutes) of my daily work time. It wasn't worth thinking about the task and becoming upset. And because I was delving into the task without avoiding it, I eventually became comfortable with reading obituaries.

I've heard similar stories from colleagues: one LNC turned a dreaded cold calling session into a game, rewarding themselves for each call completed; another set a timer for proofreading reports and found that breaking the task into short bursts made it less overwhelming. These personal experiences show that reframing your approach and sharing strategies can help demystify procrastination and make challenging tasks more manageable.

Think about your most dreaded LNC task—could you commit just four minutes a day to it this week and see what changes? Challenge yourself to try this approach and notice how your attitude shifts.

A positive mindset lays the foundation for productivity. Now let's apply it to one of the biggest stressors in LNC work: deadlines. This section offers real-world strategies for staying on track and building attorney trust.

Conquering Deadlines: A Practical Guide for New Legal Nurse Consultants

Real-Life Strategies for Staying on Track and Building Attorney Trust

Stepping into your first assignment as a legal nurse consultant is both exciting and a bit nerve-wracking. While your clinical expertise prepares you to analyze medical records and communicate findings, one of the most crucial skills you'll need is mastering deadline management. Meeting—or better yet, exceeding—deadlines not only earns attorney trust but also opens doors for future opportunities. Let's walk through practical strategies, real-life examples, and simple tools to help you stay organized and confident as you start your consulting journey.

Clarify, Don't Assume: Avoiding Last-Minute Surprises

Imagine this: Leonora, a brand-new legal nurse consultant, receives her first case. The attorney says, "I need your review by September 15th." Eager to impress, Leonora plans her analysis for the week before the deadline. However, she pauses and asks, "Is that when you need my findings, or do you need the full written report by then?" The attorney replies, "Actually, I have a deposition on the 15th—I'll need your report by the 10th to prepare." Thanks to this simple clarification, Jenny submits her report early, giving the attorney ample time to review and ask follow-up questions. She avoids the stress of a last-minute rush and earns a glowing recommendation.

Tip 1: Always Clarify Every Deadline

Never hesitate to ask for specifics about timelines. When an attorney provides a date, follow up with questions like, "Is this the date you need the completed report, or the date you'll be using my findings for a meeting or deposition?" By confirming these details, you ensure your work is both timely and valuable.

When "ASAP" Isn't Clear: Setting Realistic Expectations

Sometimes, deadlines aren't so straightforward. Let's say you're told, "We need this reviewed ASAP." What does that really mean? Does ASAP mean tomorrow, next week, or next month? Here's where good communication can make all the difference.

Consider the story of Michael, an experienced consultant who receives an "ASAP" request. He immediately asks, "What's your ideal turnaround time? Are there any key meetings or hearings I should be aware of?" The attorney clarifies that the file isn't needed until the end of the month. By seeking clarity, Michael avoids unnecessary stress and can allocate his time efficiently.

Tip 2: Pin Down "ASAP" and Know Your Commitments

Whenever you hear "as soon as possible," ask for a specific date or context. This helps you prioritize your workload and prevents misunderstandings. Transitioning to the next key point, remember to evaluate your personal schedule before agreeing to tight timelines.

Tip 3: Assess Your Own Schedule Before Accepting Rush Jobs

Take a holistic view of your commitments. If you have family obligations—like 3 school-age kids who need sports physicals, immunizations, and back-to-school clothes—or other ongoing cases, be honest with yourself about your capacity. It's better to communicate your availability upfront than to compromise quality or risk missing a deadline.

Negotiating Deadlines: Flexibility Pays Off

There will be times when you know a deadline isn't feasible. Rather than declining outright or risking a late submission, open a dialogue about alternatives. For instance, if you're juggling multiple assignments and realize you'll need more time, ask the attorney if the deadline is negotiable. Often, attorneys can adjust their timelines, especially if you give them enough notice.

Here's how one consultant navigated this: Alex was assigned a case with a two-week deadline, but the records were extensive. He explained the situation, offering a realistic timeframe and even suggesting the option of subcontracting part of the review to a trusted colleague. The attorney appreciated the proactive communication and agreed to extend the deadline, resulting in a thorough, high-quality report.

Tip 4: Open Communication for Deadline Negotiations

If you anticipate challenges, ask, "Is there any flexibility with the deadline?" If not, consider alternatives—such as bringing in a subcontractor for support. This not only demonstrates professionalism but also helps you maintain positive relationships with your clients.

Tip 5: Organize Medical Records for Efficient Review

Once you receive the records, request permission to organize them if they arrive in paper form and are out of order. Properly arranged records—by section and chronological order—will make your review faster and more accurate. Electronic medical records should already be organized in some fashion.

Tip 6: Tackle the Work in Manageable Segments

Large volumes of records can be overwhelming. Break the task into smaller parts—review nurses' notes first, then orders, and so forth. Setting mini-deadlines for each segment will keep you on track and prevent burnout.

Tip 7: Use Tools and Templates to Stay Organized

As your caseload grows, having a system is essential. Whether you prefer a paper planner, an electronic calendar, or a simple checklist, find what works for you. Here are two sample tools to get started:

Sample Assignment Tracking Checklist:

- ✓ Case Name / Number
- ✓ Attorney Contact Info
- ✓ Date Received
- ✓ Deadline Clarified (Y/N)
- ✓ Report Due Date

- ✓ Calendar Entry Created
- ✓ Subcontractor Involved (if applicable)
- ✓ Completion Status

Sample Calendar Reminder Template:

Case: [Case Name]

Review Due: [MM/DD/YYYY]

Attorney Meeting / Phone Conference: [MM/DD/YYYY]

Progress Check: [Set reminder 3 days before due date]

You're Ready to Meet—and Conquer—Your Deadlines

By proactively clarifying expectations, communicating openly, and using organizational tools, you'll not only meet deadlines but also build a reputation for reliability and professionalism. Remember, every assignment is a chance to showcase your skills and grow your consulting practice. You've got this!

Meeting deadlines requires organization, and that's where checklists shine. In the next section, we'll explore five compelling reasons every LNC should use them to stay focused and efficient.

5 Reasons for LNC Checklists

Keeping Your LNC Practice on Track

If you've ever used a preoperative checklist, you know firsthand how helpful they can be in streamlining tasks and preventing oversights. Preop checklists serve as visual reminders for nurses to complete essential steps, and this same principle can benefit legal nurse consultants (LNCs). Here are five specific reasons to incorporate checklists into your LNC practice, along with practical scenarios and expanded insights to enhance your workflow and accuracy.

1. Infrequent Tasks: When you rarely perform a particular set of tasks, a checklist can be invaluable. For example, most new LNCs don't get cases from attorneys every day. Creating a checklist for conflict of interest evaluation—such as "Review attorney list, cross-reference with known contacts, check for prior case involvement, document findings"—ensures you complete this process quickly and accurately, even if it's not part of your daily routine.

2. Variable Task Execution: Some tasks are done often but differ based on the situation. This is like surgical pick lists tailored to each surgeon's preferences. In the legal field, you may work with multiple attorneys who each want reports in different formats or styles. Maintaining individual checklists for each attorney—detailing their preferred report structure, required data, and deadlines—can help you consistently meet expectations and avoid errors.
3. Learning New Tasks: If you're still mastering a process, checklists can guide you through each step and prevent missed details. Take hiring an expert, for instance. Instead of just knowing the steps, use a sample checklist: Locate expert, verify credentials, schedule introductory call, confirm availability, negotiate fee. This actionable list gives you a concrete starting point and helps standardize your approach for future cases.
4. Tracking Completion: If you often wonder, "Did I do that?" a checklist provides clarity and peace of mind. Investing a few minutes to create a checklist saves time later by eliminating the need to mentally retrace your actions. By using a checklist, you reduce the risk of missing critical steps and improve your overall efficiency, especially when handling multiple cases at once. This systematic approach helps you stay organized and boosts confidence in your work.
5. Boosting Motivation: Checklists aren't just practical—they're motivating. The satisfaction of checking off completed tasks can spur you to keep going, even with challenging objectives like marketing your services as a new independent LNC. A weekly checklist could include items such as "Contact three attorneys, connect with five LinkedIn contacts, update portfolio." This structure helps you stay accountable and maintain consistent progress toward your goals.

Numbered lists and concise, scenario-based descriptions not only break down complex concepts into digestible pieces but also support better organization, accuracy, and workflow for LNCs. Consider implementing customized checklists in your practice to optimize your processes and achieve reliable, high-quality results.

Checklists are powerful, but they're even more effective when paired with reminder systems. Let's walk through how to set up both physical and digital ticklers to keep your practice running smoothly.

How to Set Up Tickler and Reminder Systems for Legal Nurse Consultants

Step-by-Step Guide for Beginners

As a legal nurse consultant, managing multiple case assignments, court dates, client deadlines, and business tasks can quickly become overwhelming. Effective organizational systems—like tickler and digital reminder systems—help you prioritize, stay on track, and ensure nothing falls through the cracks. Whether you're new to consulting or looking to streamline your workflow, these systems can keep your business running smoothly and professionally.

Step-by-Step: Setting Up a Physical Tickler System

You don't need a smidgen of technology to use this system. I used this tickler method for years before digital reminder systems became available.

1. Gather Supplies: Collect 43 file folders—31 labeled with each day of the month (1–31) and 12 labeled for each month (January–December). You'll also need a section of a file cabinet or an expandable file box.
2. Label Folders Clearly: Use large, easy-to-read labels. For daily folders, number them 1 through 31. For monthly folders, use the full month name.
3. Organize the Folders: Place the daily folders in order, followed by the monthly folders. For example, after folder "31," add "January," "February," and so on.
4. File Your Tasks and Documents: For tasks or documents with specific dates (such as paying a bill on the 10th or following up with a client on the 20th), place them in the corresponding daily folder. For tasks scheduled in future months (like preparing for a court date in August), put reminder notes or documents in the appropriate monthly folder.
5. Daily Review Routine: Each morning, check the folder for that day's date. Take out tasks, bills, or reminders, and move completed items out of the system. At the end of each month, move items from the monthly folder into the daily folders for the new month as their deadlines approach.
6. Concrete Example: If you need to prepare documents for a deposition on the 15th, place a checklist in folder "15." For a client follow-up scheduled three months from now, add a reminder in the folder labeled with that future month.

Step-by-Step: Setting Up Digital Reminder Systems

Reminder systems are more high-tech and can be used in lieu of a physical tickler system. Below are instructions for setting up two reminder systems, Evernote and

TeuxDeus, and common electronic calendar systems. Evernote is like having digital sticky notes and TeuxDeux is a program that lets you check off tasks as you complete them.

- Evernote[66]: Download Evernote on your computer or mobile device and create a free account. Create a notebook called "Deadlines and Reminders." Add notes for each deadline (e.g., "Submit client report by 6/05/2026") and set reminders using Evernote's built-in alert feature. Sync across devices so you receive notifications wherever you are. Example: Set a reminder for a court date, attach related documents, and get alert notifications as the date approaches.
- TeuxDeux[67]: Sign up for TeuxDeux online and log in. Enter tasks under each day (e.g., "Review medical records for new case" on November 2). Check off completed items to track progress. Unfinished tasks automatically roll forward to the next day. Example: List key case deadlines for the week and monitor completion as each day passes.
- Electronic Calendars (Outlook[68], Google Calendar[69]): Create calendar events for each project deadline, court appearance, or meeting. Set up recurring reminders for routine tasks (e.g., weekly invoice review). Sync your calendar to your phone for instant notifications. Example: Enter monthly networking meetings and receive alerts a day in advance.

Common Challenges and Practical Solutions

Legal nurse consultants may face obstacles such as forgetting to check folders or ignoring reminder notifications. Here are practical solutions:

- Consistency: Make reviewing your tickler or digital reminders part of your morning routine, just like checking email.
- Recurring Alarms: Set recurring alarms or notifications on your phone to prompt you to review your system daily.
- Overload: If folders or digital lists get too crowded, schedule a weekly "clean-up" session to reorganize and reprioritize tasks.
- Missed Deadlines: For high-priority tasks, set multiple reminders (e.g., one week and one day before the deadline).

[66] Evernote. https://evernote.com/ (accessed January 2026).
[67] TeuxDeux. https://teuxdeux.com/ (accessed January 2026).
[68] Outlook. https://tinyurl.com/ycyr43yk (accessed January 2026).
[69] Google Calendar. https://tinyurl.com/5xtxrpuf (accessed January 2026).

- Concrete Example: If you're tracking court dates for several clients, color-code folders or calendar entries by client name to avoid confusion and overlap.

Real-World Scenarios: Applying Systems in Your Practice

- Tracking Court Dates: Place court appearance reminders in both your tickler system and digital calendar. Set alerts a week in advance to prepare necessary documents.
- Managing Multiple Client Deadlines: Assign each client a color or code in your system, and schedule reminders for key milestones such as report submissions or communication follow-ups.
- Client Communications: Add notes to your tickler system to remind you to call or email clients on specific dates, ensuring consistent follow-up and excellent service.
- Networking Events: Use monthly folders or a calendar to track professional development and networking opportunities, so you never miss important growth events.

Conclusion: Make Your System Work for You

Staying organized is essential for legal nurse consultants, especially when juggling multiple responsibilities. Whether you choose a physical tickler system, a digital reminder tool, or a combination of both, personalize your setup to fit your workflow and preferences. The key is consistency—review your system daily and update it as your business grows. With these practical tools and tips, you'll be well-equipped to meet deadlines, manage cases, and deliver outstanding results for your clients.

Look Ahead Day

A Step-by-Step Guide for Legal Nurse Consultants

Staying organized is crucial for every legal nurse consultant (LNC), regardless of experience level. As nurses, we're trained to manage our time and tasks—making sure every patient receives proper care on schedule. But when I transitioned to legal nurse consulting, I quickly realized that the skills I'd honed as an RN didn't transfer perfectly. The workload is different, the deadlines are tighter, and instead of patients, you're juggling dozens of cases at various stages. Early on, I struggled to meet every deadline and attorney request. I often found myself scrambling at the last minute, wishing I had a better system. That's when I created my Look Ahead Day, which has since become my most valuable organizational tool.

The Look Ahead Day for Law Firm LNCs: Four Actionable Steps

Whether you're brand new or a seasoned law firm LNC, implementing a weekly Look Ahead Day can keep you proactive and efficient. Here's how you can break it down:

1. Review Attorney Calendars for the Next Month: Set aside time (I used Wednesdays) to scan through your attorneys' schedules one month out. Look for important dates—hearings, depositions, client meetings, and telephone conferences.
2. Cross-Reference Upcoming Events with Your Case List: For each event on the attorneys" calendars, match it with your current cases. Determine which cases are affected and what your involvement might be.
3. Identify Tasks Needed for Each Event: Create a list of actionable items. For example, if a treater's deposition is coming up, plan to review their medical records and update the medical chronology. If an attorney has a client meeting, note which records and reports need to be prepared.
4. Schedule Time for Follow-Up or Last-Minute Requests: Set aside blocks in your schedule for unexpected needs that can arise. By planning ahead, you'll have the flexibility to handle surprises without stress.

Look Ahead Day for Independent and Expert LNCs: Practical Examples

The Look Ahead Day concept is just as valuable if you're an independent or expert LNC. If you don't work in a law firm or don't have cases yet, dedicate your Look Ahead Day to moving your business forward. For example:

- Marketing Your Services: Use this time to update your website, refresh marketing materials, or compose emails to potential clients.
- Organizing Networking Activities: Plan outreach—schedule coffee chats with attorneys, attend local legal events, or connect with colleagues on LinkedIn.
- Managing Ongoing Education: Research upcoming webinars, enroll in continuing education courses, or review recent legal or medical literature.
- Client Follow-Ups: Reach out to past clients for testimonials or check in on their current needs. This keeps relationships warm and often leads to new referrals.
- Professional Development: Block time to work on certifications, attend online workshops, or join professional associations.

For example, I know one LNC who last Wednesday spent part of her Look Ahead Day updating her LinkedIn profile and drafting a newsletter for attorneys she'd worked with. She also scheduled a lunch with a local attorney, which she hoped would lead to a new consulting opportunity.

From Struggle to Success: Personal Insights

When I first started, I missed a few deadlines and felt overwhelmed by the volume and variety of requests. But after consistently using my Look Ahead Day, I found myself more prepared, less stressed, and better able to support my attorneys and clients. The difference was night and day—tasks stopped piling up, and I handled last-minute requests with ease. Even if you're not naturally organized, this process is easy to learn and adapt. With practice, you'll develop the skill and confidence to manage your workload smoothly.

Ready to Try Your Own Look Ahead Day?

Whether you're inside a law firm or running your own LNC business, adopting a Look Ahead Day can set you up for success. It's actionable, flexible, and proven to work—because I've lived the difference it makes. Give it a try, and you'll find yourself moving from chaos to control in no time!

Once your checklist system is in place, you can take it a step further with customizable cheat sheets—quick-reference tools that streamline your workflow and reinforce consistency.

LNC Cheat Sheets

Creating and Using Electronic Templates

Cheat sheets are sometimes misunderstood but can be valuable organizational tools for legal nurse consultants managing multiple medical malpractice cases. Attorneys expect you to be familiar with every detail of your assigned cases, but when your caseload grows, recalling specifics for each case becomes a challenge. Many legal nurse consultants find that structured cheat sheets are essential for efficiently accessing critical information and responding promptly to attorney inquiries.

For example, when I began my role in a defense law firm, I inherited 30 cases from a departing LNC. When questions arose, I often had to search through file cabinets to locate details—an inefficient and time-consuming process. To address this, I developed cheat sheets that allowed me to keep key information at my fingertips. Initially, I used handwritten index cards for each case, but as my caseload exceeded 100 cases, I transitioned to electronic files for improved organization and accessibility.

Step-by-Step Guide: Creating an Electronic Cheat Sheet Template

1. Set Up a Template File:
2. Open Microsoft Word and create a new document. Save this document as a Word Template (.dot) for future use.
3. Insert a Structured Table: Within the template, insert a table with two columns and eight rows. You may choose to use only outside borders for a cleaner appearance or retain all table lines based on your preference.
4. Label the Left Column: In the left column, list pertinent case details such as Case Name, Plaintiff, Defendant, Client, Co-Defendants, Adjustor, Expert, Allegations, Case Deadlines.
5. Input Case Information: When starting a new case, open the template, enter the relevant information in the corresponding cells of the right column, and save the completed sheet as a Word document (.doc) as shown on the attached sample.
6. Organize and Access Your Cheat Sheets: Store your completed cheat sheets electronically on your computer for quick retrieval. This system enables you to efficiently answer attorney questions without searching through paper files.

This streamlined process for creating electronic cheat sheets greatly improved my ability to manage a large caseload and respond to inquiries with confidence. By implementing an organized template system, legal nurse consultants can enhance their productivity and maintain professional standards in communication with attorneys.

Sample LNC Cheat Sheet

Case Name/Number:	Otis v. Little Babies Pediatrics / O-74590
Plaintiff(s):	Aibhe Otis (and parents)
Client(s)	Little Babies Pediatrics
Allegations:	Failure to timely diagnose osteosarcoma in a 6-year-old
	Resulting in AKA
	Jamie Johnson
Assigned Attorney:	Aston Beulens, MD, Zbygnev (Ziggy) Salomon, DO
Other Defendants:	

Adjustor:	Christina Blaketon, JD
Expert(s)	Kumara Vemulakonda, RN (Pediatrics), Roar (Rorie)
Deadlines:	Depo Dr. Beulens July 10, 2026

With your cheat sheets ready, the next challenge is navigating medical records efficiently. Let's explore six practical strategies for locating key information quickly and accurately.

6 Ways to Find Information in the Chart

How to Quickly Locate Specifics in Medical Records

Did you know that many law firms still print copies of electronic records? Attorneys use these printed pages for meetings with clients, depositions, and more. When working with attorneys who need to find details in medical records, I often see them glance at the chart for a nanosecond before handing it to me and saying, "Here, YOU find it." When I first started as a legal nurse consultant, searching for specific information in medical records was stressful and time-consuming. Today, I've developed techniques that allow me to locate details almost instantly.

Here are six methods I use to find information quickly and easily in medical records. Each tip includes a practical example to help you apply these strategies in your own work.

1. Make a copy of important pages. Create copies of the pages most relevant to the case. On each copy, write the name of the provider and describe how you obtained the records (e.g., "Cedar Ridge Hospital RFC Smith" for records received from a request for copies from defendant Smith). This helps you organize and access the information quickly—just look for the file labeled with the provider's name. This approach is especially useful if you do not consolidate records into a single working copy.
2. Flag important records. Use colored flags to mark key documents. Assign different colors for different defendants or roles—for example, red for treating physicians and blue for nursing staff. If you know the attorney will want to discuss certain entries, flag those pages in advance. This system works well with

working copies and makes it easy to locate and discuss critical records during meetings.

3. Note the location in a report. When summarizing medical records, always record where each piece of information is found. For instance, if referencing a pathology report, specify its location: "The pathology report from ABC Labs (found in the records of Dr. Trenton) showed adenocarcinoma." This prevents delays and confusion if someone asks to see the document later. It should also trigger you to obtain records from ABC Labs.
4. Bates stamp the records. Number each page using Bates stamping so every record is uniquely identifiable. This is invaluable for team discussions—an expert can say, "Check page 00175," and everyone can quickly locate the same document. To make this even more effective, include Bates page numbers in your report, such as: "On October 21, 2013, John Milford, MD ordered Pradaxa 75mg (00175). At 4:00 p.m. that same day, Mary Langdon, RN charted that she administered 150mg of Pradaxa (00998)." This detail streamlines finding each chart entry.

Electronically link to records. For digital medical records, add hyperlinks in your reports to specific pages or documents. Programs like CaseMap let you link directly to individual pages, but you can also create hyperlinks in Microsoft Word. As electronic records become standard, these links let you instantly open the exact page you need.

5. Bookmark important pages. Use bookmarks in electronic medical records to mark crucial documents or sections. This is similar to flagging paper records; clicking on a bookmark takes you straight to the page you're looking for. If you need help setting up bookmarks, look for tutorials specific to your software.

With these strategies, you'll be able to locate any information an attorney requests quickly and confidently from the medical records!

About the Author

Katy Jones, MSN, RN, has spent more than four decades at the intersection of healthcare and the legal system. As a Legal Nurse Consultant, she has helped attorneys navigate thousands of pages of medical records, uncover critical case details, and build stronger, clearer arguments. Her passion is teaching other nurses how to bring their clinical expertise into the legal world with confidence, clarity, and professional polish.

Katy is known for her practical, no-nonsense approach to LNC work. She has developed tools, templates, and workflows that simplify complex tasks and help consultants deliver high-quality results under real-world pressures. Her writing is clear, accessible, and grounded in decades of hands-on experience.

When she's not reviewing medical records or mentoring new consultants, Katy focuses on creating resources that make the LNC role more approachable and sustainable. The *Legal Nurse Consultant Procedure Manual (and More)* is the guide she wishes she had at the start of her own journey — and the one she hopes will support the next generation of LNCs.

www.ingramcontent.com/pod-product-compliance
Lightning Source LLC
LaVergne TN
LVHW060014210926
848481LV00013B/3708